Archaeology

Archaeology

DOWN TO EARTH *Fifth Edition*

ROBERT L. KELLY
University of Wyoming

DAVID HURST THOMAS
American Museum of Natural History

Australia • Brazil • Japan • Korea • Mexico • Singapore • Spain • United Kingdom • United States

Archaeology: Down to Earth, Fifth Edition
Robert L. Kelly and David Hurst Thomas

Publisher: Yolanda Cossio
Acquisitions Editor: Aileen Berg
Developmental Editor: Lin Gaylord
Assistant Editor: Mallory Ortberg
Editorial Assistant: Margaux Cameron
Media Editor: John Chell
Senior Brand Manager: Liz Rhoden
Senior Market Development Manager: Michelle Williams
Content Project Manager: Cheri Palmer
Art Director: Caryl Gorksa
Manufacturing Planner: Judy Inouye
Rights Acquisitions Specialist: Roberta Broyer
Production and Composition: MPS Limited
Photo Researcher: PreMediaGlobal
Text Researcher: PreMediaGlobal
Copy Editor: Heather McElwain
Illustrator: MPS Limited and Graphic World
Text Designer: Ellen Pettengill
Cover Designer: Lee Friedman
Cover Image: © David Fettes/Image Source/Corbis

Library of Congress Control Number: 2012946810

Student Edition:
ISBN-13: 978-1-133-60864-6
ISBN-10: 1-133-60864-7

Loose-leaf Edition:
ISBN-13: 978-1-133-95091-2
ISBN-10: 1-133-95091-4

Wadsworth
20 Davis Drive
Belmont, CA 94002-3098
USA

Cengage Learning is a leading provider of customized learning solutions with office locations around the globe, including Singapore, the United Kingdom, Australia, Mexico, Brazil, and Japan. Locate your local office at **www.cengage.com/global.**

Cengage Learning products are represented in Canada by Nelson Education, Ltd.

To learn more about Wadsworth, visit **www.cengage.com/wadsworth**

Purchase any of our products at your local college store or at our preferred online store **www.CengageBrain.com.**

Printed in the United States of America
1 2 3 4 5 6 7 16 15 14 13 12

For Matt and Dycus, for their love of big piles of dirt.

—R.L.K.

For LSAP(T), colleague, companion, advocate, and mother of my son. And, most significantly, still my very best friend.

—D.H.T.

Brief Contents

Contents

Featured Contents

LOOKING CLOSER

PROFILE OF AN ARCHAEOLOGIST

WHAT DOES IT MEAN TO ME?

IN HIS/HER OWN WORDS

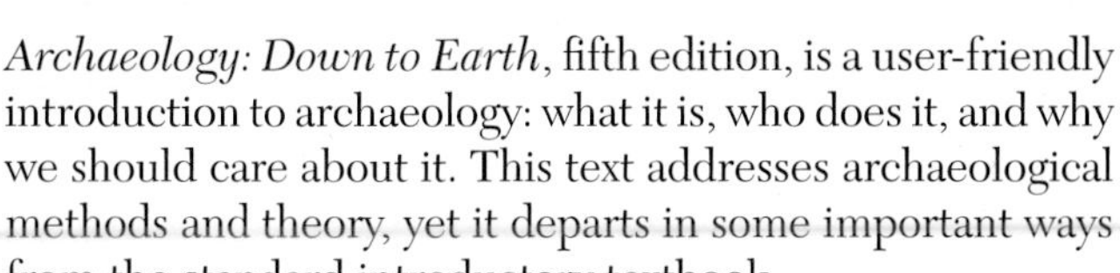

Preface

Archaeology: Down to Earth, fifth edition, is a user-friendly introduction to archaeology: what it is, who does it, and why we should care about it. This text addresses archaeological methods and theory, yet it departs in some important ways from the standard introductory textbook.

Students tell us that they sometimes don't bother reading the introductory textbooks they've purchased—whether the books are about archaeology, chemistry, or whatever. We've heard several reasons for this paradox: The instructor covers exactly the same material, using the same examples as the text—so why bother reading what you can get condensed in a lecture? Or their textbooks are deadly dull, written in arcane academic jargon that no one can enjoy reading. Still others tell us that they take an archaeology course just because it sounds like a fun way to fulfill a distribution requirement—but the text actually has nothing to say to them.

We want students to know that we've heard them. Accordingly, we picked many of the book's topics with these students in mind.

As it turns out, these are the very subjects that budding career archaeologists should know. We don't shy away from controversial subjects—in fact, the text begins with one in its introduction—that touch upon sensitive issues that influence both professional archaeologists and the public. Many archaeology texts avoid these sensitive issues, such as the excavation of the dead or what archaeology has to say about climate change. But we think that these are precisely the issues that matter most to students and to instructors, so we've not backed away from them.

In fact, instructors tell us they have used previous editions of this text precisely because their students will actually *read* it.

Personal Examples, High-Interest Topics

In most archaeology texts, the approach is fairly encyclopedic and dispassionate. But we cannot do it that way. To be sure, modern archaeology is a specialized and complicated academic discipline, with plenty of concepts, several bodies of theory, and a huge array of analytical methods—all things we'd like students to learn about. But we think that the best way for students to begin to understand archaeology (or any subject, for that matter) is through a few well-chosen, extended, personalized examples—stories that show how archaeologists have worked through actual problems in the field and in the lab. So that's the approach we take here.

Writing a textbook is not easy. We must provide a solid foundation for students who intend to become professional archaeologists. This requires a thorough review of the discipline, including all its major concepts and jargon. But we must also write for the many students who will *not* become professional archaeologists.

About This Edition

The first edition of *Archaeology: Down to Earth* was published back in 1991; succeeding editions have retained the coverage and personalized writing style that users praised, while also reflecting up-to-the-minute changes in the discipline. By the time the third edition rolled around, David Hurst Thomas decided one person simply couldn't cover the field adequately anymore, and he invited Robert Kelly to join in the project. These two first met more than 30 years ago, when Thomas was excavating Gatecliff Shelter in Nevada and Kelly was a gangly, enthusiastic high school kid. They worked together for several years, after which their careers diverged. When the time came to expand the authorship, Thomas turned to Kelly as the obvious choice for a coauthor. This partnership continues with the present fifth edition of *Archaeology: Down to Earth*. We've further streamlined this edition, keeping the same number of chapters, but removing some material from a few that seemed too long. We've continued to update the examples, especially in the areas of remote sensing and genetic analyses, and the photos and graphics for a better visual presentation that enables students to see more clearly the key points of a concept or example. We have also added several new features, upon which the following elaborates.

Aids to Learning, Old and New

What Does It Mean to Me? Throughout the text, we address issues about archaeology that should resonate with students, such as buying artifacts from online auction houses, climate change, human alteration of the environment, and the excavation of human burials. We think that students will find these topics thought provoking (and these sidebars could easily form the basis of writing assignments or group discussions).

Looking Closer

A popular feature from earlier editions, these sidebars cover ancillary topics in each chapter. In addition, some seek to be helpful to budding archaeologists, suggesting equipment students will need for survey and excavation, or what courses they might take. Others look at the lighter side of archaeology, such as how sites get their names, or give personal glimpses into fieldwork—what it's like to do survey or ethnoarchaeology.

In His/Her Own Words In several places, we found that others told their own first-person stories better than we could, so we've included their words to help personalize the text.

Profile of an Archaeologist We've kept these sidebars to emphasize the diversity of today's working archaeologists and to illustrate the varied ways in which archaeologists make a living.

These features combine with the following learning aids to help students master this complex, fascinating discipline:

- New student learning objectives provide students with the material they are expected to master after reading each chapter.
- Each chapter has a running glossary (with glossary terms defined at the bottom of the page on which the term is introduced), plus the text has an alphabetized Glossary at the end.
- Each chapter's preview contains several questions that students should be thinking about while reading.
- At the end of each chapter, we've provided brief answers to those questions to help students review the chapter's key points.
- Each chapter contains Rapid Reviews, mid-chapter bulleted or tabular features that summarize especially important key concepts.
- At the end of chapters, there is a list of media resources pertinent to each chapter.

A Distinctive Approach

The following strategies all contribute to a fuller, more up-to-date exploration of the field:

Discussions of Archaeological Objects in Context

You'll notice that we eschew an encyclopedic approach, which tends to encourage students to simply memorize a laundry list of techniques without context. Instead, we've embedded and contextualized discussions of things like stone tools and ceramics in substantive examples. These presentations ensure that students learn about these basic archaeological objects in ways that carry significance for them—so that they see why, for instance, it might be useful to know where a sherd's temper comes from.

Balanced Coverage: Depth, Breadth, Theory

The text is not encyclopedic, but it is a comprehensive review of the field. Given the background knowledge that a first- or second-year college student brings to an introductory course, this text strikes a balance among the different directions that archaeologists take. This text is thoroughly readable, not at all dumbed down, and places the thought process of archaeology within a wider context. Students learn about science and challenges to it, the Enlightenment, and evolutionary thought.

Expanded Geographic Coverage As before, many of the examples used in this text are drawn from the archaeology of western North America. Between the two of us, we've spent nearly eight decades working there and, frankly, it's what we know best. But we've continued the expanded geographic coverage of the fourth edition, drawing upon work in the eastern United States, Central and South America, Egypt and the Near East, Madagascar, France, Australia, Micronesia, and other places. Although the text is focused, it is not provincial—and should inspire classroom discussions of research projects from around the world.

All in all, we think you'll find this text is one that both instructors and students will appreciate.

Organization of the Text

We constructed this text so that various ideas build upon one another. We know that each archaeologist teaches his or her introductory course differently, but you should keep in mind that many chapters cross-reference material discussed in other chapters. We note each instance within the text.

The text begins with an introduction that focuses on the legalities that surround the Kennewick Man case—a purposeful selection because it shows both the potential of what archaeologists can learn about the past and the ethical issues that confront archaeology in doing so.

Chapter 1 addresses the history of archaeology, with an emphasis on several individual archaeologists who have defined the field. In Chapter 2, we relate archaeology to the rest of anthropology and wrestle with the diversity of theoretical paradigms evident in contemporary archaeology. We also discuss the intellectual process of archaeology in terms of low-, middle-, and high-level theory. This somewhat simplified presentation provides an easy entry into the diversity of contemporary archaeology. And rather than come down on the side of processual or postprocessual archaeology, we take a centrist position that we believe characterizes the majority of working archaeologists today.

Chapters 3 and 4 provide the nuts and bolts of archaeology, explaining how archaeologists go about doing surface survey, using remote sensing equipment, and excavating sites. In these chapters, we try to give students some sense of how much fun fieldwork can be. We also introduce the field of geoarchaeology, emphasizing formation processes, but also covering archaeological stratigraphy, showing students how a site's stratigraphy can be "read" to provide a context for the artifacts contained there. Chapter 5 covers dating methods used in prehistoric and historic archaeology. The range of dating technology seems to increase annually, and we had to make some tough choices about what to include. The major purpose of this chapter is not to write an encyclopedia of available methods, but instead to provide enough information about key techniques so that students can relate dating technology to ancient human behavior. Chapter 6 discusses various archaeological concepts—types, cultures, and phases—that help construct large-scale patterns in space and time. Our goal is to help students see the world as an archaeologist views it, as an ever-changing spatial and temporal mosaic of material culture.

Chapters 7 through 11 consider how archaeologists go about breathing some anthropological life into this spatial and temporal mosaic—how they actually use material remains to infer something about past human behavior. Chapter 7 is about middle-range theory—how it differs from standard analogy and how archaeologists construct it through taphonomic, experimental, and ethnoarchaeological research. Our goal here is to convince students that archaeologists don't just make up stuff, but instead give plenty of thought to how they infer ancient behavior from material objects and their contexts. Chapter 8 recounts how archaeologists reconstruct diet from faunal and floral remains and how they infer hunting strategies and symbolic meanings attributed to the natural world. In Chapter 9, we consider what we can learn—about diet, disease, and workload—from human skeletal remains; this chapter also explores the field of molecular archaeology. Chapter 10 shows how archaeologists can reconstruct social and political systems of the past and looks at gender, kinship, and social hierarchies. Chapter 11 presents how archaeologists address the symbolic meanings once attached to the material remains; here, we look at the nature of symbols and what archaeologists can realistically hope to learn about them.

Chapter 12 explores historical archaeology, especially those aspects that set the field apart from prehistoric archaeology—the ability to uncover "hidden history," the ability to provide a near-forensic analysis of historical events, and the ability to present alternative perspectives on U.S. history. Finally, Chapter 13 examines the legal structure of modern archaeology, emphasizing the field of cultural resource management (how it came to be and the critical role it plays in archaeology today). This chapter also covers the subjects of reburial and repatriation in some detail, and it looks at the future of archaeology, especially the ways in which archaeologists apply their knowledge to contemporary problems. We conclude by discussing the increased involvement of indigenous peoples in the archaeology of themselves and asking whether we are on the brink of another revolution—one that might produce a newer "new" archaeology.

Supplemental Materials

This text also comes with a strong supplements program to help instructors use their class time most effectively and to aid students in mastering the material. (Each item is followed by its ISBN.)

Online Instructor's Manual with Test Bank (9781133950936)

The instructor's manual offers chapter outlines, learning objectives, key terms and concepts, and lecture suggestions. The test bank consists of 40 to 60 test questions per chapter, including multiple-choice, true/false, and essay questions.

Doing Fieldwork: Archaeological Demonstrations CD-ROM, Version 2.0 (9780495604242)

Granted that students can learn field techniques only from actually participating, this CD shows professional archaeologists involved in various digs (many of which are referenced in the text), illustrates field techniques, gives students perspective about what they're learning, reinforces concepts and techniques through live examples, and encourages students to participate in a dig themselves. The presentation is organized by the main techniques that one uses on a dig. Users are taken through each step automatically or can navigate to any point via the navigation bar. Students review illustrations and video clips of each technique. After reviewing a step in the dig process, students are taken to "Check Points," which are concept questions about each step of the dig. Students can see the answers, receive their score, and e-mail the score to the instructor.

PowerLecture™ with ExamView® for Archaeology: Down to Earth, fifth edition (9781133950929)

A complete all-in-one reference for instructors, the PowerLecture CD contains Microsoft® PowerPoint® slides of images from the text, zoomable art, image library, PowerPoint lecture slides that outline the main points of each chapter, Microsoft® Word files of the Test Bank and Instructor's Manual, and ExamView testing software that allows instructors to create, deliver, and customize tests and study guides (both print and online) in minutes.

Anthropology CourseMate (www.cengagebrain.com)

Cengage Learning's Anthropology CourseMate brings course concepts to life with interactive learning, study, and exam preparation tools that support the printed textbook. Watch student comprehension soar as your class works with the printed textbook and the textbook-specific website. Anthropology CourseMate goes beyond the book to deliver what you need!

Anthropology WebTutor™ with eBook for Blackboard® and WebCT®

Jump-start your course with customizable, rich, text-specific content within your Course Management System.

- Jump-start—Simply load a WebTutor cartridge into your Course Management System.
- Customizable—Easily blend, add, edit, reorganize, or delete content.
- Content—Rich, text-specific content, media assets, quizzing, web links, discussion topics, interactive games and exercises, and more.

Case Studies in Archaeology, edited by Jeffrey Quilter

Enrich your students' study of archaeology with the many contemporary case studies in this acclaimed series. Students will learn how archaeologists study human behavior through analysis of material remains. They will learn about new interpretations and developments within the field—and the importance of the archaeological perspective in understanding how the past informs our experience of the present. These engaging accounts of cutting-edge archaeological techniques, issues, and solutions—as well as studies discussing the collection of material remains—range from site-specific excavations to types of archaeology practiced. Visit www.cengage.com/anthropology, and see "Anthropology and Archaeology Case Studies" for complete information on all case study titles available.

Who Helped Out?

Despite the personal flavor of these pages, this text was created by more than four hands. Many people helped out, and we'd like to thank them here.

The overall presentation was vastly improved by a contingent of top-notch colleagues and friends who provided advice and critical reviews of the manuscript. We are particularly grateful to several anonymous reviewers who provided comments on the fifth edition. We are most grateful for their advice and suggestions.

Paul E. Langenwalter II (Biola University)
Elizabeth A. Mancz (University of Akron)
Kenneth W. Mohney (Monroe County Community College)
Elizabeth L. Pintar (Austin Community College)

Many others commented on portions of chapters or entire chapters, answered questions, provided photographs or text for sidebars, and checked facts for us. We gratefully acknowledge timely and sometimes detailed assistance on this and previous editions from the following:

Anna Agbe-Davies (University of North Carolina)
David Anderson (University of Tennessee)
Roger Anyon (Pima County, Arizona)
Bettina Arnold (University of Wisconsin, Milwaukee)
George Bagwell (Colorado Mountain College)
Doug Bamforth (University of Colorado)
Mary C. Beaudry (Boston University)
Jeffrey Behm (University of Wisconsin, Oshkosh)
The late Lewis Binford
Michael Blakey (College of William and Mary)
Matthew Bogdanos (Manhattan District Attorney's Office)
Charles A. Bollong (University of Arizona)
The late Rob Bonnichsen
Bruce Bradley (Exeter University, UK)
Steven Brandt (University of Florida)
Robert Brooks (Oklahoma State Archaeologist)
Jack Broughton (University of Utah)
Margaret Sabom-Bruchez (Blinn College)
Jane Buikstra (Arizona State University)
Richard Burger (Yale University)
Virginia Butler (Portland State University)
Catherine Cameron (University of Colorado)
Robert Carneiro (American Museum of Natural History)
Philip J. Carr (University of South Alabama)
Beverly Chiarulli (Indiana University of Pennsylvania)
Cheryl Claassen (Appalachian State University)
C. William Clewlow (Ancient Enterprises)
Margaret Conkey (University of California, Berkeley)
John Cornelison (National Park Service)
The late Don Crabtree
George Crothers (University of Kentucky)
Jay Custer (University of Delaware)
Hester Davis (formerly Arkansas State Archaeologist)
William Davis (formerly University of California, Davis)
Kathleen Deagan (Florida Museum of Natural History)
Jeffrey Dean (University of Arizona)
Rob DeSalle (American Museum of Natural History)
Diana DiZerega-Wall (City College of New York)
William Doelle (Desert Archaeology, Inc.)
Kurt Dongoske (Zuni Heritage and Historic Preservation Office)
Robert Elston (retired)
James Enloe (University of Iowa)
Clark Erickson (University of Pennsylvania)
George Esber (Miami University)
T. J. Ferguson (University of Arizona)
Terry Fifield (U.S. Forest Service, Alaska)
Ben Fitzhugh (University of Washington)
Kent V. Flannery (University of Michigan)
Don Fowler (retired, University of Nevada, Reno)
Anne Fox (University of Texas, San Antonio)
Richard Fox (retired, University of South Dakota)
Julie Francis (Wyoming Department of Transportation)
George Frison (retired, University of Wyoming)
Robert Gargett (San Jose State University)
Ervan Garrison (University of Georgia)
Joan Gero (retired, American University)
Diane Gifford-Gonzalez (University of California, Santa Cruz)
Dean Goodman (University of Miami, Japan Division)
Martha Graham (SRI Foundation)
Donald K. Grayson (University of Washington)
David Grimaldi (American Museum of Natural History)

Donny Hamilton (Texas A&M University)
The late Marvin Harris
Charles Hastings (Central Michigan University)
Christine Hastorf (University of California, Berkeley)
Eugene Hattori (Nevada State Museum)
William Haviland (retired, University of Vermont)
Brian Hayden (Simon Fraser University)
Michelle Hegmon (Arizona State University)
Kim Hill (Arizona State University)
Matthew G. Hill (Iowa State University)
Robert Hitchcock (Michigan State University)
Richard Holmer (Idaho State University)
Andrea A. Hunter (Northern Arizona University)
Tony Hynes (Danville Area Community College)
The late Cynthia Irwin-Williams
Rosemary Joyce (University of California, Berkeley)
John Kantner (School for Advanced Research)
Barry D. Kass (Orange County Community College, SUNY)
William Kelso (Jamestown Rediscovery Archaeological Project)
Thomas King (National Park Service)
Keith Kintigh (Arizona State University)
Vernon James Knight, Jr. (University of Alabama)
Clea Koff (independent scholar)
Stephen Kowalewski (University of Georgia)
Steve Kuhn (University of Arizona)
Chapurukha Kusimba (Field Museum, Chicago)
The late Charles Lange
Clark Spencer Larsen (Ohio State University)
Mark Leone (University of Maryland)
Janet Levy (University of North Carolina, Charlotte)
Barry Lewis (University of Illinois, Champaign–Urbana)
David Lewis-Williams (University of Witwatersrand)
William Lipe (retired, Washington State University)
Dorothy Lippert (Smithsonian Institution)
Diana Loren (Peabody Museum, Harvard)
Karen Lupo (Southern Methodist University)
The late Scotty MacNeish
David B. Madsen (retired)
Joyce Marcus (University of Michigan)
Fiona Marshall (Washington University)
Patrick E. Martin (Michigan Technological University)
Patricia McAnany (University of North Carolina)
Heather McInnis (University of Oregon)
Heather McKillop (Louisiana State University)
Justine McKnight (independent archaeobotanical consultant)
Frank McManamon (retired, tDAR)
Shannon McPherron (Max Planck Institute, Germany)
David J. Meltzer (Southern Methodist University)
George Miller (California State University, Hayward)
Barbara Mills (University of Arizona)
Paul Minnis (University of Oklahoma)
Paula Molloy (National Park Service)
The late Craig Morris
Juliet E. Morrow (Arkansas State University)
Cheryl Munson (Indiana University)
Melissa Murphy (University of Wyoming)
Fraser Neiman (Monticello Archaeology Program)
Margaret Nelson (Arizona State University)
Michael J. O'Brien (University of Missouri)
James O'Connell (University of Utah)
John Olsen (University of Arizona)
Tim Pauketat (University of Illinois)
The late Christopher Peebles
Stephen Plog (University of Virginia)
Robert Preucel (University of Pennsylvania)
The late William Rathje
Elizabeth Reitz (University of Georgia)
David Rhode (Desert Research Institute)
John Rick (Stanford University)
Anibal Rodriguez (American Museum of Natural History)
Nan Rothschild (Columbia University)
Irwin Rovner (North Carolina State University)
Ralph Rowlett (University of Missouri)
Ken Sassaman (University of Florida)
Vernon Scarborough (University of Cincinnati)
Michael Schiffer (University of Arizona)
Enid Schildkrout (American Museum of Natural History)
Lynne Sebastian (SRI Foundation)
Payson Sheets (University of Colorado)
Stephen Silliman (University of Massachusetts, Boston)
Steve Simms (Utah State University)
Jeff Sommer (University of Michigan)
Stanley South (retired, University of South Carolina)
Charles Spencer (American Museum of Natural History)
Charles Stanish (University of California, Los Angeles)
Amy Steffian (Alutiiq Museum)
Vin Steponaitis (University of North Carolina)
Simon Stoddart (Cambridge University)
Elizabeth Stone (State University of New York, Stonybrook)
Todd Surovell (University of Wyoming)
The late William Tallbull
Ian Tattersall (retired, American Museum of Natural History)
Anya Taylor (John Jay College of CUNY)
Mark Taylor (Manhattan College)
The late W. W. Taylor
Lawrence Todd (retired, Colorado State University)
The late Bruce Trigger
Ruth Tringham (retired, University of California, Berkeley)
Bram Tucker (University of Georgia)
Donald Tuohy (retired)
Christy Turner (retired, Arizona State University)
Mary Vermilion (Saint Louis University)
Nicole Waguespack (University of Wyoming)
Danny Walker (Wyoming State Archaeologist Office)
Mike Waters (Texas A&M University)
Patty Jo Watson (retired, Washington University)
Gloria Cranmer Webster (U'mista Cultural Centre)
Kathryn Weedman (University of South Florida)
John Weymouth (University of Nebraska)
The late Joe Ben Wheat
Mary Whelan (University of Iowa)

Nancy Wilkie (Carleton University)
Chip Wills (University of New Mexico)
Al Woods (Florida Museum of Natural History)
James Woods (College of Southern Idaho)
John Yellen (National Science Foundation)
Amy Young (University of Southern Mississippi)

Each contributed worthwhile suggestions, which we often followed. We alone, however, are responsible for any errors of commission or omission.

Thomas also wishes to thank others in the American Museum of Natural History, especially Lorann S. A. Pendleton, Matt Sanger, Anna Semon, and Molly Trauten, each of whom cheerfully helped out with dozens of details, as well as Ginessa Mahar, Elliot Blair, and Diana Rosenthal.

Kelly is grateful to his colleagues at the University of Wyoming, many of whom supplied photographs, answered innumerable questions about archaeological and anthropological trivia, and generally provided support. He is especially grateful to Lin Poyer and her unbounded patience and thoughtfulness.

We are also grateful to the crew at Wadsworth: Senior Acquisitions Sponsoring Editor Aileen Berg, Senior Development Editor Lin Gaylord, Senior Content Project Manager Cheri Palmer, Media Editor John Chell, Assistant Editor Mallory Ortberg, and Editorial Assistant Margaux Cameron. We thank the production team: Production Editor Jill Traut of MPS Limited, and Copy Editor Heather McElwain. We also gratefully acknowledge Dennis O'Brien, who created many of the illustrations used in this edition, as well as the contributions of the illustrators Diana Salles and the late Nicholas Amorosi, both of the American Museum of Natural History.

Keeping in Touch with Your Authors

We see this textbook as an opportunity to become more available to both instructors and students. With e-mail, we can all have casual conversations with people around the globe, in more or less real time. We want to know what you think about this text and about archaeology—what you like and what you don't care for—so we can improve future editions. We encourage you to write us at the following e-mail addresses. Provided that we're not off on some remote dig somewhere, we'll get back to you right away. Drop us a line—we'd enjoy hearing from you.

R. L. K.
Laramie, Wyoming
RLKELLY@uwyo.edu

D. H. T.
New York, New York
thomasd@amnh.org
July 2011

A Note about Human Remains

In several instances, this book discusses important new frontiers of bioarchaeological research. But we also recognize the need to deal with human remains in a respectful and sensitive manner. Several Native American elders have requested that we refrain from publishing photographs or other depictions of American Indian human remains. Although we know that not all Native Americans feel this way, no images of Native American skeletal remains appear in this book. Should other groups express similar concerns, their requests will be addressed in succeeding editions as appropriate.

About the Authors

Robert Kelly began collecting arrowheads in farmers' fields when he was 10 years old and has participated in archaeological research since 1973, when he was a high school sophomore. He has worked on excavations in North and South America and conducted ethnographic research in Madagascar. He is currently conducting research into the paleoindian archaeology of Wyoming's Bighorn Mountains. A former president of the Society for American Archaeology and a past secretary of the Archaeology Division of the American Anthropological Association, Kelly has published more than 100 articles and books, including the 1996 Choice's Outstanding Academic Book *The Foraging Spectrum: Diversity in Hunter-Gatherer Lifeways*. He has been a professor of anthropology at the University of Wyoming since 1997.

David Thomas has served since 1972 as curator of anthropology at the American Museum of Natural History in New York City. A specialist in Native American archaeology, Thomas discovered both Gatecliff Shelter (Nevada) and the lost sixteenth-/seventeenth-century Franciscan mission Santa Catalina de Guale on St. Catherines Island, Georgia. Since 1998, he has led the excavation of Mission San Marcos near Santa Fe, New Mexico. A founding trustee of the National Museum of the American Indian at the Smithsonian since 1989, he has published extensively, including 100 papers and 30 books—most recently, the best-selling *Skull Wars: Kennewick Man, Archaeology, and the Battle for Native American Identity*. As an archaeologist, Thomas likes "old stuff," including his 1961 Corvette, his 120-year-old house, and the Oakland Raiders.

Introduction

July 1996: The two college students never intended to make a federal case out of the day's fun. They never meant to rock the ethical foundations of U.S. archaeology, either. All they wanted was to see hydroplane boat races for free.

The month of July in the city of Kennewick (Washington) is a series of festivals topped off by hydroplane races on the Columbia River. To avoid paying admission to the races, the two young men snuck through a brushy area of riverbank where they could get a good view, even if it meant getting wet. Trudging along the river's edge, they spied a smooth white object. One of them picked it up and jokingly pronounced it a skull. Imagine his surprise when he saw two dark eye sockets staring back at him. It *was* a skull.

After the races, the students reported their find to police, who called in the coroner to see if the remains were those of a murder victim. The coroner eventually called in archaeologist James Chatters. Although there was no evidence of a burial pit, the skull's near-pristine condition suggested that it had eroded from the riverside only days earlier; in fact, Chatters eventually found much of the skeleton in the shallow water.

Who Was "Kennewick Man"?

The analyses that followed showed that the individual was male and roughly 45 years old when he died. He stood about 5 feet 9 inches tall. Laboratory analysis showed that two-thirds of his protein probably came from fish and that he ate limited amounts of starchy foods. In his time, the man might have been considered healthy, but today we would call him a "survivor." He suffered from severe disease or malnutrition when he was about 5 years old. He had minor arthritis in his knees, elbows, lower back, and neck from a lifetime of daily, intense physical activity. As a young adult, he had damaged the nerves to his left arm. He'd also suffered a serious chest injury, a blow to the head, and an injury to his right arm and shoulder in his youth. And, as if that weren't enough, he had a stone spear point embedded in his hip. He had survived this injury, too.

Chatters knew that spear points like the one in the skeleton's hip were manufactured thousands of years ago, but he was still surprised when a radiocarbon date indicated that the man had died 9400 years ago. "Kennewick Man" was one of the oldest human skeletons ever found in the Americas.

Even more intriguing was that the skull did not look like other Native American skulls; some people even thought it might be European! It's not, but that suggestion titillated the media, which created sensationalist stories of how Europeans, rather than the ancestors of American Indians, first colonized the Americas. One group, the Asatru Folk Assembly, which says it practices an ancient Celtic religion, even claimed that Kennewick Man was their ancestor.

Who Controls Human Remains?

Many laws govern archaeology in the United States (we'll examine some of these in Chapter 13). One such law, the 1990 Native American Graves Protection and Repatriation Act (NAGPRA), provides for the repatriation of Native American human remains to their culturally affiliated tribes. Several tribes from the Kennewick area claimed the new find to be their ancestor and requested that the remains be turned over to them under this law. Kennewick Man had been discovered on lands administered by the U.S. Army Corps of Engineers, and that agency quickly agreed to halt all scientific studies and return the skeleton to the tribes.

But a group of eight archaeologists and biological anthropologists filed a lawsuit, arguing that handing over the remains would actually violate NAGPRA—because, they argued, the skeleton was not affiliated with the modern tribes, it might not be Native American, and doing so would violate the scientists' First Amendment rights.

Eventually, the Ninth District Circuit Court heard the case, which presented the judge with uncharted legal waters: Was this 9400-year-old man a Native American or not? And if so, was he culturally affiliated with the modern tribes who claimed him as an ancestor? These are tough questions, both legally and scientifically. And the answers could potentially forever change the direction of American archaeology.

Five years after the boys found the skull, the judge ruled that Kennewick Man was not Native American. And even if he were, the judge ruled, the bones could not be culturally affiliated with any modern tribe. In February 2004, the appeals court upheld the district court's ruling: Kennewick, the courts said, is not Native American.

What Does It Mean to You?

The Kennewick decision shows two facets of archaeology. It shows how much archaeologists can reconstruct about the past from remarkably limited material remains. We know what Kennewick Man ate, when he died, how old he was, what his life was like. But Kennewick Man also shows the difficult ethical issues that confront archaeology: What gives archaeologists the right to study the dead? Who owns the past, anyway? And who gets to decide? This is also what archaeologists do: They make difficult ethical and moral decisions about the past (and the present).

These sorts of questions should matter to you. Archaeologists often say that we study the past to help chart the future. But Kennewick Man points to a dilemma buried in this aphorism. By claiming the skeletal remains as their own, the Indian tribes asserted that scientists should conduct no studies. The tribes believed that they already knew their past and resented attempts by non-Indians to probe the remains of their ancestors. Although not all Native Americans agree with this position, many do, and this dispute underscores the important point that archaeology is not just about the dead; it is also about the living—you. How can we "study the past to create a better tomorrow" if scientific study is curtailed? Yet how can we pursue this laudable goal if the very act of conducting research offends the living descendants of the ancient people being studied? Archaeologists have to deal with these difficult ethical issues.

We don't expect every reader of this book to become a professional archaeologist. Many of you are probably taking this course to fulfill a distributional requirement, and because archaeology interests you. But throughout this text, we will demonstrate that *the past matters to you*. We will do this through text boxes labeled, appropriately enough, "What Does It Mean to Me?" Sometimes these ask you to confront ethical issues, such as the excavation of burials or the buying and selling of artifacts. And sometimes they show you how knowledge of the past is crucial to planning for the future. After we learn something more about the practice of archaeology, we will return to the case of Kennewick Man to explore its implications for the future of archaeology.

Meet Some Real Archaeologists

1

Christie's Images/CORBIS

"Excavation of the Sphinx" by Ernst Koerner, 1883. The Sphinx was built about 2500 BC and is the largest monolith statue in the world. It was not fully excavated until 1936.

Learning Objectives

After reading this chapter, you should be able to answer these questions:

- What makes an archaeologist an archaeologist?
- Why is the study of the past controversial?
- How was the rise of archaeology connected to the discovery of humanity's "deep" antiquity?
- Who were the antiquarians, and why include them in a history of archaeology?
- What trends have characterized archaeology over the last century?

Preview

THIS BOOK IS ABOUT what archaeologists want to learn, how they go about learning it, and what they do with that knowledge. These tasks require archaeologists to piece together a picture of the past from scraps of bone, rock, pottery, architecture, and other remains that are hundreds, thousands, or tens of thousands of years old. To further complicate this already difficult process, the very nature of archaeology carries with it some serious ethical dilemmas.

In this book, we will also look at some of the different perspectives that characterize today's archaeology. Sometimes these approaches coexist; sometimes they clash. As we discuss these various archaeological perspectives, you should keep a couple of things in mind: First, no archaeologist fits perfectly into any of these named categories, and second, there is more than one way to do good archaeology.

Introduction

Who is an archaeologist? Is it Indiana Jones, fighting Nazis and grabbing gold statues from curse-laden catacombs? Is it Lara Croft, battling all manner of beasts to retrieve some ancient treasure that holds the secret of time? Sydney Fox on *Relic Hunter*? Or was it Josh Bernstein or Hunter Ellis, on the History Channel program *Digging for the Truth*?

Of course, these are not real archaeologists. The media play up the physically thrilling side of archaeology, the mystery of discovery, and the potential threats. Archaeology is indeed exciting, even if we don't do our research with whips and guns, have a camera crew trailing behind us, or battle ancient beasts. Closer to the mark is *Time Team America*, the recent science reality series on PBS that sends archaeologists on a race against time to excavate historic sites around the nation. But even with urgency, we certainly don't just grab the good stuff and dash out of the temple. We work with notebooks and pencils, measuring tapes, calipers, graph paper, and some high-tech tools like laser transits and fluxgate magnetometers (more on those in later chapters). We document everything we find—*everything*—with a precision that we admit is often mind-numbing. But the results can be equally mind-blowing. We can extract blood from stone tools. We can determine the age of remains that are millions of years old. We can reconstruct ancient social and political organizations. We can tell if a person ate much plant food or meat based on their skeletal remains. This kind of work takes years of careful, precise analysis. But from it comes an understanding of a realm of humanity that otherwise would remain lost to us, the realm of the past. Although archaeological field research is exciting, the knowledge that comes from fieldwork provides the reason we do archaeology.

We think that the best way to introduce you to archaeology is through its history. Archaeology is a young field that has changed dramatically over the past century. As a relatively young discipline, archaeology is still experiencing some growing pains. What does not change, however, is that archaeology is about ancient objects—the **artifacts** we retrieve from sites are the primary source of our information. To borrow a phrase from archaeologist-philosopher Alison Wylie (University of Washington), archaeologists "think from things." The history of archaeology reflects a changing relationship to those things: from a fascination with objects themselves, to a concern with objects' ages, to what they tell us about the lives of ancient peoples, to a recognition of their power and ethical treatment.

Who Was the First Archaeologist?

Many historians ascribe the honor of "first archaeologist" to Nabonidus (who died in 538 BC), the last king of the neo-Babylonian Empire (see "Looking Closer: AD/BC/BP . . . Archaeology's Alphabet Soup"). A pious man, Nabonidus's zealous worship of his gods compelled him to rebuild the ruined temples of ancient Babylon and to search among their foundations for the inscriptions of earlier kings. We are indebted to the research of Nabonidus's scribes and the excavations by his subjects for much of our modern picture of the Babylonian Empire. Though nobody would call Nabonidus an "archaeologist" in the modern sense, he remains an important figure for one simple reason: *Nabonidus looked to the physical residues of antiquity—things—to answer questions about the past.* This may seem like a simple step, but it contrasted sharply with the beliefs of his contemporaries, who regarded tradition, legend, and myth as the only admissible clues to the past.

For archaeology to become an intellectual field, scholars first had to grasp the idea of "the past." Through the Middle Ages, Europeans recognized only a remote past, which they reified through myth and legend. This remote past was accessed largely through the Bible, as well as Roman and Greek texts. During the Renaissance (circa AD 1300 to 1700), however, scholars such as Francesco Petrarch

LOOKING CLOSER

AD/BC/BP . . . Archaeology's Alphabet Soup

In anything written by archaeologists, you'll encounter a blizzard of acronyms that refer to age. Let's clear the air with some concise definitions of the most common abbreviations:

BC ("before Christ"): For instance, 3200 BC; note that the letters follow the date.

AD ("anno Domini"): Meaning "in the year of the Lord," indicates a year that falls within the Christian era (that is, after the birth of Christ). Given the English translation of the phrase, archaeologists place the "AD" before the numerical age—we say the Norman Invasion occurred in "AD 1066" rather than "1066 AD." The earliest AD date is AD 1; there is no AD 0 because this year is denoted by 0 BC and double numbering is not allowed.

CE ("Common Era"): Basically the same as AD, except that it is intended to avoid religious connotations or privilege.

BCE ("Before Common Era"): The same as BC, but as with CE, it avoids the religious connotation.

BP ("Before Present"): Most archaeologists feel more comfortable avoiding the AD/BC split altogether, substituting a single "before present" age estimate (with AD 1950 arbitrarily selected as the zero point; we'll explain why in Chapter 6). By this convention, an artifact from, say, the Hastings battlefield would be dated 884 bp (AD 1950 – AD 1066 = 884 BP). We will primarily use this system in the text, or we will use the more colloquial "years ago."

(1304–1374) saw a stark difference between the present and the past. To Petrarch, the "father of humanism," the remote past was an ideal of perfection, and he looked to antiquity for moral philosophy. Of course, to imitate classical antiquity, one must first study it. This led to a rediscovery of the past by those in the Western European intellectual tradition, and Petrarch and his contemporaries began to collect ancient texts and to make systematic observations on archaeological monuments.

It remained for the fifteenth-century Italian scholar Ciriaco de' Pizzicolli (1391–1455) to establish the modern discipline of archaeology. Upon translating the Latin inscription on the triumphal arch of Trajan in Ancona, Italy, he was inspired to devote the remainder of his life to studying ancient monuments. His travels took him into Syria and Egypt, throughout the islands of the Aegean, and to Athens. When asked his business, Ciriaco is said to have replied, "Restoring the dead to life"—which today remains a fair definition of the everyday business of archaeology.

Archaeology Can Be Controversial

But not everyone wants the dead to be restored. Ever since Petrarch looked to ancient texts to provide moral philosophy (and probably even before), people have used the past to justify their actions in the present. For example, in 1572, Matthew Parker, Queen Elizabeth's archbishop of Canterbury, formed the Society (or College) of Antiquaries, devoted to the study of Anglo-Saxon law and writings. At the same time, Parliament upheld English Common Law, said to have been granted by William the Conqueror upon his conquest of England in 1066. English Common Law was based on the laws and customs of the Anglo-Saxons. Unfortunately, British kings had persistently claimed that their authority to rule—the "divine right of kings"—originated in their descent from the legendary King Arthur (who probably lived about AD 500, but no one really knows). King James therefore asserted that Common Law did not apply to the Anglican Church or the king because it originated with William rather than with Arthur. But the Society of Antiquaries used ancient documents to demonstrate that William the Conqueror did not actually create English Common Law—instead he had simply allowed it to stand and to be fused with his own ideas of justice. This was a problem for King James, for in English Common Law people had the right to rebel against an unlawful and unjust king. Seeing that meddling with the past had the potential for starting riots in the streets, King James ordered the dissolution of the Society of Antiquaries in 1614. The study of the past is often controversial.

But the die was cast, and the Society for Antiquaries (re-formed in 1707) was only the first of many British scholarly associations interested in the relevance of the past to the present. Of course, many private collectors were concerned only with filling their curio cabinets with *objets d'art*, but the overall goal of British antiquarianism was to map, record, and preserve national treasures. By the late

artifact Any movable object that has been used, modified, or manufactured by humans; artifacts include stone, bone, and metal tools; beads and other ornaments; pottery; artwork; religious and sacred items.

eighteenth century, members of Europe's leisure classes considered an interest in classical antiquities to be an important ingredient in the "cultivation of taste."

The Discovery of Deep Time

Archaeological research until the eighteenth century proceeded mostly within the tradition of Petrarch—that is, concerned primarily with clarifying the picture of classical civilizations of the Mediterranean. The eighteenth- and early nineteenth-century mind readily digested this lore because nothing in it challenged the Bible as an authoritative account of the origin of the world and humanity.

But a problem arose when very crude stone tools like that shown in Figure 1-1 were discovered in England and continental Europe. About 1836, a French customs official and naturalist, Jacques Boucher de Crèvecoeur de Perthes (1788–1868), found ancient axe heads in the gravels of the Somme River. Along with those tools, he also found the bones of long-extinct mammals. To Boucher de Perthes (as he is more commonly known), the implication was obvious: "In spite of their imperfection, these rude stones prove the existence of [very ancient] man as surely as a whole Louvre would have done."

FIGURE 1-1 Boucher de Perthes found Paleolithic handaxes like this in the Somme River gravels.

Few contemporaries believed him. Why? Some 200 years before Boucher de Perthes's discoveries, several scholars had figured the age of the earth as no more than about 6000 years. The most meticulous of these calculations were those of James Ussher (1581–1656), archbishop of Armagh, Primate of All Ireland, and vice-chancellor of Trinity College in Dublin. Using biblical genealogies and correlations of Mediterranean and Middle Eastern histories, Ussher concluded that creation began at sunset on Saturday, October 22, 4004 BC. His effort was so convincing that the date 4004 BC appeared as a marginal note in most Bibles published after AD 1700. (The precision of his date sounds silly today, but though Ussher was wrong, he followed very careful reasoning.)

This reckoning, of course, allowed no chance of an extensive human antiquity; there simply wasn't enough time. Therefore, the thinking went, Boucher de Perthes must be mistaken—his rude implements must be something other than human handiwork. Some suggested that the "tools" were really meteorites; others said they were produced by lightning, elves, or fairies. One seventeenth-century scholar suggested that the chipped flints were "generated in the sky by a fulgurous exhalation conglobed in a cloud by the circumposed humour," whatever that means.

But customs officials have never been known for their reserve, and Boucher de Perthes stuck to his guns. More finds were made in the French gravel pits at St. Acheul (near Abbeville), and similar discoveries turned up across the channel in southern England. The issue was finally resolved when the respected British paleontologist Hugh Falconer visited Abbeville to examine the disputed evidence. A procession of esteemed scholars followed Falconer's lead and declared their support in 1859; the idea that humans had lived with now-extinct animals in the far distant past was finally enshrined in Charles Lyell's 1863 book *The Geological Evidences of the Antiquity of Man*.

The year 1859 was a banner year in the history of human thought: Not only was the remote antiquity of humankind accepted by the scientific establishment, but Charles Darwin published his influential *On the Origin of Species*. Although Darwin mentioned humans only once in that book (on nearly the last page he wrote, "Much light will be thrown on the origin of man and his history"), he had suggested the process by which modern people could have arisen from ancient primate ancestors. In the beginning, though, Darwin's theory (which had to do with the transformation of species) was unconnected to the antiquity of humanity (which was a simple question of age).

Nonetheless, the discovery of deep time—the recognition that life was far more ancient than biblical scholars recognized and that human culture had evolved over time—opened the floodgates. British archaeology soon billowed out across two rather divergent courses. One direction became involved with the problems of remote geological time and the demonstration of long-term

LOOKING CLOSER

American Indian or Native American?

Some years ago, as Thomas was telling his son's third grade class what it's like to be an archaeologist, a small (but adamant) voice of protest came from the back of the room.

"How come you keep saying 'Indians'? Don't you know they want to be called 'Native Americans'?" a girl asked.

She had a good point. Many people are confused about these terms. In fact, our Native American colleagues tell us that people often correct them when they say "Indian," as if the term has become a dirty word.

Names are important because they are power; the people who name things are generally the people who control them. The word "Indian," of course, is a legacy from fifteenth-century European sailors, who mistakenly believed they'd landed in India. "Native American" arose among Indians in the 1960s and 1970s, during the civil rights movement. But many Indians point out the ambiguity in this term. Although your authors are not American Indians, both are native Americans (because we were born in the United States).

Most indigenous people of North America today simply accept the imprecision of today's terms and use American Indian, Canadian Native, First Nations, Native American (or Native Hawaiian), Indian, and Native interchangeably; we follow this lead.

Of greater concern to most Indian people is the tribal name. Many Navajo people, for instance, wish to be known as Diné (a traditional name meaning "The People"). When discussing particular tribes, we attempt to use the term preferred by the tribe in question.

human evolution. The other continued the tradition of Petrarch and focused on classical studies, particularly the archaeology of ancient Greece and Rome, a field now known as **classical archaeology**. This philosophical split has continued into modern times, although some signs suggest that these fields are coming back together.

Archaeology and Native Americans

Across the Atlantic, American archaeology faced its own vexing issues of time and cultural development. How, nineteenth-century scholars wondered, could regions such as the Valley of Mexico and Peru have hosted the civilizations of the Aztecs and the Incas while people in many other places—such as the North American West—seemed impoverished, even primitive? When did people first arrive in the New World? Where had these migrants come from, and how did they get here?

Speculation arose immediately. One idea held that Native Americans were one of the lost tribes of Israel. Another suggested that Indians came from Atlantis. Others said they were voyaging Egyptians, Vikings, Chinese, or Phoenicians.

Gradually, investigators came to recognize considerable continuities between the unknown prehistoric past and the Native American population of the historic period. As such knowledge accumulated, the profound differences between European and American archaeology became more apparent. While Europeans wrestled with their ancient flints—without apparent modern correlates—American scholars saw that living Native Americans were relevant to the interpretation of archaeological remains. In the crass terms of the time, many Europeans saw Native Americans as "living fossils," relics of times long past.

New World archaeology thus became inextricably wed to the study of living Native American people. Whereas Old World archaeologists began from a baseline of geological time or classical antiquity, their American counterparts developed within an anthropological understanding of Native Americans. The study of American Indians became an important domain of Western scholarship in its own right, and North American archaeology became linked with anthropology through their mutual interest in Native American culture (see "Looking Closer: American Indian or Native American?").

We must stress an important point here: As Europeans refined the archaeology of Europe, they were studying their own ancestors (Anglo-Saxons, Celts, Slavs, Franks, and so forth). But New World archaeology involved Euro-Americans digging up Native Americans' ancestors. This has led to some fundamental issues in the ethical treatment of archaeological remains in the New World compared to Europe. We will return to some of these issues in later chapters.

classical archaeology The branch of archaeology that studies the "classical" civilizations of the Mediterranean, such as Greece and Rome, and the Near East.

A Brief History of Archaeology

The history of archaeology is illustrated here by a few individuals whose lives and careers typify archaeology of their time. These individuals were by no means the only ones practicing archaeology over the last 200 years. However, their stories demonstrate stages in the growth of archaeology and show how goals and perspectives have changed. At their heart, though, lies an abiding interest in ancient objects as the source of information about the past.

Giovanni Battista Belzoni: Circus Strongman—and Early Archaeologist

The earliest archaeologists are like the crazy uncle that no one wants to talk about. In fact, we don't call them archaeologists at all, but refer to them as **antiquarians**, people who were fascinated by ancient objects but who rarely used those objects to reconstruct the past.

Giovanni Battista Belzoni (1778–1823) was one of the earliest antiquarians. Though Figure 1-2 suggests Belzoni was a native of the Near East, he was actually born in Italy. The son of a barber, Belzoni came to archaeology by a circuitous route. He left home at 16 to join a monastic order and study hydraulics in Rome. But with Napoleon's entry into Italy, Belzoni found his opportunities curtailed and he left, eventually settling in England in 1802. More than six and a half feet tall, with a broad, powerful torso, his physique earned him employment as a circus strongman. Billed as the "Patagonian Sampson," he traveled England and Ireland lifting heavy weights, carrying a dozen men nightly around the stage, and, using his engineering knowledge, creating stage shows featuring jets of flame and water. In 1812, Belzoni took his show on the road, leaving England to perform in Portugal, Spain, Sicily, and eventually the island of Malta.

© Topham/The Image Works

FIGURE 1-2 Giovanni Battista Belzoni, dressed in Middle Eastern garb, was an antiquarian from Italy.

In Malta, he met an agent of Mohammed Ali Pasha, Egypt's ruler. Though Mohammed Ali was Albanian, he rose to power in Egypt after a British-Ottoman force defeated Napoleon's army and left a power vacuum that Ali, a member of the conquering force, managed to fill. He immediately set about industrializing Egypt, especially the production of cotton that British textile factories were eager to buy. To do so, he needed to irrigate Egypt's deserts, and to do that, he needed someone, the agent told Belzoni, who knew hydraulics. Tired of his career as a circus performer, Belzoni saw his chance. In 1815, he traveled to Egypt and after a year demonstrated an oxen-driven waterwheel to the pasha. Though it worked splendidly, an unfortunate accident led the pasha to reject it and throw Belzoni out of the palace. Penniless, he was stuck in Egypt, with no prospects in sight.

But the past provided his future. Several European nations were looting Egypt of its antiquities to stock their museums, and the British consul in Egypt had promised associates at the British Museum that he would send antiquities for display. Many of these antiquities were huge statues, and the British consul saw how to put Belzoni's knowledge and strength to work. With Britain's financial backing, Belzoni soon became one of the best of the pillagers. His first task was to move the 8-ton head and torso of a statue of Ramesses II from Thebes. This effort required not only his great physical strength but also his engineering ingenuity, for the statue fragment had to be placed on a sledge and rolled, inch by inch, for two weeks to the Nile River, where it was loaded on a boat and floated north. It also required considerable negotiating skills, for Belzoni had to convince local leaders to provide him with the workmen needed for the effort. Sometimes this required bribery, and sometimes he simply picked up an obstinate tribal leader and "shook him like a rat." The statue of Ramesses II is still on display at the British Museum.

In only three years, Belzoni "recovered" numerous statues, mummies, and carvings. He was the first European to enter the temple at Abu Simbel, and the first European to enter the pyramids on the Giza plateau outside Cairo. He removed the 6-ton granite obelisk from Philae, and discovered five tombs in the Valley of the Kings (where 100 years later the tomb of King Tutankhamen would be found). It was Belzoni's spoils, in fact, that inspired Percy Bysshe Shelley's famous poem "Ozymandias."

Looters from various countries vied for the spoils (the French took the obelisk from Belzoni at gunpoint). Belzoni soon tired of the fighting and, in 1819, he returned to England, where he received considerable acclaim for his accomplishments (and booty). An inveterate wanderer, he left again in 1823, to seek the origin of the Nile, but was felled by dysentery, and died in Benin.

Why do we remember Belzoni, and not his rivals in what is now known as "the rape of the Nile"? Belzoni's methods were destructive enough to make modern archaeologists cringe. Once, crawling nearly naked through a mummy-filled cave, Belzoni tried to sit, but "when my weight bore on the body of an Egyptian, it crushed it like a band-box. . . . I sank altogether among the broken mummies, with a crash of bones, rags, and wooden cases." Valuable information was lost by such carelessness. And no archaeologist today would so thoughtlessly remove another country's cultural heritage. But Belzoni stands out because he bothered to take notes and to make illustrations and observations of the places he visited. To be sure, the antiquities were first on his mind, but he, and some other antiquarians, were also interested in what those things had to tell us. There was no professional archaeology at the time; there were no excavation manuals, no national laws protecting antiquities, and no idea that crucial knowledge was being lost. Nonetheless, it is from such humble (and humiliating) beginnings that the science of archaeology arose.

Courtesy National Museum of Denmark

FIGURE 1-3 Jens Jacob Asmussen Worsaae, the first professional archaeologist.

Jens Jacob Asmussen Worsaae: The First Professional Archaeologist

Many of the early antiquarians felt no shame in trashing ordinary mummies or less spectacular sites because they knew little of the potential for ancient objects to tell us something about the past. These men thought they already knew the past, or they simply didn't care. They thought *about* things, but they didn't think *from* things. This began to change in the mid-nineteenth century.

With hindsight, we can see that the antiquarians' role in the development of archaeology was to create collections of objects from which patterns eventually emerged, patterns that suggested ancient cultures were not static, but had changed over time. Trying to get a handle on the chronology of these changes, then, was the first order of business, and this is what the world's first professional archaeologist set out to do.

Jens J. A. Worsaae (1821–1885) was a toddler when Belzoni passed away (see Figure 1-3). Born in Denmark, he was fascinated by artifacts as a child, and even dug into a few mounds and barrows. Worsaae intended to study law, but before he was 20, he was volunteering for Christian Thomsen (1788–1865), who was organizing the archaeological collections at what is now the National Museum of Denmark (Thomsen had devised the now well-known typological scheme of the Stone, Bronze, and Iron Ages). Thus, Worsaae was the first person to receive training, albeit informal, in archaeology. Through connections, Worsaae received financial support from the king of Denmark to write his first book, *Primeval Antiquities of Denmark*, published in 1843, when he was only 22. Later he was appointed Denmark's first inspector for the Conservation of Antiquarian Monuments and, at age 34, became the first professor of archaeology at the University of Copenhagen.

We recognize Worsaae as the first archaeologist because, unlike antiquarians, who excavated to find things, Worsaae *excavated to answer questions*. He was interested in what artifacts tell us about the lives of ancient people; Worsaae was *thinking from things*. Moreover, he was not content with studying artifacts farmers or pillagers found. He argued that "antiquities have a value with reference to the spot in which they are found" and that it was "necessary to examine and compare with care the places in which antiquities are usually found." In other words, he knew that an artifact's archaeological *context* was as important as the artifact itself. (We'll return to the idea of context in Chapter 4.)

Here's an example. Large piles of shells once lay all along the Danish shore, and during the mid-nineteenth century some geologists argued that wave action created these piles. But Worsaae's excavations demonstrated that these were **middens**, trash heaps people created. In one of his notebooks, he wrote that the "heaps were the places where the people of the neighborhood, in that far-off time, took their meals, as witness, for example, the **potsherds**, charcoal, bones of animals, and stone implements." He also excavated sites to test Thomsen's Three -Age system, showing that the Stone, Bronze, and Iron Ages were real chronological phases, as Thomsen had hypothesized. In sum, Worsaae demonstrated two important attributes of an archaeologist: He excavated to answer questions, not just to find things; and he knew that an artifact's context was as important as the artifact itself.

antiquarians Originally, someone who studied antiquities (that is, ancient objects) largely for the sake of the objects themselves, not to understand the people or culture that produced them.

midden Refuse deposit resulting from human activities, generally consisting of sediment; food remains such as charred seeds, animal bone, and shell; and discarded artifacts.

potsherd Fragment of pottery.

Alfred Vincent Kidder: Founder of Anthropological Archaeology

Professional archaeology developed a bit later across the Atlantic, and one of its early figures was Alfred Vincent Kidder (1885–1963), shown in Figure 1-4. Kidder was born in Michigan, and his father, a mining engineer, made sure that his son received the best education available. First enrolled in a private school in Cambridge, Massachusetts, Kidder then attended the prestigious La Villa in Ouchy, Switzerland, and then registered at Harvard. Kidder joined an archaeological expedition to northeastern Arizona, exploring territory then largely unknown to the Anglo world. The southwestern adventure sealed his fate.

When Kidder returned to Harvard, he enrolled in the anthropology program and, in 1914, was awarded the sixth American PhD specializing in archaeology—and the first with a focus on North America. Kidder's dissertation examined prehistoric Southwestern ceramics, assessing their value in reconstructing culture history. Relying on scientific procedures, Kidder demonstrated ways of deciphering meaning from one of archaeology's most ubiquitous items, the potsherd. Urging accurate description of ceramic decoration, he explained how such apparent minutiae could help determine cultural relationships among various prehistoric groups. Kidder argued that only through controlled excavation and analysis could researchers draw inferences about such anthropological subjects as acculturation, social organizations, and prehistoric religious customs.

In 1915, the Department of Archaeology at the Phillips Academy in Andover, Massachusetts, was seeking a site of sufficient merit to justify a multiyear archaeological project. Largely because of his anthropological training, Kidder was selected to direct the excavations. After evaluating the possibilities, he decided on Pecos Pueblo, a massive prehistoric and historic period ruin located southeast of Santa Fe, New Mexico. Kidder was impressed by the great diversity of potsherds scattered about the ruins and felt certain that Pecos contained enough stratified debris to span several centuries. He dug at Pecos for ten summers.

The Pecos excavations were consequential for several reasons. Kidder followed and separated particular strata, distinctive layers of earth, to construct a cultural chronology. He also went beyond the pottery to make sense of the artifact and architectural styles preserved at Pecos. His intensive artifact analysis, done before the advent of radiocarbon dating or tree-ring chronology (methods that we discuss in Chapter 5), established the framework of southwestern prehistory, which remains intact today.

After joining the Carnegie Institution of Washington, DC, as director of the Division of Historical Research, Kidder launched an ambitious archaeological program to probe the Maya ruins of Central America. He directed the Carnegie's Maya campaigns for two decades, arguing that a true understanding of Maya culture would require a broad plan of action with many interrelated areas of research. Relegating himself to the role of administrator, Kidder amassed a staff of qualified scientists with the broadest possible scope of interests. His plan was a sea change in archaeological research, enlarging traditional archaeological objectives to embrace the wider realms of anthropology and allied disciplines. Under Kidder's direction, the Carnegie program supported research by ethnographers, botanists, geographers, physical anthropologists, geologists, meteorologists, and, of course, archaeologists. With the help of Charles Lindbergh, Kidder even employed aerial reconnaissance to discover new ruins and map the boundaries of various types of vegetation. Today, the interdisciplinary complexion of archaeology is a fact of life, but when Kidder proposed the concept in the 1920s, it was revolutionary.

Through his research in the Maya region and in the American Southwest, Kidder helped shift archaeology toward more properly anthropological purposes. Kidder maintained that archaeology should be viewed as "that branch of anthropology which deals with prehistoric peoples," and that archaeologists were merely a "mouldier variety of anthropologist." Although archaeologists continue to immerse themselves in the nuances of potsherd detail and architectural specifics, the ultimate objective of archaeology is to move from *things* to *people*.

FIGURE 1-4 Alfred V. Kidder (right), conducting a survey with Jesse Nusbaum at Mesa Verde, Colorado, in 1907.

Gertrude Caton-Thompson: Looking beyond Tombs

Born in England to a wealthy family, Gertrude Caton-Thompson (1888–1985) had the physical and intellectual grit required in archaeology (see Figure 1-5). Several trips to Egypt, Greece, Palestine, and Malta as a youth generated a deep interest in prehistory, but initially she led the sort of carefree existence typical of the wealthy around the turn of the century. This changed during World War I, when she volunteered for various offices and eventually attended the Paris peace talks in 1919 as a personal assistant. Here she met T. E. Lawrence ("Lawrence of Arabia"), who had done some archaeology, as well as Gertrude Bell, an archaeologist and student of Arabia (she helped found the Baghdad Museum and create the modern national borders of Iraq). Her encounter with Lawrence and Bell encouraged Caton-Thompson to return to her childhood passion, and she began studying archaeology formally in 1921. Recognizing, like Kidder, that archaeology requires a knowledge of many fields, she studied geology, zoology, paleontology, Arabic, and, of course, anthropology.

The Principal and Fellows, Newnham College, Cambridge

FIGURE 1-5 Gertrude Caton-Thompson, one of the pioneers of modern excavation in Egypt.

A quick learner, she soon found herself in Egypt working with Sir Flinders Petrie, an important figure in archaeology. Working in remote parts of Egypt or other parts of Africa was and still is difficult, but Caton-Thompson was up to the task. On one trip, she slept in an empty stone tomb—apparently with two cobras—with a revolver under her pillow for protection against hyenas. On another, she had to hike across the desert one night to find help for a crew that was running out of water. And in southern Africa, she tangled with a leopard on the edge of a cliff.

More importantly, she advanced archaeology intellectually. At the time, most archaeologists in Egypt focused their attention on tombs and temples, but Caton-Thompson thought that they were missing something by not excavating settlements. In the 1920s, she became the first archaeologist to excavate a village site in Egypt, using the same careful methods that she had learned under Petrie. A few years later, she undertook a survey of the northern Faiyum Desert in Egypt. This was a groundbreaking project because it was interdisciplinary: Caton-Thompson worked with a geologist to reconstruct the sequence of settlements and their relationships to ancient lake levels preserved in sediments and landforms.

Caton-Thompson continued to work in Egypt, as well as elsewhere, but her work in Zimbabwe (then Southern Rhodesia) shows an important element of modern archaeology. For decades, the colonial powers had known of the massive ruins of a site known as Great Zimbabwe (from which the modern nation took its name after independence). Sitting atop a hill, the site contains massive stone walls and buildings (see Figure 1-6). Several investigators (whose methods were those of the worst of the antiquarians) argued that the site was Ophir (the location of King Solomon's mines) or the palace of the Queen of Sheba. None wanted to believe that indigenous African people were capable of creating such a structure. They asserted that the Phoenicians had built the site, and used its alleged biblical connections to justify European colonization and control of southern Africa.

Robert Harding World Imagery/Passage/Corbis

FIGURE 1-6 Great Zimbabwe, a medieval-age ruin in Zimbabwe, Africa. Caton-Thompson disproved hypotheses that European or Asian peoples built it.

In 1929, the British government invited Caton-Thompson to resolve the controversy. Reasoning that previous efforts failed because they had ignored the site's **stratigraphy** (we'll discuss this concept in Chapter 6), she approached the problem with two straightforward questions: How old is the site, and was it built by Africans? Caton-Thompson carefully excavated deep trenches to bedrock in several places, and even tunneled under a massive solid stone conical tower. Studying glass trade beads, she eventually demonstrated that the site had been inhabited in the thirteenth and fourteenth centuries—far too late for its alleged biblical associations. She also found that the pottery and other implements, as well as the architecture, were little different from those of later known African peoples. By thinking from things, Caton-Thompson concluded that Great Zimbabwe was African in origin. She took considerable flak for this conclusion because it did not support colonial rule of southern Africa. The past is often used to justify the present—and archaeologists are often called upon to judge these claims. This is one of the realities of archaeology that we will touch upon in later chapters.

Archaeology at Mid-Twentieth Century

Archaeology began as a pastime of the rich, but developed into a professional scientific discipline. Most professional archaeologists were affiliated with major museums and universities; others joined the private sector, working to protect and conserve America's cultural heritage. This institutional support not only encouraged a sense of professionalism and fostered public funding, but also mandated that public repositories care for the archaeological artifacts recovered. Twentieth-century archaeologists were not collectors of personal treasure: All finds belonged in the public domain, available for exhibit and study.

We can also see a distinct progression toward specialization in our target archaeologists. Scholars accumulated knowledge of the past so rapidly that by the early twentieth century, archaeologists specialized in particular regions. It is difficult today to find someone like Caton-Thompson doing seminal work in Egypt while simultaneously tackling challenging issues in southern Africa. Possibly the greatest change, however, has been the quality of archaeologists' training. Worsaae was more or less self-taught, but Kidder and Caton-Thompson received more formal training, much of it hands-on. American archaeologists were also well versed in the broader field of anthropology, although this was less true for European archaeologists.

Archaeologists by mid-century wanted to transcend mere cultural chronology, but classifying artifacts and sorting out their patterns in space and time left little opportunity for more anthropological objectives, such as reconstructing society. By the middle of the twentieth century, most archaeologists were practicing what is called **culture history**, documenting how material culture changed over time and space. Their main goal was to track the migrations and development of particular prehistoric cultures. Some archaeologists tried to explain changes by relating them to climatic change, for example, or to vague ideas about cultural evolution. But for the most part, archaeologists attributed differences in artifact frequencies between sites to the presence of different cultures or ideas. Changes in artifact frequencies over time, such as the types of pottery found in different layers of earth at a site, were attributed to the diffusion of ideas from other cultures or the replacement of one culture by another. Worsaae, for example, thought that the Stone, Bronze, and Iron Ages marked the diffusion of new ideas or the migration of new people into Denmark, rather than a technological evolutionary sequence.

By the 1950s, the basic prehistory of many world regions was sufficiently well understood that some archaeologists could move beyond simple documentation to more in-depth reconstructions of prehistory. Worsaae wanted to paint a picture of life alongside the growing shell middens of Denmark. Caton-Thompson excavated village sites because she knew that she could not draw a complete picture of life in ancient Egypt by excavating tombs alone. But only later, as methods and basic cultural chronologies developed, could archaeologists move on to more anthropological goals and seek explanations for the prehistory they were reconstructing.

H. Marie Wormington: Ancient Man in North America

Born in Denver, Colorado, H. Marie Wormington (1914–1994) was part of the generation that began to take archaeology further (see Figure 1-7). Like many archaeologists before her, she had originally intended to

FIGURE 1-7 Marie Wormington, a female pioneer in American archaeology.

pursue another career—zoology or medicine, in her case. But while taking an archaeology class at the University of Denver, she discovered her passion. "Once I discovered there was such a thing as archaeology," she later said, "I just never looked back." Wormington continued her education in France, working on a cave excavation in the Dordogne in 1935, and then joined the staff at what is now the Denver Museum of History and Science. She left temporarily to obtain her doctorate from Radcliffe, but remained employed at the museum until 1968, when she left to occupy several teaching positions. She was among the first American anthropologists to enter the former Soviet Union, as well as the People's Republic of China.

This vignette exposes some of archaeology's dirty laundry. The many women involved in the earliest days of archaeology faced a difficult time and hard decisions because women were often considered unsuited for the rigors of archaeology. Some, such as Caton-Thompson, sacrificed marriage and family. Marie Wormington once had to sit in the corridor because, as a woman, she was prohibited from entering the lecture hall at Harvard. She signed her work "H. M. Wormington," concealing her gender because the director of the Denver museum feared that no one would read a book on archaeology by a woman. Into the late 1960s, many male archaeologists refused to take women on their field crews.

Times have changed—fully half of the several thousand archaeologists in the United States today are female—but in the 1930s, women like Marie Wormington were in the vanguard. She was only the second woman admitted to study in Harvard's anthropology department, and was the first female president of the Society for American Archaeology. Though remembered as eminently polite and diplomatic, she was no shrinking violet: She once told the dangerous Nicaraguan dictator Anastasio Somoza Debayle that a site in Nicaragua was not as old as he hoped.

Wormington worked in many places and on various research topics, but her first love was "paleoindian" archaeology—the archaeology of pre-8000-year-old North America. In 1939, at the age of 25, she published *Ancient Man in North America*, which went through four editions, the last published in 1957. These editions demonstrate how archaeology matured over time. In 1939, the American scientific community was only able to estimate how long people had lived in the New World; by 1957, radiocarbon dating gave certainty to those estimates. The last edition contains discussions of genetic data (blood typing), geology, skeletal data, and comparisons to archaeological material in South America and Siberia. Importantly, Wormington wrote *Ancient Man* (as well as *Prehistoric Indians of the Southwest*, 1947) for the general public, anticipating the present-day concern that the results of archaeology be accessible to the public that supports the field.

The various editions of *Ancient Man* chronicle not only the astonishing growth in the amount of information available, but also the progress in interpreting archaeological data in terms of technology, subsistence, migratory routes, and age. The book evolved from a straightforward catalog of sites and finds to a discussion of what those finds *mean* in terms of the lives of the ancient people who left them behind. That is, the various editions of *Ancient Man* demonstrate the shift from a concern with *things* to a concern with *thinking from things*. "Artifacts themselves are not important," Wormington once said, "it's the information they can provide about cultures and about people." She closed *Ancient Man in North America* with a clear statement of why modern archaeology abandoned the misguided confidence of the antiquarians in favor of a more rigorous concern for methods and techniques:

> To the casual observer the growing list of unanswered questions regarding the ancient inhabitants of North America may seem appalling; actually it should be regarded as encouraging. With a new subject the tendency is to oversimplify through lack of knowledge. Only with increased knowledge comes the realization of the complexity of the problem, for with each solution which is reached new fields are opened and new perplexities arise. To find an answer one must first have sufficient knowledge to formulate the question.

As the knowledge of prehistory accumulated, the methods and objectives of archaeology changed, as archaeologists who were trained in the 1960s demonstrated.

Lewis R. Binford: Archaeology's Angry Young Man

If archaeology has ever had an "angry young man," it was Lewis R. Binford (1931–2011; see Figure 1-8). After a period of military service, Binford enrolled in 1954 at the University of North Carolina, wanting to become an ethnographer. But by the time he entered the graduate program at the University of Michigan, Binford was a confirmed archaeologist.

The 1960s were a watershed time for American college campuses. Baby-boom demographics and the GI Bill inflated enrollments. Campuses became the focal point for the waves of social and political confrontation that roiled the nation. Clashes over the war in Vietnam and civil rights created a revolutionary atmosphere. Archaeology was firmly embedded in this intellectual climate. Everyone, including archaeologists, braced for the change.

stratigraphy A site's physical structure produced by the deposition of geological and/or cultural sediments into layers, or strata.

culture history The kind of archaeology practiced mainly in the early to mid-twentieth century; it "explains" differences or changes over time in artifact frequencies by positing the diffusion of ideas between neighboring cultures or the migration of a people who had different mental templates for artifact styles.

Lewis R. Binford, photo by Grant Spearman

FIGURE 1-8 Lewis R. Binford (right) at Tulugak Lake in Alaska in 1999 with a Nunamiut friend, Johnny Rulland. Binford helped develop the "new archaeology" of the 1960s.

Binford thrived in this cultural climate. He could lecture, sometimes for hours, with the force and enthusiasm of an old-time southern preacher, and he rapidly assumed the role of archaeological messiah. His students became disciples spreading the word: As the study of cultural change, archaeology has obvious relevance to modern problems. To fulfill this role, Binford argued, archaeology must transcend potsherds and spear points to address larger issues, such as cultural evolution, ecology, and social organization. Archaeology must take full advantage of modern technology by using scientific methods and sophisticated, quantitative techniques. Archaeology must study the remaining preindustrial peoples to scrutinize firsthand the operation of disappearing cultural adaptations. And archaeology must be concerned with its methods for reconstructing the past. In the 1960s, this became known as the **new archaeology** (see "In His Own Words: The Challenge of Archaeology" by Lewis R. Binford). Archaeology had, in Marie Wormington's words, sufficient knowledge to start asking more complex and difficult questions.

The new archaeology (a now-antiquated term for us all, and especially to today's student) emphasized a new way of studying the past and a new agenda for doing archaeology. The master plan was set forth in a series of articles published through the 1960s and early 1970s, many by Binford and his students.

Binford asked why archaeology had contributed so little to general anthropological theory. His answer was that archaeologists interpreted material culture too simplistically. He believed archaeologists lavished too much attention on artifacts as passive traits that "blend," "influence," or "stimulate" one another. Binford proposed that artifacts be examined in their cultural contexts and interpreted instead as reflections of technology, society, and belief systems. That is, Binford underscored the need to change from thinking *about* things to thinking *from* things.

Binford also emphasized the importance of precise, unambiguous scientific methods. Archaeologists, he argued, must stop waiting for artifacts to speak up. They must formulate hypotheses and test these on the remains of the past. Binford argued that, because archaeologists always work from samples, they should acquire data that make the samples amenable to statistical analysis. He urged archaeologists to stretch their horizons beyond the individual site to the scale of the region; in this way, they could reconstruct an entire cultural system (as we discuss in Chapter 3). Such regional samples must be generated from research designs based on the principles of probability sampling. Random sampling is commonplace in other social sciences, and Binford insisted that archaeologists apply these scientific procedures to their own research problems.

Binford's ideas about methodology fostered projects designed to demonstrate how this approach can help comprehend cultural processes. Intricate statistical techniques were applied to a variety of subjects, from the nature of Mousterian (some 150,000 years old) stone tools to the archaeology of historic forts. He proposed new ideas, rooted in the field of human ecology, to explain the origins of plant domestication. These embroiled Binford in factual, substantive debate, and so his goals and methods gained credibility among field archaeologists because he was arguing about specifics, not just theory. Binford also conducted his own ethnographic fieldwork among the Nunamiut Eskimo, the Navajo, and the Australian Aborigines, testing the utility of archaeological concepts and methods on the trash of living peoples.

Binford and his students set off a firestorm that quickly spread throughout the archaeological community. A 1970s generation of graduate students and young professionals was greeted with the inquisition, "Are you a new archaeologist, an old archaeologist, or what? Make up your mind!"

The "new archaeology" of the 1960s has today evolved into so-called processual archaeology. In subsequent chapters, we explore the tenets of this position and also examine how yet another wave of archaeological criticism—postprocessual archaeology—finds fault with Binford's approach and suggests some alternative directions.

Archaeology in the Twenty-First Century

So, what about today? Who is a mover and a shaker of the twenty-first century?

Perhaps in another 50 years or so, hindsight will suggest one person who truly captures the spirit of these times. But right now, we do not detect a single, defining trend that dominates archaeology; instead, the discipline has several branches, each growing and intersecting with the others in interesting ways.

Many of these diverse approaches result from new techniques and perspectives; others arise from the nature of employment in archaeology. Archaeologists

IN HIS OWN WORDS

The Challenge of Archaeology

by Lewis R. Binford

As I was riding on the bus not long ago, an elderly gentleman asked me what I did. I told him I was an archaeologist. He replied: "That must be wonderful, for the only thing you have to be to succeed is lucky." It took some time to convince him that his view of archaeology was not quite mine. He had the idea that the archaeologist "digs up the past," that the successful archaeologist is one who discovers something not seen before, that all archaeologists spend their lives running about trying to make discoveries of this kind. This is a conception of science perhaps appropriate to the nineteenth century, but, at least in the terms in which I myself view archaeology, it does not describe the nature of archaeology as it is practiced today. I believe archaeologists are more than simply discoverers. . . .

Archaeology cannot grow without striking a balance between theoretical and practical concerns. Archaeologists need to be continuously self-critical; that is why the field is such a lively one and why archaeologists are forever arguing among themselves about who is right on certain issues. Self-criticism leads to change, but is itself a challenge—one which archaeology perhaps shares only with paleontology and a few other fields whose ultimate concern is making inferences about the past on the basis of contemporary things. So archaeology is not a field that can study the past directly, nor can it be one that merely involves discovery, as the man on the bus suggested. On the contrary, it is a field wholly dependent upon inference to the past from things found in the contemporary world. Archaeological data, unfortunately, do not carry self-evident meanings. How much easier our work would be if they did!

still work in museums and universities, but most today are employed by federal agencies and especially private "cultural resource management" firms (companies that arose in response to federal legislation passed in the 1960s, designed to protect the nation's archaeological resources—more about these in Chapter 13). Before the 1970s, most American archaeologists were white and male; today the archaeological profession comprises equal numbers of men and women, and more minorities, including Native Americans, are actively involved in the field. Throughout these pages, we will meet some archaeologists who exemplify those trends (in boxes labeled "Profile of an Archaeologist"). For now, we'll present just one more archaeologist as a way to introduce modern archaeology.

FIGURE 1-9 Kathleen Deagan, a contemporary archaeologist, excavating at St. Augustine, Florida.

Kathleen A. Deagan: Archaeology Comes of Age

Kathleen Deagan (b. 1948) helped fulfill Binford's call for a better archaeology (see Figure 1-9). Deagan received her doctorate in anthropology from the University of Florida in 1974. Still a curator at the Florida Museum of Natural History, she specializes in Spanish colonial studies. She has pushed the frontiers of historical archaeology (see Chapter 12), especially the archaeological investigation of disenfranchised groups, and remains actively involved in bringing archaeology to the public. She is concerned with the people and culture behind the artifact and with explaining the social and cultural behaviors that she reconstructs from archaeology—that is, she thinks from things.

Deagan is perhaps best known for her long-term excavations at St. Augustine (Florida). Continuously occupied since its founding by Pedro Menéndez in 1565, St. Augustine is the oldest European enclave in the United States (see "In Her Own Words: The Potential of Historical Archaeology" by Kathleen Deagan).

new archaeology An approach to archaeology that arose in the 1960s, emphasizing the understanding of underlying cultural processes and the use of the scientific method; today's version of the "new archaeology" is sometimes called processual archaeology.

IN HER OWN WORDS

The Potential of Historical Archaeology

by Kathleen Deagan

From its emergence as a recognized area of research in the 1930s, historical archaeology has advanced from providing supplemental data for other disciplines, through an anthropological tool for the reconstruction of past lifeways, to a means of discovering predictable relationships between human adaptive strategies, ideology, and patterned variability in the archaeological record.

Because it can compare written accounts about what people said they did, what observers said people did, and what the archaeological record said people did, historical archaeology can make contributions not possible through any other discipline. Inconsistencies and inaccuracies in the written records may be detected and ultimately predicted. Insights into conditions provided by such written sources may be compared to the more objective archaeological record of actual conditions in the past in order to provide insight into cognitive processes.

The simultaneous access to varied sources of information allows the historical archaeologist to match the archaeological patterning of a given site against the documented social, economic, and ideological attributes of the same site to arrive at a better understanding of how the archaeological record reflects human behavior.

The unique potential of historical archaeology lies not only in its ability to answer questions of archaeological and anthropological interest, but also in its ability to provide historical data not available through documentation or any other source. Correcting the inadequate treatment of disenfranchised groups in America's past, excluded from historical sources because of race, religion, isolation, or poverty, is an important function of contemporary historical archaeology and one that cannot be ignored.

Deagan addressed the processes and results of Spanish-Indian intermarriage and descent, a topic dear to the hearts of many anthropologists and ethnohistorians. The fact that mestizos, people of Spanish-Indian descent, constitute nearly the entire population of Latin America brought this issue to the forefront long ago. Similar processes took place in Spanish Florida, but the Hispanic occupation left no apparent mestizo population in La Florida, what Deagan called "America's first melting pot." Accordingly, when she began her doctoral research, we knew virtually nothing about early race relations in North America.

Deagan hypothesized how the mestizo population fit into this colonial setting. Given the nature of the unfortunate interactions that characterized eighteenth-century Florida, she expected the burdens of acculturation to have fallen most heavily on the Indian women living in Spanish or mestizo households. Because no mestizo people survive here, the tests for her hypothesis were necessarily archaeological. If her hypothesis is true, then acculturation should affect mostly the Native American women's activities visible in archaeological sites (food preparation techniques, equipment, household activities, basic food resources, child-related activities, and primarily female crafts such as pottery manufacture). Conversely, male-related activities (house construction technology and design, military and political affairs, and hunting weapons) should show less evidence of Spanish infusion.

To explore these processes, Deagan began a series of archaeological field schools at St. Augustine in 1973. This long-term, diversified enterprise excavated sites whose inhabitants represented a broad range of incomes, occupations, and ethnic affiliations. Hundreds of students have learned their first archaeology at St. Augustine, where a saloon long sported a placard celebrating the years of "Digging with Deagan."

It was not long before her explorations into Hispanic–Native American interactions led Deagan to the Caribbean, where she headed interdisciplinary excavations at Puerto Real, the fourth-oldest European New World city (established in 1503). As she steadily moved back in time, Deagan's research eventually led her literally to the doorstep of Christopher Columbus.

In northern Haiti, Deagan discovered La Navidad, the earliest well-documented point of contact between Spanish and Native American people. On Christmas Eve, 1492—following two nights of partying with local Taino Arawak Indians—Columbus's flagship *Santa Maria* ran aground. He abandoned ship, moved to the *Nina*, and appealed to the local Native Americans for help. This disaster left the explorers one boat short. When Columbus sailed home with his world-shattering news, he left 39 unfortunate compatriots behind, protected by a small stockade built from the timbers of the wrecked *Santa Maria*. Returning a year later, Columbus found the settlement burned, his men killed and mutilated.

Columbus soon established the more permanent settlements of La Isabela and Puerto Real—sites of the first sustained contact between Europeans and Native Americans—and Deagan has also conducted important field excavations there. With a population of nearly

RAPID REVIEW

Key Elements of Modern Archaeology

- Linked to the larger field of anthropology; interested in the people behind the artifacts
- Multidisciplinary, incorporating specialties of the natural and physical sciences
- Uses scientific methods, but concerned with communicating results to the public
- Concerned with ethics, especially the relationship between archaeology and the descendants of those whose past is studied

1500 people, La Isabela was home to soldiers, priests, stonecutters, masons, carpenters, and nobles. Although this first Columbian town lasted only four years, several critical events took place here: the first intentional introduction of European plants and animals; the first expedition into the interior; and the first Hispanic installation of urban necessities, such as canals, mills, roads, gardens, plazas, ports, ramparts, and hospitals.

The biological aftermath of the Columbian exchange soon overtook La Isabela. Europeans and Native Americans alike suffered from dietary deficiencies, an excessive workload, and contagious disease. Influenza struck during the first week, affecting one-third of the population. When Columbus ordered the settlement abandoned in 1496, fewer than 300 inhabitants were left. Deagan extended her research to investigate daily life in the initial colonial period, including the ways in which European colonists coped with their new and largely unknown New World environment.

Beyond new directions in historical archaeology, Deagan's research demonstrates the degree to which contemporary archaeology is played out in the public arena. Her work creates headlines, and she was featured in consecutive years in *National Geographic* magazine. She has also published, with Venezuelan archaeologist José María Cruxent, two books on La Isabela—one a data-laden professional monograph, the other a readable volume for the public. Deagan knows that archaeologists cannot afford to isolate themselves in ivory towers or archaeology labs. One way or another—whether through federal grants, state-supported projects, tax laws, or private benefaction—archaeology depends on public support for its livelihood. Consequently, it owes something back to that public.

Decades ago, Margaret Mead (1901–1978), one of the nation's first anthropologists, recognized the importance of taking the work of anthropologists to the public. Mead kept anthropology alive in the print and electronic media. Today, archaeology enjoys unprecedented press coverage, and archaeologists like Deagan know that without such publicity, archaeology has no future.

Conclusion: Archaeology's Future

Archaeology does indeed have a future, however, and it's a lively and vibrant one. Archaeology enjoys enormous public interest, as shown by the popularity of places such as Mesa Verde National Park, expanding television programming, and popular college courses. This level of public support suggests that more, not less, archaeology will be needed in the future.

Archaeology has evolved from a pastime of the wealthy to an established scientific discipline. But with these changes has come the realization that studying the human past raises numerous ethical issues. Nobody can practice archaeology in a political or cultural vacuum. We argue that archaeology remains a science that insists on high standards of evidence and must continue to examine how we make inferences from evidence. Science in this sense is self-correcting, making it essential to most inquiry (including archaeology). But we also recognize that scientific inquiry is susceptible to cultural biases. We think that archaeologists must continue to work closely with indigenous peoples and descendant communities, attempting to recognize and correct cultural biases (as in Figure 1-10, which shows a working example of this compromise). We'll return to this matter in the text's final chapter.

David Hurst Thomas

FIGURE 1-10 Archaeology today confronts both scientific and ethical challenges, yet there are many signs that archaeology need not be antagonistic to indigenous peoples. Here, Bryceson Pinnecoose (Hopi/Cheyenne, on right) and Ron Winters use a power sifter to screen archaeological deposits at Mission San Marcos, New Mexico.

Summary

- What makes an archaeologist an archaeologist?
  - Archaeologists reconstruct and explain the past by "thinking from things," using their analyses of material remains as the basis for knowledge of the past.
- Why is the study of the past controversial?
  - People typically use their vision of the past to justify their actions in the present. The assumption that Europeans built Great Zimbabwe justified Europeans' taking southern Africa. Archaeologists can (and should) question such mistaken beliefs.
  - New World prehistory is largely studied by people of European descent, setting up inevitable and important disagreements about the past and its use in the present.
- How was the rise of archaeology connected to the discovery of humanity's "deep" antiquity?
  - Studying the past depends on *recognizing* a past.
  - Although many early scholars were aware of the classical civilizations, the discovery in France of human artifacts with extinct animals made evident the need to study that past in great detail, without ancient documents as a guide.
- Who were the antiquarians, and why include them in a history of archaeology?
  - For better or worse, these looters helped spark an interest in the ancient world. They built museum collections that inspired later generations to create the profession of archaeology (which would reject the methods and attitudes of antiquarians).
- What trends have characterized archaeology over the last century?
  - The evolution from antiquarianism to professional archaeology has involved the movement from thinking *about* things to thinking *from* things.
  - Archaeologists have always sought to build cultural chronologies, reconstruct ancient societies, and explain why cultures change over time. Today, we can see they were initially successful with the first objective, then the second, and eventually the third. Along the way, archaeologists have increasingly borrowed information and techniques from many fields—geology, zoology, mathematical statistics, astronomy, climatology, and others—as they develop ways of making solid inferences from material remains using solid scientific methods.
  - Archaeology is today a diverse field that covers both prehistoric and historical eras. Archaeology is concerned with bringing knowledge to a broader public, with making research relevant to contemporary society, and with understanding the opinions and needs of indigenous and descendant communities.

Media Resources

Doing Fieldwork: Archaeological Demonstrations CD-ROM 2.0

This CD, developed by the authors, shows professional archaeologists involved in various digs, many of which are referenced in the text. The presentation is organized by the main techniques used on an archaeological dig, reinforcing concepts and techniques via live examples. The CD takes you through each step automatically, or you can navigate to any point via the navigation bar. After reviewing a step in the dig process, you are taken to Check Points, which are concept questions about each step of the dig. Then you can see the answers, receive your score, and even send your scores to your instructor.

See the "What Is the Question?" section of the CD-ROM to learn about topics covered in this chapter.

CourseMate

Access chapter-specific learning tools including learning objectives, practice quizzes, videos, flash cards, and glossaries, as well as web links, and more in your Archaeology CourseMate. Login to www.cengagebrain.com to access the resources your instructor has assigned and to purchase materials.

The Structure of Archaeological Inquiry

2

Southeast Archaeological Center, National Park Service, photo by David G. Anderson.

Excavation of a 500-year-old Mississippian Mound at Shiloh National Military Park.

Learning Objectives

After reading this chapter, you should be able to answer these questions:

- What is an anthropological approach?
- What two paradigms do anthropologists use to study culture, and how are these different ways of thinking reflected in archaeology?
- What is science and how does it explain things?
- What three levels of theory does a scientific approach in archaeology entail? How do these relate to paradigms?

Preview

IN THIS CHAPTER we consider how archaeologists relate to the broader field of anthropology and how archaeologists go about trying to reconstruct the past. The concept of culture is crucial to anthropology, and archaeologists study it in different ways. We'll also see how scientific approaches work in archaeology.

Archaeologists use theories at all levels of their research; we are especially concerned with the concept of *paradigms*, the overarching frameworks used to help us understand the human condition. Finally, we'll examine the cyclical structure of archaeological inquiry.

Introduction

More than 50 years ago, archaeologist Philip Phillips (1900–1994) declared that "Archaeology is anthropology or it is nothing." Especially within the United States, archaeology remains a subfield of anthropology. Although both of us are archaeologists, our multiple degrees are all in anthropology, and we both work in departments of anthropology. In fact, there are few U.S. departments of archaeology (the most prominent is at Boston University). Outside the United States, however, archaeology is often more closely aligned with the humanities, such as history, classics, or art history (and it sometimes appears in these departments at U.S. universities). But the boundaries between these various archaeologies and these former alliances are crumbling. Archaeology will always change, but we believe that good archaeology will always be closely aligned with an anthropological approach.

What's an Anthropological Approach?

Everyone knows what anthropologists do: They study native people and fossils and chimpanzees. They grin from the pages of *National Geographic* magazine and show up on the Discovery Channel. But few people know everything that anthropologists actually do, or even what makes them anthropologists at all. **Anthropology** is tough to pin down because anthropologists do so many different things.

So, what makes an anthropologist an anthropologist? The answer is surprisingly simple: All anthropologists believe that the best understanding of the human condition arises from a global, comparative, and holistic approach. It's not enough to look at a single group of Americans, Chinese, or Bushmen to find the keys to human existence. Neither is it enough to look at just one part of the human condition, as do economists, historians, political scientists, and psychologists. Because looking at part of the picture gives you just that—only part of the picture.

What holds anthropology together is its insistence that every aspect of every human society, extant or extinct, counts. This broad-based approach qualifies anthropology as uniquely capable of understanding what makes humankind distinct from the rest of the animal world. This isn't to say that all anthropologists study everything. The Renaissance anthropologist—the individual who does everything—has faded into folklore. Today, nobody can hope to do everything well.

So, anthropologists specialize. Archaeologists are anthropologists who specialize in ancient societies. But archaeologists still draw upon each of the other subfields of anthropology (and several other sciences). Before examining how modern archaeology articulates with the rest of anthropology, let's first see how anthropologists carve up the pie of human existence.

Kinds of Anthropologists

Anthropology embraces four subfields: **biological anthropology**, **cultural anthropology**, **linguistic anthropology**, and **archaeology** (Figure 2-1).

Biological anthropologists study humans as biological organisms. Some work with human fossils to reconstruct the biological evolution of humans. Others study modern human biological (genetic) variability or work in forensic anthropology (featured in all those TV programs such as *CSI* and *Bones*); others study the biology and behavior of nonhuman primates, such as chimpanzees; still others are bioarchaeologists, who study human biological variability in the ancient past. Archaeologists overlap with biological anthropologists because they often encounter human skeletons, and biological anthropologists are essential in the recovery and analysis of these remains (see Chapter 9).

Cultural anthropologists describe and analyze the culture of living human groups. Cultural anthropologists commonly employ the method of **participant observation**, gathering data by personally questioning and observing people while actually living in their society. Anthropologists study rituals, kinship, religion, politics, art,

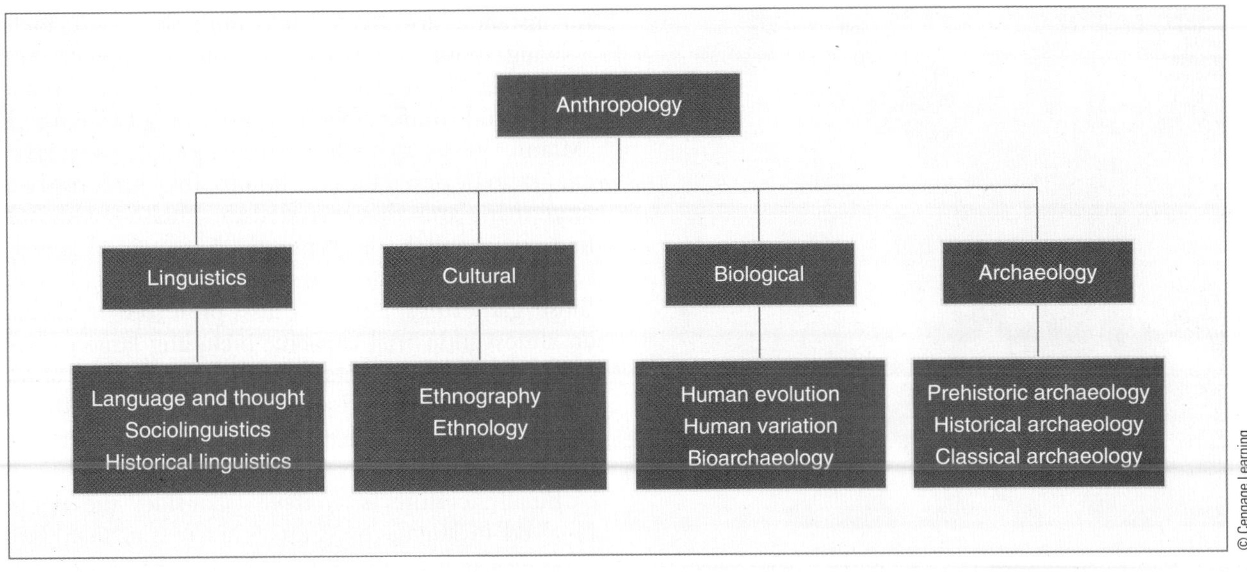

FIGURE 2-1 The four subfields of anthropology and their areas of study.

oral histories, medical practices—anything and everything that people in contemporary societies do, say, or think. Archaeology overlaps with cultural anthropology in that some archaeologists conduct research with living peoples to understand the relationships between behavior and material remains (see Chapter 7). And all archaeologists look to ethnographic research for ideas about how to interpret the things they find in sites.

Anthropological linguists evaluate language: how sounds are made, the relationship between language and thought, how linguistic systems change through time, and the basic structure of language. Anthropological linguists also chart historical relationships and track ancient migrations between now separate, but linguistically related, populations. Many modern linguists study how people acquire second languages and work with native peoples to revive dying languages. Archaeology overlaps with linguistics when language helps reconstruct when and from where modern populations migrated.

Archaeologists study human culture as well, but their technology and field methods differ from those of cultural anthropologists. Without living, breathing informants, archaeologists acquire their data through the recovery of material remains—stone tools, broken bones, potsherds, pollen, plant parts, and so on—commonly by careful excavation (see Figure 2-2). They analyze these material remains using a powerful array of techniques. As we will see, these methods produce information and insights that living, breathing informants probably never would (or could) provide.

Today, archaeology is a major component in many graduate programs in anthropology. Undergraduates often tell us that archaeology is the liveliest and most exciting program within anthropology. Cultural resource management (see Chapter 13) is the most employable kind of archaeology, even for undergraduates. Look for archaeology to continue making significant contributions to the overall mission of anthropology.

The Culture Concept

We have said that a global, comparative, and holistic perspective unites the diversity within anthropology. But even more than that, it is the concept of **culture** that brings together the subfields of anthropology. Sir Edward Burnett Tylor (1832–1917), whom many consider to be the founder

anthropology The study of all aspects of humankind—biological, cultural, and linguistic; extant and extinct—employing a holistic, comparative approach and the concept of culture.

biological anthropology A subdiscipline of anthropology that views humans as biological organisms; also known as physical anthropology.

cultural anthropology A subdiscipline of anthropology that emphasizes nonbiological aspects: the learned social, linguistic, technological, and familial behaviors of humans.

linguistic anthropology A subdiscipline of anthropology that focuses on human language: its diversity in grammar, syntax, and lexicon; its historical development; and its relation to a culture's perception of the world.

archaeology The study of the past through the systematic recovery and analysis of material remains.

participant observation The primary strategy of cultural anthropology, in which data are gathered by questioning and observing people while the observer lives in their society.

culture An integrated system of beliefs, traditions, and customs that govern or influence a person's behavior. Culture is learned, shared by members of a group, and based on the ability to think in terms of symbols.

© Ofer Bar-Yosef

FIGURE 2-2 Hayonim Cave in Israel, where careful excavation has allowed archaeologists to make important discoveries in human evolution.

of modern anthropology, offered the classic definition of culture. Tylor's definition of "culture" appeared in 1871 on the first page of anthropology's first textbook: "Culture . . . taken in its wide ethnographic sense is that complex whole which includes knowledge, belief, art, morals, law, custom, and any other capabilities and habits acquired by man as a member of society."

Culture in Tylor's sense is *learned*—from parents, peers, teachers, leaders, and others. Note that culture is not biological or genetic; any person can acquire any culture. And under this anthropological definition, all peoples have the same amount of culture. Somebody who can recite Shakespeare and listens to Beethoven is no more "cultural" than one who reads *People* magazine and prefers Lady Gaga. If a baby born to European parents were raised in China, that individual's appearance would come from its genes (as moderated by environmental factors), but he or she would speak Mandarin or Cantonese and act and think as other Chinese do.

Culture creates our different conceptions of life, about what is proper and what is not. Tribal people in New Guinea think it laughable that American women wear earrings, but believe it's normal to wear bone or shell nose ornaments for ceremonies. Cultures change over time; material factors (such as nutrition) and historical factors (such as contact with other peoples) affect this process. Because archaeology is concerned with how cultures change over time, the concept of learned culture is essential to archaeology.

Culture is also *shared*. Although everyone is an individual with his/her own values and understandings, members of a human group share some basic ideas about the world and their place in it. Anthropology focuses on such shared ideas, rather than on individual variations of those ideas. Many Euro-American homes, for instance, are divided into multiple rooms, including a living room, a smallish kitchen, a family room, and bedrooms. Most Euro-Americans consider this pattern normal and comfortable. But, according to George Esber (Miami University), when Apache people were given the chance to design their own homes, they preferred a single large living area that included the kitchen, with only the bedrooms and baths separate. The central living area was to accommodate large social gatherings. To cook for those gatherings, Apaches also preferred kitchens with an almost industrial capacity, including large cabinets to hold large cooking pots. Clearly, shared ideas about life are reflected in shared social behaviors that in turn result in patterned sets of material remains—the sort of things that archaeologists recover.

Finally, culture is *symbolic*. Consider the symbolism involved in language: There is no reason that the word "dog" in English means "a household pet," any more than does "chien," "perro," or "alika" (French, Spanish, and Malagasy). What's more, dogs are not inherently pets. Indeed, in many places, such as Micronesia and Southeast Asia, dogs are feast foods. Though this disturbs many Americans, the idea of "pet" is not inherent in a dog—it is a socially constructed, symbolic meaning that a culture gives to dogs. Symbolic meanings of behavior condition what we do—for example, what we eat—which in turn affects the material traces of those behaviors, such as which bones wind up in ancient middens.

So, culture is learned, shared, and symbolic. Culture provides you with a way to interpret human behavior and the world around you; and it plays a key role in structuring the material record of human behavior—which archaeologists recover.

How Do Anthropologists Study Culture?

To oversimplify a bit, anthropologists study culture in two basic ways. An **ideational perspective** focuses on ideas, symbols, and mental structures as driving forces in shaping human behavior. Alternatively, an **adaptive perspective** emphasizes technology, ecology, demography, and economics as the key factors defining human behavior. Let's examine each of these.

Culture as Ideas

The ideational perspective holds that culture is a complex set of conceptual designs and shared understandings that govern the way people act. This perspective on culture emphasizes ideas, thoughts, and shared knowledge and sees symbols and their meanings as crucial to shaping human behavior. It encompasses material culture insofar as material things manifest symbolic ideas.

The ideational theorist insists on "getting inside a person's head" to seek out the shared meanings of a society. According to the ideational view of culture, one cannot comprehend human behavior without understanding the symbolic code for that behavior.

Culture as Adaptation

An adaptive perspective privileges "culture as a system." Social and cultural differences are viewed not as reflections of symbolic meanings, but rather as responses to the material parameters of life, such as food, shelter, and reproduction. Human behaviors are also seen as linked together systemically, meaning that change in one area, say technology, will result in change in another area, such as social organization. It is the cultural system—technology, modes of economic organization, settlement patterns, forms of social grouping, and political institutions—that articulates the material needs of human communities with their ecological settings.

In the adaptive perspective, culture keeps societies in equilibrium with their ecosystems. Change results from those elements of technology, subsistence economy, and social or political organization most closely tied to life's material needs. Archaeologists working with the adaptive perspective link cultural behaviors largely to the environment, demography, subsistence, or technology.

Which perspective is better? In a word, neither. Each perspective sees the world differently, privileging some aspects and downplaying others. An adaptive perspective recognizes that humans must respond to the material conditions of their environments; it helps account for why the potlatch occurred where and when it did. An ideational perspective shows how humans respond through particular, symbolically charged behaviors; it helps account for the particular ways in which the potlatch was conducted. We need both perspectives to understand human diversity and history. Both perspectives fall within an overarching scientific approach.

What's a Scientific Approach?

Science (from the Latin "to know") refers, in its broadest sense, to a systematic body of knowledge about any field. Although the beginnings of modern science are generally traced to the European Renaissance and, earlier, to Islamic scholars, the origins of scientific thinking extend far back in human history. Archaeological sites preserve examples of early scientific reasoning: astronomical observations, treatment of disease, and calendrical systems. Cave paintings and carvings in bone or stone are often cited as early instances of systematizing knowledge.

Science as a distinct intellectual endeavor began in the seventeenth century, when Sir Francis Bacon codified the scientific method in his book *Novum Organum* (1620). Anthropologist Lawrence Kuznar (Indiana-Purdue University at Fort Wayne) provides several characteristics of a scientific approach:

- **Science is empirical, or objective.** Science is concerned with the observable, measurable world. Questions are scientific (1) if they are concerned with the detectable properties of things, and (2) if the result of observations designed to answer a question cannot be predetermined by the biases of the observer.
- **Science is systematic and explicit.** Scientists try to collect data relevant to solving a problem, and they try to specify their procedures, so that any trained observer under the same conditions would make the same observations.
- **Science is logical.** Scientists work not only with data, but also with the ideas that link data to interpretations, and with the ideas that link the ideas together. These linkages must be grounded in previously demonstrated principles; otherwise an argument is a house of cards.
- **Science is explanatory and, consequently, predictive.** Science is concerned with causes. It seeks theories—explanatory statements that not only predict *what* will happen under a specified set of conditions, but also explain *why* it will happen.
- **Science is self-critical and based on testing.** Many people think that science is about white lab coats, supercomputers, and complex equations. Although science may involve such things, it's really about honesty. Scientists propose hypotheses, and then they say, "Here is my idea; here is the evidence that will prove it wrong; and here is my attempt to collect that evidence." Scientists acquire understanding *not* by proving that an idea is right, but by showing that competing ideas are wrong. The best scientists are professional skeptics, always asking themselves: *How do I know that I know something?* Science, in this sense, becomes the right to be wrong.
- **Science is public.** Scientific methods, the observations, and the arguments linking observations with conclusions are explicit and available for scrutiny by the public. The origin or political implications of ideas are irrelevant. What matters in science is that ideas can be tested by objective methods.

Taken together, these characteristics of science produce scientific methods, elegant and powerful ways to understand the workings of the material world. Archaeologists have been doing scientific research for a long time. The public, however, frequently misunderstands science (see "What Does It Mean to Me? Does Archaeology Put Native Americans on Trial?"). To understand how the scientific method works, let's see how it was used to solve the "mystery" of the Moundbuilders.

ideational perspective A research perspective that focuses on ideas, symbols, and mental structures as driving forces in shaping human behavior.

adaptive perspective A research perspective that emphasizes technology, ecology, demography, and economics as the key factors in defining human behavior.

science The search for answers through a process that is objective, systematic, logical, predictive, self-critical, and public.

WHAT DOES IT MEAN TO me?

Does Archaeology Put Native Americans on Trial?

Many American Indians do not trust anthropologists, including archaeologists. This seems odd because anthropologists have long been the champions of Native American legal and cultural rights. For example, many anthropologists testified on behalf of tribes when Indian land claims were decided in courts in the 1950s and 1960s, and many today work to maintain Indian rights and languages.

One problem is that anthropologists often take a scientific perspective toward American Indian culture, and many Native Americans see a "scientific" approach to understanding their history as denigrating their own indigenous versions of history. This disconnect is particularly evident in the research regarding American Indian origins—one of the major questions in American archaeology. As early as 1589, the Jesuit missionary José de Acosta wrote in *Historia Natural y Moral de las Indias* that Indians had walked to the New World via a land route that connected the New World with Asia. He was prescient: Genetic data demonstrate that the ancestors of Native Americans indeed migrated from Asia at least 13,500 years ago.

This position contrasts with most Native American origin stories. In many of these, the first people emerged from a hole in the earth, having traveled up from successive layers of worlds that lie below this one. Traditional Hopi beliefs, for example, hold that the modern world is the fourth world (with more to come).

No Native American religion explicitly states that "people came from Asia," and many American Indians see this suggestion as insulting, an affront to their religious beliefs (just as the idea of evolution is insulting to fundamentalist Christians). Some scholars agree, suggesting that archaeologists have no right to ask questions that put Native American religion on trial.

We disagree with this implied censorship; no one can deny another the right to ask questions. But more to the point, asking questions about Native American origins does not challenge American Indian (or any other) religion. Science evaluates claims about the *material* world, and religion is fundamentally about the *nonmaterial* world. Religions do sometimes make claims about the material world: How old is the earth? Where did people come from? What's the relationship between humans and animals? Because these are claims about the material world, we can subject them to scientific scrutiny.

So, what does it mean that scientific archaeology holds that the ancestors of Native American people came from Asia? Does this prove that Native American religions are wrong?

Absolutely not. Nobody can prove or disprove claims of the nonmaterial world using a method that evaluates claims about the material world. Archaeologists can prove only that a religious claim about the material world cannot be taken at face value. Some might think this means that the religion is false, but it might also mean that a religion's claim about the material world, even if unsubstantiated by science, holds deeper truths. From such a perspective, science encourages one to look deeper into religious beliefs, to find a significance that goes beyond issues of mere space and time.

How Science Explains Things: The Moundbuilder Myth

Sixteenth-century Europeans arriving on the North American continent confronted a serious intellectual challenge: Who were the people already living here? This was an important question because its answer begged another, more practical one: Did Europeans have the right to take the land?

Colonial Americans justified the taking of Native American lands in several ways, and one involved archaeology. Colonists settling the eastern woodlands encountered thousands of mounds and earthworks, especially in the Ohio and Mississippi River valleys. Some mounds were modest, only a few meters in diameter, but others were enormous: Monks Mound at the site of Cahokia (just across the Mississippi River from St. Louis) stands nearly 70 feet tall, with a footprint larger than the largest pyramid in Egypt. Some mounds were conical in shape; others were truncated pyramids. Some were "effigy mounds," fashioned in the shape of animals such as serpents and birds (Figure 2-3 shows an example); others were precise geometric embankments enclosing many acres.

Colonial farmers plowed many of the mounds, finding curious things inside. Many contained human skeletal remains, but some mounds produced remarkable, eye-catching artworks such as copper and antler headdresses and stone pipes crafted into birds and other animals. They also found sheets of intricately shaped mica, carved shells, massive log tombs, spear points, incised pottery, copper ornaments, and polished stone disks (see Figure 2-4). Today, we understand that some mounds were constructed as early as 5500 years ago in the southern Mississippi River valley; by 3000 years ago, the practice was widespread across the eastern United States.

FIGURE 2-3 Aerial photo of Serpent Mound, an effigy mound in Ohio.

Inspired by such finds, colonial scholars dreamed up several ideas to explain who built the mounds. The favored interpretation held that the Moundbuilders were a superior race wiped out by Indians. Some thought this pioneering race was Viking; others nominated the Egyptians, Israelites, Chinese, Greeks, Polynesians, Phoenicians, Norwegians, Belgians, Tartars, Saxons, Hindus, Africans, Welsh, or residents of the lost continent of Atlantis. An Ohio minister even suggested that God had created the Serpent Mound in southern Ohio to mark the site of Eden.

The Moundbuilders, it seemed, might have been anyone—except the ancestors of American Indians. Nineteenth-century scholars saw the Indians as late-arriving marauders, destroyers of a magnificent civilization. After all, weren't the mounds full of human bones, evidence of past battles? Thus arose the myth of a Moundbuilder civilization.

This view of history provided colonists with a sense of innate superiority and the right to avenge the Moundbuilders by dispossessing Native Americans of their land. Handy history—but was it true?

Ephraim Squier (1821–1888), a Connecticut civil engineer, surveyor, and journalist, teamed up with Edwin Davis (1811–1888), an Ohio physician. In their 1848 monograph, *Ancient Monuments of the Mississippi Valley*—the first publication by the newly formed Smithsonian Institution—they provided a thorough description of mounds across the eastern United States (see Figure 2-5).

Squier and Davis claimed that they did not seek to "sustain" any particular hypothesis, only "to arrive at truth" and to avoid "speculation." But in their final pages, they suggested that the Moundbuilder population was related to the "semicivilized" nations of Mexico and Central America (such as the Aztecs), providing more support to the Moundbuilder hypothesis. By 1873, the president of the Chicago Academy of Sciences thought it "preposterous" that Indians could have built the mounds. And in his 1872 book, *Ancient America*, J. D. Baldwin considered any relationship between the Moundbuilders and Indians to be "absurd."

Because the Moundbuilder issue captivated public interest, Congress insisted that the Bureau of American Ethnology spend $5000 a year—one-fifth of the bureau's budget—on mound exploration. Cyrus Thomas (1825–1910), a lawyer, merchant, and entomologist was

FIGURE 2-4 An etched slate from Moundville, Alabama. Artifacts such as these convinced nineteenth-century scholars that the Moundbuilders were a superior culture.

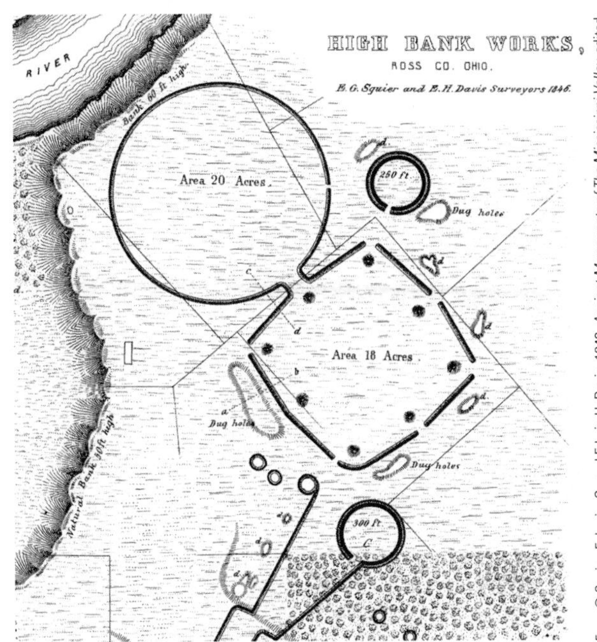

FIGURE 2-5 A portion of one of Squier and Davis's maps, showing a mound group in Ohio.

hired to lead the inquiry. Working through the Bureau of American Ethnology, Cyrus Thomas began his own program of survey and excavation. Over the next 12 years, with the aid of local affiliates, he compiled data on some 2000 sites in 21 states, finally publishing a 700-page report in 1894. In the beginning, Thomas was a proponent of the Moundbuilder hypothesis, but he nonetheless collected the empirical data to test the idea that someone other than Native Americans built the mounds.

Reporting the results of his thorough investigation, Thomas quietly but definitively concluded that "the author believes the theory which attributes these works to the Indians to be the correct one." There was no lost race of Moundbuilders. They had not been overrun by Native Americans. The myth that had helped perpetuate a racist attitude toward Native Americans was simply that—a myth. Sadly, by 1894, the truth about the Moundbuilders had come too late. The Indian Wars were officially over, virtually all Native Americans were confined to reservations, and a change in racist attitudes toward Indians was still decades away.

The Scientific Method

The history of the Moundbuilder myth provides a simple example of some characteristics of the **scientific method**, which we can reduce to six steps:

1. Define a relevant problem.
2. Establish one or more hypotheses.
3. Determine the empirical implications of the hypotheses.
4. Collect appropriate data through observation and/or experimentation.
5. Test the hypothesis by comparing these data with the expected implications.
6. Reject, revise, and/or retest hypotheses as necessary.

This is an idealized summary, and scientific research does not always progress neatly through each of these steps. Nonetheless, this framework remains the goal of modern science.

The Role of Inductive Reasoning

The first two tasks (Steps 1 and 2) involve defining a relevant question and translating it into an appropriate **hypothesis**. The idea is to build upon a simple description of the known facts and create a hypothesis to account for them. Such hypotheses are generated through **inductive reasoning**, working from specific facts or observations to general conclusions. The known facts serve as premises in this case; the hypothesis should not only account for the known facts but should also predict properties of as yet unobserved phenomena. No rules exist for induction (just as there are no rules for thinking up good ideas). It does not matter where or how one derives the hypothesis. What matters is how well the hypothesis accounts for unobserved phenomena.

Squier and Davis worked in the inductive phase (Steps 1 and 2) of Moundbuilder research. Because no one knew much about the mounds, the first order of business was to gather some facts: How many mounds were there? What sort of variability was present among the mounds? What exactly was in the different types of mounds? How old were they? What were they made of? From these data, Squier and Davis inductively derived a conclusion: The living Indians of the United States were not descendants of the Moundbuilders.

Science Is Self-Correcting

Squier and Davis, as it turned out, were completely wrong, but the beauty of the scientific method is that it is self-correcting. Science insists that we always ask, "Do we really know what we think we know?" Squier and Davis thought they were at Step 6 in the process, but in hindsight, we can see that they had only inductively formulated a hypothesis. It was left to Thomas to test this idea. This is how science sometimes proceeds, by backtracking and rethinking things that others thought were over and done with.

How does one test a hypothesis (Steps 4 and 5)? The first step is to translate the hypothesis into testable form. Curiously, *hypotheses can never be tested directly* because they are abstract statements. In fact, scientists don't verify hypotheses; instead, they verify the logical material consequences of their hypotheses (the empirical implications established in Step 3).

Deductive reasoning is required to uncover these logical outcomes. A deductive argument is one for which the conclusions must be true, given that the premises are true. Deductive arguments generally take the form of "if . . . then" statements: *If* the hypothesis is true, *then* we expect certain outcomes. Bridging the gap from *if* to *then* is a tricky step.

Although Thomas was never explicit about this, we can see the simple deductive reasoning he employed for his version of Step 5. *If* American Indians did not know about mound building, *then* there should be no explorer accounts of mound building by Indians. *If* the mounds were built by a long-vanished race, *then* they should be considerably older than the known age of Indian culture. *If* the metal artifacts in mounds were signs of a "superior" Moundbuilder culture, *then* the manufacturing technology associated with them should be absent from later Indian culture. This is how Thomas laid out the criteria whereby he could claim the Moundbuilder hypothesis to be false.

For Thomas, "testing" meant collecting data, analyzing it, publishing it, and openly evaluating it against the competing hypotheses. The **testability** of a hypothesis is critical. *A hypothesis is testable if different observers can measure its implications with the same results.* We have to know that you would make the same observations that we would make.

Science Is Reiterative

The scientific method is really more of a cycle. Step 6 (testing, rejecting, or revising the hypothesis) normally leads back to Step 1 (redefining the problem at hand).

Scientific cycles commence in the world of facts. Through the process of induction, these facts are probed, and hypotheses are devised to account for what is already known. But because hypotheses are general declarations, they cannot be tested against further facts until they are translated into their logical consequences.

The scientific cycle thus begins and ends with facts. But these newly discovered facts themselves suggest new hypotheses, and once again inductive reasoning leads from the world of facts to the world of abstraction, initiating a new cycle of investigation.

Scientific thinking applies at many different levels, from questions such as "What's this red stain in the soil?" or "What was this stone tool used for?" to questions such as "Why did humans switch from hunting and gathering to agriculture?" or "What is human nature?" Sometimes the cycle is played out over the course of a day, sometimes over the course of many lifetimes (as in the Moundbuilder controversy).

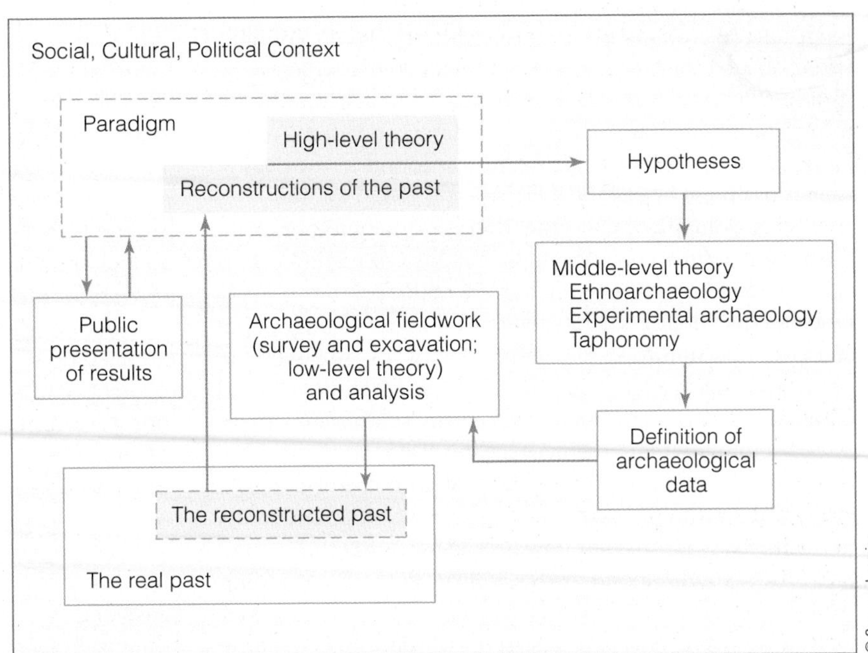

FIGURE 2-6 A model of archaeological inquiry.

Science Is Not Infallible

Because science is a human venture, it is subject to false starts, dead ends, preconceived notions, and cultural biases. It's clear, for instance, that the Moundbuilder hypothesis was not drawn directly and inductively from sterile archaeological facts. The idea was widespread well before anyone knew much about the mounds because the myth facilitated and justified what colonists wanted—seizure of Indian land. Science is embedded in the scientist's culture and never free of cultural biases. The social, cultural, and political context of archaeology influences its theories. A scientific approach does not always deliver the right answer on the first try, or even the second or third. Sometimes we only see what we have learned in hindsight. But we generally find, in the end, that we've learned something—and that is what science is all about.

With this background, let's consider the specific application of scientific methods to the archaeological enterprise.

The Structure of Archaeological Inquiry

Figure 2-6 translates the generic scientific cycle into a format specific to archaeology. You'll see that the term **theory** crops up three times. In science, "theory" refers to statements that purport to explain observed, empirical phenomena. In this sense, theories answer the "why" questions, which occur at a low level, a middle level, and a high level. We distinguish the different levels not by complexity or difficulty, but by their place in the process of archaeological inquiry.

Low-Level Theory

Low-level theory begins with archaeological objects and generates relevant facts or data about those objects. Some data are physical observations. For example,

scientific method Accepted principles and procedures for the systematic pursuit of secure knowledge. Established scientific procedures involve the following steps: (1) define a relevant problem; (2) establish one or more hypotheses; (3) determine the empirical implications of the hypotheses; (4) collect appropriate data through observation and/or experimentation; (5) compare these data with the expected implications; and (6) revise and/or retest hypotheses as necessary.

hypothesis A proposition proposed as an explanation of some phenomenon.

inductive reasoning Working from specific observations to more general hypotheses.

deductive reasoning Reasoning from theory to predict specific observational or experimental results.

testability The degree to which one's observations and experiments can be reproduced.

theory An explanation for observed, empirical phenomena. It seeks to explain the relationships between variables; it is an answer to a "why" question.

low-level theory The observations and interpretations that emerge from hands-on archaeological field and lab work.

"Artifact 20.2/4683 is (a) made of obsidian, (b) 21.5 mm long, and (c) weighs 2.1 grams." This statement contains three observations made on an archaeological object (the number 20.2/4683 is the item's unique catalog number—more on that in a later chapter). Other observations might be contextual: "Artifact 20.2/4683 was found in excavation unit B-5, 56 cm below the surface."

Before going further, we need to consider another term, **data**. You might consider "data" to be a straightforward concept, but it's actually much more complex.

Gatecliff Shelter is a Nevada **rockshelter** where people camped, now and then, beneath a shallow overhang over a period of some 7000 years (see Figure 2-7). Thomas found Gatecliff in 1970, and excavated the site's deposits with an interdisciplinary team throughout the 1970s.

Gatecliff is nearly 40 feet deep, with cultural deposits stacked up within a floor area of about 300 ft^2. Thousands of artifacts were buried inside Gatecliff Shelter: stone projectile points, bone awls, willow basketry, grinding stones, small pieces of slate incised with enigmatic geometric designs, woven sagebrush bark mats, stone scrapers, and shells and turquoise used as ornaments. Gatecliff also contained objects not made by humans—**ecofacts**, which are items relating to the natural environment, such as bighorn sheep bones, charcoal, piñon nut hulls, and pollen. We also encountered **features**—pits, hearths, rodent burrows—which are nonportable cultural and noncultural things that archaeologists measure, draw, photograph, and sample.

FIGURE 2-7 Gatecliff Shelter, late in the excavation: removing deposits through a bucket brigade method.

The point here is simple but important: After nearly a decade of excavating at Gatecliff, Thomas excavated no data at all. So why, you might ask, would an archaeologist waste a decade digging holes that produce no data? The reason is that data don't lie out there waiting for somebody to pick them up, like Easter eggs on the lawn. *Data depend on theory*, much as *theory depends on data*.

Thomas found no data at Gatecliff because archaeologists don't excavate data. Archaeologists excavate objects; data are *observations* made on those objects. Those observations enable archaeologists to make *interpretations* of the objects: Is this grubby little black thing a piece of pottery? To answer that simple question, we need to ask if it contains the characteristics of pottery: Does it contain clay and temper (material added to the clay to give it strength)? Does it look as though it had been fired (heated)? If the answers are yes, then we "interpret" the grubby little black thing to be a piece of pottery.

Data, then, become the observations that allow us to make interpretations. Data tell us *why* something is what we think it is. This means that the observations we make on objects, as well as the interpretations of those observations, are all *theory-driven*. This is what low-level theory is all about.

Why are these observations that create data theoretical statements? Because each is based on a "why" question: Why do we know that something is obsidian? Because the stone has certain characteristics that fit a definition of obsidian (a dark volcanic glass), and this knowledge derives from a theoretical understanding of how rocks form. Why do we know the length, weight, and provenience? Because these measurements were made using digital instruments whose ability to measure things reliably is based on theories from physics.

Here's another example: While excavating, a student comes upon a curving red band in the sediment. On the concave side of the red band are some black flecks that turn out to be charcoal. The student calls to her crew chief, "I've got a hearth over here!" How does she know it is a hearth—and not a filled-in rodent burrow, an ancient posthole, or something else?

The charcoal was a clue, but archaeological sites often contain scattered charcoal. She also observed the feature's properties (its diameter, depth, and fill), and interpreted those. Apparently, she knows that heat has a predictable effect on sediments with high iron content: The iron is oxidized (bonded with oxygen) and turns red. Our student may be unaware of the theory that accounts for the oxidation and color change, but her interpretation is still based on that theory.

This kind of archaeology is "low-level" theory, not because it is simple or unimportant, but because archaeologists normally give little thought to the theories that stand behind their basic observations in the field or lab. We record that we found something—a hearth or bison femur or potsherd—without presenting the geochemical, evolutionary, or other theory that gives us the ability to identify something as a hearth or a bison bone.

We can make an infinite number of observations on any single archaeological object. Many of these are made on the object itself: length, width, thickness, weight, angle measurements, material, color, curvature, chemical composition, manufacturing techniques, and so forth. Others might be observations on the object's context—that is, where it was found in a site. Overall, the important dimensions of low-level theory are the classical ones in archaeology: form and context.

Low-level theory remains critical because it allows archaeologists to know that their data are comparable. However, these basic observations can become the focus of scrutiny if, for instance, archaeologists try to determine when humans began to use fire intentionally (perhaps some hundreds of thousands of years ago). In this case, what constitutes an *intentional* hearth becomes of more than passing interest. The same is true when archaeologists try to determine whether some chipped stones are tools or simply rocks that Mother Nature has broken in fortuitous ways (more than one archaeologist has been fooled). When archaeologists give this sort of attention to inferences made from observations, they move into the realm of middle-level theory.

Middle-Level Theory

Middle-level theory links some specific set of archaeological data with the human behavior or natural processes that produced them. At this middle level, we make a critical transition, moving from the archaeologically observable (the low-level theoretical facts) to the archaeologically invisible (relevant human behaviors or natural processes of the past). How does this transition actually take place?

Keep in mind that the archaeological record is the *contemporary* evidence left by people of the past. Strictly speaking, the archaeological record is composed only of static objects—the artifacts, ecofacts, and features that have survived the passage of time. Those objects are the products of both human behavior and natural processes. Our job is to infer the long-gone behavior and natural processes from the static results—the objects we recover from archaeological sites. Figure 2-8, for example, shows a large scatter of bison bone at a site in Wyoming. All that the archaeologist can record is the kind of bones that are present and their arrangement and condition. But how does the archaeologist infer from these observations whether people killed and butchered these bison?

Archaeologists conducting middle-level research seek situations in which they can observe (1) ongoing human behavior or natural processes and (2) the material results of that behavior or those processes. This requires that

FIGURE 2-8 The Horner site in Wyoming. The bones are those of dozens of bison. How would we know if these animals had been hunted?

archaeologists step out of their excavation trenches and turn to experimental archaeology, ethnoarchaeology, or taphonomy. We'll discuss these fields in detail in Chapter 7. For now, it's only important to remember that middle-level theory is necessary to infer human behavior and natural processes from archaeological data. Middle-level theory allows archaeologists to create the "if . . . then" statements in Step 3 of the scientific method discussed earlier. This can take the form of experimenting with the manufacture of stone tools or pottery to determine the material results—the things that might be left behind. It could also entail studying living populations to see how their behaviors are translated into material remains. Or it might require the study of natural processes to see, for example, how carnivores break bones of their kills, or how rivers move bones and artifacts in patterned ways.

data Relevant observations made on objects that then serve as the basis for study and discussion.

rockshelter A common type of archaeological site, consisting of a rock overhang that is deep enough to provide shelter but not deep enough to be called a cave (technically speaking, a cave must have an area of perpetual darkness).

ecofact Plant or animal remains found at an archaeological site.

feature Nonportable archaeological evidence such as fire hearths, architectural elements, artifact clusters, garbage pits, and soil stains.

middle-level theory Hypothesis that links archaeological observations with the human behavior or natural processes that produced them.

High-Level Theory

High-level theory is archaeology's ultimate objective; low- and middle-level research are necessary steps to attain this goal. High-level theory goes beyond the archaeological specifics to address the "big questions" of concern to many social and historical sciences. High-level theory applies to all intellectual inquiry about the human condition, raising questions such as: Why did we humans become cultural animals? Why did hunter-gatherers become agriculturalists? Why did social stratification arise? Why did human history take the particular course it did in the New World as opposed to the Old World? Why did aboriginal hunter-gatherers in California not take up agriculture? Why did large civilizations develop in some parts of the world and not in others?

Some general theories stress environmental adaptation, some emphasize biological factors, and some involve only cultural causality; others try to combine these.

Paradigms

Paradigms provide the overarching framework for understanding "how the world works" that each researcher brings to a particular question or problem. This is the most abstract and yet the most important of our concepts.

Paradigms are a lot like culture—both are learned, shared, and symbolic. Archaeologists sharing the same paradigm can converse with one another and leave a lot unstated; an archaeologist following another paradigm might have to ask many questions, seeking definitions of basic concepts and terms. Like culture, your paradigm influences how you frame your research questions, and how you interpret the answers. Paradigms contain some *a priori* notions of which variables are relevant and which are not. And, like culture, a paradigm can give you both correct and incorrect answers. Paradigms are not open to direct empirical verification or rejection; they just turn out to be useful or not.

Just as all humans participate in a culture, all archaeologists operate within a paradigm, whether or not they are aware of it. Without a paradigm, nothing would make sense. So, although a paradigm can give you an inaccurate bias, the goal isn't to become paradigm-free. Rather, we simply must be aware of the paradigm we're using.

The two basic paradigms in modern archaeology—the processual and the postprocessual paradigms—closely mirror the adaptive and ideational approaches previously discussed. We will deliberately simplify our presentation of these paradigms because the history of any intellectual field resembles more a braided stream than a simple river of thought. No archaeologist today, for example, falls neatly into either category, and we intend to give you only the basic differences between these two ways of thinking to show the range of ways in which archaeologists think about the past.

Processual Archaeology

The **processual paradigm** includes the new archaeology of Lewis Binford and his generation (see Chapter 1) and extends to the evolutionary approaches practiced today. Processual archaeology takes its name from its concern with "process"—that is, with the ways that cultures change over time. Processual archaeologists search for a "grand narrative" about how culture changes.

The processual paradigm has several key characteristics. First, *processual archaeology emphasizes evolutionary generalizations, not historical specifics, and often downplays the importance of the individual.* In the early days of the processual paradigm, archaeologists viewed history as the opposite of science, as description rather than explanation. The processual paradigm claims to be scientific, not historical. It focuses on regularities, correlations, and patterns among different historical cases to point to causal variables. An interest in developing cultural (as opposed to biological) evolutionary theory directed the processual paradigm away from ideology and history and toward environmental change, population growth, food production, trade, and conflict over limited resources as the forces driving cultural evolution.

Processual archaeology saw particular historical sequences as individual "experiments" from which one could construct theory and law-like generalizations. Early on, processual archaeologists did not consider culture history by itself to be important.

Reflecting the processual paradigm's focus on historical regularities and correlations, Binford and others rejected "great man" explanations of history—explanations that attribute major changes in economy or social or political organization to a single person who had a "great idea." Archaeologists, for instance, once thought that the origin of agriculture was one of these great ideas, a hypothesis that has since been disproven.

Second, *processual archaeology views culture from a systemic perspective and takes an adaptive approach to the study of human culture.* Because culture provides the nonbiological system through which people adapt to their environment, processual archaeology could (and briefly, did) tap into a much larger body of established external theory, often called **general systems theory**. The theoretical premise is that various complex entities—thermostats, computers, glaciers, living organisms, and even human societies—are most profitably viewed as systems composed of multiple parts that interact in a number of predictable ways. Depending on the application, the rules governing all systems (such as positive feedback, negative feedback, and equilibrium) could explain the behavior of the major parts of any system—regardless of its specifics. (Although many processual archaeologists today view human societies as systems, they no longer explain them in the sterile terms of general systems theory.)

Processual archaeology focuses attention on technology, ecology, and economy and takes an adaptive rather than ideational perspective on culture. Consequently, processual archaeology focuses on behavior rather than on the cultural ideas that stand behind that behavior. Religion and ideology are seen as "epiphenomena"—cultural add-ons with little long-term explanatory value.

Third, *explanation in processual archaeology is explicitly scientific.* Procedures in processual archaeology depend on deductive models grounded in the hard sciences (math, chemistry, physics) and emphasize the importance of being objective. By objective, we mean that processual archaeologists believe that they can see the world "as it really is," not through a filter that colors their perception of the world.

The processual paradigm initially championed the view that predicting events (even those in the past) is equivalent to explaining them. More recent approaches, however, stress the interplay between induction and deduction, the *relative* objectivity of observations, and the probabilistic nature of explanation in the social sciences.

Fourth, *processual archaeology attempts to remain ethically neutral and claims to be explicitly nonpolitical.* Processual archaeology tries to generate evidence about the past that is deliberately disconnected from the present. Politics of the present, processual archaeologists argue, should have nothing to do with the study of the ancient past. Archaeology should avoid subjectivity, and its conclusions should not be influenced by modern politics. Processual archaeology is not interested in passing moral judgments on people of the past.

Processual archaeology does wish to be relevant to the modern world and to provide an understanding of cultural evolution that is useful in directing the world's future. Archaeology should influence politics, the thinking goes, but politics is not to influence archaeology.

Perhaps half of archaeologists today pursue the processual paradigm in one form or another (although many of them also agree with some tenets of the postprocessual paradigm, as discussed next). Why does processualism hold such appeal for archaeologists? One reason is that it emphasizes technology, economy, environment, and demography—those aspects of human existence that leave the clearest traces in the archaeological record. Processualism may also be popular because it suggests that the world and cultural change result from orderly processes—an idea challenged by the postprocessual paradigm.

Postprocessual Archaeology

The **postprocessual paradigm** is embedded within the larger arena of postmodernism. It arose in archaeology largely in Great Britain and Europe, nurtured by archaeologists such as Ian Hodder (Stanford University), but adherents today can be found on both sides of the Atlantic. We will characterize postprocessual archaeology in contrast to the points we just made about processual archaeology.

First, *postprocessual archaeology rejects the processual search for universal laws and emphasizes the role of the individual.* The postprocessual paradigm holds that universals of human behavior do not exist (or that they are banal) and that scientific explanations are inadequate because they downplay historical circumstances in their search for universals. Processual archaeology saw the particulars of history—such as a certain culture's ideas about men and women or specific religious beliefs—as playing no significant role in the grand scheme of history. Postprocessual archaeologists see the grand scheme, if it exists at all, as uninteresting; instead, they see the trajectory of particular societies as heavily influenced by that society's particular cultural ideas, so much so that the search for a grand narrative is rendered meaningless. Some postprocessual archaeologists think archaeology should be more closely allied with history than with anthropology.

In fact, postprocessual archaeology often emphasizes the role of the individual in human society. We do not mean that postprocessual archaeology aims to see particular individuals in archaeology—for example, to find the name of the person who made a particular pot. Instead, postprocessual archaeology argues that large social change results from individuals going about their daily lives. In this view, societies are not animated strictly by change from the "outside" (such as environmental change). More specifically, postprocessual archaeology tends to see social tension—for example, competition between men and women, elites and nonelites, or regional groups—as especially important in generating (or negotiating) social change. Postprocessual archaeology is keenly interested in how cultural change results from the process of individuals negotiating their daily lives around issues of power.

Second, *postprocessual archaeology rejects the systemic view of culture and focuses more on the ideational approach to culture.* Postprocessual archaeology discredits the systems approach as a "robotic view of humans."

high-level theory Theory that seeks to answer large "why" questions.

paradigm The overarching framework, often unstated, for understanding a research problem. It is a researcher's "culture."

processual paradigm The paradigm that explains social, economic, and cultural change as primarily the result of adaptation to material conditions. External conditions (for example, the environment) are assumed to take causal priority over ideational factors in explaining change.

general systems theory An effort to describe the properties by which all systems, including human societies, allegedly operate; Popular in processual archaeology of the late 1960s and 1970s.

postprocessual paradigm A paradigm that focuses on humanistic approaches and rejects scientific objectivity. It sees archaeology as inherently political and is more concerned with interpreting the past than with testing hypotheses. It sees change as arising largely from interactions between individuals operating within a symbolic and/or competitive system.

Postmodernism in general distrusts any deterministic perspective that reduces individual humans to the status of a historical droid, not significantly different from conditioned laboratory rats.

Postprocessualists argue that the systemic view of human society suggests a coordinated, uniform organism responding only to outside pressures, mainly the environment and demography. But recall that postprocessual archaeologists see society as composed of conflicting individuals, groups, genders, and classes, whose goals are not necessarily identical and whose interests and actions are often in conflict with the adaptive success and functional needs of the cultural system as a whole. How can we reconcile a vision of society as a well-oiled adaptive machine with the fact that specific individuals, such as dictators, whose interests are maladaptive for others, often control a society?

Postprocessualists tend to look at artifacts differently than do processual archaeologists. Processual archaeologists generally see things, such as the pot shown in Figure 2-9, in terms of functions: Was the pot used for cooking? Food or water storage? Is it a serving vessel? But postprocessual archaeologists remind us that things also carry symbolic meanings: Did this pot "stand for" women, or hospitality, or the Raven clan? Thus, postprocessualists argue that we cannot understand what artifacts mean simply by looking for their functions; we must also consider their symbolic meanings.

Third, *postprocessual archaeology sees knowledge as "historically situated," and not as objective as processual archaeologists argue.* By "historically situated," postmodernists mean that our understanding of the world reflects the specific time and place in which we live. This is demonstrated through the method of deconstruction. Coined by French philosopher Jacques Derrida (1930–2004), **deconstruction** refers to efforts to expose the assumptions behind the allegedly scientific search for knowledge.

Anthropologist Richard Wilk (Indiana University), for instance, has shown that explanations for the demise of Maya civilization are linked to the larger cultural and political context of archaeologists. The Maya civilization flourished in portions of Central America and Mexico, reaching a zenith about 1300 years ago. The Maya constructed magnificent centers with stone pyramids, surrounded by thousands of households. These complexes were the center of a rich ceremonial life, places where kings recorded their exploits in hieroglyphs on stone monuments called **stelae** (see Figure 2-10). The society ran according to a set of complex calendars and supported its agriculture with water storage systems. But the Maya civilization collapsed about 1100 years ago (although the Maya people never disappeared, of course; they are still there today). People abandoned the ceremonial centers, which were gradually consumed by the jungle. Why?

Processual archaeologists proposed many explanations for the collapse of Maya civilization, especially war, environmental degradation, and the abuse of power by political elites. Wilk argues that these explanations waxed and waned in popularity in relation to major U.S. political events. Warfare as an explanation began in 1962, the beginning of the Vietnam War, and grew in popularity until the end of that war. During the ecology movement

FIGURE 2-9 An Inca-style aribalos vessel from the site of Puruchuco-Huaquerones. Processual archaeology focuses on its function, postprocessual archaeology on its meaning.

FIGURE 2-10 Stela B at Copán, Honduras. Erected in AD 731, it depicts the ruler, 18-Rabbit.

of the mid-1970s, explanations turned to environmental degradation. And after 1974, in the aftermath of the Watergate fiasco and historic resignation of Richard Nixon, some archaeologists favored the abuse of government power as an explanation.

By deconstructing archaeological thinking about the Maya collapse, Wilk demonstrated the degree to which modern events can influence our understanding of the past. There is nothing new in suggesting that archaeologists are products of their own culture; scientists (like Wilk) have always tried to discover biases, remove their effects, and move on. Although some postmodernists argue that objectivity is impossible and that truth is subjective, most postmodernists adhere to a weaker version of this thesis, seeing the effects of cultural biases as difficult but not impossible to remove. Deconstruction helps achieve that goal.

Fourth, *postprocessual archaeology argues that all archaeology is political.* Processual archaeologists wanted to be "relevant" to modern society but politically neutral. But postprocessual archaeology argues that all research is inescapably political. The Moundbuilder researcher Ephraim Squier, for example, was a confirmed polygenist—meaning that he did not believe that Indians originated in the same act of creation as did people of European ancestry, and this belief probably clouded his interpretation of the archaeological evidence. Likewise, postprocessualism argues that the evolutionary approaches processual archaeologists favor are based on Western notions of progress and hence are potentially (some would say fundamentally) racist.

Processual-Plus

Is there a middle road? Absolutely. Intellectual change occurs through the process of "thesis–antithesis–synthesis." The clock is a useful analogy here. One paradigm pulls the clock's pendulum far to one side and in response another paradigm pulls it the opposite way. Eventually, the pendulum will come to rest in the middle. In recent years, many (perhaps most) archaeologists have listened to debates and settled on the compromise that Michelle Hegmon (Arizona State University) calls "processual-plus."

Most archaeologists today adhere to some form of scientific inquiry as a way to evaluate ideas about what happened in the past; few subscribe to the extreme postmodern idea that we cannot know anything true about the past. And most still believe that material factors such as technology, subsistence, and environment play critical roles in how human societies have changed. But few seek universals; instead, many seek generalities, patterns that point to how material factors may constrain or channel, but not determine, cultural change.

We also recognize the importance of other factors. All archaeologists know that artifacts carried symbolic meanings for people in the past and that humans respond to situations through their cultural understandings of the world. And all archaeologists view history as the combined result of the actions of individuals, individuals who actively made decisions grounded in material concerns and cultural ideas simultaneously. Especially important has been a trend to look at gender, at the roles that men and women played in ancient societies (we'll return to this topic in Chapter 10). Most modern archaeologists also recognize the linkage between politics and research. Although few approach their research for purely political purposes, archaeologists today are taught to understand the political context and implications of their research.

Those, in a nutshell, are the important components of archaeological inquiry. How might these different elements work together in a research project? How would you start thinking like an archaeologist?

How Archaeological Inquiry Works

Take another look at Figure 2-6 on page 25. Notice first that the entire process of archaeological inquiry takes place within a box labeled "Social, Cultural, Political Context." The idea here is that scientists cannot step outside their culture; if we tried to do that, we'd cease being human, and lose our ability to analyze and understand the world. This fact can lead to bias, but by constantly checking ourselves, over time we should be able to distinguish between what is cultural bias and what is actually true.

The dotted line defining the "Paradigm" box symbolizes this interplay between one's research agenda and cultural context. Both paradigm and culture provide (often vague) understandings of the world, and each points researchers toward a question's answer. These biases are not necessarily wrong. Richard Wilk's analysis, for instance, suggests that Vietnam War–era experiences encouraged 1960s researchers to privilege war as the primary cause of the Maya civilization's collapse. Although these contexts are relevant, they do *not* mean that war did *not* cause the Maya collapse.

Paradigms provide specific guidelines for high-level theory—general statements such as, "Agriculture occurs when a human population grows to the point where it exceeds the natural carrying capacity of the local environment." Paradigms also generate more specific claims about a region's prehistory, such as, "In the Mimbres Valley of southern New Mexico, there was a change in social organization as evidenced by a shift from pithouse to

deconstruction Efforts to expose the assumptions behind the alleged objective and systematic search for knowledge; a primary tool of postmodernism.

stelae Stone monuments erected by Maya rulers to record their history in rich images and hieroglyphic symbols. These symbols can be read and dated.

RAPID REVIEW

Some Contrasts between Processual and Postprocessual Archaeology

Processual Archaeology	Postprocessual Archaeology
Emphasizes evolutionary generalizations and regularities, not historical specifics; downplays the importance of the individual	Rejects the search for universal laws and regularities
Views culture from a systemic perspective and defines culture as adaptation	Rejects the systemic view of culture and focuses on an ideational perspective
Explanation is explicitly scientific and objective	Less enthusiastic about scientific methods and denies possibility of objectivity
Attempts to remain ethically neutral; claims to be explicitly nonpolitical	Argues that all archaeology is unavoidably political

pueblo villages about 1000 years ago." Both statements are linked to the overarching paradigm by directing researchers to measure some variables (such as demography and changing social organization) and to set other variables (such as religion) aside. Such propositions tend to occur to archaeologists operating within a processual paradigm.

By contrast, an archaeologist operating within a postprocessual paradigm might suggest "Agriculture originated from the need to create goods to give away at competitive feasts" or "In the Mimbres Valley, a new symbolic order appeared about 1000 years ago, as evidenced by an art style involving painted naturalistic designs on bowls that are ritually 'killed' and placed in human burials."

Testing Ideas

In either case, hypotheses must be constructed to test the competing propositions. For each hypothesis, we can frame one or more "if . . . then" statements that build upon the research proposition and predict some presently unknown aspect of the archaeological record. Figure 2-6 shows this as "Hypotheses" resulting from high-level theory.

Take, for example, the question relating population growth and agriculture. Suppose we already know that an agricultural economy began about 4000 years ago in our research area. We might hypothesize: If our proposition is true—that is, if population is the driving force behind agriculture—then signs of population growth and subsequent pressure on the food base should appear prior to 4000 years ago.

Here is where hypotheses lead to middle-level theory (as shown in Figure 2-6). Testing this proposition requires some way of inferring population numbers from archaeological data. Because we can't measure population directly—the people in question died a long time ago—a bridging argument is required to infer changes in population over time from archaeological variables. Perhaps we need to survey existing ethnographic data or conduct original ethnoarchaeological research to find correlates between population size and things that archaeologists could record, such as house, cemetery, or village size.

Likewise, how do we measure "stress" on the food base? Maybe we can find ethnographic evidence that people under conditions of stress use foods that are more difficult to harvest. We might then have to conduct experiments, gathering foods with aboriginal technologies and measuring the efficiency with which they are collected. Such research might tell us that very small seeds are less efficiently harvested than large seeds, and their use might signal subsistence stress.

With adequate middle-level theory, we can define what constitutes relevant archaeological data (shown at lower right in Figure 2-6). If house size is a good measure of population, then we should measure a sample of houses from sites that date to time periods before and after 4000 years ago to see if there is evidence of population growth *before* the appearance of an agricultural economy. And if decreasing seed size is a good way to monitor stress on the food base, then let's recover and measure seeds from the appropriate archaeological sites.

Having done this background work, we can state the hypothesis in a more specific way: If agriculture appears because population exceeds carrying capacity, then (1) house size should increase before 4000 years ago, and (2) seeds found in trash associated with those houses should become smaller over time.

Here's the fun part: the archaeological fieldwork required to collect the data necessary to test our hypothesis (shown in the center of Figure 2-6). As archaeologists, we

PROFILE OF AN ARCHAEOLOGIST

An Academic Archaeologist

Michelle Hegmon is a professor of anthropology at Arizona State University. Reprinted by permission.

© Michelle Hegmon

Michelle Hegmon

Two tenets are key to my brand of archaeology, processual-plus. The first is open-mindedness, a willingness to set theoretical egos aside, and the second is recognition of the power of theory, words, and labels to shape our understanding of the past.

I work in the Mimbres region of New Mexico, a place that is famous for its pottery, but it was analysis rather than artifacts that originally drew me to archaeology. I don't remember my first piece of pottery, but I definitely remember the Introduction to Archaeology class in which Steve Plog described how ceramic designs could tell us about the social lives of people 1000 years ago. That's what caught my interest: solving puzzles and learning from artifacts.

I began graduate school in 1981 at the University of Michigan—renowned for its processual approach—and in 1982, postprocessualism appeared. Those were heady days for me and my fellow students (including [author] Kelly). Born too late to be a real hippie, I tried to rebel intellectually. No ecology or evolution for me, I was going to be a real postprocessualist. I cringe when I think back on my young theoretical ego, passionately identifying with labels, and now appreciate the patience of my teachers (especially Henry Wright and Richard Ford). By the time I finished my dissertation, which returned me to my early interest in pottery design, I had developed much of what I now call processual-plus: a melding of postprocessual interest in symbols and meaning with processual concerns regarding systematic generalizations.

At the conclusion of my PhD defense, my committee stood to congratulate me. I stood, and (I am only 5'3") literally looked up at the tall men surrounding me. Until then, I had paid little attention to gender. My mother, a physicist and feminist, had fought those battles for me; her generation made it possible for women in mine to move ahead with relative ease. For me, Southwest archaeology was a supportive environment. At a seminar on engendering Southwest archaeology, I joined a group of colleagues who pushed the intellectual envelope. As my mother's daughter, I assumed prehistoric women's domestic labor (such as corn grinding) was drudgery, but others assumed it was highly respected. This disagreement made clear the importance of labels and of prior experience. Gender research—a key component of processual-plus—also taught me that feminism still has much to do.

I've done most of my professional research as part of the Eastern Mimbres Archaeological Project (EMAP), which Peggy Nelson and I began in 1993. The rich floodplain of the Mimbres River of southwest New Mexico is known for its Classic Mimbres villages, many of which were depopulated at a time of low rainfall around 870 BP. Unfortunately, looters have destroyed many of those sites, searching for pottery. In contrast, the eastern Mimbres region is drier but more remote. Landowners (including Ted Turner) have protected sites and supported our research. One of EMAP's most important conclusions is that the eastern area sustained a more continuous occupation than the Mimbres Valley. We documented a post-870 BP regional reorganization, when people changed their lifestyle and their pottery but remained in their homeland.

EMAP is, above all, a collaboration, and becoming part of it is one of the best things I have ever done. Peggy Nelson's specialties include lithic technology and ecology, while mine are ceramic style and social theory, but rather than dividing these realms we have brought our perspectives together to delve into issues such as socioecology and the technology of style. Together we also have more fun. For many years we have run a large fieldschool, in which we teach our students the importance of collaboration and the many skills—ranging from tire changing to soils analysis—that are part of archaeological research. We also prepare a generation of young scholars to move ahead in a world of both women and men. Finally, our collaboration has taught me the importance of relinquishing some degree of control, trusting that Peggy and our students know what they are doing.

This lesson is key to a new direction in our research. Together with our colleagues at Arizona State University, we are embarking on several interdisciplinary projects that, by their very nature, draw on data and theory more vast than any of us can master single-handedly. These projects must be collaborations in which we set our theoretical egos aside.

must design fieldwork to generate adequate samples of house floors and seeds from the right time periods. Low-level theory is required to identify house floors (through the presence of postholes, packed clay floors, hearths, and so forth) and to identify seeds (we'll discuss fieldwork much more in the following chapters).

Reconstructing the Past

Hypothesis testing requires that we reconstruct the past, that we figure out what actually happened back in time (as shown at the lower left in Figure 2-6). Perhaps we will find that houses became larger over time (or maybe not); perhaps we learn that seeds became smaller through time (or maybe not). Notice that in Figure 2-6, the dotted line enclosing "The reconstructed past" is itself inside a larger box labeled the "The real past." We did this to emphasize that we cannot hope to reconstruct the complete past. Although we're getting better at recovering and extracting information from material remains, a complete picture of the past will always elude us.

As the postprocessual critique makes clear, our experiences in the present heavily color our vision of the past. Our sample hypothesis looks to demography (rather than religion or social change) to explain a change in subsistence. The implication from this hypothesis is that to reconstruct the past, some issues are important and others can be downplayed. Had we hypothesized a religious cause to agricultural origins, then we would have generated very different data during our fieldwork. We might have looked, for example, for evidence of how plants were used in different rituals, and we would probably have excavated religious structures instead of houses.

Back to the Beginning

Let's return to the original propositions to see whether we confirmed or falsified them: Did the fieldwork and ensuing analyses find evidence of population growth and resource stress prior to 4000 years ago, or did it not?

At this point, the archaeological narrative goes public. This presentation necessarily begins with scientific monographs or papers that other archaeologists will scrutinize. But modern archaeologists know that results need to be conveyed to a broader public through books or magazine articles written in lay terms, public lectures, television presentations, or museum exhibitions. This is how the public can learn from and comment on the research. This professional and public feedback might require the archaeologist to revisit the research propositions and maybe even start the process all over again. Sometimes, through this recursive process (shown at left in Figure 2-6), archaeologists recognize a poor fit between their ideas and the archaeological record—maybe it's time to discard one paradigm for another, and begin anew.

Conclusion

Archaeology is firmly embedded in anthropology, drawing upon the methods and approaches of the other subfields of anthropology. The differing perspectives of anthropologists on culture are reflected in archaeological research as well. Although archaeologists can approach their subject in many different ways (which we've characterized as processual and postprocessual paradigms), most archaeologists believe that they conduct scientific research as we've described it: Define a specific problem, then conduct objective research to test the hypotheses.

Few archaeologists can do every step in the process of archaeological inquiry; almost everyone specializes. Some emphasize middle-level theory, doing experimental or ethnoarchaeological research. Others concentrate on the public side, presenting their research and that of others to a broader audience. Others work mostly with theory or critiques of paradigms, and still others spend most of their time doing fieldwork. But, however archaeologists spend their time, it's critical that each understands the role that he or she plays in the overall process of archaeological inquiry.

Summary

- What is an anthropological approach?
  - Anthropologists believe that a true understanding of humankind can arise only from a perspective that is comparative, global, and holistic. Anthropology includes four subfields: biological, cultural, and linguistic anthropology, and archaeology. The concept of culture unites these diverse fields. Culture is a learned, shared, and symbolically based system of knowledge that includes traditions, kinship, language, religion, customs, and beliefs.
- What two paradigms do anthropologists use to study culture, and how are these different ways of thinking reflected in archaeology?
  - There are two major approaches to the study of human culture. The ideational perspective deals with mentalistic, symbolic, cognitive culture; it sees culture as an instrument to create meaning and order in one's world. The adaptive perspective emphasizes those aspects of culture that most closely articulate with the environment, technology, and economics,

and sees culture as the way in which humans adapt to their natural and social environment.

- These approaches are reflected in the two major paradigms of modern archaeology: processual and postprocessual archaeology. The former takes a scientific approach and focuses on the material factors of life; the latter emphasizes symbolic meanings, power relationships, individual actions, and gender.

◎ What is science and how does it explain things?

- Science is a search for answers through a process that is objective, systematic, logical, predictive, self-critical, and public. It works through a cyclical process that entails constructing hypotheses, determining their empirical implications, and testing those hypotheses with empirical data. For more than a century, archaeology has been firmly grounded in a scientific perspective, which provides an elegant and powerful way of allowing people to understand the workings of the visible world.

◎ What three levels of theory does a scientific approach in archaeology entail? How do these relate to paradigms?

- Low-level theory involves the observations that emerge from archaeological fieldwork; this is how archaeologists get their "data," their "facts."
- Middle-level theory links archaeological data with human behavior or natural processes; it is produced through experimental archaeology, taphonomy (the study of natural processes on archaeological sites), and ethnoarchaeology (the study of living peoples to see links between behavior and material remains).
- High-level theory provides answers to larger "why" questions.
- Paradigms are frameworks for thinking that interrelate concepts and provide research strategies. They apply to intellectual inquiry in general and are not specific to archaeology.

Media Resources

Doing Fieldwork: Archaeological Demonstrations CD-ROM 2.0

This CD, developed by the authors, shows professional archaeologists involved in various digs, many of which are referenced in the text. The presentation is organized by the main techniques used on an archaeological dig, reinforcing concepts and techniques via live examples. The CD takes you through each step automatically, or you can navigate to any point via the navigation bar. After reviewing a step in the dig process, you are taken to Check Points, which are concept questions about each step of the dig. Then you can see the answers, receive your score, and even send your scores to your instructor.

See the "What Is the Question?" section of the CD-ROM to learn more about topics covered in this chapter.

CourseMate

Access chapter-specific learning tools including learning objectives, practice quizzes, videos, flash cards, and glossaries, as well as web links, and more in your Archaeology CourseMate. Login to www.cengagebrain.com to access the resources your instructor has assigned and to purchase materials.

Doing Fieldwork: Surveying for Archaeological Sites

3

© IRA BLOCK/National Geographic Stock

Chaco Canyon, in northwestern New Mexico, contains several massive pueblos that were occupied in the eleventh century, including Pueblo Bonito (lower right); many smaller sites were revealed by surface survey, and a road system by remote sensing.

Learning Objectives

After reading this chapter, you should be able to answer these questions:

- Why do archaeologists "survey"?
- What is the main principle of survey? Why does this matter?
- What limits surface survey? What are the basic remote sensing techniques and their benefits?
- What is "landscape archaeology"?

Preview

NOW THE FUN BEGINS! The next two chapters will show you what it's like to do real archaeology. For many in the discipline—ourselves included—fieldwork is why we became archaeologists in the first place. That said, we must begin this introduction to archaeological field techniques with two important warnings:

- There is no one "right" way to find and excavate sites (but there are plenty of wrong ways).
- Nobody ever learned how to do proper archaeological fieldwork from a book (including this one).

Despite recent advances, archaeological fieldwork remains as much art as science. All we can do here is examine some common techniques, list some archaeological standards and principles, and give you a sense of what it feels like to participate in an archaeological exploration.

Introduction

Every archaeologist is eventually asked the same question: "How do you know where to dig?"

There are many answers. We've known about some **archaeological sites**, such as Egypt's pyramids, for centuries—they were never lost. The locations of other sites have been handed down through the generations, preserved in oral and written traditions. For example, archaeologists identified the site of Tula in northern Mexico as the prehistoric Toltec capital by tracing and testing Aztec traditions. Sites are sometimes deliberately discovered in large-scale systematic surveys, during which large regions are scanned for the remains of previous habitation. And some of the most important archaeological sites in the world were found by accident, hard work, and luck.

Good Old Gumshoe Survey

In Chapter 2, we mentioned Gatecliff Shelter in Nevada, where both of us excavated in the 1970s. But before we could dig at Gatecliff, the site had to be found. How did that happen?

Gatecliff was found by a fortunate combination of happenstance, hard work, and luck, a process that James O'Connell (University of Utah) calls old-fashioned "gumshoe survey."

In the summer of 1970, Thomas was in central Nevada's Reese River Valley conducting a systematic archaeological survey (a technique we discuss later in this chapter). Basically, this fieldwork entails mapping and collecting archaeological materials found on the ground. The survey went well, but it could not answer all the questions. Thomas needed to know, for example, something about prehistoric subsistence and the chronology of different artifact types. Such information can only come from buried sites, where food remains (bones and seeds) might be preserved and where artifacts can be dated. Rockshelters and caves often contain the necessary buried deposits, but despite the Reese River crew's best efforts, they could not locate one.

At the end of the first field session in Reese River, Thomas assembled the crew for steak dinners in the town of Austin, about an hour's dusty ride away. Austin is a pocket-sized Nevada mining town with fewer than 250 citizens, a picturesque little desert dive. Writer Oscar Lewis described it as "the town that died laughing," and William Least Heat Moon called it "a living ghost town: 40 percent living, 50 percent ghost and 10 percent not yet decided."

When two dozen grubby archaeologists come to such a town for steaks and beverages, word gets around quickly. Thomas soon found himself talking with the waitress's husband, Gale Peer, a mining geologist who had prospected central Nevada for 40 years. There are few places Gale Peer had not been, so Thomas asked if he knew of any caves or rockshelters.

Indeed, Mr. Peer did know of a cave—in Monitor Valley, about 20 kilometers east of Austin. He had not been there in years, but the details were fresh in his mind.

"You take the main dirt road south in Monitor Valley, then turn west, up one of the side canyons. I don't remember which one. As you drive along, oh, let's see, maybe 10 or 15 miles, there's a large black chert cliff. At the bottom of the cliff is a cave. Some time, a long time ago, the Indians painted the inside of the cave. There are pictures of people and animals, plus a lot of writing I don't understand. Top of the shelter's caved in. Maybe in an earthquake. There's not much of the cave left. Drive out there when you get a chance. I'd like to know what's in that cave." He sketched a map on his business card.

archaeological site Any place where material evidence exists about the human past. Usually, "site" refers to a concentration of such evidence.

LOOKING CLOSER

How Do Archaeological Sites Get Their Names?

It's an archaeologist's prerogative to name new sites. Many are named after a prominent topographic feature, such as the canyon in which the site is located, or a nearby mountain, river, or town—or a rock formation, as in the case of Gatecliff Shelter.

Sites on private land are commonly named after the landowners; some become the namesakes of the amateur archaeologists who find them. And sometimes the archaeologist can have fun with a site's name. Robert Bettinger (University of California, Davis) named one California cave site Gimme Shelter (after the Rolling Stones tune).

Some names have stories attached to them. Danger Cave, on the edge of Utah's Great Salt Lake, for example, was originally called Hands and Knees Caves by locals, to describe how it was entered. But during Elmer Smith's 1941 excavation, a huge piece of the lip broke off and crashed into the excavation, narrowly missing several crew members and, according to legend, landing right where some had just finished lunch. This incident resulted in a permanent name change. During Jesse Jennings's excavations there in the 1950s, the students elected to change the name to Lamus Cave, after Blair Lamus, a superintendent of the potash plant in nearby Wendover, to recognize the help he had given to the project (which apparently included small amounts of dynamite). Jennings apparently nixed the suggestion.

So sites acquire their names in many different ways. There is, in fact, only one cultural rule to follow: A professional archaeologist can *never* name a site after him- or herself.

The next summer Thomas and his crew returned, hoping to find the cave that Mr. Peer had described. They knew that the rockshelter was several miles up a canyon, on the north side—but there were 15 such canyons.

Beginning at the southern end of Monitor Valley, the crew drove up and down each side canyon, working their way northward. They were hampered by spring snow and washed-out roads—typical fieldwork conditions in central Nevada.

Each of the canyons had potential. The crew would see something, stop the truck, and skitter up the hillside. But each time, the "something" turned out to be a shadow, an abandoned mine shaft, or just a jumble of boulders.

After a week, Thomas came to Mill Canyon, just the next one on the list, with no greater potential than the ten canyons they had already combed. The road was a little worse than most and, even in four-wheel drive, the truck lurched down a steep ridge into the rocky canyon. Finally, as the crew moved up the flat canyon bottom, a black cliff loomed ahead, riddled with small caves and rockshelters.

As had happened many times before, the shelters were empty, unless you count coyote scats and pack rat nests. Finally, the crew spied a dim shadow where the black dolomite formation was swallowed up beneath the Mill Canyon bottomland.

The paintings were invisible until you stood right in the mouth of the shelter. But there they were, just as Mr. Peer had said: small human figures, painted in red and yellow. On the other wall were cryptic motifs in white and black. And, yes, the roof had caved in years before. One boulder dwarfed the pickup.

There was nothing "archaeological" on the surface, but a small test pit turned up telltale signs that people had once lived in the shelter: several pieces of broken bone, a few of them charred, and a dozen stone flakes (probably debris from resharpening stone knives or **projectile points**).

Across the campfire that night, the crew assayed the finds. The rock art was intriguing; only two similar sites were known in central Nevada. The stones and bones were suggestive, but the shelter seemed hardly the deep site they were seeking. Thomas named the site after the rock formation, Gatecliff, in which they found it (see "Looking Closer: How Do Archaeological Sites Get Their Names?").

On the strength of this meager evidence, they decided to dig some—a good decision, it turned out, because the deposits inside Gatecliff Shelter proved to be 12 meters deep, making it one of the deepest rockshelters in the Americas. And the strata were spectacularly layered, not jumbled up as in most sites in the area. Flash floods had periodically inundated the shelter, the surging waters laying down thick layers of rock-hard silt. This flooding occurred at least a dozen times, separating the deposits into clean occupational "floors."

Gatecliff had what textbooks—including this one—describe as "layer-cake stratigraphy." Sandwiched between these sterile flash-flood deposits was a wonderful 7000-year record of human activity and environmental change in Monitor Valley. And it was found only because a waitress's husband in Austin, Nevada, remembered an interesting place from years before.

In fact, many important sites have been found by ranchers, cowboys, sheepherders, farmers, geologists, and amateur

FIGURE 3-1 Students conducting a site survey in the Carson Desert.

archaeologists—anyone who spends a lot of time wandering about outdoors. This is the essence of gumshoe survey—hanging out in coffee shops, bars, and gas stations, listening to those who know more about the landscape than you do.

Finding interesting sites is only one goal, however. The other is discovering a region's archaeological character. For that, we need to consider how to adequately sample a region's archaeology.

Surface Archaeology in the Carson Desert

The Great Basin is best known for vast stretches of sagebrush and arid mountain ranges, but it also contains several substantial wetlands. Anthropologist Julian Steward's Depression-era research documented the lives of those Shoshone and Paiute people who lived in areas *without* wetlands. So, without much ethnographic data, archaeologists in the 1970s debated how the wetlands were incorporated into the **seasonal round** of the region's native peoples.

One hypothesis held that the wetlands provided a permanent, sedentary home for hunter-gatherers; an opposing view held that the wetlands served as only one element in a broader seasonal round. Both hypotheses were grounded in the processual paradigm, but the first argued that wetlands provide abundant, high-quality foods; it also assumed that people would become sedentary (that is, stay in one location year-round) wherever food was abundant. The second viewed wetland food resources as lower in quality and more difficult to gather than others, such as piñon and large game. And it assumed that hunter-gatherers became sedentary when lack of food elsewhere forced them to do so. Expressed as research questions, the hypotheses were: Did prehistoric peoples settle down and focus exclusively on the wetlands, or did they incorporate the wetlands' resources into a more diversified seasonal round?

One of the Great Basin's largest wetlands lies in the Carson Desert, about 100 kilometers east of Reno, Nevada. A large basin filled with sand dunes and alkali flats, the Carson Desert is also the terminus of several large rivers that created a vast, slightly alkaline wetland. This wetland is host to many species of plants and animals that provided ancient peoples with food and various kinds of raw material for clothing, houses, and tools: cattail, bulrush, and other plants; fish; muskrats and other small mammals. Piñon pine nuts grow in the piñon-juniper forest of the Stillwater Mountains that form the eastern edge of the Carson Desert, and foragers could find tubers, seeds, and bighorn sheep there as well. Previous research suggested that people had lived in this region off and on for more than 9000 years.

In the late 1970s, we were excavating Hidden Cave, a site located at the south end of the Stillwater range, which overlooks the Carson Desert. The site was used primarily between 5000 and 1500 years ago as a place to cache hunting gear and as an escape from the desert's extreme summer heat. Hidden Cave is an intriguing site, but because we knew that people had lived in the Carson Desert for at least 9000 years, we assumed that Hidden Cave documented

projectile points Arrowheads, dart points, or spear points.

seasonal round Hunter-gatherers' pattern of movement between different places on the landscape, timed to the seasonal availability of food and other resources.

only a portion of the region's prehistory. Furthermore, the site obviously gives us limited insight into the lives of the people who lived in this area—like trying to reconstruct someone's life by looking only at that person's safe deposit box or back porch. (We'll have more to say about Hidden Cave in Chapter 8.)

To understand ancient life in the Carson Desert, we therefore needed to explore the regional archaeological record. What kind of archaeological remains are found near the marsh, in the dunes, in the low foothills of the Stillwater Mountains, and, higher in the mountains, in the piñon-juniper forest? We hypothesized that if a sedentary population exploited the wetland, then we should find evidence of large, year-round populations living near the marsh. There should be little evidence of use of the mountains, except perhaps by hunting parties seeking bighorn sheep. People should have made far less use of the dunes and alkali flats, because their economic potentials are low compared with that of the wetland. If, on the other hand, the wetlands were just one stop on a broad-scale seasonal round, then we should find evidence of more transient use of the wetlands and more intensive use of the mountains.

With these alternative hypotheses in mind, we generated some archaeological expectations for each. Because we would rely strictly on surface archaeology, where organic remains are not preserved, we focused on stone tools (pottery is rare in this region) and the waste flakes from their manufacture and resharpening. We'll talk more about these kinds of artifacts in Chapters 6 and 7.

The point is this: Long before taking to the field, we had a good idea of what we should find if one hypothesis was correct and the other was incorrect. If a sedentary population had used the wetlands, then we expected to find dense scatters of waste flakes and broken tools (the remains of villages occupied for years at a time) in the wetland. In the uplands, we expected to find only evidence of hunting activities, small campsites containing broken projectile points. If, instead, the second hypothesis were correct, then we should find smaller, less dense settlements on the valley floor and, in the mountains, evidence not only of hunting but also of tuber, seed, and piñon gathering, as shown by the **manos** and **metates** (grinding stones) used for processing seeds and nuts.

Some Sampling Considerations

You can see that the fieldwork appropriate to test our hypotheses must explore the character of archaeological evidence across a large region. But what should that region be? And did we need to search every square inch of it? Given the practicalities of desert archaeology, it was obvious that we could not look everywhere. We must *sample*, but capricious and biased sampling methods can lead archaeologists astray. What if we looked only in places where we thought sites would be located? Not being Great Basin hunter-gatherers, we would surely not see the landscape as past foragers did. We would undoubtedly overestimate the importance of some places and overlook others, generating a biased image of the region's archaeology.

The best way to ensure unbiased results is through judicious use of **statistical sampling**. We'll cover only the basic principles of this large and complex subject here. (But note that any students contemplating a career in archaeology will need to take several statistics courses, because statistical analysis is as indispensable to archaeologists as their trowels.)

To acquire a statistical sample, you must first define the **statistical population** that you wish to characterize. In this case, that population is the observations we could make on the stone artifacts and waste flakes found in the archaeological sites of the Carson Desert and Stillwater Mountains.

Statistical sampling also requires that we define a relevant **sample universe**, the archaeological sites that will provide the sample population. Because the research question concerned the relationships between sites on the valley floor (in particular, those in the wetland) and sites in the mountains, our sample universe had to contain both of these regions.

The result was a sample universe—a survey area—of some 1700 square kilometers that looks like the head of a large, barking dog (shown in Figure 3-2). The size and shape of a survey area result from the research question and practical considerations. In this case, the survey area's odd shape was a product of the need to encompass the wetland, dune area, and alkali flats, as well as the northern Stillwater Mountains, where there is a piñon-juniper forest today, and the southern mountains, which are covered primarily by sagebrush. But we also needed to avoid (1) the town of Fallon, (2) a large wildlife refuge that lies in the dog's "mouth," and (3) in front of the dog's ear, a large naval bombing range that contained unexploded ordinance. (Fallon is home to one of the U.S. Navy's elite fighter pilot schools—portions of the film *Top Gun* were filmed there.)

Because soil formation in deserts is often slow and vegetation is sparse, many archaeological remains still lie on the surface, where people dropped or discarded them hundreds or even thousands of years ago. Doing surface archaeology in such places means that you simply spot an artifact, plot its location in your field notes, pick it up, and label it—no digging!

But who could survey all 1700 square kilometers? That could take lifetimes! This is where statistical sampling theory helps out, providing a set of methods to characterize a population without having to record data on every item in that population. We draw upon the same set of methods and theory that pollsters use to take the nation's political pulse by interviewing only a thousand people.

You begin by selecting a **random sample** of the site population. The word "random" here is critical, for it specifically means that *each site has an equal chance of being selected for the sample.* If there are 100 sites, say, then each

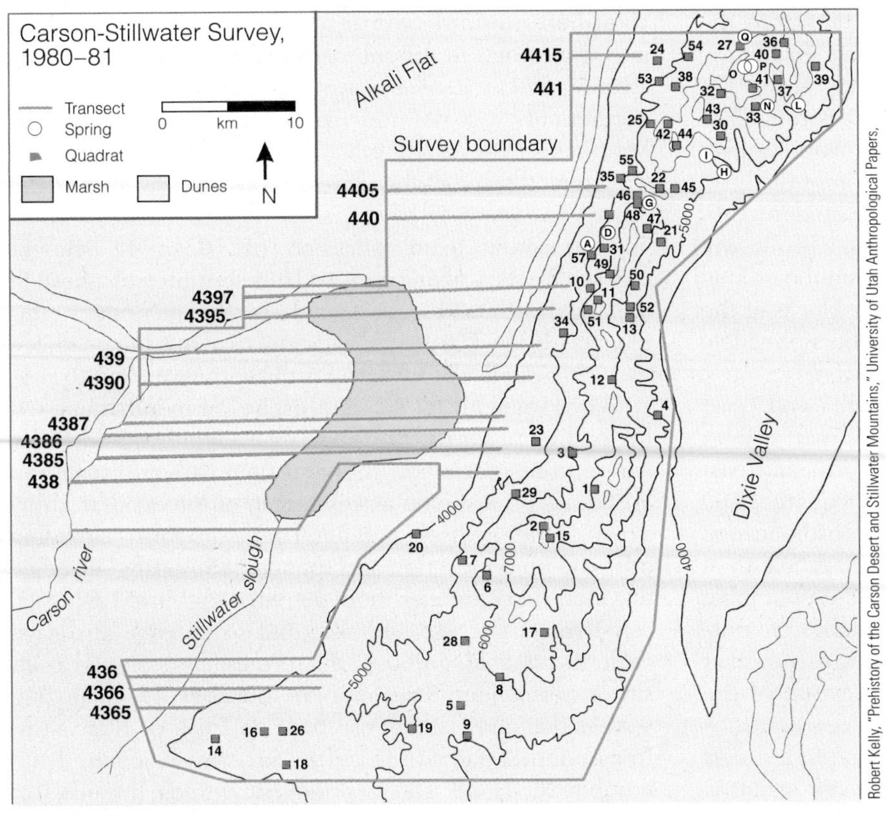

FIGURE 3-2 Map of the Carson Desert and Stillwater Mountains (Nevada), showing the locations of survey transects, quadrats, and spring surveys.

site must have a 1/100 = 1 percent chance of being included in the sample. If the sample is not selected in a random manner, then some sites may be overrepresented and others underrepresented in the sample. And that could bias the final results.

Random sampling provides the only way for archaeologists to collect meaningful negative evidence. This is important because, in addition to knowing what activities took place where, archaeologists want to know which activities did *not* occur in a particular area or biotic community. As you will see, the requirement for negative evidence imposes severe yet necessary requirements on survey fieldwork.

Randomly selecting the samples also permits us to analyze the results statistically. Because statistical analysis generally requires a random sample, archaeologists who use a biased sampling design will never know if their results are meaningful or not.

Getting the Sample

Once we have decided on the sample universe, the next task is to select the sample. The first step is to decide on the **sample fraction**. What portion of the sample population will be included—1 percent of the sites? 5 percent? 50 percent? Archaeologists are somewhat hampered in this regard because the size of the sample depends on characteristics of the statistical population, which in this case is unknown.

One solution is to start with a small uniform sample across the region and then use the findings to decide whether some regions need more intensive sampling. So, we began in 1980, with a 1 percent sample of the entire region and then increased the sample fraction in particular areas the following summer.

The second step is more pragmatic: How do you actually acquire the sample? We solved this problem by using randomly selected **sample units**. Sample units can be many different shapes, but squares, circles, and transects (long, narrow rectangles) are the most commonly used; all three were employed in this survey. The choice of which to use depends on the research questions, but also on practical considerations.

In the mountains, we used 500 × 500 meter squares (we called them quadrats) as the sample unit. Kelly selected this size because Thomas's previous experience in other Nevada surveys had shown that they were

mano A fist-sized, round, flat, handheld stone used with a metate for grinding foods.

metate A large, flat stone used as a stationary surface upon which seeds, tubers, and nuts are ground with a mano.

statistical sampling The principles that underlie sampling strategies and provide accurate measures of a statistical population.

statistical population A set of counts, measurements, or characteristics about which relevant inquiries are to be made. Scientists use the term "statistical population" in a specialized way (quite different from "population" in the ordinary sense).

sample universe The region that contains the statistical population and that will be sampled. Its size and shape are determined by the research question and practical considerations.

random sample A sample drawn from a statistical population such that every member of the population has an equal chance of being included in the sample.

sample fraction The percentage of the sample universe that is surveyed. Areas with a lot of variability in archaeological remains require larger sample fractions than do areas of low variability.

sample units Survey units of a standard size and shape, determined by the research question and practical considerations, used to obtain the sample.

a manageable size, given the exigencies of survey in the mountains and the number of crew members at hand.

We located these squares randomly using the **UTM** (Universal Transverse Mercator) grid. What is the UTM grid? Simply put, mapmakers divide the world into a grid of 1 × 1 meter squares; each intersection in that grid has north and east coordinates. Look at a standard U.S. Geological Survey (USGS) topographic map, and you will see these coordinates written in small black numbers along the map's margins that label 1 × 1 kilometer blocks of the UTM grid drawn in black lines. These numbers provide a handy, preexisting way to sample a landscape.

We randomly selected sets of north and east coordinates (by putting the UTM coordinates in a hat—nothing fancy here!). Each set of north and east coordinates defined the northwest corner of a 500 × 500 meter sample square; for example, the coordinates of Quadrat 36 were 4416000 North, 407500 East. We then located these squares on the appropriate topographic map and drew them in. We selected a number of units from predefined portions of the mountains to ensure that survey units were spread throughout the extent of the Stillwater Mountains.

Water is critical for hunter-gatherers living in a desert environment. In the Stillwater Mountains, water is mostly present as springs that create a small seep or a short creek. In his Reese River Valley survey, Thomas found that sites tended to occur within about 450 meters of a water source, so we chose to survey a 500-meter radius around a sample of the springs. These 500-meter radius circles were then completely surveyed for sites.

On the valley floor (defined as all land below 1340 meters [4400 feet] in elevation), we used 100-meter-wide transects (instead of 500-meter squares) to sample the area. We chose this width because we had 10 to 12 students working on the project, and this meant that they could be spaced about 10 meters apart—an interval that previous experience told us was the maximum distance surveyors should walk to avoid missing small sites.

We located the first transect by randomly selecting a UTM north coordinate from near the north end of the valley survey and using that coordinate to define the middle of the 100-meter transect width. To increase the sample to the desired fraction, we then selected additional transects at 10-kilometer intervals south of the first. Later, additional transects were selected by placing them between these existing ones.

Doing the Work

We completed the Carson-Stillwater survey in two summers. During the first summer, we found that archaeological remains were most dense and variable in the piñon-juniper forest of the mountains and in the dune area. Site density and variability were somewhat less in the wetland region of the valley floor and in the unforested portion of the mountains. So, during the second summer, we pursued a **stratified random sample**, dividing the sample universe into five strata, or sub-universes: the wetland, the dune area to the west of the wetland, the south valley, the northern Stillwater Mountains, and the southern Stillwater Mountains. As a result of the first summer's survey sample, we sampled some of these areas more intensively than the others.

The survey team consisted of 10 to 12 student archaeologists, walking at 8- to 10-meter intervals through the sagebrush and greasewood. In the mountains, this team made five 100-meter-wide passes across the quadrats; we used a similar procedure for the spring surveys.

When someone found a site, each crew member marked his or her place on the line (so everyone would know where to resume surveying) and then gathered together. We located the site on a sketch map of the quadrat, drew a map of the site itself, and filled out a site form (including information on location and topographic setting; distance to water; vegetation; erosion; potential for buried deposits; estimates of site age and size; and so on). We also gave each site a field number, but eventually assigned each site a permanent **Smithsonian number**—a cataloging system that most states use to keep track of their sites. For example, one site found in our survey acquired the number 26CH798: The 26 stands for Nevada, because it is the 26th state alphabetically (excluding Alaska and Hawaii, which acquired statehood after this system was in place; they are now 49 and 50). The CH stands for Churchill County, and 798 means it was the 798th site recorded in that county.

After two summers, we had surveyed 57 quadrats, 8 springs, and 260 kilometers of transects—about 47 square kilometers, or a sample fraction of the total survey universe of about 3 percent; some strata were sampled more intensively than others.

We recorded 160 sites and collected some 10,400 stone tools and more than 70,000 manufacturing and resharpening waste flakes. We analyzed these over the next several years.

What We Learned

Recall that our first hypothesis held that if sedentary peoples used the wetlands then the highest site density should be in the wetland. But our survey found that the highest site densities occurred in the dunes, the south valley region, and the northern forested portion of the mountains.

This hypothesis also predicted that sites in the wetlands should contain evidence of long-term habitation. But the archaeological survey recovered stone tools and evidence of stone tool manufacturing techniques suggesting that wetland sites were short-term camps. This evidence is more in line with the second hypothesis, which argued that the wetland was but one stop on a seasonal round (and, in fact, the sites in the dune region contained tools and waste flakes that suggested even more transient stays than those in the wetland).

But the second hypothesis also suggested that the piñon forests should have been included in the seasonal round. Although we found evidence of hunting there, evidence for plant collecting, in the form of grinding stones, was almost nonexistent.

In sum, neither hypothesis seems to provide an adequate reconstruction of ancient life in the Carson Desert and Stillwater Mountains. We have come full circle in the research cycle and are now back at the beginning, proposing new hypotheses that take into account what we have learned.

GPS Technology and Modern Surveys

Surveys today are assisted by **global positioning system (GPS)** technology. This system did not exist when we surveyed the Carson Desert; if it did, it would have made the work easier and more accurate.

The GPS consists of 27 satellites (24 active ones and 3 spares) that circle the earth in 12-hour evenly distributed orbits at an altitude of about 14,000 kilometers. These orbits repeat the same ground track (because the earth turns beneath them) twice each day. Each satellite carries a computer and very accurate atomic clocks.

Handheld GPS units operate by picking up the continuously broadcast signals from at least four satellites. The GPS receiver triangulates a position fix using the interval between the transmission and reception of the satellite signal. Even inexpensive units ($150) will give 5-meter accuracy within seconds, and expensive devices can give sub-centimeter accuracy. GPS technology has made fieldwork easier, and no archaeologist today would take to the field without a GPS unit.

Looking below the Ground

The archaeological surveys we have discussed so far recorded only evidence that is visible with a pedestrian survey. In places like the Carson Desert, important archaeological remains can lie on a stable desert surface for millennia. But elsewhere, artifacts can be washed away or deeply buried (as at Gatecliff Shelter).

This issue cropped up in the Carson Desert project after we finished our survey in 1981. Two years later, and about 300 kilometers away, torrential rains and heavy snows began falling across the headwaters of the Humboldt River, which eventually drains into the Carson Desert. The heavy precipitation kept up until the Carson Desert—that barren basin of sand dunes and alkali flats—became a 40-mile-wide lake.

During the summer of 1986, as floodwaters receded, they stripped away the tops of dunes and exposed hundreds of human burials and archaeological sites containing shallow houses (Figure 3-3 shows an example), storage pits, bones, stone tools, beads, and grinding stones (we discuss these sites and burials in Chapters 8 and 9). When the U.S. Fish and Wildlife Service (the agency that manages the Carson Desert's wetland) plotted the newly exposed finds, their maps showed that our survey crews had literally walked right over some of these sites. We missed them because there was no surface indication of what lay buried below.

Surface archaeology documents only what lies on or near the ground surface. Although you can never be absolutely certain about what lies below, there are ways to get a pretty good idea. Archaeologists working in the eastern United States, Europe, and elsewhere confront this problem all the time, because these areas witness considerable soil buildup, and artifacts rarely lie on the undisturbed ground surface. In agricultural regions, archaeologists do **plow-zone** archaeology, walking through plowed fields after spring tilling (and especially after a rain), because the plow will turn up shallowly buried archaeological remains.

In other areas, archaeologists use **shovel testing**. Survey crews carry small shovels and sometimes a backpacked screen with them. As the crew moves across a survey unit, each member stops at a predetermined interval, digs a shallow hole, and screens the dirt, looking for evidence of buried archaeological remains. It's slow going, and it obviously cannot locate remains that are more than about a meter deep.

Looking for more deeply buried remains, some archaeologists use backhoe trenches or hand or mechanical soil augers, but the former can be very expensive (as well as destructive) and the latter very slow. We normally use them in areas that previous research suggests are good places to prospect for buried remains. In other cases, archaeologists use natural exposures, such as arroyos or riverbanks, which sometimes expose deeply buried deposits.

UTM Universal Transverse Mercator, a grid system in which north and east coordinates provide a location anywhere in the world, precise to 1 meter.

stratified random sample A survey universe divided into several sub-universes that are then sampled at potentially different sample fractions.

Smithsonian number A unique catalog number given to each site; it consists of a number (the state's position alphabetically), a letter abbreviation for the county, and the site's sequential number within the county.

global positioning system (GPS) Handheld devices that use triangulation from radio waves received from satellites to determine your current position in terms of either the UTM grid or latitude and longitude.

plow-zone The upper portion of a soil profile that has been disturbed by repeated plowing or other agricultural activity.

shovel testing A sample survey method used in regions where rapid soil buildup obscures buried archaeological remains; it entails digging shallow, systematic pits across the survey unit.

© Robert Kelly

FIGURE 3-3 An archaeological crew excavating a semi-subterranean house pit in the Stillwater Marsh (Nevada). Surface survey missed dozens of sites like this because they were not visible beneath sand and saltgrass.

Archaeologists also can use some pretty high-tech ways to "see" belowground. Next, we will consider how surface survey was combined with some of these new techniques to find Mission Santa Catalina, a Spanish Franciscan mission lost in Georgia's Sea Islands for more than 300 years.

At its seventeenth-century zenith, Spanish Florida had three dozen Franciscan missions, satellite settlements each heavily dependent on the colonial capital at St. Augustine. To the west lived the Timucuan, Apalachee, and Apalachicola Indians; to the north, toward St. Catherines Island, lay the province of the Mocamo and the Guale. Although a dozen sixteenth- and seventeenth-century missions once existed in the present state of Georgia, archaeologists and historians had not identified a single one when Thomas began his search for Santa Catalina.

Historians and archaeologists have long thought that the lost mission of Santa Catalina lay along the western margin of St. Catherines Island, a 1400-acre tract 80 kilometers south of Savannah. Unlike the other so-called Golden Isles, St. Catherines Island hasn't been subdivided and developed. The Georgia-based, not-for-profit St. Catherines Island Foundation owns the island and sponsored a comprehensive program of research and conservation. This land management policy ensured that Mission Santa Catalina was not destroyed beneath the crush of condos and fast-food joints that typify so many southern barrier islands.

Surface Survey

In 1974, when Thomas first visited St. Catherines Island, the combined French, English, and Spanish historic documentation supplied only vague geographic clues, and although several first-rate archaeologists had previously worked on the island, none had successfully located this important mission site.

Virtually uninhabited, St. Catherines Island is today blanketed with dense forest, briar patches, and almost impenetrable palmetto thicket. When Thomas began his search for Santa Catalina, he was overwhelmed by the vastness of the area involved. So little was known about the landscape that he could not overlook any portion of the island.

Archaeological fieldwork is slow and tedious—and nobody could (or should) excavate an entire island—so Thomas began by random sampling. He calculated that 30 east-west transects, each 100 meters wide, would provide a 20 percent sample of the island (see Figure 3-4). This sample allowed him to characterize the island's archaeology; but random sampling, even with a relatively large 20 percent sample, is not good for finding rare sites—and there was only one Santa Catalina de Guale.

In systematic archaeological surveys, the idea is to walk the straightest line possible, climbing over rocks and deadfalls, skirting along the sides of steep ridges—looking even in places where you don't expect to find anything.

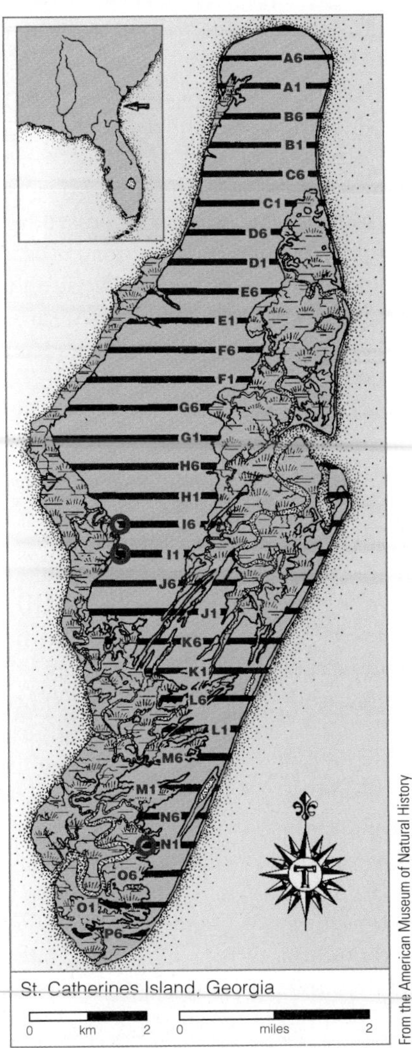

From the American Museum of Natural History

FIGURE 3-4 Systematic transect research design used to derive a 20 percent regional randomized sample on St. Catherines Island (Georgia). All surveyed transects (the darker stripes) have a letter + number designation. Occurrences of sixteenth- and seventeenth-century Spanish ceramics have been circled.

In Nevada's wide-open spaces, it's fairly easy to keep your bearing even without a compass: Just keep walking toward that peak, mesa, or other landmark in the distance. But on densely vegetated St. Catherines Island, it was impossible to see past the palmetto bush directly in front of you (see Figure 3-4). The field crew was experienced in desert survey and carried compasses, but even then, some veered off their paths as they wound their way through bushes and briars. Palm-sized orb spiders hung down from Spanish moss–draped oaks; an occasional scream told others that someone had taken one in the face. Orb spiders are not dangerous, but cottonmouths and canebrake rattlesnakes are, and the crew quickly learned about tides and alligators.

In Nevada, we could see sites on the ground surface—but on St. Catherines, the sites are almost always buried. We searched for them partly by using probes—meter-long sharpened steel rods. We would push the probe down into the ground every few steps and see if we hit something. This was effective because St. Catherines Island is one huge sand dune—there is no natural stone on the island. Eventually, we learned to tell the difference between the feel of a tree root and rock or shell—the last two suggesting a buried archaeological site. We recorded 135 sites, ranging from massive shell middens to isolated shell scatters. We investigated each site with several 1-meter square test units (see Chapter 4); we excavated more than 400 such test pits.

Subsurface Testing

The surface survey and testing told us that sixteenth- and seventeenth-century Spanish ceramics occurred only at 5 of the 135 archaeological sites, all but one along the western perimeter of the island. The ruins of Mission Santa Catalina almost certainly lay buried in a target area the size of 30 football fields along the southwestern margin of the island.

But 30 football fields is a huge area to dig with dental pick and camel hair brush. Moreover, although our confidence was growing, we had to admit almost complete ignorance of what we were looking for. Did Santa Catalina survive merely as heaps of sixteenth- and seventeenth-century garbage? Or could we realistically hope to find buried evidence of buildings as well? Clearly, it was time to scratch the surface.

Looking around for better ways to find the needle hidden in this haystack, Thomas learned about Kathleen Deagan and her successful search for sixteenth-century St. Augustine. Deagan and her students used a gasoline-powered posthole digger and excavated hundreds of round holes on a grid system. Following her lead, Thomas did the same on St. Catherines Island for the area that the survey had identified as most likely to contain the mission. With the noisy, nasty auger, two people could dig a 3-foot-deep hole in less than a minute. The power auger threw up a neat doughnut of dirt that was hand-sifted for artifacts. We dug hundreds of such holes.

Once the field testing was complete, we identified all materials recovered and plotted the distribution in a series of simple maps. The power auger allowed us to focus further field evaluation on a single 100 × 100 meter square in the overall sampling grid where diagnostic mission-period artifacts were found.

Although this area contained absolutely no surface evidence to distinguish it from the surroundings, judicious use of surface and subsurface sampling had narrowed the search from an entire island to a relatively small area. And this is indeed where we eventually discovered the remarkably well preserved ruins of Mission Santa Catalina de Guale.

But where to dig? In the past, we might have excavated a trench across the 10,000 square meters and hoped for the best. But just as medical science can use CAT scans and ultrasound to see inside your body, archaeologists today can see below the ground, map subsurface features in detail, and execute pinpoint excavations, minimizing damage to the rest of the site.

Remote Sensing

Remote sensing refers to an array of photographic and geophysical techniques that rely on some form of electromagnetic energy—it might be raw electricity, light, heat, or radio waves—to detect and measure characteristics of an archaeological target. This greatly enhances our ability to see, quite literally, given that the human eye can detect less than one ten-millionth of the entire electromagnetic spectrum. We'll say more about photographic techniques later; here we consider how other kinds of remote sensing helped find Mission Santa Catalina on St. Catherines Island.

Thomas used transect survey and power auger testing to narrow down the location of the mission. One of the survey units in this area, Quad IV, was an undistinguished piece of real estate covered by scrub palmetto and live oak forest. Although we could see aboriginal shell midden scatters here and there, Quad IV betrayed absolutely no surface clues as to what lay below. We'd driven over it dozens of time. At this point, Thomas shifted the field strategy from preliminary subsurface testing to noninvasive, nondestructive remote sensing.

Choosing the right method depends on what you expect to find. So what, exactly, were we looking for? For more than a century, Santa Catalina had been the northernmost Spanish outpost on the eastern seaboard, and this historical fact implied considerable size and permanence. The seventeenth-century mission must have had a fortified church and some buildings to house soldiers and priests, plus enough granaries, storehouses, and dwellings for hundreds of Guale Indian neophytes.

We figured that the mission buildings were built of wattle and daub. Freshly cut timbers were probably set vertically along the walls and reinforced with cane woven horizontally between the uprights. This sturdy wattlework was then plastered (daubed) with a mixture of marsh mud, sand, and plant fibers (probably Spanish moss). Roofs were thatched with palmetto.

So constructed, wattle-and-daub buildings are totally biodegradable. The thatch roof will eventually rot and blow away. And once directly exposed to the weather, mud and twig walls will simply wash away. Archaeologists seeking such a dissolved mission would soon be out of business.

But thatched roofs often burn, and if that happened at Santa Catalina, the heat would have fired and hardened the daub walls, like a pot baking in a kiln. Fired daub, nearly as indestructible as the ubiquitous potsherd, thus became a key in our search for the mission.

So, how do you find chunks of burned mud buried beneath a foot of sand without excavating thousands of square meters?

The Proton Magnetometer

The marsh mud used in daub plaster contains microscopic iron particles. Normally, these are randomly oriented to all points of the compass. But when intensely heated, the particles orient toward magnetic north—like a million tiny compass needles. To pinpoint these magnetically anomalous orientations, we relied upon a **proton precession magnetometer**. The theory behind this device is complicated, but the principle is simple: Magnetometers measure the strength of magnetism between the earth's magnetic core and a sensor the archaeologist controls. If hundreds of these readings are taken across a systematic grid, we can generate a magnetic contour map reflecting both the shape and the intensity of buried magnetic anomalies.

Many subsurface anomalies are archaeologically irrelevant magnetic "noise"—interference from underlying rocks, AC power lines, or hidden iron debris. The earth's magnetic field fluctuates so wildly on some days that the readings are meaningless, and electrical storms can hopelessly scramble magnetometer readings. Even minor interference, such as the operator's wristwatch or eyeglasses, can drive a magnetometer crazy.

But when everything works just right, the magnetometer provides the equivalent of an MRI, tipping off archaeologists to what's going on beneath the earth's surface. Many archaeological features have characteristic magnetic signatures—telltale clues that hint at the size, shape, depth, and composition of the archaeological objects hidden far below. Shallow graves, for instance, have a magnetic profile vastly different from, say, a buried fire pit or a wattle-and-daub wall.

Working with Ervan Garrison (University of Georgia) and a team from Texas A&M University, we conducted a magnetometer survey of Quad IV. As they were packing up their field equipment to work up the data in their lab, they shared a couple of hunches, based strictly on their raw magnetometer readings: "If we were y'all, we'd dig in three places: here, over yonder, and especially right

FIGURE 3-5 Systematic archaeological survey on St. Catherines Island (Georgia).

here." We took their advice and explored all three magnetic anomalies in the few days remaining in our May field season. One anomaly—"especially right here"—turned out to be a sixteenth-century iron barrel ring. Excavating further, we came upon another ring, and more below that. At about 3 meters down, we hit the water table. Digging underwater, we encountered a well-preserved oak well casing.

Archaeologists love wells because, like privies, they can be magnificent artifact traps. After removing the bones of an unfortunate fawn (which had long ago drowned), we found an array of distinctive Hispanic and Guale Indian potsherds and a metal dinner plate dropped (or tossed) into the well. All artifacts were typical of the sixteenth and seventeenth centuries. We had indeed found Mission Santa Catalina, and we pressed on to see what else the magnetometer might have turned up.

© American Museum of Natural History, photo by Ginessa Mahar

FIGURE 3-6 Christina Friberg and Rachel Cajigas performing a magnetometer (fluxgate gradiometer) survey on St. Catherines Island. Rachel is walking the survey transect with the gradiometer and Christina is recording significant magnetic readings.

Our second magnetic anomaly—the one "here"—was a small mound. After removing the overburden, we came across a burned daub wall that, as it fell, had crushed dozens of Spanish and Guale domestic artifacts: imported tin-enameled glazed cups, painted ceramic dishes, a kitchen knife, and at least two enormous pots for cooking or storage. Charred deer and chicken bones littered the floor, and dozens of tiny corncobs lay scattered about. This time, the magnetometer had led us to the kitchen (in Spanish, *cocina*) that seventeenth-century Franciscan friars used at Santa Catalina.

Finally, we began digging the "over yonder" anomaly, which proved to be a linear daub concentration more than 12 meters long—obviously the downed wall of yet another, much larger mission building. Here excavations turned up none of the everyday implements and debris so common in the scorched *cocina*. Instead, we found a complete buried sixteenth-century mission church.

The search was over. We had discovered the paramount house of worship at Santa Catalina de Guale. Our magnetometer survey provided trustworthy directions to the buried daub walls and iron barrel hoops. Even lacking computer processing, the magnetometer took us to the very heart of Mission Santa Catalina.

We spent two decades excavating the church ruins. The lateral church walls were constructed of wattle and daub that, when encountered archaeologically, consisted of a densely packed linear rubble scatter; this is what the magnetometer "saw" in Quad IV. It's among the very oldest Christian churches in North America.

Geomagnetic survey has progressed considerably since we searched for Mission Santa Catalina de Guale. Today, we use an instrument called a fluxgate gradiometer to monitor magnetism in buried deposits (see Figure 3-6). The new instruments are quicker to use, more accurate, and less expensive, but the basic principles remain unchanged. As we discuss in the next section, we have recently conducted extensive geomagnetic surveys at several sites on St. Catherines Island, including Mission Santa Catalina de Guale and the McQueen Shell Ring site, combining the gradiometer results with another technique known as soil resistivity.

Soil Resistivity

Proton magnetometry was just one of the techniques used to locate and define Santa Catalina de Guale. **Soil resistivity survey** monitors the electrical resistance of soils in a restricted volume near the surface of an archaeological site. In part due to its relatively low cost, soil resistivity survey has become a popular technique of geophysical prospecting over the past four decades.

The degree of soil resistance depends on several factors, the most important of which is the amount of water

remote sensing The use of some form of electromagnetic energy to detect and measure characteristics of an archaeological target.

proton precession magnetometer A remote sensing technique that measures the strength of magnetism between the earth's magnetic core and a sensor controlled by the archaeologist. Magnetic anomalies can indicate the presence of buried walls or features.

soil resistivity survey A remote sensing technique that monitors the electrical resistance of soils in a restricted volume near the surface of an archaeological site; changes in the amount of resistance registered by the resistivity meter can indicate buried walls or features.

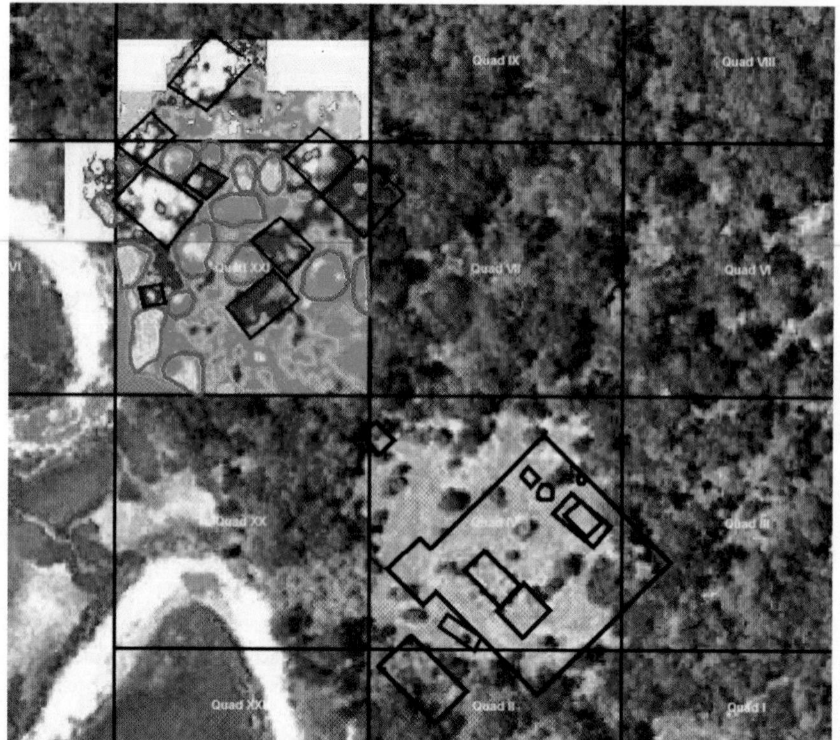

FIGURE 3-7 This aerial view of Mission Santa Catalina de Guale has been enhanced with the results of both geophysical prospection and archaeological excavation. The light square (lower right) is a one-hectare (100 m 3 100 m) clear-cut around the mission church and outlying buildings (outlined in black). The multicolored inset shows projected outlines of shell middens (in red) and of buildings (in black) erected in the Pueblo part of the mission complex; these outlines are conjectural, based on the results of noninvasive soil resistivity surveys.

retained in the soil—the more water, the less resistance to electrical currents. Compaction such as occurs in house floors, walls, paths, and roads tends to reduce pore sizes and hence the potential to retain water; this registers as high resistance. When electricity is sent through the soil, buried features can often be detected and defined by the differential resistance to electrical charge caused by their differential retention of groundwater.

The aggregation of fill in pits, ditches, and middens also alters resistivity. Foundations or walls, particularly those in historic-period sites, generally have *greater* resistivity than surrounding soil, whereas the generation of humus by occupation activity increases the ion content of the soil, *reducing* resistivity.

After the initial discovery of the mission and a pilot resistivity survey, Mark Williams and the late Gary Shapiro returned to St. Catherines Island to help us conduct a more comprehensive study. We measured soil resistance by setting four probes in line at 1-meter intervals, each probe inserted to a depth of 20 centimeters. We conducted one of the preliminary resistivity surveys in a 15 × 15 meter area that straddled a test excavation of Structure 2 at Santa Catalina, initially located by the proton magnetometer survey. From our test excavations, we suspected that this building was probably the kitchen, but we had no idea of the building's configuration. The resistivity diagrams clearly identified the margins of the unexcavated building. Later excavations confirmed the accuracy of the soil resistivity diagram.

Today, resistivity survey has been streamlined with new instruments and sophisticated ways to analyze the data. The earliest resistivity survey at Mission Santa Catalina took two days; we can now conduct the same survey in two hours. Figure 3-7 shows the results of modern resistivity surveying at Mission Santa Catalina, remote sensing results that disclose the presence of several still-buried buildings constructed around the mission core.

Figure 3-8 combines the results of geomagnetic and resistance surveys at the McQueen Shell Ring, another archaeological site on St. Catherines Island. The McQueen ring is a circular construction made entirely of marine shell (clam, oyster, mussel, and the like). It stands about 1 meter high and forms a perfect circle 70 meters across. The inside is perfectly clean, and large enough to play a full-court game of basketball—but it is completely buried; virtually no trace remains on the surface. The McQueen shell midden dates between 4000 and 5000 years old, and contains hundreds of pieces of fiber-tempered ceramics (the oldest pottery complex known in North America). As shown in Figure 3-7, we conducted a gradiometer survey across the entire surface, with a follow-up resistivity survey as well. Figure 3-8 combines the results of both remote sensing surveys, providing a detailed road map of what lies there. For the past three years, we have used these geophysical surveys to guide our pinpoint testing of this important site.

Ground-Penetrating Radar

Yet another method of geophysical prospecting is **ground-penetrating radar (GPR)**. Although this method tends to be expensive, its cost is offset to some degree by its speed. But neither operating the radar equipment nor interpreting the results is simple, and the assistance of trained specialists is required.

In GPR, radar pulses directed into the ground reflect back to the surface when they strike targets or interfaces within the ground (such as a change in the density of dirt, groundwater, buried objects, voids, or an interface between soil and rock). As these pulses are reflected, their speed to the target and the nature of their return are measured. The signal's reflection provides information about the depth and three-dimensional shape of buried objects.

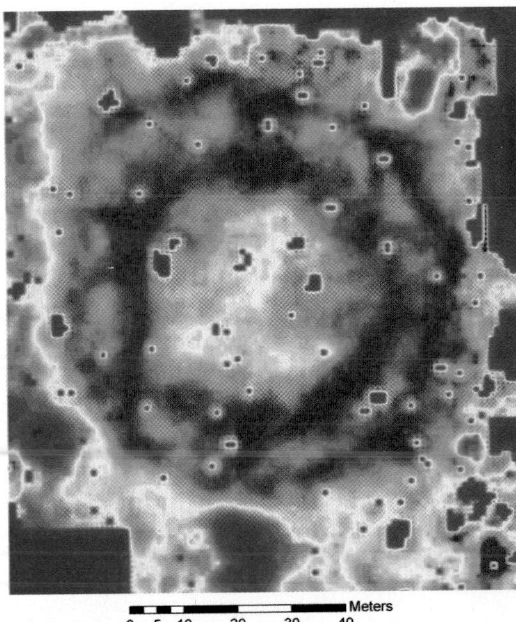

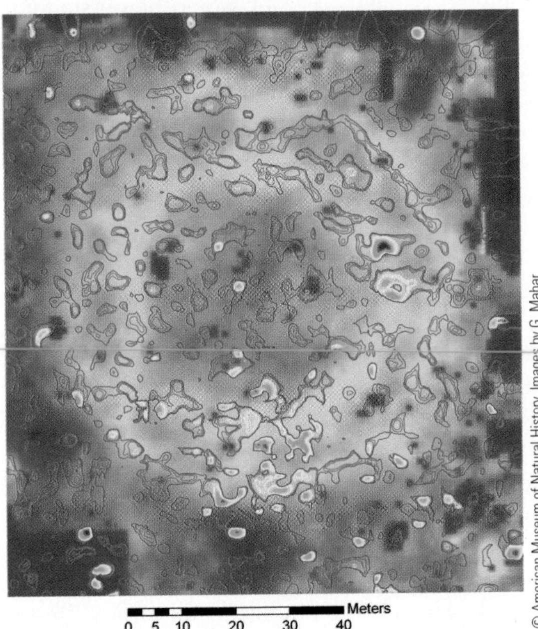

FIGURE 3-8 Remote sensing data can be arrayed in several ways. Top: A soil resistance map of the McQueen Shell Ring (St. Catherines Island), coded with high resistance indicated by purple and low resistance by dark orange. Bottom: Also the McQueen Shell Ring, but the resistivity data are arrayed in grayscale, and gradiometry results are rendered as an overlay contour. Magnetic anomalies with a weaker signature are shown here as warm-colored contours, while stronger anomalies are shown as steep contour arrangements of warm and cool colors.

FIGURE 3-9 David Hurst Thomas (right) and Lawrence Conyers (University of Denver) conduct a ground-penetrating radar survey on the site of San Marcos, a Spanish mission and pueblo site in New Mexico.

With *transducers* (devices that convert electrical energy to electromagnetic waves) of various dimensions, a researcher applying GPR can direct the greatest degree of resolution to the depth of specific interest. A pulsating electric current is passed through an antenna, inducing electromagnetic waves that radiate toward the target and return in a fraction of a microsecond to be recorded. As the antenna is dragged across the ground surface, a continuous profile of subsurface electromagnetic conditions is printed on a graphic recorder (see Figure 3-9). The location and depth of subsurface targets can be inferred from, and tested against, this graphic record.

Why did we begin using GPR at Santa Catalina? Historical documents suggested that the Spanish had fortified the mission as a precaution against British attack, perhaps by building a stockade-and-moat complex to protect the buildings immediately adjacent to the central plaza. Yet, after three years of using magnetometer and resistivity surveys and limited test excavations, we had failed to locate any trace of defensive fortifications, such as palisades, bastions, or moats encircling the central mission zone. Given that these features might not have burned and because they could be as saturated with water as the surrounding sediment, they might have eluded the magnetometer and resistivity instruments. However, these features might have differed from the background sediment in terms of their compaction, and that suggested to us that GPR might help locate them.

We ran a number of systematic north-south transects at 20-meter intervals, locating significant anomalies on the ground by means of pin flags. We then ran a third set of transects at a 45° angle, to intercept buried anomalies at a different angle. Directed by these radar profiles, our test excavations led directly to the discovery of the

ground-penetrating radar (GPR) A remote sensing technique in which radar pulses directed into the ground reflect back to the surface when they strike features or interfaces within the ground, showing the presence and depth of possible buried features.

palisade-and-bastion complex encircling the central buildings and plaza at Santa Catalina. Although this defensive network could surely have been located by extensive test trenching, the radar approach proved to be considerably more cost effective and less destructive than conventional archaeological exploration.

The Benefits of Noninvasive Archaeology

It is clear from these examples that remote sensing can help archaeology in very significant ways. One drawback has been that remote sensing techniques are expensive, but the cost has been going down as the machinery becomes more widely available. And remote sensing can pay for itself, given that the alternative—hand excavation—is also costly. By targeting excavation efforts, remote sensing can actually reduce a project's cost.

Some form of remote sensing can work almost anyplace, though not everywhere (at least not yet). Where there is a lot of background noise—such as a high groundwater table, considerable background rock, or natural subsurface features—it is often difficult for the geophysical devices to pick out which anomalies are worth investigating. But with increasing refinements to the technology, remote sensing has become an indispensable tool facilitating both archaeological survey and excavation.

The advances in geophysics have implications that reach to the core of archaeological thinking. For years, archaeologists analyzed only those artifacts that they could hold in their hands or excavated archaeological features that they could see with their eyes. Remote sensing has changed that focus, allowing us to construct robust linkages between the larger things that archaeologists find—walls, structures, and features—and the way that they are remotely perceived by the sensors of geophysical machinery and remote imagery.

In effect, remote sensing allows modern archaeologists to transcend an "archaeology by capture" approach—the only real truth is the artifact in your hand—opening the door to a less invasive, conservation-oriented archaeology of the future.

Geographic Information Systems

Archaeological data are inherently spatial, and archaeologists map things all the time. Maps show where things are and, more important, how they relate to each other. Archaeologists use maps to plot the results of remote sensing, such as artifact distributions within a site and distributions of sites across a region, a state, or even a continent.

But in their traditional form, maps are difficult to update with new information, and the resulting distributions are often unwieldy to analyze.

This all changed in the late 1980s, with the advent of **geographic information systems (GIS)**, computer programs designed to store, retrieve, analyze, and display cartographic data. GIS lets you view information—any geographically related information—visually. The most common programs in use today are ArcView and ArcInfo.

Every GIS consists of three primary components: a powerful computer graphics program used to draw a map, one or more external databases that are linked to the objects shown on the map, and a set of analytical tools that can graphically interpret or statistically analyze the stored data. Most of the United States is in the process of putting all their archaeological site records into a GIS. Clearly, GIS is a basic skill that any student contemplating a career in archaeology should learn.

In true GIS format, the earth's various features are not depicted visually—as they would be on standard two-dimensional maps—but as digital information. Virtually every standard USGS topographic map is now available digitally (some high-end GPS units contain them already). Data stored digitally, of course, can be manipulated and displayed in numerous ways.

In GIS, a database is composed of several themes, or layers. Envision a base topographic map—that's one theme. Now envision laying a clear sheet of plastic over that map (this is how we used to do it!). You plot on the sheet all the archaeological sites you just found in a survey. This layer is another theme. Over the first sheet, you lay another on which you draw in all the water sources; this is a third theme. On yet another sheet, you draw the distribution of different vegetation communities. On another, you plot the results of high-altitude imagery; on still another, the region's different soils . . . you get the picture.

Mapping like this with physical plastic sheets is unwieldy, and the resulting patterns are difficult to analyze statistically. However, by inputting all these different data digitally into a single **georeferenced** database, we can call up one or more of the layers and analyze the distributions. "Georeferenced" means that data are input using a common mapping reference, such as the UTM grid system mentioned previously. Because the data are digital, we can do spatial analyses in minutes that previously might have taken weeks or longer. Each of the data points is linked to a database, which can include complete information on that point. A site record, for example, might contain information on a site's artifacts—how many projectile points or potsherds were found there—plus other data such as its size, its slope, and the kind of architecture that were present.

We can ask myriad questions of this database. For example, we might ask, "How far away from water sources are pueblo sites found?" With a GIS database, we can quickly *buffer* springs and streams at some standard distance, say 1-kilometer intervals. Think of this as drawing concentric circles around the springs with radii of 1 kilometer, 2 kilometers, 3 kilometers, and so on. Likewise, we would trace out land areas within 1, 2, and 3 kilometers of rivers and streams. We could then ask the program to tell us how many pueblo sites versus other kinds of sites are in the various buffers. We could also see if sites are more frequently associated with a particular kind of vegetation community or soil type—in fact, with any data set that has a spatial dimension to it.

FIGURE 3-10 Pueblo Bonito, photo by Charles Lindbergh, 1929.

Landscape Archaeology

GIS opens up new ways to analyze spatial data. Partly because of this new ability, archaeologists have developed a new approach called **landscape archaeology**. Although the word "landscape" has a colloquial meaning, Carole Crumley (University of North Carolina) defines landscape as "the material manifestation of the relation between humans and their environments."

In a sense, landscape archaeology has been around since the 1940s, when Gordon Willey (1913–2002) conducted the first regional archaeological study in Peru's Virú Valley. Although landscape archaeology is similar to the study of a seasonal round we discussed earlier, it adds a concern with how people use and modify their environment. The case of the "Chacoan roads" shows how GIS, combined with remote sensing, can help test hypotheses about how ancient peoples used a landscape.

The Chacoan Roads: Discovery

Chaco Canyon was the center of a vast social and political network between 950 and 850 years ago, when two distinct kinds of sites appeared in the region. Throughout the Four Corners area, numerous smaller pueblo sites dotted the landscape. But huge sites—the Great Houses such as Pueblo Bonito (see Figure 3-10, and the chapter's opening photo)—appeared in Chaco Canyon and a few other places on the Colorado Plateau. The Great Houses were centrally located amid a cluster of smaller sites, defining a "community." By 900 years ago, the Great Houses had developed into large, formal ancestral Pueblo towns.

In the 1970–1971 field season , archaeologist R. Gwinn Vivian (Arizona State Museum) was mapping what he thought was a series of ancient canals in Chaco Canyon. As he began excavating, Vivian realized that the linear features were like no canals he'd ever seen. Instead of having a U-shaped cross-section, the Chaco "canal" appeared to be a deliberately flattened and carefully engineered *roadway*.

Vivian described his curious find to Thomas Lyons, a geologist hired to experiment with remote sensing possibilities in Chaco Canyon. Together, Vivian and Lyons started looking at the available aerial photographs of the area. Some of these photographs dated to the 1960s, but others had been taken in the 1930s by Charles Lindbergh (1902–1974), the famous American aviator and explorer, before grazing was permitted at Chaco.

Looking carefully at these black-and-white photos, Vivian and Lyons saw unmistakable traces of a prehistoric road network. They commissioned new flights, and road segments were field-checked against the aerial photographs. By 1973, Vivian and Lyons had identified more than 300 kilometers of prehistoric roads (diagrammed in Figure 3-11).

geographic information system (GIS) A computer program for storing, retrieving, analyzing, and displaying cartographic data.

georeferenced Data that are input to a GIS database using a common mapping reference—for example, the UTM grid—so that all data can be spatially analyzed.

landscape archaeology The study of ancient human modification of the environment.

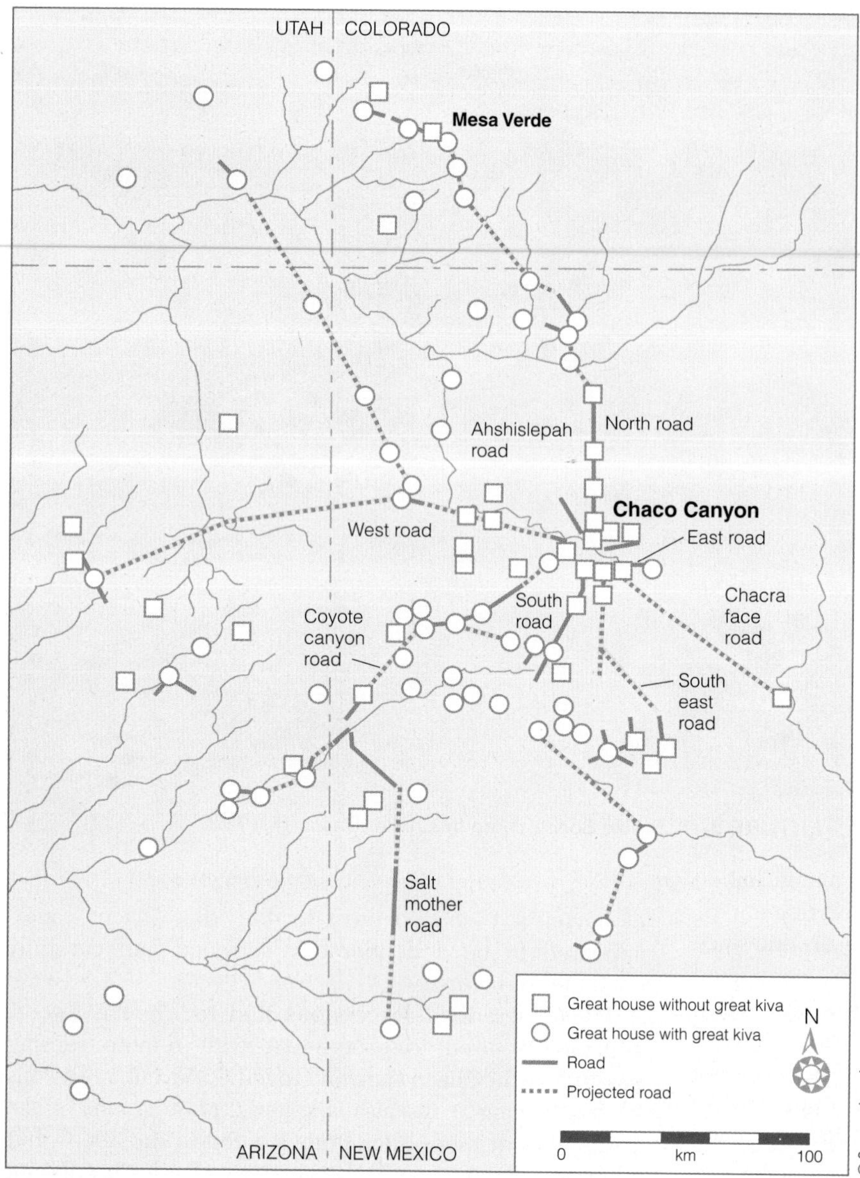

FIGURE 3-11 A diagram of the Chaco road system as it may have appeared 950 years ago.

Early photographic techniques were restricted to the visible portion of the electromagnetic spectrum, and cloud cover was a problem. But new photographic techniques capture portions of the electromagnetic spectrum that the naked eye cannot see, and they are unaffected by cloud cover.

One technique that NASA used at Chaco in the 1980s was **thermal infrared multispectral scanning**, or **TIMS**. TIMS measures infrared thermal radiation given off by the ground; it is sensitive to differences as small as 0.1° centigrade. Although we've had the ability to make infrared photographs for some time—the Landsat satellite did it in the 1970s—TIMS produces photographs of higher quality.

All photographs consist of pixels, and an instrument cannot record anything smaller than the size of a particular technique's pixel. In early satellite imagery, the pixels were 30 meters on a side, so these techniques could not record anything smaller than about 900 square meters. Such photos were of limited use to archaeology. The resolution of TIMS images depends on the altitude at which the photos are taken, but photos with a resolution of 8 meters, or even 1 to 2 meters, can be quite useful to archaeology.

TIMS images require a very complex kind of camera, and the data—the sensed infrared radiation—are transformed via a computer program into so-called false-color images. False-color images map the ground in terms of infrared radiation—rendering terrain in garish red, blue, and purple.

Because the Chacoan roads are more compacted than the surrounding matrix (even if their compacted surface is buried), they reflect more radiation than the surrounding sand. In false-color images, the roads appear as clear, tan lines against a backdrop of red sand. The Chaco experiment proved that TIMS can detect features such as buried road systems, even if they are invisible to an archaeologist standing on top of them.

Today, analysis of aerial and high-altitude photographs has revealed possibly as many as 600 kilometers of ancient roadways around Chaco Canyon. These roads are only 5 to 10 centimeters deep, yet sometimes 7 to 10 meters wide. Often they turn suddenly in doglegs, and they are occasionally edged by low rock berms. Sometimes they are littered with potsherds. Some were cut into the earth, and others were made by clearing away the surface rock and vegetation.

The longest and best-defined roads, probably constructed between 925 and 860 years ago, extend some 50 kilometers outward from Chaco Canyon. Sometimes the roads are just short segments, and it is unclear if they were intended to be segments, if they were unfinished, or if portions of the road have disappeared through erosion. In places, the Chacoans constructed causeways, and elsewhere they cut stairways into sheer cliffs. The generally straight bearings suggest that the people laid out the roads prior to construction.

Why did the Chaco people build these roads across the desert? This elaborate road system covered more than 250,000 square kilometers, yet these ancestors of modern Pueblo peoples had no wheeled vehicles or even beasts of burden.

The Chacoan Roads: Interpretation

One hypothesis is that the Chaco roads facilitated movement of foods and other goods across the landscape. The roads radiate outward from Chaco Canyon, so perhaps they were a way to provision the inhabitants of the canyon's Great Houses with maize, timber, and other supplies.

But the landscape carries symbolic meanings as well as economic potential. Perhaps the roads were not economic at all, but instead served some ceremonial function with symbolic meanings. In fact, because the roads tend to cut straight across hills, rather than skirt around their bases, and make inexplicable sharp turns in the middle of the desert, many archaeologists favor a noneconomic interpretation. To hypothesize what this purpose might be, we can look to the descendants of Chaco.

Among the likely descendants of the people who inhabited Chaco Canyon are the Keres, the Puebloan peoples who live along the northern Rio Grande in New Mexico in the pueblos of Cochiti, San Felipe, Santa Ana, Santo Domingo, and Zia. In traditional Pueblo theology, the world consists of several nested layers, surrounded at the edges by four sacred mountains. As James Snead (California State University, Northridge) and Robert Preucel (University of Pennsylvania) describe them, these nested layers center on a village, and different directions are associated with different powers, societies, and supernatural beings, as well as with maleness and femaleness (see Figure 3-12). Direction is important in this view of the world.

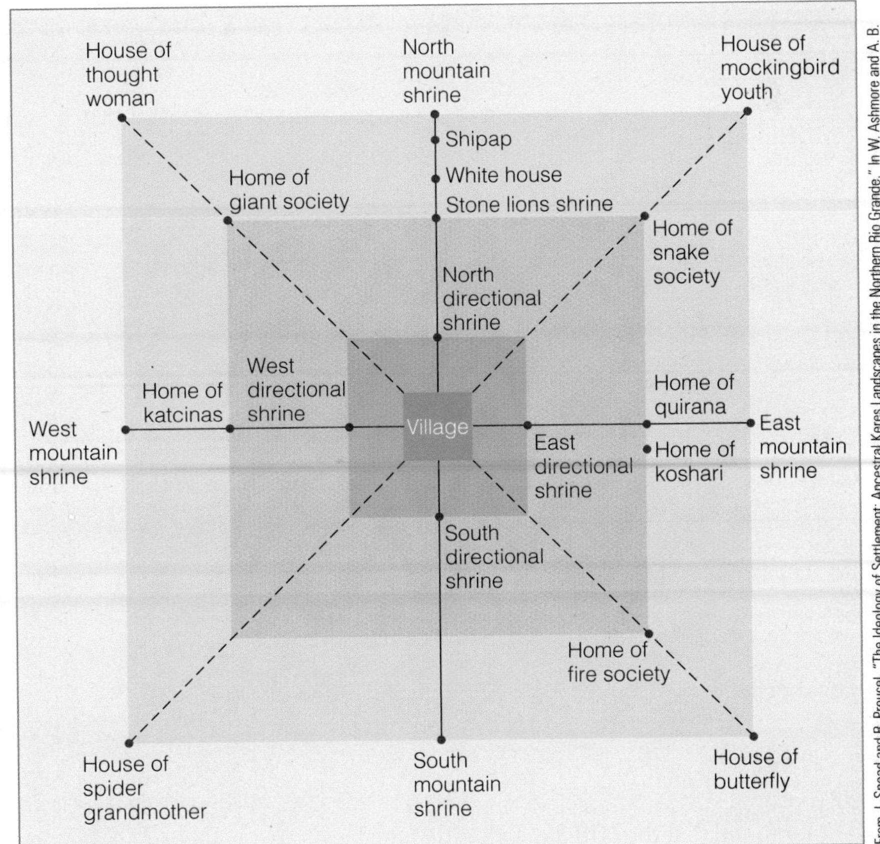

FIGURE 3-12 A schematic representation of the Keres symbolic landscape.

This symbolic landscape is physically manifested by different kinds of shrines. The shrine on Mount Taylor, for example, the west mountain shrine for Laguna Pueblo, is a shallow pit where people still come to pray. Directional shrines may be located closer to the villages and are often found in caves or near springs. One important directional shrine is two mountain lions carved from bedrock and surrounded by a circle of stones. Closer to the village are directional shrines that mark a village's boundaries. Located in the four cardinal directions, they are often keyhole-shaped stone structures with openings to the north or east. Other shrines are found within the village itself, especially in plazas where important dance rituals take place.

So, it is clear that in the Puebloan world, the landscape has both economic and symbolic meanings. Direction, in particular, seems to hold special symbolic significance in Pueblo religion. Although the ancient Chacoans probably did not share the Keres worldview exactly, they may have had a similar one, or at least one in which shrines marked significant places and directions on the landscape.

Working just south of Chaco Canyon, John Kantner (School of Advanced Research) used a GIS to test whether the roads were linked to the economic or symbolic aspects of the desert landscape. He reasoned that if the roads were for purely economic purposes, then they should follow the path of least resistance between Pueblo villages; if they did not, then perhaps the roads fulfilled a more religious purpose that was driven by the ancient peoples' symbolic interpretation of the landscape.

Using a digital elevation model, Kantner asked the GIS to do a straightforward task: Find the easiest walking route between settlements that are connected by roads. The easiest walking route would be the shortest route between two villages as well as one on which a person gained the least amount of elevation. Although it would take an archaeologist many days to walk out the possibilities in the field or even to trace them out on topographic maps, the GIS could quickly calculate the "path of least resistance" for someone walking from one settlement to another.

thermal infrared multispectral scanning (TIMS) A remote sensing technique that uses equipment mounted on aircraft or satellites to measure infrared thermal radiation given off by the ground. Sensitive to differences as small as 0.1°C, it can locate subsurface structures by tracking how they affect surface thermal radiation.

RAPID REVIEW

Remote Sensing Methods

Method	What Does It Measure?	Where Does It Work Best?
Soil resistivity	Sediment's resistance to electrical current	In damp sediments; useful to locate compacted surfaces that retain less water and hence are more resistant to electrical current; also looser fill in pits that will retain water and increase conductivity
TIMS (a technique of aerial photography)	Thermal radiation given off by the earth's surface	Where the archaeological features of interest are fairly large, 8 to 10 meters in size
Proton magnetometer	Magnetic anomalies	Burned buildings and hearths; significant subsurface disturbance such as buried ditches or pits
Ground-penetrating radar (GPR)	Strength and speed of radar pulses directed into the earth	Buried surfaces that differ in their compaction from surrounding sediments

Kantner found that the GIS did *not* predict the locations of the roads. In fact, some of the roads crossed terrain that is substantially different from that predicted by the GIS. The Chacoan roads do not follow the path of least resistance. We assume that anyone as familiar with their landscape as the Chacoans were would know the easiest way to walk from one settlement to another. But perhaps this assumption was wrong—perhaps people did *not* know or did *not* use the easiest paths between settlements. To test this hypothesis, Kantner asked whether there were any archaeological remains associated with the GIS-predicted paths.

In fact, he found that small stone shrines occur along the predicted footpaths; it appears that someone was using the predicted paths, probably on a regular basis. In contrast, large circular stone shrines, ones that required more effort to construct, were almost always found with the roads, not the predicted footpaths.

From this, Kantner concluded that the roads did not serve simply as part of the Chacoan economy. Although food and other goods may have been moved along the roads, this was not their primary purpose. Instead, people probably routinely moved food and goods along trails that followed the paths of least resistance between villages, footpaths marked by small shrines today. But the formal roads' association with large shrines suggests that they performed some other role. Perhaps they were religious paths; some, in fact, lead directly to places on the landscape that figure prominently in modern Puebloan religion. Or perhaps they helped to integrate the small far-flung pueblos with the Great Houses in Chaco Canyon. We still don't know the purpose of the roads for sure, but GIS clearly casts doubt on the economic hypothesis.

Conclusion

We began this chapter by talking about "gumshoe survey"—looking around for a good site to excavate by talking with lots of people, most of whom are not archaeologists. This is a good way to find rare or spectacular sites because those are the kinds of places that nonarchaeologists remember. Few would note, or even notice, small scatters of potsherds or stone flakes.

But archaeologists are interested in more than the big, spectacular sites. They are trying to understand the whole range of human settlement—from the showy, spectacular pueblos to the small scatter of a single broken pot. Systematic surveys arose in the 1960s, not as a way to find sites, but as an unbiased means to characterize a region's archaeology. Spectacular sites are always informative, but their value increases dramatically when we know something about their regional context. And sample survey provides that context.

A complete, 100 percent sample is preferable because it alone can guarantee the discovery of rare sites. But complete surveys are expensive, and, as we have shown here, research questions can be addressed with a far smaller sample.

WHAT DOES IT MEAN TO me?

I'm Not a Professional Archaeologist, but Can I Still Play a Role?

There are thousands of avocational archaeologists in the United States—individuals who are interested in archaeology but have no academic credentials. Many of these people collect artifacts on their own. They are often important sources of information for gumshoe survey. Some professionals love them, others begrudgingly tolerate them, and others won't deal with them at all because they feel that any association with collectors condones looting.

Most archaeologists differentiate between the weekend collector of surface artifacts and those who dig for profit. They condemn the latter, but find relationships with avocationals to be productive. George Frison, professor emeritus at the University of Wyoming, a member of the National Academy of Sciences, and past president of the Society for American Archaeology, says, "I think you gain a hell of a lot more by cooperating with amateurs . . . than if you deride them and chase them underground. Then they'll really do you some damage."

As an avocational archaeologist, is there a role for you in professional archaeology? According to Hester Davis, retired state archaeologist, Archaeological Survey, Fayetteville, Arkansas, the answer is yes:

> The greatest potential for site protection is through statewide avocational groups. The secret weapon held by these organizations is their ability to influence their own members, politicians, landowners, teachers, schoolchildren, and even pothunters (looters). By their very numbers and the fact of their organization, avocational archaeological societies should be the real advocates for site protection.
>
> Avocational archaeological groups have the greatest potential for making a real difference in which sites and how many sites are protected in the future. All archaeologists, in my use of the term, must coordinate, communicate, organize nationally, and become pro-protection. Legislation protecting unmarked graves must hit hard on the looters and vandals; ordinances at the local level must become commonplace. The names and faces of archaeological organizations speaking for less wanton destruction must be on educational television and the evening news.
>
> There are probably four or five times as many avocational archaeologists as there are professional ones, and dozens more avocational archaeological organizations than professional ones. Since their interests are supposed to be the same, they must all become strong active advocates for site protection, from the individual site where the shopping center is going in, to the national historic landmarks still in private ownership.

Archaeology is also constrained by a conservation ethic. Because only a finite number of sites exist, we excavate only what we must to answer a particular research question, saving portions of sites, or entire sites, for future researchers. By giving archaeologists a cost-effective means of making observations on objects and features that have not yet been excavated, remote sensing can obviate the need for excessive excavation and permit archaeologists to preserve more for the future. This is today an important consideration for many American Indian tribes and for any ethical archaeologists.

GIS has likewise become a critically important tool. One of archaeology's strengths is the ability to use spatial patterns to test hypotheses about ancient cultural behavior. GIS is also extremely useful to federal and state agencies that must manage the archaeological sites on their properties. For these reasons, it is likely that GIS will become as indispensable to archaeologists as their trowels. However, these methods will never replace our need to excavate sites. And this realization brings us to the next chapter.

Summary

- Why do archaeologists "survey"?
  - We do survey because no single site reveals everything about an ancient society.
- What is the main principle of survey? Why does this matter?
  - The main principle of archaeological survey is to generate a representative sample of a landscape; sometimes a survey is randomized to ensure that every site has an equal chance of being included in the sample.
  - This matters because if we only look in the "logical" places, we will almost certainly bias the sample and our reconstruction of the past.
- What limits surface survey? What are the basic remote sensing techniques and their benefits?

- Survey can only find what lies on the ground; remote sensing helps us understand what lies below the ground.
- The proton magnetometer detects magnetic anomalies in the ground, such as pieces of metal, and burned sediments (e.g., hearths).
- Soil resistivity measures how readily an electric current passes through sediment, detecting areas of looser or more compact materials based on differences in water content.
- Ground-penetrating radar detects features, especially architecture, using radar waves.
- Remote sensing can help preserve sites by targeting excavations.

What is "landscape archaeology"?

- Landscape archaeology is similar to settlement pattern archaeology because of its interest in the regional record of human behavior, but it focuses on human modification of the environment.

Media Resources

Doing Fieldwork: Archaeological Demonstrations CD-ROM 2.0

This CD, developed by the authors, shows professional archaeologists involved in various digs, many of which are referenced in the text. The presentation is organized by the main techniques used on an archaeological dig, reinforcing concepts and techniques via live examples. The CD takes you through each step automatically, or you can navigate to any point via the navigation bar. After reviewing a step in the dig process, you are taken to Check Points, which are concept questions about each step of the dig. Then you can see the answers, receive your score, and even send your scores to your instructor.

See the "Remote Sensing" and "Beginning to Excavate" sections of the CD-ROM to learn more about topics covered in this chapter.

CourseMate

Access chapter-specific learning tools including learning objectives, practice quizzes, videos, flash cards, and glossaries, as well as web links, and more in your Archaeology CourseMate. Login to www.cengagebrain.com to access the resources your instructor has assigned and to purchase materials.

Doing Fieldwork: Why Archaeologists Dig Square Holes

4

Students excavating the 300,000-year-old level at Gran Dolina, Spain, in 2008.

Learning Objectives

After reading this chapter, you should be able to answer these questions:

- Why does context matter? How is it recorded?
- What determines preservation?
- What is the difference between arbitrary and natural levels? Why do these matter?
- How do archaeologists recover the smallest artifacts and ecofacts?
- What is the difference between systemic and archaeological contexts, and why does this difference matter?

Preview

ASK MOST PEOPLE what archaeologists do, and they'll tell you this: "They dig." And that's true. Despite what we saw in the preceding chapter about archaeological survey and remote sensing technology, digging up old stuff remains at the heart of archaeology—and probably always will.

But excavation is a more complex and sophisticated venture than throwing a shovel into a pickup and heading off for the mountains. Archaeologists are well aware that as they gather data from a site, they are also destroying that site, because once a site is excavated, it can never be excavated again. Therefore, it's essential that archaeologists record as much detail as possible, so that future archaeologists can reconstruct what earlier archaeologists did and use the records to answer new questions. This means that you dig slowly and take excruciatingly careful and detailed notes. Nonetheless, as Kent Flannery (University of Michigan) once said, "Archaeology is the most fun you can have with your pants on." And he's right, as anybody who has ever participated in a dig will tell you. Co-author Thomas joined his first archaeological expedition as a college junior; and Kelly joined his first as a high school sophomore. We were both hooked from the start.

We warned earlier about the problems of learning archaeological field techniques from a book (even this one): You just can't do it. But in this chapter, we describe common archaeological field methods, and we do hope to show you how fieldwork is done and what it really feels like.

Introduction

In the last chapter, we talked about how archaeologists go about finding sites, such as Gatecliff Shelter. But locating sites is only the beginning; excavating these sites can be far more time-consuming. Along with fields such as geology and paleontology, the science of archaeology destroys data as they are gathered—for once we excavate a site, nobody can ever dig it again. This is why archaeologists are compulsive about field notes—recording, drawing, and photographing everything we can about an artifact or a feature before removing it. This is also why we usually try to leave a portion of a site unexcavated for the future.

This chapter can be reduced to one simple point: An artifact's **provenience**—its location within a site—is the most important thing about that artifact. Some might even say it is more important than the artifact itself. The reason is that provenience is essential to recording an artifact's *context*—its relationship to other artifacts, features, and geologic strata in a site. This information is crucial to knowing what an artifact has to tell us. The following account demonstrates this fundamental principle.

The Folsom Site and Humanity's Antiquity in North America

In Chapter 2, we discussed how eighteenth-century scholars were preoccupied with the question of where Native Americans came from. A closely related question was, "How long have Native Americans been here?" As we saw in the Moundbuilder controversy, many scholars believed that American Indians arrived in the Western Hemisphere only shortly before European colonists. This matter was politically important: If archaeology showed that American Indians were longtime inhabitants of the New World, then their claim to the land was strengthened; if Indian people were only recent immigrants, their hold on the land could be minimized in favor of the Europeans.

So, from the earliest colonial times, scholars debated the antiquity of humanity in the New World (and they still do). Some claimed that the discovery of apparently crude stone tools demonstrated that humans had been in the New World for thousands of years, since the last phase of the Ice Age, but others showed that these crude artifacts could be mere quarry rejects, unfinished pieces that the artisans deemed too flawed to complete, and had nothing to say about how Indians had lived in the New World.

Interestingly, the argument over the antiquity of humanity in the New World came down to animals. This is not as odd as it sounds. Nineteenth- and early twentieth-century archaeologists had no way to date their sites absolutely. But they knew that the world had experienced a great Ice Age in the distant past. And they reasoned (quite accurately, it turns out) that this Ice Age, more properly called the **Pleistocene**, had ended about 10,000 years ago. Scholars also knew that different kinds of animals lived in North America during the Pleistocene—mammoths, mastodons, a large species of bison, giant bears, ground sloths, horses, camels, and so on. Anybody who found artifacts in undisputed association with the bones of such extinct fauna would prove that humans had been in North America for at least 10,000 years. Thus, the quest relied heavily on *context*: seeking ancient artifacts in unquestionable association with the bones of extinct fauna.

In the last chapter, we mentioned that some of the most important archaeological sites are found by nonarchaeologists. A hard-rock miner found Gatecliff Shelter, and an ex-slave named George McJunkin (1851–1922) found the Folsom site—the place that proved the extent of human antiquity in the Americas.

The Black Cowboy

Born into slavery, McJunkin acquired his freedom at age 14, "borrowed" a mule from its former owner, and left his home on a Texas plantation in search of work. By 1868, he was breaking horses for a Texas rancher and later held down a string of ranch jobs in Colorado and New Mexico. He became an expert cowboy and knew just about all there was to know about horses and cattle.

McJunkin also learned a lot about many other things. Although he never received a formal education, he taught himself to read and play the fiddle. He was curious about everything, especially natural history, and one of his prize possessions was a wooden box filled with rocks, bones, fossils, and arrowheads. McJunkin never married and lived most of his life as the only African American in his community.

Early in the 1890s, McJunkin's talents were recognized by the owner of the Crowfoot Ranch, in northwestern New Mexico near the town of Folsom. Soon, McJunkin was ranch foreman and proved himself an able leader of men, as well as cowpuncher and wrangler.

One day in August 1908, torrential rains fell on the Crowfoot Ranch, creating a flash flood that destroyed much of Folsom. (Many people were killed, but more would have died had not the local telephone operator, Sarah Rooke, remained at her post, calling people to warn them until the floodwaters claimed her life.) After helping to search for the dead, McJunkin began checking the Crowfoot's fences. Up Wild Horse Arroyo, he found a line that dangled across a now deep, muddy gully. Pondering how to fix it, he spotted bones protruding from the walls of the arroyo, some 15 feet down the embankment.

McJunkin had seen plenty of cow bones in his day, and these were definitely not cow. The bones seemed too large even for bison. McJunkin returned to the site over the years to collect bones that he then stacked on his mantle at home. He would talk to anyone about them and showed the site to several townsfolk.

A Spear Point between the Ribs

Eventually, the site was brought to the attention of Jesse Figgins, director of the Colorado Museum of Natural History (now the Denver Museum of Nature and Science), who was looking for skeletons of the extinct Pleistocene bison, *Bison antiquus*, for a museum display. Sadly, McJunkin had died a few years before Figgins's arrival, so he did not live to see the day that his site made archaeological history.

Some of the townsfolk who had visited the site with McJunkin had occasionally found an artifact or two among the bones (now identified as ancient bison), but they did not document their finds, meaning that the context of these artifacts was unknown. And in 1926, Figgins's crew also found a beautifully made spear point with a distinct central groove or channel (what we now call a "flute"). But, unfortunately, they could not tell whether the artifact was found with the bison skeletons or had fallen from a later, higher level—meaning that the newest find still lacked the necessary context.

Figgins telegrammed the crew to leave any artifacts exactly where they were discovered so that he could personally observe them in place. So, when excavators located similar spear points the following summer, they left the artifacts **in situ** (in place) to record their context. One of these points lay between the ribs of a bison. Figgins sent telegrams to prominent members of the archaeological community, including the skeptical A. V. Kidder, who was excavating at Pecos only 100 miles away.

After joining other archaeologists at the excavation site, Kidder solemnly pronounced that the association between the spear points and the extinct bison remains was solid. There was no evidence that rodents had burrowed into the deposit, carrying later artifacts from higher in the ground down to the bison skeletons. There was no indication that streams had redeposited the artifacts on top of the remains. Everyone present saw undeniable evidence that the spear points had killed the extinct bison.

For the first time, the association between extinct fauna and human artifacts was confirmed: People had been in the Americas since at least the end of the Pleistocene, some 10,000 years ago. Today, we know McJunkin's site as the Folsom site, and the distinctive spear points found there are called "Folsom points" (see Figure 4-1)—both named after the nearby town that was almost destroyed by the deadly flood that first exposed the site.

provenience An artifact's location relative to a system of spatial data collection.

Pleistocene A geologic period from 2 million to 10,000 years ago, which was characterized by multiple periods of extensive glaciation.

in situ From Latin, meaning "in position"; the place where an artifact, ecofact, or feature was found during excavation or survey.

FIGURE 4-1 A fluted Folsom spear point lying between the ribs of an extinct species of bison at the Folsom site.

As you can see, *context* was everything at the Folsom site. And this is true for any site. In fact, other than "When's lunch?," what you hear most frequently on any archaeological dig is, "Show me exactly where that came from."

Excavation: What Determines Preservation?

Excavation procedures depend on several factors, beginning with the kind of materials that have survived the passage of time. Some sites have wonderful preservation of organic materials, including basketry, leather, and wood; in other sites, only ceramics, stones, and bones survive; and in the earliest archaeological sites, only stone tools remain. Here are some examples that demonstrate the various conditions under which organic remains are preserved.

The Duck Decoys of Lovelock Cave

Lovelock Cave (Nevada) sits on a barren hillside, just north of the Carson Desert that we described in the last chapter. But thousands of years ago, anybody sitting in the cave's mouth would have looked out upon a vast wetland just a few kilometers away. Lovelock Cave was first excavated in 1912 (by Llewellyn Loud, a museum security guard at the University of California, who was sent by anthropologist Alfred Kroeber to gather museum specimens) and again in 1924 by Mark Harrington of New York's Museum of the American Indian.

The dry and dusty interior of Lovelock Cave was better suited for storing things than for shelter, and Loud and Harrington found several caches of gear. One that Harrington found, Pit 11, held a buried basket that contained 11 duck decoys. Cleverly crafted from tule reeds twisted to simulate the body and head of a duck, some had plain tule reed bodies, and others were adorned with paint and feathers. As artifacts, the decoys are striking. Even *Sports Illustrated* has extolled the creativity and craftsmanship of these prehistoric duck hunters (see Figure 4-2).

Someone buried this basket of decoys (in fact, they were interred beneath the pit's false bottom), intending, evidently, to use them on a later duck hunt. Although the person who buried the decoys never retrieved them, it was wise to cache them inside Lovelock Cave because they were perfectly preserved; they are usable even today. We now know from radiocarbon dating (discussed in the next chapter) that these decoys were made about 2000 years ago.

The Houses of Ozette

Equally remarkable, yet strikingly different, preservation is seen at the site of Ozette on Washington's Olympic Peninsula. Ozette was a major beachside village once occupied by the ancestors of the Makah people. In fact, some Makahs remained at Ozette into the 1920s, and their oral traditions helped lead Richard Daugherty (then at Washington State University) to the site in the first place.

FIGURE 4-2 A 2000-year-old duck decoy from Lovelock Cave, Nevada.

FIGURE 4-3 The archaeological site of Ozette on the coast of Washington.

Ozette was once a lively village stretching for a mile along the Pacific Coast, home to perhaps 800 people who lived in massive split-plank cedar houses (see Figure 4-3). They hunted, gathered berries in the forest, collected shellfish along the coast, and fished for halibut, salmon, and other species. They even hunted killer whales.

Part of Ozette village lay along the bottom of a steep hill. Some 300 years ago, during an especially heavy rain (or possibly a tsunami), the hillside above the village became saturated and, with a roar, an enormous mudslide descended on the village, shearing the tops off five houses and burying their interiors. Some people escaped, but others were caught inside. Because the coast of Washington is so wet, the destroyed portion of Ozette remained waterlogged and the mudslide capped it with a thick layer of clay.

The saturated dirt and the clay cap preserved entire houses with all their furnishings and gear. During the 1970s, Richard Daugherty excavated the houses, recovering some 42,000 artifacts, including baskets, mats, hats, halibut hooks, bowls, clubs, combs—even an entire cedar canoe. The archaeological team worked closely with the Makah people, and many of the artifacts from Ozette village are now on display at the Makah Cultural and Research Center in Neah Bay, Washington. These displays highlight the remarkable degree of preservation at this important waterlogged site.

The Ice Man of the Alps

Our third example demonstrates yet a different kind of archaeological preservation. In 1991, two skiers in the Alps came upon the body of a man lying in a pool of icy glacial water at 10,000 feet. The body was so well preserved that the authorities thought he was perhaps a mountaineer who had perished in a blizzard a few years earlier. But today, we know this man as Ötzi, the "Ice Man," who died some 5300 years ago. His body was remarkably well preserved—even tattoos are clearly visible on his skin—because he froze shortly after he died, and a small glacier then sealed his body in the shallow depression where it had come to rest. Here he freeze-dried and lay undisturbed until the warmth of recent decades caused the glacier to recede, exposing his remains (see Figure 4-4).

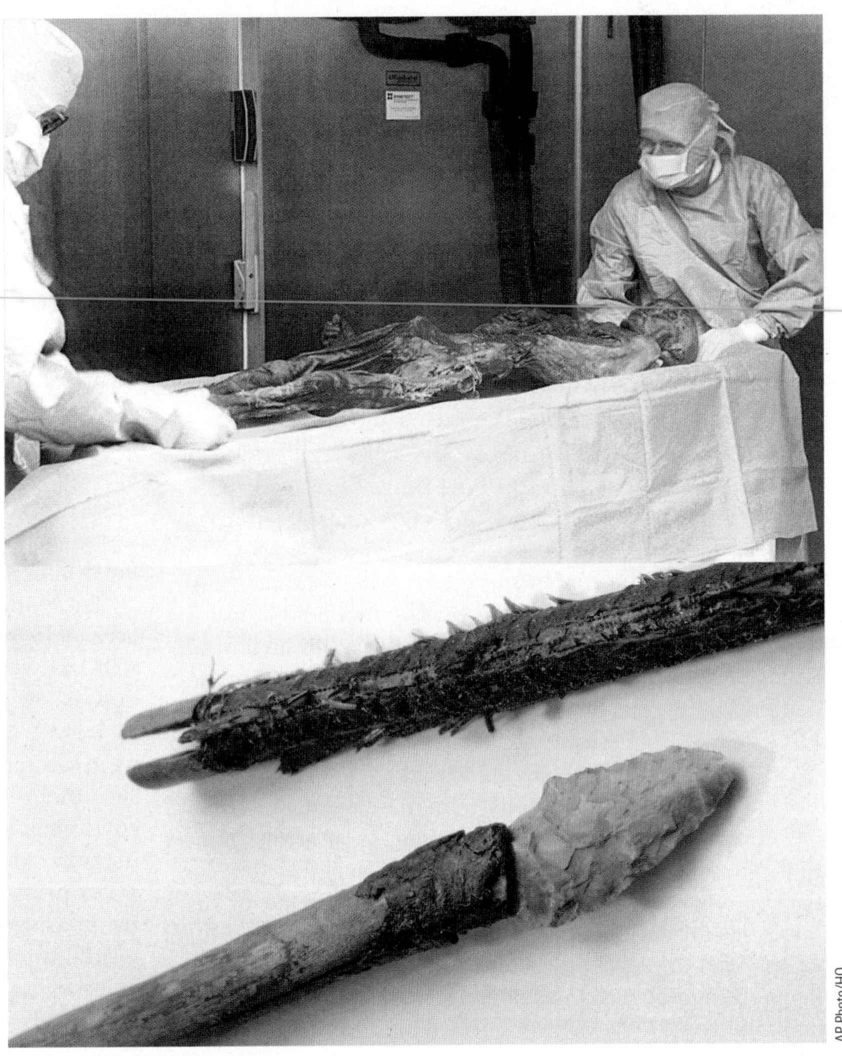

FIGURE 4-4 Ötzi, the "Ice Man" (above) and portions of some of his tools (below).

LOOKING CLOSER

The Excavator's Toolkit

Here we list things that well-equipped excavators should carry in their excavation toolbox:

- A 4- to 5-inch trowel (Marshalltown brand only, accept no substitute! Sharpen the edges and cut a V-notch in one of the back edges—it's useful for cutting roots. It's also useful to have both a pointed and a square-ended kind—the latter is especially helpful when cleaning stratigraphic profiles.)
- A metal file (for sharpening that Marshalltown)
- A 2-meter and a 25-meter tape measure (metric only)
- Work gloves
- A builder's line level and string (nylon, yellow)
- A builder's angle finder (to take artifact inclinations)
- A compass (to take artifact orientations)
- Pencils (regular and mechanical), pencil sharpener, and Sharpie pens
- Spoon (a very useful excavation tool and handy at lunchtime)
- Jackknife (one with a serrated edge is useful against larger roots)
- Nails (of various sizes—for example, to hold a level string for drawing a stratigraphy)
- Straight-edge ruler with metric markings
- Torpedo level (to maintain good vertical profiles)
- Root clippers
- Small wire cutters (to cut root hairs to prepare a stratigraphic profile for photos)
- Empty film canisters (for various sorts of samples)
- A variety of small Ziploc bags
- Toilet paper (for wrapping delicate artifacts)
- Dental tools (dentists throw them out after a limited number of uses)
- Brushes (whisk broom and 1- to 2-inch paintbrushes)
- Bamboo slices (whittle the ends to a rounded tip; essential for excavating bone)
- Aluminum foil (for radiocarbon and other samples)
- Toothpicks (useful for temporarily marking artifact locations or strata in a profile)

Realizing the significance of the Ice Man, archaeologists scoured the site and recovered portions of his clothing—a belt to hold up a leather breechcloth and leggings, a coat of deerskin, a cape of woven grass, a leather fur-lined cap, and calfskin shoes, filled with grass. They also recovered tools, including a hafted copper axe, a bow and a quiver of arrows, bone points, extra bowstrings, a wooden pack frame, birch-bark containers, a stone scraper, a hafted knife, and a net.

By analyzing the contents of the Ice Man's stomach and intestine, scientists determined that he had not eaten for at least eight hours before his death and that his final meal had included barley, wheat, and deer. Pollen analysis of the contents of his intestine suggests that he died in the spring. DNA analysis suggests he was lactose intolerant, had brown eyes, Type O blood, and suffered from Lyme disease.

Why did this 30-year-old man die at such a high elevation, far from any village or camp? An arrow point that penetrated past his shoulder blade suggests that he had been attacked shortly before his death. One of his hands also bears unhealed cuts, as though he warded off an assailant armed with a knife. One guess is that he was fleeing, stopped to rest in a depression away from the wind, and quietly passed away from his wounds.

The Preservation Equation

So, why were the Lovelock duck decoys, the houses of Ozette, and the Ice Man so well preserved?

Decomposition is carried out by microorganisms that require warmth, oxygen, and water to survive. In each case, one of these was lacking: Lovelock Cave lacked moisture, the wet deposits beneath the clay cap at Ozette were anaerobic (oxygenless), and the Ice Man's glacial environment lacked warmth.

These different preservation conditions present the archaeologist with both opportunities and challenges. At Ozette, for example, the waterlogged archaeological deposits were a muddy gumbo that was almost impossible to trowel or shovel. And because the wooden artifacts were saturated with water, a misplaced shovel stroke could slice them like a knife through butter. To cope with these conditions, Daugherty assembled a complex system of pressurized hoses to wash away the mud. By adjusting the water pressure, his team could use fire hoses to clean off the massive house posts and wall planks, switching to a fine misting spray when exposing delicate basketry.

Likewise, sites such as Lovelock Cave offer a wealth of artifacts not normally found, but such sites tend to be extremely complex. They are favorite places for rodents and carnivores, whose actions can move artifacts up and down, making it difficult to sort out what belongs with what. This means that they require especially slow excavation.

And although the Ice Man contributed enormously to our knowledge of the past, his preservation now requires a sophisticated storage chamber (at Italy's South Tyrol Museum of Archaeology), where museum personnel control the temperature and humidity.

Preservation, of course, is only one factor conditioning how we excavate a site; other determinants include the site's depth, time and financial constraints, accessibility, and, most important, the research questions being pursued. We have excavated with backhoes, shovels, trowels, dental tools, and garden hoses (see "Looking Closer: The Excavator's Toolkit"). We even used a jackhammer once (to remove several massive blocks of stone that had fallen from the roof in Gatecliff Shelter).

Sometimes archaeologists can rely on the latest technology; other times, financial constraints or remote conditions require the use of less elegant methods. Archaeologists excavate ancient Pueblo sites in New Mexico that contain well-defined room clusters very differently from high-altitude caves in Peru. Peeling off sequential levels of a Maya temple in Guatemala differs radically from excavating through seemingly homogeneous shell midden deposits in Georgia. Submerged sites, such as ancient shipwrecks, require their own special brand of archaeology.

There are many ways to excavate a site, and each is appropriate if it allows archaeologists to achieve the project's research goals within the constraints of time, funding, and technology. The important thing is that *the excavation techniques must record an artifact's context as precisely as possible.*

Principles of Archaeological Excavation

The key to maintaining information about an artifact's context is to record its provenience. *Provenience* means an artifact's location, but location is both hierarchical and relative.

Location is hierarchical because an artifact's provenience is simultaneously a particular country, a particular state in that country, a particular county in that state, a particular site in that county, a particular excavation unit in that site, a particular vertical level in that unit, and a particular position and orientation in that level. Obviously, the last levels in this hierarchy are more useful than the first levels. Figgins's excavators found some spear points at the Folsom site, but it was not until they were found in situ, lying between the bison's ribs, that their provenience became meaningful to a particular question.

Location is relative because we measure an artifact's position relative to a spatial system. We could use the UTM grid (mentioned in Chapter 3), or we could use a site-specific format. The key is to find a procedure that will allow a future archaeologist to reconstruct, in great detail, where you found things in the site.

How do we go about excavating a site so that we recover an artifact's provenience? Let's return to Gatecliff Shelter to see how this is done.

Test Excavations

From day one, Thomas wanted to learn two things: how long people had used Gatecliff Shelter, and whether the buried deposits could tell us about how human life had changed over time in this part of the Great Basin. The initial goal, then, was to decide if Gatecliff could help answer these questions. This meant that Thomas had to know what kind of historical record Gatecliff preserved. Was it a short or long record? Was it nicely stratified or a jumbled mess?

For this reason, the initial **test excavation** strategy was vertical, designed to supply, as expediently as possible, a stratified sequence of artifacts and ecofacts associated with potentially datable materials. Consequently, Thomas "tested" Gatecliff with two test pits. Like most archaeologists, we dig metrically, typically in 1-meter squares, for practical as well as scientific reasons: Squares much smaller would squeeze out the archaeologist, and larger units might not allow sufficient accuracy and would remove more of the site than necessary to answer the initial questions.

Test pits are quick and dirty because we must excavate them "blind"—that is, without knowing exactly what lies below. But even when digging test pits, archaeologists maintain three-dimensional control of the finds, recording the x and y axes (the horizontal coordinates) and the z axis (the vertical coordinate) for each one. This is one reason why archaeologists dig square holes. Provided the pit sidewalls are kept sufficiently straight and perpendicular, excavators can use the dirt itself to maintain horizontal control on the x and y axes by measuring directly from the sidewalls. Here the horizontal provenience is relative to the sidewalls of the pit.

What about vertical control? At Gatecliff, Thomas dug the test pits in arbitrary, but consistent, 10-centimeter levels. Everything of interest—artifacts, ecofacts, soil samples, and so forth—was kept in separate level bags, one for each 10-centimeter level. The z dimension for each level was usually designated according to

test excavation A small initial excavation to determine a site's potential for answering a research question.

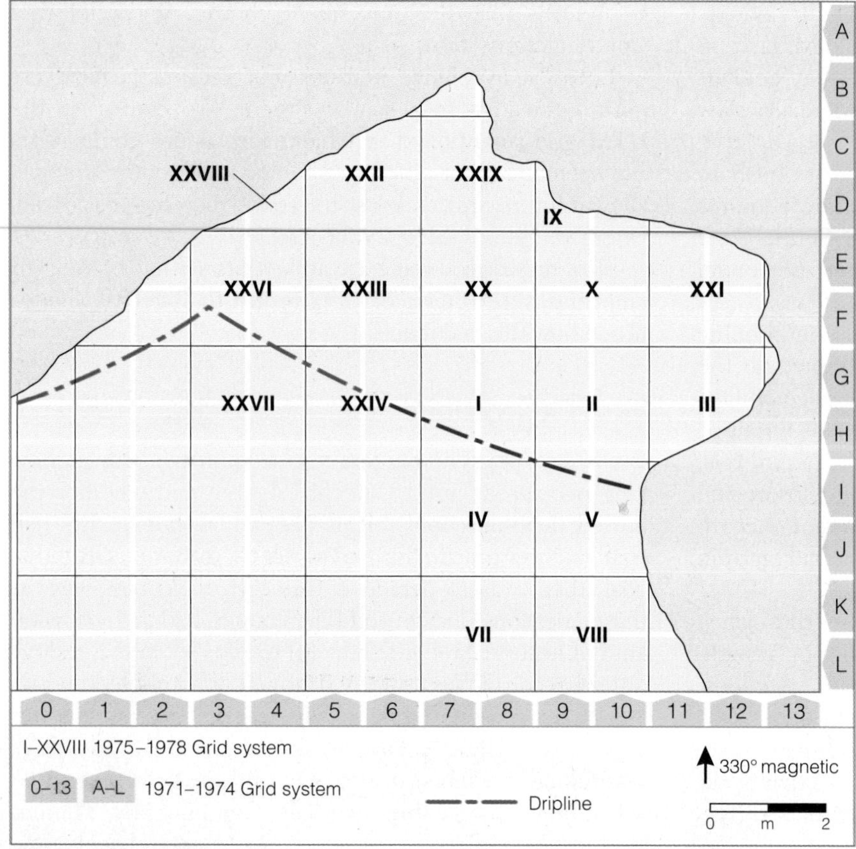

FIGURE 4-5 Plan view of the two grid systems used at Gatecliff Shelter. The alphanumeric system (consisting of letters and numbers) defined 1-meter excavation squares used in the first four seasons. Roman numerals designate the 2-meter squares used later, when large horizontal exposures were excavated. Courtesy American Museum of Natural History.

distance below the ground surface: Level 1 (surface to 10 centimeters below), Level 2 (10 to 20 centimeters below), and so forth. Thus, the excavators measured vertical provenience relative to the ground surface. This also can be a problem, given that the ground surface can change over time and make it potentially difficult for future archaeologists to correlate their levels with those of a previous archaeologist. But every project requires trade-offs, and there is no point to investing much effort in a site before knowing if it will provide the necessary information. This is why test pits often record only minimal levels of provenience.

Expanding the Test Excavation

The test pits at Gatecliff told Thomas that the site warranted a closer look, and he returned the next year to do just that. He first divided the site into a 1-meter grid system, oriented along the long axis of the shelter, recording the compass orientation of this grid. He assigned consecutive letters to each north-south division and numbered the east-west division (see Figure 4-5). Each excavation square could then be designated by a unique alphanumeric name (just like Bingo—for example, A-7, B-5, and the ever-popular K-9). Other archaeologists use different systems; the point is to establish a grid system that provides horizontal control on artifact provenience.

At Gatecliff, the east wall of the "7-trench" (so named because it contained units B-7 through I-7) defined a major profile that exposed the site's stratigraphy. Stratigraphy, you recall from Chapter 1, is the structure produced by the deposition of geological and/or cultural sediments in layers, or strata. The stratigraphy is a vertical section against which the archaeologists plot all artifacts, features, soil and pollen samples, and radiocarbon dates.

A **datum point** was established at the rear of the shelter and assigned an elevation of zero. All site elevations from this point on were plotted as "*x* centimeters below datum," rather than below surface (important because the surface almost never has the same elevation across any given site). Using an altimeter and a U.S. Geological Survey topographic map, Thomas determined the elevation of the datum point to be 2319 meters (7607 feet) above sea level. All archaeological features—fire hearths, artifact concentrations, sleeping areas, and the like—were plotted on a master site map, and individual artifacts found in situ were plotted in three dimensions—their x and y coordinates based on the map, and their z coordinates (that is, their elevation) based on the datum point.

This is how we did things in the 1970s. Today, we would have placed the datum many meters off the site in an area that would remain undisturbed by construction, natural processes, or future excavation. The datum would be an aluminum or brass cap marked with the site's Smithsonian or other identifying number, set in concrete or on top of a long piece of concrete reinforcement bar driven into the ground. Today, we would also use a global positioning system (GPS) instrument to determine the datum's elevation and UTM location. Once the datum is tied into the UTM grid, a future archaeologist could recreate its location even if the marker were destroyed.

How Archaeologists Dig

Despite what action-hero characters like Indiana Jones or Lara Croft might lead you to believe, archaeologists do not dash in, grab the goodies, and then run for their lives. We don't even mindlessly shovel dirt into a bucket. Instead, we excavate within horizontal excavation units in

natural levels and **arbitrary levels**. Natural levels are the site's **strata** (singular, **stratum**), which are more or less homogeneous or gradational material, visually separable from other levels by a change in the texture, color, rock or organic content, or by a sharp break in depositional character (or any combination of these).

Excavators prefer to excavate by natural levels wherever possible. Where these natural levels are thicker than 10 centimeters, they excavate in arbitrary levels no more than 10 or even 5 centimeters in thickness within the natural levels. At Gatecliff, excavators carefully troweled the deposit, and then passed it outside the cave for screening (we say more about this later); artifacts and ecofacts found in the screen were bagged by level. Individual excavators kept field notes at this stage in bound, graph-paper notebooks. Good field notes record everything, whether or not it seems important at the time. Remember, the excavators' goal is to capture the detail that will allow future archaeologists to "see" what the excavators saw as they were digging. Today, field notes employ standardized forms (unique to each excavation) so that excavators record the same detailed information for each level. Depending on how much they find, excavators may need a week to complete this one form (but usually it takes less than a day). This information includes the date, the excavator's name, a map of the unit showing where artifacts and features were found, and a detailed description of the sediments ("rock-hard clay, grading from brown to reddish-orange" or "loose, and dusty, with a lot of pack rat feces and cactus spines"). A geologist's Munsell soil color chart is often used to record sediment colors.

Excavators also record the level's beginning and ending elevations, observations on how this level was different from that above it ("There is more charcoal in this level"), whether any samples were taken (soil, carbon, plant materials), and so on. In addition, copious photographs (black and white, color slides, and digital) are taken of all unit profiles, all significant finds in situ, and all features. Nowadays, we often make a video recording of all excavation units at the end of each day, or during the excavation of important features and finds. The overriding purpose of all of this is to record an artifact's context.

Expanding Gatecliff's Excavation

The vertical excavation strategy at Gatecliff was a deliberately simplified scheme designed to clarify chronology. By the end of the fourth field season, Trench 7 had reached a depth of 9 meters below the ground surface. We had learned a good deal about the cultural sequence of Gatecliff Shelter, but our vertical excavation strategy had also left us with a series of extremely steep and hazardous sidewalls. Even though the excavation was stair-stepped to minimize the height of these sidewalls, they were still dangerous. Today, deep excavation trenches are heavily shored. Unshored walls higher than 4 feet are a violation of federal OSHA (Occupational Safety and Health Administration) regulations. And with good reason: More than one archaeologist has been nearly killed by collapsing profiles. Clearly, a change was in order for reasons of safety.

Change was required for conceptual reasons as well. The early excavations demonstrated that Gatecliff could contribute much more than chronology. As described in the last chapter, flash floods periodically filled the shelter with thick beds of silt. Eventually, the shelter dried out, and people used it once again. The result was that layers of sterile silt neatly separated **living floors**, or occupational surfaces, inside the overhang. This was a rare opportunity to study discrete living surfaces within a rockshelter environment.

Few archaeologists have such a chance, so we shifted away from the initial chronological objectives to concentrate on recording the spatial distributions of artifacts and features on the living floors. The goal now was to reconstruct what activities took place in the shelter as indicated by the distribution of artifacts across the living floors sandwiched between the silt layers. With the stratigraphy suitably defined, extensive vertical sections were no longer necessary, and we concentrated on opening entire (horizontal) living surfaces.

We switched to 2 × 2 meter units, but excavated the living floors more slowly than in the previous vertical excavations, and excavators tried to recover and map all artifacts in situ. We excavated and screened features such as hearths separately, and we retained soil samples for laboratory processing. We plotted artifacts, scatters of waste flakes from stone tool manufacture, concentrations of bone—anything found in situ—on master living floor maps.

This horizontal strategy required significantly more control within contemporary layers. A single excavator carefully worked each 2 × 2 meter unit, attempting to find

datum point The zero point, a fixed reference used to keep control on a dig; usually controls both the vertical and horizontal dimensions of provenience.

natural levels A vertical subdivision of an excavation square that is based on natural breaks in the sediments (in terms of color, grain size, texture, hardness, or other characteristics).

arbitrary levels The basic vertical subdivision of an excavation square; used only when easily recognizable "natural" strata are lacking and when natural strata are more than 10 centimeters thick.

strata (singular, **stratum**) More or less homogeneous or gradational material, visually separable from other levels by a discrete change in the character of the material—texture, compactness, color, rock, organic content—and/or by a sharp break in the nature of deposition.

living floors A distinct buried surface on which people lived.

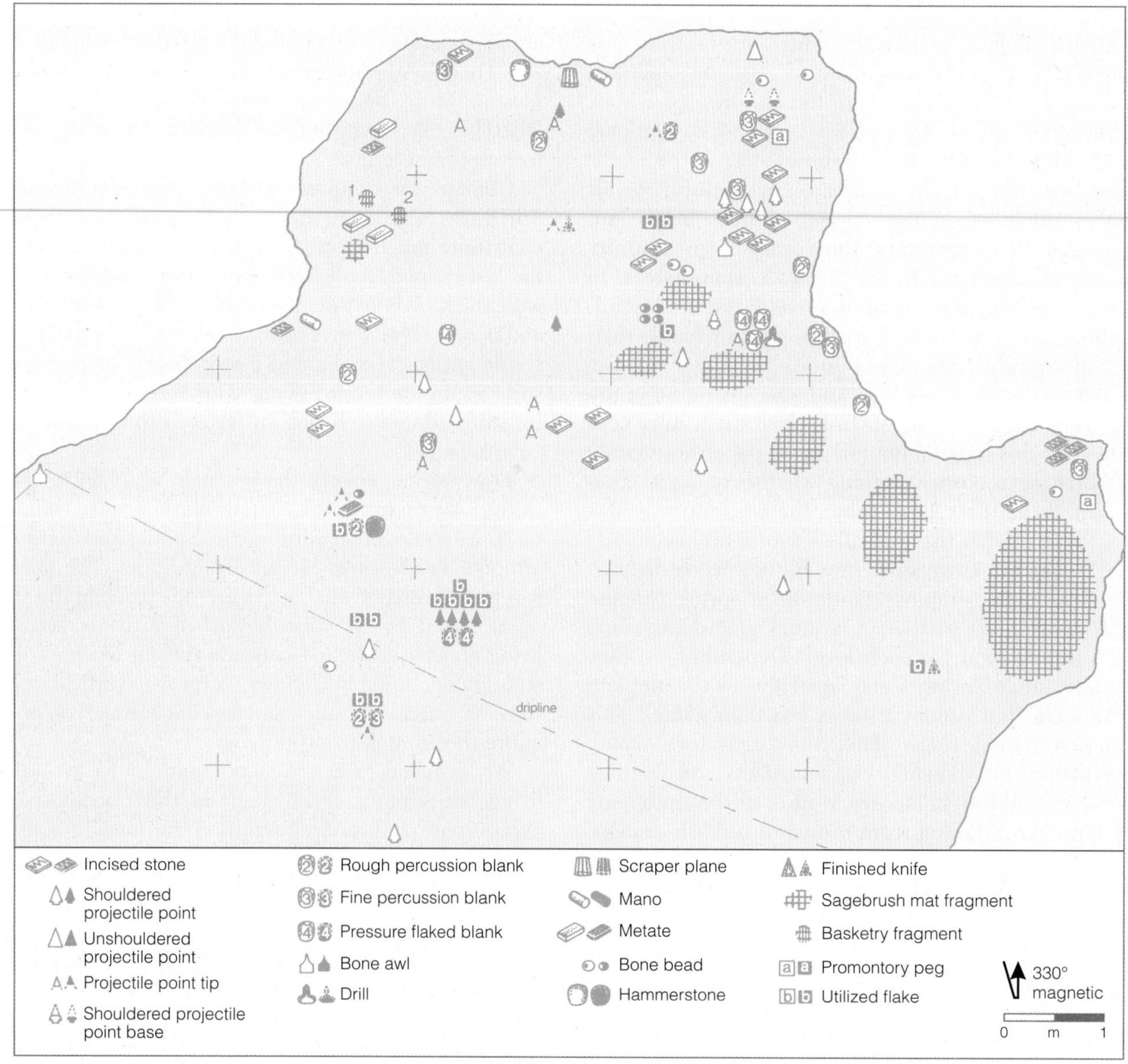

FIGURE 4-6 A living floor map showing the distribution of artifacts and hearths on Horizon 2 (deposited about AD 1300) at Gatecliff. Courtesy American Museum of Natural History.

as many artifacts as possible in situ. We plotted all artifacts, features, and large ecofacts onto the large-scale living floor maps for each surface. The result was a set of living floor maps that are rare among rockshelter excavations in the world (see Figure 4-6).

Precision Excavation

This description of the Gatecliff excavation provides a general sense of what goes on at archaeological sites. But excavation has become an even more exact science since Thomas excavated Gatecliff in the 1970s. Given the importance of an artifact's context, archaeologists continue to devise ways to record provenience for more objects with greater precision.

For example, at Gatecliff, we first used string line levels tied to the datum and tape measures to determine an artifact's vertical provenience (its depth below datum); we later switched to a more precise builder's level and measuring rod. We recorded horizontal provenience by measuring distances from two of a unit's sidewalls. Today, many archaeologists, ourselves included, use **total stations** to record provenience (see Figure 4-7). New instruments cost a pricey $5000, but they are necessary for state-of-the-art excavation.

How do total stations work? The devices are set up on a tripod over the site's datum. After workers input the correct data, the total station "knows" where it is on the grid system and which direction it is pointing. When an artifact is found, a glass prism is held on the artifact's location, and the total station is turned and aimed at the

© Robert Kelly

FIGURE 4-7 Harold Dibble (center) and Shannon McPherron (right) record data on-site while excavating Pech de L'Azé IV in France; the student at the far left is using a total station.

prism. Push a button, and the station shoots a beam of infrared light. By measuring the time it takes the light to bounce back from the prism, the total station calculates and records the artifact's x, y, and z coordinates—its provenience. This information is later downloaded to a database for mapping and analysis. Total stations take only a second or two to make measurements that are accurate to ± 3 *millimeters*. These instruments can be used at distances of hundreds of meters, so a site may need only one rather than the several datums that other measurement systems may require.

Some archaeologists record the provenience of virtually every item found in situ (a practice sometimes called "piece plotting"). Others set a cutoff, recording provenience on everything found in situ that is larger than, say, 3 centimeters (about an inch) in any dimension. As we said before, there are always trade-offs. Recording the provenience of every item found in situ provides archaeologists with a very accurate record of where they found things, but it takes much more time—meaning that less gets excavated (this is a special problem if the site is threatened with destruction). How much you piece-plot depends on how much time you have for the excavation and the questions you need the data to answer.

Is that all there is to it? No, there is more to recording provenience than simply location. Today, archaeologists sometimes record not only an artifact's x, y, and z coordinates, but also which side of the artifact was "up" when it was found, the compass orientation of its long axis, and its slope or inclination (recorded with a builder's angle finder or *clinometer*). We would also note whether the artifact is burned, has calcium carbonate or a particular kind of sediment adhering to it, or possesses other characteristics. Although this can make excavation mind-numbing, the resulting information is critical to understanding how a site was formed and, consequently, for inferring what people did there.

Sifting the Evidence

Digging is just the beginning of excavation. No matter how carefully you excavate, it is impossible to see, map, and recover everything of archaeological interest; this is why we use sifters to find things that hand excavation misses. This is also the second reason why we excavate in square units—sometimes only .5 × .5 meter in size. If the excavator misses something, the sifting process can at least tie its provenience down to a particular level in a particular unit—a very small area of the site.

At Gatecliff, excavators removed deposit with a trowel and whisk broom or paintbrush, carefully sweeping it into a dustpan. When excavators found an artifact in situ, they recorded the artifact's provenience; sometimes they photographed it in place and drew a sketch in the field notes before placing the artifact in a separate bag and labeling it with an identifying number.

They then poured the dustpan of dirt into a bucket and tagged it with a label identifying the unit and level. When the bucket was full, the day's "gopher" took it to the screening area, outside the shelter in the hot sun (the gopher is the person whose daily assignment was to "go for" this and "go for" that). Here the bucket was poured onto a screen with 1/8-inch mesh (to give you some idea of the size, standard window screen is 1/16-inch mesh), where workers sifted and carefully checked for any artifacts the excavators missed, including stone tool manufacturing waste flakes, fragments of bone, and anything else of importance.

Although archaeologists agree that Marshalltown makes the only trowel worth owning, there are many opinions on screens. Many archaeologists manufacture their own, and the design and workmanship of screens varies from dig to dig (a few are shown in Figure 4-8). Some are suspended from tripods, some are mounted on rollers, and others are driven by gas engines to speed things up. When Thomas dug Alta Toquima, a village located at 12,000 feet in the

total stations A device that uses a beam of light bounced off a prism to determine an artifact's provenience; it is accurate to ± 3 millimeters.

FIGURE 4-8 A few of the innumerable sifter designs that archaeologists use.

FIGURE 4-9 Water screening in the Stillwater Marsh, Nevada.

mountains of central Nevada, he invented a "backpacker" design for the screens. At Gatecliff, we used the most common kind—a shaker screen mounted on two pivoting legs.

Exactly what kind of screen you use is far less important than the mesh. Many archaeologists prefer 1/8-inch hardware cloth, but the choice of mesh size varies with the circumstances. The important point is that *screen size affects what you recover and how fast you can recover it.* Use 1/4-inch mesh and you can process dirt faster, but you will lose a surprising number of important objects. Use 1/16-inch mesh and the recovery rate goes up—but so does the time to process the dirt.

Thomas did an experiment some years ago to see how different screen sizes might affect the recovery of animal bones in archaeological sites. He built a three-decker screen with superimposed layers of 1/4-inch over 1/8-inch over 1/16-inch mesh screens. He then ran a set of faunal remains recovered from a site through the screens.

As you might guess, he found that 1/4-inch mesh was adequate for recovering bones of large animals such as bighorn or bison. But he also found that significant numbers of bones of medium-sized animals, such as rabbits and rodents, were lost. The 1/8-inch mesh screen was better for recovering the bones of these small mammals. But, in fact, significant amounts of small mammal bones are even lost through 1/8-inch screens! One needs 1/16-inch mesh (or flotation, discussed later) to recover the remains of animals the size of, say, pack rats, small birds, and especially fish.

Water Screening and Matrix Sorting

Archaeologists sometimes use **water screening**, especially when the artifacts and ecofacts are expected to be very small. The dirt is simply poured onto a screen (usually 1/8- or 1/16-inch mesh) and sprayed with a garden hose until all the sediment is washed through. The screen will then be set aside and, once dry, searched. Kelly used water screening at a site in the Stillwater Marsh in the Carson Desert (see Figure 4-9). Because the site was located on a clay dune that contained no natural rock, he simply water-screened the deposits through 1/16-inch mesh, dried what was left, and bagged it all. He saved literally everything—flakes from the manufacture of stone tools, burned pieces of mud, fish and bird bones, and shell fragments—and sorted it later in the field camp.

You should always use the finest mesh screen possible. But sometimes this isn't possible, because of time constraints or the presence of sediments that can clog even a 1/4-inch screen quickly. For this reason, we sometimes use a larger screen mesh in the field, but take bulk sediment samples from each level. These samples are processed in the lab and sorted by hand to separate stone from small stone tool waste flakes, shells, bits of ceramics, and bones. This is known as **matrix sorting** and, along with writing catalog numbers on artifacts, is often one of the first tasks a novice may be assigned in a lab.

Flotation

In some archaeological sites, like the upper parts of Gatecliff Shelter, the deposits are sufficiently protected from moisture that plant remains simply dry up and can be recovered by screening. But in other kinds of deposits, plant remains may be preserved only if they were burned and carbonized. These remains are often quite small and nearly impossible to collect by hand in the field.

The most common method of recovering such plant remains is **flotation**. Several procedures exist for floating archaeological samples, but all are based on the same principle: Dirt doesn't float, but carbonized plant (and some animal) remains do. By using water flotation, archaeologists can float most burned plant remains out of samples of archaeologically recovered dirt.

In one of the earliest applications, Stuart Struever (retired, former president of the Crow Canyon Archaeological Center) floated soil samples from 200 features attributable to the Middle Woodland component at Illinois's Apple Creek site. The samples were hauled to nearby Apple Creek, where they were placed in mesh-bottomed buckets and then water-separated by students who worked midstream. More than 40,000 charred nutshell fragments, 2000 carbonized seeds, and some 15,000 identifiable fish bones were collected in this manner. Standard dry-screening techniques would have missed most of these.

While excavating at Salts Cave in Kentucky, Patty Jo Watson (retired) and her associates were not blessed with a nearby stream, so they improvised. Sediments were placed in double plastic bags and carried outside the cave. They first spread the samples (weighing a total of 1500 pounds) in the shade to dry. They then filled two 55-gallon drums with water, and placed the dry samples in metal buckets whose bottoms had been replaced with window screen. They submerged the buckets in the 55-gallon drums.

After a few seconds, the investigator skimmed off the charcoal and carbonized plant remains that had floated to the surface, using a small scoop made from a brass carburetor screen (cloth diapers and aquarium nets work well, too). They spread the debris that floated to the top (called the "light fraction") and the stuff that sank (the "heavy fraction") on labeled newsprint to dry again. These flotation samples yielded carbonized remains of hickory nuts and acorns, seeds from berries, grains, sumpweed, chenopods, maygrass, and amaranth.

Today, flotation is not an expensive or even a particularly time-consuming process. Flotation techniques can (and should) be fitted to the local requirements. At Mission Santa Catalina, Thomas also used a converted 55-gallon drum, and one person could process dozens of samples each day. Some elaborate power-driven machines are equipped with aeration devices and use *deflocculants* or chemicals to remove clays that adhere to and sink carbonized plant remains. The technology is available to fit any budget.

RAPID REVIEW

Principles of Archaeological Excavation

- Record artifact context by recording provenience in detail.
- Structure excavation methods to level of preservation.
- Follow natural stratigraphy wherever possible; use arbitrary levels only where necessary.
- Excavate in the smallest practical horizontal and vertical units to maintain provenience of artifacts not found in situ.
- Utilize sieving, water screening, and sediment samples to recover small items.

But accuracy, not technology, is the issue. For a long time, archaeologists saved only bone (and even then, just the large, identifiable pieces) but ignored plant remains. This frequently led archaeologists to deemphasize the plant component of the economy. Now that flotation techniques have come into their own, we are discovering new things about the past. For example, from those seemingly innocuous burnt seeds of sumpweed, chenopods, may grass, and amaranth that Patty Jo Watson and others collected through flotation, archaeologists made the important discovery that Native Americans had domesticated some indigenous plants of North America's eastern woodlands at least 4000 years ago—more than 1000 years before maize appeared on the scene. Those tiny bits of burnt plant material floating on the water turned out to be very important.

Cataloging the Finds

Excavating objects is just the beginning; in fact, excavation is only about 15 percent of a project—most of our time is spent in the lab analyzing the finds. And before the artifacts and field data can be analyzed, the

water screening A sieving process in which deposit is placed on a screen and the matrix washed away with hoses; essential where artifacts are expected to be small and/or difficult to find without washing.

matrix sorting The hand sorting of processed bulk soil samples for minute artifacts and ecofacts.

flotation The use of fluid suspension to recover tiny burned plant remains and bone fragments from archaeological sites.

objects must be cataloged. In many cases, archaeologists assign artifacts their catalog numbers in the field, as they are excavated. We do this by printing up sheets of sequential catalog numbers on peel-off return address forms (we've used the format 48BH3178/xxxx, where the 48BH3178 is the site's Smithsonian number and the xxxx is a sequential number). When an artifact is found, it is piece-plotted and placed in a small Ziploc bag. The excavator peels a catalog number off the sheet (ensuring that there can be no duplicate numbers) and places it inside the bag (in case the label peels off, it will still be in the bag with the artifact). A crew member then records the number in the total station's data log and on the excavation level form.

Back in the lab, archaeologists catalog the artifacts. Most archaeologists are fanatical about cataloging their finds, because it's easy for one distracted lab worker to mess up an artifact's record of provenience. The catalogers work through the field bags, writing the catalog number onto the artifact itself with an archival pen, and sealing the number with clear fingernail polish; numbered tags are sometimes tied to some artifacts, such as small beads. Some archaeologists preprint the catalog numbers on minute labels and glue them to artifacts with archival glue. Even those items that were not found in situ or otherwise assigned a catalog number in the field are given a number in the lab. The catalog number is what ties a particular artifact back to observations made in the field. Thus, although cataloging can often take hundreds of person-hours, it is necessary to ensure that an artifact's original provenience, and consequently its context, is never lost.

Lab workers then enter the cataloged artifacts' information into a computer database, usually including rudimentary observations (such as weight, condition, color), collection date, its provenience (for example, unit, level, and x, y, z coordinates), and contextual data (for instance, stratum, inclination, and orientation). A digital photo may be attached to the data record. Copies are then made of the database so that the artifacts' all-important contextual data will not be lost.

Site Formation Processes: How Good Sites Go Bad

Every archaeological site is unique. Some sites are remarkably well preserved; others are not. Some lie on the surface; some are deeply buried; and others lie underwater. Some are frozen; others are dry. Casual observers may think of an "archaeological site" as stable and unchanging, but every archaeologist knows better. Sites are complex, and things can move around after they are buried. It's the archaeologist's job to draw inferences about human behavior from sites, but to do that we have to know how a site formed over time.

To accomplish this important task, we must always bear in mind that *the archaeological record is only the contemporary evidence left over from past behavior.* Artifacts are the static remains of past dynamic behavior. However, because both natural and cultural factors impinge on these remains, the archaeological record is rarely a *direct* reflection of past behavior.

The archaeological record is a contemporary phenomenon. Although the objects and their contexts may have existed for centuries or millennia, observations and knowledge about those objects and contexts are as contemporary as the archaeologists who do the observing. Archaeological strata are "leaky," and artifacts can move around quite a bit from where they were originally deposited.

To interpret the archaeological record more accurately, Michael Schiffer (University of Arizona) distinguishes between archaeological and systemic contexts. Artifacts, features, and residues were once part of an ongoing, dynamic behavioral system. Arrowheads were manufactured, used for specific tasks, broken, repaired, and then lost or discarded. Potsherds were once part of whole pots, which were manufactured and decorated according to prescribed cultural criteria. People used the pots for cooking or storage or ceremonial functions. The pots broke or were intentionally broken or discarded, perhaps as part of a ritual. Food bones and plant remains are the organic residues of a succession of activities—hunting or gathering, butchering or processing, cooking, and eating. While these materials are being manufactured and used, they exist in their **systemic context**. These items are part of a living behavioral system.

By the time such materials reach an archaeologist's hands, they have long since ceased to participate in this behavioral system. The artifacts, features, and residues archaeologists encounter are recovered from their **archaeological context**, where they may continue to be affected by human action, but where they are also affected by the natural environment.

Formation Processes in the Systemic Context

Using Schiffer's distinction between systemic and archaeological context, we can discuss **formation processes**—how artifacts enter the archaeological record and how they are modified once they are there (see Table 4-1). For our purposes, we distinguish among four distinctive processes in the systemic context that influence the creation of archaeological sites: cultural deposition, reclamation, disturbance, and reuse.

Cultural Depositional Processes

Cultural depositional processes constitute the dominant factor in forming the archaeological record. Artifacts enter the archaeological record in four primary ways:

TABLE 4-1 Site Formation Process Summary

Systemic Context	Archaeological Context
Cultural Deposition	Floralturbation (plants)
Discard	Faunalturbation (animals)
Loss	Cryoturbation (freezing)
Caching	Argilliturbation (wet/dry cycles)
Ritual interment	Graviturbation (hillslopes)
Reclamation	
Cultural Disturbance	
Reuse	

1. *Discard.* Tools, clothing, structures—everything eventually breaks or wears out and is discarded. When this happens, the object ceases to function in the behavioral system and becomes part of the archaeological context.
2. *Loss.* Other things are inadvertently lost, such as an arrow that misses its target or a necklace or pot left at an abandoned camp. In this case, the items are most likely small and still in usable condition.
3. *Caching.* Still others are intentionally cached. The Lovelock duck decoys we mentioned were intentionally buried. They remained part of the archaeological record because the person who cached them never returned.
4. *Ritual Interment.* Burials and their associated grave goods are the most obvious example of ritual interment, but other examples include offerings left at a shrine or, alternatively, deliberate destruction and burial of a shrine or religious site.

Reclamation Processes

Part of an archaeologist's job is to figure out whether the artifacts entered the archaeological record through discard, loss, caching, or ritual interment. This task is made difficult because artifacts can move back and forth between the systemic and archaeological contexts through **reclamation processes**. Archaeologists frequently find artifacts that were scavenged by later peoples. Pueblo peoples, for example, believed that ancient stone arrow and spear points contained power. If they happened to encounter a point while out working, they might keep it and later make a ritual offering of it. In this case, the arrowhead has moved from a context where it was (perhaps) unintentionally lost to one in which it was intentionally interred. It has also moved from the context of an earlier time period to one of a later time period, as well as from a context that records its original everyday function to one that records another culture's ritual!

Whenever a discarded projectile point is resharpened, a potsherd picked up and used to scrape hides, or an old brick reused in a new fireplace, reclamation has occurred.

Likewise, all archaeologists must cope with the fact that nonprofessionals (amateur archaeologists and looters) often collect artifacts from sites. If we ignore this fact, we run the risk of misinterpreting archaeological data. In the Carson Desert, for example, we knew that local people had collected projectile points from sites in the wetland for decades. One man had covered the walls of his dining room with picture frames full of points, and he lined his driveway with large stone mortars and metates. The fact that our survey recovered relatively few projectile points from sites in the marsh probably reflected this reclamation process—otherwise known as looting—and not necessarily a lack of hunting.

Cultural Disturbance Processes

Reclamation processes are the transfer of materials from the archaeological to the systemic context. But the archaeological record is also heavily conditioned by transformations *within* the archaeological contexts through **cultural disturbance processes**. Disturbance changes the contexts of materials within the archaeological site itself. Examples include such diverse cultural mechanisms as dam building, farming, and construction of houses, pits, and hearths.

Reuse Processes

An object can also move through a series of **reuse processes** before it enters the archaeological record. This can entail the recycling of some objects. Potsherds, for example, are sometimes ground up and used as temper in manufacturing new vessels. Broken arrowheads are sometimes rechipped into drills and scrapers. Beams from one building are sometimes pulled out and reused in another. The point here is that an object can be created for one purpose

systemic context The living behavioral system in which artifacts were originally manufactured, used, reused, and discarded.

archaeological context Once artifacts enter the ground, they become part of the archaeological context, where they can continue to be affected by human action but are also affected by natural processes.

formation processes The ways in which human behaviors and natural actions operate to produce the archaeological record.

reclamation processes Human behaviors that result in artifacts' moving from the archaeological context back to the systemic context—for example, scavenging beams from an abandoned structure to use them in a new one.

cultural disturbance processes Human behaviors that modify artifacts in their archaeological context—for instance, digging pits, hearths, canals, and houses.

reuse processes Human behaviors that recycle and reuse artifacts before the artifacts enter an archaeological context.

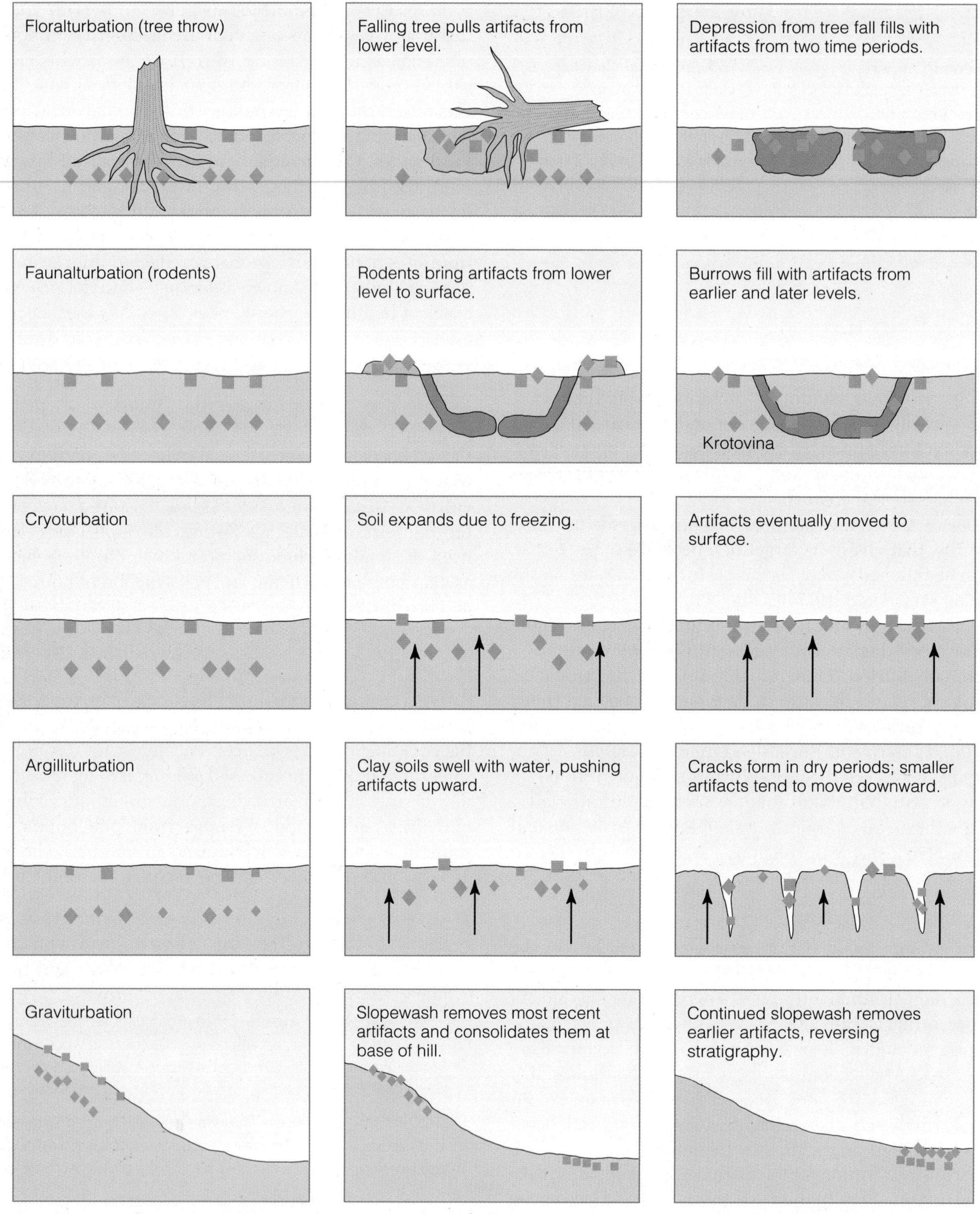

FIGURE 4-10 The effects of some natural formation processes on the distribution of artifacts in a hypothetical archaeological site.

but then modified and deposited in an entirely different context than a similar object that has not been reused.

The difference between reuse and reclamation has to do with whether the archaeological context is involved. If beams are taken from a currently occupied building, it is an instance of reuse; if they are taken from a building long abandoned, then it is reclamation. The distinction seems trivial, yet it tells us something about the potential difference in the age of the items being reused. Items that are reclaimed are probably moving from an archaeological context considerably older than the systemic context they enter; reused items, on the other hand, are probably moving between systemic contexts that are much closer in age.

This review of cultural formation processes shows that archaeologists need to be aware that human activities frequently move things from their original depositional provenience to another. This can make archaeological sites very complicated and difficult to interpret. And natural processes can complicate matters even more.

Formation Processes in the Archaeological Context

Once an object enters an archaeological context, a host of natural as well as cultural formation processes takes place. These natural processes determine not only whether organic material will be preserved, but also where objects will be found. Following are a few major categories of natural site formation processes (summarized in Figure 4-10). This assortment of processes is only a brief introduction; its purpose is to help you conceptualize just how complex an archaeological site can be. Additionally, this discussion shows that natural processes can both disrupt patterns that would otherwise tell us something about human behavior and, at the same time, create their own patterns, which can be misinterpreted as the result of human behavior. It warns us, then, that *there is no simple correspondence between the distribution of artifacts in a site and human behavior*. We give an example of how important an understanding of site formation processes can be when we revisit this important aspect of archaeology in Chapter 7.

Floralturbation

If you walk down almost any sidewalk, you'll see how tree roots can dislocate concrete slabs. **Floralturbation** refers to all the things that plant growth does to archaeological sites. Roots can tear buried ancient walls apart. By loosening soil, roots promote the downward movement of artifacts from their original stratigraphic context. And when a tree falls over, it can also move artifacts upward as the roots pull up large amounts of sediment—something known as "tree throw."

Faunalturbation

Faunalturbation refers to the things that animals do to archaeological sites. Burrowing animals can push artifacts that were originally deposited in lower layers up to the surface, placing old artifacts in a younger stratigraphic context. Burrowing can also *size-sort* artifacts vertically, moving larger artifacts downward and smaller artifacts upward. For example, pocket gophers dig their burrows around objects larger than about 5 centimeters; anything smaller they push out of their burrows. The larger artifacts and rocks left behind eventually tumble to the bottom of the burrows. Repeat this process over hundreds or thousands of years, and you end up with a site in which the small artifacts and stones are near the top and the large artifacts and stones are near the bottom. Some might conclude that people changed from using large to small tools over time, but they would be wrong: The pattern only tells us about pocket gophers, not people.

Sometimes these burrows are filled with rock and earth washed or blown in from above, forming a feature called a **krotovina** (pronounced "kro-toe-*vee*-na"; the term comes to us from Russian soil science and means "mole hole"). If so, then archaeologists can excavate the burrow separately from the surrounding sediments. But if the burrows simply collapse, they can be difficult or impossible to see.

Cryoturbation

In northern climates, freeze/thaw processes, or **cryoturbation**, can also move buried artifacts up to the surface. As soil freezes, it expands, pushing artifacts upward. As the soil thaws, soil particles move down, partially or completely filling the void below artifacts, ensuring that the artifacts cannot move back down. Thus, freeze/thaw cycles move large artifacts upward (sometimes at a rate of several centimeters a year). This can create a site in which artifacts are vertically size-sorted, with the smallest artifacts at the bottom of the sediment and larger ones near the top (an effect opposite to that of burrowing animals).

Argilliturbation

A similar process, known as **argilliturbation**, happens in clay-rich soils that undergo wet/dry cycles. As these soils become wet, they expand and push larger artifacts upward for the same reason as cryoturbation. But as these soils dry, they form cracks—sometimes several meters in depth—down which artifacts can fall. Run this process over and over for hundreds or thousands of years, and a site's stratigraphy can become thoroughly churned.

floralturbation A natural formation process in which trees and other plants affect the distribution of artifacts within an archaeological site

faunalturbation A natural formation process in which animals, from large game to earthworms, affect the distribution of material within an archaeological site.

krotovina A filled-in animal burrow.

cryoturbation A natural formation process in which freeze/thaw activity in a soil selectively pushes larger artifacts to the surface of a site.

argilliturbation A natural formation process in which wet/dry cycles push artifacts upward as the sediment swells and then moves them down as cracks form during dry cycles.

PROFILE OF AN ARCHAEOLOGIST

An African Archaeologist

Chapurukha (Chap) M. Kusimba is curator of African archaeology and ethnology at the Field Museum of Natural History in Chicago. Reprinted by permission.

Chap Kusimba/Chicago Field Museum of Natural History

Chap Kusimba.

I became interested in the natural history of East Africa when, as a youth in Kenya, I learned of the discoveries of Louis and Mary Leakey in Olduvai Gorge in neighboring Tanzania. I was intrigued by claims that East Africa was the cradle of humankind and fascinated by the idea that all humankind ultimately traced its beginnings to Africa. The fact that there was so much to discover in my own backyard shaped the way I viewed my heritage and encouraged my interest in becoming a scientist.

The study of social complexity has long been contentious in Africa. Assuming that Africans could not be innovative, previous scholars credited the origins of social complexity and "high culture" to immigrants from Southwest Asia. Today, African archaeologists have rejected diffusion as the initiator of cultural and technological transformations in Africa, and look instead to the specific processes of development.

My research focuses on the role of technology, economy, and interregional interaction in the development of chiefdoms and states in East Africa. In so doing, it evaluates the roles of Indian Ocean trade, ironworking technology, and interregional interaction in the development of social complexity in East Africa. I have conducted regional archaeological surveys, defined settlement patterns, and augmented these with problem-oriented excavations in key locales and sites in southeastern Kenya. The results are published in a number of research articles and in my book, *The Rise and Fall of Swahili States*, a text on the archaeology of social complexity in Africa.

With a few exceptions, all thoroughly investigated sites on the Kenya coast are large urban centers with monumental structures composed of elite residences, chiefly courts, and mosques. The focus on large urban sites inevitably introduced significant biases in data collection and influenced the rendering of regional history. But African archaeologists cannot ignore the relationship between urban areas and their trading partners in the hinterlands. And so, beginning in 1998, Dr. Sibel Barut Kusimba (Northern Illinois University) and I began to examine the role of trade in shaping East Africa's diverse ethnic identity. We did this by surveying areas in the Tsavo National Park and surrounding area, 150 kilometers from Kenya's eastern coast. We described more than 200 sites, from the Early Stone Age into the historic era, including hunter-gatherer rockshelter camps and residences, pastoral, agropastoral, and agrarian villages and chiefdom-level settlements, fortified stockades, market centers, and iron production areas. So far, we have excavated 12 of these sites and conducted intensive interviews with local communities called the Wataita, Somali, and Waata.

An important pattern emerging from our research is the web of social interactions among peoples of diverse origins and languages practicing and inventing different ways of life. The Tsavo region was a mosaic of political and economic alliances, an example of regional systems that exist in many areas of the world but are not completely understood. Understanding the development of social complexity in Africa requires attention to such regional interactions. Indeed, the mosaic is important to us not just as grist for the archaeologist's mill, but as a reservoir for potentially understanding Africa's future, because Africa's modern dynamics of ethnicity, social, and political power are rooted in these earlier interactions.

Graviturbation

Archaeological materials deposited on hillsides eventually move downslope. **Graviturbation** is accomplished through slopewash and gravity. The result is that archaeological materials originally deposited on a hillside move downslope and eventually come to rest in a context completely different from the one where they were originally deposited.

Some sites (like Gatecliff) have a high degree of stratigraphic integrity—meaning that artifacts are found where they were lost, discarded, cached, or ritually interred. Other sites are complex, with little stratigraphic integrity. In these sites, a range of cultural and natural formation processes have moved artifacts from their initial archaeological context. These processes do *not* make archaeology impossible. They do mean, though, that one of our first tasks is to establish just how the artifacts got to where the archaeologists found them. Although how we do this is different for each site, the objective is the same: Understanding the effects of site formation processes is the first step in knowing what an archaeologist can realistically accomplish with the information from a site. Archaeologists need to keep in mind all the processes that affect how artifacts and ecofacts enter the ground—and everything that can happen to them once they are there. In so doing, archaeologists have to think of the site not only as a record of human behavior, but also as a record of natural processes. They must think of the site as a geological record, as well as an archaeological record. Increasingly, archaeologists find that extremely careful and meticulous data, such as the orientation and inclination of plain old rocks as well as of artifacts, are needed to accomplish this goal. Thus, this realization of the importance of formation processes requires even greater precision and care in site excavation.

Conclusion

Archaeologists have traditionally protected their excavations against vandals and pothunters. Excavation often draws unwanted attention, and vandals have been known to attack sites during the field season at night. On Thomas's first job in archaeology, a 24-hour guard (armed, appropriately enough, with bow and arrow) was posted to protect the open excavation units from looters. At Gatecliff, we tediously backfilled the site by hand every year to protect the archaeology from the curious public, and the public from the dangers of open-pit archaeology.

On St. Catherines Island, the problem is somewhat different. The only visitors are scientists, who realize the research value of archaeological sites and leave the excavations untouched. It is thus possible to open a few test units on several sites, process the finds, and then return next year to the more promising sites for more intensive excavation.

On strictly research projects—like our work at Mission Santa Catalina—where the sites are not threatened by outside incursions, one must adopt a conservative excavation strategy. Archaeologists never excavate more of a site than is needed to answer their research questions; extensive excavations are undertaken only in the case of sites threatened by development or erosion. Most archaeologists leave as much of a site intact as possible for later investigators, who undoubtedly will have different questions and better techniques. As we have seen, remote sensing technology and archaeological survey techniques sometimes provide archaeologists with low-impact ways of learning without digging at all.

Regardless of whether we use high-tech instruments or old-fashioned elbow grease, our personal responsibility for site conservation remains unchanged and fundamental. Archaeology is a destructive science. We said it at the beginning of this chapter and it is worth repeating: Sites can be excavated only once, so it is imperative we do things right. Sometimes those sites have remarkable preservation and sometimes not. The degree of preservation affects what kind of excavation techniques we use and how quickly the excavation proceeds. But how much or how little we find does not change the fact that we must take any step necessary to ensure that provenience for virtually every artifact, ecofact, and feature is acquired during the excavation and recorded. We excavate in controlled units using a systematic grid system; we excavate in natural levels where possible, and, even if natural strata are present, in levels no more than 10 or even 5 centimeters thick; we record everything we can about an item before we pull it from the ground; and we assign catalog numbers to everything found so that each item can be related back to information gathered on its context. Once we have this information in hand, we are prepared to move on to the next chore of archaeology: making sense of everything we have found.

graviturbation A natural formation process in which artifacts are moved downslope through gravity, sometimes assisted by precipitation runoff.

Summary

- Why does context matter? How is it recorded?
  - Context matters because information comes from what artifacts are associated with each other, with features, and with particular strata. It's not enough to know that an artifact came from a particular site; we need to know how it relates to everything else found at the site.
  - Context is recorded by recording the provenience of artifacts, features, and ecofacts.
- What determines preservation?
  - Preservation is enhanced in continuously dry, continuously wet, and/or very cold environments—anyplace where conditions prevent the existence of the microorganisms that promote decay.
  - Diverse excavation strategies respond in part to different preservation conditions, constraints, and objectives to record provenience. From test-pit to full-scale excavation, archaeologists maintain records of the three-dimensional provenience of the objects being recovered. Archaeological records record an excavation in such a way that another archaeologist can "see" what the original excavator saw.
- What is the difference between arbitrary and natural levels? Why do these matter?
  - Natural levels follow the site's geologic stratigraphy; arbitrary levels are normally 5 or 10 centimeters thick and are based on depth below the datum point.

Arbitrary levels are normally used only in test pits when the natural stratigraphy is unknown or when natural layers are more than 10 centimeters thick.
  - Arbitrary levels could mix artifacts from different natural levels, of different geologic contexts.
- How do archaeologists recover the smallest artifacts and ecofacts?
  - We use screening, flotation, and bulk matrix processing to recover extremely small artifacts and ecofacts.
- What is the difference between systemic and archaeological contexts, and why does this difference matter?
  - The systemic context refers to artifacts as people are using or manipulating them; the archaeological context refers to natural processes that act on artifacts and features once they are deposited in the ground.
  - Artifacts leave the systemic context (and enter the archaeological context) through cultural depositional processes, including loss, discard, caching, and ritual interment.
  - Once in the archaeological context, artifacts can continue to be moved and altered by a variety of natural site formation processes, including landslides, burrowing animals, earthworms, tree throw, and the actions of water and climate.
  - This difference matters because in most sites, stratigraphy results from a complex interplay between natural and cultural processes, and because recognizing this interplay tells us how an artifact in the ground relates to the human behavior that is our ultimate interest.

Media Resources

Doing Fieldwork: Archaeological Demonstrations CD-ROM 2.0

This CD, developed by the authors, shows professional archaeologists involved in various digs, many of which are referenced in the text. The presentation is organized by the main techniques used on an archaeological dig, reinforcing concepts and techniques via live examples. The CD takes you through each step automatically, or you can navigate to any point via the navigation bar. After reviewing a step in the dig process, you are taken to Check Points, which are concept questions about each step of the dig. Then you can see the answers, receive your score, and even send your scores to your instructor.

See the "What Is the Question?" "Beginning to Excavate," "Excavation," and "Stratigraphy" sections of the CD-ROM to learn more about topics covered in this chapter.

CourseMate

Access chapter-specific learning tools including learning objectives, practice quizzes, videos, flash cards, and glossaries, as well as web links, and more in your Archaeology CourseMate. Login to www.cengagebrain.com to access the resources your instructor has assigned and to purchase materials.

Chronology Building: How to Get a Date

5

The site of Betatakin, a thirteenth century cliff dwelling in the Navajo National Monument in northern Arizona.

Learning Objectives

After reading this chapter, you should be able to answer these questions:

- What is the difference between relative and absolute dating?
- What are the major dating techniques, what materials do they date, and what is their time range?
- What do archaeological dates date?

Preview

THIS CHAPTER IS ABOUT dating archaeological sites—how archaeologists get a grasp on time. Here, you'll find a broad range of dating techniques: tree-ring dating, radiocarbon dating, thermoluminescence dating, and others that allow us to date organic material, rocks—even dirt itself. The chemical and physical underpinnings of these techniques can be mind-boggling, but you need to have at least a basic understanding of them to understand when you can and cannot use a particular technique.

You also need to understand the basis of these techniques to know just what the "date" is actually telling you, because *dates in and of themselves mean nothing*. Demonstrating the *validity of associations* between dates and human behavior is the key issue in archaeological dating.

Introduction

The Fourth Egyptian Dynasty lasted from 2613 to 2494 BC. The Roman Colosseum was constructed between AD 70 and 82. The Battle of the Little Big Horn took place on June 25, 1876. Each date represents the most familiar way of expressing chronological control: the **absolute date**. Such dates are expressed in specific units of scientific measurement—days, years, centuries, or millennia—but no matter what the measure, all such absolute determinations pinpoint a specific year or a specific range of years.

In the early days, archaeologists did not have absolute dating methods. Before the 1950s, most dates were instead **relative dates** involving unspecified segments of time, expressed as relationships or comparisons. The stepped pyramid at Saqqara in Egypt is *earlier* than Khufu's pyramid; the historic settlement of Williamsburg is *later* than the pueblos of Chaco Canyon; Folsom spear points are *earlier* than Chupadero black-on-white pottery. Relative dates are obviously not as precise as absolute dates, but before the 1950s, they were the best that archaeology had.

Relative Dating

The key to relative dating is the **index fossil concept**.

Developed in the early nineteenth century, the index fossil concept is often attributed to British geologist William "Strata" Smith (1769–1839), although it was in circulation throughout Europe at the time. Geologists of Smith's day wrestled with the problem of how to correlate the ages of widely separated exposures of rock. Smith observed that forms of life changed over time, so different fossils characterize different rock strata. Thus, widely separated strata could be correlated and assigned to the same time period if they contained the same fossils. It seems like a simple idea, but it allowed Smith and others to make the first geological maps, and these radically altered the way that geologists conceived of the landscape. Now they could see broad patterns that told a story of ancient seas, mountain building, and ice ages.

The Index Fossil Concept in Archaeology

Archaeology faced a similar problem. Geology's **law of superposition** could indicate which artifact types or styles were older than other forms in particular sites—the older ones are at the bottom and the younger ones near the top—but how could the individual site chronologies be chronologically related to one another? The index fossil concept provided the answer. In archaeology, however, artifacts replace fossils: Strata in widely separated sites that contain the same distinctive artifact forms—called **time markers** in archaeology—are assumed to be of similar age.

What is really needed, of course, is a *master sequence*—a site with a deep stratigraphic profile that would permit the law of superposition to demonstrate the changing sequence of artifact types and styles. Early twentieth-century archaeologist Nels Nelson (1875–1964) searched for just such a master sequence for the American Southwest during his excavation at Pueblo San Cristobal (New Mexico). Nelson knew that there were deep deposits at San Cristobal, and he hoped that a carefully controlled excavation into them would show whether certain artifacts could act as time markers (see Figure 5-1).

Selecting an area with minimal disturbance, Nelson isolated a block of debris measuring 3 feet by 6 feet wide and nearly 10 feet deep. Clearly, the midden had accumulated over a long interval, and several distinctive kinds of pottery were buried there. Because the dusty black midden lacked sharp stratigraphic divisions, Nelson personally excavated the block in 1-foot arbitrary levels, cataloging the potsherds recovered by level. Imposing arbitrary levels on an undifferentiated stratigraphy seems almost pedestrian today, but in 1914, Nelson's stratigraphic method was revolutionary; New World archaeologists immediately seized the method as a fundamental of excavation (for the record, Nelson got the idea from his European colleagues).

Nelson then applied the law of superposition to look for culture change within the midden column. All else

FIGURE 5-1 General view across Nels Nelson's excavations at San Cristobal (New Mexico). The 700-year-old walls of this huge pueblo are clearly evident. Note also that no screens appear anywhere; sifting of archaeological deposits did not become standard practice until almost 50 years after this picture was taken.

being equal, the oldest trash should lie at the bottom, capped by more recent accumulations. Even though the dense midden lacked tangible stratigraphy, Nelson searched for time markers in the form of distinctive pottery types.

This is how Nelson applied the index fossil concept to the prehistoric ceramics of San Cristobal. Just as geologists learned to distinguish certain extinct life forms as characteristic of various rock strata, so too could archaeologists use distinctive artifact forms to characterize and correlate strata between archaeological sites. Pottery was a natural choice, given that potsherds were common cultural debris and Nelson knew that ceramic styles varied considerably across the American Southwest.

More than 2000 potsherds turned up in the 10-foot test section at San Cristobal. Nelson first grouped the potsherds into obvious types and then plotted their distribution according to depth below the surface (we discuss the principles of creating types in Chapter 6). Table 5-1 summarizes his results. Column 1 contains the frequency of corrugated pottery, the most common everyday cooking ware. Because the relative frequency of corrugated potsherds remained more or less constant throughout the occupation of San Cristobal, Nelson rejected Column 1 as a potential time marker. For the same reason, he also rejected biscuit ware, a dullish whitish-yellow, as a potential time marker (see Column 2).

Nelson then turned to the three remaining kinds of pottery—which he termed Types I, II, and III—and discovered, just as the Europeans had with their fossils, that certain forms were associated with specific stratigraphic levels (see Figure 5-2). The most ancient levels at San Cristobal contained a predominance of Type I painted pottery, black designs on a white background. Type I potsherds were most numerous at and below the 8-foot mark and were only rarely recovered above 7 feet. Type II pottery—red, yellow, and gray potsherds ornamented with a dark glaze—occurred most commonly at and above the 7-foot mark. In other words, Type I potsherds characterized the lower strata, and the Type II potsherds characterized the upper deposits.

The Type III pottery, three-colored glazed ware, was rare at San Cristobal and appeared only in the uppermost levels of Nelson's column. This made sense, given that Pueblo peoples were making three-colored wares when the Spaniards arrived in New Mexico in the sixteenth century.

Nelson's arbitrary levels made possible the definition of three important ceramic time markers. Not only did he document the specific ceramic changes at San Cristobal, but more important, his controlled stratigraphic excavation provided a master sequence with which to place other sites, strata, or features in the region into a relative chronological sequence.

absolute date A date expressed in specific units of scientific measurement, such as days, years, centuries, or millennia; absolute determinations attempting to pinpoint a discrete, known interval in time.

relative dates Dates expressed relative to one another (for instance, earlier, later, more recent) instead of in absolute terms.

index fossil concept The idea that strata containing similar fossil assemblages are of similar age. This concept enables archaeologists to characterize and date strata within sites using distinctive artifact forms that research shows to be diagnostic of a particular period of time.

law of superposition The geological principle that in any pile of sedimentary rocks that have not been disturbed by folding or overturning, each bed is older than the layers above and younger than the layers below.

time markers Artifact forms that, as with index fossils in geology, research shows to be diagnostic of a particular period of time.

TABLE 5-1 Potsherds at San Cristobal

Depth below Surface	Corrugated Ware 1	Biscuit Ware 2	Type I: Black-on-White Glaze 3	Type II: Two-Color Glaze 4	Type III: Three-Color Glaze 5	Total
1st foot	57 (36.7)	10 (6.5)	2 (1.3)	81 (52.2)	5 (3.2)	155
2nd foot	116 (31.3)	17 (4.6)	2 (.01)	230 (62)	6 (1.6)	371
3rd foot	27 (15.3)	2 (1.1)	10 (5.7)	134 (76.1)	3 (1.7)	176
4th foot	28 (21.3)	4 (3)	6 (4.5)	93 (70.9)	0 (0)	131
5th foot	60 (17.3)	15 (4.3)	2 (.01)	268 (77.6)	0 (0)	345
6th foot	75 (18.6)	21 (5.2)	8 (1.9)	297 (73.8)	1? (.01)	402
7th foot	53 (23.1)	10 (4.3)	40 (17.5)	126 (55)	0 (0)	229
8th foot	56 (24.6)	2 (.01)	118 (51.9)	51 (22.4)	0 (0)	227
9th foot	93 (45.4)	1? (.01)	107 (52.5)	3 (1.4)	0 (0)	204
10th foot	84 (54.4)	1? (.01)	69 (44.8)	0 (0)	0 (0)	154
Total	649	83	364	1283	15	2394

Source: Nelson, Nels. 1916. Chronology of the Tano Ruins, New Mexico. *American Anthropologist* 18: 159–180.
Figures in parentheses are row-wise percentages

FIGURE 5-2 Examples of Nels Nelson's Types I (bottom), II (middle), and III (top) pottery from San Cristobal Pueblo.

The Next Step: Seriation

The index fossil concept was essential to archaeology in the early twentieth century. The law of superposition permitted archaeologists to produce a chronology of cultural change at a particular site, and the index fossil concept allowed archaeologists to date sites *relative* to one another. Given this discovery, archaeologists could date other southwestern Pueblo sites based on the type of pottery found in them. A site with predominantly black-on-white pottery would be older than one that contained red glazed pottery. Archaeologists did not know *how much* older the first site was than the second, but they could nonetheless still place sites into a relative chronological sequence based on their ceramics. This was a tremendous advance for the time.

This advance became the basis of **seriation**, a relative dating technique that was crucial to archaeology in the mid-twentieth century. European archaeologists first developed the technique in the late nineteenth century, and Alfred Kroeber (1876–1960) introduced it to the New World. Seriation is grounded in the readily observable fact that styles change over time. In ancient times, just as now, most new ideas are slow to catch on, with only a few pioneers participating in the fad. Eventually, a new idea may become chic and replace earlier vogues, only to fall gradually into disuse and be replaced by the next "new thing." The index fossil concept relied primarily on the presence or absence of distinctive kinds of artifacts. Seriation refined this by using changes in the *frequencies* of artifacts or styles to date sites relative to one another (paleontologists, by the way, do the same thing with fossils).

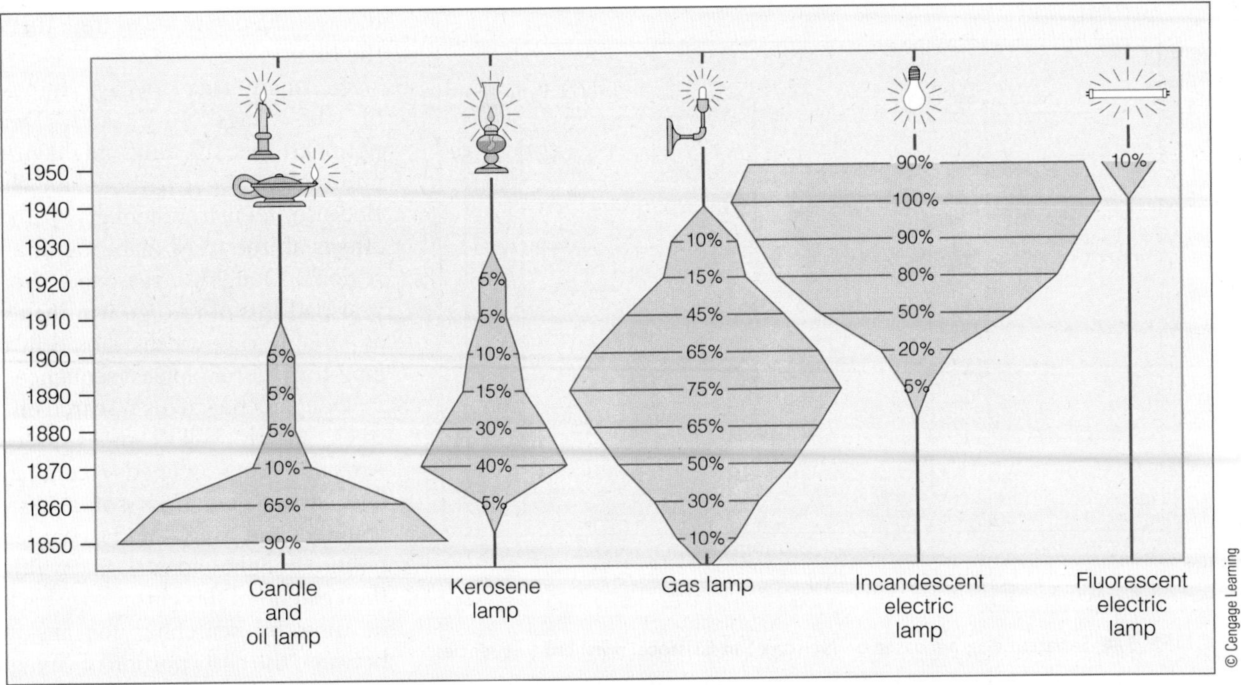

FIGURE 5-3 Seriation diagram showing how methods of artificial illumination changed in Pennsylvania between 1850 and 1950. Redrawn from Mayer-Oakes 1955, Figure 15.

To get a sense of how seriation works, look at Figure 5-3, which shows changes in lighting technologies in late nineteenth-century Pennsylvania. At mid-century, most houses were illuminated by candles and oil lamps; only a few households had gas lamps. Over the next 50 years, more and more families switched to gaslights. Those who could not afford such installations used kerosene lamps (made possible by the growing petroleum industry in Pennsylvania and elsewhere). By 1900, however, electric lights were replacing gaslights and, by 1940, gaslights had all but disappeared. By that year, virtually everyone used incandescent lightbulbs—which were already being replaced by fluorescent lamps by 1950.

The shape of such popularity curves, which James Ford termed "battleship curves" because they often look like a warship's silhouette from above, is the basis for seriation. By arranging the proportions of temporal types into lozenge-shaped curves, one can determine a relative chronological sequence.

This phenomenon is evident in Nelson's potsherd counts from San Cristobal Pueblo (Figure 5-4 translates the frequencies from Table 5-1 into a seriation diagram). As we've already noted, when San Cristobal was first built, ceramics were most commonly decorated with black designs painted on a white background; corrugated ware was also fairly common. Moving up Nelson's stratigraphic column, however, two-color glaze rapidly takes over in popularity, with black-on-white pottery fading out. In the top half of the column, three-color pottery comes into use. The midden at San Cristobal faithfully preserved these changes in ceramic "fashion."

This sequence can help archaeologists date other archaeological sites in the American Southwest. Instead of just using the presence or absence of a particular artifact type, we use frequencies of those different artifacts to place sites into a finer chronological sequence. For example, sites with high percentages of black-on-white ceramics would be older than sites with high percentages of two-color glaze and small percentages of black-on-white pottery. These sites, in turn, would be older than sites with high percentages of two-color glaze, small percentages of corrugated ware, and only trace amounts of black-on-white pottery. And these sites would be older than sites dominated by two-color glaze with trace amounts of three-color glaze.

We can use the seriation method based on a single master stratigraphy, or we can compile one analytically by linking several overlapping stratigraphies at different stratified sites. Thus, seriation takes the index fossil concept and refines it to permit a more fine-grained relative sequence. Nonetheless, seriation still cannot tell us *how old* a site or stratum is, only whether it is older or younger than another.

Seriation was a common technique in the mid-twentieth century, but today it is used mostly where absolute dating methods cannot be employed or are not sufficiently specific. And archaeologists still use the index

seriation A relative dating method that orders artifacts based on the assumption that one cultural style slowly replaces an earlier style over time. With a master seriation diagram, sites can be dated based on their frequency of several artifact (for instance, ceramic) styles.

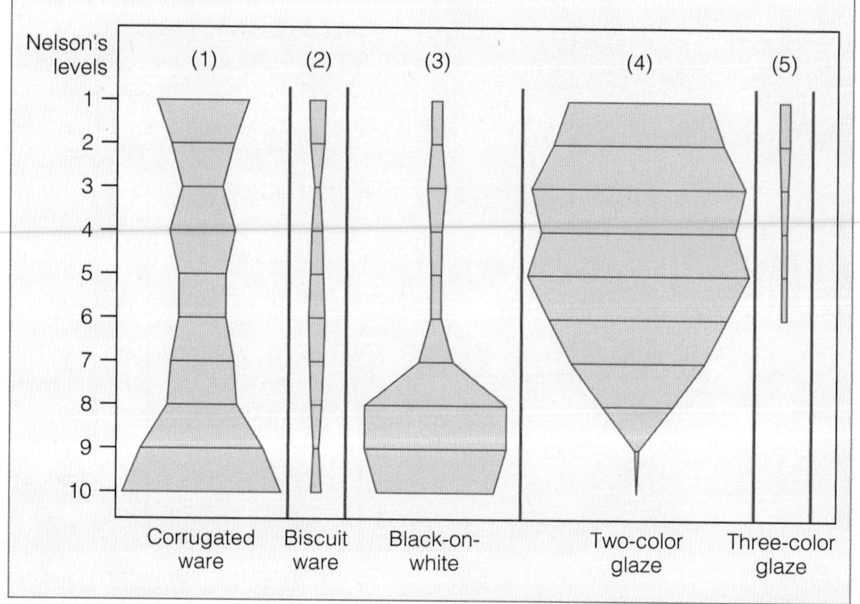

FIGURE 5-4 Seriation diagram based on Nelson's San Cristobal potsherd frequencies.

fossil concept, but only as a rough guide. For example, excavations have shown that Folsom spear points, like those found at the Folsom site mentioned in Chapter 4, date to around 12,300 to 12,900 years ago. If we excavated a site with Folsom points in it, we would gleefully tell our colleagues that "we had a Folsom site," and they would know how old the site is. But we would *always* try to refine that estimate by using one of the absolute dating techniques discussed next.

Absolute Dating

Absolute dating gave archaeology an incredibly powerful tool and helped shape it into the science that it is today. In this chapter, we only highlight the most commonly used techniques among the many that are available. We give special attention to radiocarbon dating as a way to demonstrate the issues that archaeologists must consider when determining what a date actually means.

Tree-Ring Dating

Tree-ring dating, also called **dendrochronology**, was developed by Andrew E. Douglass (1867–1962), an astronomer interested in the effect of sunspots on the earth's climate. Douglass knew that trees growing in temperate and arctic areas remain dormant during the winter and then burst into activity in the spring. This results in the formation of the familiar concentric growth rings, alternating light and dark. The light rings are a year's spring/summer growth, and the dark rings are that year's late summer/fall growth. Because each set of rings represents a single year, it's a simple matter to determine the age of a newly felled tree: Just count the rings.

In many tree species, the widths of the rings vary, and Douglass reasoned that the rings might preserve information about past climatic change. Because environmental patterning affects all the trees maturing in a given region, Douglass reasoned, year-by-year patterns of tree growth manifested as variable ring widths should fit into a long-term chronological sequence.

Douglass began his research on living trees, mostly yellow pines in central Arizona. He examined recent stumps and cores taken from still-living trees, counted the rings, and recorded the pattern of light and dark ring widths. He then extended this chronology backward in time by searching for an overlap between the early portion of young trees with the final years of growth of an old tree or stump. In doing so, he created a master sequence of tree rings extending back in time. But this sequence of stumps and living trees went back only about 500 years.

Douglass worked in the American Southwest, where arid conditions enhance preservation. Sampling ancient beams in pueblo sites, he slowly constructed a prehistoric "floating chronology," which spanned several centuries but was not tied into the sequence based on modern samples (see Figure 5-5). Eventually, Douglass was able to bridge this gap between these two sequences of ancient and modern trees, giving southwestern archaeology a reliable, year-by-year dating tool.

Methodology of Tree-Ring Dating

In practice, tree-ring dating works like this: An archaeologist digs up a sample of charcoal or wood of the appropriate species that bears at least 20 rings. He or she then sends it to a lab, such as the University of Arizona's Laboratory of Tree-Ring Research, with appropriate contextual data. There, an analyst cuts or sands the sample so that the rings are easily visible, then measures the widths individually.

Then the hard work begins. Normally, the archaeologist has some idea of how old the site is—perhaps less than 500 years old, or between 750 and 1000 years old. A lab analyst tries to match the sample to the appropriate portion of the regional sequence. This can be a slow, laborious process, because the analyst is looking for a segment of the master sequence that has the same order of variable-width rings as the archaeological sample—say, a pattern of four thick summer rings, followed by three thin ones, then three thick rings, two thin rings, and finally four not-quite-so-thick rings. Computer programs can assist in this task, but the matching often requires visual comparison because some samples have oddities, such as missing rings or partial rings, that only a trained technician can detect.

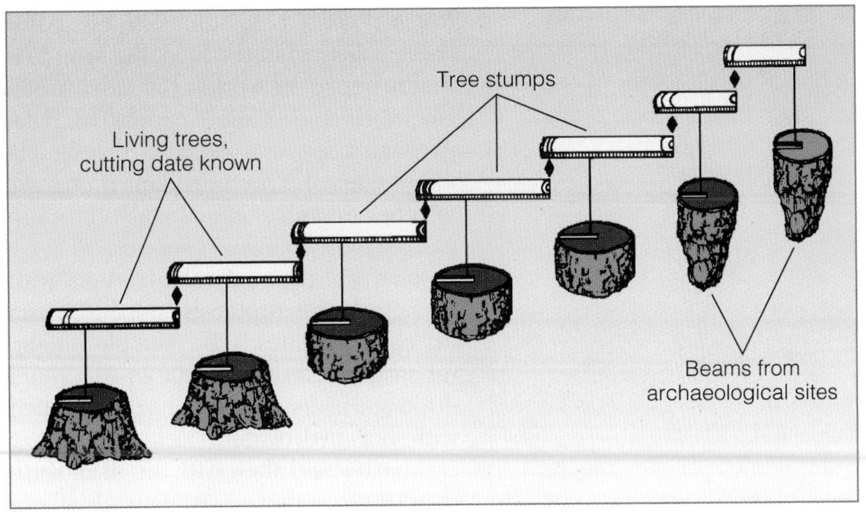

FIGURE 5-5 How a tree-ring chronology is built up by matching portions of tree-ring sequences from known-age living trees (lower left) to older archaeological samples; the diamonds indicate the portions of the sequences that overlap.

For tree-ring dating to work, the analyst has to make several adjustments and consider several factors. For example, trees grow more quickly when they are young than when they are old. Thus, absolute tree-ring width is a function of climate and a tree's age. Dendrochronologists solve this problem by using the estimated curvature of the rings on a sample along with a mathematical function that converts ring widths into a standardized index that takes the tree's age into account.

Additionally, a sample's age is the age of the last (outermost) ring. But if that ring is not present—if the outer portion of the sample was adzed off or burnt away—we won't know what year the tree died. By looking for markings that are diagnostic of the outer edge of a tree—such as signs of bark or beetle activity—a trained analyst can determine whether the outermost ring on the sample was the tree's final ring. If so, then you have what is known as a *cutting date*; if not, then your date is only a maximum age (that is, we could say that a specimen was cut down after, say, AD 1225, but we would not be able to say *how many* years after).

Finally, the sample sent to the lab must have at least 20 rings visible on it to increase the chance that the sample will match one and only one segment of the master sequence. A sample with fewer rings might match to several segments, leaving the archaeologist guessing which match is the correct one.

We can apply tree-ring dating to many tree species as long as the species reflects climatic change. The most commonly used are piñon pine, ponderosa pine, Douglas fir, juniper, and white fir. Limber pine, bristlecone pine, oak, red cedar, and the giant sequoia are also useful. But some species are unsuitable. Cottonwood, for example, grows only near water sources and taps into a more continuous supply of groundwater. As a result, its rings do not reflect local climate very well, and without climatically induced variation in ring width, we cannot link individual samples and build a chronology.

Dendrochronological sequences have been developed in many areas, including the American Southwest, the Arctic, the Great Plains, the American Midwest, the American Southeast, Germany, Great Britain, Ireland, New Zealand, Turkey, Japan, and Russia. In the American Southwest alone, more than 60,000 tree-ring dates have been established for some 5000 sites. Here the logs used to make pueblo rooms and pithouses allow the tree-ring sequence to extend back some 2300 years; using oaks preserved in ancient bogs, one sequence in Germany extends back almost 10,000 years.

Tree Rings and Climate

Dendrochronology also provides climatic data. Because tree-ring width is controlled by precipitation as well as temperature, trees preserve a record of past environmental conditions. Although tree metabolism is complex, analysts have made great progress in such ecological reconstructions. In the American Southwest, for instance, detailed models can tell us how much rain fell in, say, northwestern New Mexico, year by year, even season by season. For example, these data demonstrate that catastrophic floods occurred there in AD 1358. These detailed climatic reconstructions can provide archaeologists with fine-grained paleoenvironmental chronologies—provided an appropriate dendrochronological sequence is available locally.

Radiocarbon Dating: Archaeology's Workhorse

In 1949, physical chemist Willard F. Libby (1908–1980) announced to the world that he had discovered a revolutionary new dating technique: radiocarbon dating. For his efforts, Libby deservedly received the Nobel Prize in chemistry in 1960. Although dendrochronology is a more precise technique, radiocarbon dating is more widely applicable and is the workhorse in archaeology's stable of dating methods.

How It Works

There are three principal isotopes of carbon: ^{12}C, ^{13}C, and ^{14}C. The isotope ^{14}C (read this as "carbon-14") is of interest here, even though it is the rarest: Only one ^{14}C atom exists for every trillion atoms of ^{12}C in living

tree-ring dating (dendrochronology) The use of annual growth rings in trees to assign calendar ages to ancient wood samples.

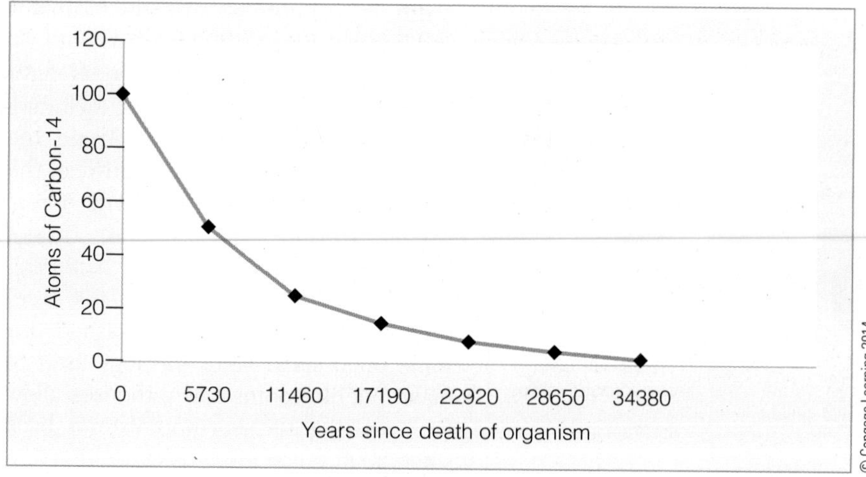

FIGURE 5-6 The amount of ^{14}C in the remains of an organism is reduced by half every 5730 years, radiocarbon's so-called half-life.

material. The ^{14}C is produced in the upper atmosphere, where cosmic radiation creates neutrons that replace one of nitrogen's (^{14}N) protons to create ^{14}C. This ^{14}C is oxidized to form carbon dioxide, which is dispersed throughout the atmosphere by stratospheric winds. About 98 percent of all ^{14}C enters the oceans; plants take up much of the rest through photosynthesis. From plants, radioactive carbon enters herbivores and carnivores—and you.

All radioactive isotopes are unstable and break down, or "decay," over time. The ^{14}C breaks down through beta emissions (the loss of a negatively charged electron) into ^{14}N. The amount a living organism loses through decay is replaced from the environment, so as long as an organism is alive, the amount of ^{14}C in it remains in equilibrium with the atmosphere. But once the organism dies, it ceases to take in ^{14}C, and hence the amount of ^{14}C in its body begins to decrease through decay (see Figure 5-6).

But not very quickly. In fact, we now know that after 5730 years, half of the ^{14}C available in a sample will have converted to ^{14}N; this number is termed the **half-life** of ^{14}C.

What do we mean by "half-life"? Imagine a sample of charcoal that contains 100 atoms of ^{14}C (actually, it would contain much more, but let's keep it simple). After 5730 years, 50 of these atoms would have decayed into ^{14}N. After another 5730 years, half of the remaining 50 ^{14}C atoms (that is, 25 atoms) would have converted to ^{14}N, leaving us with only 25 ^{14}C atoms. After another 5730 years (a total of 17,190 years), this amount would be halved again to about 12 ^{14}C atoms. As you can see, after a long time, very few ^{14}C atoms remain. Theoretically, radiocarbon dating should extend far back in time, but current technology places a practical limit on it: *Radiocarbon dating is good only for organic remains that are no more than about 45,000 years old.*

Radiocarbon dating can be run on any organic material, although some materials are better sources of dates than others. Carbon, or charcoal, is perhaps the most common material dated in archaeology. After being collected in the field, the sample is sent to one of the world's 130 radiocarbon labs with appropriate contextual data. Archaeologists first examine the sample microscopically for intruding root hairs or other organic contaminants; they also try to identify the wood species.

The lab pretreats the carbon with one of several protocols, depending on its characteristics. The sample might, for instance, be physically crushed and dispersed in deionized water, then washed with hot hydrochloric acid to remove carbonates and then with an alkali wash (NaOH) to remove organic acids (these could make the date younger or older if not removed). Such pretreatment is important because even a small amount of contamination can greatly alter the measured date of a sample.

After pretreating, the lab counts the amount of ^{14}C in the sample by using a scintillation or ionization detector (devices akin to very sophisticated Geiger counters), which counts the number of beta emissions over a measured interval of time. The rate of emissions will be high if the sample is young and low if the sample is very old. By using an established equation, the lab converts the measured rate of beta emissions to an age.

What the Lab Can Tell You

Archaeologists who submit a sample will eventually receive a detailed report from the radiocarbon lab. Here's one date we received on a carbon sample from the Pine Spring site in southwestern Wyoming:

Beta–122584 6510 ± 70 BP

The alphanumeric string records the laboratory and sample number: Beta Analytic (the world's largest radiocarbon lab) and sample number 122584 (in our reports, we always publish this number with the date so that another archaeologist could consult data in the lab's sample logbook). The second part estimates the age of the sample in radiocarbon years BP (before present—*present* being defined as 1950). Therefore, the radiocarbon lab told us this about the Pine Spring sample: A plant died and burned about 6510 *radiocarbon years before* AD 1950.

Why "radiocarbon years"? Labs measure samples in radiocarbon years, not calendar years. As we will see, radiocarbon dating has certain biases, and the laboratory date must be corrected to reflect actual calendar years. We return to this later.

Why 1950? In radiocarbon dating, the present is defined as the year AD 1950—the year Libby invented the method. The reason for this is that "the present" keeps becoming the past, so we need a standard that keeps still. This means that a date of, say, 1000 BP obtained in the year 1960 is actually about 1060 years old in the year 2010 (add 60 years because 2010 is 60 years after the BP "baseline" year, AD 1950).

Can You Handle the Uncertainty?

So far, so good. But remember that the lab report attached ± 70 to the age estimate. The decay process of ^{14}C is a statistical process, and the number of beta emissions is not constant over short periods (but the rate does average out over the half-life). For this reason, the lab measures the amount of beta emissions over several lengths of time and then averages those emissions to get an age. In Beta-122584, the number 6510 estimates the actual age of the sample; it is the mean of a number of measurements made by the lab.

That counting process also produces a standard deviation, read as "plus or minus," which estimates the degree of consistency among the counting runs. The standard deviation expresses the range within which the true date falls. We know from statistical theory that there is a 68 percent chance that the true date falls within one standard deviation on either side of the mean date. By both adding and subtracting 70 years from the age estimate, we know that there is a 68 percent chance that the true age of the carbon falls between 6440 (6510 – 70) and 6580 (6510 + 70) radiocarbon years BP. If you want to be even more certain, statistical theory tells us that there is a 95 percent chance that the actual age falls within *two* standard deviations of the mean date, which in this case means between 6370 and 6650 radiocarbon years BP.

The standard deviation must never be omitted from the radiocarbon date, because without it one has no idea how precise a date is. When archaeologists get a date back from a lab, they first look at the mean date, but they evaluate that date's utility by looking at the standard deviation. If it is very large, the date may be worthless (although it depends on the specific research question).

Are All Organics Created Equal?

The simple answer is no.

Bone, for example—especially very old bone (> 5000 years)—can create problems. Bone is very complex chemically and contains nonorganic as well as organic components. In addition, it can be easily contaminated by younger carbon percolating in from the surrounding sediments. For these reasons, bones can give dates that are quite a bit older or younger than their actual ages. One way around this problem is to extract the amino acids chemically and date the carbon that is part of those organic molecules.

Plant remains are also tricky. All plants take in carbon through the process of photosynthesis, but different plant species do it through one of three **photosynthetic pathways**. The first such pathway converts atmospheric carbon dioxide into a compound with three carbon atoms. This so-called C_3 pathway is characteristic of many plants in temperate climates. A second pathway converts carbon dioxide from the air into a complex compound with four carbon atoms. This C_4 pathway is used by plants in arid and semiarid regions, including maize, sorghum, millet, yucca, and prickly pear. A third, the CAM ("crassulacean acid metabolism") pathway, is found in succulents, such as cacti.

These different photosynthetic pathways are important because C_4 plants end up taking in *more* ^{14}C relative to the other isotopes of carbon than do C_3 and CAM plants. Because Libby developed radiocarbon dating before this diversity in photosynthesis was known, his system uses the photosynthetic process of C_3 plants as the standard. This can create problems.

Imagine a maize plant growing next to an oak; the maize, being a C_4 plant, will take in more ^{14}C than the oak, a C_3 plant. If both die at the same time, and both are later dated, the maize sample will appear to be *younger* than the oak tree by 200 to 300 years, because the maize began the decay process with more radiocarbon than did the oak.

Fortunately, radiocarbon labs can correct this problem by measuring the ratio of ^{13}C to ^{12}C and using that value to normalize the resulting date on the sample. This is why archaeologists should always try to identify the kind of plant that they are dating.

The Reservoir Effect

A second problem concerns the **reservoir effect**. Libby's method was based on the abundance of ^{14}C in the atmosphere, but some organisms obtain their carbon from sources whose carbon content may be significantly different from that of the atmosphere. Snails that live in lakes in areas of limestone will incorporate "dead" carbon (meaning that the carbon source is so old that no discernible ^{14}C remains) by incorporating the limestone's carbonate into their shells. If dated, a snail that died yesterday in such a situation can appear to be hundreds, or even thousands, of years old.

Marine organisms present a similar challenge. Fish and shellfish take in carbon from the water, not the

half-life (of ^{14}C) The time required for half of the carbon-14 available in an organic sample to decay, or 5730 years.

photosynthetic pathways The specific chemical processes through which plants metabolize carbon. Because the three major pathways discriminate against carbon-13 in different ways, similarly aged plants that use different pathways can produce different radiocarbon ages.

reservoir effect When organisms take in carbon from a source that is depleted of or enriched in ^{14}C relative to the atmosphere; carbon dating of such samples may return ages that are considerably older or younger than they actually are.

atmosphere. The ocean is another reservoir of carbon containing more "old" carbon than the atmosphere at any given time. Given that the radiocarbon method is based on an atmospheric standard, marine organisms also tend to date somewhat older than they actually are—by about 400 years. This creates an ancillary problem in dating skeletal remains of humans or animals who relied heavily on seafood; their skeletons will reflect the composition of the foods they consumed and hence also appear to be older than they actually are. Again, labs can correct this problem if they have sufficient background information on the sample.

Tree Rings Refine Radiocarbon Dating

Libby assumed that the amount of ^{14}C in the atmosphere remains constant through time, but we now know that this is not correct.

The first investigator to find fault with the atmospheric assumption was Hessel de Vries of the Netherlands. In the 1950s, de Vries cut several beams from historic buildings and determined the age of the wood by counting the rings. When he dated the known-age specimens by radiocarbon assay, he found the ^{14}C dates to be 2 percent older than expected for the known-age wood. Scientists at the time generally dismissed the work, because the errors de Vries discovered were relatively small—just barely outside the limits of expected error.

But the specter of larger errors finally inspired several radiocarbon labs to look more closely into the problem. In one landmark study, Hans Suess (University of California, San Diego) analyzed wood from bristlecone pine trees. Native to the western United States, bristlecones are the world's oldest living organisms (some living specimens are 4600 years old). Working from live trees to ancient stumps, investigators had already extended the bristlecone tree-ring sequence back nearly 8200 years (by the tree-ring technique discussed previously). Suess radiocarbon-dated dozens of known-age samples and compared the results obtained by each method. When he did so, it became clear that significant fluctuations, now known as **de Vries effects**, occurred in the atmospheric ^{14}C concentrations. There have been at least 17 such fluctuations over the past 10,000 years, produced, we believe, by pulses in sunspot activity.

This tree-ring research led to the discovery that the production of ^{14}C has not remained constant over time as Libby had assumed. This is generally not a big problem for dates younger than about 3500 years, but it becomes progressively worse as we move farther back in time. In fact, a piece of carbon that gives a radiocarbon date of around 10,000 radiocarbon years is actually closer to 12,000 calendar years old.

So the bad news is that *radiocarbon years are not the same as calendar years.* The good news is that we can fix the problem.

Using tree-ring chronologies from several places in the world, researchers have extended the calibration curve to 11,800 calendar years. Other methods push the calibration curve back even farther, to 45,000 years, the limit of radiocarbon dating. We can now convert radiocarbon dates into calendar dates through easy-to-use online programs.

Accelerator Dating: Taking Radiocarbon to the Limit

Some scholars see archaeology as an odd science because it progresses through unique and unrepeatable experiments. Digging remains our primary "experimental" method, and all archaeologists know that, as they dig, they are destroying data that no one has even yet thought of collecting. Before 1950, for example, archaeologists rarely saved charcoal—how could they have anticipated radiocarbon dating? This is why, today, we slowly excavate only that portion of a site necessary to answer a question, and it's why we compulsively save at least a sample of everything we find. We know that future technologies will enable us to learn things that we cannot even imagine now. New methods of radiocarbon dating demonstrate this principle.

Recall that labs obtain conventional radiocarbon dates by counting beta emissions. To do this effectively, you need to submit a fairly large sample of carbon. Back in the 1970s, in fact, archaeologists sometimes said you needed a good "double handful" of carbon for a decent date. But often all we find are small, isolated bits of carbon; we cannot simply combine them because we'd then risk combining carbon of vastly different ages—which would produce a date that would be useless.

The development of **accelerator mass spectrometry (AMS)** for radiocarbon dating in the 1980s changed this by drastically reducing the quantity of datable material required. Accelerator technology does not count beta emissions as conventional technology does. Instead, it uses an electrostatic tandem accelerator and a technique known as mass spectrometry to count the *proportion* of carbon isotopes in a sample. Given that a single gram of modern organic material contains some 59 *billion* atoms of ^{14}C, a much smaller amount of material is required by AMS. *In fact*, it requires only a few milligrams of carbon—a sample about the size of a sesame seed.

This new radiocarbon method allows archaeologists to test old ideas by enabling us to date sites or objects that previously defied adequate dating. In some cases, AMS dating has corrected some significant errors (see "Looking Closer: Is the Shroud of Turin the Burial Cloth of Christ?").

But AMS dating is not a panacea. Archaeologists initially thought that AMS would push the radiocarbon barrier back to 100,000 or more years, but that hasn't happened—at least not yet. Although researchers keep trying, today AMS cannot reliably date anything that is older than about 45,000 years. To do this, we need other methods.

LOOKING CLOSER

Is the Shroud of Turin the Burial Cloth of Christ?

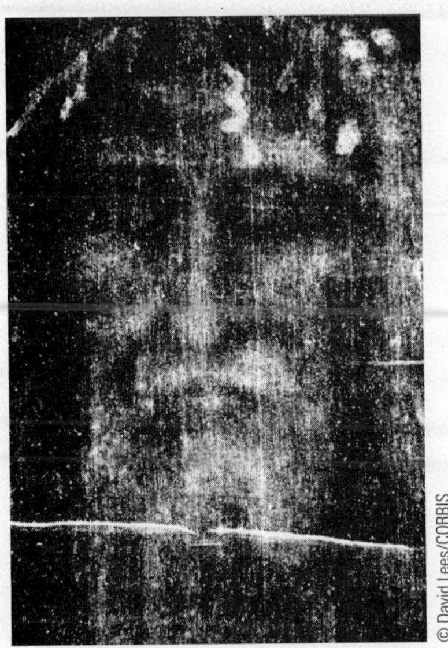

The face on the Shroud of Turin.

Accelerator dating has uses beyond its original one. Antiquarians and musicians, for instance, are turning to AMS technology to detect fakes, such as fraudulent Stradivarius violins.

AMS dating grabbed headlines when it was applied to the Shroud of Turin, thought by many to be the cloth in which Christ's crucified body was wrapped. Although the Roman Catholic Church never officially proclaimed the shroud to be Christ's burial cloth, 3 million of the faithful filed past the shroud when it was displayed in the Cathedral of St. John the Baptist in 1978. Many believed they had looked into the face of Christ. What did they see?

The shroud itself is a simple linen cloth, slightly more than 14 feet long and a yard wide. On it appears a pale sepia-tone image of the front and back of a naked man about 6 feet tall. Pale stains of presumed blood mark wounds to the head, side, hands, and feet. Believers take the shroud to be a true relic of Christ's Passion. But since the fourteenth century, critics have argued that the shroud is a cruel, if clever, hoax.

The mystery deepened when scientists from various research centers examined the shroud in detail, photographing it under ultraviolet and infrared light, bombarding it with x-rays, peering at it microscopically. But the scientists could not come up with a clear conclusion either way. If the shroud was a fraud, it was a very clever one.

For nearly 40 years, scientists had argued that radiocarbon dating might help settle the issue, because for the shroud to even possibly be Jesus's burial cloth, it had to be about 2000 years old. If it were a fourteenth-century hoax, then it would only be some 600 years old. Unfortunately, conventional radiocarbon methods would have destroyed a handkerchief-sized piece of the shroud, and church authorities rejected all such requests. But because AMS requires only a minuscule sample of linen, the Pontifical Academy of Sciences agreed in 1984 to such dating.

After years of squabbling about the ground rules, each of three laboratories (at the University of Arizona in Tucson, the British Museum in London, and the Swiss Federal Institute in Zurich) finally received a postage stamp–size piece of the shroud plus control specimens of various known ages. Only British Museum officials, who coordinated the research, knew which specimen was which. When the owner of the shroud, Pope John Paul II, was informed of the outcome, his response was simple: "Publish it."

And so they did. In October 1988, a gathering of ecclesiastical and technological specialists hosted a news conference at which Cardinal Anastasio Ballestrero, archbishop of Turin, solemnly announced that all three laboratories agreed that the flax plants from which the linen in the shroud was made had been grown in medieval times—between AD 1260 and 1390—long after the death of Jesus.

Although a certain degree of mystery still surrounds the shroud, particularly because nobody can explain how such an image was created using medieval technology, one thing is clear: Radiocarbon dating unambiguously resolved a controversy that spanned five centuries. The Shroud of Turin could not possibly be the authentic burial cloth of Jesus.

Trapped Charge Dating

Those other methods include three—thermoluminescence, optically stimulated luminescence, and electron spin resonance—that are jointly known as **trapped charge dating**. Although rarely applied 25 years ago, trapped charge dating methods are increasingly common in archaeology today. Their ultimate age ranges are unknown, but they extend back at least 300,000 years.

The geochemical basis for these methods is complex, so we'll simplify. The same principle underlies all three techniques: Over time, background gamma radiation in sediment causes some electrons of the atoms of certain minerals, notably quartz and feldspar, to move to a different

de Vries effects Fluctuations in the radiocarbon-dating calibration curve produced by variations in the atmosphere's carbon-14 content; these can cause radiocarbon dates to calibrate to more than one calendar age.

accelerator mass spectrometry (AMS) A method of radiocarbon dating that counts the proportion of carbon isotopes directly (rather than using the indirect Geiger counter method), thereby dramatically reducing the quantity of datable material required.

trapped charge dating Forms of dating that rely upon the fact that electrons become trapped in minerals' crystal lattices as a function of background radiation; the age of the specimen is the total radiation received divided by the annual dose of radiation.

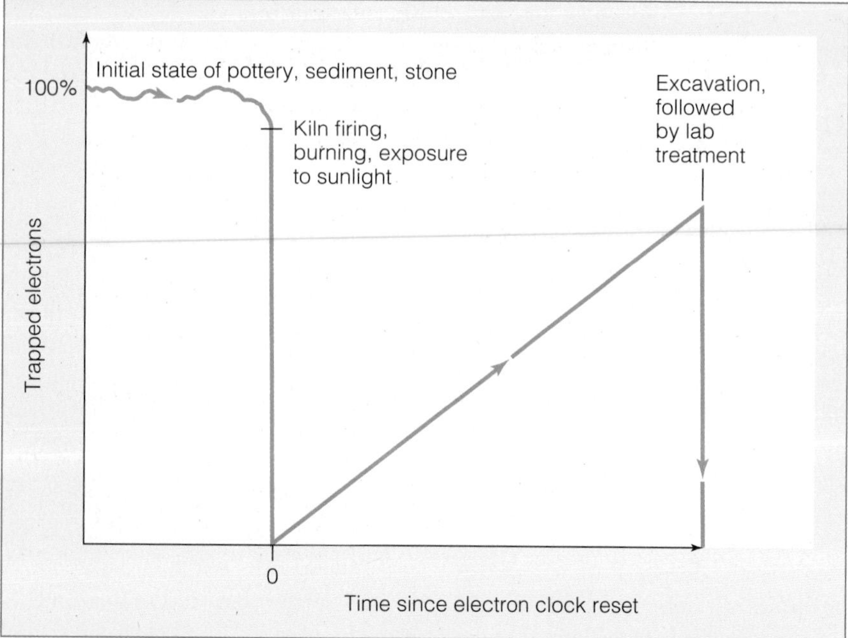

FIGURE 5-7 The process of setting an object's clock to zero in trapped charge dating. An object begins with some number of trapped electrons that is "reset" to zero when the object is heated or exposed to sunlight. The object then slowly gathers more trapped electrons through time due to background radiation. Its clock is again reset in the lab, where the number of trapped electrons is estimated to calculate the object's age.

energy state. When this happens, some electrons are "trapped" in atomic imperfections in the minerals' crystal lattices. As time passes, an increasing number of electrons are trapped in this way.

Assuming that the radiation dose is constant over time, electrons become trapped at a constant rate. If we could somehow measure the number of electrons trapped in the crystal lattice, we would have an estimate of the *total* radiation dose the specimen has received over time. If we then knew the *annual* background radiation dose, we could calculate a specimen's age simply by dividing the first measure by the second. How do we calculate these values?

We figure the annual dose by burying a radiation-measuring device, called a **dosimeter**, in an archaeological site and retrieving it a year later. The device records how much radiation it was exposed to in a year's time.

To determine a specimen's total radiation dose, we need to measure the number of trapped electrons in that specimen. Obviously, we can't just count them. But several methods accomplish this task, and the three techniques are partially distinguished by the methods used to determine the total radiation dose, as well as the kinds of material that they date. To understand *how* we can measure the total radiation dose, you must first understand *what* it is that trapped charge techniques measure.

Electrons that are moved *out* of their orbits (that is, are trapped) by background radiation are *returned* to their orbits by sufficient heat (500°C) or by exposure to even a few minutes of sunlight. Through the application of heat or light, the specimen has its clock reset to zero, so to speak, and the slow trapping process will begin again (see Figure 5-7). So, strictly speaking, *trapped charge dating identifies the last time a specimen had its electron traps emptied.* Knowing this tells us how to apply the different techniques.

Thermoluminescence (TL) measures the total radiation dose by heating a specimen rapidly to 500°C. Trapped electrons in quartz and feldspar crystals slip free and move back to their orbits. When they do, they release energy in the form of light. The lab measures the amount of light released as the specimen is heated; this gives us the needed measure of the total radiation dose. Like radiocarbon dating, trapped charge dating produces a mean date with a standard deviation.

Archaeologists have used TL to date ceramics. Imagine a ceramic pot, consisting of clay with some sand added to give the pot strength. The sand contains quartz and feldspar that have been slowly accumulating trapped electrons. When that pot is fired, however, those traps are emptied, and the pot's clock is reset. Eventually, the pot breaks and its sherds are discarded. Once those sherds become buried, the quartz and feldspars are exposed to gamma radiation and begin to collect trapped charges again. When the sample is reheated under laboratory conditions (a small portion of the specimen has to be destroyed for analysis), the intensity of the light emission measures the number of electrons that were trapped between the two episodes of heating—in the original fire and in the lab. The method is also used to date burned stone artifacts, because heat resets the TL clock of the minerals in the stone. (Museums often use the method to detect ceramic forgeries, because TL can quickly distinguish between an ancient clay figurine and a twentieth-century fake.)

The artifact's context is therefore especially important, because what interests archaeologists is the age of the artifact, which may or may not coincide with the events that trapped charge methods date. For instance, if a stone tool was accidentally burned 1000 years after its manufacture, TL will date the age of the burning, not the age of the artifact's manufacture—and it's usually the latter that interests archaeologists. Nonetheless, if careful attention is paid to context, trapped charge dating has the potential to rewrite prehistory, because it can date objects that radiocarbon cannot and because it can date objects that are beyond the range of radiocarbon.

For example, archaeologists Ofer Bar-Yosef (Harvard University) and Bernard Vandermeersch (University of Bordeaux) employed this technique to challenge our understanding of human evolution. The transition between

Neanderthals and modern *Homo sapiens* was for many years based on the chronology of western Europe. There, *Homo sapiens* replaced Neanderthals about 40,000 years ago. But for various reasons, Bar-Yosef suspected that "archaic *Homo sapiens*" (called such because their skulls appear to be transitional between earlier hominins and biologically modern humans) appeared earlier in the Near East. Excavating the site of Qafzeh in Israel, Bar-Yosef and Vandermeersch found strata containing skeletal remains of archaic *Homo sapiens* along with stone tools, some of which had burned in hearths. These strata were beyond the range of radiocarbon dating and hence must be at least 45,000 years old—older than the western European counterparts.

But how much older? TL dating provided the answer. Dating a series of the burnt stone tools, Bar-Yosef found that the artifacts had burned some 92,000 ± 5000 years ago, much earlier than the European chronology. Although the date's standard deviation might seem large, note that it is only about 5 percent of the mean date. And even allowing for the large standard error, the TL date on the tools suggests that modern humans may have first appeared in the Near East rather than in Europe.

Optically stimulated luminescence (OSL) has many uses in archaeology because it can date the most common material in archaeological sites—dirt.

OSL dating relies on the fact that some of the trapped electrons are sensitive to sunlight as well as to heat. Sand grains of quartz and feldspar have their clocks reset (referred to as *bleaching*) in a matter of minutes as they blow through the air and are exposed to sunlight; once buried, they begin accumulating trapped electrons again. *OSL therefore dates the time when the sands were buried.* Although OSL can be used on a variety of sediments, wind-blown sands are best because they are more likely to have been sufficiently bleached by sunlight than, say, sands deposited by a river.

Instead of measuring luminescence through the application of heat, OSL measures it by passing light of a particular wavelength over the specimen. This causes light-sensitive electrons to emit their own light as they return to orbit; the intensity of that light is a measure of the total radiation dose. Incidentally, when we take sediment samples for OSL dating, we must be sure not to expose them to sunlight.

Electron spin resonance (ESR) is primarily used to date tooth enamel. Ninety-six percent of tooth enamel consists of the mineral hydroxyapatite, which contains no trapped charges when formed. Once the tooth is deposited in the ground, however, it accumulates charges from the background radiation. To measure those trapped charges, a portion of the specimen is exposed to electromagnetic radiation, which resets the electrons. In this case, the total radiation dose is proportional to the amount of microwave energy absorbed by the specimen.

ESR dating, too, has challenged our understanding of human evolution. As we noted previously, the European chronology showed that modern humans rapidly replaced Neanderthals about 40,000 years ago. But when ESR was applied to tooth enamel of animals found in strata containing evidence of *Homo sapiens* and Neanderthals at Qafzeh in Israel, as well as at three nearby cave sites (Tabun, Skhul, and Kebara), the dates suggested that *Homo sapiens* existed as early as 120,000 years ago, and Neanderthals as late as 60,000 years ago. This means that for a long period of time, perhaps as much as 60,000 years, modern humans and Neanderthals existed side by side—a different scenario than in western Europe, where they overlapped for much less time.

Trapped charge dating techniques can date objects that are beyond the range of radiocarbon dating. But we must remember that what we are dating is *the last time that the clock was reset*—by light in the case of OSL and by heat in the case of TL (neither seem to affect ESR measurements). Like radiocarbon dating, these techniques date accurately to a range of years, not a single year.

Argon-Argon

Archaeologists have a variety of other radiometric dating techniques that, like radiocarbon dating, are based on the fact that radioactive isotopes decay at known rates. These techniques are useful for dating the age of the formation of a particular layer of volcanic rock. Because the radioactive isotopes used have extremely long half-lives, they are useful for dating materials that are hundreds of thousands or millions of years old. These dating methods are important for archaeologists who work in Africa and Asia where early human remains are found.

Many rocks, including volcanic minerals, contain traces of potassium, which, like carbon, occurs naturally

dosimeter A device to measure the amount of gamma radiation emitted by sediments. It is normally buried in a stratum for a year to record the annual dose of radiation. Dosimeters are often a short length of pure copper tubing filled with calcium sulfate.

thermoluminescence (TL) A trapped charge dating technique used on ceramics and burnt stone artifacts—anything mineral that has been heated to more than 500°C.

Neanderthals (or Neandertals) An early form of humans who lived in Europe and the Near East about 300,000 to 30,000 years ago. Biological anthropologists debate whether Neanderthals were in the direct evolutionary line leading to *Homo sapiens*.

optically stimulated luminescence (OSL) A trapped charge dating technique used to date sediments; it measures the time elapsed between the last time a few moments' exposure to sunlight reset the clock to zero and the present.

electron spin resonance (ESR) A trapped charge technique used to date tooth enamel and burnt stone tools; it can date teeth that are beyond the range of radiocarbon dating.

in several isotopic forms. One of these, potassium-40 or ^{40}K, decays slowly, with a half-life of 1.31 *billion* years, into argon-40 (^{40}Ar), an inert, stable gas. By comparing the relative proportions of these potassium and argon isotopes in a sample, we can determine its age. As with radiocarbon dating, the principle is simple: The more ^{40}Ar in a sample relative to ^{40}K, the older the sample is.

For potassium-argon to work, there must have been no argon trapped at the time of rock formation. As with all trapped charge dating methods, a rock's argon-accumulating clock must have been reset to zero, so that all argon is the result of potassium decay. Fortunately, during a volcanic eruption, high temperatures drive all gases—including ^{40}Ar—out of the microscopic rock crystals. Such episodes set the potassium-argon clock to zero, meaning that all ^{40}Ar present in the ash today has accumulated since the ash was ejected from the volcano. In addition, all argon must be retained in the rock structure without loss to the atmosphere. Some rocks "leak" argon, so care must be exercised in deciding which rock types to subject to potassium-argon dating.

This is why volcanic ash deposits are so useful. If an archaeologist finds human fossils or stone tools just *below* a layer of volcanic ash, the law of superposition tells us that the potassium-argon method will provide a *minimum* age estimate for the tools and fossils contained in the archaeological stratum below. Find fossils between two layers of volcanic ash deposits, and you bracket the age of the archaeological material (although you cannot date the archaeological material itself).

The maximum age range of potassium-argon dating is theoretically the age of the earth. Although this method is not as precise as radiocarbon dating, its results are close enough, and it provides dates for some critically important early sites in Africa and elsewhere.

For example, potassium-argon dating was used to estimate the age of **Homo erectus**, an early hominin, in Asia (see Figure 5-8). For decades, investigators believed that *Homo erectus* evolved exclusively in Africa, the earliest fossils being slightly less than 2 million years old. Then, sometime after 1.5 million years ago, *Homo erectus* expanded out of Africa, colonizing other parts of the Old World.

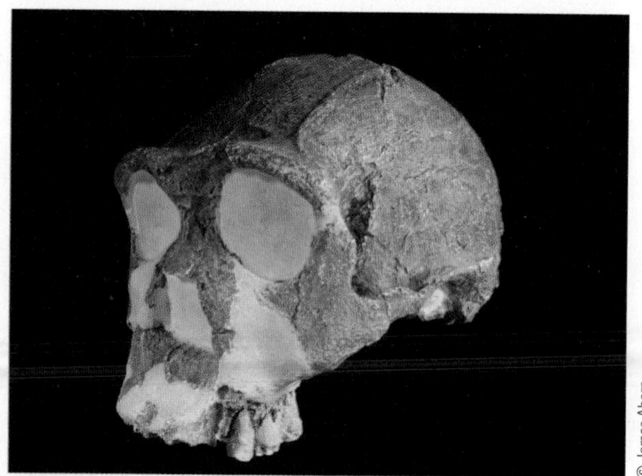

FIGURE 5-8 A 1.8-million-year-old Homo erectus skull (KNM-ER 3733, from Koobi Fora, Kenya).

© James Ahern

Human paleontologists were shocked in 1971, when Garniss Curtis (University of California, Berkeley) used potassium-argon dating to date the sediments associated with an infant *Homo erectus* skull from Mojokerto, Java. Because Java is a long way from Africa, most investigators thought that the Mojokerto skull should be much younger than a million years. But Curtis estimated that it was nearly twice that age: 1.9 million years old. Most paleontologists rejected this extraordinarily ancient age because they were convinced that the only hominins in the world at that time lived in Africa.

Both this early date and the technique itself came under criticism. Although potassium-argon dating had been around for decades, the laboratory methods were cumbersome, and the process required a large sample that increased the chance for contamination.

So Curtis teamed up with Carl Swisher (Rutgers University) to develop a new dating method. The **argon-argon dating** method simplifies the lab process and avoids the contamination problem by using small samples. The method works by irradiating the volcanic crystals. When a neutron penetrates the potassium nucleus, it displaces a proton, converting the potassium into ^{39}Ar, an "artificial" isotope not found in nature. The minute quantities of artificially created argon and naturally occurring ^{40}Ar are then measured to estimate the ratio of potassium to ^{40}Ar. This high-precision method, which has replaced potassium-argon dating, allows investigators to focus on single volcanic crystals, which can be dated one by one; thus, any contaminants can be discarded.

In 1992, Curtis and Swisher used the argon-argon method to date some white volcanic pumice obtained from the matrix inside the braincase of the Mojokerto fossil. The result was virtually the same as the "old-fashioned" potassium-argon date: 1.8 million ± 40,000 years. These dates remain controversial, but it is clear that dating techniques such as the argon-argon method will be increasingly important in evaluating fossil evidence in the years to come.

What Do Dates Mean?

These are just some of the ways that archaeologists can date sites—there are many others. It is important to keep in mind what materials the different techniques date, how far back in time they can extend, and what events the techniques actually date (summarized in Rapid Review), because these factors are necessary to answering the most important question of all: What do the dates mean?

© Charles & Josette Lenars/CORBIS

FIGURE 5-9 The pyramids at Giza.

We can never date archaeological sites by simple equivalences. The radiocarbon lab, for instance, takes a chunk of charcoal and tells you how long ago that tree died. By itself, this date says nothing important about your site. However, if we can show that the charcoal came from a tree used as a roof beam in a pueblo, then we have a date that matters.

In every case, you have to show that the dated event is contemporaneous with a behavioral event of interest—such as building a house, cooking a meal, killing a deer, or making a pot. We can drive this point home by examining a common issue of radiocarbon dating: the **old wood problem**.

How Old Are the Pyramids?

When most people hear the word "archaeology," they think about Egypt's pyramids (see Figure 5-9)—and with good reason. They are impressive structures, especially the three that stand watch over modern Cairo on the Giza Plateau. One of these, the pyramid of Khnumkhuf ("the god Khnum is his protection"; often abbreviated to Khufu or, in Greek, Cheops) is the largest in Egypt. Khufu began building his tomb soon after his reign began in 2551 BC. Made of some 2,300,000 blocks of stone, each weighing an average of 2.5 tons, the pyramid measures 230 meters (756 feet) on a side and is oriented only 3 minutes 6 seconds off true north. It contains several interior passageways and three chambers—one at the end of a tunnel cut into the bedrock deep below the structure. The burial chamber, in the center of the pyramid, has several roofs above it; the Egyptians specifically engineered this roof to distribute the weight of the overlying rock outward and prevent the chamber from being crushed. The pyramid's exterior was originally covered in polished white limestone—making it a landmark that would have shone above the horizon for miles around (the limestone was scavenged by later rulers). At 146 meters (481 feet),

Homo erectus A hominin who lived in Africa, Asia, and Europe between 2 million and 500,000 years ago. These hominin walked upright, made simple stone tools, and may have used fire.

argon-argon dating A high-precision method for estimating the relative quantities of argon-39 and argon-40 gas; used to date volcanic ashes that are between 500,000 and several million years old.

old wood problem A potential problem with radiocarbon (or tree-ring) dating in which old wood has been scavenged and reused in a later archaeological site; the resulting date is not a true age of the associated human activity.

Khufu's pyramid remained the world's tallest building for 4440 years—until the Eiffel Tower was built in 1889! It is a remarkable piece of architectural engineering.

But how old is it really? The ages of the pyramids are based on historical documents—the hieroglyphs that cover the insides of tombs and temples (and that are found on papyrus used to stuff the bulls, crocodiles, ibexes, and other animals that were mummified and buried in the pyramids and other structures). The hieroglyphs give us the dates of the reigns of kings and document their accomplishments. The Egyptian civilization is probably one of the best dated in the world, and the pyramids on the Giza Plateau outside Cairo are among the oldest in Egypt.

But some people speculate that the pyramids are actually thousands of years older, built by a civilization some 10,000 years ago. To check the ages based on historical documents, a consortium of archaeologists, led by Shawki Nakhla and Zahi Hawass (of the Egyptian Supreme Council of Antiquities) in 1984, decided to date the pyramids through radiocarbon dating. But what could they date? The pyramids are made of stone, and the organic remains buried in them were often treated with tar and chemicals that make them unreliable for radiocarbon dates.

But Nakhla and Hawass knew of another source of carbon. Contrary to popular belief, the pyramids were put together with mortar. Workmen made this mortar by burning gypsum, apparently on the work platforms that were erected around the pyramid as it was being constructed. They mixed the resulting ash with water and sand and then slopped the mortar into the cracks between the massive blocks of stone. Inadvertently, pieces of carbon from the fires were caught in the mortar, trapped there for eternity.

In 1984 and 1985, the Egyptian archaeological teams scrambled over the pyramids like ants on an anthill, looking for fingernail-sized bits of carbon. They found quite a few pieces, dated them using the AMS method, and then calibrated the dates. They found not a shred of evidence that the pyramids were 10,000 years old. But what they found still surprised them. The radiocarbon dates on Old Kingdom (4575 to 4134 BP) pyramids were from 100 to 400 years *older* than the documentary dates suggested. Yet dates on later Middle Kingdom pyramids (4040 to 3640 BP) were not far off from their accepted ages. Why were the Old Kingdom dates "too old"?

The first explanation was the old wood problem: In desert (or high-altitude or arctic) environments, wood can lie around without decaying for a long time. In California's White Mountains, you can make a fire today from bristlecone wood, send a piece of the charcoal to a lab, and be told that your fire was 2000 years old. The wood is 2000 years old—but the fire that made the charcoal is not.

Egyptian archaeologists thought this old wood problem was unlikely. By Old Kingdom times, the Nile River valley had been occupied for millennia, and by a large population. Excavations near the pyramids reveal a community of stoneworkers, builders of the pyramids, that housed 20,000 people. All the Nile's people cooked over wood and used wood in house construction. And there is not much wood to begin with along the Nile; the floodplain is rich, but it's a narrow strip of green in a vast, treeless desert. For these reasons, the archaeologists postulated that there could not have been any old wood lying along the Nile.

But perhaps Egyptians found another source of old wood. The Old Kingdom's construction projects at Giza were massive: three huge and several small pyramids, associated temples, boat docks on the Nile, the Sphinx, and the workers' quarters. These projects required massive amounts of wood—for construction; for ovens to bake bread for the workers; for levers, wedges, and sledges to move the stone blocks; for scaffolding; and for firewood to produce the mortar.

To get all the wood needed, it is likely that Khufu and other pharaohs scavenged older settlements or looted their predecessor's temples and tombs for wood—which Egypt's dry climate would preserve for hundreds, even thousands, of years. We know that pharaohs raided earlier temples and tombs for construction material and jewelry. Perhaps for these Old Kingdom projects, they also sought out firewood. This may account for the early dates on Old Kingdom pyramids.

But then, why were the Middle Kingdom radiocarbon dates not "too old"? By Middle Kingdom times, Nakhla and Hawass reasoned, earlier construction projects had depleted the sources of old wood, and Middle Kingdom builders had to make do with the wood at hand—which would not have been very old.

The more general point here is important: Every absolute dating technique dates a particular event, but archaeologists must decide how a date relates to the age of human behavior.

The Check, Please

How archaeologists excavate a site depends on several factors, one of these being cost. None of these dating methods is cheap. Right now, a standard radiocarbon date runs about \$300; an AMS date costs about \$600. Tree-ring dates are cheaper—the University of Arizona's Tree-Ring Lab charges about \$25 per sample. TL and OSL dates may cost \$800 apiece. There are no commercial rates for the other trapped charge and radiometric dating methods, but they have hidden costs. Because so much background information is required for their successful implementation, it is often necessary to finance a visit to the site by the specialist and cover additional sediment and dosimetry studies.

Archaeologists try to get as many dates as they can for a site, but they always have to do so within budget limitations.

RAPID REVIEW

Summary of Absolute Dating Methods

Technique	Target Material	Range of Accuracy	Comments
Dendrochronology	Wood, as carbon, roof beams, firewood	Depends on length of sequence; back to about 2000 years in the American Southwest	Only useful on particular species of trees. Sequence cannot be extended beyond the region it was developed in.
Carbon-14	Any organic material; carbon the most common	To 45,000 BP	Requires calibration; calibration curve only reliable to about 11,000 years. Accelerator mass spectrometry permits dating of minute samples.
Thermoluminescence	Ceramics, burnt stone	Unknown, but perhaps back to 300,000 years	Dates the last time an object was heated to 500° C.
Optically stimulated luminescence	Quartz, feldspars in wind-blown sands	Unknown, but perhaps back to 300,000 years	Dates the last time sand was exposed to sunlight sufficient to empty the electron traps. Samples must avoid sunlight; lab must date individual grains.
Electronic spin resonance	Tooth enamel, burned stone tools, corals, shells	10,000 to 300,000 or more years	Dates when a tooth was buried. Electron traps reset by exposure to electromagnetic radiation in the lab.
Argon-argon	Volcanic ash	Several million years	Dates the eruption that produced the ash. Needs small sample.

Conclusion

In Chapter 1, we pointed out that archaeology underwent a revolution of sorts in the 1960s, notably through the efforts of Lewis Binford. Binford, however, claimed the widespread availability of absolute dating methods in the 1960s, notably radiocarbon dating, brought the change in how we do archaeology.

As you have seen, relative dating techniques helped to lift the fog of time that obscures the past. They were a significant advance because they made it possible to place objects and cultures into a historical sequence. Absolute dating techniques were an even more significant advance, because they could assign artifacts to a particular year or a specific range of years. Absolute dating techniques allow us to see not only the order of events, but the rate of change as well. Why did this permit Binford's generation to change archaeology?

One reason is that absolute dating techniques freed archaeologists to do other things with their data. Instead of spending time on seriation diagrams, an archaeologist could simply send a piece of carbon to a lab for a radiocarbon date.

A more significant reason is that absolute dating techniques allowed archaeologists to control a major dimension of their data—age—in a more rigorous and absolute manner. Seriation was grounded in an often unspoken theory of culture change—material items appear, grow in popularity, and then disappear. No one knew, or cared, why this happened; all that mattered was that the technique provided a way to build a chronology. But for archaeologists to transcend chronology, they needed to know more. They needed to know how rapidly an item became prevalent, or how rapidly another replaced it. They needed to know how long a piece of material culture was used—50 years, 500 years, 5000 years? They needed to know whether an item first appeared in a particular region and then spread to others, or whether it had multiple centers of origin. Relative dating methods could not answer these questions very precisely, but absolute dating could. This is why absolute dating techniques had a large effect on archaeological paradigms.

In recent years, technology has afforded us increasingly sophisticated ways to date artifacts, sites, and strata, and this progression shows no sign of stopping. We can expect, then, that continual advances in dating methods will not only permit a greater understanding of the chronology of the past, but will also help create new paradigms, new ways of understanding the past.

Summary

- What is the difference between relative and absolute dating?
  - Relative dating places sites, strata, features, and artifacts in relative order, without saying how much older or younger one site, stratum, feature, or artifact is than another.
  - Absolute dating provides specific ages or specific age ranges. Absolute dating methods are absolute in the sense that they provide a particular age range at a known level of probability.
- What are the major dating techniques, what materials do they date, and what is their time range?
  - Tree-ring dating (dendrochronology) dates wood of particular species; it is limited to relatively small regions and usually cannot date samples that are more than 2000 years old.
  - Radiocarbon dating dates any organic material using the known rate of decay of ^{14}C; it is useful for materials less than 45,000 years old.
  - Trapped charge dating techniques—thermoluminescence (TL), optically stimulated luminescence (OSL), and electron spin resonance (ESR)—date ceramics or burned stone tools, eolian sediments, and tooth enamel, respectively. They date an object by calculating the amount of background radiation the object has been subjected to since the object's electron "clock" was last reset by heat (TL) or sunlight (OSL). These techniques can extend back several hundred thousand years.
  - Argon-argon dating helps determine dates on volcanic rock, especially ash. This technique can date volcanic layers that are millions of years old.
- What do archaeological dates date?
  - Dating techniques tell us nothing *directly* about cultural activities. Radiocarbon dating, for example, tells us when a plant or an animal died—it is up to archaeologists to relate the event being dated to a behavioral (cultural) event of interest.

Media Resources

Doing Fieldwork: Archaeological Demonstrations CD-ROM 2.0

This CD, developed by the authors, shows professional archaeologists involved in various digs, many of which are referenced in the text. The presentation is organized by the main techniques used on an archaeological dig, reinforcing concepts and techniques via live examples. The CD takes you through each step automatically, or you can navigate to any point via the navigation bar. After reviewing a step in the dig process, you are taken to Check Points, which are concept questions about each step of the dig. Then you can see the answers, receive your score, and even send your scores to your instructor.

See the "Dating" section of the CD-ROM to learn more about topics covered in this chapter.

CourseMate

Access chapter-specific learning tools including learning objectives, practice quizzes, videos, flash cards, and glossaries, as well as web links, and more in your Archaeology CourseMate. Login to www.cengagebrain.com to access the resources your instructor has assigned and to purchase materials.

The Dimensions of Archaeology: Time, Space, and Form

6

left, © Werner Forman/CORBIS; right, © Bowers Museum of Cultural Art/CORBIS; (four projectile points), center: © Art Resource, NY; © (projectile point) center bottom: National Park Service, Chaco Culture National Historic Park

A collection of artifacts that can provide key time markers in archaeology.

Learning Objectives

After reading this chapter, you should be able to answer these questions:

- What are the principles of archaeological typology?
- What is the strength of archaeology?
- What role does typology play in archaeology's strength?
- What are archaeological cultures, site components, and phases?

Preview

IN THE NINETEENTH CENTURY, archaeological sites were viewed as little more than mines in which to prospect for artifacts. But professionally trained archaeologists, such as Kidder and Wormington, shifted their objectives to focus more on understanding the person behind the artifact rather than the artifact itself. And in the 1960s, archaeology further refined that focus, wishing not only to reconstruct what happened in the past, but also to explain that past.

To achieve these objectives, archaeology analyzes how artifacts and features fall into changing patterns over space and time; this chapter shows how archaeologists identify those patterns. We first consider classification—the ways that archaeologists divide the many kinds of objects found into reasonable and useful artifact types. We then discuss the concepts of archaeological cultures, periods, phases, assemblages, and components—all of which are used to organize archaeological data into what is called *space-time systematics*.

Introduction

The title of this chapter comes from an article by archaeologist Albert Spaulding (1914–1990), who pointed out that archaeology is all about patterns in artifact and feature *form* through *time* and across *space*. We divide the spatial and temporal continuum of reality into parcels of space and time based on differences in material culture. For example, the kinds of houses found in much of the American Southwest at 2200 BP were semi-subterranean pithouses, usually round, covered with heavy log roofs and a layer of sod. They were warm in the winter and cool in the summer. At the same time, but in a different place—farther north in the Great Basin—houses were more ephemeral, consisting of simple windbreaks or shade structures for summer houses and conical log structures for the winter. Returning to the Southwest, we see a dramatic change in house form around 1300 BP. At that time, many people lived in square, aboveground masonry homes—the familiar pueblos—rather than pithouses. Back in the Great Basin, however, people continued to live in the same sort of houses they had occupied in 2200 BP. Archaeologists have spent the greater part of the last century documenting such patterns in how material culture changes through time and across space; these patterns are what archaeologists seek to explain. How we go about organizing data into meaningful spatial and temporal patterns is the subject of this chapter.

This organization is vital to the field, because *archaeology's major strength is its access to tremendous quantities of time and space*. Although many ethnologists study cultural evolution and culture change, they are restricted to short-term study if they deal exclusively with ethnographic evidence. And even if they include oral history or historical documents, ethnologists cannot go back in time more than a century or two. Archaeology, on the other hand, can address the entire history of humanity based on the things that people left behind, from 2.5-million-year-old stone tools in Africa to World War II submarines on the bottom of Pacific lagoons. No other social science has so much time at its disposal.

Archaeologists also deal with worlds of "space." Many ethnologists study entire societies for years on end, but none can realistically employ the tools of ethnography to study an entire region such as the American Southwest, to say nothing of continents or hemispheres. So, what archaeology loses in detail it makes up for by recording what the ethnologist cannot: patterns of human behavior as they were manifested over vast reaches of space, far beyond the confines of a single community.

The goal of archaeology is to reconstruct and explain the past: What did people do, and why did they do it? But to reach this goal, we must first gain a firm grasp on artifact patterning in time and space. You must know the when and the where in broader terms before contemplating the how, the who, the what, and especially the why. Defining a spatial and temporal framework requires that archaeologists date the physical remains, classify archaeological objects into useful categories, and explore their distribution across time and space. In previous chapters, we've discussed the fieldwork of archaeology. In this and succeeding chapters, we move into the other half of archaeology: the part that goes on after the excavation.

After the Excavation: Conservation and Cataloging

Suppose that you've just completed a regional survey and have excavated a sample of the sites discovered. You did the survey and excavations by the book, dated the sites, studied the sites' formation processes, and so on. You've

LOOKING CLOSER

Preserving the *Hunley*

© The Granger Collection, New York

The Hunley submarine in drydock in Charleston, South Carolina, 1863. Oil painting by Conrad Wise Chapman (1842–1910).

In 1864, the Confederacy was losing the Civil War and in need of desperate measures to destroy the Union Navy, whose blockades were strangling the South. The Confederacy thought it had found the answer in a secret weapon: a small submarine designed to destroy Union vessels from beneath the waves.

The South had planned submarine warfare from the war's beginning. Funded by Horace Hunley, whose name would grace the third model, the subs were bold designs, but early versions had leakage and control problems (the *Pioneer* was destroyed to prevent its capture by the Union, and the *American Diver* sank off Alabama's coast on a test run). Even the *Hunley*'s first voyages were catastrophes. It capsized on its first and second runs, losing half the first crew and the entire second crew, including Hunley himself. Nonetheless, the submarine was recovered, and a third crew stepped forward.

Crammed into a space 18 feet long and 4 feet wide, seven men propelled the *Hunley* by manually turning a crankshaft while the captain guided the sub and worked the ballast tanks that controlled depth. Two 15-inch manholes, fore and aft, were the only escape routes; a single candle lit the captain's depth gauge.

The tactic was to approach a Union ship, dive, and then ram a long, barbed spar equipped with a 90-pound explosive charge into the enemy's hull. As the sub backed away, a rope played out. At 150 feet, the rope tightened and detonated the charge.

This design worked perfectly on February 17, 1864, when the *Hunley* met the USS *Housatonic*. The Union's largest ship sank within minutes.

The *Hunley* surfaced, signaled shore, and started home. But she never made it. For reasons still unknown, she sank, killing all eight men aboard. A submarine did not sink a ship again until World War I.

The *Hunley*'s location remained a mystery until persistent efforts by author Clive Cussler and archaeologists Ralph Wilbanks, Wes Hall, and Harry Pecorelli located her in 1995 (using a magnetometer towed behind a research vessel) only 30 feet below the surface. The submarine's hatches were unopened (only one viewport was broken) and the hull unbreached. Buried beneath 3 feet of silt, the sub was protected from the saltwater currents that normally destroy iron ships.

Once removed from the water, however, the ship would have quickly corroded. Chlorides from the seawater had infiltrated the iron hull; if they dried, they would form crystals that would expand and destroy the metal. To prevent this, the hull was sprayed with water from the moment it was raised until it was placed into a specially designed water-filled tank. A lab now keeps the tank's fresh water at 10°C to prevent the growth of fungus and algae and to reduce the rate of corrosion. The lab also monitors the tank for pH, temperature, chlorides, conductivity, and oxygen.

After the vessel was stabilized, its interior, which had filled with silt, was excavated, and the human remains and personal effects removed (the human remains were buried in April 2004 in Charleston, South Carolina). The next question was how to preserve the *Hunley*.

Through microbial and electrochemical reactions, the vessel had developed a carbonate coating that prevented oxygen from reaching the sub's metallic surface. Without this carbonate coating, the sub would see more corrosion in six months than in the previous 136 years. Keeping this carbonate layer intact is thus critical to preservation of the vessel. But how do we preserve the *Hunley* indefinitely?

Metal artifacts are normally preserved through electrolysis—that is, by running an electric current through the water, which then removes oxygen. But this technique may not work on a long-term basis, and it may be ineffective for large objects, especially ones in which many surfaces are welded, bolted, or riveted together and made of different metals. One solution would be to dismantle the entire sub; but this option, understandably, does not excite the *Hunley*'s conservators.

An alternative is to anneal the sub through hydrogen reduction. This means baking the sub in a hydrogen furnace over a week or more, slowly raising the temperature to 1060°C. This, too, has its problems, the first being locating a furnace that is large enough and that can withstand the hydrochloric acid that is a by-product of this process. Clearly, the preservation of this important piece of American history will puzzle conservators for years to come.

returned home with many, many carefully labeled bags full of bones, stone tools, ceramics, beads, and figurines. What happens to all the stuff now that the fieldwork is over?

The first step is to conserve the recovered materials. Once this meant little more than washing off the artifacts with water (except for things that water would obviously damage, such as basketry). But today, many archaeologists hesitate to wash some artifacts because even this simple operation might destroy some information. Stone and ceramic artifacts, for example, can contain pollen or residues of blood, plants, or other materials that can be identified and used to reconstruct tool use and diet—but not if a scrupulous lab worker has thoroughly scrubbed the piece. In general, though, a simple cleaning is in order.

Other artifacts may require more attention, especially organic or metal artifacts recovered from wet deposits (see "Looking Closer: Preserving the *Hunley*"). Conservation on wooden artifacts recovered from the Ozette site (see Chapter 4) began as soon as excavators removed them from the muddy matrix, because wet wooden artifacts quickly crumble as they dry out. Richard Daugherty preserved Ozette's wooden artifacts by soaking them in vats of Carbowax—polyethylene glycol—melted and diluted with water. He needed huge vats to soak the houses' cedar timbers. Some of the artifacts, especially those made of hardwoods (which have small pores and soak up liquid slowly), had to soak for years.

During an excavation near New York's Wall Street, archaeologists found several Revolutionary War–era cannons lying on the bottom of what was once the East River. The first task in preserving these artifacts was to replace the brackish water that had impregnated the metal with fresh water. Looking for watertight containers large enough to hold the bulky cannons, project directors Roselle Henn (U.S. Army Corps of Engineers) and Diana diZerega Wall (City College of New York) finally settled on metal coffins! The conservation of artifacts has become a significant specialty within archaeology.

It may also be necessary to reconstruct broken pieces. This is frequently required with pottery because ceramics are often found in pieces, and reconstruction obviously tells us more about vessel shape, size, and decoration. Piecing together a broken pot is like trying to put together a three-dimensional jigsaw puzzle with no picture on the box and some of the pieces missing. It requires a particular personality—somebody who can stay put for long hours—and a sculptor's eye. Some people can do this with ease; others are lucky if they get two pieces to fit.

The cataloging procedure, which starts at the excavation, continues in the lab after the field season is over. Every single item must be accounted for, and its provenience retained through a catalog. The novice's first job in a lab is almost always cataloging: writing all those minute numbers on artifacts or labels and entering the information into a database. This can take a great deal of time. In fact, as a rule of thumb, for every week spent excavating, archaeologists spend 3 to 5 weeks or more cleaning, conserving, and cataloging the finds. Sometimes it seems mindless, but cataloging is essential because provenience is lost without the catalog, and without provenience an artifact's value to future researchers is greatly reduced.

Archaeological Classification

Cataloging and conservation are just the beginning, because at the end of those tasks you are faced with thousands of artifacts that differ in terms of function, style, raw material, provenience, and condition. This is where the really time-consuming part of archaeology begins. Archaeologists spend far more time analyzing their finds than they do excavating them.

Archaeologists begin to get a handle on variability in artifacts through **typology**, the classification of artifacts into types. Even before cataloging and conservation begin, archaeologists will have begun to classify the objects. When things turn up in the sifter, a screener will sort the finds into simple categories of stone, bone, shell, ceramic, organic, brick, cloth, wood, metal, or some other category depending on the nature of the site. Sometimes, objects cannot be identified and sorted in the field; the on-site rule is always "When in doubt, send it to the lab."

In the lab, the cataloged artifacts are further separated into even finer categories. The stone tool analyst might sort the stone artifacts into waste flakes and retouched pieces (flakes that have been chipped into tools) and then sort each of those into even narrower categories. Ceramics may be sorted into decorated and undecorated sherds, or into rim sherds (those that preserve a bit of the vessel's rim or mouth) and body sherds. And so forth.

But then what? How should you deal with all this stuff?

Here's a clue: *The archaeologist's first responsibility is to simplify*. Generations of archaeologists have found it unrealistic, even preposterous, to cope simultaneously with all the variability that turns up in even the simplest batch of archaeological objects. You could write a detailed paragraph on each artifact that you found. Although that might produce a wonderful descriptive catalog, it would teach us little, because meaning lies not in endless data, but in *patterns within those data*. And patterns appear only when you isolate some aspect of the variation and ignore the rest (for the time being).

So you simplify to reveal meaningful patterns. Because archaeology's twin strengths are time and space, we first develop the categories necessary to reveal patterns in material culture through time and space. Such patterning is known in archaeology as **space-time systematics**. And our first step in that direction is identifying types of artifacts.

Types of Types

Archaeology's basic unit of classification is termed a **type**. Be careful here because "type," like "culture," is an everyday word appropriated by anthropology and reassigned a very specific, nonintuitive meaning.

Archaeologists can classify the same object in many different ways. Think about a familiar set of modern artifacts—say, a workshop of woodworking tools. Carpenters classify their tools by function—hammers, saws, planes, files, drills, and spokeshaves. But when insuring a carpenter's workshop, the insurance agent uses another classification, sorting these same tools into new categories, such as flammable and nonflammable, or perhaps according to replacement value: "under $10," "between $10 and $25," and so on. Should the carpenter relocate, the furniture movers will group these same tools into another set of divisions, such as heavy or light, bulky or compact, or perhaps fragile or unbreakable. While storing the tools, the carpenter may classify them into "things my kids can touch" and "things my kids should not touch."

This discussion serves to make two important points. First, *types are abstractions* archaeologists impose on a variable batch of artifacts. We saw in Chapter 2 how cultures classify the world differently. Dogs are considered food in some cultures, pets in others. There is nothing inherent in dogs that makes them "really" food or "really" pets. And there is nothing inherent in an artifact that makes it belong to one and only one type.

As we've said before, your analysis (and the types you create) will depend on your research question. Suppose, for instance, we wanted to learn whether everyone in an ancient society made pots, or if only specialized potters made them. To do this, we might develop a way to classify pots into those novices made and those experts made, maybe by classifying pots according to the quality of their construction or painting. On the other hand, if we were interested in the household functions carried on in different rooms, then we might classify a site's ceramics into cooking vessels, water jars, serving vessels, and storage containers. We can classify the same object in many different ways.

Do *not* think that our goal is to classify things the way ancient peoples would have classified them. Archaeologists may divide stone scrapers into many different types based on their shape (to see if any could be useful time markers), but ancient peoples may have recognized only two kinds: ones that were still useful and ones that were used up. Both classifications have their purpose, and both are valid.

This brings us to our second point: We formulate a classification with a specific purpose in mind. Archaeology has no general, all-purpose classification. As Irving Rouse (1913–2006) put it, "Classification—for what?"

In Chapter 5, you saw one answer to this question: to create time markers. At San Cristobal, Nelson sought distinctive types of pottery that he could use to assign strata or sites to a relative chronology. We began that discussion with some pottery types, such as biscuitware and

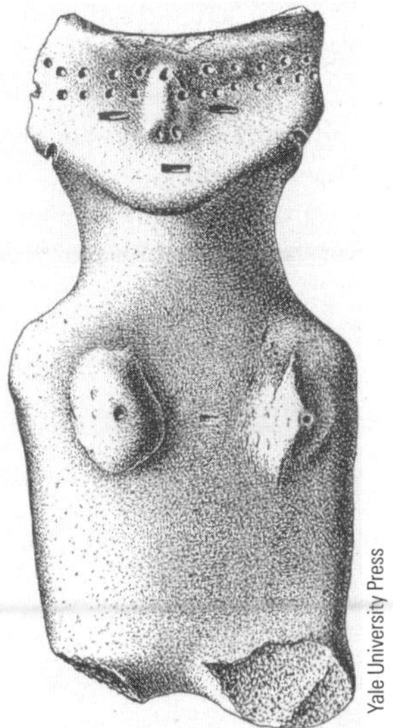

FIGURE 6-1 A Clay Type 2-A figurine from Pecos Pueblo.

three-color glaze pottery. Nelson was not concerned with the pots' functions, or quality, or anything else; he simply wanted to know if some types were earlier or later than other types. Another researcher with a different purpose might create a different typology.

But where do such types come from? To answer this question, let's first consider three major types of types.

Morphological Types

Modern observers exploring the range of material remains an extinct group left will encounter many unfamiliar artifacts. To make sense of the past using these remains, the first analytical step is to describe the artifacts carefully and accurately by grouping them into **morphological types**.

From Chapter 1, you'll recall Alfred Kidder and his early twentieth-century excavations at Pecos Pueblo in New Mexico. From these excavations, Kidder recovered many different kinds of artifacts, including many clay figurines. He classified these into four major types, with two of those types having several subdivisions. Here's how he described Type A-2 (see Figure 6-1), "flat bodied with protruding legs":

typology The systematic arrangement of material culture into types.

space-time systematics The delineation of patterns in material culture through time and across space. These patterns are what archaeologists will eventually try to explain or account for.

type A class of archaeological artifacts defined by a consistent clustering of attributes.

morphological type A descriptive and abstract grouping of individual artifacts whose focus is on overall similarity rather than function or chronological significance.

> The bodies are . . . broad and flat; the arms are either entirely ignored or suggested by very slight extensions of the square shoulders. The legs, however, are (to stretch the term) realistically modeled, being one-half to one-third as long as the body, and round in cross-section. The thighs set forward, there is a bend at the knee, and the lower leg, a mere stump with no attempt to depict the foot.

Note that Kidder did not speculate on how people used the figurines; he simply illustrated and described them in enough detail so that other archaeologists could visualize the artifacts without having to view them firsthand. Such bald description is the primary function of a morphological type (sometimes termed a "class" in archaeological literature).

Morphological types have a second, basic property: They are abstract. Types are not the artifacts per se; they are composite descriptions of many similar artifacts. This means that every morphological type must encompass a certain range of variability: Several colors may have been applied; the quality of manufacture may vary; absolute size may fluctuate; and so forth.

Morphological types are purely descriptive. We ascribe no function to them at this point, and they don't necessarily have any chronological significance. No set rules exist for creating morphological types, although basic raw material (pottery, stone, shell, bone, and so on) is normally the first criterion, followed by shape. Morphological types help communicate what the archaeologists found without describing every single specimen.

Temporal Types

Temporal types are morphological types that have specific chronological meaning for a particular region. In other words, they are time markers. If morphological Type B, for instance, occurs only in strata dating between 1500 and 1000 BP, then it can be elevated to the status of a temporal type. This promotion is important because when artifacts belonging to temporal Type B turn up in an otherwise undated context, the time span from 1500 to 1000 BP becomes the most plausible hypothesis for their age.

Functional Types

Functional types reflect how objects were used in the past. Functional types can crosscut morphological types. A set of stone scrapers, for instance, might have all been used to prepare hides (that is, they all had the same function), so they are a functional type. But some are big and others are small; some are thin and others are thick; some are made of chert, but others are of quartzite and obsidian; some are sharpened on the ends of stone flakes, others along their sides. Yet all these objects are the same with regard to their function. The remaining variability is (for now) irrelevant.

Functional types can also crosscut temporal types. Sometimes, pots are painted with distinctive designs for a limited period (like some of the pottery types that Nelson defined at San Cristobal). These distinctive styles of finish make the ceramics a temporal type. But all the differently decorated pots may be of the same functional type—they may all be cooking vessels, water jars, or seed storage pots.

Projectile Point Typology at Gatecliff

Let's recap. Good typologies have two crucial characteristics:

1. Regardless of its final purpose, *a typology must minimize the differences within each created type and maximize the differences between types*. If a lot of overlap or ambiguity occurs in the types, then they cannot reveal any significant or meaningful patterning.
2. *The typology must be objective and explicit*. This means that any trained observer should be able to replicate the result. If it is not replicable, then your methods cannot be duplicated (and your work is therefore not scientific).

Once you've created your typology, you can focus on placing it in time and across space.

To show you how typology works, we're going to take you step by step through Thomas's classification of Gatecliff Shelter's projectile points. By now, you know that the first question to ask is this: What was the goal of Thomas's classification?

Thomas asked several research questions at Gatecliff Shelter. One of these was whether the shelter would allow him to create and test a projectile point typology that would provide temporal types—time markers. Once defined, these temporal types could be used to estimate the age of surface assemblages (where radiocarbon dates could not be processed). That was the goal—the research question—of the Gatecliff typology.

Choosing Criteria

Great Basin archaeologists knew that projectile points were made out of different types of stone, such as chert, quartzite, obsidian, and rhyolite. But experience showed that the raw material did not change over time in a systematic way; in fact, it mostly told archaeologists what kind of material was locally available. A typology based on raw material would not help construct temporal types.

But archaeologists who worked in the Great Basin also knew that projectile point *shape* changed over time. Small points, for example, tended to occur in upper (later) strata; larger points occurred in lower (earlier) strata. And small points that were notched from the side seemed to occur stratigraphically above small points notched from the corners. These observations suggested that a typology based on shape and size could be used to construct temporal types.

The first step in applying your criteria can be informal, sometimes just separating superficially similar artifacts into piles on the laboratory table. We can ignore variables like stratigraphy, time depth, cultural affiliation, and even provenience because (for now) the primary concern is to reduce the complexity to our primary criteria—shape and size.

Look at the projectile points in Figure 6-2. These are just a few of the 400 points recovered from Gatecliff Shelter.

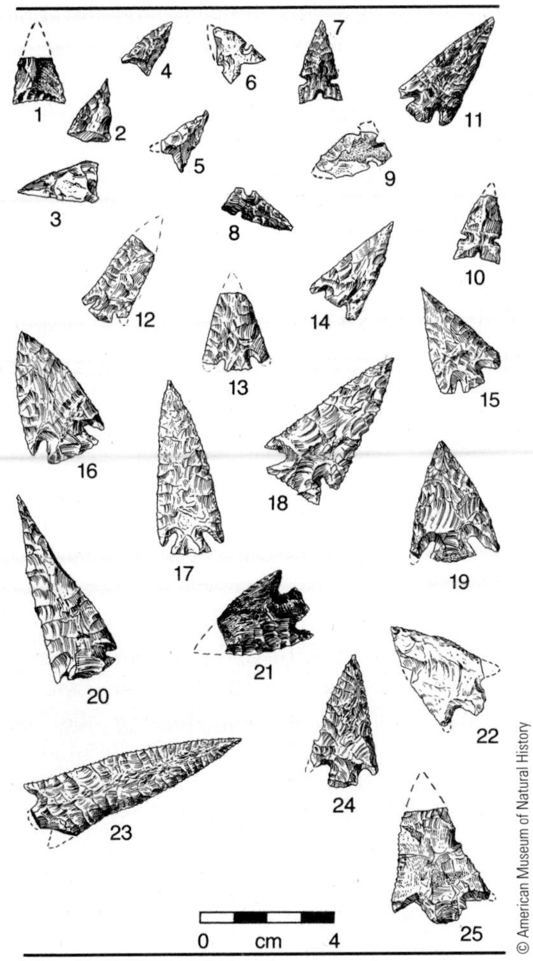

FIGURE 6-2 An unsorted batch of stone projectile points recovered at Gatecliff Shelter (Nevada).

If you are any kind of observer at all, you will distinguish some important similarities and differences among them. The points at the top of the figure, for instance, are smaller than those at the bottom. Another difference is in how the points are notched for hafting. Some are notched from the side (for example, 7, 8, and 9), and others from the base (for instance, 14 and 15); some are notched from the corner (16 and 24), and some are not notched at all (1 and 3).

Defining Attributes

Differences like size and notch position are called **attributes**, which are measurable or observable qualities of an object. We could make an infinite number of observations and take an infinite number of measurements on a projectile point, a few of which are shown in Figure 6-3. There are no rules governing the number of attributes to record; in general, we try to use as few as seem necessary to accomplish the purpose of the typology.

The two attributes of size and notching are sufficient to create workable morphological types. But it is insufficient simply to say "size" and "notch position." To define adequate attributes, we must explain precisely what we mean by the terms, so that another observer could make identical observations.

Take size. We all know what size means, but it can be recorded in several ways. Measure the length of a projectile point and you know something about its size. The width also reflects size. Or you can weigh something to find its size. So, what size are we talking about?

Weight is a good measure of projectile point size (although it is necessary to estimate the original weight of broken specimens). Other attributes that measure size (such as length, width, and thickness) all correlate with weight: As a point gets longer, wider, and/or thicker, it also becomes heavier. But weight is the easiest to measure, and so it was one of the first attributes Thomas used to define morphological types. The lightest point in the Gatecliff sample weighs only 0.4 gram (about the weight of a paper clip) and the heaviest, more than 5 grams (about the same as a nickel). The weights for the 25 Gatecliff Shelter points in Figure 6-2 are presented in Table 6-1.

You can see that these weights are patterned, with certain natural breaks defining three projectile point sizes in this collection (this is even clearer when you look at the data on all 400-plus points):

Small points: Weight less than 1.0 gram
Medium points: Weight between 1.0 and 2.5 grams
Large points: Weight over 2.5 grams

These projectile point weights are variable because flintknappers cannot erase their mistakes; they must work around errors, creating some variation in the finished products. Points also break when they are used. If they are not too severely broken, they can be reshaped into usable points—but this too makes them smaller than the maker initially intended (this can have an effect on typology; see "Looking Closer: The Frison Effect"). But for each of the three weight categories, the point's maker had a mental template of what the "proper" point's size should be. By and large, the three size categories reflect natural breaks in the distribution of weights.

The second attribute is notch position. Among the small points (Points 1 to 10 in Figure 6-2), some have notches and others do not. Two categories are hence apparent: small, unnotched points and small, side-notched points. Thomas was hardly the first archaeologist to notice this distinction, and the literature of Great Basin archaeology refers to these two morphological types in this way:

temporal type A morphological type that has temporal significance; also known as a time marker or index fossil.

functional type A class of artifacts that performed the same function; these may or may not be temporal and/or morphological types.

attribute An individual characteristic that distinguishes one artifact from another on the basis of its size, surface texture, form, material, method of manufacture, or design pattern.

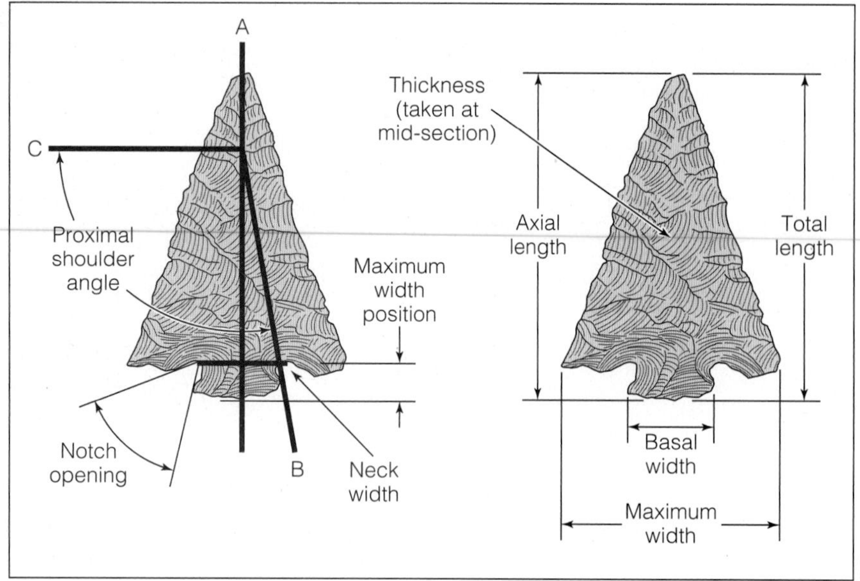

FIGURE 6-3 A Great Basin projectile point and some of the data that can be recorded from it. These observations are only a few of all that could be made on a projectile point.

Cottonwood Triangular (Points 1 through 5)
 Weight: less than 1.0 gram
 Notching: absent
Desert Side-Notched (Points 6 through 10)
 Weight: less than 1.0 gram
 Notching: present (from the side)

So the smallest points—Points 1 through 10—belong to already recognized morphological types.

Points 11 through 15 are medium sized (weighing between 1.0 and 2.5 grams) and have notches creating a small base (or stem). Thomas described them as follows:

Rosegate series (Points 11 through 15)
 Weight: between 1.0 and 2.5 grams
 Notching: present

Archaeologists get to name the point types they define. The first name generally refers to the site or region where they were first distinguished. The last name describes some morphological characteristic. Thomas's term "Rosegate" is a combination of "Rose Spring," a site in southeastern California, and "Eastgate," a small overhang near Eastgate, Nevada. Originally, two different point types were defined, one named after each site, but Thomas could find no significant difference between the two, so he combined them. (In this case, he modified the naming convention somewhat, combining the two original place names into a single term.) Points 11 through 15 have now been "typed."

The larger points are more complicated. Numbers 16 through 25 weigh more than 2.5 grams. Some have

TABLE 6-1 Attributes for Gatecliff Shelter Projectile Points

Specimen Number	Weight in Grams	Proximal Shoulder Angle	Specimen Number	Weight in Grams	Proximal Shoulder Angle
1	(0.9)	—	14	1.5	85
2	0.8	—	15	2.5	80
3	0.9	—	16	4.1	110
4	0.4	—	17	3.5	120
5	(0.9)	—	18	3.9	130
6	(0.4)	200	19	3.5	120
7	0.8	180	20	(4.2)	150
8	(0.6)	180	21	(2.8)	80
9	0.7	180	22	(3.4)	85
10	(0.8)	190	23	(5.5)	80
11	2.3	100	24	2.7	100
12	(1.5)	100	25	(5.5)	60
13	(1.4)	95			

Note: Weights in parentheses are estimates on broken points.

LOOKING CLOSER

The Frison Effect

Stone tools are important because they are ubiquitous in prehistoric sites. But as they are used, stone tools are resharpened and become smaller and change shape. This can affect tool typologies.

François Bordes (1919–1981) was a well-known French archaeologist (a member of the French underground during World War II, Bordes also wrote science fiction novels under the pen name Francis Carsac). The stone tools found in Neanderthal cave sites especially intrigued Bordes. These assemblages, dating from 130,000 to 35,000 years ago, are referred to as **Mousterian**, after Le Moustier, the site where they were first found. Bordes divided these stone tools into 63 types, including a variety of points, scrapers, knives, handaxes, and denticulates (flakes with crenulated edges). He created these types simply by laying assemblages out and then sorting them into morphological categories. Tabletop typology was common in Bordes's day, though statistical analysis later supported his findings.

Bordes then looked at Mousterian sites and found something interesting: The 63 tool types co-occurred in set frequencies, creating four majors kinds of assemblages. For example, the Mousterian of Acheulean Tradition contained many handaxes, denticulates, and backed knives, but only moderate numbers of scrapers; the Typical Mousterian contained few handaxes and backed knives.

Bordes found that the four assemblages often alternated with one another throughout a site's strata. From this, he argued that the four assemblages reflected different cultural groups of Neanderthals, just as different car and architecture styles reflected different groups of Europeans. Bordes's typology was successful because it allowed him to see a higher level of patterning.

His interpretation of this patterning assumed that the stone tools were in their final intended form. Different scrapers, he thought, had different shapes because their makers had different ideas about what a "proper" scraper should look like. But scrapers wear out, often quite quickly, and are rejuvenated by removing a few flakes along their edges. In the 1960s, George Frison (University of Wyoming) pointed out that stone artifact shape can change considerably during use through such resharpening.

Harold Dibble (University of Pennsylvania) investigated whether the "Frison effect" was responsible for at least some of the variation in Bordes's Mousterian scraper types. Undertaking some experimental and archaeological studies, he eventually concluded that resharpening accounts for some of Bordes's scraper types. For example, "single edge scrapers" turn into "transverse scrapers" simply by resharpening.

Does this mean that Bordes was wrong? Not necessarily. He saw and categorized morphological variation, and that process allowed him to see patterning. His interpretation of the patterning may be wrong or incomplete, because some differences in tool form reflect only how heavily some tools were used. Assemblages with many transverse scrapers, for example, were probably produced by longer occupations than assemblages dominated by single-edge scrapers. Archaeologists proceed in exactly this way—they sort through variability, removing those parts explained by humdrum factors so that they can determine the more intriguing parts. Classification is an important step in that process.

expanding bases (that is, the neck is narrower than the base), and others have contracting bases. But "expanding" and "contracting" are ambiguous terms, and on given points, archaeologists often disagree about just which stems expand and which contract. Look at Point 24: We call this stem contracting, but you might think that it is expanding. Who's right? Neither, because we have yet to define the attribute—a necessary step toward replicability.

The stem is created by the notches—the two slits added so that the point can be tied more securely to a shaft. The lower edge of this notch forms an angle with the major longitudinal axis of the point, and angles are useful because they can be measured.

To measure the angle, draw an imaginary line along the long axis of the point (Line A in Figure 6-3). Now draw another line (Line B) along the bottom of the point's notch, extending it to where it intersects the line you drew down the axis. Finally, draw a line perpendicular to that point of intersection on the opposite side of the point (Line C) and measure the angle between Line C and Line B.

Thomas called this attribute the proximal shoulder angle (PSA), because this side of the notch is nearest ("proximal to") the point shaft. Table 6-1 lists the proximal shoulder angles for the ten large points (Points 16 through 25) from Gatecliff Shelter. Now the difference between expanding and contracting stems is apparent: Points 16 through 20 have PSAs greater than 110°, and Points 21 through 25

Mousterian A culture from the Middle Paleolithic ("Middle Old Stone Age") period that appeared throughout Europe after 250,000 and before 30,000 years ago. Mousterian artifacts are frequently associated with Neanderthal human remains.

have PSAs smaller than that. On this basis, Thomas separated them into the following morphological types:

Elko Corner-Notched (Points 16 through 20)
Weight: Greater than 2.5 grams
PSA: ≥110° and ≤150°

Gatecliff Contracting Stem (Points 21 through 25)
Weight: Greater than 2.5 grams
PSA: <100°

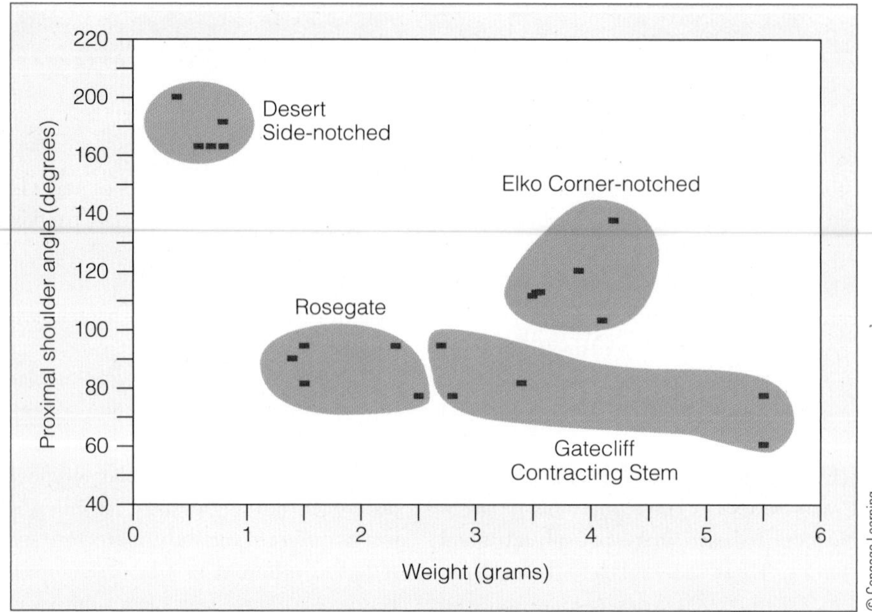

FIGURE 6-4 The relationship between the attributes of weight and proximal shoulder angle for the 20 notched projectile points in Figure 6-2.

Elko points were initially recognized at sites in Elko County, Nevada, and Thomas first defined Gatecliff points from data recovered at Gatecliff Shelter. As morphological types, they differ only in basal form, as described by the PSA measurements.

We have now classified all 25 points. This example is purposely simplified, but it demonstrates the first step in projectile point classification. Although a number of additional attributes were necessary to deal with the more than 400 points found at Gatecliff, the fundamental procedures are the same.

Memorizing endless type names may seem meaningless, but dealing with these five descriptive names is many times better than coping with 25 individual artifacts—to say nothing of the 400 individual points at Gatecliff, or the thousands found throughout the Great Basin. And that is the function of morphological types.

What Did the Typology Do?

Our typology has now organized the jumble of projectile points into groups based on measurable characteristics. But before we use the typology to think in broader terms—those crucial dimensions of time and space—we must first ask if it has fulfilled the two necessary characteristics of a typology.

Consider the first characteristic: *Minimize the differences within each type and maximize the differences between types.*

In the past, archaeologists accomplished this goal simply by placing artifacts on a table and sorting them into piles. However, most typologies today make use of statistical analyses (with names like cluster and discriminant analysis) that are designed to take a set of measured attributes and provide an objective measure of how well a typology accomplishes this goal. We've avoided the statistical detail of the Gatecliff typology, but you can get a sense of where such an analysis might go by looking at Figure 6-4. In this figure, we plotted the 20 notched points in terms of their weight and PSA. The Desert Side-notched, Elko Corner-notched, and Rosegate points are clearly different from one another in terms of both weight and notching—the differences within each group are minimized and the differences between them maximized. Rosegate and Gatecliff Contracting Stem points are less easily distinguished. They are similar in terms of PSA, and their difference in weight is less clear. However, Gatecliff points are more frequently resharpened than are Rosegate points—making them smaller than they were originally. The difference is subtle here, but a larger sample would separate these two point types more clearly in terms of weight. Therefore, the typology meets the first criterion: It minimizes the differences within groups and maximizes the differences between groups.

The second characteristic was that *the typology must be objective and explicit*. Thomas's typology actually made use of more attributes than simply weight and proximal shoulder angle, and he defined more than the four projectile point types discussed here. By examining patterning in attributes, Thomas was able to organize the resulting Great Basic projectile point types into a flowchart, shown in Figure 6-5. To see how this typology is objective and explicit, let's take an "unknown" projectile point and classify it according to the Gatecliff criteria.

Figure 6-3 (page 102) illustrates Artifact 20.4/2010, a projectile point recovered during Kelly's survey of the Carson Desert. Projectile point 20.4/2010 has the following attributes:

Total length: 37.5 mm
Axial length: 37.5 mm
Basal indentation ratio: 1
Maximum width: 18 mm
Maximum width position: 4 mm
Basal width: 7 mm
Neck width: 7 mm
Proximal shoulder angle: 100°
Notch opening: 40°
Weight: 1.6 grams

To type this point, a few definitions of Thomas's other attributes are needed.

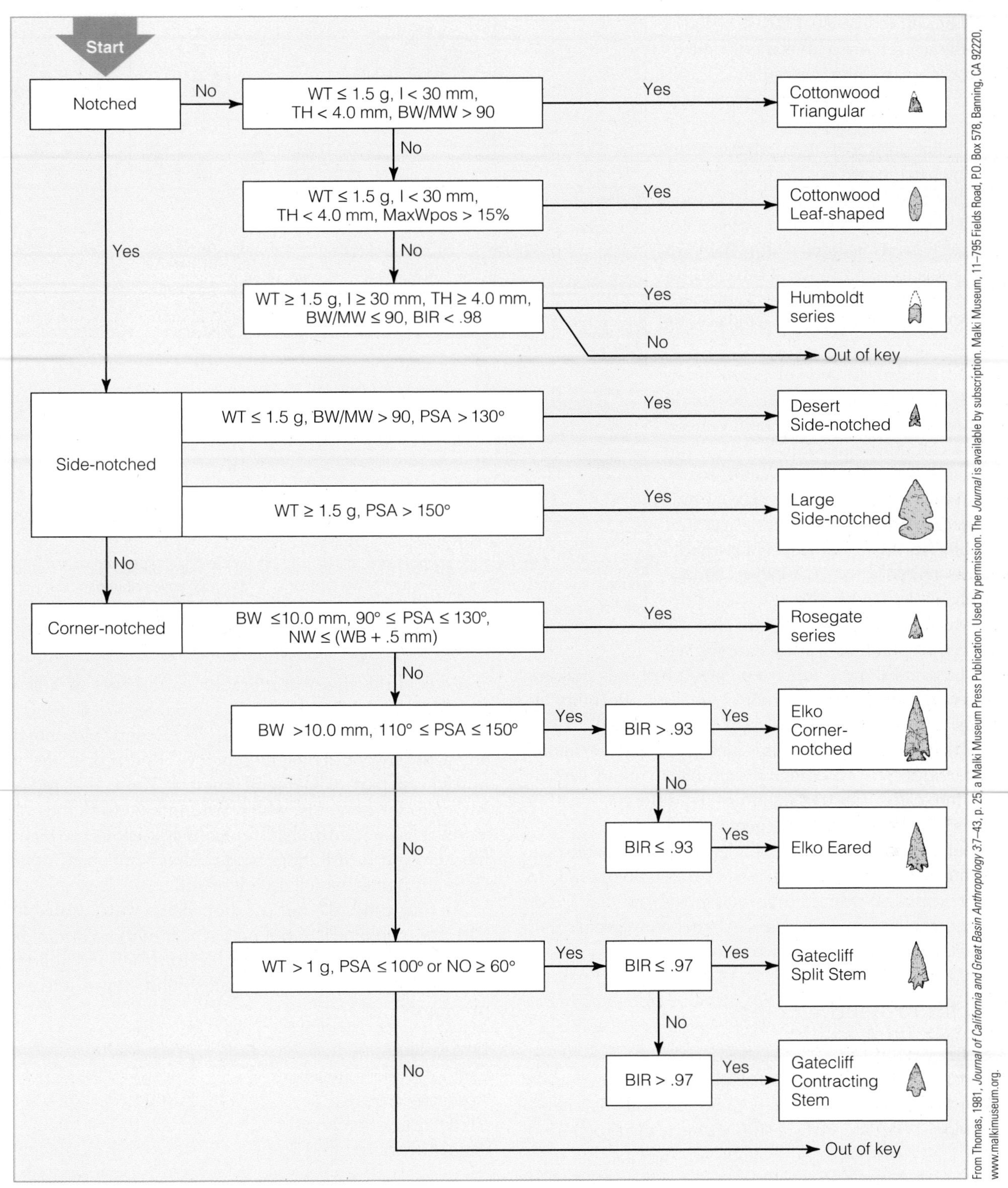

FIGURE 6-5 The central Great Basin projectile point key.

Total length is obvious; axial length, however, is the length from the point's tip to the basal concavity. For Artifact 20.4/2010, there is no basal concavity, so the axial length equals the total length. (If this point had a concave base, the axial length would be somewhat shorter than the total length.) The utility of this measurement is that, by dividing the axial length by the total length, we have a measure of how concave the base is, what Thomas called the "basal indentation ratio." A high ratio means a shallow concavity; a low ratio means a deep concavity.

The maximum width position is simply the distance from the point's base to the point's greatest width. By dividing the maximum width position by the total length, we have one measure of a point's shape. A high ratio indicates a more triangular point (like 20.4/2010); a lower ratio indicates a more leaf-shaped point.

With these attributes, we can now classify Artifact 20.4/2010 using the flowchart. We begin with the question: Is the point notched? The answer is yes, so we follow the arrow down to the next box. Is the point side-notched? No, so we move on to the corner-notched box. We are now faced with a set of three questions: Is its basal width (BW) less than or equal to 10 mm? Yes, it is. Is its PSA between 90° and 130°? Also, yes. Is the neck width (NW) less than the basal width plus .5 mm? Yes.

If the answer to any of these three questions had been no, then we would have moved to the following box. But the answer to all these questions is yes, so the point is typed as a Rosegate. With this key, any trained student would classify this point as accurately as the most seasoned archaeologist. By using an explicit and objective typology, archaeologists know that when they talk about a "Desert Side-notched" or "Rosegate" or some other type of point, all of them are talking about the same thing. We have created attributes that are objective and explicit—and that is what "replicability" is all about.

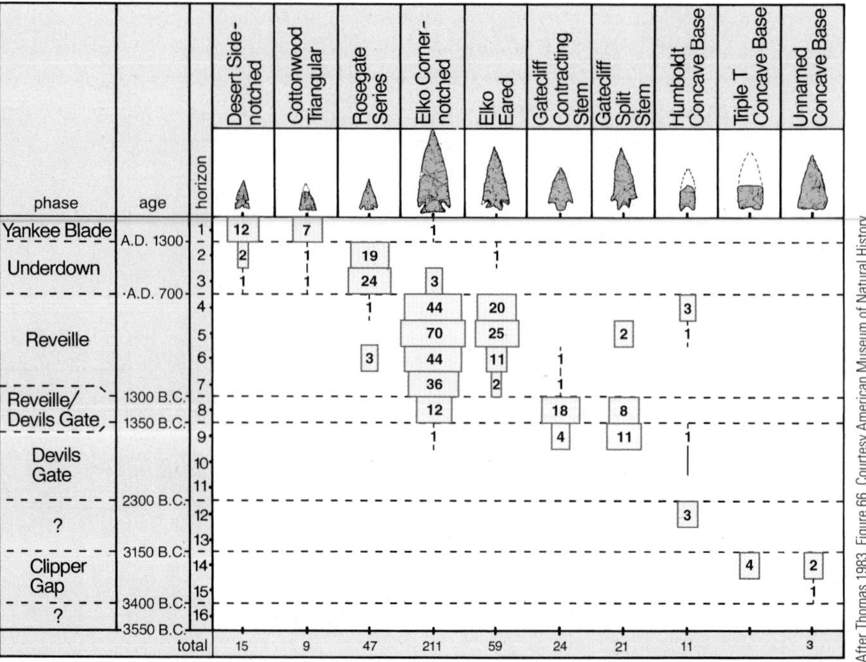

FIGURE 6-6 Relative proportions of selected projectile point types across the stratigraphic units of Gatecliff Shelter. Note that one or two extremely abundant temporal types seem to dominate most strata.

So this typology fulfills both of the essential characteristics: It sorts things using objective and explicit criteria into categories that minimize the differences within them and maximize the differences between them.

So far, we've only been talking about morphological types, but remember that the goal of this typology was to create temporal types, or time markers. Now that we've identified the types occurring at Gatecliff, we can see if they have any temporal significance.

Gatecliff Projectile Points as Temporal Types

As the name implies, temporal types help archaeologists monitor time; they provide us with index fossils that allow archaeologists to date surface sites and strata within buried sites.

In Chapter 3, we compared the stratigraphy of Gatecliff Shelter to a giant layer cake stacked 40 feet high. Geology's law of superposition tells us that, all else being equal, the oldest artifacts lie at the bottom, with later artifacts showing up in progressively higher strata. The Gatecliff deposits thus provide extraordinary temporal control over the past 7000 years. When we plot the vertical distribution of the more than 400 classifiable projectile points from Gatecliff Shelter, we arrive at the distribution shown in Figure 6-6. (This figure includes all the types used to classify the entire Gatecliff collection.)

Look at the sharp stratigraphic differences (which, you should note, exhibit the battleship curves like those in the seriation diagrams of Chapter 5). Desert Side-notched and Cottonwood Triangular points occurred in the very uppermost part of Gatecliff Shelter. These had replaced Rosegate series points, which are confined to slightly older strata. These, in turn, had replaced Elko points, which are found lower, in still older strata. Elko points had replaced Gatecliff points, which are older still.

At that time, 47 radiocarbon dates were available to date the geological sequence at Gatecliff (we now have many more), and it was possible to assign the following time ranges to the projectile point types discussed previously:

Desert Side-notched	post-700 BP
Cottonwood Triangular	post-700 BP
Rosegate series	1500 to 700 BP
Elko Corner-notched	3500 to 1500 BP
Gatecliff Contracting Stem	4500 to 1500 BP

With this critical step, several of our morphological types have become temporal types. Each time similar points are found in undated contexts, we now have a clue (a hypothesis, really) to their time of manufacture.

Note what has happened in this example:

1. Individual artifacts were initially grouped strictly on formal criteria; all that mattered for morphological types was that the artifacts looked alike.
2. These morphological categories were then tested against independent evidence—specifically, the

layer-cake stratigraphy and the chain of 47 radiocarbon dates available from Gatecliff Shelter.

3. All five morphological categories were significantly restricted in time, so they were elevated to the status of temporal types.

Not every morphological point type from Gatecliff made the grade. The frequencies of some morphological types (especially the larger, concave base points) did not change significantly through time, and these types flunked the test for graduating to the level of temporal type. Maybe somebody, eventually, will demonstrate that concave base points are indeed time markers in the Great Basin; but until that demonstration, these types remain merely "morphological," without temporal significance.

We began with the simplifying assumption that change through time reflects shifts in ancient peoples' "mental templates" for an idealized projectile point shape. Never mind what the artifacts meant to the makers, whether they were spear or arrow points, or how they were made. For now, we care only about whether some cluster of measurable attributes (which we call types) changed through time.

The seriation-like diagram for Gatecliff projectile points shows us what changes over time and what does not, which permits us to pose more interesting questions. For instance, although we now know that Desert Side-notched and Cottonwood Triangular points postdate 700 BP, we do not know *why* two morphological types existed simultaneously. Are two social groups living at Gatecliff after 700 BP? Are Desert Side-notched points designed for hunting bighorn, whereas Cottonwood points are for rabbits? Are Cottonwood points for "war arrows"—left unnotched so that they remain embedded in a body even if the shaft is pulled out? Or perhaps the difference is technological: Could the Cottonwood Triangular points be unfinished, intended to be later notched (and thereby becoming Desert Side-notched points)? Notching is often the last thing done to a point, and if done incorrectly, it can ruin the point. Were Cottonwood Triangular points made by novices who were not adept at notching points? All these guesses are hypotheses at present untested—and they would have been impossible without first creating projectile point temporal types.

Space-Time Systematics

So far we have been talking only about the temporal dimension of archaeology, change in artifacts over time. We now shift and consider the spatial dimension of these temporal changes.

Archaeology has adopted a relatively standardized framework for integrating the kind of chronological information just discussed into a regional framework. Gordon Willey (1913–2002) and Philip Phillips (1900–1993) initially set out this regional infrastructure in their influential book *Method and Theory in American Archaeology* (1958). Since then, the nomenclature has varied somewhat from region to region, some terms have been discarded because they reflect outdated theoretical paradigms, and others do not have quite the significance that they once carried. Nonetheless, the 50-year-old Willey-Phillips framework remains the most generally accepted system in North America.

Archaeological Cultures: Dividing Space

To begin, however, we must go back to before Willey and Phillips's day, to the early twentieth-century concept of *culture areas*. Long before anthropology existed as a discipline in the United States, scholars recognized that not all Native American societies were alike. Some people were nomadic; others lived in large pueblos. Some hunted bison; others were maize farmers. Those in California relied heavily on acorns for their food; Northwest Coast peoples fished and hunted sea mammals. By the late nineteenth century, American anthropology had formalized these observations into culture areas (see Figure 6-7), large regions defined primarily in terms of what people ate (which of course had a lot to do with the environment). The theory that attempted to explain these geographic patterns is no longer important to

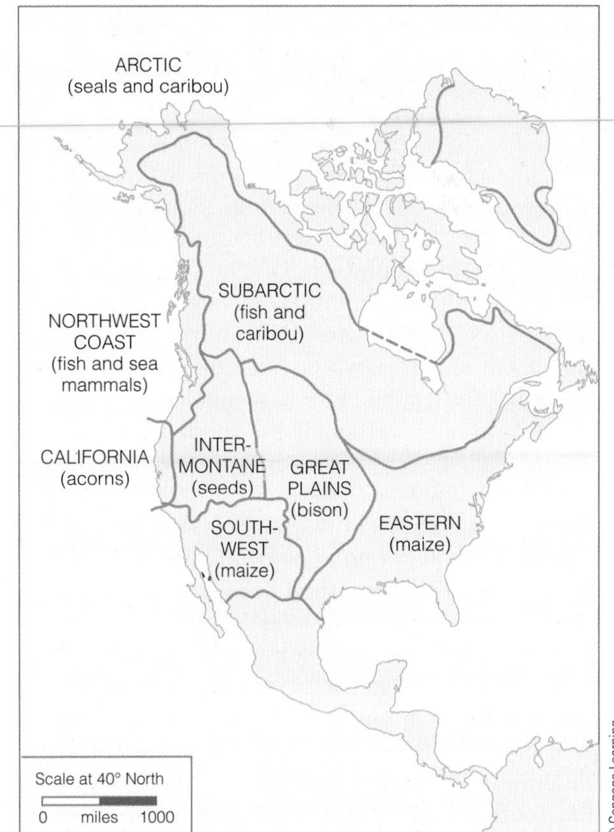

FIGURE 6-7 North American culture areas. Such areas were important to nineteenth-century anthropology, but are less so today.

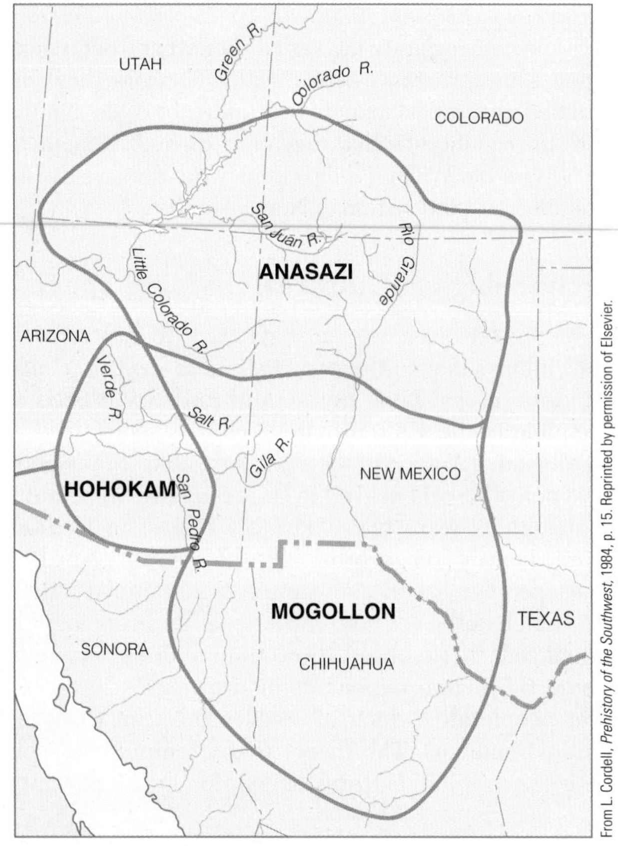

FIGURE 6-8 Southwestern archaeological cultures, or traditions. The theory that lay behind these areas is outdated today, but the patterns that stand behind these traditions still demand explanation.

anthropology, but the culture areas left a legacy in that archaeologists who study the prehistory of North America tend to focus on one of these culture areas. They work on the Plains, or in the southeastern United States, California, or the Southwest.

Working with the prehistory of one of these regions, archaeologists quickly saw "subculture areas"—regions within a culture area whose material culture (such as house styles, settlement patterns, ceramics, or subsistence) differed from one another. These subdivisions of culture areas are called "traditions" or *archaeological cultures*. Figure 6-8 shows the location of the three major archaeological cultures of the Southwest culture area: the Hohokam, Mogollon (*muh*-gee-own), and Anasazi. These three regions are distinguished from one another in terms of pottery and architectural styles.

But these archaeological cultures are *not* ethnographic cultures. If we could go back in time to, say, the Mogollon region and travel around, we would probably encounter several different languages, as well as different customs in different villages. In all likelihood, people in a village at the southern end of the Mogollon region considered themselves different from those who lived at the northern end. By drawing lines around areas on a map and labeling them archaeological cultures, we are simply drawing attention to spatial differences in the kinds of artifacts that are found in those regions. The *meaning* of these differences is another matter.

Periods: Dividing Time

As archaeologists began to investigate the prehistory of regions, they also discovered that the Native American culture that ethnographers documented (and that formed the basis for maps of culture areas) had not always been there. People living in the American Southwest some 5000 years ago, for example, were nomadic hunter-gatherers who never knew maize or built pueblos. As the chronologies of different culture areas were worked out, prehistory was organized into slices of time that were given different names.

Archaeologists divided prehistory into **periods** based on gross changes in easily observable archaeological remains, such as subsistence or house forms. The concept of periods is still used to organize archaeological thinking about time. For example, pick up a text on Southwestern archaeology and an early chapter will be on the "Paleoindian Period" (from 13,000 to 7500 BP), a period of time in which the distinctive Pueblo archaeological cultures, such as the Mogollon, did not exist, and people were nomadic hunters of large game and gatherers of wild plant foods. The next chapter might be on the "Archaic Period" (from 7500 to 1900 BP). This is a time when people made heavier use of plant foods, began to develop distinctive regional traditions in material culture, and, toward the end of the period, experimented with agricultural crops, most notably maize. This may be followed by chapters that describe "Early Village" and "Pueblo" periods.

The concepts of archaeological cultures and periods helped map out major spatial and temporal patterns in material culture. Periods record change over time; archaeological cultures record change over space. Knowing *how* and *when* material culture changed over time and space is an obvious first step toward explaining *why* those changes occurred.

Phases: Combining Space and Time

As archaeologists learned more about the time markers of a region, they found that different regions in a culture area did not all change in lockstep with one another. Pottery, for example, may first appear at different times in different areas; likewise, from a common base, pottery styles may differentiate over time at different rates and in different ways in different regions. In other words, there are temporal and spatial changes in material culture of which periods were just a first approximation.

A **phase** is a block of time that is characterized by one or more distinctive artifact types—a particular kind of pottery, housing style, and/or projectile point, for example. The phase has become the practicable and intelligible unit

PROFILE OF AN ARCHAEOLOGIST

A Federal Archaeologist

Terry Fifield is the archaeologist for the Prince of Wales Island Districts, Tongass National Forest, Alaska. Reprinted by permission.

© Terry Fifield

Prince of Wales Island, in the southern portion of southeast Alaska's Alexander Archipelago, is an archaeological frontier.

In 1994, I moved my family to the Craig/Klawock area on the west coast of Prince of Wales Island. I was the first Forest Service archaeologist to live there, and the first to have the opportunity to get to know the residents and become familiar with the land and seascape.

During my first summer, Dave Putnam, a Quaternary geologist/archaeologist working with me, spotted a scrap of spruce root basketry eroding from a muddy riverbed in the estuary of the Thorne River. Dave and I worked closely with the state of Alaska (on whose land the discovery was located), other Forest Service resource groups, the Alaska State Museum, and local tribal people. Within a few days, having assembled a small team and having received a lot of advice, we excavated a pedestal of mud containing the oldest example of spruce root basketry known from North America's Northwest Coast.

I made mistakes in that situation, especially in the area of consulting with Native Americans. Being new to the island, I was unfamiliar with clan and tribal boundaries and failed to locate the correct clan leaders for advice.

But I did try to make the contacts and we did one thing right: After preserving the basket in isopropyl alcohol–laced water, we invited local weavers to come view it. We did not know the basket's age then, but the site's stratigraphy suggested it was several thousand years old. The scene that played out in the Forest Service conference room over the next few days was a powerful one. Weavers from Klawock, Craig, and Hydaburg came by to study the 11- × 13-inch swatch of woven fabric. Haida and Tlingit alike saw the similarities between this ancient basket and the craft they had learned from their aunts and grandmothers.

Before the basket was hand-carried to the Alaska State Museum in Juneau for curation, the Forest Service conference room was host to a small but moving ceremony affirming the importance of this artifact to its people and place of origin.

Study of the Thorne River basket eventually revealed it to be a collecting basket woven of spruce root almost 6000 years ago. In 1998, the basket and its discovery were the subject of the Alaska Archaeology Week poster. The poster, featuring Margaret Davidson's technical drawing and watercolor reconstruction, was popular with Native American weavers all over southeast Alaska. People again imagined the chain of knowledge linking 300 generations of women over nearly six millennia.

This important discovery provided tangible proof to today's subsistence-oriented residents that the lifeways and traditions of the island's native people extend deeply into the past.

Here on Prince of Wales Island, where many people are of Native American ancestry, there is widespread interest in studying and understanding the past. But there is also some apprehension about where archaeological specimens go, and perhaps more important, what happens to the knowledge that scientists draw from research. I believe an essential part of what we do as archaeologists must be to communicate what we have learned to the people most affected, to the public at large, and to our professional colleagues. As with most situations involving people, it's all about communication, in this case sharing information and the excitement of learning about the past.

---

of archaeological study, defined by Willey and Phillips as "an archaeological unit possessing traits sufficiently characteristic to distinguish it from all other units similarly conceived . . . [and] spatially limited to the order of magnitude of a locality or region and chronologically limited to a relatively brief interval of time."

How do we construct phases? Phases are defined by temporal types (like our Gatecliff points), items of material culture that show patterned changes over time. We have already seen how to derive temporal types: You group individual artifacts into morphological types, and then test them against independent data (such as a dated site stratigraphy, correlation with other known sites, or direct dating of the artifacts themselves). We recognize those types

period A length of time distinguished by particular items of material culture, such as house form, pottery, or subsistence.

phase An archaeological construct possessing traits sufficiently characteristic to distinguish it from other units similarly conceived; spatially limited to roughly a locality or region and chronologically limited to the briefest interval of time possible.

of artifacts that change systematically and observably through time as time markers.

The next analytical step is to see how the time markers themselves cluster to reflect site chronology. Here we have to define a few other terms that archaeologists commonly use.

Archaeological sites consist of **assemblages**, collections of artifacts recovered from some unit of provenience. We could talk about a site's stone tool or ceramic or projectile point assemblage. In this case, the provenience might be the site itself. We could also talk about the assemblage of a particular stratum—say, the stone tool assemblage of Stratum 22 at Gatecliff. In a well-stratified and carefully excavated site like Gatecliff, there could be many assemblages.

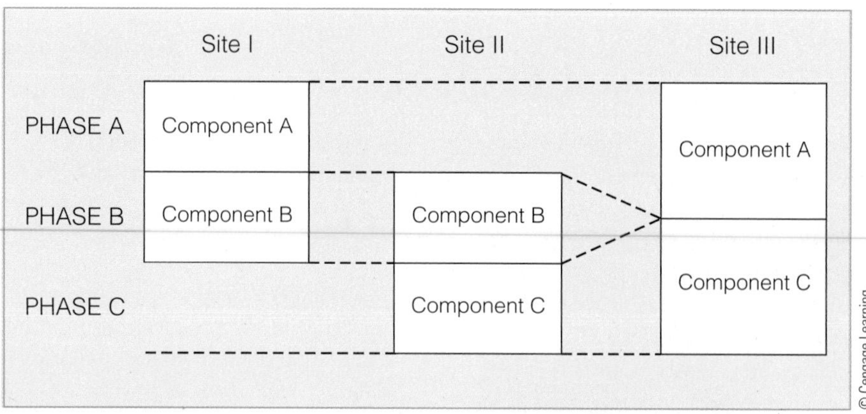

FIGURE 6-9 Relationship of archaeological sites to the analytical concepts of component and phase.

We might then analytically cluster these assemblages into **components**. A component is considered a culturally homogeneous unit within a single site. By "culturally homogeneous," we mean that although the assemblages that go into a component might have been deposited during different years and by different individuals, they were deposited by people who were the same culturally. Some small archaeological sites may contain only one assemblage representing a single component; some may contain multiple assemblages that nonetheless still represent one component; others may contain multiple assemblages representing several components; and some sites may be too badly mixed to sort out assemblages or to define components at all.

Defining archaeological components involves the intangible factor of cultural homogeneity; there can be no firm rules for their construction. But it helps if the strata are obvious from the stratigraphic profile, as at Gatecliff, where numerous strata of non-artifact–bearing silts separated the deposits into discrete living floors. During analysis, we could keep the floors distinct (as individual assemblages) or group them together on the basis of shared similarities. Although Gatecliff contained many living surfaces, Thomas decided that it contained only five distinct cultural components, each incorporating the assemblages from one to six living surfaces. Components are thus site-specific—a given component is, by definition, from a single site.

Each component at Gatecliff is defined by its associated array of dates and its particular set of characteristic artifacts, including our much-analyzed projectile points and artifacts such as incised slates and carved wooden pegs (used to construct snares to trap small mammals).

How do these observations help create phases? By comparing Gatecliff's components with those of other nearby sites, we define the spatial and temporal range of particular artifact types, and from this comparison archaeologists construct a regional chronology of phases. Briefly, assemblages (all items of one kind from one stratum or location) are grouped into site-specific components (differentiated in culture and in time). Components from nearby sites are grouped into phases. These building blocks therefore identify similarities across space and time.

To see how this works, consider the three hypothetical archaeological sites in Figure 6-9. These three hypothetical sites are located in the same geographic region. They have been carefully excavated and analyzed and, as is often the case, no single site contains the complete cultural sequence. The first site has Components A and B; the second site contains Component B plus a new component called C; and the third site has Components A and C but lacks Component B. By analyzing the temporal types shared among the components and comparing the absolute dates, a regional sequence of phases can be constructed from evidence at these three sites.

To give a more concrete example, archaeologists working in the central Great Basin divide the post-5550 BP era into five phases, each defined by one or more temporal projectile point types (as well as other artifact types). You can see these in Figure 6-6 (page 106), which showed how different morphological point types at Gatecliff sort out in time. These phases were defined on the basis of the analysis of assemblages from many stratified sites and the consistent association of particular morphological artifact types with particular spans of time.

The latest of these, the Yankee Blade phase (named after a nineteenth-century silver mine in the town of Austin) is typified by Desert Side-notched and Cottonwood Triangular points, as well as simple pottery. This phase began about 700 BP and lasted until Euro-American contact, about 1850 (100 BP) in central Nevada. The other phases were similarly defined, each composed of different kinds of artifacts (primarily projectile points) and spanning other episodes of time.

Phases: The Basic Units of Space-Time Systematics

The phase is archaeology's basic unit of time-space systematics, combining both spatial and temporal patterns in the material culture we dig up. Phases are defined by time, but also by space. There is no Yankee Blade phase in Georgia, or New Mexico, or even Utah because the nature and tempo of change in material culture in these areas was not the same as in the central Great Basin. Even within the Great Basin, phases are not synchronous. Figure 6-10 shows some of the phase names used in the western and central Great Basin. Time and periods appear at left, along the vertical axis; space appears along the horizontal axis. This diagram is one result of archaeologists' efforts to create space-time systematics. Each phase, or block, in this figure—Cowhorn, Early Lovelock, Grass Valley—is defined by particular artifact types that have particular temporal ranges in their particular regions.

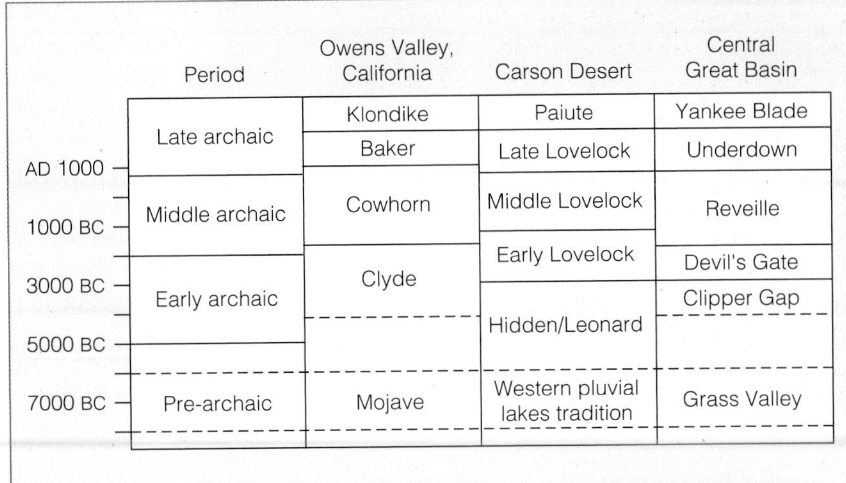

FIGURE 6-10 Time-space systematics: some of the phases used in three regions of the Great Basin, with period names. Dashed lines indicate phase boundaries that are not well dated.

So that's how the temporal boundaries work within the central Great Basin. But where are the geographic "edges" of this chronology? At the town of Austin, in central Nevada? Or 100 miles west at Fallon in the Carson Desert? It's hard to say. Phases are a lot like pieces of a three-dimensional puzzle with fuzzy edges. Neighboring regions do not necessarily have the same phases, because they did not see the same progression of change in material culture.

Constructing phases lets archaeologists synthesize reams of data into (admittedly simplistic) time slices that, in turn, can be compared and contrasted with similar schemes from neighboring areas. They allow us to see, in a rough way, differences and similarities in the spatial and temporal scale of artifact change over time. Because we presume that artifacts reflect behavior, phases are ultimately ways to track spatial and temporal change in human cultural behavior. Phases are the first step toward developing ideas about regional patterns and trends—ideas that can be tested, refined, and expanded.

Phases can last a few generations or thousands of years. This depends in part on the kind of archaeological remains involved and on our contemporary knowledge of those remains. If pottery styles changed rapidly, then we can, with sufficient study of tightly controlled and well-dated stratigraphic excavations, develop short phases using seriation. Chronological control tends to be better for younger material, so young phases tend to be shorter than old phases. One of the phases preceding the 550-year-long Yankee Blade phase is the Reveille phase, from 3300 to 1300 BP—some 2000 years. The Reveille phase is longer simply because the material remains used for its definition (including Elko series projectile points) were used over a longer span of time than the artifacts used to define the Yankee Blade phase (Desert Side-notched points, Cottonwood Triangular points, and pottery). Phases covering the most recent prehistory of the American Southwest may be only 25 to 50 years long.

The phase concept is vague, and deliberately so. Archaeology needs to impose a set of minimal units on time. The phase is that minimal unit. Phases allow archaeologists to provisionally define time, which is actually a continuous variable, as if it were a discrete set of temporally ordered points. When we discuss the Yankee Blade phase, we are treating the time span from 700 to 150 BP as if it were an instant. By definition, two components of the Yankee Blade phase are simultaneous, provided that "simultaneous" is understood to last 550 years.

Keep in mind that phases are always defined *provisionally*. As knowledge of the Yankee Blade phase expands, we may be able to recognize divisions within the phase—for instance, to distinguish an early Yankee Blade component from a late Yankee Blade component. When this happens, the initial phase is divided into *subphases*. This increasing subdivision reflects the amount of research accomplished on each phase and underscores the degree to which our knowledge of the archaeological record is a contemporary phenomenon. This is why we leave the concept of phase vague, so that it can accommodate new findings and help us learn more, rather than place blinders on our ability to see new patterns in prehistory.

assemblage A collection of artifacts of one or several classes of materials (stone tools, ceramics, bones) that comes from a defined context, such as a site, feature, or stratum.

component An archaeological construct consisting of a stratum or set of strata that are presumed to be culturally homogeneous. A set of components from various sites in a region will make up a phase.

RAPID REVIEW

Principles of Archaeological Classification

- Decide what the purpose of the typology is.
- Choose attributes that will achieve this purpose.
- Define the attributes objectively so that they can be replicated by others.
- Construct types that minimize differences within types and maximize differences between types.

Conclusion

We began this chapter with the simple observation that patterning in archaeology falls along three dimensions: space, time, and form (of artifacts). The construction of space-time systematics requires a simplification of the enormous variation in material culture over time and space into some meaningful patterns, and you now appreciate how we go about doing that. But building space-time systematics is not the goal of archaeology; it's the means to an end. Because the goals of archaeology are to reconstruct and explain the past, it's fair to ask how space-time systematics help achieve this goal.

To answer this question, let's look at the case of Shoshone ceramics, which appeared suddenly in many parts of the Desert West about 700 BP and which Shoshone people made until about 150 BP. Shoshone pottery thus implies certain limits: time (700 to 150 BP, the Yankee Blade phase in the central Great Basin) and space (the Desert West).

With its temporal parameters estimated, Shoshone pottery becomes a useful time marker. Sites containing these potsherds in the Desert West can be provisionally assigned to the 700 to 150 BP interval.

But we're not nearly finished. We've just begun because as a time marker, the concept "Shoshone pottery" leaves many questions unanswered. Was this pottery introduced by migrating Shoshone-speaking peoples, or did the idea of pottery simply spread across the Desert West? Did the various peoples of the Desert West independently invent the idea of pottery, or were the vessels traded in from elsewhere?

Each of these is a research question that could inspire years of investigation: Is it possible to document a population movement across the Desert West 700 years ago? If so, where did these newcomers come from? And what happened to the pre-700 BP inhabitants of the Desert West? Are there signs of trading activity or warfare beginning 700 years ago?

Questions like these can pile up without end. Although we cannot reconstruct what happened in the past by looking only at time markers, we don't even know the relevant questions to ask or hypotheses to test until we know something about the when and the where of the past.

And reconstructing *what* happened in the past is itself but one step in the process. As we pointed out in Chapter 1, archaeologists today are equally interested in *why* prehistory took the particular course that it did; we are interested in explaining the past as well as in reconstructing it. The time marker of Shoshone pottery tells us that distinctive potsherds occur in archaeological deposits dating from 700 to 150 BP across the Desert West. But viewed as a time marker, Shoshone pottery tells us nothing about *why* pottery was introduced in 700 BP. For some reason, one segment of the Desert West cultural system changed, and people began manufacturing pottery. This complex issue can be studied only by pursuing related shifts in the lifeway, drawing evidence from the settlement pattern and demography, cultural ecology, social organization, and religion.

Let's just say, for instance, that research eventually leads us to conclude that the pottery was introduced by a migrating Shoshone population. The next question would be: Why did this population migrate in? What gave it the ability to replace the existing (pre-700 BP) population? Did climate change render the pre-700 BP adaptation untenable, thereby enabling the Shoshone to invade the Desert West? Did the ecological adaptation change to make ceramic vessels more efficient after 700 BP? Did population growth drive the migration, or was it warfare, or some environmental calamity?

By definition, we base our time markers on selected aspects of shared culture; time markers deliberately ignore much cultural behavior. Obviously, questions such as diffusion, migration, invention, and adaptation are complex, reflecting changes in the underlying cultural systems. Time markers, grounded only in shared behavior, are patently inadequate for unraveling the mechanics of cultural systems.

In many respects, the space-time systematics of archaeology have been worked out, especially for North American archaeology, and they no longer preoccupy archaeology the way they did in the first half of the twentieth century. Nonetheless, space-time systematics were and are a crucial first step in the archaeological process. Only after documenting temporal and spatial change in selected that we can set about reconstructing what people actually did in the past. In the following chapters, we will discuss how archaeologists go about doing exactly that.

SUMMARY

- What are the principles of archaeological typology?
  - We create groups (based on one or more attributes of form) that minimize the differences within each group and maximize the differences between groups.
  - We construct these groups through an objective, explicit, and replicable process.
  - We recognize that there is no single "correct" typology. A typology's usefulness is judged relative to the question it is used to answer.
- What is the strength of archaeology?
  - Although surrendering some of the detail available to ethnographers, archaeologists can focus on mega-patterns spanning vast reaches of space and time—across continents and millennia.
- What role does typology play in archaeology's strength?
  - Seeking changes across space and time—so-called space-time systematics—archaeologists can find important patterns in the form of material culture. Because this cannot be done by focusing on artifacts individually, archaeologists address "types" of material culture—projectile points, pottery, architecture, and so on—across spans of space and time.
  - By testing morphological types against solidly dated contexts, archaeologists define temporal types, the backbone for building cultural chronologies.
- What are archaeological cultures, site components, and phases?
  - Spatial patterning in material culture defines archaeological cultures, but these are not the same as ethnographic cultures.
  - By seeking out clusters of temporal types, we construct site components, which are culturally homogeneous units within a single site that can be synthesized into phases—archaeological units of cultural homogeneity that are limited in both time and space.
  - Phases are the basic archaeological building blocks for regional synthesis, capturing temporal and spatial similarity in material culture.

Media Resources

Access chapter-specific learning tools including learning objectives, practice quizzes, videos, flash cards, and glossaries, as well as web links, and more in your Archaeology CourseMate. Login to www.cengagebrain.com to access the resources your instructor has assigned and to purchase materials.

Taphonomy, Experimental Archaeology, and Ethnoarchaeology

7

Mikea women pounding maize in southwestern Madagascar (and watching the anthropologists).

Learning Objectives

After reading this chapter, you should be able to answer these questions:

- What is the difference between analogy and middle-level theory?
- What is the principle of uniformitarianism?
- What do taphonomy, experimental archaeology, and ethnoarchaeology study?

Preview

WE HAVE NOW EXPLORED how archaeologists locate and excavate sites, how they date those sites, and how they construct cultural chronologies. Now it is time to move a step up the theoretical ladder and examine the role of middle-level research in modern archaeology.

We have already discussed the various natural and cultural processes that combine to create the archaeological record. Low-level theory enables us to generate data from this record. Now, we can apply theory developed in middle-level research to relate these data to past human behaviors. If you flip back to the model of archaeological inquiry in Figure 2–6 (page 25), you'll recall that archaeologists sometimes put down their trowels, climb out of their trenches, and conduct research designed to give them the tools they need to interpret the data they have generated. That is what this chapter is about.

Here, we concentrate on three areas of middle-level research that we introduced in Chapter 2:

1. Taphonomy studies the role that natural processes play in creating the archaeological record.
2. Experimental archaeology uses controlled experiments to replicate the past under different conditions to look for links between human behavior and its archaeological consequences.
3. Ethnoarchaeology studies living societies to see how behavior is translated into the archaeological record.

Introduction

Archaeologists are often compared to detectives, and this comparison is both appropriate and instructive. Both are concerned with what happened in the past, and both make inferences about the past based on recovered material remains. But, ideally, detectives deal with crime scenes that are found and sealed off as soon as after the crime as possible. Imagine detectives confronted by a crime scene that is several thousand years old, in which nothing organic survives and burrowing rodents have jumbled the evidence. Even Sherlock Holmes would have a hard time making his conclusions stand up in court. Yet this is what archaeologists deal with all the time.

Archaeologists also face the complication that, unlike detectives, they commonly recover objects whose function and meaning are unknown. Imagine if our detectives first had to figure out that the metallic cylinder lying on the floor was a spent cartridge (and not a piece of jewelry, a child's toy, or the ever-popular ritual object). Detectives routinely use "common sense"—knowledge of their own culture, actually—to decide if something "doesn't look right" at a crime scene. Imagine how much more slowly investigations would proceed if those detectives first had to decide if the distribution of furniture in the room—a chair lying on its side, dishes strewn about the floor—was culturally normal or an aberration.

It is important to realize that archaeological sites are contemporary phenomena. Many of you might think that archaeological sites are like Pompeii, the Roman city covered by volcanic ash in AD 79, which seemingly preserved a moment in time (horrific as it was). But the truth is that all sites, even Pompeii, are the complex result of natural and cultural processes that make each site unique. Interpreting archaeological evidence is *never* straightforward because low-level facts cannot explain themselves. Middle-level research aims to provide archaeology with the crucial tools needed to infer behavior from the contemporary archaeological record.

Middle-Level Research: What Is It?

Archaeologists develop such tools by observing behavior and its material correlates simultaneously, yet independent of one another. Archaeological sites contain only material remains. Behavior must be inferred from those remains; it cannot be observed independent of them. So where do archaeologists get the means to make these inferences?

Let's consider how archaeology's sibling discipline, geology, solved this problem. Like the archaeological record, the geological record consists of two things: objects and the relationships among them. A *geological fact* is a contemporary observation a geologist makes on objects from the geological record. How do geologists go from contemporary observations to meaningful inferences of the remote geological past?

Geologists addressed this question in the eighteenth century. James Hutton (1726–1797), a Scottish doctor and farmer, was also a self-taught geologist. He formulated a simple principle that is one of the cornerstones of modern geology. What became known as the **principle of uniformitarianism** asserts that the processes now operating to modify the earth's surface are the same as those that operated in the geological past. It's that simple: Geological processes in the past and the present are assumed to be *identical.* This assumption provides us with a tool to make interpretations.

We know from modern observations, for instance, that as glaciers move, their massive weight leaves *striations*—that is, scratches—on bedrock deposits. They also deposit rock and earth at their fronts and sides, often in distinctive formations called *moraines.* Study of modern geology shows that moraines and striations are formed only through glacial action.

Now suppose a geologist finds moraines and striated rocks in New England, where no glaciers exist today. Armed with knowledge of contemporary glacial processes, a geologist can confidently interpret those features as evidence of past glaciers.

The same logic applies to archaeology. Archaeologists recover the material remains of past human behavior. And, like geologists, archaeologists must also look to the contemporary world to provide them with hypotheses that account for the formation and deposition of these physical remains. This is an important point: Observation of the contemporary world provides the information necessary to infer past human behavior and natural processes from observations on archaeological objects.

Some Bones of Contention

Perhaps you are thinking that, sure, this makes sense—but shouldn't the meaning of remains still be relatively obvious?

Consider a simple problem in the interpretation of animal bones (also known as **faunal** remains) from archaeological sites. As we discuss in Chapter 8, archaeologists study animal bones to learn about past diets, hunting and butchering practices, how animals were domesticated, the season in which the hunt occurred, and other related issues.

Most of these faunal studies begin by considering the relative frequencies of animal bones in a site. When analyzing the bones from Suberde, an 8500-year-old Neolithic village in Turkey, Dexter Perkins and Patricia Daly observed that the upper limb bones of wild oxen were usually missing. Perkins and Daly suggested that the frequencies of the different bones resulted from how people had butchered the oxen. They must have first skinned the animals, then stripped the meat from the forequarters and hindquarters, and then thrown away the defleshed upper limb bones. Perkins and Daly presumed that the meat was piled on the skin and that the lower limb bones were used to drag the hide bearing the meat back home. Calling this the "schlepp effect," they believed their interpretation explained why only lower limb bones were discarded at the habitation site.

Now jump across Europe to England, where R. E. Chaplin analyzed the bones recovered from a late ninth-century Saxon farm. The facts in this case also included a shortage of the limb bones of sheep and cattle, but Chaplin suggested that these bones disappeared because the carcasses were dressed and exported to market.

Across the Atlantic, archaeologists working on American Plains Indian sites also discovered that the upper limb bones of food animals were often missing. Theodore White decided that the bones were destroyed during the manufacture of bone grease. Relying on ethnographies of Plains Indians, White argued that the limb bones were pulverized and boiled to render their grease to make pemmican (a mixture of dried meat, fat, and berries), which was stored for the winter.

We could cite other examples, but the point should be clear: Three different teams made three different inferences from exactly the same archaeological facts—the lack of upper limb bones in habitation sites.

Archaeologists face such problems daily: several competing hypotheses accounting for the same body of facts. And all the hypotheses are reasonable.

Scientific protocol stipulates how to select among the competing hypotheses (for the present, we restrict our attention to the three just described). Each one is a generalized statement about human behavior. But a contemporary archaeologist can never observe a Neolithic villager butchering a wild ox, and none of us will ever watch nineteenth-century American Plains Indians making bone grease. Archaeologists must therefore concentrate on finding the material *consequences* of activities like butchering Neolithic oxen or making bison bone grease.

We do this by constructing a series of logical *if . . . then* statements: *If* bone grease were manufactured from bison bones, *then* we should find artifacts X, Y, and Z and physical residues M, N, and O; bones should be distributed in patterns C, D, and E; and bone elements J, K, and L should be missing. Similarly, to test the second hypothesis, we must generate some *if . . . then* statements regarding the trading of meat and bones. Before we can do that, we need answers to some very specific questions: Which are the best cuts to trade? How far can meat be transported before it spoils? Is meat marketed only in the winter months? Are carcasses butchered in special ways so that certain cuts can be traded? Then we can create arguments like "*If* these carcasses were being dressed for market, *then* we should see marks A and B on bones X and Y, and the site should include features G or H and implements K and L."

These *if . . . then* statements become *bridging arguments*, a concept we first mentioned in Chapter 2, that translate hypotheses into specific expectations that can be tested using archaeological evidence. These bridging arguments are essential to testing ideas with archaeological evidence, and their construction is one of the most difficult things that archaeologists do.

But—we hope you are wondering—how do we know these things? Why do archaeologists surmise that making bone grease requires artifacts X, Y, and Z? And how do we know which bone elements are destroyed in the process? Hypothesis testing is only as robust as these *if... then* bridging arguments. If we generate incorrect implications, then our hypothesis testing will be worse than useless, because it will lead us to specious or erroneous conclusions. For instance, if we assume that the lack of limb bones *always* means that people were rendering grease from bones, we would make a completely incorrect inference if the lack of limb bones in a particular site was really the result of the schlepp effect.

Here is where the notion of middle-level research comes into play. Because the facts cannot speak for themselves, archaeologists must provide bridging arguments that breathe behavioral life into the objects of the past. Properly formulated, middle-level theory links human behavior to empirical data that are archaeologically observable. Although it has been an important aspect of archaeological inquiry for more than a century, Lewis Binford's call for middle-level research served to focus additional attention on this neglected area of archaeology.

To create relevant bridging arguments, archaeologists must observe the workings of a culture in its systemic context, much as geologists defined their processes through observation of the contemporary world—such as streams carrying silt to a delta or the wind blowing sand across dunes. Archaeologists do the same: They study modern analogies to understand the processes that created the archaeological record.

© Robert Kelly

FIGURE 7-1 Looking down into an unroofed kiva at Mesa Verde National Park. Note the square opening for the ventilation shaft (at the top of the photo), the upright stone between the ventilation shaft and the central hearth, and the sipapu—the small hole near the bottom of the photo.

Analogy versus Middle-Level Theory

We used the term "analogy" in the previous paragraph, and you may be asking yourself if there is a difference between analogy and middle-level theory. The answer is that *middle-level theory is a particularly rigorous analogy.*

To see what we mean by this, let's first consider what a simple analogy is. An **analogy** notes similarities between two entities—for example, an archaeological feature and an ethnographic description of a similar feature—and infers from those facts that an *additional* attribute of one (the ethnographic feature) is also true of the other (the archaeological feature). Following Nicholas David (University of Calgary) and Carol Kramer (1943–2002), we can describe a simple analogy as taking the following form:

- An archaeological object is characterized by attributes A, B, C, and D.
- The ethnographic analogy is characterized by A, B, C, and D and has the function or property E.
- Therefore, the archaeological object also has the function or property E.

Archaeologists, for instance, who excavate ancient pueblo ruins in the American Southwest often uncover **kivas** in the settlements. Kivas are religious structures where native peoples of the American Southwest held various rituals. They are usually round and semi-subterranean, with massive log roofs that were covered by dirt. They were entered via a ladder placed in a central opening in the roof that also served as a smokehole.

Many kivas share certain features: an exterior, stone-lined vertical shaft that opens near the kiva floor, a central fireplace, and an upright stone slab (or a small masonry wall) between the fireplace and the shaft's opening. These features (shown in Figure 7-1) are probably functional.

principle of uniformitarianism The principle asserting that the processes now operating to modify the earth's surface are the same processes that operated long ago in the geological past.

faunal In archaeology, animal bones in archaeological sites.

analogy Noting similarities between two entities and inferring from that similarity that an *additional* attribute of one (the ethnographic case) is also true of the other (the archaeological case).

kiva A Pueblo ceremonial structure that is usually round (but may be square or rectangular) and semi-subterranean. They appear in early Pueblo sites and perhaps even in the earlier (pre–AD 700) pithouse villages.

The fireplace provided light and warmth. The shaft provided ventilation, and the upright stone deflected wind blowing down the shaft and prevented smoke and embers from annoying the ritual's participants.

Along the wall opposite the ventilator shaft, archaeologists usually find a very small pit or simply a depression called the **sipapu** (a Hopi term meaning "place of emergence"). Unlike the fireplace, ventilator shaft, and deflector stone, the sipapu has no apparent material function. To interpret this recurrent feature, archaeologists turned to living Pueblo societies, such as the Hopi, who use kivas today for rituals.

Hopi kivas also contain this small, innocuous pit, and its size belies its cultural significance, for the sipapu symbolizes the place where the Hopi emerged from the underworld. In traditional Pueblo theology, the world consists of several levels, and oral histories recount stories of people moving from one level to the next by crawling through a small opening. The current world, the Hopi say, is the fourth world, with more worlds above it. The kiva's sipapu is a reminder of these stories, providing a portal through which the natural and supernatural worlds communicate. Archaeologists infer that sipapus in archaeological kivas had the same function as they do in modern kivas.

Does this inference fit the definition of an analogy? Let's put it into the David and Kramer definition:

- Archaeological kivas are semi-subterranean with entry through the smokehole; they have a central fireplace, a ventilator shaft, a deflector stone, and a small pit opposite the ventilator shaft.
- Hopi kivas are semi-subterranean with entry through the smokehole; they have a central fireplace, a ventilator shaft, a deflector stone, and a small pit (the sipapu) opposite the ventilator shaft. The sipapu represents the hole where the Hopi emerged into the current world; it allows communication between the natural and supernatural worlds.
- Therefore, the sipapus in archaeological kivas also represented the place where ancient peoples say they emerged from a previous underworld, and the sipapus also allowed communication between the natural and supernatural worlds.

This seems straightforward enough, but such analogies must be used cautiously. Why? Because just as we enumerated the similarities between the Hopi and the archaeological kivas, we can also list the *differences* between them: Hopi kivas are often square, not round; they are often placed in open plazas or streets between room blocks, rather than incorporated into blocks of residential rooms as they were at many prehistoric pueblos. We could list the similarities between Hopi and archaeological kivas and stack those up against the differences. But how similar do ethnographic and archaeological cases have to be for the analogy to hold true?

Formal and Relational Analogies

To answer this question, we introduce two kinds of analogy, which Alison Wylie (University of Washington) terms **formal** and **relational analogies**. Formal analogies rely on similarities in form between the archaeological and ethnographic cases, regardless of whether the analogies come from the same culture. For example, we infer that stone projectile points are in fact projectile points because they are so similar to the stone tips found on the projectiles of many ethnographically known peoples the world over. Formal analogies are, of course, strengthened (1) if many ethnographic cases demonstrate the same pattern and (2) if the archaeological and ethnographic cases have many attributes in common. But no rules exist to tell us how *many* ethnographic cases make a strong analogy, or how *many* similarities between the archaeological and ethnographic cases are needed to justify the analogy. We only know that more of each is better.

Relational analogies entail formal similarities, but the archaeological and ethnographic cases are *related* in some fashion. By "related," we mean that they both come from societies with similar settlement systems, economies, or environments—for instance, they may both be desert-adapted hunting-and-gathering societies, or the ethnographic society that serves as an analogy may be a cultural descendant of the archaeological case. In addition, relational analogies may entail "natural" relations—that is, a causal and hence necessary link between the attributes of an object or a feature and their interpretation. We come back to this aspect of relational analogies in a moment.

The kiva example involves elements of both formal and relational analogies because (1) there are formal similarities between the archaeological and Hopi kivas, and (2) modern Hopi culture is clearly related to ancient Puebloan culture. Analogies such as this have been and always will be important to archaeological inference.

But analogy entails certain risks. Suppose you are studying a prehistoric horticultural and pastoral society in the deserts of Kenya. In your site, you've excavated many stone scrapers. You are interested in inferring who used these tools—men or women. As we will see in Chapter 10, inferring the activities of different genders from archaeological data is a difficult task. Analogy is one option for making the inference.

Knowing that analogies are safer the closer they are in time and space to the archaeological case, you look around Africa for a contemporary society that is roughly comparable to the archaeological one—one that lives in a similar environment with a similar economy and a similar culture. Doing so, you encounter the ethnographic research of Steven Brandt (University of Florida) and Kathryn Weedman (University of South Florida) with several Ethiopian peoples. Among these people today are individuals who work cattle skins to manufacture bedding and bags (see Figure 7-2). About a third of those who work hides use stone tools.

© Steven Brandt/Kathryn Weedman

FIGURE 7-2 Sokati Chirayo, a Konso woman in Ethiopia, working a hide with a stone scraper mounted in a wooden handle.

This would seem to have terrific potential for building an analogy, but which Ethiopian group should you use? If you pick the Gamo, you'll find that men do all the hide working and tool manufacture. The Gamo-based analogy would imply that men also did the hide working in your archaeological society. But among the Konso, *women* do virtually all the stone tool manufacture and hide working, so the Konso analogy would obviously lead to a very different conclusion.

Like dynamite and backhoes, analogies are part of the archaeologist's toolkit, but they must be used with caution.

One solution to this problem is to determine the relative strength of the analogy. By increasing the number of formal similarities between an ethnographic and archaeological case, we increase the probability that the formal analogy is correct. Still, though, we wouldn't know if an analogy that relies on ten attributes is twice as good as one that relies on only five. Even the best analogy is no more than a probability—and retains the chance that it could be wrong.

Drawing the analogy from an ethnographic case that is culturally related to the archaeological one improves the analogy, but what if recent events caused cultural discontinuity between the past and the present? And what happens with archaeological cases that have no clear ethnographic referent, such as the 10,000-year-old Folsom site we mentioned in Chapter 4?

Middle-Level Theory as Powerful Analogy

As we noted earlier, relational analogies can rely not just on cultural continuity but also on "natural" relationships, by which Wylie means causal linkages between attributes of a thing and the inference to be made from it.

Analogies based on such casual linkages are considered middle-level theory, a special kind of analogy simply because it *is* theory. As you recall from Chapter 2, theories explain things; they answer *why* questions. Middle-level theory tries to make an analogy more certain by explaining why there is a *necessary* relationship between an object's or feature's attributes and an inference made from those attributes. Relying on the principle of uniformitarianism, middle-level theory attempts to explain *why* an inference should necessarily be true.

This isn't easy. In fact, establishing such *necessary* relationships might be the archaeologist's most difficult chore. Consider the hypothetical example in which the archaeologist wished to know if men or women used stone scrapers. What theory would *necessarily* link some observable attribute of a scraper—such as length, width, thickness, raw material, or context—to the gender of its user? It's hard to imagine.

Absolute certainty will forever elude archaeological inference, but archaeologists have been able to make new and more secure inferences from archaeological remains by constructing their middle-level theories through taphonomy, experimental archaeology, and ethnoarchaeology.

Taphonomy

The word "taphonomy" (from the Greek *tapho*, meaning "death" or "tomb") was coined by the Russian paleontologist I. A. Efremov; it refers to the study of how organisms become part of the fossil record. Archaeologists use the term to refer to the study of how natural processes contribute to the formation of archaeological sites. In Chapter 4, we discussed site formation processes—how

sipapu A Hopi word that loosely translates as "place of emergence." The original sipapu is the place where the Hopi are said to have emerged into this world from the underworld. Sipapus are also small pits in kivas through which communication with the supernatural world takes place.

formal analogies Analogies justified by similarities in the formal attributes of archaeological and ethnographic objects and features.

relational analogies Analogies justified on the basis of close cultural continuity between the archaeological and ethnographic cases or similarity in general cultural form.

© Diane Gifford-Gonzalez, photo by Michael J. Mehlman

FIGURE 7-3 Diane Gifford-Gonzalez collecting data for a taphonomic study in Africa.

human behavior and natural processes affect the creation of the archaeological record. Taphonomy is an important aspect of the study of site formation processes because it considers how human behavior and natural processes incorporate bones and plants into sites.

Taphonomists study some bizarre stuff. One might record how large animal carcasses decompose on an African savanna (see Figure 7-3). How long does it take the carcass to disarticulate? Which bones separate first? Which ones are carried away by carnivores? And how far? Is decomposition in the rainy season the same as in the dry season? Others might examine lion kills and ask what telltale markings lions leave behind. How do these differ from the evidence that human hunters leave behind?

Another might climb to raptor nests along a cliff and collect their feces or vomit (many raptors eat prey whole and then regurgitate the bones and hair). What do rodent bones look like after they have passed through a raptor? Or what do fish bones look like that have passed through a dog? How about through a human? Depending on your perspective, taphonomic research is either gross or really cool.

In archaeology, taphonomy has expanded from paleontology's traditional concern with bones to include plant remains. What are the various ways that seeds, leaves, twigs, and pollen enter archaeological sites? Here you might study the feces of various herbivores, the plant-collecting behavior of pack rats, or the way that wind or water carries leaves, pollen, and sediments.

Recall that taphonomy tries mostly to understand the natural processes that contribute to a site's formation. Although still difficult, it's easier to infer natural processes from artifacts and ecofacts rather than human behavior because natural processes are more mechanistic and hence more predictable than human behavior. This observation is useful to archaeology for two reasons: First, recall that data are *observations* on objects, and that archaeologists seek *patterns* in their data. Therefore, one strategy for understanding an archaeological site is first to *remove all the patterns that are the result of natural processes.* Once we do this, we know that the remaining patterns are the ones that need to be explained in terms of human behavior.

Second, knowing how a site formed is crucial to understanding not just the human behavior that took place there, but also the *environmental context* of that behavior. This information can tell us if the climate was temperate or tropical, if a landscape was eroding away or aggrading, if streams were running or were dry, if forest fires were prevalent, and so on.

Archaeologists use taphonomic research to develop bridging arguments by simultaneously (yet independently) observing natural processes in action and their material results. By trying to explain *why* those natural processes produce the particular material results that they do, you move from simple analogies into middle-level theory. The Hudson-Meng bison **bonebed** provides an example of taphonomic research in archaeology.

Taphonomy at the Hudson-Meng Bison Bonebed

The Hudson-Meng site lies in a low swale in windswept northwest Nebraska, where the remains of at least 500 bison are crowded into an area of about 1000 meters square (see Figure 7-4). Twenty-one spear points (or point fragments) were found among the remains. Accelerator mass spectrometry dates indicate that the site is about 9500 radiocarbon years old.

Paleontologist Larry Agenbroad (Northern Arizona University) was the first to dig at Hudson-Meng, in the 1970s. Using the standard conventions of the day, he inferred human behavior from *patterns* he observed in the faunal remains. One clear pattern was that the tops of the crania were missing. Mandibles were present along with some cranial fragments, but the top of nearly every single skull was missing. Agenbroad knew that modern Plains Indians often broke bison skulls open to remove the brains and use them in tanning hides. Using this as an analogy, he reasoned that the skull tops at Hudson-Meng were missing for the same reason and therefore that humans must have killed the animals.

Agenbroad then made several more inferences. How could people on foot, armed only with spears, have killed 500 bison? People without horses, Agenbroad decided, could not control such a large herd. So he inferred that there

© Lawrence C. Todd

FIGURE 7-4 Students excavating a small portion of the Hudson-Meng site, Nebraska. A weatherport covers this excavation.

must be a low cliff nearby that is now buried beneath the sand that blows daily across western Nebraska. The hunters drove the bison over the cliff and then dragged some 500 of them to a processing area. Calculating that 500 bison could produce nearly 10,000 kilograms of dried meat, Agenbroad further inferred that the ancient hunters were a large group and that they had a sophisticated storage system.

So Agenbroad had made inferences about (1) the presence of humans, (2) hunting strategy, (3) group size, and (4) food storage from patterning—the missing skull tops—evident in the skeletal assemblage. These inferences were based on an analogy with historically known Plains Indians, one that had elements of both formal and relational analogies:

- This was formal analogy because it relied on the similarity in bison skull form (the missing top of the cranium), and similarities between the site and ethnographically documented butchering practices.
- This was relational analogy because it took a known practice of Plains Indians and extrapolated back in time to their ancestors.

But this is not middle-level theory because Agenbroad did not try to explain the character of the skulls he found in light of what might happen to bison crania butchered by known Plains Indian practices. The necessary bridging argument was assumed, not demonstrated. From a taphonomic perspective, modern archaeologists look at the foundation of Agenbroad's inferences—the missing crania—and wonder: Could a natural process create the same pattern?

Hudson-Meng has always presented some troubling facts. For example, comparing it with similar bison kill sites, we might expect something closer to 150 points and point fragments, not just 21. And why are there no cut marks on the bones? In the process of butchering 500 bison, it seems likely that a stone knife would occasionally have cut to bone as it sliced through tendons and meat. Archaeologists have encountered thousands of such telltale nicks at other kill/butchery sites, but only carnivore tooth marks appear on the bones at Hudson-Meng. Finally, many of the skeletal remains are in anatomical position, lying in the ground as if the bison had simply died there and were buried undisturbed. If ancient hunters had butchered these animals, we'd expect them to have removed at least some of the meaty portions of the body, such as the upper rear leg (containing the femur).

Lawrence Todd (retired) and David Rapson (Wyoming State Historic Preservation Office) were bothered by these facts, so they excavated a portion of the Hudson-Meng site using a battery of high-precision excavation techniques. They also applied the perspective of taphonomy, and began by asking this simple question: How do bison fall apart?

For years, taphonomists have studied the carcasses of large animals as they lay decomposing on North America's high plains, Africa's Serengeti, and elsewhere. Some of these animals had been shot; others had frozen to death or simply died of old age. Some were ravaged by carnivores; others were undisturbed. Some died on hillsides; others died in gullies. Some died in the winter or wet season; others in the summer or dry season. Sometimes the hide dried to form an armor-like case, holding the bones together years after death, sometimes the rotting carcass burst from the maggots within. In other words, taphonomists had documented what actually happens to large animal carcasses under a variety of natural circumstances.

Are there any patterns in how these large animal skeletons fall apart? Absolutely. Andrew Hill (Yale University) and Anna Behrensmeyer (Smithsonian Institution) found that the first joint to disarticulate is where the scapula attaches to the vertebral column, allowing the entire front limb to drop away. Then the caudal (tail) vertebrae-to-sacrum joint goes, followed by the scapula-humerus joint, and then the "elbow," where the humerus articulates with the radius and ulna. The last joints to disarticulate tend to be those of the vertebrae. Such documented sequences of natural disarticulation provide a baseline against which to judge the distinctiveness of human butchering practices.

bonebed Archaeological and paleontological sites consisting of the remains of a large number of animals, often of the same species, and often representing a single moment in time—a mass kill or mass death.

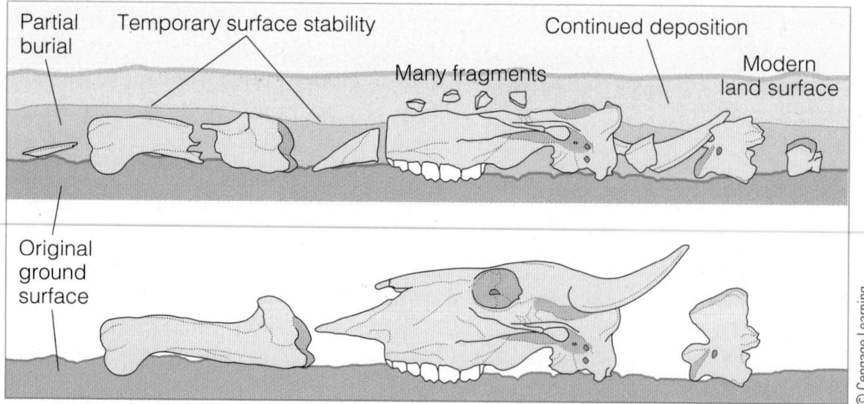

FIGURE 7-5 Todd and Rapson's reconstruction of how taphonomic processes, rather than human butchering, created the pattern of incomplete crania at the Hudson-Meng site. The animal dies and decomposes; as the body collapses into a pile of bone (bottom), it continues to trap sediment until it is mostly buried, although the skull's top remains exposed. The cranium weathers (top), and the small bone fragments that flake off are blown away by the wind.

A decomposing bison carcass will eventually collapse into a flat pile of bones (see Figure 7-5). The skull often ends up resting on its mandibles (the lower jaw). Carnivores may drag some limb bones away and, eventually, the entire skeleton lies flat on the ground—with the skull poking up above all the other bones.

This bone pile effectively becomes a sediment trap, catching blowing dust and sand. It takes 10 to 15 centimeters of sediment to cover the now collapsed limb bones and rib cage, but 30 to 40 centimeters to cover the skull. This means that much of the skull is left sticking up above the ground surface after the rest of the bones are buried. And once leg bones, vertebrae, and ribs are buried—thus covering most of the irregular surface that traps blowing sand—sediment accumulates less quickly, leaving the top of the skull exposed for a longer period of time than the rest of the skeleton.

Then the sun goes to work. Sunlight is quite destructive of bone, and the exposed top of the skull quickly flakes away. Eventually, the top of the skull is destroyed and the rest is buried.

Taphonomy and Uniformitarianism

So the incomplete crania, the basis of Agenbroad's analogy, are readily explained by natural processes, not human behavior. This is more than simple analogy—it is middle-level theory, because we understand *why* bison bones disarticulate, become buried, and weather the way that they do. But this understanding is based on observations of modern animals. Can we trust these observations to explain archaeological remains?

The principle of uniformitarianism applies here, because ancient animals, like the bison that died at Hudson-Meng, had the same anatomy as the animals observed in taphonomic studies. Bison disarticulation is governed by the amount of cartilage and tendons holding bones together and the amount of muscle tissue around them. The more cartilage, tendon, and muscle in a joint, the more resistant the joint is to disarticulation. If skeletal disarticulation is largely a product of anatomy, and if bison anatomy has not changed over the past 10,000 years (and it hasn't), then modern observations are relevant to the interpretation of archaeological data.

Likewise, the effect of sunlight on bone is a product of the nature of bone and the nature of sunlight. And given that neither sunlight nor bone composition has changed over time, we have gone beyond analogy to explain *why* particular natural factors have particular predictable effects on bone.

This is middle-level theory. And the implication is that humans played little role, if any, in the deaths of the 500 bison at Hudson-Meng. But if humans did not dispatch the bison—what happened? Todd and Rapson hypothesize that a summer storm sparked a massive prairie fire that drove the bison herd into the swale for protection (many of the bison lie with their heads to the southeast, which, using analogy with modern bison behavior, suggests that they were responding to a northwest wind). None of the bones are burned, so these animals were not burned to death. But the fire could have jumped the swale and asphyxiated the bison by sucking up all the oxygen for a few critical minutes. This hypothesis remains to be tested.

And what of the 21 projectile points found there? As you have seen in previous chapters, archaeological sites are often reoccupied. In their careful excavations, Todd and Rapson found several thin soils containing a few archaeological remains *above* the bison. In fact, Agenbroad

RAPID REVIEW

Characteristics of Middle-Level Theory

- Middle-level theory creates bridging arguments that link material remains to human behavior or natural processes.
- It uses the structure of analogy, but adds the principle of uniformitarianism.
- The principle of uniformitarianism argues that relationships observed in the present were true of the past because they are inherent to the objects or actions being observed.
- The principle of uniformitarianism is essential to giving middle-level theory its power of inference.

found fewer than ten points *among* the bones. The spear points, then, were probably discarded or lost long after the bison had died, decomposed, and become buried, and a few points moved downward through rodent burrowing and sediment processes into the bonebed.

Experimental Archaeology

Taphonomy uses observations of modern processes to help make inferences from archaeological data. But what if this is impossible? What if we want to know the material effects of behaviors that *no longer exist*? This is especially relevant to human behaviors, because people did things in the past that they no longer do today. Understanding the material remains of these behaviors requires **experimental archaeology**.

How Were Stone Tools Made?

Many prehistoric techniques died with their practitioners, and experimental archaeologists have been forced to rediscover them. Making stone tools is one such technique, and many archaeologists have experimented by manufacturing their own.

To make a stone tool, you must first locate and collect the appropriate raw materials—rocks that break with a glassy fracture such as obsidian, quartzite, or chert. This may require excavating into bedrock, because frost fracturing and sunlight can ruin surface specimens. Some ancient peoples excavated major quarries into bedrock using only fire, wooden wedges, and stone mallets.

If the stone is chert or quartzite, you might improve it by **heat treatment**—burying large **flakes** or small **cores** in about 5 centimeters of sand, and then burning a fire on top for a day or so. Ancient flintknappers learned that they could more easily chip and shape stone treated in this way. The problem is that, over the millennia, plenty has been forgotten about the detailed technology required to make good stone tools from a pile of rocks.

Fortunately, a school of experimentalists—many of them dedicated amateur archaeologists—has rediscovered some of this technology. One of the best known, Don Crabtree (1912–1980) spent a lifetime experimenting with stone tool manufacturing methods. One of his projects was to rediscover the techniques used to fabricate Folsom spear points. Remember from Chapter 4 that Folsom points, such as those found at the Folsom site in New Mexico, date to 12,300 to 12,900 calendar years ago. These exquisite points turn up in many sites on the Great Plains and in the Rocky Mountains where, mounted on spears or darts, they brought down game, including bison. Although the points are often only about 6 to 8 centimeters (2 to 3 inches) long, Crabtree counted more than 150 minute sharpening flakes removed from their surface.

The most distinctive property of Folsom artifacts are the **flutes**—wide, shallow, longitudinal grooves on each face of the point (see Figure 7-6). Flutes are made by removing **channel flakes** from the point's base on both sides. Nobody is sure why these artifacts were thinned in this fashion, but everybody agrees that fluting is an extraordinary feat of flintknapping.

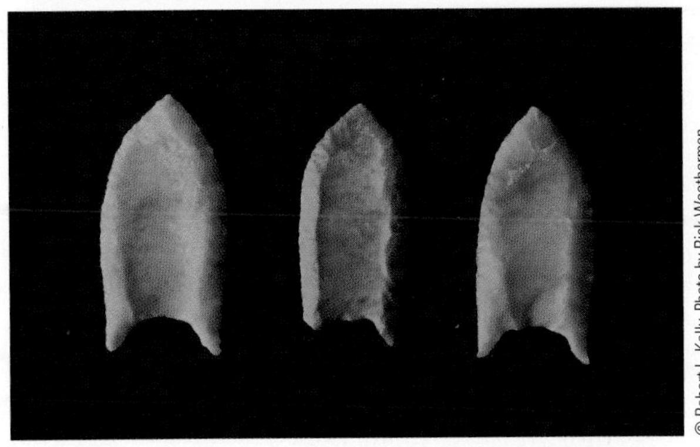

FIGURE 7-6 Folsom-style spear points manufactured by Eugene Gryba. Note the large "fluting" flakes that were removed from the points. Points are about 5 centimeters long.

The technical quality of Folsom points intrigued Crabtree. With enough practice, one can learn to quickly fashion many projectile points. But making Folsom points must have required hours, assuming that one understood how to do it in the first place. And in the twentieth century, nobody did.

Archaeologists have long speculated how ancient peoples removed the channel flakes. And for 40 years, Crabtree tried every way he could think of to manufacture Folsom replicas. He described 11 different methods he had tried to remove channel flakes. Most simply didn't work: Either the method was impossible with primitive tools or the resulting flute was different from those on the Folsom points. One method succeeded only in driving a copper punch through his left hand.

Crabtree eventually concluded that channel flakes could be removed in only two ways. In one experiment, he

experimental archaeology Experiments designed to determine the archaeological correlates of ancient behavior; may overlap with both ethnoarchaeology and taphonomy.

heat treatment A process whereby the flintknapping properties of stone tool raw material are improved by subjecting the material to heat.

flake A thin, sharp sliver of stone removed from a core during the knapping process.

core A piece of stone that is worked ("knapped"). Cores sometimes serve merely as sources for raw materials; they also can serve as functional tools.

flute Distinctive channel on the faces of Folsom and Clovis projectile points formed by removal of one or more flakes from the point's base.

channel flake The longitudinal flake removed from the faces of Folsom and Clovis projectile points to create the flute.

placed an antler shaft, known as a "punch," on the bottom of the unfinished artifact and then struck the punch with a sharp upward blow. Because placement of the antler punch was critical, this technique required two workers. A second technique was based on the seventeenth-century observations of Juan de Torquemada, a Spanish Franciscan friar who traveled through the Central American jungles in 1615. This method used a chest crutch, with padding at one end and an antler tine hafted to the other, to drive flakes off a core. So, Crabtree manufactured one following Torquemada's description. He then tied an unfinished experimental Folsom point into a wood-and-thong vise, which he gripped between his feet. Bracing the crutch against his chest and pressing downward, he successfully detached channel flakes, time after time. The resulting artifacts were almost identical to prehistoric Folsom points.

Crabtree's research unleashed an avalanche of experimentation in the fluting problem. These efforts show that some ten different methods can successfully remove channel flakes and produce the distinctive flutes of Folsom points.

Experimental Archaeology and Uniformitarianism

Archaeologists have used replicative experiments in several ways. Some have experimented with ways of moving enormous blocks of stone, such as the huge statues on Easter Island in the Pacific Ocean. They have experimented with ways to manufacture just about everything that is found in archaeological sites—stone tools, pottery, basketry, metal tools, houses, and so on. Some have even built structures and then burned them down to see how destruction translates into archaeology.

But what do these experiments prove? Researchers found many ways to remove channel flakes from Folsom points, but which method was actually used in Folsom times? Where's the element of uniformitarianism?

Sometimes, a variety of methods will work successfully. Crabtree demonstrated that it was *not impossible* to use a chest crutch to replicate Folsom points. But experiments show that other methods were also possible. None of the experimental flintknappers demonstrated conclusively how Folsom points were *actually made.* Replicative experiments often only demonstrate that a given technique could have been used in the past—that it was *not impossible.*

Determining which method (or methods) Folsom flintknappers actually used requires further research, experiments comparing the characteristics of ancient Folsom points and the waste flakes from their manufacture with experimentally produced Folsom points and waste flakes. Because we know that stone breaks according to certain principles of fracture mechanics, we know that the characteristics of flakes produced today in experiments can help us infer what techniques were used in the past.

But even lacking these findings, experimental archaeology can still teach us something about the past. For example, experimental archaeology has taught us three important things about Folsom spear point manufacture. First, regardless of which technique is used, it's difficult to flute points; it takes years of practice. Second, fluting results in a rather high breakage rate near the end of the manufacturing sequence, regardless of the technique. And third, fluting appears to have no specific function. In fact, after Folsom times, similar but unfluted spear points were made for another thousand years. Presumably, these were as effective as Folsom points.

The uniformitarian element of experimental archaeology often comes in the guise of telling us what *could* or *could not* have happened in the past. Although this may not pinpoint the precise technique that was actually used, it can provide powerful tests of hypotheses.

Here's another example.

Building the Pyramids

Swiss author Erich von Däniken has long argued that aliens from outer space built the world's prehistoric wonders, including the pyramids. Von Däniken looked at those engineering marvels (see Chapter 5) and asked, "How is it possible that a primitive people working with the simplest of tools could have built structures of such astounding size and sophistication?" In fact, he asked, "How could the Egyptians have even moved the large stones and statues without the aid of advanced technology?" His conclusion? They must have had help from extraterrestrial aliens!

Von Däniken's hypothesis can be tested using experimental archaeology: Can stones that weigh several tons be moved using only the tools and materials that the ancient Egyptians had available to them? If not, then perhaps von Däniken's hypothesis has some merit. But if such stones *can* be moved with Egyptian technology, then his hypothesis is undermined.

Had von Däniken done his homework, he would have quickly discovered paintings within tombs that depict men hauling stones and statues. One shows 172 men pulling a statue of Djehutihotep (a Middle Kingdom noble) estimated to weigh some 58 tons (thus, each man is pulling about 650 pounds). The statue rides on a wooden sledge accompanied by a man who pours a liquid onto the runway in front of the sledge—no doubt to ease the workmen's burden.

But does this method really work? Can it haul stone up ramps hundreds of feet long? Maybe the Egyptian tomb painters just made it up.

More than a decade ago, experimental archaeology answered this question. Archaeologist Mark Lehner (Oriental Institute of the University of Chicago and Harvard Semitic Museum) and stonemason Roger Hopkins staged an experiment to see whether they could really move large blocks of stone in this manner. Working with Egyptian quarrymen and masons, they built a pyramid 20 feet high using ancient Egyptian technology. A TV crew from the series *NOVA* filmed the experiment, so Lehner and Hopkins had to complete the pyramid on a tight schedule—3 weeks.

Lehner experimented with several possible techniques to move and lift stone. One entailed the method depicted in Djehutihotep's tomb, but with the loaded sledge resting on wooden rollers. As the sledge was pulled, workmen would pick up the rollers behind the sledge and move them to the front. Although this idea seemed sound, Lehner's experiment showed that, if the rollers were not placed perfectly, the sledge would veer off course. The same error happened if the rollers were not perfectly lathed. Lehner concluded that moving large stones over long distances with this method might have been more trouble than it was worth.

Another idea was using wooden levers to lift the stones up high. In this method, one side of the block is levered up, and planks are placed beneath it. Then the block's opposite side is levered up, and planks are placed below that side. The workers then repeated the process until they raised the stone to the desired height. This idea worked for small rises but, as the block rose higher, levering became difficult and the stone's balance became precarious.

Lehner then turned to ramps. Archaeologists have found remnants of ramps at several Egyptian sites, including the stone quarry beside the Giza Plateau. These ramps consist of two parallel retaining walls, the area between them filled with rubble and topped with a coat of sand or crushed gypsum. In this top layer, the Egyptians set planed logs, perpendicular to the retaining walls, about 50 centimeters apart.

Egyptologists speculate on the kinds of ramps the ancient Egyptians used. Some suggest a straight ramp—although, by the time the pyramid reached its peak, the ramp would have been hundreds of meters long. Other suggestions include ramps that formed a spiral up the sides of the pyramid or multiple ramps built at different levels during construction.

Lehner built his ramp with an incline of about 7 percent. He found that a 2-ton stone, similar to those used in the pyramids, resting on a sledge could easily be hauled up by 20 men. Once the stone was on top of the pyramid, 4 or 5 men using levers could roll it. With this method, Lehner built his pyramid within the 3 weeks allotted for the task.

As in the Folsom fluting experiments, researchers found many ways to build a ramp, and perhaps the Egyptians used all of them. But the precise technique does not matter. The principles involved in simple machines like levers and wedges have not changed from the days of the pharaohs; their capabilities today are the same as they were in the past. This is the important element of uniformitarianism that allows Lehner's experiments to test von Däniken's hypothesis. With no more than dirt ramps, wooden sledges, rope, and plenty of strong backs, the ancient Egyptians were well equipped to move the stones necessary to build their pyramids and temples. Aliens from outer space were not required.

Ethnoarchaeology

What if we want to know about ancient kinship, social, or political organizations that no longer exist? These questions are the sort that archaeology in the 1960s wished to answer; unfortunately, the answers require a type of behavioral inference that archaeologists at the time had no ability to make.

Binford Takes Off for Points North

In the 1960s, the ways to infer social behavior from archaeological remains were little more than simple rules of thumb that were often culturally biased. Archaeologists began to test them through **ethnoarchaeology**, with the understanding that if generalizations cannot cover *contemporary* behavior, then they cannot be used to interpret the evidence of *ancient* behavior.

Binford was concerned with this inferential problem and, to help solve it, he conducted ethnoarchaeological research in the 1970s among the Nunamiut Eskimo of Alaska. Binford's real interest lay in the Middle Paleolithic archaeology of Europe, especially France. Why would he study living Eskimos in Alaska if he were interested in the 200,000-year-old archaeology of France?

Recall from Chapter 6 (see "The Frison Effect") that the French archaeologist François Bordes argued that different stone tool Mousterian assemblages were products of different Neanderthal cultures. These assemblages often alternated throughout the strata of some key French sites, and Bordes argued that this meant that different "tribes" of Neanderthals alternately used the caves.

Binford saw things differently. He suspected that the different assemblages were the by-products of different activities, not different tribes. He argued that Bordes's inference (different tool assemblages = different Neanderthal tribes) needed to be evaluated. But we cannot evaluate an inferential argument using archaeological data, because the systemic context (the behavior) cannot be observed independently of the archaeological data. Binford had to find a place where he could observe living hunting peoples and see what residues their activities left behind. The Nunamiut's Arctic environment was somewhat analogous to the French Middle Paleolithic environment, and the Nunamiut hunted large game (caribou and sheep), as had the Neanderthals. But Binford was not as interested in animal bones or the Nunamiut as he was in evaluating the concepts that archaeologists of the time employed to understand the past.

Binford accompanied Nunamiut hunters on their hunting trips, recording what they did at each locality and

ethnoarchaeology The study of contemporary peoples to determine how human behavior is translated into the archaeological record.

what debris was left behind. In so doing, he demonstrated that the same people—the same individuals, in fact—leave different kinds of tools and bones at different locations on a landscape. What Nunamiut hunters left behind were not just products of their culture, but also of tasks being performed, the season of the year, the distance back to camp, the availability of transportation, the amount of food already in camp, the weather, and other factors. Although culture plays a significant role in determining what kinds of artifacts are left behind, Binford demonstrated that archaeologists couldn't uncritically *assume* that a difference in artifacts reflects *only* a difference in culture. Other hypotheses, such as site function, have to be tested and discarded before inferring that different tool assemblages in a site's strata indicate use of the site by different cultures.

Ethnoarchaeologists have frequently provided such cautionary tales. But ethnoarchaeology can also be a powerful tool for creating middle-level theory. It can do so (1) if it focuses on aspects of ethnographic data that are archaeologically observable, and (2) if it attempts to explain why a relationship between behavior and archaeologically observable remains should necessarily hold true. As we will see, however, the principle of uniformitarianism is harder to implement in ethnoarchaeology than in taphonomy or experimental archaeology. Here we describe one ethnoarchaeological project that author Kelly conducted in Madagascar.

Ethnoarchaeology in Madagascar

Kelly was trained as an archaeologist working in western North America. He was particularly interested in how nomadism factored into people's lives. In some cultures, especially hunting-and-gathering societies, people are highly nomadic, moving as often as every week. In others, especially part-time farming cultures, people change their residence less frequently, perhaps only once or twice a year. Some people return seasonally to a settlement for several years in a row, and some stay year-round in sedentary villages.

Kelly wanted to discern different levels of nomadism archaeologically, so he looked for an ethnographic situation in which he could see variation in nomadism and study its material consequences. He finally learned of the Mikea, a little-known society in the forest of southwestern Madagascar whose people grow maize and manioc, raise cattle, and do some hunting and gathering.

If you know anything about Madagascar, it probably involves lemurs leaping through a tropical forest, but such forests actually make up only a small part of Madagascar. The southwest part of the island, where the Mikea live, is drier and more open. It has distinct wet and dry seasons, and the wet season is blisteringly hot. The forest contains dense vine-covered thickets, stands of 5-meter-high cacti, and baobab trees. There are no rivers in the Mikea Forest and only a few wells. Bordering the forest on one side is the Mozambique Channel and on the other, a vast savanna.

Mikea live in four major kinds of settlements that differ in how long they are occupied (see Figure 7-7). Many have houses in large, permanent villages of 1000 people or more located on the edge of the forest. Here, they grow manioc and other crops and raise cattle, pigs, and chickens. These villages frequently host weekly markets that people attend from many miles around.

Other Mikea live most of the year in forest hamlets, in kin-related groups of about 40 people. Most people who live in these hamlets also maintain a house in the larger villages. Around these forest hamlets are **slash-and-burn** maize fields. As the arable land around the settlement becomes exhausted, the hamlet is moved, about every 3 to 10 years.

Some Mikea who live in the villages also occupy seasonal hamlets in the forest during the growing season so that they can tend to their maize fields. These are much like forest hamlets, but they are generally occupied for a much shorter period of time—only during the growing season.

Finally, Mikea who live in the forest hamlets as well as some who live in the villages move away from their homes and into the forest during the dry season. Here they live in foraging camps of a few families, staying in camp for a week or so. While in these camps, people collect tubers and honey and search tree hollows for estivating hedgehogs.

Mikea Settlements from an Archaeological Perspective

Kelly asked, "Are the different lengths of stay reflected in the material remains left behind at these sites?" To answer this question, he recalled that ethnoarchaeology's first objective is to relate behavior to *archaeologically observable phenomena*. Over time, the only things that might remain of the Mikea settlements are features, such as postholes, hearths, and pits, and scattered trash, such as burnt maize, bone fragments, and broken tools.

Accordingly, Kelly and his associates collected data on houses, features, and the distribution of trash in some 30 settlements; for some, they recorded data over a 3-year period (see "Looking Closer: Doing Ethnoarchaeology in Madagascar"). They also counted the number of posts in houses and measured their diameter—an activity that amused their Mikea hosts (and once sparked an accusation of witchcraft). They mapped the settlements, showed the locations of houses and features, as well as the placement of trash deposits. Through interviews, Mikea reported the history of each settlement, how they were used, why they were abandoned, and other information. What did Kelly find out?

Trash Disposal

Ethnoarchaeologists often begin by observing what people do with their trash. In foraging camps, people unceremoniously toss ash from fires and other trash into bushes, only 1 to 2 meters away from the family hearth. In the forest and seasonal hamlets, trash is disposed in an arc some 3 to 9 meters in front of the house door. Unlike the foraging camps, hamlets

FIGURE 7-7 Mikea habitations. Clockwise from upper left: A family sits around a hearth outside a lean-to in a temporary forest camp; a wattle-and-daub house in a permanent village (note the lack of trash); a house with shade structure in a forest hamlet; and a set of houses lacking shade structures in a seasonal hamlet.

were periodically swept clean. This meant that larger items would end up in the trash arc, whereas smaller pieces missed by the palm-frond broom were trampled into the sand.

As people occupied their hamlets for longer periods of time, they deposited their trash farther away from their house's door. For example, Kelly visited one settlement the year it was established and found that trash was deposited some 3 to 4 meters from houses. A year later, trash was deposited some 8 meters away. Why? Early in a settlement's life, bushes grow near the house, and they are a convenient place to toss trash. Eventually, however, these bushes are destroyed (for firewood, by children playing, and by goats and cattle foraging), and trash is swept into bushes farther from the house. In hamlets occupied for several years, in fact, periodic cleanings create a second trash deposit, this time as a ring around the entire settlement.

The permanent villages exhibit a major change in the disposal of trash. Here one cannot simply sweep trash to the side of one's household, because this would mean sweeping trash into a neighbor's space. Consequently, people throw trash into pits next to the houses (the pits were excavated to make mud for the wattle-and-daub houses), or they collect trash in baskets inside the houses and periodically dump it at the edge of the settlement, as much as 30 or 40 meters away.

By the way, this discussion doesn't imply that Mikea settlements are filthy or reeking of rotting garbage. Much of the trash, in fact, is maize husks and other dry plant material. Any wet garbage—including almost all bones—is eaten by the ever-hungry dogs.

House Posts

After trash, the next things ethnoarchaeologists might notice are the houses. Other ethnoarchaeological studies have found, not surprisingly, that people invest more labor and care in houses that they expect to inhabit for a long time, and the Mikea are no different. But how is that investment reflected archaeologically?

In the villages, Mikea often build wattle-and-daub houses about 10 square meters in size. They first set posts upright in the ground, 75 centimeters deep, and then weave smaller saplings horizontally between these posts. They pack this lattice with coarse mud, smoothing the surface. The house has a door made of planks, usually with a lock, and one or two windows, with wooden shutters. The floors are packed clay. Most of these houses have thatch roofs

slash-and-burn A horticultural method, used frequently in the tropics, in which a section of forest is cut, dried, and then burned. This returns nutrients to the ground and permits the land to be farmed for a limited number of years.

LOOKING CLOSER

Doing Ethnoarchaeology in Madagascar

By Robert Kelly

I conducted ethnographic work in Madagascar with my wife, Lin Poyer, a cultural anthropologist. On our first trip we flew to Washington, D.C., then to Paris, Cairo, Nairobi, and finally to the capital of Madagascar, Antananarivo. The entire trip took nearly 48 hours. After meeting officials and finalizing permits, we flew to the provincial capital of Toliara, where we met our Malagasy colleagues, Jean-François Rabedimy and Jaovola Tombo.

You do archaeology with a trowel and ethnography with a pencil and notebook, but that's just the beginning of the differences. In Madagascar, all educated people speak French, and few speak English. And the Mikea spoke only their dialect of Malagasy. So our daily language was a mixture of French, Malagasy (as we learned the dialect), and English.

There's also no schedule—an ethnographer is always "on the job." One time we arranged to leave "early in the morning." Our guide arrived at 3 a.m., so we got up, packed, and left. Another time, the men in the village, armed with spears, went after cattle rustlers at midnight, and we stayed up all night to learn the result (they got the cattle, but not the rustlers).

We spent several weeks, on and off, living in Mikea hamlets and foraging camps. It was the dry season, and we joined the Mikea in walking many kilometers to the nearest well or digging up *babo* (a wonderful water-engorged tuber) and eating it. Meals were tubers, white rice with a dollop of peanut butter, and the occasional scrawny chicken or dried fish.

The Mikea wanted virtually everything that we owned, especially clothing (which is hard for them to come by). We avoided such dunning by carrying no spare clothing. But we freely handed out tobacco; occasionally offered gifts of food, money, and clothing; and, when possible, provided medical assistance.

The Mikea were curious and a little suspicious about why we were there. They couldn't believe that foreigners would travel so far just to measure house posts, draw maps, and weigh tubers. They were remarkably patient with us.

An ethnographer tries to immerse him- or herself in another culture and to participate in it as much as possible. We witnessed trance dances, spirit possession ceremonies, and a goat sacrifice. Like the Mikea, we traveled on foot or by oxcart, often in the cool of the night. We dug tubers, hunted hedgehogs, ate honey from a hive while bees buzzed about, and slept on the ground around a fire.

Ethnoarchaeology is the best way for archaeologists to learn firsthand how difficult it is to interpret human behavior from static material remains. But even more, it is an extreme growth experience: You learn as much about your own limits and prejudices as you do about another culture.

Kelly (in middle) interviewing a Mikea man.

that extend beyond the walls, forming a narrow veranda around the house. A wattle-and-daub house takes a month or more to build, but if the owner maintains the roof, the house should last 25 years or more.

In the forest hamlets, Mikea have more modest pole-and-thatch houses. About half the size of village houses, they are made of thinner posts not so deeply set and have roofs of baobab bark slabs and walls of bark, grass, or reeds. A cold wind blows nightly in the dry season, so the door is on the north wall, and the south wall is woven tightly. There is a hearth just inside and to one side of the door. Two to three meters outside the door is another hearth, covered by a shade structure, the top of which serves to store dried corn and tools. These forest hamlet houses can be built in a week and need repair every year or so. Some are used for only a year.

The houses in seasonal hamlets look similar to those in forest hamlets, but they appear to a Westerner's eye to be shabbier. They are often shorter and have fewer shade structures outside the front door.

Because foraging camps are used in the dry season and it rarely rains at that time of the year, houses are rare in

TABLE 7-1 Summary of Differences in Mikea Settlements

Settlement Type	House Size	Post Variability	Secondary Posts	Distance to Trash (Meters)	Feature Diversity
Villages	Various, but can be large	Low	Many, closely spaced	10–40+	High
Forest Hamlets	Small	Low-Medium	Fewer, farther apart	4–9	Medium
Seasonal Hamlets	Small	High	Fewer, farther apart	3–4	Medium-low
Foraging Camps	Lean-tos or "boxes," if present at all	N.A.	N.A.	1–2	Low

N.A. = not applicable.

foraging camps; when they are present, they are no more than lean-tos or simple boxlike structures, fashioned from whatever wood is handy, and built in an hour or two.

The amount of labor involved in each of these houses is reflected in a house's roof and walls, but these things disappear. However, the amount of labor is also reflected in the postholes. And these features are familiar to most archaeologists, because they are often all that remain of ancient houses. What can they tell us?

Plenty, and all of it is pretty commonsense. Although wattle-and-daub and reed or grass houses are about the same size, the long wall of village wattle-and-daub houses contained *twice* as many posts as did the same wall in houses in seasonal hamlets. In addition, the posts used in seasonal hamlets had more variable diameters than the posts used in the more permanent settlements—especially the wattle-and-daub houses. In seasonal hamlets, people used whatever wood was handy, often scavenging poles from abandoned houses. Consistency in post diameters reflect the fact that people are more selective about the wood they use when building houses that are more permanent.

Features Outside Houses

Recall from Chapter 2 that features are artifacts that cannot be removed from a site—things like hearths, houses, pits, and postholes. In Mikea settlements, these features include different kinds of houses, fenced compounds, animal corrals, wash areas, cook houses, public troughs, drying racks, stores, wells, ceremonial enclosures, maize threshers, bellows, and storage bins and racks. The particular kinds of features found in a settlement are not so useful to the development of universal middle-level theory. But differences in the *range* of diversity of features among the different settlement types are useful.

Briefly, the more permanent a Mikea settlement, the greater the range of features it contains. When people intend to stay in or seasonally use one place for years, they invest more time in features that have a single purpose, rather than "making do" with temporary facilities. Washhouses, for example, are never found in foraging camps: People are basically "camping" at both, and water is a rare commodity in dry-season forest camps. People bathe back at the forest hamlet or village. Washhouses are also rarely found in forest hamlets—where the small, related community means that people can expect privacy without bothering to build a separate facility. However, washhouses are common in the densely populated villages, where privacy is more difficult, and where investment in a facility is worthwhile.

Table 7-1 summarizes these differences among Mikea settlements. In this table, we related some archaeologically recoverable variables (trash distribution, postholes, features) to human behavior (the length of occupation). Simply by recording the way trash is distributed, the range of features present, the number of postholes per house, and the variation in posthole diameter, we could place a new settlement into one of the four categories with a high degree of accuracy. This fulfills the first criterion of a middle-level study—it focuses on aspects of ethnographic data that are archaeologically observable. But does it explain why the relationship between behavior and archaeologically observable remains is necessarily true? What do such ethnoarchaeological studies do for archaeology?

Ethnoarchaeology and Uniformitarianism

As we have pointed out, middle-level theory tries to *explain* patterning between behavior and material remains. Such explanations depend on the principle of uniformitarianism. It is relatively easy to see how this principle applies in both taphonomy and experimental archaeology, because both study natural processes and mechanical relationships.

But the principle of uniformitarianism is tougher to apply in ethnoarchaeology, because human behavior is anything but mechanical. We conducted our study of the Mikea within the materialist paradigm (explained in Chapter 2); more specifically, it relied upon a theoretical framework known as "human behavioral ecology." One of the tenets of this framework is that because people have many demands on their time, they make choices that maximize the utility of their decisions. Choices about what kind of house to build reflect this fact. Why would someone in a forest hamlet invest more than a month in building a wattle-and-daub house when a pole-and-thatch one built in less than a week would suffice for the time that the hamlet would be occupied? The "extra" three or four weeks can be used for clearing another maize field, building a ceremonial enclosure, or some other important task. Indeed, the Mikea themselves said that the longer they intended to remain in a settlement, the more care they put into constructing houses and facilities such as maize-threshing bins and outhouses. They also said they would be more selective in their building material, choosing poles of a particular diameter for posts and even searching out certain species of wood, such as ones known for their ability to resist destruction by insects.

These seem like logical choices, and several ethnoarchaeological studies have found similar patterns in trash disposal, house form, and feature diversity in other societies in the world. Combined with these other studies, the Mikea research helps form a strong formal analogy; combined with the theoretical framework of human behavioral ecology, it also contains elements that make it middle-level theory.

But the issue of culture can make ethnographic analogies, even ones strong enough to qualify as middle-level theory, problematic. We have discussed, for instance, the disposal of trash among the Mikea as being simply a function of how long a settlement is occupied. The longer it is occupied, the farther away from a house trash is removed. But cultural ideas about trash may come into play.

Ian Hodder, a postprocessual archaeologist, conducted ethnoarchaeological research with the Moro and Mesakin in Sudan. Both groups raise various grains, as well as pigs, cattle, and goats. In both, families live in household compounds. But the Moro's compounds are relatively free of trash, whereas the Mesakin's are messier; in particular, the Moro keep pig bones out of the compounds.

Hodder argues that some of the difference between the two societies and the way they deal with trash lies in different ideas about women. Moro men see contact with women as potentially "polluting" their strength and authority. Because Moro women take care of pigs, they are associated with these animals; men are associated with cattle. As a result, Moro men consider pig remains to be foul, and Moro women take care to remove pig bones from the trash and dispose of them separately. The Mesakin do not share the Moro's beliefs about women, and they treat pig bones the same as any other animal remains. Thus, Hodder argues, archaeologists need to consider the symbolic meanings of material culture to appreciate how it will be treated as trash.

But the "cultural" component is very difficult to study archaeologically. And this means that the principle of uniformitarianism remains difficult to implement in ethnoarchaeology. For some archaeologists, this means that ethnoarchaeology can provide us only with strong analogies, not middle-level theory.

For others, ethnoarchaeological studies conducted across a spectrum of societies provide archaeology with analogies that, taken together, suggest some important principles of human behavior. These principles could *provisionally* be taken as uniform for the purpose of creating and testing hypotheses; this approach can permit ethnoarchaeology to act as middle-level theory to support archaeological inferences.

Conclusion

Archaeology is all about making inferences from artifacts, ecofacts, features, and their contexts. Middle-level theory is what allows archaeologists to know that they really do know something about the past. It lies at the heart of archaeology, because archaeology is the study of the past based on material remains. As you have seen in this chapter, archaeologists go about constructing all-important middle-level theory through taphonomy, experimental archaeology, and ethnoarchaeology. It requires that archaeologists step out of their excavation trenches and conduct a different kind of research. Some archaeologists, in fact, have permanently hung up their trowels and devoted their careers to the development of middle-level theory. And this is good, because without middle-level theory, our inferences from archaeology would be little more than just-so stories, with no more credence behind them than silly ideas like aliens building pyramids. In the following chapters, we see how archaeologists have put studies in taphonomy, experimental archaeology, and ethnoarchaeology to use in reconstructing the past.

Summary

- What is the difference between analogy and middle-level theory?
  - Analogy and middle-level theory both seek to make inferences about human behavior from archaeological remains.
  - Analogy is one way to reconstruct the past but is limited to societies that have very close geographic and cultural counterparts (preferably ones with a historical connection) or to fairly low-level inferences. The greater the number of similarities, the greater the probability that the analogy is correct.
  - Middle-level theory uses modern data from taphonomy, experimental archaeology, and ethnoarchaeology to explain why particular natural processes or human behaviors can be inferred from

particular material remains. Middle-level theory relies on the principle of uniformitarianism.

- What is the principle of uniformitarianism?
  - The "facts" of archaeology are incapable of speaking for themselves; therefore, archaeology follows geology's principle of uniformitarianism, studying ongoing processes and their material consequences to develop ways of making inferences from archaeological data.
  - The principle of uniformitarianism does not assume that the past and the present are the same; it does assume that the processes of the past and the present are the same. This is why we can use modern observations, such as the material effect of sunlight on bone, or the relationship between house posts and house permanence, to help us interpret the archaeological record.
- What do taphonomy, experimental archaeology, and ethnoarchaeology study?
  - Taphonomy studies the natural processes that help produce archaeological sites.
  - Experimental archaeology re-creates behaviors that no longer exist today, such as stone tool manufacture, or replicates behaviors, events, or processes that need controlled observation.
  - Ethnoarchaeology studies living peoples to see how human behavior is translated into material remains.

Media Resources

CourseMate

Access chapter-specific learning tools including learning objectives, practice quizzes, videos, flash cards, and glossaries, as well as web links, and more in your Archaeology CourseMate. Login to www.cengagebrain.com to access the resources your instructor has assigned and to purchase materials.

People, Plants, and Animals in the Past

8

The remains of a partially butchered bison at the Agate Basin site, Wyoming.

Learning Objectives

After reading this chapter, you should be able to answer these questions:

- What does a zooarchaeological study involve?
- How do animal bones and plants help establish a site's season of occupation?
- How do plants help to reconstruct ancient diets?
- How can pollen help reconstruct past environments?

Preview

ARCHAEOLOGISTS HAVE PLENTY of methods and techniques for reconstructing how people made a living in the past; in this chapter, we discuss a few of them. We begin with faunal analysis, the identification and interpretation of animal remains recovered in an archaeological context. Animal bones not only enable archaeologists to study ancient hunting methods and diet, but they also assist in reconstructing past environments. Of course, getting at the meaning behind the bones is neither easy nor straightforward. This chapter provides you with the basics for understanding what we can do with a bunch of animal bones.

Plant remains are also valuable to archaeology. We have already seen how the study of tree rings provides archaeologists with a trustworthy way of dating specific events of the past—when a certain Pueblo dwelling was built, for example. We learned also that tree-ring analysis indicates something about past climates, environments, and the local history of forest fires. Archaeological plant remains—pollen, seeds, charcoal, and phytoliths—also tell us about what wild plants people collected, the crops they grew, the fuels they burned, and even the roles plants played in rituals. Plant and animal remains can also tell us in what season of the year people occupied a site.

Introduction

So far, we have talked mostly about artifacts and features—objects humans created. Archaeological sites also contain ecofacts—plant and animal remains. Some of these are food refuse left by humans, but sometimes ecofacts enter sites through natural processes (as when plants and animals die on a site). As you recall, taphonomic studies figure out how plant and animal remains accumulate in archaeological sites. In this chapter, we are more concerned with what plant parts and animal bones tell us about human behavior.

Archaeologists use many methods to recover and interpret animal and plant remains—so many, in fact, that we can present only a few here. Rather than blanket the field, we introduce some of the major categories of data and provide a sense of how archaeologists go about interpreting them. We begin with the skeletal remains of animals.

Studying Animal Remains from Archaeological Sites

A **faunal assemblage** consists of the animal bones recovered from an archaeological site. Faunal assemblages differ from paleontological assemblages because humans *may* have had a hand in their formation. We find animal bones at **kill sites**, where bones may lie more or less the way they were when the hunters left, affected by carnivore scavenging, weathering, and other natural processes. We also find them in camps, villages, and larger settlements where people butchered game and/or domesticated animals. Sometimes a site might contain tens of thousands of bones, including those of animals killed on site, some transported from kill sites elsewhere, and many noncultural remains—bones of animals that simply died in the site or that carnivores or raptors brought in after people abandoned a camp.

After recovering a faunal assemblage, a **zooarchaeologist** commonly performs a **faunal analysis**, studying and interpreting the animal remains. To show you how this is done, let's look at how one zooarchaeologist analyzed the faunal assemblage of the Folsom component at Wyoming's Agate Basin site.

The Agate Basin Site

Sometime around 1916, rancher William Spencer was riding across the broken terrain of his ranch in eastern Wyoming. Visiting a spring, he noticed some large bones protruding from the edge of an arroyo (just as George McJunkin did at the Folsom site in New Mexico). His curiosity piqued, he returned to the spring several times, eventually collecting a number of large, beautiful spear points as well as bison bones from the site.

Years later, after more bison bones and spear points had turned up, Frank H. H. Roberts (deceased) started excavating

faunal assemblage The animal remains recovered from an archaeological site.

kill sites Places where animals were killed in the past.

zooarchaeologist (*also faunal analyst*) An individual who studies the faunal (*animal*) remains recovered from archaeological sites.

faunal analysis Identification and interpretation of animal remains from an archaeological site.

WHAT DOES IT MEAN TO me?

Zooarchaeology and Biological Conservation

By Virginia Butler

Virginia Butler is professor of anthropology at Portland State University.

Habitats and species around the world are being lost with increasing speed in the face of human population growth and habitat destruction. Under legislation such as the Endangered Species Act (1973), recovery plans are being developed to save or reestablish species and environments. Drawing from recent records, decisions are made on which species should be targeted for recovery, and which should be disregarded. In stark terms, these decisions determine which organisms "belong on the ark." But with access to faunal records dating back hundreds and thousands of years, zooarchaeology brings a much-needed historical perspective to wildlife management policy.

Zooarchaeological research demonstrates the ways past human predation and landscape alteration affected animal populations, and this has important implications for wildlife management. Environments that early European explorers encountered were not free of human influence—they were occupied by Native Americans. Contemporary policy that creates preserves without considering past human actions is trying to re-create environments that never existed. Management of wapiti (elk) in Yellowstone National Park provides a case in point. In the 1990s, more than 60,000 wapiti lived in the greater Yellowstone area, yet wapiti remains are rare in archaeological sites. The rarity of wapiti remains suggests that humans kept this animal's populations low through hunting. Charles Kay (Utah State University) argues that this means the "hands off" management policy in Yellowstone, which allows wapiti populations to increase unchecked, does not duplicate pre–AD 1900 conditions, and has led to serious overgrazing of the park.

My own research in California's Owens Valley helps us understand the effects of habitat loss and exotic (introduced) species on the loss of native fish species in the American West. The Owens Valley contains four indigenous species of fish—pupfish, chub, a minnow, and the Owens sucker—the first three of which are in severe decline. Analyzing an 8000-year zooarchaeological record, Michael Delacorte (California State University, Sacramento) and I found that both the size and abundance of the different species changed over time in response to changes in climate that affected the size of the valley's lakes. But none of them was in danger of extinction. The only thing that changed in the last 100 years was the introduction of exotic species, predatory fish against which the indigenous species cannot compete. With this information, managers can make informed decisions about how to save the indigenous species from extinction.

Zooarchaeological research is aiding conservation measures in many other ways. For example, when wildlife biologists reestablish a species, they try to do so with animals from a source population that is closely related to the original native stock. Because new techniques allow genetic data to be extracted from skeletal remains, genetic analysis of zooarchaeological remains can provide the genetic signature of the locally extinct native stock. In Oregon, for example, biologists wanting to reintroduce the sea otter turned to archaeological remains to determine whether Alaskan or southern California sea otters were a closer genetic match to the population that formerly inhabited Oregon's waters.

Through these and other approaches, zooarchaeology promises to help us understand long-term animal population dynamics so we can take the necessary steps to stop the loss of species diversity and conserve environments for future generations to enjoy.

at the "Agate Basin site." Eventually, William Bass (then at the University of Kansas), George Frison (University of Wyoming), and Dennis Stanford (Smithsonian Institution) all excavated there. And more recently, Matt Hill (Iowa State University) took a close look at the bison and antelope faunal assemblage contained in the site's Folsom component.

Let's begin with Hill's conclusions. About 10,780 radiocarbon years ago, a small group of Folsom hunters camped at the Agate Basin site in late March or early April. They killed at least 11 bison (*Bison antiquus*) and 5 pronghorn antelope (*Antilocapra americana*), probably not too far from their camp. They partially butchered the bison at the kill site and, for the most part, brought entire limbs back to camp. They field-dressed the antelope at the kill site and brought the nearly intact carcasses back to the camp. Despite their success, the hunters may have had a hard time making ends meet; unlike later hunter-gatherers on the Plains, these Folsom hunters seem not to have relied heavily on meat storage.

How did Hill extract all this information from a bunch of broken bones?

Identifying Bones

Hill first identified bones from the Folsom component, working through the cataloged collection, piece by piece, and assigning each bone or bone fragment to a species, if possible.

"Identifying the bones" is more complicated than it might sound. Field archaeologists know, at least in a rough way, what mammal, bird, reptile, and fish bones look like, but far more detailed information is needed in faunal analysis.

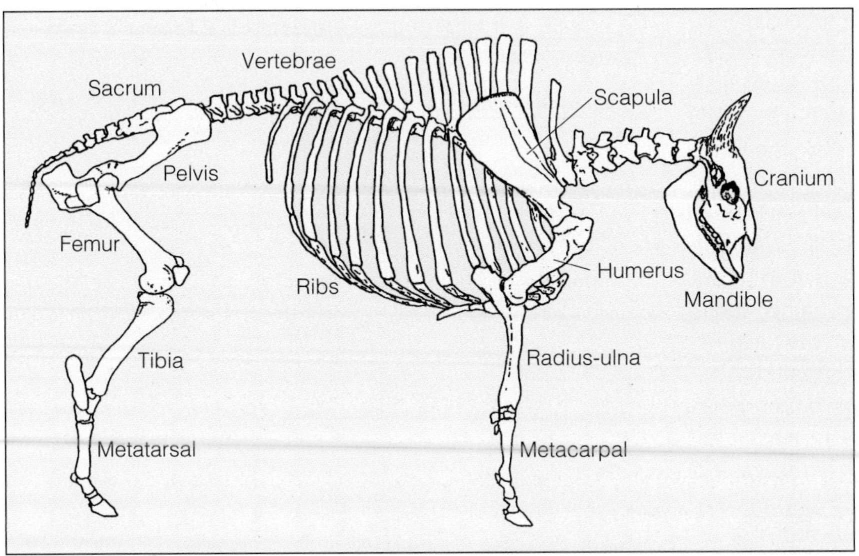

FIGURE 8-1 Bison skeleton showing major elements.

The first step is to assign each specimen to **element** (the anatomical part of the body). Is this bone a rib splinter, part of the pelvis, or a skull fragment? A femur, tibia, or calcaneus (the heel bone)? Identifying elements requires a solid working knowledge of comparative anatomy (see Figure 8-1).

But conventional comparative anatomy classes are insufficient because they deal with whole bones—not the dirty fragments that archaeologists confront. Classroom experience helps, but you really learn faunal analysis by handling a lot of bones yourself.

The next step is to identify the specimens to **taxon** (kind of animal). Success here depends on the condition of the specimen and the expertise of the analyst. The aim is to identify each bone to species, but sometimes the bones are so fragmentary that you can only identify them to higher-order groups, such as family or class. One can rarely determine, for instance, whether a long bone fragment (that is, a small piece of one of the limb bones, such as a femur shaft) came from a deer or a bighorn sheep—but anyone can see that it's not a mouse bone. In this case, the analyst might only be able to identify the fragment to the order Artiodactyla (because deer and sheep are in different families, the next broader level of classification is used). Identification to taxon, therefore, often means "narrowing down the possibilities," rather than identifying the exact species—although that is always preferred.

Sometimes, a specimen might be so difficult to identify that you can only assign it to one of five standard animal **size classes**. Rodent- and rabbit-size animals are in size class 1; wolf- and pronghorn antelope–size animals are in class 2; animals the size of mule deer and bighorn sheep are in class 3; bison- and elk-size animals are in class 4; and in class 5 are large animals such as giraffes, hippos, and elephants.

So, how did Hill know whether a scrap of bone was a piece of a bison femur, a pronghorn radius, a flat-headed peccary tibia, or a striped skunk skull? Zooarchaeologists make these identifications through a **comparative collection**. The standard zooarchaeology lab commonly contains box after box of modern animal skeletons—everything from elephants to deer mice. Each box is labeled with the species, the individual's approximate age at death, its sex, and where and when it was collected. A comparative collection contains examples of young and old, as well as male and female, members of a species. These collections are put together by hunting or trapping the animals, picking up road kills (you need a license to do these things in most states), or acquiring carcasses from a state fish and game office (sometimes confiscated from poachers).

This is stinky business because once collected the specimens must be defleshed and cleaned. Sometimes the remains are buried and nature is allowed to take its course. Other methods include simmering the bones in a solution of detergent or placing the greasy bones in a colony of dermestid beetles, which, over a few weeks' time, will literally pick the bones clean of all tissue.

Using a comparative collection, Hill identified the archaeological bones to taxon. Measurements taken on some adult bones helped determine if the bone was from a male or female.

Hill eventually assigned all the Agate Basin bones to element and taxon (or size class). Most bones were bison or pronghorn; other species included wolf, striped skunk, and frog. But because there were only a few bones from most of these species, Hill focused on the bison and pronghorn.

Natural or Cultural?

Recalling the discussion of taphonomy in Chapter 7, you might be wondering how Hill could be certain (1) that the bison and pronghorn remains were deposited by humans and (2) that they were deposited during the same occupation of the site.

element In faunal analysis, a specific skeletal part of the body—for example, humerus or sternum.

taxon In faunal analysis, the classification of a skeletal element to a taxonomic category—species, genus, family, or order.

size classes A categorization of faunal remains, not to taxon, but to one of five categories based on body size.

comparative collection A skeletal collection of modern fauna of both sexes and different ages used to make identifications of archaeofaunas.

For one thing, the bones bore some stone tool cut marks (which we know how to distinguish from carnivore tooth marks), some were burned, and some of the larger ones had impact fractures—distinctive breaks that resulted when the Folsom people smashed the bones open to retrieve the fatty, calorie-rich marrow. Frison and Stanford also found a cluster of antelope bones, some of them burned, around a hearth.

A few of the bones did show evidence of carnivore gnawing. But tooth marks appeared on only a few bison humeri and femora, and on only three antelope specimens. So, the evidence pointed to humans as the agents responsible for the antelope and bison bones at Agate Basin.

Hill also thinks that the antelope and bison bones were deposited during the same occupation of the site. The Folsom assemblage is not large, nor is it widely dispersed; some of the remains, in fact, still lie in anatomical position. This is what we would expect to see in a one-shot use of the site. Also, we might expect all the bones to be equally weathered, just as we saw at the Hudson-Meng site in Chapter 7—an "instantaneous" herd death, where nearly all the skulls were weathered in the same way.

To reach this conclusion, Hill took bone size into account. Because antelope bones are smaller than bison bones, they are more easily broken (by carnivores and also by hunters, who broke the bones for their marrow). And also, because they're smaller, sediment will cover antelope bones more quickly than the larger bison bones. So, even if all the faunal remains were deposited at about the same time, the bison bones should be slightly more weathered than the antelope bones. This was the case at Agate Basin, and Hill concluded that the bison and antelope bones in the Folsom component were animals killed by the same people during the same occupation.

TABLE 8-1 NISP Counts for the Folsom Component at the Agate Basin Site

Common Name	Scientific Name	NISP
Bison	*Bison antiquus*	1033
Pronghorn antelope	*Antilocapra americana*	297
Wolf	*Canis lupus*	7
Coyote	*Canis latrans*	3
Red fox	*Vulpes vulpes*	1
Striped skunk	*Mephitis mephitis*	1
Flat-headed peccary	*Platygonus compressus*	1
Dog	*Canis* sp. (possibly domestication)	5
Jackrabbit	*Lepus* cf. *townsendii* or *californicus*	10
Rabbit	*Sylvilagus* cf. *mutallii* or *audubonii*	4
Grouse	*Centrocercus urophasianus*	2
Frog	*Rana pipiens*	Few
Elk	*Cervus elaphus* (antler only)	2
Camel	*Camelops* sp. (possible tool)	1

Source: Hill (2001). The "sp." in some scientific names means that although the genus is certain, the species is not. The "cf." in other cases means that the specimen compares very well with one or two species within a genus, but that the researcher is not certain of the identification. Camel became extinct about 11,200 radiocarbon years ago, and there is no good evidence that humans ever hunted them; the specimen here might be a piece that a Folsom hunter picked up someplace.

What To Count?

To reconstruct human behavior at Agate Basin, Hill needed to search for meaningful patterns in the bone data, and this required that he count the bones.

Zooarchaeologists count bones in two ways, depending on their objective. One method involves the **number of identified specimens**, or **NISP**. This count is simply the total number of bone specimens that are identified to a particular taxon. Table 8-1 shows the NISP for the Folsom component at the Agate Basin site. NISP is useful for comparing large numbers of collections from different sites, but it has a severe limitation in reconstructing human behavior at a single site.

Table 8-1 suggests that bison were more important than pronghorn at Agate Basin. But what if the 1033 bison specimens came from a single highly fragmented skeleton, whereas the 297 antelope bones came from 297 different individuals? If so, then antelope would be many times more important than bison.

Problems like this have led archaeologists to another way of counting bones, called the **minimum number of individuals**, or **MNI**. Developed by paleontologists, MNI is the *minimum* number of individuals that are necessary to account for all the skeletal elements of a particular species found in the site. Suppose, for instance, that you excavated 100 fragments of bison bone from a site. The NISP equals 100, but what is the MNI? That is, what is the minimum number of individual bison required to account for those 100 bone fragments?

To figure this out, you must tabulate bone frequency by element (left femur, right tibia, hyoid, and so on) to determine the most *abundant* skeletal element. This process requires that you not only assign the specimens to their correct *element*, but also to their correct *side* for those bones that come in pairs. If four right femurs show up in the 100 bone fragments, then you know that *at least* four bison account for the fragments.

MNI has some limitations as well. When bones are fragmented, it is possible that the "four right femurs" are really fragments from the same upper leg bone. To eliminate this possibility, you must compare the bone fragments, one by one, to see whether two fragments could have come from the same bone. In our hypothetical example, if we found that two of the four right femur fragments could have come from the same femur, then the MNI would only be three.

Calculating MNI also depends on how you divide your site. Agate Basin was probably occupied only once by Folsom hunters for a few weeks. But what if the assemblage is the result of many different occupations, covering decades or even longer? In that case, we could compute the minimum number of individuals, but this might have the unfortunate consequence of reducing hundreds of bone fragments to a possibly misleadingly very few MNI. Ultimately, the decision depends on the site's specific characteristics. In general, MNI is most useful and accurate when fine stratigraphic divisions are used and when bones are not overly fragmented. The Folsom component at Agate Basin meets these criteria.

Where did Hill go from here? Of the 1033 bison bones, Hill could identify 843 to element; likewise, he could identify 198 of the 297 antelope bone fragments. Although the antelope specimens were fragmented, Hill identified one left and four right humeri (upper arm bones). This might suggest an MNI of four (given that the single left humerus could be a match to one of the right humeri). But the single left humerus was not the same size as any of the right humeri, so Hill concluded that *at least* five antelope were brought to the site.

Because they are larger and heavier, the bison bones were more intact. Taking the humeri, radii, femora, and tibiae, Hill assigned each to a side and then decided, using a comparative collection, whether they were male or female (or indeterminate; young animals don't exhibit characteristics that allow assigning to a sex). He then compared their sizes to see if the rights and lefts of each sex could possibly have come from the same animal, or whether the femora and tibiae, and the humeri and radii could *anatomically refit* (that is, would they fit together in their usual anatomical positions; femora and tibiae, for example, articulate at the patella, the knee cap). If they did refit, then they could have come from the same animal (see Figure 8-2).

From this comparison, Hill determined that there were *at least* four males, four females, and three immature bison brought to the site.

So now we know the minimum number of animals that Folsom hunters killed at the Agate Basin site: 11 bison and 5 pronghorn antelope.

Reconstructing Human Behavior at Agate Basin

By looking at which specific elements were present, Hill found that elements of the **axial skeleton** (the head, mandibles, vertebrae, ribs, sacrum, tail) for both bison and pronghorn were rare compared with bones from the **appendicular skeleton** (everything else). Bison limb bones were more common than other bison bones, but antelope lower leg bones (especially for the front legs) and toes were rare.

What accounts for these patterns? Viewed as food, bones function two ways: as a support for meat and as a container of marrow. Experimental research can quantify how much food value a bone represents in terms of these two entities. Bison long bones, for instance, rank high in both meat and marrow content, suggesting that hunters brought back only the high-utility portions of the bison and left the axial skeleton at the kill site.

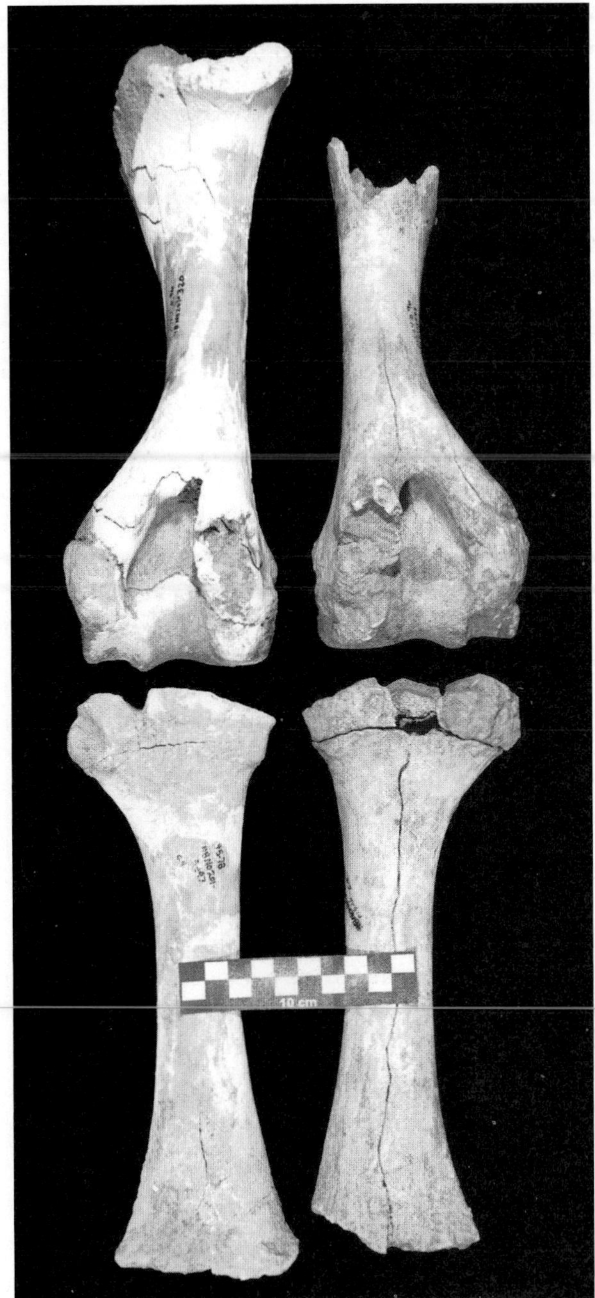

FIGURE 8-2 Anatomically refit calf bison humeri (top) and radii (bottom). Carnivore gnawing has removed the proximal (upper) end of the humerus on the right.

number of identified specimens (NISP) The raw number of identified bones (specimens) per species; a largely outmoded way of comparing archaeological bone frequencies.

minimum number of individuals (MNI) The smallest number of individuals necessary to account for all identified bones.

axial skeleton The head, mandibles, vertebrae, ribs, sacrum, and tail of an animal skeleton.

appendicular skeleton All parts of an animal excluding the axial skeleton.

The pronghorn skeletons at the Agate Basin site were more complete than the bison skeletons. Apparently, the antelope were gutted and field-dressed by removing the feet and lower limb bones, which contain little marrow and have little meat wrapped about them. The hunters then carried the more or less complete carcasses back to camp. The ribs and vertebrae may have been crushed for bone grease or eaten by dogs and carnivores, as suggested by taphonomic research.

Ethnoarchaeological studies suggest some other possibilities. Hunters consider several factors when deciding which parts of an animal to transport home: the distance back to camp, the number of hunters present, weather, terrain, and food needs of the household. If the animal is killed near camp, women and children might come out to help carry the entire carcass of a large animal back. If so, then the entire skeleton might end up in the camp rather than at the kill site. If an animal is killed far from camp, the hunters might eat some of it immediately and then butcher the animal, bringing only meat and a very few bones back to camp. In this case, most of the skeleton would remain at the kill site.

Based on these ethnoarchaeological observations, Hill suggested that the Agate Basin hunters killed the animals individually, relatively close to camp. The smaller antelope were carried back with minimal field butchery. However, because the bison could not be carried whole, it is likely that the Agate Basin hunters (and perhaps their wives and children) ate some of the meat attached to the vertebrae and ribs at the kill site and then transported the legs—with their large meat packages and high marrow content—to camp, using the lower limbs as convenient handles.

What Do Broken Toes Mean?

Although relatively rare, some bison metapodials (portions of the foot) at Agate Basin, as well as bison and antelope phalanges (toe bones) were broken open, presumably to extract the marrow. But foot bones contain little marrow, and there is no meat attached to them. Why did the hunters bother with toes, when they apparently had bison haunches and antelope tenderloin roasting on the fire?

Hill interprets the foot bones as evidence that, despite the 11 bison and 5 antelope, the Agate Basin Folsom hunters were experiencing some hard times. From paleoclimatic data, we know that the average annual temperature was much colder during Folsom times. Perhaps late winter or early spring storms—which can strike with a vengeance on the high plains—made that day's hunt impossible. Or perhaps the meat stored in camp was frozen, leaving the camp's inhabitants with no choice but to extract marrow from low-utility elements, such as metapodials and phalanges.

Hill also concluded that these Folsom hunters were living more hand to mouth than did later hunter-gatherers on the high plains. The late winter and early spring is a tough season for hunter-gatherers, because game animals are lean (and lean meat is difficult to digest) and plants are not yet ripe. Many foragers survive the spring by relying on food stored from a previous fall hunt. But these Folsom hunters probably lacked stored food, because they were hunting on a weekly or even daily basis during the spring that they occupied the site.

This interpretation depends on knowing that the Folsom hunters camped at Agate Basin in the spring. How did Hill know this?

In What Season Was Agate Basin Occupied?

Recall from the discussion of seasonal rounds in Chapter 3 that hunter-gatherers do not spend the entire year in a single camp or village. Folsom hunters moved across the landscape; so did the nineteenth-century Shoshone in Nevada, and so do Mikea forager-horticulturalists. To understand what life was like in the past, we must pay attention to **seasonality**, the time of year that a site was used.

Hill determined the seasonality of Agate Basin by knowing that modern bison give birth during the last two weeks of April and the first two weeks of May. Hill assumed that bison in the past did likewise. This uniformitarian assumption seems justified because giving birth in the early spring allows calves the maximum time to mature before the next winter arrives. Even considering climate change, it is likely that the birthing season of modern bison approximates that of their ancient cousins.

Bone development and tooth eruption in modern bison also follow quite predictable schedules (as they do for all animals, including humans). Young animals are important here; indeed, once all their teeth have erupted, adults lose their value as seasonal indicators. The teeth of the youngest bison at Agate Basin showed that it was about 11 months old when it died. A second young bison had teeth that suggested an age of about 23 months. In other words, these two animals were just one month shy of their first and second birthdays, respectively. Assuming that these two bison were born in late April–early May, then they probably died in late March or early April. The presence of some fetal bison bones (either a late-term fetus or a newborn) supports this inference. With this information, Hill concluded that Folsom hunters occupied Agate Basin at the tail end of winter or the beginning of spring.

The Zooarchaeology of a Peruvian Civilization

Now that we know something about the basics of faunal analysis, let's jump to Peru, to see how these techniques work in a very different context.

The site of Chavín de Huántar (pronounced "cha-*veen* day *whan*tar") is one of the most celebrated ceremonial centers in the Andes. It flourished from 2850 to 2200 BP, making it one of the earliest civilizations in South America. Located at an elevation of nearly 3150 meters (10,000 feet) above sea level, Chavín de Huántar is ringed by snow-covered mountains (with peaks rising more than 5500 meters [18,000 feet]).

The initial settlement was a small ceremonial center surrounded by domestic structures that made up a

FIGURE 8-3 The main temple at Chavín de Huántar.

vigorous highland community. Its location on a key trade route midway between the Peruvian coast and the lowland tropical forest to the east made Chavín de Huántar a natural trade center.

The site has given its name to the famous Chavín art style, which contains a range of fantastical and representational figures, usually combining the features of humans, snakes, jaguars, caymans (alligators), and birds with intricate geometrical and curvilinear motifs. The most elegant expression of the Chavín style is in the 150 stone carvings of the huge Chavín de Huántar temple complex (we discuss these images in Chapter 11).

The site's ceremonial buildings are honeycombed with rooms, passageways, stairways, vents, and drains (see Figure 8-3). Inside the largest structure is a knife-shaped monolith 15 feet tall, set into a narrow, interior gallery. The top of the elaborately carved sculpture reached through the ceiling, into a gallery above, where the priests of Chavín de Huántar, acting as the voice of an oracle, may have spoken to the worshippers below.

Chavín's art and temple architecture attracts the attention of Andean archaeologists, but we also need to know something about the more mundane aspects of the Chavín lifeway.

What, for instance, did the Chavín people eat? We could look to the stone iconography expressed in their sculpture, but it is unlikely that people living at 10,000 feet in the Andes dined on alligator and jaguar. Religious iconography is not a very accurate reflection of everyday diet.

George Miller (California State University, Hayward) and Richard Burger (Yale University) took a more direct approach to the problem by looking at the trash of the center's several thousand inhabitants.

When Burger excavated at Chavín de Huántar, he encountered subsistence remains in the domestic structures and refuse heaps around the ceremonial center, including some 12,000 fragments of discarded food bone. These bones were identified, first to body part and then to taxon. Next, Burger computed the MNI for each of the three major cultural phases. He then estimated the "usable meat values" for each phase by multiplying the MNI figures per phase by the average animal's butchered weight for each taxon.

Early Patterns at Chavín de Huántar

Four kinds of camelids (animals of the family *Camelidae*) live today in the Andes. The llama is used mostly as a pack animal, and secondarily for its coarse hair. The alpaca is valued mostly for its fine and abundant fleece. Both of these domesticated species play important roles in religious rituals. *Guanacos* (wild llamas) are hunted as a source of meat. Finally, the vicuña, also a wild species, has been hunted mostly for its extremely fine hair.

seasonality An estimate of the part of the year a particular archaeological site was occupied.

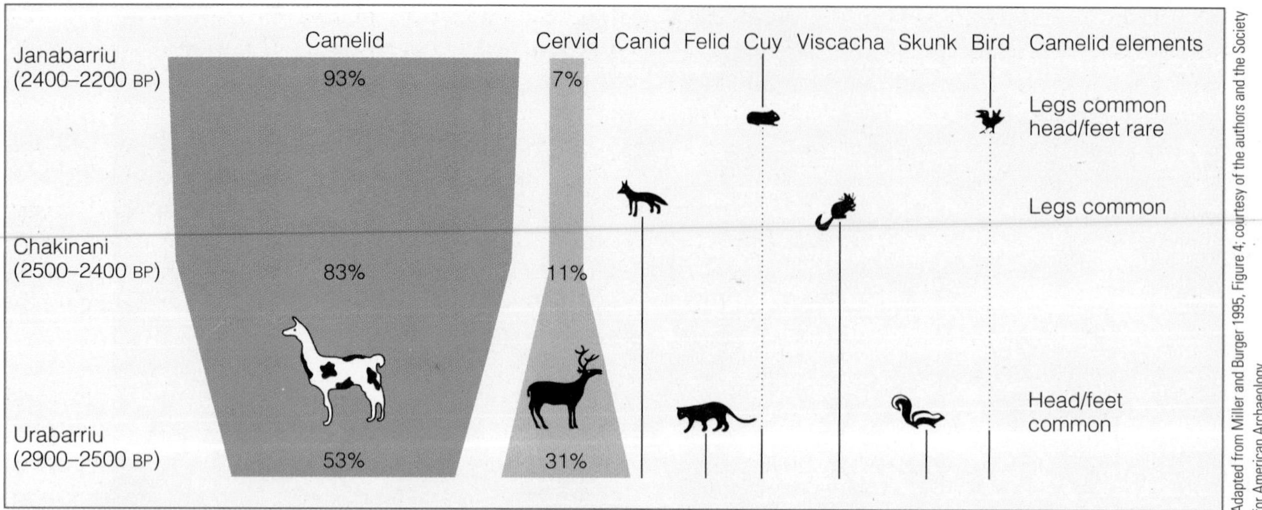

FIGURE 8-4 Changing relative abundance of the major animal groups in faunal remains at Chavín de Huántar.

During the earliest or Urabarriu phase (2900 to 2500 BP), more than half the meat came from camelids (see Figure 8-4), and most of these were llamas. Stable isotope analysis (a technique we discuss in Chapter 9) of their bones suggests that these early llama herds consumed considerable quantities of maize and therefore were probably domesticated. The other camelids were mostly vicuña.

White-tailed deer came in second (31 percent of the available meat). Skunk, large cat (either jaguar or puma), fox (or dog), and guinea pig bones also turned up in small numbers. The bones of some of these rarer animals may have been used for tools, rather than for food (although guinea pigs are today considered a delicacy in highland Peru). In other words, the Urabarriu phase bones strongly suggest a transitional pattern of mixed hunting and herding.

The Later Fauna at Chavín de Huántar

Things changed markedly during the subsequent Chakinani phase (2500 to 2400 BP). Deer frequencies drop off dramatically, and camelid frequencies jump to 83 percent, with llama bones becoming considerably more common than those of vicuña.

The large faunal sample from the terminal Janabarriu phase (2400 to 2200 BP) continues this trend: Camelid bones constitute 93 percent of the assemblage. During this phase, the rapidly expanding population had virtually abandoned hunting in favor of domesticated llamas. This much seems clear.

Recall that Miller and Burger identified the bones from Chavín de Huántar to both taxon and element. The taxonomic changes through time indicated that subsistence activities changed markedly at Chavín de Huántar. But by looking at differential representation of elements (that is, body parts), Miller and Burger explored the ways in which the various animal products entered the community.

They found a curious pattern: The early Urabarriu camelid assemblage consisted mostly of head and foot bones. During the two subsequent phases, however, leg bones become considerably more frequent, with cranial and foot bones becoming rare. What does this intriguing pattern mean?

Camelid Taphonomy

As we pointed out in Chapter 7, interpretation requires middle-level theory, and one source of such theory is ethnoarchaeology. George Miller had conducted ethnoarchaeological research on contemporary South American pastoralists in the **puna**, the high grassy plateau of southern Peru. This experience helped him to analyze the remains excavated by Burger. Interestingly, Miller found that the bone refuse in modern herding communities mirrored almost exactly the early pattern from Chavín de Huántar: plenty of head and foot bones, and not many leg bones. Why?

Miller first considered the matter of bone survival. He conducted experiments on camelid bones to see which ones survive and which ones disappear. Not surprisingly, he found that the dense foot bones and enamel-covered teeth lasted much longer than the hollow leg bones and the relatively porous vertebrae.

Miller then looked at how butchering patterns might create a different representation of skeletal parts. Put simply, the process of modern camelid butchering accelerates the skewing effects already suggested from the bone density studies. Because people commonly break up leg bones to get at the marrow inside, such long bones often enter the archaeological record fragmented, and hence are more difficult to identify to element and taxon. Like other taphonomists, Miller discovered that when dogs gnaw on camelid remains, they consume spongy bones (such as vertebrae) almost entirely, but repeated gnawing leaves dense teeth and foot bones marked, but intact. In other words, the processes involved in differential preservation—bone density, butchering patterns, and carnivore gnawing—all operated to bias the modern faunal assemblage in precisely the manner observed from the early deposits at Chavín de Huántar.

But another factor is at work here, what Miller calls the "ch'arki effect." Today, herders of the puna preserve llama and alpaca meat by alternately drying it out in the intense Andean sun, then freezing it during the cold, high-altitude nights. The product of this freeze-drying process—called **ch'arki** in the native Quechua language—has made its way into English as "jerky."

But unlike the overpriced beef jerky peddled in gas stations throughout the United States, Peruvian ch'arki consists of meat dried on the bone. In general, the head and feet are cut off in the ch'arki-making process and eaten at home by the local herding communities. Ch'arki is a major trade item between the highland puna herders and those living in the intermontane valleys and along the Pacific coast today.

So, what is the archaeological evidence of ch'arki making?

The pattern depends entirely on whether you are making or receiving the ch'arki. If you're in the puna, where the Quechua herd llamas and make ch'arki, you will find lots of cranial and foot bones. These are the heavy, dense bones (without much meat attached) that nobody wants to drag around the Andes. So they are cut off and discarded, entering the archaeological record of the puna. But if you are on the receiving end of the ch'arki trade network—in the downhill intermontane valleys and along the coast—then the pattern is the opposite. The camelid bones you receive from the uplands are those still left adhering to the ch'arki chunks. So, your garbage will contain lots of leg bones and vertebrae, but not many skull parts or foot bones.

Given this simple taphonomic patterning based on behavior of modern camelid-herding communities, we can return to the bone assemblages from Chavín de Huántar and look at the bones in a more informed manner.

The Behavior behind the Bones

Remember that the faunal remains from the Chakinani (2500 to 2400 BP) and Janabarriu (2400 to 2200 BP) phases contained mostly camelid bones—llama and some vicuña, with deer frequencies dropping off markedly from earlier times. The rapidly expanding population at Chavín de Huántar had forsaken hunting in favor of camelid herding. Miller and Burger also found that, whereas the camelid assemblage from earlier deposits consisted mostly of head and foot bones, leg bones dominated the later archaeological record, with cranial and foot elements rare.

Middle-level studies also tell us that three of the major taphonomic factors—differential bone densities, fracturing of long bones, and carnivore gnawing—all *decrease* survival of leg bones. Although these factors influenced the composition of this assemblage, the observed superabundance of leg bones suggests that taphonomy alone cannot account for the faunal distributions.

Instead, we must look to the ch'arki effect. The ethnoarchaeological findings indicated that the late-phase pattern at Chavín de Huántar is the *opposite* of what we see among contemporary alpaca herders living on the puna. Thus, high-altitude herding communities traded ch'arki to the valley residents of Chavín de Huántar. In return, the inhabitants of Chavín de Huántar may have sent maize to the puna's villages. This worked to everyone's advantage, for Chavín de Huántar lacks the cold, dry weather needed to produce ch'arki, and maize will not grow on the puna, which is better suited to llama herding.

From the faunal evidence, Miller and Burger concluded that the earliest occupants of Chavín de Huántar used llamas mostly as pack animals, camelid meat being a by-product of culling the herds. Meat was also obtained by hunting vicuña and white-tailed deer. People living on the valley floor were self-sufficient in the Urabarriu phase, acquiring their own meat as needed.

Then, the ritual importance of Chavín de Huántar increased through time, and the local community grew in size. The associated increase in agricultural production on the valley floor made hunting of local wild species less productive, and thereafter meat was derived almost exclusively from domesticated llamas. Because the valley was poorly suited for llama herding, there was an increased need for long-distance trade with the high-altitude regions. Ch'arki was traded in, and agricultural products were traded out during the later Janabarriu phase.

The differential distribution of camelid bones thus reflects important economic and social relationships between Chavín de Huántar and surrounding communities. These exchange relationships were probably reinforced by a shared participation in the Chavín religious cult, both at the massive valley floor temple and at small shrines located in high-altitude villages. With time, the residents of Chavín de Huántar shifted from a generalized economic system with only loose ties to their upland neighbors to a more specialized subsistence pattern that depended heavily on long-distance exchange with herders in the puna.

Recall that this interpretation of Chavín de Huántar's faunal assemblage is based partially on ethnographic analogy. Lidio Valdez (Trent University) points out that the analogy employed for ch'arki production is only one of several that could be drawn from the Andes. Ch'arki is made in other ways throughout the Andes, and each leaves a different faunal signature. Did Miller and Burger pick the right analogy? Peter Stahl (State University of New York, Binghamton) suggests Chavín de Huántar's local environment actually could have permitted ch'arki production. But even if Miller and Burger's hypothesis is eventually modified or rejected, their work illustrates the utility of combining ethnoarchaeological and taphonomic research to understand patterning in archaeological faunal data.

These two examples, the Agate Basin site and Chavín de Huántar, show some of the ways archaeologists pursue faunal analysis and what it can contribute to our understanding of the past. Bones, however, are only half the story.

puna Native American (Quechua) term for the treeless, windswept tablelands and basins of the higher Andes.

ch'arki Native South American (Quechua) term for freeze-dried llama and alpaca meat.

Studying Plant Remains from Archaeological Sites

Although plants are particularly vulnerable to decomposition, many archaeological sites contain well-preserved **macrobotanical remains** (readily recognizable plant parts): caches of corncobs, pine nuts, a hearth's charcoal, or acorn mush adhering to the inside wall of a food bowl. A counterpart to the zooarchaeologist, **paleoethnobotanists** are archaeologists who specialize in recovering and identifying these plant remains, focusing on the world of plant–people interactions.

Archaeologists also find plant remains in curious places, such as inside ancient human stomachs (preserved through mummification) and in human **coprolites** (desiccated feces); this evidence of past diets is about as direct as one could hope for. Evidence of past plant consumption is also preserved in the chemistry of human bone (we discuss this in Chapter 9). And it comes in a microscopic form too, as pollen and phytoliths.

Palynology

Palynology, the analysis of ancient plant pollen and spores, has long been useful to the study of prehistoric ecological adaptations by helping to reconstruct past environments. Its basics are easy to understand.

Most plants shed their pollen into the atmosphere, where the wind rapidly disperses it. Pollen grains are abundant; a single pine branch, for example, can produce as many as 350 million pollen grains. Pollen grains are tenacious and under the right conditions can survive for tens of thousands of years.

The initial steps in extracting and identifying pollen are straightforward. Sometimes pollen is recovered by core sampling, in which a circular tube is forced downward by a mechanical drilling rig into a sediment record. Lake bottoms are often good places to prospect for pollen.

We can also take pollen samples manually from archaeological stratigraphic profiles. The surface of the excavation profile is first scraped with a trowel (that has been cleaned with distilled water), and 0.2 to 0.3 liter of material is then extracted from the stratum with a clean trowel and placed in a sterile, sealable container. Samples are often taken at 5- or 10-centimeter intervals to provide a continuous record of the pollen rain throughout the period of deposition. Pollen samples can also be taken from sealed deposits within architectural features (such as ancient floors or the fill found in pits), and they can be retrieved from artifacts such as grinding stones by washing the surfaces in distilled water. Occasionally, we find pollen in human burials, on the inside of ceramic vessels, trapped inside the weave of ancient baskets, or even adhering to the working surface of a stone tool. Analysts must always be certain that they have collected the sample from a recently exposed surface so that the modern pollen rain does not contaminate it.

In the laboratory, pollen grains are isolated from the sediment with repeated hydrofluoric acid baths and centrifuging (pollen survives the acid baths that destroy most everything else in the sample). A sample of the solution is then placed on a microscope slide, which is scanned at magnifications between 400X and 1000X.

Palynology is possible only because different plants produce pollens that look very different under a microscope. Pine pollen, for example, has two "wings" that carry it long distances on the wind. Elm pollen, on the other hand, is a lumpy round ball. This difference means that the individual grains can be identified, sometimes to species, and tabulated until the analyst records a statistically significant number, say 400 to 500 grains per slide. (A skilled analyst can do this in 2 or 3 hours.) The palynologist then converts the counts to percentages and creates a **pollen diagram** that shows the proportional shift in pollen frequencies between stratigraphic levels within a site.

Fluctuations in pollen percentages reflect changes in plant densities, and a primary application of palynology is to reconstruct past environments. Peter Mehringer's (retired) research at the Lehner Ranch site shows how this works.

Reconstructing Past Environments at the Lehner Ranch Site

The question of when people first arrived in North America is still hotly debated. The people who made Folsom points were among the earliest peoples in the New World, but earlier still were people who made a different kind of fluted point, known to archaeologists as **Clovis** points. The name "Clovis" comes from an important site near Clovis, New Mexico, where, a few years after the discoveries at the Folsom site, these distinctive spear points were found lying stratigraphically beneath diagnostic Folsom artifacts. Clovis artifacts date to 13,200 to 12,900 BP and, at about a dozen sites, they are associated with the bones of extinct mammoths and mastodons.

One of those sites is the Lehner Ranch site in southern Arizona's San Pedro Valley, excavated by C. Vance Haynes (retired), among others. Here, Haynes found Clovis fluted points and stone butchering tools in association with mammoth remains. It is hard to imagine mammoths plodding among the creosote and ocotillo of the southern Arizona landscape today. Clovis hunters clearly lived in a different environment, and Peter Mehringer turned to the fossil pollen record to help Haynes reconstruct what that environment was like.

Figure 8-5 shows the pollen diagram from the Lehner Ranch site, a composite made from several localities with overlapping records.

Pollen diagrams can look daunting, but don't let them put you off. Along the left edge in Figure 8-5 is the sample number and, in the next column to the right, the stratigraphic unit, accompanied by the sample's depth. In this case, samples were taken at 10-centimeter (cm) intervals. (Because this diagram is a composite, some of the stratigraphic units appear more than once.) Running

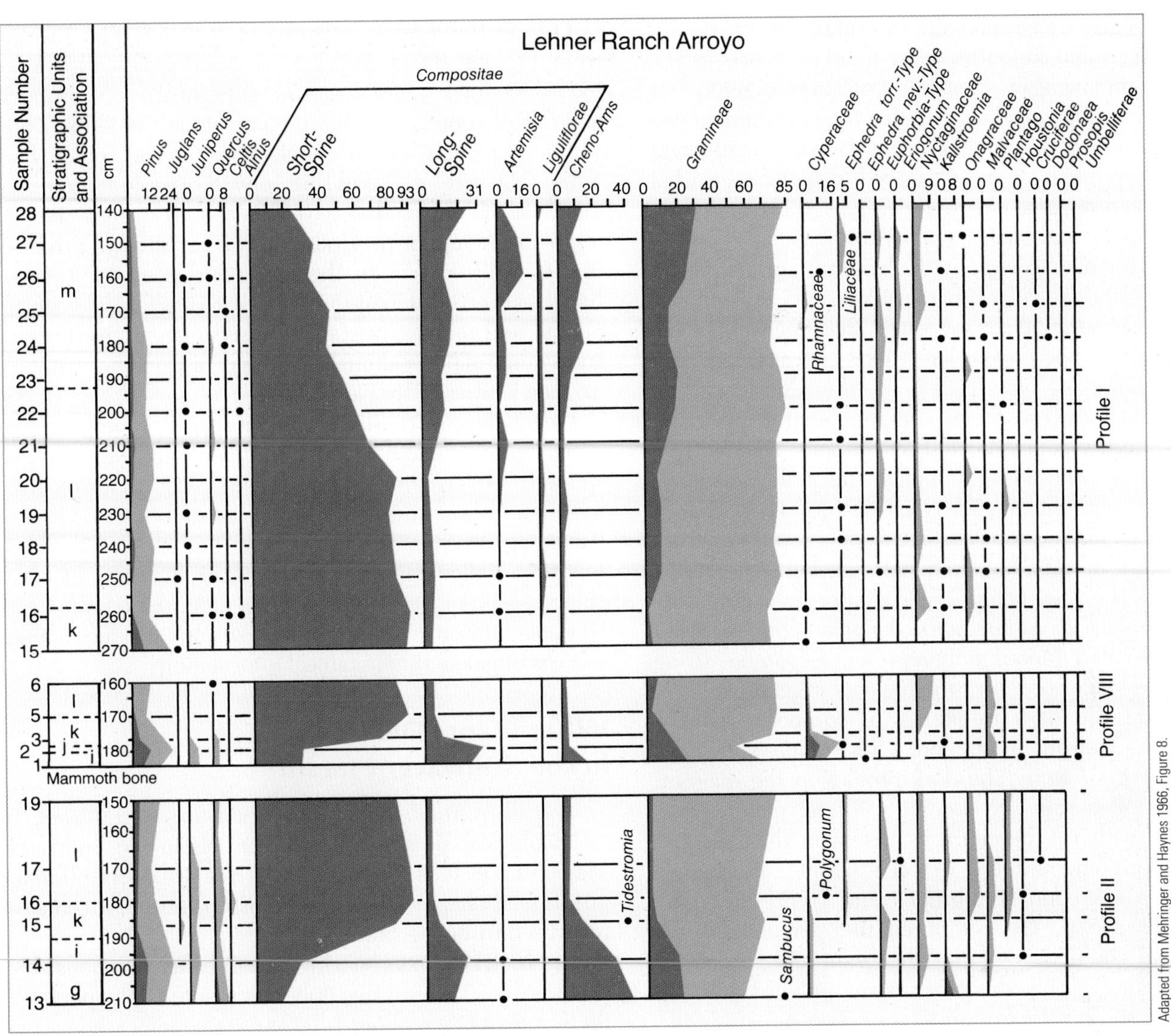

FIGURE 8-5 Pollen diagram from the Lehner Ranch site (Arizona).

along the top of the chart are the plant taxa—*Pinus* is pine, *Juniperus* is juniper, *Quercus* is oak, and so on. The horizontal scales below these are the percentages of the different kinds of pollen—for instance, *Artemisia* constituted about 16 percent of the plants found at 160 cm in Profile I. The shaded areas show the changing frequencies of different pollen. For example, pollen of cheno-ams (chenopodiaceae and amaranthaceae, closely related plants of the goosefoot family and amaranth) is most common at the lowest levels of the site (look at Samples 13 and 14 in stratigraphic Units g and i). It becomes less common through time, until stratigraphic Unit m (Samples 23 through 28), where it begins to pick up. The assumption is that pollen mirrors the local abundance of the plant species producing it; thus, goosefoot and amaranth were common early in the sequence, became less common, and later became more abundant again.

To go further, you must recognize the difference between *local* and *regional* environments. Look around at any landscape, and you will see microenvironments that do *not*

macrobotanical remains Nonmicroscopic plant remains recovered from an archaeological site.

paleoethnobotanist An archaeologist who analyzes and interprets plant remains from archaeological sites to understand the past interactions between human populations and plants.

coprolite Desiccated feces, often containing macrobotanical remains, pollen, and the remains of small animals.

palynology The technique through which the fossil pollen grains and spores from archaeological sites are studied.

pollen diagram A chart showing the changing frequencies of different identified pollens through time from samples taken from archaeological or other sites.

Clovis The earliest well-established Native American culture, distributed throughout much of North America and dating 11,200 to 10,900 BC.

reflect the regional environment. A flowing spring in a desert, for example, might support a dense stand of spruce, aspen, and mountain mahogany. Analysis of pollen from sediments near such a spring would suggest that the environment was a dense forest, when in fact the regional environment might be a vast sagebrush steppe. We need to understand what both local and regional environments looked like and, even more, we must avoid confusing the two.

Mehringer had to cope with this problem at Lehner Ranch. A distinctive "black mat" marker bed in the stratigraphy at Lehner Ranch suggested that the immediate area was a wet bog during late Clovis times. Was that a local condition, or was it true for the larger regional environment? Pollen from composites (for example, ragweed and sagebrush) and cheno-ams (plants that prefer wetter conditions) dominate the pollen diagram, suggesting that the region was wetter. This pattern characterizes many post-Pleistocene pollen profiles from southwestern deserts, but it creates a problem because it could mask the presence of less common yet ecologically sensitive indicators. Although the dominant cheno-am and composite pollen undoubtedly represent *locally* occurring species, they may not reflect the *regional* vegetation.

To offset the high frequency of composite cheno-am pollen, Mehringer applied a technique known as the *double fixed sum*. The dark profiles in the diagram are based on a standard summary for all pollen types identified, with the percentages based on the first 200 pollen grains encountered in each sample. Mehringer then made a second, 100-grain count (represented by the lighter areas). He computed the percentages for the second count by ignoring cheno-am and composite pollen, counting only the other, rarer pollen types. By comparing the results of both counts, one can study the gross frequencies of the dominants as well as fluctuations in the densities of the rarer but more environmentally sensitive species.

The pollen from stratigraphic Units i, j, and k at the Lehner Ranch reflect the climatic conditions that prevailed during Clovis times. Look carefully at the frequencies of Samples 15 and 16 in Profile I, Samples 1, 2, and 3 in Profile VIII, and Samples 14 and 15 in Profile II. The environment of the time these samples represent is "read" by moving across the diagram. Notice that the normal pollen counts—the dark portions of the figure—show a significant jump in short-spine *compositae* pollen in stratigraphic Unit k. The double fixed sum count shows slightly greater abundances of pine, oak, and juniper pollen. For trees such as pine, oak, and juniper to grow on the valley floor, the regional environment must have been somewhat moister and/or cooler before and during the deposition of the lower part of Unit k. Somewhat later, during the deposition of upper stratigraphic Unit k and Unit l, a sharp increase in the *compositae* categories and a decline in tree pollen signal a shift to fully modern conditions.

Overall, the vegetation represented by the pollen spectra from Lehner Ranch suggests a desert-grassland, which today occupies slightly wetter sites nearby. Mehringer and Haynes concluded that the climate at the Lehner site 11,000 years ago was only slightly wetter and cooler than today, followed by a rapid shift toward drier conditions. As many palynology studies have found, only a small shift in temperature and/or precipitation was required to produce dramatic differences in the environment at the Lehner Ranch site. And it may have been that slight change in rainfall and temperature that caused mammoths, horses, and a range of other animals to disappear from the southern Arizona landscape forever.

One major contribution of pollen analysis to archaeology is the reconstruction of environmental change. Properly applied, pollen studies can also help archaeologists understand past human behavior (see "Looking Closer: Palynology of Shanidar Cave: Why Formation Processes Matter"). Pollen can also play a role in figuring out what plants were important in prehistoric diet. An example from Nevada's Stillwater Marsh shows how and introduces other sources of paleoethnobotanical information.

What Plants Did People Eat in the Stillwater Marsh?

You recall from Chapter 3 that floods exposed dozens of archaeological sites and human burials in the Stillwater Marsh of Nevada's Carson Desert. We discuss the burials in the next chapter; here we focus on the plant remains recovered from one site.

Site 26CH1062 sits on a low clay dune and contains pits, postholes, and at least two ephemeral houses. People lived there at least twice, about 1400 and 1000 radiocarbon years ago.

We water-screened all the sediments, and recovered a large number of stone tools, manufacturing waste flakes, shells, and faunal remains. We also floated sediment samples from several of the features and retrieved many carbonized macrobotanical remains. We sent these to paleoethnobotanist David Rhode (Desert Research Institute). Looking at the samples under a microscope, Rhode identified the carbonized seeds and charcoal using a comparative collection; most of the charcoal was reed (*Phragmites australis*), greasewood (*Sarcobatus* sp.), and willow (*Salix* sp.). These plants are found today in the Carson Desert, and they could have been firewood, or used in housing or tools.

Rhode also found the carbonized seeds of cattail, dock, seepweed, chenopods, pickleweed, silverscale, heliotrope, saltbush, and goosefoot. The site's inhabitants could have gathered any of these as food, and all, again, occur in the area today.

One of the most abundant seeds was that of bulrush (*Scirpus* sp.), one of the many plants that the indigenous

LOOKING CLOSER

Palynology of Shanidar Cave: Why Formation Processes Matter

Neanderthal skull as it was being exposed at Shanidar Cave (Iraq). This person was probably killed by rooffall inside the cave.

Whether Neanderthals intentionally buried their dead remains a hotly contested issue. The palynology of Shanidar Cave has played an important role in this debate.

Shanidar Cave (Iraq) was occupied sporadically over the past 100,000 years. Ralph Solecki (then of Columbia University) discovered several Neanderthal skeletons (one of which was the inspiration for the shaman in Jean Auel's novel *The Clan of the Cave Bear*). One area, Shanidar IV, was very fragile, and the entire block was removed in a plaster jacket and shipped to an Iraqi museum, where it sat for two years. Investigators eventually found that Shanidar IV contained three adults and an infant.

French palynologist Arlette Leroi-Gourhan (Musée de l'Homme, Paris) tested the Shanidar IV samples for pollen and—to everyone's surprise—found large amounts of well-preserved pollen near the feet, the shoulders, and the base of the spine of one individual. The ancient pollen concentrations came from at least seven species of brightly colored wildflowers, including grape hyacinth, bachelor's button, and hollyhock. Leroi-Gourhan suggested that the fresh flowers (which bloom in late May through early July) had been woven into the branches of a pinelike shrub. The pollen data suggested that this Neanderthal burial was a formal interment, with a degree of "humanness" that few were willing to grant Neanderthals at the time.

Some asked whether the pollen grains could have blown into the cave, and are merely "background pollen rain." If so, then flower pollen should have been typical of all of the cave's deposits, not just the grave. But it was not: The sediments outside the grave not only contained far *less* flower pollen than the burial pit, but the pollen grains in the burial fill were clumped (as if they had fallen from flowers laid into the grave). Some pollen even lay in the form of the flowers' anthers, suggesting that the entire flower was once present. None of these patterns should exist if the pollen had simply blown into the cave.

But archaeology is never simple. Perhaps the pollen came into the site on flowers, but does this mean that the flowers were laid in the grave by the hands of a grieving Neanderthal?

Jeffrey Sommer (University of Michigan) suggests another possibility: rodents. Solecki noted that all the burials at Shanidar were riddled with rodent burrows. In fact, Solecki thought he could locate burials by tracing rodent burrows through the deposits. Many of the rodents died in the cave; their skeletons were identified as *Meriones persicus*, the Persian jird.

Jirds store large numbers of flower heads, neatly clipped from their stems, in the side tunnels of their burrows. Sommer points out that these rodent stores would be more than enough to account for the amount of pollen that Leroi-Gourhan found.

Thus, an alternative explanation for the Shanidar burial "bouquets" is that they were placed there by humble jirds. So the search for convincing evidence of ritual and religion among Neanderthals must continue.

Paiute Indians gathered and ate in the nineteenth century. Experimental data show that bulrush seeds are an efficiently gathered and nutritious resource.

But *did* people collect bulrush for food? Maybe the seeds were attached to bulrush plants that were used to build shelter or baskets, and were accidentally burned. Were bulrush plants, and not just their seeds, present on the site? To answer this question, we looked at another source of plant data in archaeological sites.

Phytoliths

Phytoliths, literally "plant stones," are microscopic plant opals. As plants take in water, they also take in silica and deposit it between cells, within cell walls, or in the cells themselves. Phytoliths occur in various grasses, as well as in rushes, sedges, palms, conifers, and deciduous trees. When plant material decays, the almost indestructible phytoliths are left behind.

Phytoliths take the shape of the cells in which they were deposited, and because different grasses have different cell shapes, their phytoliths also have different shapes. This means that we can identify the presence of certain kinds of plants long after those plants have decayed and disappeared. Phytolith analysis, therefore, is similar to pollen analysis, although phytoliths are not quite as identifiable to species as pollen.

Phytolith analysis was extremely useful in the Stillwater Marsh. Our sediment samples contained abundant, well-preserved phytoliths. Most of these were from *Phragmites*,

phytoliths Tiny silica particles contained in plants.

a common marsh grass. What was most intriguing, however, was the *absence* of sedge phytoliths (phytoliths produced by plants such as bulrush). This means that no bulrush plants decayed on the site.

Perhaps, then, there was no bulrush in the Stillwater Marsh 1000 years ago. Perhaps a visitor brought some bulrush seed cakes from another wetland, such as Winnemucca Lake to the west. This is a question about the *regional* vegetative environment, and it is best answered through pollen data. So, we also took pollen samples from several of the site's features. Analysis showed these to contain pollen that is little different from the modern pollen rain; in fact, bulrush pollen was abundant.

So, now we know (1) that burnt bulrush seeds were present on the site, (2) that bulrush plants were not on the site, but (3) that bulrush was abundant in the wetland. We conclude that bulrush seeds were brought to the site to be eaten.

The macrobotanical remains were also interesting because of what was *not* present. Completely missing were the seeds of upland plants such as ricegrass or piñon pine nut hulls, both important food sources to the nineteenth-century Paiute. This suggests that when people lived in the Carson Sink, they got their plant food exclusively from the wetland. They did not travel even a few kilometers into the low foothills to gather ricegrass, nor did they hike another 20 kilometers into the hills to gather piñon.

Site Seasonality

The seasonality of the Agate Basin site was determined using faunal remains, but we used the macrobotanical remains at 26CH1062. Establishing seasonality from plant remains is a matter of determining the plant foods' seasons of availability. Recall that we found seeds of bulrush, cattail, seepweed, dock, chenopods, pickleweed, heliotrope, silverscale, saltbush, and goosefoot. We know that most of these seeds ripen in mid- to late summer and into the early winter, although dock and heliotrope are gathered throughout the summer only. All of these resources, therefore, are only available in the late summer, and that is probably the best estimate of when the site was occupied, although an occupation from mid-summer into the late fall cannot be ruled out.

Coprolites of Hidden Cave

Human coprolites are another source of information on prehistoric diet. Paleontologists first used the term "coprolite" (from the Greek *kopros,* "dung," and *lithikos,* "stone") about 1830, to describe fossilized dinosaur feces. Archaeologists use the term, but the feces we analyze are desiccated, not fossilized. Although not commonly found, human coprolites are, for obvious reasons, an excellent source of information on human diet.

David Rhode studied the human coprolites found in Hidden Cave, which overlooks the Stillwater Marsh. This cave's original opening was very small, barely large enough to crawl into; and even though the cave itself is a spacious chamber, it was a lousy place even to spend the night. The cave is dark and dusty and, if you made a fire, the chamber would soon fill with smoke. Thus, we were not surprised to find no hearths, stone tool waste flakes, or bones left over from meals. People did not live in Hidden Cave; instead, they used it as a place to cache various kinds of gear in pits.

But there were also many quids—expectorated pieces of plants (such as cattail and bulrush) that people had chewed for their juices. And found nearby were bits of cordage, made from strips of bark rolled together. This suggests that people also used the cave as a place where they could escape the summer afternoon's heat, passing the afternoon by chewing succulent stalks of bulrush and cattail in the cave's cool interior while rolling bark together to make cords to tie together bundles, or to repair sagebrush bark sandals or torn baskets.

Many of the artifacts found in Hidden Cave were projectile points; these might suggest that men were the primary visitors to the cave (we deal with such gender assumptions in Chapter 10). Rhode investigated the coprolites to see what the men who used the shelter were eating. He was surprised by what he found.

Rhode prepared the 19 coprolites by first soaking them in a solution of trisodium phosphate to reconstitute them. He then washed each specimen through fine mesh screens and dried the residue. Next, he examined and sorted this material under a microscope.

A small macrobotanical remain from each coprolite was AMS radiocarbon-dated. In so doing, Rhode found that the coprolites fell into two time periods: one batch dated between 3800 and 3400 BP, the other from 1900 to 1500 BP. All of the coprolites contained abundant evidence of plants, fish, and bird remains (people may also have eaten large mammals, but obviously their bones would not appear in coprolites).

Bulrush seeds were common, as was cattail pollen. Rhode also found small waterfowl feathers, as well as the bones of tui chub, a minnow that lives in the Stillwater Marsh. In fact, fish cranial (head) and caudal (tail) bones tell us that these small fish were eaten whole. Insects showed up too, as well as snails.

Curiously, only one coprolite contained a piñon pine nut hull. Even more curiously, this coprolite also contained cattail seeds and pollen. This is important because piñon nuts ripen in late September or early October, but cattail pollen is collected in July. Clearly, one of these resources must have been stored, and it was most likely the piñon.

All this was intriguing enough, but then came the surprise. We can determine if a man or woman voided a coprolite depending on the abundance of the sex hormones estradiol, progesterone, and testosterone. This is done using a complex technique known as high-pressure liquid chromatographic analysis. After applying this technique, Rhode found that the coprolites' levels of sex hormones indicated that women had voided the coprolites. We don't know if it was also

RAPID REVIEW

Classes of Data from Plant and Animal Remains in Archaeological Sites

Faunal Remains	Plant Remains
• NISP (number of identifiable specimens), provides measure of abundance and diversity of animals	• Macrobotanical remains, provide measures of abundance and diversity of plant remains; usually retrieved as burnt remains, or in coprolites
• MNI (minimum number of individuals), another measure of abundance, most useful where stratigraphic associations are very clear	• Phytoliths, used to reconstruct the presence of particular plants on a site
• Butchering patterns, based on cut marks and breakage; reconstruct diet and trade	• Palynology, used to reconstruct past environments from pollen
• Seasonality, using ages of animals based on tooth eruptions	• Seasonality, based on plants' schedules of growth and maturation

women who cached the projectile points, spit out the quids, and spun the cordage. But coprolite analysis clearly opens up new approaches to diet as well as new approaches to reconstructing the ancient lives of men and women.

The Symbolic Meaning of Plants: The Upper Mantaro Valley Project

So far, we have talked about plants, animals, and people from a strictly economic perspective: What did people eat, and when did they eat it? But more can be done with archaeofaunas and macrobotanical remains. They can tell us not only how people interacted materially with their environment, but also how they interacted with it symbolically. The Upper Mantaro Valley Project in Peru is one example.

The Upper Mantaro Valley sits at 3300 meters (about 10,800 feet) above sea level in the central Andes of Peru. The intensively settled and cultivated valley floors are surrounded by rocky hillsides, supporting a few rocky fields, but mostly grasses, a few shrubs, and small trees. And it has probably been that way since humans first moved in, several thousand years ago.

The Upper Mantaro Archaeological Project excavated numerous house compounds from six archaeological sites spanning the period 1500 to 500 BP (divided into six phases: Pancán 1 through 4, and Wanka II and III). During the Wanka II phase, the population of the Upper Mantaro aggregated into large, walled towns located on protected knolls just above the plains. This was a time of fighting between villages, and land use was restricted to areas close to the walled settlements. After the Inca conquest during Wanka III times, the population was relocated into villages on the valley floor.

As part of the excavations, researchers collected more than 900 6-liter sediment samples from the floors, middens, pits, and hearths encountered in each excavation unit. These contained thousands of pieces of charcoal and plant fragments, recovered by both dry-screening and flotation. The recovered plant remains were classified into three simple categories: grass, stem (small-diameter twig fragments), and wood (pieces of mature wood). The wood category was further subdivided if the tree species could be identified.

Paleoethnobotanists Christine Hastorf (University of California, Berkeley) and Sissel Johannessen (U.S. Army Corps of Engineers) examined these flotation samples to analyze the changing patterns of fuel use. People can burn many different things to cook food and to heat their homes. Grass tied in tight bundles, small twigs, dung from herbivores, and, of course, mature wood can all be used. What does it mean if people use one source rather than another?

Hastorf and Johannessen found that grass, twigs, and mature wood were all used for fuel, and that mature wood was always the dominant fuel source. But it is the relative frequencies, rather than the absolute figures, that matter. Figure 8-6 graphs the ratio of wood to stems and wood to other fuel sources (stems and grass) for the six phases that cover the 1000-year-long sequence of the Upper Mantaro Valley. Prior to 700 BP (during the Pancán phases), the relative proportion of mature wood fragments dropped, meaning that over time people used more grass and stems, rather than mature wood, as fuel. Then, during Wanka II and III times, this trend reversed, with stems and grass remains decreasing.

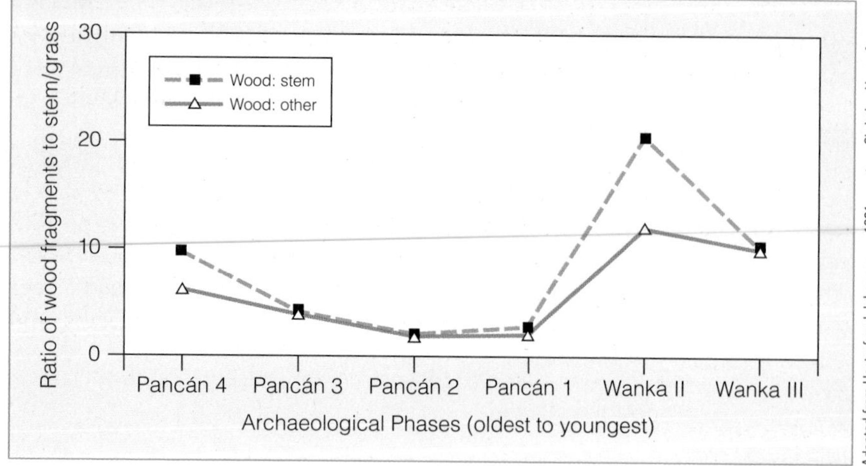

FIGURE 8-6 The changing ratios of wood to other fuel types through time in the Upper Mantaro Valley of Peru.

Hastorf and Johannessen also noted that the species composition of the mature wood shifted through time. Up to 40 different kinds of wood are present in the Upper Mantaro Valley samples, with no particular taxa being especially dominant. But the most common taxa did change in relative frequency through time. The five most popular wood types during the early Pancán phases (from yet unidentified trees) dropped out entirely by Wanka II times, and new wood types appeared beginning around 700 BP. One notable example is *Buddleia* sp. (known as *quishuar* in Quechua), a high-elevation tree that became the most popular fuel source during Inca (Wanka III) times.

What Explains Wood Use?

Let's work through the analysis step by step, following the arguments developed by Hastorf and Johannessen. First, we must consider whether the charcoal distributions in the diagram in Figure 8-6 can be attributed to factors other than fuel use—to changes, for instance, in house construction materials, subsistence, or differential plant preservation through time.

Hastorf and Johannessen rejected all these possibilities. They noted that most of the charcoal comes from fire refuse accumulated over a span of several months or years. Although some of the charcoal may have come from inadvertent fires (such as accidental burning of thatch roofs), the investigators assume that the majority of the charcoal reflects intentional fuel use for heating and cooking. They also note that the composition of the house compounds (mud and stone), the general subsistence remains, and the depositional contents are basically constant throughout the 1000-year sequence. And there is little reason to believe that rates of preservation changed significantly through time.

Hastorf and Johannessen then moved to interpret the charcoal distributions strictly in terms of changing fuel use patterns. Beginning their paleoethnobotanical analysis in standard fashion, they first determined whether the archaeological patterning of fuel use revealed long-term shifts in the relationship between these highland people and their environment.

From this strictly economic perspective, the increased reliance through time on twigs and grasses during the Pancán sequence is just what one might expect in a relatively treeless landscape. Through time, the growing human population and more intensive agricultural land use patterns made fuel wood scarce. It makes sense that as people denuded their landscape of trees, they turned to less desirable fuels such as small shrubby plants, twigs, and grasses.

But if this is so, then why would this trend reverse during later Wanka times? Contrary to strictly ecological expectations, the archaeologically recovered plant remains show that the use of high-quality fuels actually *increased* after 700 BP.

Perhaps the evidence from settlement pattern archaeology provides a clue. Beginning in Wanka II times, an elite class began social and political consolidation of the area. Maybe this elite class mandated some sort of fuel management program, perhaps in the form of tree cultivating, resulting in a greater availability of mature wood sources. This scenario is certainly possible, because we know that tree cultivation was practiced during Inca times.

Fuel, of course, has an important economic role in Andean life, especially at an elevation in excess of 3300 meters where the days, to say nothing of the nights, are cold. The increased fuel management/tree cultivation explanation provides a workable, rational answer in economic terms, but leaves several questions unanswered:

- Why does the change take place in Wanka II times? Why not earlier (when the population first increased) or later (when the Inca took over and restructured the location of the production system)?
- Why would cultivation be chosen to alleviate the fuel shortage? Why not simply go farther afield to gather fuel? Or why not just shift to lower-quality fuels?
- And why do certain tree taxa show up during Inca times, when they were absent before?

At this point, Hastorf and Johannessen decided to explore explanations that went beyond conventional economic and ecological factors. They delved into the ethnographic and ethnohistoric records to document the relationships among Andean people, the upland forest, and traditional fuel sources. In so doing, Hastorf and Johannessen found that wood is more than simply fuel in the Andes. It also has an important symbolic dimension.

Collecting fuel was an important aspect of Inca life, consuming up to four hours each day for some segments of the population. We know from documentary accounts that logs, kindling, and straw were also important tribute items in the Inca state.

But trees also had important symbolic connotations in Andean cosmology. Certain sacred trees were planted at administrative sites. Others were symbolically linked with deities. In fact, the Inca burned *quishuar,* the wood that appeared during Wanka III times, in large quantities at festivals and ritually burned human figures carved of *quishuar* as sacrifices to the divine ancestor of the Inca dynasty. Trees were also symbolically associated with water, as well as with women, clouds, winter, and the moon.

From these and other ethnohistoric and ethnographic examples, Hastorf and Johannessen concluded that wood played a strong symbolic as well as economic role in Inca life, being used to cement social relations (perhaps because it was so important and so rare). Brothers-in-law, for instance, sometimes provided wood and straw to relatives at a wake.

Relating Ideology to the Past

Hastorf and Johannessen supplemented their ecological perspective with a new appreciation of the cultural relationship between ancient Andean people and their environment. But why did the change take place in Wanka II times?

Hastorf and Johannessen argue that the ideology associated with the planting of certain trees could have been a factor in establishing the local political consolidation occurring at the time: The tree symbolized family continuity on the land, with the roots symbolizing ancestors and the fruits, the children. In fact, a ritual step in contemporary marriage ceremonies is termed "to bring the branch" and involves bringing forth ritual offspring. The dramatic increase in the use of *quishuar* might thus be attributed to its ritual significance in bringing social groups together into larger entities, rather than simply its mundane use as firewood.

These investigators believe that the act of planting trees—which could be interpreted as a purely economic response to a fuel shortage—was chosen from the other available alternatives because of cultural values concerning the ways in which cultivation and trees functioned as symbols of life and lineage, socially and politically.

Conclusion

This chapter has illustrated how archaeologists go about investigating the relationships among people, plants, and animals. From these remains, we can determine what plants and animals people ate, what seasons of the year they were taken, and what sorts of tactics were used to hunt or gather them. They can help reconstruct trade relations. Often, archaeologists view information from plant and animal remains as evidence of ancient peoples' purely materialistic and mundane relations with their environment. And often, that is correct.

But the final example from Peru suggests that our interpretations of the past may often be layered, and that material interactions with the environment may have symbolic importance as well.

Summary

- What does a zooarchaeological study involve?
  - Establish that the bones are "cultural"—left behind by people (by looking for cut marks, impact fractures, and burning).
  - Identify the bones to element, taxon, sex, and age using a comparative collection.
  - Count the bones using NISP (number of identifiable specimens) and MNI (minimum number of individuals). NISP is simply a count of the number of bones of a particular taxon; MNI is the minimum number of animals required to account for those bones.
  - The specific elements present and their breakage patterns suggest how the animals were hunted and butchered; this also suggests whether they were hunted close or far away, whether meat was stored or traded, or if people were pressed for food.
  - The links between patterns in the faunal assemblage and interpretations depend on experimental archaeology and ethnoarchaeology.
- How do animal bones and plants help establish a site's season of occupation?
  - The age of animals represented in a faunal assemblage coupled with assumptions of their season of birth help establish a site's "seasonality."
  - Likewise, the modern fruiting schedules of plants represented in sites by their seeds or other edible components suggest when a site was occupied.
- How do plants help to reconstruct ancient diets?
  - The sources include macrobotanical remains (for example, charred seeds recovered by flotation), phytoliths (silica nodules found in some plant stems), pollen, coprolites (preserved human feces), and lipids extracted from pottery.

- Each source has its strengths and weaknesses. Macrobotanical remains can be abundant, but it is not always clear if they represent food; coprolites clearly contain the remains of meals, but they are very short-term records.
- People's interaction with the environment has an economic basis, but culture may place layers of symbolic meaning on top of that interaction.

How can pollen help reconstruct past environments?

- Because different plant species produce differently shaped pollens, we can identify ancient vegetation by identifying pollen in archaeological sites.
- Samples are prepared and the pollen counted under a microscope.
- The varying percentages of pollen in the samples roughly track the varying percentages of the different plant species that produced them.
- Pollen is good at reconstructing the regional environment; palynologists must take measures to ensure that the results are not biased by a local environment's pollen.
- Other sources of information, such as wood rat nests, provide evidence of local vegetation.

Media Resources

Doing Fieldwork: Archaeological Demonstrations CD-ROM 2.0

This CD, developed by the authors, shows professional archaeologists involved in various digs, many of which are referenced in the text. The presentation is organized by the main techniques used on an archaeological dig, reinforcing concepts and techniques via live examples. The CD takes you through each step automatically, or you can navigate to any point via the navigation bar. After reviewing a step in the dig process, you are taken to Check Points, which are concept questions about each step of the dig. Then you can see the answers, receive your score, and even send your scores to your instructor.

See the "Reconstructing the Past" section of the CD-ROM to learn about topics covered in this chapter.

CourseMate

Access chapter-specific learning tools including learning objectives, practice quizzes, videos, flash cards, and glossaries, as well as web links, and more in your Archaeology CourseMate. Login to www.cengagebrain.com to access the resources your instructor has assigned and to purchase materials.

Bioarchaeological Approaches to the Past

9

Archaeologists excavate two women, presumably nuns, at the medieval nunnery in Yorkshire, England.

Learning Objectives

After reading this chapter, you should be able to answer these questions:

- How do bioarchaeologists contribute to a study of the past?
- How do bioarchaeologists determine age and sex of a skeleton?
- How do bioarchaeologists use paleopathology and bone chemistry to reconstruct the lives of ancient peoples?
- How are genetic data used to reconstruct population relationships and the ages of migrations?

Preview

THIS CHAPTER EXAMINES bioarchaeology, a specialty that straddles the fields of archaeology and biological anthropology. Bioarchaeologists study the human biological component of the archaeological record. Some bioarchaeologists study the origin and distribution of ancient diseases; others reconstruct human diets, analyze the evidence for biological stress in archaeological populations, and reconstruct past demographic patterns—all of this by exploring human bone, bone chemistry, and the DNA preserved in human tissues.

The analysis of human remains today is a sensitive subject in many parts of the world. Handling, photographing, and sampling the physical remains of a once living human being upsets many Native Americans (and plenty of other Americans, too). These concerns surfaced in the Kennewick case discussed previously. Here, we discuss the astonishing amount of information that scientists can learn from human skeletal remains (and this chapter merely scratches the surface). In the process, we demonstrate how scientists can conduct such studies in a respectful and sensitive manner. No skeletal remains of Native Americans are portrayed in this or any other chapter.

Introduction

In Chapter 3, we described Kelly's archaeological survey project in the Carson Desert of western Nevada. We mentioned that the survey had failed to find many archaeological sites in the marsh because they were obscured by sand and vegetation. However, in the mid-1980s, the greatest floods to strike the Carson Desert in a millennium exposed many sites in the marsh.

More was exposed than arrowheads and faunal remains. Kelly visited the marsh in the summer of 1986, while the Nevada State Museum was recording the new archaeological sites for the U.S. Fish and Wildlife Service (on whose lands most of the new sites were located). Many of the newly exposed sites were accessible only by airboat. Jetting up to the shore of one site, Kelly saw several human skulls rolling about in the wake. The flood had exposed not only many new sites, but also dozens of human burials as well.

In 1987, after the floodwaters had receded, Kelly returned to the Stillwater Marsh to excavate one of the habitation sites (Site 26CH1062, mentioned in Chapter 8) and to survey the marsh for burials and human bone. To assist in this task, Clark Spencer Larsen (Ohio State University), a noted bioarchaeologist, joined the team. Larsen had received graduate training in biological anthropology, with a focus on the human skeleton as a record of past human activity. And because he worked with skeletal remains recovered from archaeological sites, Larsen was aware of the complex nature of archaeological data as well.

When modern archaeologists expect to encounter Native American human remains—as did Kelly when he approached the Stillwater Marsh—they involve the appropriate Native American community. So, before proceeding further, we'd like you to know that all the data collection discussed in this chapter was approved beforehand by the local Shoshone-Paiute tribe (see "Looking Closer: Native Americans and the Stillwater Burials").

In 1987, Kelly surveyed the previously flooded portions of the wetland, looking for new archaeological sites and human remains. Along with the Nevada State Museum, he recovered the remains of more than 500 individuals. This was significant because the Stillwater finds *tripled* the number of known prehistoric human burials from the entire state of Nevada. These remains were studied by Larsen and a team of bioarchaeologists he assembled to handle specific analyses.

Skeletal Analysis: The Basics

Larsen first had to confirm that all the bones the survey team collected were in fact human. After all, the flood had washed out plenty of archaeological midden, scattering ancient and recent animal bone among the human remains. Although human bone is distinctive, archaeological skeletal remains are often fragmented and weathered, making them difficult to identify. We have seen surgeons who were unable to identify a bone scrap as a piece of a human femur. But archaeologists are accustomed to seeing things in their broken, dirty, smashed forms. Larsen had learned how to identify bone through classes in human anatomy and **osteology**, but his real skill was acquired simply by handling thousands of human bone fragments. Figure 9-1 shows some of the major bones of the human skeleton, including ones mentioned in this chapter.

Bioarchaeologists working with bones from grave sites are accustomed to working with well-defined sets of remains, each from a single individual; this is why, unlike

LOOKING CLOSER

Native Americans and the Stillwater Burials

Looters first found the Stillwater burials while looking for skulls to decorate their fireplace mantels. But dedicated amateur archaeologists raised a cry, and soon the local Fallon Paiute-Shoshone tribe asked that the U.S. Fish and Wildlife Service (USFWS) protect their heritage. The USFWS increased patrols of the marsh, began a public education campaign to reduce looting, and with the Nevada State Museum, collected and recorded more than 4000 human remains exposed by the flooding.

Although no legislation at the time protected American Indian burials, in the 1980s, archaeologists were sensitive to the issue, and everyone felt the need to do the right thing. But what would that be?

The first right thing was to involve the local Fallon Paiute and Shoshone Indian community. Local solutions always work better than those a distant government imposes, and it helps if those involved are genuinely respectful of the other side. USFWS archaeologist Anan Raymond was the right person for this task, and he consulted with the tribe immediately. At first, the tribe wanted the remains to stay where they were found. But knowing about the looters, the tribe agreed that endangered burials should be excavated and less threatened burials would be covered over (with their location plotted on a USFWS map, so they could be monitored). The chair of the Fallon tribe, Richard Hicks, inspected every burial located during our archaeological survey, and we excavated only those for which he gave permission.

Initially, the tribe hesitated to approve nondestructive analyses such as radiocarbon dating, stable isotope analysis, or the cutting of long bones to obtain cross-sections. But because tribal members were interested in what these analyses might tell them, they permitted destructive analyses provided that (1) the tribe approve the studies, (2) such analyses be kept to a minimum, and (3) we use already broken bones.

Although the tribe requested that all remains be reburied, Raymond wanted the remains preserved for the future. Working together, they eventually decided on a novel approach: a subterranean crypt that satisfied the tribe's wish to reinter the remains, but that would safely store the burials for future analyses. Today, the Stillwater burials rest in small, individual redwood coffins in a large, ventilated concrete vault buried on USFWS land. The vault's door has two locks; the USFWS has one key, and the tribe has the other.

The tribe had the power to shut off any analysis, but it elected not to and, as a result, some good scientific research was completed. This outcome was achieved because (1) the tribe was involved from the start (rather than as an afterthought), (2) the scientific issues were described in terms that everyone could understand, and (3) most important, the tribe had a seat at the table—one of genuine authority, respect, and power.

zooarchaeologists, bioarchaeologists are rarely concerned with issues of minimum number of individuals (MNI) or number of identified specimens (NISP).

Instead, bioarchaeologists are concerned with whether the human remains constitute a **burial population**, individuals who came from a specific area and who died over a relatively short period of time (as might be found in a historic period cemetery). The Stillwater burials, however, came from a 16-square-kilometer area of marsh, not a single, well-defined cemetery. Few of the burials contained any grave goods (meaning that we could not use temporal types to place the burials within archaeological phases). And only a few of the burials were dated by accelerator mass spectrometry (AMS) radiocarbon determinations. But the projectile points found at nearby sites provided at least some rough parameters for the living population that this skeletal population represented.

Good preservation conditions provide bioarchaeologists with a nearly complete human skeleton. But sometimes, only the hardest bones survive—parts of the skull, the central portions of the limb bones, and—the hardest portion of the human skeleton—the teeth. We've seen burials where nothing remained except for an eerie smile in the sand.

Ancient cultural practices can also mix human skeletal remains together and make it difficult to group skeletal remains by individual. Many eastern Native American tribes, for example, laid bodies out in a **charnel house**, where the body was allowed to decompose in the open. Eventually, the bones were cleaned of remaining flesh, bundled together, and ritually placed into a communal grave (these are known as **bundle burials**). Over time, the

bioarchaeology The study of the human biological component evident in the archaeological record.

osteology The study of bone.

burial population A set of human burials that come from a limited region and a limited time period. The more limited the region and the time period, the more accurate will be inferences drawn from analysis of the burials.

charnel house A structure that eastern Native Americans used to lay out the dead where the body would decompose. The bones would later be gathered and buried or cremated.

bundle burial Burial of a person's bones, bundled together, after the flesh has been removed or allowed to decay off the bones.

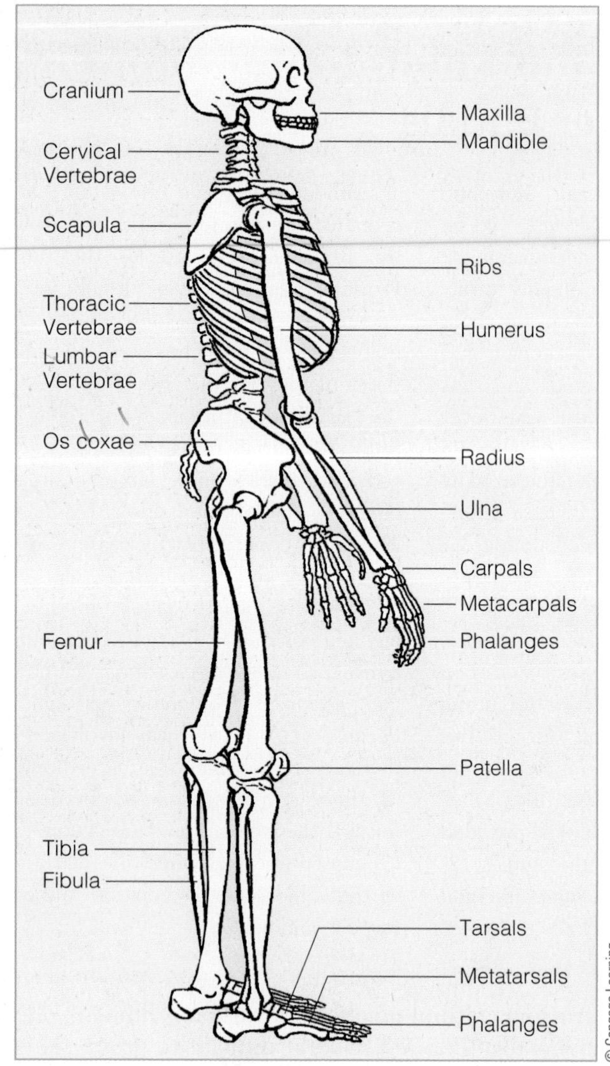

FIGURE 9-1 Some major bones of the human skeleton.

bones of various individuals would commingle. Careful excavation might be able to regroup bones by individual, but sometimes this is impossible. In other cases, as at the Stillwater Marsh, post-depositional processes scatter the once intact burials. In fact, of the 500 individuals recovered, only 54 were encountered as intact burials. In this chapter, we focus on the analysis of those remains.

Determining Sex

After removing any nonhuman bones from the collection, Larsen assigned sex and age to the intact burials. How can we determine sex from bones? One obvious place where men and women differ is the pelvic area. Evolution designed women's hips (the hips are technically composed of two halves, the right and left *os coxae* or *innominates*) to birth children; as a result, the **sciatic** (pronounced "sy-*a*-tik") **notch**, a U-shaped indentation in each os coxa's posterior (rear) portion, is wider in women than in men. There is variation among the world's population in *how much* wider, but within a burial population, one can usually see a clear difference between those os coxae with wide and those with narrow sciatic notches.

Unfortunately, the os coxae are porous, making them some of the first bones to decompose. So, if preservation is not excellent, bioarchaeologists must look elsewhere.

That usually means turning to the skull. Adult male skulls tend to be more robust than female skulls, with heavier brow ridges over the eyes, larger mastoid processes (two protrusions of bone on the bottom of the skull, one beneath each ear), and more rugged muscle attachments. Male skulls also tend to have squarer chins and eye orbits. Skilled bioarchaeologists can often "sex" an *adult* skull simply by its feel. The sex of a child, however, is difficult to determine because the sexually distinctive characteristics of bone do not develop until young adulthood.

Larsen found that the Stillwater collection contained almost twice as many males as females, but sex could not be assigned to a large number of the burials (some of the adult burials were poorly preserved or were missing key elements; others were the skeletons of children).

Determining Age

Age at death is the next goal. Like a zooarchaeologist, Larsen used osteological standards based on comparative collections. Because the pattern and timing of crown formation and tooth eruption is consistent among human populations, teeth are extremely useful for telling the age of younger individuals. Larsen determined age by recording which teeth had formed their crowns and/or erupted through the mandible or maxilla (the lower and upper jaw bones, respectively).

Patterns of bone fusion are also useful for determining age in skeletons of youths and young adults. At birth, many bones are actually several different pieces. The long bones, such as the femora or humeri, are made up of the central shaft and the two **epiphyses**—the ends that articulate with other bones. The epiphyses fuse to the shaft at known rates. For example, the proximal epiphysis of the radius (*proximal* refers to the end of a long bone that is closest to the body's center, in this case, the end of the radius closest to the elbow; *distal* refers to the end of the long bone farthest from the body) completely fuses by about age 19, whereas portions of the scapula do not fuse until age 23. Noting to what extent various bones are fused can help us estimate an individual's age at the time of death.

By age 25, most bones are fully fused and most teeth have erupted. Therefore, other methods are required to age the skeletons of mature adults, and these are more difficult to implement. The first is bone wear. After age 30, bones begin to wear down. Much of the wear is related to a person's activity level (as well as diet). But some bones tend to wear no matter what. One particularly sensitive area is the **pubic symphysis**, the place where the right and left os coxae meet in a person's groin area. As the cartilage between the two halves erodes with age, the symphysis undergoes distinct changes. At age 20, for example, the symphysis has a distinct set of surface ridges that look like ocean waves. By age 35, these ridges have disappeared, and a rim has formed along the edge of the symphysis. By age 50, the rim has disappeared, and the symphysis looks like a shriveled prune. But because the os coxae are among the first bones to decay, this useful method of determining skeletal age is not applicable to many archaeological skeletons.

Degree of tooth wear and loss also help estimate a skeleton's age at death. Because teeth wear down continually with age, bioarchaeologists have generated standardized tables (from nonindustrial populations) to estimate age from the extent of tooth wear. But caution is required here too, because the rate of tooth wear and loss is strongly related to diet. People who depend on food processed on grinding stones will have higher rates of wear because of the grit in their diet. And if their diet is high in carbohydrates, people may also experience a higher rate of tooth loss from cavities.

Using these methods, Larsen determined that the Stillwater burials ranged in age from fetuses to individuals of more than 50 years old (it's difficult to pin down the age of individuals older than 50 years). But because the skeletal indicators of age are not accurate to a year, Larsen followed standard procedure and placed skeletons into five-year age classes (0 to 5 years, 6 to 10 years, 11 to 15 years, and so on).

How Well Did the Stillwater People Live?

Eventually, Larsen derived the basics of the Stillwater population: He knew how many men, women, infants, and adolescents there were, and he knew these individuals' approximate ages. Now he could turn to questions he wanted to ask of this population, such as: How well did the people of Stillwater Marsh people live? He did not ask this question out of idle curiosity. Instead, he wanted to use the Stillwater population to shed light on a major dilemma of anthropology.

Prior to the 1960s, many anthropologists assumed that the lives of ancient hunter-gatherers were, to use the words of seventeenth-century philosopher Thomas Hobbes (1588–1679), "nasty, brutish, and short." In this view, hunter-gatherers had to work excessively hard, lived hand to mouth with barely enough food, suffered from high rates of infant mortality, and lived short lives.

But research with the Ju/'hoansi of southern Africa's Kalahari Desert and other foragers in the 1960s suggested that hunter-gatherers actually had plenty of leisure time, an adequate diet, and low levels of disease. Anthropologist Marshall Sahlins (University of Chicago) went so far as to label hunter-gatherers the "original affluent society." In the 1960s, this image of prehistoric peoples resonated with those seeking an alternative to the perceived excesses of modern industrial life.

Both of these characterizations were based on ethnographic data, but the observers might have been predisposed to see hunter-gatherers in one way rather than the other. Larsen thought that the skeletal data of an archaeological population could provide a more objective assessment of the nature of this foraging lifeway. Larsen wanted to see whether the Stillwater foragers of 1000 years ago were closer to the "nasty, brutish, and short" or the "original affluent society" image of hunter-gatherers.

To do this, Larsen turned to **paleopathology**, the study of ancient disease, disorders, and trauma. This specialization includes the identification of specific diseases, but few specific diseases can be identified from bones (syphilis [venereal and nonvenereal], tuberculosis, and leprosy are the major ones that leave distinctive lesions and other characteristics on bone). Broken bones, even if healed, are also easy to identify; unhealed breaks are usually evidence of trauma that was the immediate cause of death.

But bioarchaeologists can glean more from human skeletons if they look at human bone as being formed by complex interrelationships among the environment, behavior, and physiology. Larsen used this perspective to look for *nonspecific* indicators of stress, particularly those caused by nutritional deficiencies and/or nonspecific infectious disease in the Stillwater burial population. Though challenging, the study of biological stress has become an important area of bioarchaeology.

Disease and Trauma at Stillwater

Larsen found little trace of specific diseases among the skeletal remains from Stillwater Marsh—no evidence of syphilis, tuberculosis, or leprosy. He did, however, find some telltale signs of iron deficiency anemia.

Iron is essential for adequate transport of oxygen by red blood cells. But sometimes iron is limited, perhaps by a lack of red meat in the diet (a primary source of easily absorbed iron), chronic diarrhea, or parasites (such as hookworm, which can cause internal bleeding and the loss of a body's iron stores). Regardless of the specific cause, whenever iron is limited, the body tries to produce more

sciatic notch The angled edge of both halves of the posterior (rear) side of the pelvis. Measurement of this angle is used to determine sex in human skeletons. Although its width varies among populations, narrow notches indicate a male and wider notches indicate a female.

epiphyses The ends of bones that fuse to the main shaft or portion of bone at various ages. Most bones are fused by age 25; this fact can be used to age skeletons of younger individuals.

pubic symphysis Where the two halves of the pelvis meet in the groin area. The appearance of its articulating surface can be used to age skeletons.

paleopathology The study of ancient patterns of disease and disorders.

red blood cells. Because red blood cells are produced in the marrow cavities of bone, these cavities enlarge. When this happens in the cranium, the surface of the skull takes on a spongy appearance, a characteristic known as **porotic hyperostosis**. The same phenomenon can happen to bone in the eye sockets (where it is known as **cribra orbitalia**). Larson documented evidence of iron deficiency in only 4 of the 54 burials from the Stillwater Marsh.

The Stillwater group also showed little evidence of physical trauma. Sheilagh Brooks (1923–2008), who also studied the Stillwater materials, found only 18 individuals with bone breaks (all healed); 6 of these (5 males and 1 female) had broken noses. In general, then, the Stillwater population seemed to have been relatively healthy, suffering from few broken bones (but perhaps the occasional fistfight).

These observations were made largely on adult skeletons, but many anthropologists will tell you that to understand overall quality of life, you must look at the children. Because they are fragile, children's skeletons are rarely well preserved, making it more difficult to find appropriate samples to study. But human bone has a "memory," and some childhood events leave a telltale record on the adolescent and adult skeleton.

Growth-Arrest Features

Childhood growth may be periodically arrested because of disease, trauma, or malnutrition. Whenever this happens, bones record the cessation of growth. In long bones, such as the tibia and femur, this growth arrest appears as a thin line of bone, known as **Harris lines**, perpendicular to the bone's long axis. These lines are not visible on the outside of the bone, but they do appear in x-rays. These lines form in childhood, but disappear later in life, as the bone is remodeled as it grows.

Teeth likewise register the cessation of growth. Adult teeth form, of course, in the mandible and maxilla during childhood. When a child becomes severely ill or is malnourished, tooth growth stops. If the child recovers, growth starts up again, but the episode of growth arrest is forever encoded as shallow grooves, known as **enamel hypoplasias,** across the front of the teeth (see Figure 9-2). Because teeth grow at known rates, bioarchaeologists can measure the distance from the hypoplasia to the tip of the root to estimate at what age the growth-arrest event took place. Likewise, the width of a hypoplasia indicates the duration of the period of stress.

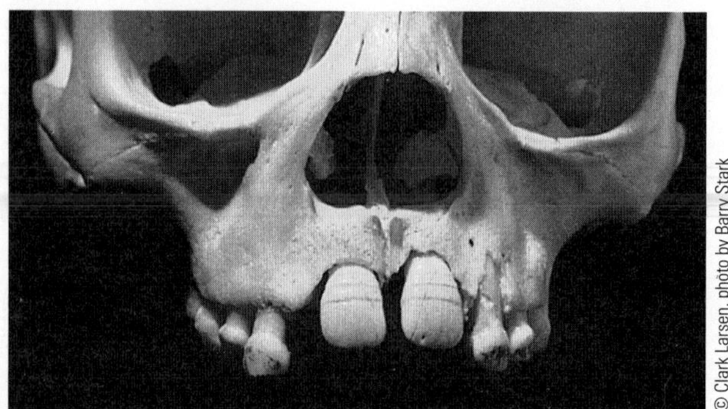
© Clark Larsen, photo by Barry Stark

FIGURE 9-2 Enamel hypoplasias.

Because enamel hypoplasias are more permanent than Harris lines, Larsen focused on them. (He could also analyze them without the cost of x-rays and with minimal disturbance to the bone.) Working with Dale Hutchinson (University of North Carolina), Larsen found that two-thirds of the individuals had hypoplasias, and that most of these occurred between the ages of 3 and 4. But the number of hypoplasias per tooth, and the average width of the grooves, was less than for other Native American populations. Larsen and Hutchinson concluded that the children of Stillwater Marsh had seen some hard times, but conditions were by no means as bad as they might have been.

The specific cause of the Stillwater hypoplasias, however, is more difficult to determine. They could have resulted from physical trauma to the face, parasitic infection, or malnutrition. We know that trauma was relatively rare (and restricted to adults), and the evidence for extensive infections was limited. Larsen and Hutchinson concluded that fluctuations in the food supply from the marsh—subject to the vagaries of local climate—most likely caused periods of malnutrition for young children.

In fact, the young population might be especially hard hit by a fluctuating food supply. Among hunter-gatherers, children are often not fully weaned until they are 3, 4, or even 5 or 6 years old. This means that, if the 3- or 4-year-olds at Stillwater Marsh were in the process of being weaned during a severe winter or a lean spring, the children might very well have suffered a limited period of malnutrition.

That the individuals survived to adulthood, however, demonstrates that this hard time was not insurmountable.

Workload

To this point, Larsen had discovered that the people who lived in the Stillwater Marsh enjoyed a relatively healthy life. But other skeletal data show that this life came at a cost.

As we said before, bones have a memory—they are lifetime diaries that record whether a person lived life as a hotshot fighting forest fires or as a couch potato. Bones can be hard to read, but they do not lie.

Bioarchaeologists use a variety of ways to determine how much physical labor a person saw in his or her lifetime. When working with the Stillwater collection, Larsen relied on patterns of osteoarthritis and the study of bone biomechanics.

Osteoarthritis

Osteoarthritis is a joint disorder created by the loss of cartilage, often caused by mechanical stress. This condition appears as a bony growth (known as an **osteophyte**) that forms a lip around the edge of an articular surface of a long bone's epiphysis (for example, at the elbow or knee) or between vertebrae, as shown in Figure 9-3. When the cartilage disappears completely, the articular surfaces rub

FIGURE 9-3 A vertebra with osteoarthritis.

against one another, creating a polish known as **eburnation**. Eburnated joints are extremely painful to move.

Larsen found that *every single adult* skeleton in the Stillwater collection had osteoarthritis in at least one joint. In fact, this was the most severe osteoarthritis that Larsen had ever seen in any skeletal population. The people of Stillwater Marsh may have lived a healthy life, but they apparently had to work—and suffer aches and pains—for it.

Males were slightly more osteoarthritic than females, and not in all the same places. Men suffered from osteoarthritis more in the hip, ankle, and foot; women, more in their lumbar vertebrae—their lower back. Larsen suggested that the males in the Stillwater population probably did more walking—and more difficult walking—than did women. This makes sense, because women probably foraged for plants, fish, and small game within a short distance of camps within the marsh itself, while the men probably traveled farther, into the rougher terrain of the Stillwater Mountains, in search of large game. The women were hardly taking it easy, though. They, too, had osteoarthritis that indicated they did a great deal of difficult walking, no doubt carrying children and gear when they moved camp. But men evidently did even more walking.

Why the high incidence of osteoarthritis in the lower backs of women? Larsen pointed to two likely factors: child rearing and food processing. Because hunter-gatherer children breast-feed until they are several years old, children must stay with their mothers. And if the Stillwater women were to complete their daily foraging tasks, they probably had to carry the children with them (just as many hunter-gatherer women do). If so, then the Stillwater women probably carried children throughout most of their adult lives—with resulting strain on the lower back.

In addition, the seeds and tubers that women collected in the marsh were ground on metates. A lifetime of such seed grinding could have led women to overuse their lower vertebrae and given them a higher incidence of osteoarthritis there.

Biomechanics

Larsen also worked with Christopher Ruff (Johns Hopkins University) to transfer knowledge from civil engineering to the analysis of **long bone cross-sections**. Civil engineers know that the type of supports used in a building is a function of how much stress the building will place on the beams (which is largely a function of the building's height). Bones are the same, except that, unlike a building's support beams, bones change their cross-section over time as they respond to stress. Although the specifics are complex, the principle is simple: When femora are placed under heavy mechanical stress (for example, by routine walking over difficult terrain while carrying a heavy load), they tend to develop a more oval cross-section. The cross-sections of the femora of a couch potato, on the other hand, are more rounded.

Larsen and Ruff obtained cross-sections of the femora through CAT scans at the Veteran's Administration hospital in Reno, Nevada. Although the overall bone mass was relatively low in the Stillwater femora, bone strength was among the highest that Larsen and Ruff had ever seen. As was true for osteoarthritis, the femur cross-sections indicated that men did more—and more strenuous—walking than women. This could be because the Stillwater folk, especially the men, were generally robust, with large, heavy bones. But when Larsen and Ruff looked at the cross-sections of the humeri (the upper arm), they found no difference between men and women, and no real difference between the Stillwater and other populations of native North Americans. This suggests that the difference

porotic hyperostosis A symptom of iron deficiency anemia in which the skull takes on a porous appearance.

cribra orbitalia A symptom of iron deficiency anemia in which the bone of the upper eye sockets takes on a spongy appearance.

Harris lines Horizontal lines near the ends of long bones indicating episodes of physiological stress.

enamel hypoplasias Horizontal linear defects in tooth enamel indicating episodes of physiological stress.

osteoarthritis A disorder in which the cartilage between joints wears away, often because of overuse of the joint, resulting in osteophytes and eburnation.

osteophyte A sign of osteoarthritis in which bones develop a distinct "lipping" of bone at the point of articulation.

eburnation A sign of osteoarthritis in which the epiphyses of long bones are worn smooth, causing them to take on a varnish-like appearance.

long bone cross-sections Cross-sections of the body's long bones (arms and legs) used to analyze bone shape and reconstruct the mechanical stresses placed on that bone—and hence activity patterns.

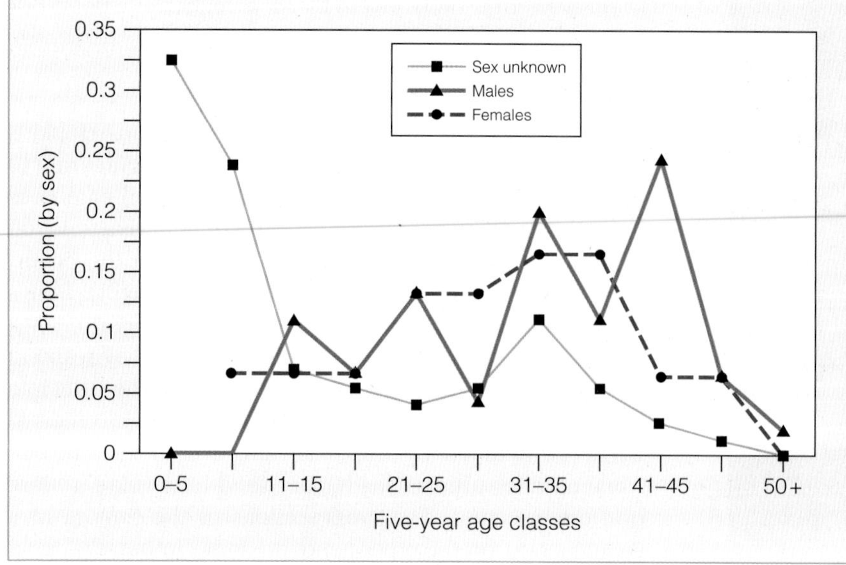

FIGURE 9-4 The Stillwater mortality profile.

in men's and women's femoral cross-sections was produced by a difference in men's and women's behavior and not simply by differences in the size of men and women.

In sum, the femur cross-sections and the patterns in osteoarthritis indicated that the people living at Stillwater Marsh walked a great deal to make a successful living, and that men did more walking than women. Neither of these conclusions was particularly striking, but it was conclusive proof that the people who lived at Stillwater were nomadic, and it gave Larsen a clearer picture of the differences between men's and women's lives.

Paleodemography

Still another way to judge quality of life is to examine patterns of mortality. **Paleodemography** reconstructs parameters such as life expectancy at birth, the age profile of a population, and patterns in the ages at death. Bioarchaeologists do this by constructing various sorts of **mortality profiles** for a prehistoric population based on the age and sex data of burials. Mortality profiles show at what age adult males, adult females, and children died.

Paleodemography works best with well-defined cemetery populations (that is, for a skeletal sample derived from the same biological population over a few years or decades). Although radiocarbon dates suggested that the Stillwater burials dated to the Underdown phase, this phase covers 600 years. For this reason, the Stillwater population is not an ideal candidate for a paleodemographic study.

paleodemography The study of ancient demographic patterns and trends.

mortality profiles Charts that depict the various ages at death of a burial population.

Still, bioarchaeologist Sheilagh Brooks was able to derive some useful data from mortality profiles for the Stillwater burials. One of these profiles (see Figure 9-4) shows the burial data sorted into five-year age classes by sex. Note first that the 0 to 5 age category is composed mostly of "unknowns"; as we mentioned earlier, it is almost impossible to determine the sex of very young children.

Why did so many children die so young? Ethnographic data show that the mortality of newborns and toddlers is very high among hunting-and-gathering populations: Of all children born in most foraging populations, 50 to 60 percent do not survive to 5 years of age. The Stillwater mortality profile reflects this sad fact.

There are no strong peaks in female age at death. Girls may have had a slightly higher chance of dying at a young age compared with boys, and men may have had a slightly greater chance of surviving into their 40s than women. The female mortality profile shows an increase in deaths beginning at age 21, the early child-bearing years; this is also similar to other foraging populations. Finally, notice that few individuals are assigned to the 46 to 50 and 50+ age categories; this reflects a shorter overall life expectancy. Although we might regard the late 40s as the prime of life, a 48-year-old person in Stillwater was an elder.

Stature

Measuring stature is yet another way to assess quality of life. Bioarchaeologists estimate stature with equations that relate the length of certain long bones to an individual's height. These equations were created, incidentally, from measurements on individuals who donated their bodies to science.

The femur is the best bone for computing stature (because tall people tend to have long femora and short people tend to have short femora). But because the relationship between height and femur length varies from population to population, it is important that bioarchaeologists apply the appropriate equation. Here, for instance, is the stature formula, which has an error factor of ± 3.5 centimeters, for ancient populations in central Mexico:

$$\text{living height} = (2.26 \times \text{femur length}) + 66.38$$

This equation tells us that, if a femur excavated in central Mexico measures 40 centimeters in length, it likely

PROFILE OF AN ARCHAEOLOGIST

A Native American Archaeologist

Dorothy Lippert is an archaeologist with the Smithsonian Institution. Reprinted by permission.

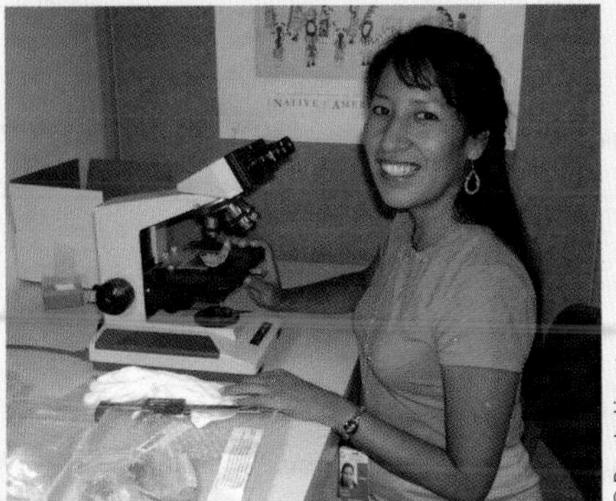

© Dorothy Lippert

Dorothy Lippert.

Deciding to become an archaeologist was the easy part. I had no fixed ideas about what such a career would consist of other than that I would be participating in the scientific process of understanding our human past. I was unaware of the extent to which my own Native American heritage would play a role; in the beginning, I didn't realize that this part of my identity would so closely focus both my career and my beliefs about what we are meant to do as archaeologists. My reasons for choosing this discipline initially centered on a love of history and science, although I had little patience for understanding history as a simple series of dates and even less for reducing science to sterile sets of data. Archaeology, for me, has always been a humanistic endeavor, one in which we come to know and respect people of the past in the same way we should people of the present day.

I find that archaeologists who are also Native American seem to have similar views of the discipline, particularly when talking about prehistoric archaeological work in North America. This is most likely because we know these people as our ancestors and in the course of practicing archaeology it becomes our privilege and our responsibility to care for them and to speak about their lives. A common thread within indigenous cultures is a respect for our elders and this permeates archaeology as it is practiced by Native Americans.

In 2003, there were 11 Native Americans with doctorates in archaeology. It is my suspicion that this number reflects both the small numbers of Native Americans who hold doctorates in any subject as well as the emotional and scholarly hazards that archaeology holds for us. The impression that many tribal people have had up to now of archaeology is that it is something that is done to Native peoples by outsiders. Those of us who try to practice archaeology from a Native perspective are still caught by this impression and, in some people's eyes, have become outsiders ourselves. Tribal people have insinuated to me that I must not be truly Native if I can bring myself to practice archaeology. I also have the added burden of having studied human osteology. Frequently, when I meet other Native people, I don't mention that I'm an archaeologist until late in the conversation, in hopes of forestalling a negative response.

Other Natives are more supportive, saying that it's about time that we (indigenous people) have started doing this work. Many understand just how difficult a career this can be and encourage me to continue. In their minds, as in my own, archaeology is a way to work for Native Americans, both the ancestors and present-day communities.

I think that many nonnative archaeologists are unaware of these kinds of reactions. Some seem convinced that archaeology done with a Native perspective will somehow be less scientific, as if their cultural heritage plays no role in their own studies. While I am a firm believer in maintaining scientific rigor in our analyses, I see no reason not to illuminate these studies with the cultural legacy that was maintained, sometimes at horrendous cost, by our ancestors. As Natives begin to participate fully in archaeology, I think the discipline will become broader in its approach and more open to combinations of different knowledge bases in order to understand a more human past.

When I speak with other Native Americans about the practice of archaeology, I find that we all tend to use this discipline to answer questions that are influenced by our cultural background. For instance, in my own studies of health and medical theory, I was interested in the ways that these were experienced by a small community whose inhabitants lived and died some 400 years ago. I could never quite see my research as the simple practice of collecting data; rather, I felt myself to be engaged in communication with these ancient ones. Their cold, white bones used my breath and mind to tell this world their long forgotten story. Through the practice of this science, I became their voice.

Even when reading archaeological reports and looking through pages of dry, scholarly text, I find that I am searching for the humanity of the people whose remains or material objects are being studied. I have also realized that this perspective is not limited only to indigenous archaeologists. There are a number of nonnatives who seem to intuitively approach our science with a very humanistic flair. I believe that in the years to come, more and more archaeologists will begin to appreciate just how much more fun it is if we see our discipline as dealing with fellow beings. Shakespeare summed it up well. "You are not stones, nor bones, but men." While archaeology frequently encounters both stones and bones, it is best if we keep in mind that what we are really meeting up with are human beings.

RAPID REVIEW

Classes of Basic Data from Human Skeletons

Information	Based on:
Age	Teeth, bone fusion, pubic symphysis
Sex	Skull, pelvis observations
Life expectancy	Analysis of age distributions in burial populations
Stature	Femur measurements
Disease	Manifested in different bones depending on specific type
Growth arrest	Dental hypoplasias, Harris lines in long bones
Workload	Bone joint osteoarthritis records which joints were heavily used; long bone cross-sections

belonged to an individual who stood about 157 centimeters tall (5 feet 2 inches), give or take 3.5 centimeters. Different formulae are available for skeletons recovered from other parts of the world.

Height provides a useful measure of overall health, because it is closely related to diet. However, because different populations have different genetic capacities for height, it is best to use this variable as a measure of health when looking at data for one burial population across time. Larsen did not calculate height estimates for the Stillwater burials, because most of the burials dated to the same phase, and no good comparative population data were available.

However, Larsen did use height estimates to track health changes in another project that examined individuals who lived on St. Catherines Island and elsewhere along the coast of Georgia. Here he was interested in testing hypotheses about the effect of maize agriculture on a human population's health. He estimated the heights from skeletons of the hunting-and-gathering population (pre–950 BP) and of the agricultural population (post–950 BP). Contrary to what you might expect, he found that the average male in an agricultural population was 1 percent and the average female in an agricultural population was 3 percent *shorter* than their foraging ancestors. In this case, agriculture was a poorer diet than the hunting-and-gathering one, and it hit women harder than men.

Reconstructing Diet from Human Bone

The people who lived at Stillwater were hunter-gatherers. But can we go beyond this general statement to talk more specifically about what people ate? Following the old adage "You are what you eat," diet can be reconstructed from human bone in several ways. We discuss two of these methods here.

Cavities

Dental **caries** (cavities) can help differentiate between agriculturalists and hunter-gatherer populations. Caries result when simple carbohydrates, especially refined sugar but also starchy foods like maize or tubers, remain on your teeth. Bacteria that feed on the carbohydrates produce a by-product of acid that dissolves tooth enamel. If you ate mostly meat, you would have few caries—regardless of whether you brushed your teeth.

The prevalence of caries, then, serves as an indicator of starchy diets (which, in ancient North America, generally means the consumption of maize). Skilled bioarchaeologists, in fact, can glance at a subject's teeth and make a good guess as to whether the person was an agriculturalist or a hunter-gatherer—just by looking for caries.

The people at Stillwater Marsh were strictly hunter-gatherers; they did not grow or eat maize. Because their diet was low in simple carbohydrates (and obviously did not include refined sugar at all), only 3 percent of the Stillwater skeletons had dental caries—a remarkably low figure.

But they were hardly free of dental problems. The Stillwater folks lost many of their teeth by middle age, generally because of excessive tooth wear—a product of the grit in their diet from seeds and tubers ground on metates. They also suffered from abscesses, which appear as large voids in the mandibles and maxillas. In fact, some teeth had shallow grooves worn into their sides, where a person had habitually twirled a toothpick-sized twig to overstimulate the nerves and alleviate the pain of an abscess.

Bone and Stable Isotopes

We can also reconstruct ancient diets by analyzing the carbon and nitrogen stable isotopes preserved in human bone.

We encountered the concept of isotopes when discussing radiocarbon dating (in Chapter 5). Carbon, you remember, has both stable and unstable isotopes. One stable form, ^{12}C, makes up about 99 percent of the world's carbon; another stable isotope, ^{13}C, accounts for less than 1 percent. Remembering that plants take in carbon through one of three photosynthetic pathways (C_3, C_4, and CAM), you'll recall that C_4 plants (such as maize) take in more ^{13}C and ^{14}C isotopes than do C_3 and CAM plants. Because human bone reflects the isotopic ratios of plants ingested during life, bioarchaeologists can reconstruct the dietary importance of certain classes of plants by measuring the ratio of carbon isotopes contained in bone **collagen**, the organic component of bone. A diet rich in C_4 plants (such as maize), for example, can produce bones with a higher ratio of ^{13}C to ^{12}C than diets low in C_4 plants.

Nitrogen also has two stable isotopes, ^{14}N and ^{15}N. Some plants obtain their nitrogen from the air and others absorb nitrogen from the soil. These diverse mechanisms result in different ratios of ^{15}N to ^{14}N in various plants. Using this information, bioarchaeologists analyze a bone's stable isotope composition to determine which plants were eaten and which were not. In addition, we know that carnivores tend to lose ^{14}N through their urine, but they retain ^{15}N. This means that humans who consume large amounts of meat have a higher ratio of ^{15}N to ^{14}N than those who eat mostly plants. To complicate things further, marine plants tend to have ^{15}N to ^{14}N ratios that are 4 percent higher than terrestrial plants. These differences are passed up the food chain, so marine mammals also tend to have higher ratios of ^{15}N to ^{14}N than do terrestrial mammals. You cannot interpret the values blindly, but used properly, differences in nitrogen values tell us whether people relied more heavily on marine than terrestrial foods or had more or less meat in their diets.

Larsen submitted samples of human bone from 39 of the individuals recovered at Stillwater Marsh to Margaret Schoeninger (University of California, San Diego). With the human bone samples, Larsen also submitted several modern plant specimens and animal bones (identified to species) to act as controls.

The actual measurement of a bone's carbon and nitrogen isotope ratios is a complex process involving a mass spectrometer and need not concern us here. But Schoeninger's findings are not difficult to understand. To make her point, Schoeninger compared the results of the analysis of the Stillwater materials to two very different populations: the skeletal remains from Pecos Pueblo in New Mexico, a maize-dependent population, and the skeletal remains of a foraging population from Ontario, Canada, which was heavily dependent on meat. In Figure 9-5, the horizontal axis plots the ratio of ^{13}C to ^{12}C—higher ratios are farther to the right (indicating more C_4 plants like maize in the diet) and lower ratios to the left (meaning fewer C_4 plants in the diet). Don't let the negative numbers confuse you. To make measurements comparable, Schoeninger reports the stable isotope values calibrated as deviations from an agreed-upon standard (the fossil *belemnitella*, in the Pee Dee limestone formation of South Carolina). The vertical axis plots the ratio of ^{15}N to ^{14}N; higher ratios are at the top (more carnivorous diet) and lower ratios are at the bottom (less carnivorous diet).

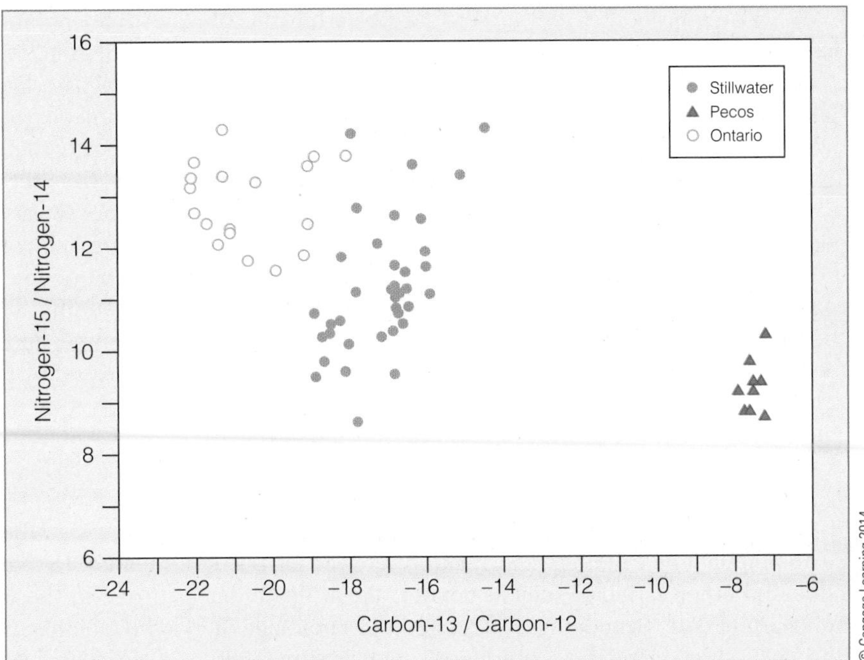

FIGURE 9-5 Stable carbon and nitrogen isotopes for the Stillwater burial population compared with those of Archaic Ontario hunter-gatherers and of Pecos Pueblo maize horticulturalists.

As Figure 9-5 shows, the Pecos population has a high ratio of ^{13}C to ^{12}C and a low ratio of ^{15}N to ^{14}N. This means that the Pecos population ate plenty of maize and very little meat. At the upper left part of the graph, the Ontario hunting population has a high ratio of ^{15}N to ^{14}N, with virtually no C_4 plants in its diet; this makes sense, because the Ontario foragers lived in an environment unsuitable for horticulture and relied primarily on fish, moose, and caribou for food. The Stillwater ("Carson Desert") population lies between these two extremes, with very

caries Cavities.

collagen The organic component of bone.

few C_4 plants in its diet, but a diet that was a mixture of plant and animal foods.

Schoeninger took her results even further. Remember that she also analyzed some modern plant samples; one of these was piñon pine. It turns out that piñon has a very low ratio of ^{15}N to ^{14}N. Schoeninger figured that if piñon was important to the Stillwater diet, then the bones of this population should have a much lower nitrogen ratio than the graph indicates. Because they do not, Schoeninger concluded that piñon could not have been an important component of the Stillwater diet. Instead, by looking at the values for the other plant and animal control samples, Schoeninger concluded that a strictly marsh-based diet could readily account for the observed carbon and nitrogen isotope ratios in the Stillwater remains.

Note in Figure 9-5 that the Stillwater population has a greater *range* of nitrogen values than either the Ontario or Pecos populations. Finding no correlation between nitrogen value and other variables such as gender, age at death, or radiocarbon date, Schoeninger suggested that the range of nitrogen values might be a product of dietary variability. Although bone chemistry is a lifelong average of one's diet, the period of youth and adolescence is particularly important because this is when bone collagen forms. If foods available in the wetlands varied from decade to decade because of flooding, fires, climate change, or other factors, then perhaps people ate different suites of food over the years. In some years, perhaps jackrabbits were commonly roasted over the fire; in other years, bulrush seed cakes might have been the daily fare. If this dietary variability accounts for the differential nitrogen ratios, then it suggests that the Pecos farmers and Ontario foragers had far more monotonous diets than did the people living at Stillwater Marsh.

Lives of Affluence? Or Nasty, Brutish, and Short?

We can now return to Larsen's original research question: Does the Stillwater burial population reflect human lives that were "nasty, brutish, and short" or those of an "affluent society"?

The answer is "both" and "neither." The people of Stillwater Marsh consumed a varied diet that probably went beyond their minimal nutritional needs. They were relatively healthy, generally free of serious disease, disorders, broken bones, and infections. This part seems to fit the "original affluent society" image.

But the Stillwater people also worked hard, and some had good reason to complain about aching knees and backs. Some youngsters suffered periods of malnutrition, and a large proportion of the Stillwater children did not live to their 5th birthday. Nobody lived much beyond 50 years. These data conform more to the "nasty, brutish, and short" model.

The point is not to pigeonhole the Stillwater burial population, per se, but to learn what life was like for people in the past. We seek to understand the various factors that influenced their diet, their rates of infection and bone breakage, their workloads, and their dental health. In some ways, the Stillwater people had a good life; in other ways, it was not so easy. The past can almost never be characterized in simple black-and-white terms.

The people of Stillwater lived lives that were physically demanding, but not very violent. Not all people were so fortunate, and in some places, ancient lives of violence are witnessed by the bones.

Archaeology and DNA

How was the world colonized? Are modern humans related to Neanderthals? When did Native Americans arrive in the New World (see Looking Closer: Coprolites and Colonization of the New World)?

Archaeologists once used artifacts alone to talk about ancient migrations and the historical relationships among the world's populations. But modern genetic technology provides another avenue to reconstructing the past. By using genetic material—DNA from human skeletal remains and living peoples—geneticists and archaeologists have joined forces to create a new approach to reconstructing the past known as **molecular archaeology**. As is so often true, this new approach raises as many questions as it attempts to answer.

A Little Background on DNA

Most of our genetic information exists as about 3 billion nucleotide base pairs grouped into some 50,000 genes on the 46 chromosomes inside the nucleus of each cell in our bodies. This stuff, called **nuclear DNA** (deoxyribonucleic acid, or nDNA), makes each of us unique and is inherited from our biological parents. Your nDNA contains the recipe for your biological composition, telling your body to create blue or brown eyes, to be short or tall, to have straight or curly hair. A **gene** is a segment of a chromosome, one small piece of the recipe that codes for particular biological attributes.

Although nDNA is extraordinarily useful to the genetics of living populations, it is not so useful to archaeology. It degrades fairly quickly, and by the time the human body decomposes, nDNA is no longer intact (although sections of about 200 nucleotide base pairs can survive for thousands of years).

But another form of DNA, known as **mitochondrial DNA (mtDNA),** is found in the cells' mitochondria (organelles responsible for the cell's energy metabolism)—outside the nucleus. Mitrochondrial DNA contains only about 0.0006 percent of the genetic material of nDNA, which would seem to limit its use, but mtDNA has

WHAT DOES IT MEAN TO me?

Should We Excavate and Analyze Human Remains?

In many places in the world, archaeologists have no qualms about excavating human skeletal remains. But in the United States, conducting research on American Indian remains is a sensitive issue indeed. In fact, archaeologists who do field research in the United States today generally excavate human remains only if they are in the way of a construction project that cannot be rerouted. And no archaeologist would excavate a burial without consulting at least the nearest tribe (in fact, such consultation is mandated by law if the excavation is on federal land). Sometimes this consultation works out well, as it did in Stillwater. But tribal attitudes change, and if the Stillwater remains were exposed today instead of nearly 20 years ago, it's possible that their excavation and analysis would be blocked. It has become increasingly difficult for bioarchaeologists to work with extant collections; those involved with the Kennewick case had to file a lawsuit to get access to that skeleton.

All of this raises major ethical questions. Some modern archaeologists believe that we should simply forgo the analysis of human skeletons and accept that as the price to be paid for showing respect and sensitivity to modern Native Americans who find the excavation and analysis of ancestral remains disrespectful. Many other Americans would agree with them.

Although many museums curate both Indian and non-Indian skeletal remains, the proportion of Native American skeletons often outweighs the non-Indian remains—reflecting, in large measure, the historical interest of American archaeology in excavating American Indian burial sites. And reburying non–Native American remains often seems to be the obvious, and respectful, thing to do. Those Civil War dead who are discovered today are sometimes studied, but always reburied. From the outset, archaeologists agreed to rebury the remains of those who died in the *Hunley*, the Confederate submarine that sank on its first mission (see "Looking Closer: Preserving the *Hunley*," page 97).

Archaeologists have long curated Native American remains in museum collections, in case new techniques enable us to learn more about the past. Such breakthroughs do occur: Who, in 1965, would have thought that within two decades we would be extracting genetic material from 7000-year-old human skeletons? This chapter gives only a glimpse of what we can learn from human skeletons, and each year brings new techniques. There is so much more to learn.

Scientists wish to learn more about the past to increase our understanding of the history of humanity. This is a good thing. But Native Americans wish to see their ancestors, and themselves, treated with respect. This is also a good thing.

Which should we choose? Does science trump every other concern? Answer yes, and you appear ethnocentric. Do some people have the right to shut the door on an area of knowledge? Answer yes, and you would seem to condone book burning.

What is knowledge worth? What is knowledge *for*? Every archaeologist, especially those who study human skeletal remains, must carefully consider these questions today.

three interesting properties. First, although it contains only a limited segment of the total genetic recipe, each cell contains thousands of copies of it (in contrast to just the two in the nucleus). This translates to a greater probability of retrieving mtDNA than nDNA. But don't think that there are gobs of mtDNA just lying around in archaeological sites. Its recovery is made possible through the technique of *polymerase chain reaction* (PCR), which enables researchers to create billions of copies of a very small sample of mtDNA, so that this genetic material can be more readily studied.

The second intriguing property of mtDNA is that you inherit yours *only* from your mother. If you are female, you pass along your mtDNA to your children. If you are male, none of the mtDNA that you inherited from your mother is passed on to your biological offspring. This makes it possible to define molecular "family trees" and to trace the movement of female lineages.

Finally, although mtDNA is probably not completely free from the pressures of natural selection, it appears to be under less selective pressure than nuclear DNA. And because it is transferred from mother to offspring as a chunk, it does not recombine (as does nuclear DNA). Instead, mtDNA appears to change over time largely as a result of random mutations. Nuclear DNA can also change as a result of random mutation (this is, in fact, one of the main ways that new genetic material appears). But compared with nuclear DNA, mtDNA mutates rapidly, about 2.8 to 6.6 mutations per 10,000 years. Although this

molecular archaeology The use of genetic information in ancient human remains to reconstruct the past.

nuclear DNA Genetic material found in a cell's nucleus; this material is primarily responsible for an individual's inherited traits.

gene A unit of the chromosomes that controls inheritance of particular traits.

mitochondrial DNA (mtDNA) Genetic material found in the mitochondria of cells; it is inherited only from the mother and appears to mutate at a rate of 2 to 4 percent per 1 million years.

LOOKING CLOSER

Coprolites and Colonization of the New World

Given the vagaries of preservation, archaeologists cannot afford to be picky about their sources of information: data are where you find them. At Paisley 5 Mile Point Caves in Oregon, crucial information on the colonization of the New World came from . . . coprolites.

You'll recall that coprolites are desiccated feces. In the dry caves of the desert West, coprolites of many different species of animals are often preserved, including those of humans. At one of the Paisley caves, Dennis Jenkins (University of Oregon) recovered more than a dozen human coprolites, three of which returned radiocarbon dates in excess of 12,000 radiocarbon years, meaning that they were *1000 or more years older* than the oldest known dates for Clovis. To confirm the dates, Jenkins submitted samples to another lab, which returned the same ages. The coprolites were indeed old. But many creatures defecate in caves. The coprolites *looked* human, but Jenkins needed to be certain.

Jenkins tested six of the coprolites using crossover immunoelectrophoresis (CIEP), a standard test used in crime labs to detect human proteins in stains of unknown origin; two of the three oldest coprolites tested positive. All three also tested positive when samples were reconstituted using trisodium phosphate, which turns a dark brown when applied to human coprolites. These tests were encouraging, but Jenkins needed to be certain. And so he turned to Danish geneticist Eske Willerslev.

Willerslev found that all six coprolites tested positive for human mtDNA. Further testing also found evidence of Native American haplogroups (specifically, subgroups of A and B). Again, encouraging, but ancient DNA samples are extremely prone to contamination, so how could Willerslev be certain that the DNA was ancient? For starters, he had the work replicated in two other labs that use slightly different techniques. Both of these labs returned the same results. Thus, contamination in Willerslev's lab could be ruled out. But perhaps the coprolites had been contaminated during fieldwork. Many people worked at and visited the site. Maybe some of their DNA—transmitted through dead skin cells, or a sneeze, had contaminated the samples. To check for this, Willerslev took samples from everyone who worked at or visited the site (and even from all the workers in his lab), regardless of whether they handled the coprolites or not, and compared it to the sequences found in the coprolites. None matched. So far, so good.

But perhaps the coprolites were contaminated by later humans who visited the cave. The archaeological data show that this site was used for thousands of years by later people. Perhaps some of their DNA—transmitted through bodily fluids, hair, or dead skin cells—had contaminated the coprolites. This is an even more difficult factor to rule out, but Jenkins and Willerslev came up with an ingenious solution. Wood rats used the cave more than people did. If human DNA was moving around through the sediments, then certainly wood rat DNA would, too. So, Willerslev tested the coprolites for wood rat DNA. But the tests were negative. So, for the time being, the most definitive evidence of a pre-Clovis human presence in North America comes from the most humble of human artifacts—coprolites.

Excavation in progress at Paisley 5 Mile Point Cave.

may seem slow, it is *6 to 16 times faster* than nuclear DNA's mutation rate. If one assumes that this rate of change has been constant through time, then differences in the mutations between related mtDNA samples can be used to estimate how much time has elapsed since the branches of the family tree diverged. For this reason, mtDNA is sometimes used as a "clock" to date the timing of human population movements in the remote past.

Think of it this way: Imagine a population of interbreeding humans. Women in this population are closely related and, consequently, all members of the population (not just the women) share the same mutations in their mtDNA. Now imagine that this population splits apart, and one group migrates to a region far enough away that the two groups no longer interbreed. Both will share the mutations they had prior to the migration, but chances are that future mutations in their mtDNA will not be the same. If the population has three mutations in common and three that are different, then, assuming the clock is accurate, the population split into two about 5,000 to 10,000 years ago (at roughly 3 to 6 mutations every 10,000 years).

This might be a very useful tool for archaeology, if we could recover ancient DNA (or, as it is now known, **aDNA**) from organic remains recovered in archaeological sites.

Prospecting for aDNA

In 1984, Allan Wilson (1934–1991) and his student Vince Sarich (University of California, Berkeley) were the first to identify aDNA. When they cloned DNA from the 140-year-old skin of quagga—a recently extinct, zebra-like African beast—the Berkeley team showed that DNA could indeed survive after the death of an organism.

At about the same time, Swedish researcher Svante Pääbo (Max Planck Institute for Evolutionary Anthropology, Germany) cloned aDNA from a 4400-year-old Egyptian mummy. This was the first time that anyone had applied PCR techniques to ancient humans. Not long after, Pääbo pushed the barrier back another 2600 years by extracting aDNA from 7000-year-old human brain tissue preserved at the waterlogged Little Salt Spring site in Florida.

Initial excitement over this new frontier was tempered by the realization that it is extraordinarily difficult to prevent aDNA samples from being contaminated with modern human DNA. Let's face it: DNA is *really* small and you can't just sweep a lab clean of it. This is not such a large problem when studying DNA extracted from faunal remains—the presence of human DNA would be a dead giveaway that something was amiss in the lab. But separating modern from ancient human DNA is far more difficult. As a result, labs must use some very strict protocols to prevent contamination. For example, geneticists take samples from every person who came into contact with the ancient remains to demonstrate that the sample is uncontaminated by modern DNA.

An African Eve?

Wilson's work did not stop with the quagga. Instead, he and his colleagues moved on to explore the human past as well.

Wilson and his team (including Rebecca Cann, University of Hawaii, and Mark Stoneking, Max Planck Institute for Evolutionary Anthropology, Germany) collected 147 mtDNA samples from around the world (from human placentas) and compared the human data with that of a chimpanzee (as a control). The most striking fact about mtDNA is how much of it we all share. At the molecular level, all living human groups share all but about 0.6 percent of mtDNA. As you might expect, humans and chimpanzees share somewhat less, humans and horses share even less, and so forth. The 0.6 percent figure is important because it suggests a way to determine the relatedness among all living individuals and groups.

By examining the mtDNA from various modern human populations, Wilson could see what a close-knit species we really are. This was a surprise because mtDNA is supposed to evolve fairly rapidly. Components of the modern global sample turned out to be remarkably alike—both within geographical populations and between continental groups. The result was a family tree for all of (surviving) humanity. Africa provided the longest branch on the tree, suggesting this is where human mtDNA began to differentiate. Those of African descent also showed the most variability among themselves (in fact, Bushmen peoples have the most diverse DNA of any living human population) and were the most distinct from other populations of the world. Wilson argued that this pattern is precisely what one would expect *if all modern humans had descended from a single population in Africa.*

These investigators went a step further, suggesting that all the genetic composition evident in living human populations could be traced to a single ancient African ancestor. Because mtDNA is passed down strictly through the maternal line, this fictive ancestor must have been female. She was quickly nicknamed Eve, after the biblical first woman and wife of Adam.

Even more controversial than Eve's African origin was the molecular clock that Wilson and his group derived. Because geneticists assume that mtDNA changes at a constant rate, the 0.6 percent figure is important for another reason: It provides a relatively precise way to gauge the first appearance of *Homo sapiens* (modern humans). Although this so-called **molecular clock** does not keep perfect time,

aDNA Ancient DNA recovered from organic materials in archaeological sites.

molecular clock Calculations of the time since divergence of two related populations using the presumed rate of mutation in mtDNA and the genetic differences between the two populations.

it does suggest some genetic limits within which human evolution may have taken place.

Wilson's molecular clock suggested that Eve must have lived about 200,000 years ago. If so, then the first descendants of Eve (early modern humans) must have fanned out of Africa to supplant other hominins about this time. This theory, which has come to be known as the "out of Africa" hypothesis, had, it turned out, also been framed independently on the basis of the fossil evidence alone.

To call the Eve hypothesis controversial is an understatement. Some biological anthropologists, such as Milford Wolpoff (University of Michigan), see strong continuity between pre- and post-200,000-year-old skulls from various parts of the Old World. To these anthropologists, the skeletal data offer arguments for continuity in various parts of the Old World (humans had not yet colonized the New World by this date) rather than recent replacement by a migrating population from Africa. (Although Africa is still the homeland of humanity, as we saw in Chapter 5, the question here is whether *all* modern humans derive from a later African expansion.)

What Happened to the Neanderthals?

Others charged that the Eve hypothesis was based on modern genetic distributions and that it needed to be tested by using DNA extracted from ancient bone. One particularly controversial area is whether the Neanderthals of Europe and the Near East are related to modern humans or if they are an evolutionary dead end.

Neanderthals were present in Europe by at least 500,000 years ago; they also appear in the Near East and in parts of Asia. They probably coexisted with modern humans in the Near East for several tens of thousands of years, but they appear to have quickly disappeared by roughly 30,000 years ago in Europe—about the time that biologically modern humans appear there. Did modern humans drive Neanderthals to extinction, or did they interbreed with them so thoroughly that the population's distinctive appearance was genetically swamped?

Based on skeletal data, Neanderthals are strikingly different biologically from modern humans. Popularly, they are thought of as short, slump-shouldered, beetle-browed, slack-jawed brutes; calling someone a "Neanderthal" is not considered a compliment! But this says more about our cultural biases than it does about skeletal biology, for these features were probably part and parcel of an anatomy that was adapted to the cold, near-glacial environment of Europe. Neanderthals had arms and legs that were shorter relatively to the length of their torsos than modern humans, the result of selective pressure to reduce heat loss. And although they had sloping chins and foreheads, and a more projecting face, their cranial capacity was probably comparable to that of modern humans. They also had especially powerful hands

FIGURE 9-6 A reconstruction of a Neanderthal woman.

and arms, and were generally more robust and muscular than modern humans. One genetic study of Neanderthal remains found the genes coding for light skin and red hair (see Figure 9-6).

Looking at the skeletal data, some biological anthropologists see continuity between the Neanderthals and modern Europeans, and argue that Neanderthals are part of the human line. Others see skeletal differences too large to place Neanderthals in the ancestry of modern humans. Which is it? Are Neanderthals in the human family tree, or an ancient offshoot that went extinct in the face of competition with modern humans?

Recently, several studies have extracted aDNA from Neanderthal skeletal remains. An initial study looked only at mtDNA and found no overlap between Neanderthals and modern humans. But in 2010, a team of geneticists led by Svante Pääbo sequenced the nDNA genome from three Neanderthals. This is nothing short of remarkable given how easy it is for nDNA to degrade, and how easy it can be contaminated with DNA from bacteria and microbes, as well as with the DNA of the many people who have handled the remains over the years.

Pääbo and his colleagues could sequence about two-thirds of the Neanderthal genome. They then compared this genome to that sequenced from living peoples in sub-Saharan Africa, Europe, and Asia. They found no trace of Neanderthal genes in the sub-Saharan African population—which makes sense because there never were any Neanderthals in sub-Saharan Africa. But the other populations carried from 1 to 4 percent of Neanderthal DNA. Neanderthals and humans interbred some 40,000 to 50,000 years ago and produced fertile offspring, most likely in the Near East where those two populations overlapped for a long period of time. They probably did not "hook up" frequently, however; otherwise, we might expect the overlap to be greater than 1 to 4 percent.

One suggested explanation for the lack of much interbreeding was that Neanderthals were not just physically different from modern humans, but mentally different as well. Specifically, some people have suggested that Neanderthals were unable to speak and communicate in the way that modern humans can. Geneticists know that one gene, the $FOXP_2$ gene, is crucial for the development of language because it controls the muscles that permit us to articulate speech. This gene, found only in humans, is absent from all other primate genomes. But Pääbo found the $FOXP_2$ gene in the Neanderthal sequence. This means that Neanderthals had the same physical capacity for speech as modern humans. Still unanswered, however, is whether they had modern humans' remarkable ability to use symbols, to speak using metaphors and similes, that is such a hallmark of human communication.

We are still a long way from relying on genetic evidence to reconstruct the past. But the advances that have been made in only the past 20 years are sufficiently intriguing to suggest that, whatever the answer may be, molecular archaeology provides a major new source of information on the past. If nothing else, these data will force archaeologists to reconsider whether they really do know what they think they know. And that, as we have said, is what science is all about.

Conclusion

Studying human skeletal remains provides an up-close way for archaeologists to understand the people of the past. Where burial populations are available, our knowledge of the past can grow by leaps and bounds. By analyzing skeletal morphology and bone chemistry, bioarchaeologists can learn a great deal about men's and women's workloads, diets, patterns of disease, trauma, and quality of life. And the field of bioarchaeology is in its infancy, each year producing new ways to analyze human bone and promising to expand our knowledge of the past considerably.

Molecular archaeology has great promise to help reconstruct human migrations, if we can figure out how to use genes as clocks. This is an area of middle-level theory that will require considerable attention in the future.

The next two chapters will move us into questions about aspects of past human lives that are even more difficult to reconstruct: understanding social and political behavior and the meaning of symbols.

Summary

- How do bioarchaeologists contribute to a study of the past?
  - Bioarchaeology is the study of the human biological component evident in the archaeological record; it examines the health and workload of ancient populations. This specialty requires expertise in the method and theory of both biological anthropology and field archaeology.
- How do bioarchaeologists determine age and sex for a skeleton?
  - We use characteristics of several bones, notably the pelvis and skull, to determine an individual's sex.
  - An individual's age can be determined by tooth eruption; patterns of bone fusion, tooth wear, and bone wear are used to age individuals over the age of 25.
- How do bioarchaeologists use paleopathology and bone chemistry to reconstruct the lives of ancient peoples?
  - Paleopathology is the study of those ancient diseases that leave skeletal traces. Iron deficiency, for example, leaves a distinctive spongy appearance on the skull and the interior of the eye orbits. In addition, growth-arrest features, such as Harris lines and enamel hypoplasias, indicate periods of severe disease or malnutrition in childhood.
  - Bones respond to the routine mechanical stresses placed upon them; patterns of osteoarthritis and long bone cross-sections can point to different patterns of workload between the sexes or to changes through time.
  - Stature estimates can track changes in the quality of diet.
  - Bioarchaeologists can also reconstruct diet: High frequency of dental caries indicates a diet high in simple carbohydrates and sugars. The ratios of carbon and nitrogen isotopes in bone can reconstruct the dietary importance of various kinds of plants and animals.
- How are genetic data used to reconstruct population relationships and the ages of migrations?
  - Molecular archaeology uses data from living and ancient peoples to reconstruct population migrations. Especially useful is mitochondrial DNA. Although we still have much to learn about the rates at which DNA mutates, current studies show that DNA studies are important to reconstructing the past.

Media Resources

Access chapter-specific learning tools including learning objectives, practice quizzes, videos, flash cards, and glossaries, as well as web links, and more in your Archaeology CourseMate. Login to www.cengagebrain.com to access the resources your instructor has assigned and to purchase materials.

Reconstructing Social and Political Systems of the Past

10

© Douglas Peebles/CORBIS

A portion of Nan Madol, a ceremonial center of a chiefdom on the island of Pohnpei in Micronesia. The walls were constructed of massive basalt columns transported from the opposite side of the island.

Learning Objectives

After reading this chapter, you should be able to answer these questions:

- What concepts help archaeologists to reconstruct past social and political organizations?
- What archaeological remains are important in reconstructing political organization, especially those involving inherited social inequities?
- What archaeological remains help reconstruct social organization, especially kinship?
- What techniques help reconstruct ancient trade networks?

Preview

SO FAR, WE have talked about how archaeologists learn about human diets, foraging activities, site seasonality, and settlement patterns—not easy business, but readily grounded in the bedrock realities of archaeology. Now, we'll venture into new territory, exploring ancient social and political organization—what these are, and how archaeologists find out about them.

This chapter looks at three key components of human society: gender, kinship, and social status. Each brings its own interpretive problems and middle-level difficulties. What men and women did in the past is essential to understanding how a society operates, yet assigning specific artifacts to men and women is difficult. Kinship is a major structuring principle of human social organization, but it leaves ambiguous traces. The archaeological record reflects social status a bit more clearly, but many ancient societies may have been organized politically in ways that have no simple ethnographic analogies today. Trade, we will see, is an important component of political and social systems, and archaeologists have various ways of tracing the movement of food and goods across a landscape. Although we are entering a more difficult realm of archaeology, we will show that reconstructing past social and political systems is not impossible.

Introduction

Recall from Chapter 2 that archaeology is firmly situated within the broader field of anthropology. Right now, we must return to archaeology's roots in anthropology to define some terms and concepts.

Social Vocabulary

Social organization refers to the rules and structures that govern relationships between individuals within a group of interacting people. These relationships are never simple because people belong to groups on many different levels; some of these crosscut one another, and others are hierarchically organized.

You, for example, simultaneously belong to one or more families (as a son or daughter, husband or wife, brother or sister) and to a town, a state, and a country. You are biologically male or female, and you may be a member of or hold office in a sports club, political party, or community organization. In other words, you play various roles in a variety of social groups. Which identity is currently operating depends upon the situation.

Some social groups are residential, consisting of domestic families or households, territorial bands, or community-level villages. Residential groups tend to be physical, face-to-face associations of people. Residential groups appear in the archaeological record as households and villages.

Other groups are nonresidential; these are groups in the abstract sense and may never actually convene. Nonresidential groups are usually manifested archaeologically through the use of symbols, ceremonies, mythologies, or insignias of membership that appear as particular styles of material culture, such as ceramics, architecture, rock art, or burials. Although the residential group regulates discrete spatial matters, the nonresidential group binds these territorial units together.

A related concept is **political organization**, the formal and informal institutions that regulate a society's collective acts. Sometimes, control rests primarily at the level of the residential group; in other cases, the nonresidential group exerts a powerful influence. The nineteenth-century Great Basin Shoshone and Paiute, for example, lived in nuclear families, three or four of which came together in a residential group. Such groups were ephemeral, and families would come and go in an ever-changing set of associations. Clusters of families would sometimes come together for a communal jackrabbit or antelope drive. When they did, one individual, recognized for his hunting ability, would take charge, but his authority would disappear when the drive was over. Shoshone families did not "do as they pleased," but neither did they participate in a formal, permanent level of political integration above the family. This means that although behaviors such as murder and theft were considered antisocial, punishment varied depending on the particular circumstances and families involved.

Contrast this with eighteenth-century Tahitian society. At the time of European contact (in 1767), Tahiti—an island in the South Pacific with a population of some 100,000—had a horticultural economy of taro, breadfruit, yams, and coconuts. People also raised pigs and chickens, caught fish, and collected shellfish. Families lived in small villages along the coast and in the island's interior.

Unlike Shoshone bands, the membership of Tahitian villages was more or less permanent, with several strong and overarching levels of control. Tahitian villages were organized into about 20 competing **chiefdoms**. A "sacred chief" ruled each of these chiefdoms. Below the sacred chiefs were "small chiefs," and under the small chiefs were sub-chiefs. Below the sub-chiefs were the commoners. Sacred chiefs claimed to be descended directly from the gods, whereas commoners were said to exist only to provide for the needs of chiefs. A man had to marry a woman in his own class. Chiefs owned the land in their respective villages, and they had larger houses and canoes than commoners, as well as distinctive clothing. Some chiefs had craft specialists in their employ, and chiefs controlled communal fishing gear and village production.

The sacred chief also controlled the distribution of food and goods among villages. Periodically, he demanded tribute for special feasts and demonstrated his authority by redistributing food and goods to all who attended. The chief always retained some portion of the tribute for use by his household; chiefs also handed out punishments for social transgressions.

The Great Basin and Tahiti provide extreme examples of social and political organizations. To understand such differences, we will restrict the present discussion to four broad areas of human social and political behavior: gender, kinship, social status, and trade.

From Artifact to Symbol

Before doing this, we must re-emphasize the importance of middle-level theory. As you know, archaeologists use material remains to reconstruct past human activities; in Chapter 1, we talked about "thinking from things." People butcher an animal and leave behind stone tools and the bones. They make, use, and break a pot, leaving the sherds behind in a trash midden. Natural processes work on those remains, and discarded artifacts are sometimes reclaimed or recycled. Archaeologists need to consider all these dimensions of artifact use and reuse when interpreting the archaeological record.

Now we add another dimension that's especially important to understanding social and political organization. Although it might seem that archaeologists act as if artifacts only reflect human behavior, we know that artifacts are not just things—they are also *symbols*. Bringing flowers or a bottle of wine to dinner is a standard American way to thank a host. But such gestures would be meaningless to the Mikea (see Chapter 8), who expect their guests to show up with tobacco.

This fact—*that material culture reflects symbolic meanings as well as functional behaviors*—makes archaeological patterning even more difficult to understand because only rarely can we tell if objects are best interpreted in terms of their functional or symbolic meanings. Archaeologists are finding new ways to infer ancient social and political organization from artifacts, and this chapter provides several examples of how this works. We will return to the symbolic dimension of artifacts in Chapter 11.

Archaeology and Gender

Anthropologists distinguish between sex and gender, and between **gender roles** and **gender ideology**. Sex refers to inherited, biological differences between males and females. But gender refers to culturally constructed ideas about sex differences. Humans have only two sexes, male and female—but there can be more than two genders. In some Plains Indian tribes, for example, **berdaches** (also known as "two-spirits") were men who chose to live as women, performing women's traditional roles, and even marrying men (although marriage in this case did not imply a sexual relationship).

This leads us to the difference between gender *role* and gender *ideology*. Gender role refers to the differential participation of males and females in the various social, economic, political, and religious institutions of a group. These roles describe culturally appropriate behavior for men and women. In some societies, women can play very public roles, for example, in politics; in others, women's public participation may be limited. Gender ideology refers to the culturally specific meaning and value assigned to terms such as "male," "female," "sex," and "reproduction." In some societies, men and women generally share equal footing. In some, men are considered of greater importance, and in others, the activities of men and women are so differently valued that adult men and women interact very little. In some traditional New

social organization The rules and structures that govern relations within a group of interacting people. Societies are divided into social units (groups) within which are recognized social positions (statuses), with appropriate behavior patterns prescribed for these positions (roles).

political organization A society's formal and informal institutions that regulate a population's collective acts.

chiefdom A regional polity in which two or more local groups are organized under a single chief (who is the head of a ranked social hierarchy). Unlike autonomous bands and villages, chiefdoms consist of several more or less permanently aligned communities or settlements.

gender role The culturally prescribed behavior associated with men and women; roles can vary from society to society.

gender ideology The culturally prescribed values assigned to the task and status of men and women; values can vary from society to society.

berdaches Among Plains Indian societies, men who elected to live life as women; they were recognized by their group as a third gender.

© William S. Webb Museum of Anthropology

FIGURE 10-1 The site of Indian Knoll (Kentucky). In the days of Works Progress Administration (WPA) archaeology, a huge portion of the site was excavated, and hundreds of human burials uncovered.

Guinean societies, for example, men spend much of their leisure time in a communal men's house, rather than in their separate family homes.

These facts are important to understanding other societies, and also to understanding archaeological inference. Recognition of gender ideology led Margaret Conkey (University of California, Berkeley) and Janet Spector (retired) to accuse archaeology of a strong **androcentric** bias. Archaeologists at the time were mostly male, and they viewed the world largely in terms of men's activities and perceptions—and, in fact, in terms of white, middle-class, European male understandings of the world. Conkey and Spector found that most archaeologists failed to identify the sources of their assumptions and rarely tried to confirm or validate them. In other words, the only middle-level theory operating was the archaeologists' culturally biased view of gender roles.

As an example, consider the site of Indian Knoll in western Kentucky, a large, 2.5-meter-deep **shell midden** along the Green River (see Figure 10-1). This midden accumulated over a long period, from about 6100 to 4500 years ago. It was first excavated in 1916, by the self-trained archaeologist C. B. Moore (1852–1936) and then in the 1930s and 1940s by William Webb (1882–1964; formally trained as a physicist, Webb was almost certainly the only archaeologist to help develop the atomic bomb).

Indian Knoll is a shell midden—the remains of tens of thousands of shellfish meals are preserved there—but it was also a burial place. Between the two of them, Moore and Webb excavated some 1200 burials. They found that men were generally buried with axes, fishhooks, and other tools, whereas women were buried with beads, mortars, and pestles.

Some burials were accompanied by beautifully polished stones, a few inches long, somewhat triangular in cross-section, with slightly convex sides (see Figure 10-2). A hole was drilled neatly lengthwise down the middle of the stone. With these stones were often found pieces of whittled, slightly curved antler, a neat hook at one end.

Moore was puzzled by these enigmatic objects. He thought the stones might have served to hold cords the appropriate distance apart when weaving fishing nets; the antlers he thought might be netting needles.

But having seen well-preserved examples from dry caves in Texas and Arizona, Webb recognized these artifacts as parts of atlatls, or spear-throwers. The stones were slid onto one end of the wooden atlatl arm, perhaps 2 feet long, and the antler hook was fixed to one end, held in place by pitch or tree resin. The hook held the atlatl dart in place as the hunter took aim, and the stone weight increased the centrifugal force of the weapon as the hunter swung the atlatl overhead, launching the dart. The wooden atlatl arm and darts had decayed in the midden, but the stone and antler remained.

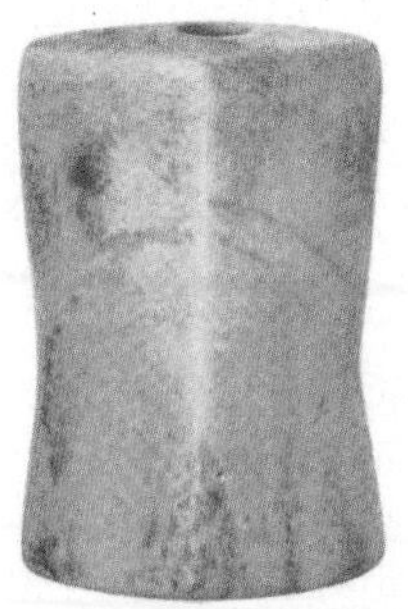
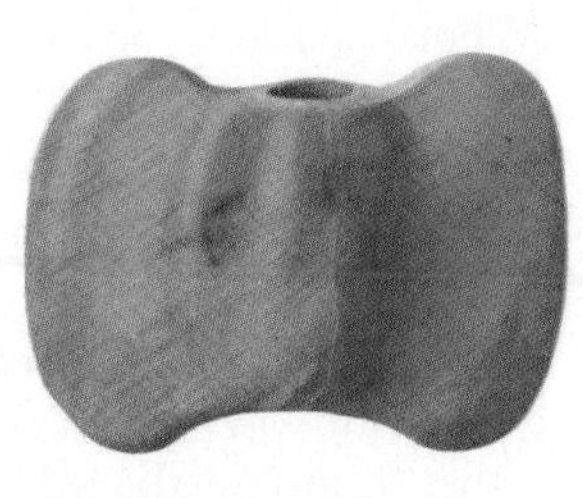
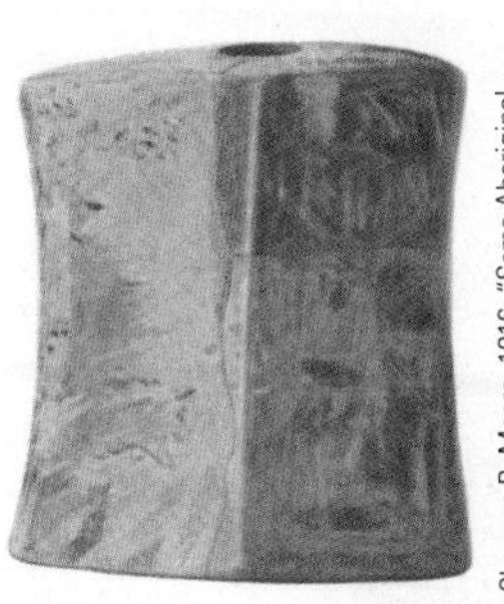

From Clarence B. Moore, 1916, "Some Aboriginal Sites on Green River, Kentucky," *Journal of the Academy of Natural Sciences of Philadelphia*, Vol. XVI, Plate XI.

FIGURE 10-2 Three atlatl weights from the Indian Knoll site.

Webb was curious about the distribution of these atlatls. Of the 76 burials that held atlatl weights, 31 were adult males, 13 were adult females, and 18 were children (the sex of the other 14 adults could not be identified). Why, Webb wondered, did people place hunting weapons in the graves of women and children? In 1946, he wrote, "It is hardly to be supposed that infants, children, *and women* would have any practical use in life for an atlatl" (emphasis added).

Trying to explain this apparent conundrum, Webb noted that the people of Indian Knoll often buried these beautifully made atlatls intact, but they also sometimes intentionally broke the spear-throwers at the time of burial, as evidenced by the presence of all the fragments of an atlatl weight in grave fill. Knowing that atlatls were also buried with children and women, Webb argued that the artifacts reflected an intentional burial ritual, rather than grave goods for use in the afterlife. We know that in some Native American societies, people cut their hair as a symbol of mourning. Perhaps thousands of years ago at Indian Knoll, the destruction and burial of atlatls carried a similar symbolic meaning—a way for men to express their grief for a deceased child, wife, sister, or mother in a culturally appropriate way.

Notice how Webb's argument is grounded in the assumption—by no means illogical—that atlatls were interred with adult males because they were tools men used (hence they would need them in the afterlife). This reasoning would, of course, assume that some women at Indian Knoll also hunted. But because Webb could not conceive of women as hunters, he searched for another explanation for the inclusion of atlatls in women's graves. Although Webb's final explanation could still be right, his underlying logic demonstrates the caution needed to detect our own cultural biases, especially when it comes to matters of gender roles.

Before looking at how archaeologists reconstruct what men and women did in the past, let's consider whether this difficult task is even necessary. Do we really need to know whether men or women did the hunting, or plant gathering, or other tasks? Is this concern with gender simply an imposition of the *current* American culture of political correctness? We don't think so, and the following ethnographic example demonstrates why.

Hunting in Africa's Rain Forest

Popularly known as "Pygmies," the BaMbuti are hunter-gatherers who live in the Ituri Rain Forest of central Africa. Living in small temporary camps, they hunt a variety of animals and gather wild plants and honey in the forest. Nearly all these groups exchange meat for agricultural produce with their neighbors, Bantu horticulturalists. They also sometimes work for them in their fields.

Years ago, Colin Turnbull (1924–1994) observed that some BaMbuti hunt individually with bows and arrows whereas other groups hunt communally with nets (see Figure 10-3). Among net hunters, women and children drive game (such as the duiker, a small antelope) through the forest into the nets, where men (and sometimes women) club the animals. Bow hunters shoot monkeys and other prey that seek refuge in treetops, but they, too, hunt the duiker. They sometimes hunt communally, but they also hunt alone.

These two kinds of BaMbuti societies differ in their hunting technology, and they should leave different archaeological signatures—one should leave behind nets and evidence of their manufacture; the other, projectile points, bows, and arrows. Such differences in technology are precisely the sort of patterning that archaeologists seek to document and explain.

Why do the BaMbuti use different hunting methods? Turnbull attributed the difference to simple cultural preference, but other anthropologists weren't satisfied. Some argued that Bantu horticulturalists introduced net hunting to the forest and that it spread because it was more efficient than bow hunting. Those who lived close to the Bantu had already benefited from this technology, whereas those living farther away had yet to acquire it. Others suggested that net hunting was a response to the crowding created by Bantu emigration; nets were a way to extract more food from limited portions of the forest. The bow hunters, on the other hand, worked in Bantu fields, receiving produce through their labor rather than by trading meat, so they eschewed net hunting.

Others argued the reverse—that net hunting was less efficient than bow hunting and net hunters sacrificed efficiency for volume, using nets to harvest a surplus of meat for trade. Yet another explanation was that the

androcentric A perspective that focuses on what men do in a society, to the exclusion of women.

shell midden The remnants of shellfish collecting; some shellfish middens can become many meters thick.

© Barry Hewlett

FIGURE 10-3 A young Aka girl removes a blue duiker caught in a net.

thick undergrowth of the net hunters' environment made archery an impractical hunting technique there.

Anthropologists Robert Bailey (University of Illinois, Chicago) and Robert Aunger (University College, London) tested these competing hypotheses. Drawing upon ethnographic and environmental records, they found that (1) no significant differences exist between the environments of net hunters and those of archers, (2) net hunting is no more or less efficient than bow hunting, and (3) bow hunters do not live nearer to or trade more with Bantu peoples than net hunters. In other words, the evidence contradicted every available hypothesis.

Bailey and Aunger observed that whereas women participate in net hunts, they rarely hunt in archer groups. So the question, perhaps, is not why some BaMbuti hunt with nets and others with bows and arrows, but rather *how women decide whether to participate in hunts*.

Recall that many BaMbuti trade meat with Bantu horticulturalists for produce. Some women also work as laborers for horticulturalists, and they receive some of the produce as payment. Bailey and Aunger argued that women decide to hunt or to work in fields depending on which activity gives them the greatest return for their effort. Testing this hypothesis, Bailey and Aunger found that net hunters live near Bantu with *small* gardens whereas bow hunters live near Bantu with *large* gardens.

Where gardens are small, Bantu women do not need BaMbuti women as laborers and, because they cannot work for produce, BaMbuti women help with the hunting. Presumably, net hunting is a better way to utilize this extra labor. Where gardens are large, however, Bantu women need assistance. They hire BaMbuti women, who apparently make a greater return as workers than as hunters. Without the extra labor, men hunt individually, with bows and arrows.

The key to BaMbuti hunting technology, then, may depend in large measure on women's choices. This example demonstrates that options, decisions, and activities by men and women condition the larger patterns in material culture that archaeology excels in revealing.

Reconstructing Male and Female Activities from Archaeology

One reason for archaeology's androcentric bias was the fact that, for decades, the field was male-dominated. Another was that archaeologists were simply unaware of the extent to which their own culture affected the way they viewed and understood the world. We believed that, as true scientists, we could be objective about the past.

This attitude has changed significantly in recent years. Half of all professional archaeologists in the United States today are women, and few modern archaeologists would blithely make such simplistic assumptions as atlatl = male, or pottery = female. We recognize the biases of past archaeological research and understand that knowing what men and women did in the past is not a matter of political correctness; it is important to understanding prehistory.

Some feminist archaeologists believe that it is unnecessary to ascribe particular tasks to men or women in order to take a gendered perspective on prehistory. But others argue that we cannot answer important anthropological questions unless we know, for a particular archaeological case, whether men or women used this or that artifact.

Is this possible? Can we reconstruct what men and women did in the past? If so, how?

These questions raise some difficult problems of middle-level theory. In Chapter 9, we explored one approach. Skeletal analysis can tell us something about the different mechanical stresses placed on men and women, but the cause of these stresses still requires some guesswork.

And human skeletal evidence can take us only so far. What about everything else found in archaeological sites? How would we know if a man or a woman made or used a particular stone tool, pot, or basket? Because archaeologists lack an established method for objectively deriving this sort of information from material remains, most investigators are forced to rely on ethnographic analogy or historic documents, with all their inherent limitations (see Chapter 7).

Were Ceramics Made by Men or Women?

Ceramic technology provides a case in point. There are two basic ways to make a pot. In the first method, the potter constructs the vessel by hand, either by molding the clay or by rolling it into a long "snake" and then coiling it up to build the pot's base and walls; the pot's walls are then smoothed by hand.

The other technique is to work a lump of clay onto a wheel that is rotated manually by the potter (and today by a powered device). The potter then uses the spinning clay's centrifugal force to shape it by hand. The method used on a given pot is relatively easy to determine from characteristics of potsherds.

Working from this simple baseline, Prudence Rice (Southern Illinois University) surveyed ethnographic data from a variety of societies around the world and discovered that when pottery is fashioned by hand, it is usually manufactured by women. In contrast, men usually manufacture pottery made on a wheel. Archaeologists can draw on this kind of strong analogy to infer past behavior with a high (but not absolute) degree of certainty: If archaeological evidence shows that pottery was made by hand, then we infer that the pottery was *probably* made by women. By contrast, if we find evidence that pottery was made on a wheel, then we say that the potter was *probably* male.

FIGURE 10-4 A Maya carving from the site Yaxchilán, Lintel 1. The figure at the right carrying a textile bundle is identified as a woman by the clothing (a huipil) she is wearing.

As we cautioned in Chapter 8, this sort of analogy can be made stronger if we can actually *explain* the inferred pattern; but in this case, the explanation is not easy. There is, of course, no inherent reason why women could not have used the wheel to produce pottery (and, indeed, many female potters do so today). The uniformitarian assumption that we discussed in Chapter 8 fails in this instance.

Perhaps the reason lies in the *purpose* of pottery made on the wheel versus that made by hand. Archaeologists know that the pottery wheel is associated with craft specialization and the marketing of pottery. Thus, it appears that when pottery moves from production for the residential group to production for the nonresidential group, the task shifts from women to men. *Why* this should happen, however, is much harder to say.

An alternative approach is to use an ethnographic analogy that is historically linked to the archaeological population being studied. Rosemary Joyce (University of California, Berkeley) used this approach to create some deeper understanding of Maya men and women.

Gender in Maya Iconography

In previous chapters, we have mentioned the Maya civilization of southern Mexico and Central America. The Maya developed a remarkable art style and often depicted themselves on stone stelae, on polychrome (multicolored) pottery, in paintings and carvings on lintels inside temples and tombs, and in books called *codices*, which were long strips of paper, many meters in length when unfolded, made of pounded inner tree bark. (The Spanish considered them heretical and destroyed all they could find; only four survive today.)

The images commonly depict Maya wearing intricate, complex costumes (see Figure 10-4). To the Western eye, these costumes appear flamboyant, even outlandish. But to the Maya, ways of dressing encoded immense amounts of cultural information (this is true of us, too). These figures rarely have overt sexual characteristics, in large part because of the elaborate costuming. Women are sometimes identified with a particular glyph, but not always.

Because Maya epigraphers can read Maya hieroglyphic writing, we know much of what is going on in these images. And the images themselves tell us something about Maya sex roles. For example, women are often portrayed (especially on polychrome pottery) weaving, preparing maize for meals, and serving food to others. Rosemary Joyce and others, notably Tatiana Proskouriakoff (1909–1985), used these images to discover that Maya iconography displays women wearing three distinctive dress styles: a simple wrapped garment that covers the breasts, body, and legs, but leaves the arms bare; a woven *huipil*, a housecoat-like garment that covers the entire body; and, more rarely, a jade-bead skirt, often with a fish-monster-and-shell belt (a belt depicting an open shark's mouth and a bivalve shell). Some interpret this last style as an impersonation of the male maize god, who is always depicted with such costuming.

Joyce used these clothing styles to identify women on the carved stelae, despite the lack of overt sexual characteristics. Women are seen holding and offering ceramic vessels, bundles of cloth, or paper and bloodletting instruments (the Maya believed that rulers had to sacrifice their blood, often by cutting their tongues, to communicate with the gods and renew the world). The remaining figures, the male ones, often hold weapons, shields, or scepters that represent double-headed axes—the instruments of war.

Although one might interpret the women in the images simply as servants, Joyce wondered if there was a deeper interpretation, so she turned to ethnographic data gleaned from the codices, early Spanish observations, and modern ethnography.

The modern Maya participate in what anthropologists call a **cargo system**, in which a responsible, married man is selected annually to direct the ceremonial system (today this system is a combination of Catholicism and the indigenous religion). This individual is responsible for holding a number of feasts that accompany rituals; his wife, who acts as his assistant, takes on the title "mother of" the man's named position. Other elderly women are responsible for preparing food, tending to incense for purification ceremonies, and ensuring that everyone observes appropriate manners and protocol during the feasts. In this way, men and women occupy complementary roles in the important feasts of the cargo system.

Joyce argues that women depicted in the Classic Maya stelae may have occupied similar complementary, rather than subservient, roles. She points out that Maya ethnographers discuss the complementarity of men and women, and the need for rulers to "assert claims to represent in themselves the split and complementary totality that they would like to control." Joyce suggests that the pairing of male and female figures on stelae in culturally appropriate ways could symbolize a ruler's need to combine male and female elements to acquire and maintain political power. This could include not only a claim to male/female prerogatives and powers, but might also extend to the right of male rulers to claim the products of female labor, such as weaving.

Interpretations such as this are impossible without adequate ethnographic analogy and are therefore subject to both the potentials and the pitfalls of such analogies (as discussed in Chapter 7). For example, other archaeologists might point out that the cargo system is a poor analogy for interpreting Maya stelae because many of the women shown on stelae are partners in marriages between royal families—marriages that created key military alliances, as they did in Europe. Thus, the purpose of women in these images is starkly different from that entailed in the cargo system.

One way to probe the strength of an analogy is to look for additional formal similarities between the analogy and the archaeological case, and there is at least one in this instance: Joyce found that women are often paired with men on stelae—sometimes on the "backs" of stelae (that is, the stelae's side that faces away from the largest public area), whereas male figures occupy the more public sides. Sometimes, the women are depicted in a spatially lower position than their male counterparts.

Joyce points out that, when viewed from prominent vantage points in a ceremonial center, women depicted on the stelae are more frequently to the left of the male images. Ethnographic data show an association between Maya women and the left hand as well as lower elevations, whereas men are associated with the right hand and upper elevations. This ethnographic pattern may hold true for Maya stelae as well and, if it does, might strengthen the analogy.

Nonetheless, modern archaeologists still find it difficult to say much with certainty about gender roles in the past, let alone move beyond such relatively mundane activities to an understanding of gender ideology. Doing so may be limited to those instances in which a close, historically linked analogy is available.

Archaeology and Kinship

Kinship refers to the socially recognized network of relationships through which individuals are related to one another by ties of descent (real or imagined) and marriage. A kinship system blends the facts of biological descent and relatedness with cultural rules that define some people as close kin and others as distant kin, or not kin at all. These groupings are important because they strongly condition, and sometimes dictate, the nature of relationships between individuals.

Kinship may not seem very significant to you. We don't mean that you don't care about your family, but on a day-to-day basis, most of the people you interact with are not kin. Instead, they are friends, teachers, representatives of the government, bosses, subordinates, and so on. But in the nonindustrial world, most people interact on a daily basis with people who are kin. The same was true of much of the ancient world.

So, if you fail to understand a society's kinship pattern, you might misread a lot of their behavior. For example, a woman from the island of Pingelap in Micronesia once casually listed the members of her household to Kelly: "That child there is my son, and that girl is my daughter. The young woman over there is my sister and the man next to her is her husband. Of course, my father over there [pointing to a man splitting open coconuts] is my mother's brother." If her last statement brings images of incest to mind, we assure you that you are wrong, and understanding the kinship system shows why.

Forms of Kinship

The world of kinship is incredibly complex; we will simplify matters here by concentrating on three basic forms of kinship. The first of these, **bilateral descent**, should be familiar because it is the standard kinship in North America, as well as in many other industrialized nations. In bilateral descent, an individual traces his or her relatives *equally* on the mother's and father's sides. Although you might be closer to your mother's or father's side (because of geography, divorce, or personalities), neither side of the family is *a priori* more important than the other. Evidence of this is the fact that names applied to relatives on either side of the family are the same. Father's brother and mother's brother, for example, are both "uncles" (in English).

Kinship in cultures with bilateral descent tend to lack "depth"—meaning that few individuals know who their great- or great-great-grandparents are, much less their great-great-grandparents' siblings' offspring's offspring. This is because *in bilateral descent, the nuclear family is the important economic unit.*

The next two kinds of kinship systems are strikingly different from bilateral descent because they privilege one side of the family over the other. These *unilineal* descent systems are depicted in Figure 10-5. In this figure, the triangles stand for males and the circles for females. The equal sign (=) stands for marriage, the solid horizontal lines connect siblings, and the vertical lines indicate offspring. The square (indicating either sex) places you within the kinship diagram.

In **patrilineal descent**, the nuclear family may constitute the residential unit, but the most important group is the **patrilineage**, people to whom you are related *through the male line*. The top portion of Figure 10-5 portrays this system, with the shaded individuals belonging to "your" patrilineage. These are all the people who are biologically related to you through a male—your father and his siblings, your father's father and his siblings, your father's brothers' children, and your father's father's brothers' children; we could extend the same to your great-grandfather's and great-great-grandfather's generation, and so on. These individuals are members of one patrilineage.

In patrilineal descent, you acquire your patrilineage from your father. The other people in the diagram belong to other patrilineages. Societies with unilineal descent commonly forbid marriage between members of the same lineage. So, your mother belongs to a different patrilineage than your father and, consequently, to a patrilineage other than yours.

Patrilineal societies make up about 60 percent of the world's known societies. They are associated with a wide range of conditions, including hunting-and-gathering, agricultural, and pastoral societies. They are also associated with internal warfare—that is, war with close neighbors.

Keep in mind that patrilineages contain both males and females—because anyone biologically linked to you through a male is a member of your lineage (such as your father's brother's daughters). Your father's sister is included, but not her offspring. And don't think that members of patrilineal societies are confused about matters of human reproduction. They understand the biological facts of life completely, and they do not ignore "kin" on their mother's side. In patrilineal descent, your mother's side is simply less important. In contrast to bilateral descent, *in unilineal descent systems, the lineage is the important economic unit.* The lineage, rather than the nuclear family, normally owns or controls land and other resources. The lineage makes decisions about whether to move a village, go to war, or dig irrigation ditches. Although the nuclear family matters in unilineal descent systems, it is secondary to the interests and concerns of the patrilineage.

This difference is reflected in kin terms. Men call their biological father by a term meaning "father," but they may also call their father's brother "father," and consequently, they may call their father's brother's offspring "brother" and "sister," rather than "cousins." In patrilineal descent, your mother's brothers' children belong to another lineage (*their* father's lineage), so they are called by a term that we might translate as "cousin," but not "brother" or "sister." Your father's and mother's siblings are the same kind of relative in a bilateral descent system, but not in a patrilineal descent system.

The bottom chart in Figure 10-5 contains the same biological facts as the top one, but they are now organized into **matrilineal descent**. Here, you trace relatives through the

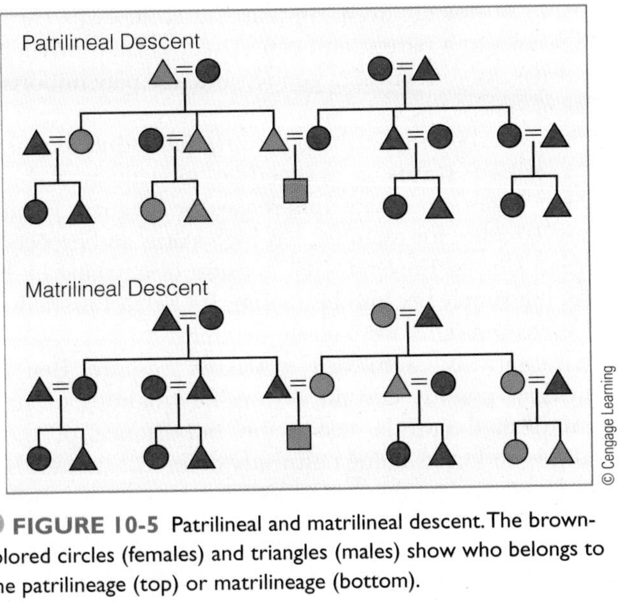

Patrilineal Descent

Matrilineal Descent

FIGURE 10-5 Patrilineal and matrilineal descent. The brown-colored circles (females) and triangles (males) show who belongs to one patrilineage (top) or matrilineage (bottom).

cargo system Part of the social organization found in many Central American communities in which a wealthy individual is named to carry out and bear the cost of important religious ceremonies throughout the year.

kinship A socially recognized network of relationships through which individuals are related to one another by ties of descent (real or imagined) and marriage.

bilateral descent A kinship system in which relatives are traced equally on both the mother's and father's sides.

patrilineal descent A unilineal descent system in which ancestry is traced through the male line.

patrilineage Individuals who share a line of patrilineal descent.

matrilineal descent A unilineal descent system in which ancestry is traced through the female line.

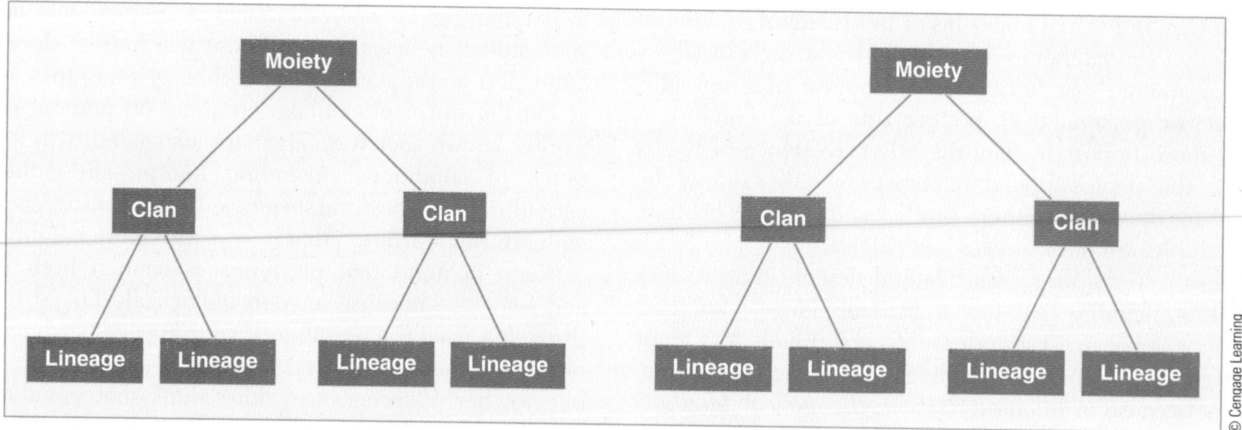

FIGURE 10-6 The relationships among lineages, clans, and moieties. (If moieties are present, there are two, and only two.)

female line, forming **matrilineages**. In matrilineal societies, you get your lineage from your mother. Your lineage includes you, your mother, her siblings and her sisters' offspring, your mother's mother, her siblings and her sisters' offspring, and so on. As in patrilineal societies, nuclear families exist, but the primary unit is the matrilineage.

By now, you can probably guess why the Pingelapese woman said that her mother's brother was her father: In matrilineal societies, the mother's brother is a "fictive" father. The biological father, in fact, may have little to do with his biological offspring; instead, he spends his time with his sister's children. Because they are members of his lineage, it is they, not his biological offspring, who will inherit whatever resources, knowledge, or privileges he possesses.

Matrilineal societies are rare, composing only about 10 percent of the world's societies. They appear to be associated with horticulture, long-distance hunting, and warfare with distant enemies.

matrilineage Individuals who share a line of matrilineal descent.

clan A group of matri- or patrilineages who see themselves as descended from a (sometimes mythical) common ancestor.

moieties Two groups of clans that perform reciprocal ceremonial obligations for one another; moieties often intermarry.

status The rights, duties, privileges, powers, liabilities, and immunities that accrue to a recognized and named social position.

ascribed status Rights, duties, and obligations that accrue to a person by virtue of his or her parentage; ascribed status is inherited.

achieved status Rights, duties, and obligations that accrue to a person by virtue of what he or she has accomplished in life.

Finally, to complicate things even more, we must note that lineages are sometimes clustered into **clans**. A clan is a set of lineages that claim to share a distant, often mythical, ancestor (see Figure 10-6). Clans, in turn, may be clustered into **moieties** (*moy*-i-tees; from the French word meaning "half"; in any society with moieties, there are only two). Moieties often perform reciprocal ceremonial obligations for each other, such as burying the dead of the other or holding feasts for one another. These various social groupings can be reflected in how people place themselves "on the ground" (see "Looking Closer: Kinship and Residence among the Mikea"). We will come back to these terms later.

Archaeology and Social Status

Status consists of the rights, duties, privileges, and powers that accrue to a recognized and named social position. In our own society, the status of "mother" is determined both by the duties she owes to her son or daughter and the responsibilities she can legitimately demand of her children. Similarly, a child owes certain obligations to a parent and can expect certain privileges in return. As you will see, gender and age play important roles in status.

Status can be assigned through *ascription* and *achievement*. An **ascribed status** is assigned to individuals at birth, without regard to innate differences or abilities. Britain's Prince Charles, for example, has high status and expects to become king of England—not because of anything he has done, but simply because his mother is Queen Elizabeth II. His status and rights were ensured at birth.

Alternatively, **achieved statuses** require that an individual possess certain admirable qualities or have accomplished certain tasks (the importance of these qualities and tasks being culturally defined). Rather than being assigned at birth, achieved statuses are earned through individual effort. A Shoshone man who proved

LOOKING CLOSER

Kinship and Residence among the Mikea

To see whether descent systems can be detected archaeologically, we return to the Mikea of Madagascar, a patrilineal society that also practices *patrilocal residence* (in which a wife lives with her husband in his original village). Look at the kinship chart and map showing where people live in one particular Mikea forest hamlet; sometimes, young children and single, elderly individuals lived in small, separate houses. (The lines drawn through some of the kinship symbols indicate deceased individuals.)

Several patterns emerge regarding Mikea kinship and settlement. Note that the houses are arranged in a linear, north-to-south scatter, with doors facing north. The hamlet contains two primary house clusters, marked by trampled areas of vegetation around the houses, and an untrampled belt of vegetation and trash (mostly maize husks) between the two. A path (shown with broken lines) connects the two clusters.

The kin diagram likewise demarcates two patrilineages at this hamlet, each with an older man and his wife, with their sons and their wives, and their unmarried children and grandchildren. These two patrilineages are linked by virtue of several marriages between the sons of one of the elder couples and the daughters of the other.

This arrangement is typical of Mikea forest hamlets, where members of two patrilineages live together, united by marriage ties or a link through a woman. There is usually some tension between these two clusters, and the sharing of tools and labor typically occurs *within* each of these clusters, but is rarer *between* the two.

Notice how the patrilineages map onto the ground: The northern cluster of houses contains men (and unmarried sisters) who belong to the same lineage along with their wives and children; similarly, the southern cluster contains brothers who belong to another lineage, with their wives and offspring. The same social relationships mapped out in virtually every settlement we visited: The closer a social relationship is between two people or two groups, the closer they live to one another.

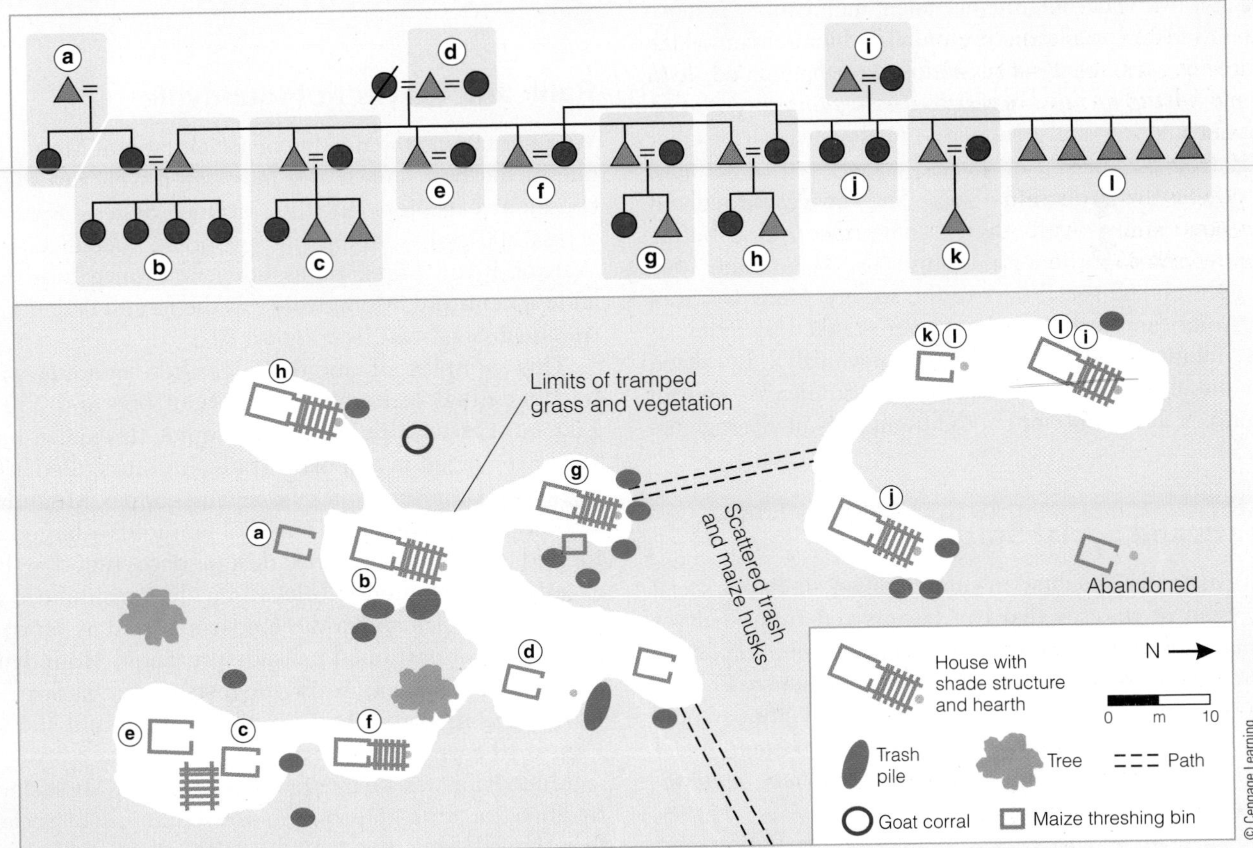

Mikea hamlet map with kinship chart. Notice how the patrilineages are linked by marriage, yet separated on the ground.

to be a good hunter might achieve status as a leader in hunts, but upon his death, no one would automatically fill his former position.

FIGURE 10-7 Moundville (Alabama), looking south over Mound B; Mound A is in the center of the clearing.

Egalitarian and Ranked Societies

The concept of status allows us to bridge from the level of the individual to that of the society. A society is termed **egalitarian** when there is no fixed number of positions of status; instead, the number of valued statuses is equal to the number of people with the ability to fill them. No one individual wields complete authority over another. The important features, then, are that status is achieved and that *members of egalitarian societies generally have equal access to critical, life-sustaining resources*. Gender and age are the primary dimensions of status in egalitarian communities. The nineteenth-century Great Basin Shoshone people we described previously were egalitarian.

Ranked societies limit the positions of valued status so that not everyone of sufficient talent can actually achieve them. Such a social structure entails a hierarchy in which relatively permanent social stations are maintained, *with people having unequal access to life-sustaining resources*. Gender and age still play a role in the division of labor in ranked societies. But ranked societies tend to have economies that redistribute goods and services throughout the community, with those doing the redistributing keeping some portion for themselves. This creates one or more ranked social tiers to the society. Many tribes of the American Northwest Coast were ranked societies, as was Tahitian society (mentioned previously). Localized residential kin groups (such as a patrilineage) control resources, and economic goods flow in and out of a regional center.

Death and Social Status

The categories "egalitarian" and "ranked" define a social spectrum of statuses that can be inferred from analyses of material culture. Mortuary remains are one important source of information on extinct political systems. For the past three decades, archaeologists have used ethnographic data to show that *societies that have important social distinctions among living individuals also have material distinctions among the dead.*

Death, in a sense, is a period of separation and reintegration for both the deceased and those they leave behind. The deceased are separated from the living and must be properly integrated into the world of the dead. Social ties existed between the living and the once living, and the ceremonial connections at death reflect these social relations. Mortuary rituals reflect who people were and the relationships they had with others when they were alive. Therefore, they should reflect a person's social status.

Rank and Status at Moundville

We can examine the ranking of social status at Moundville, one of the best known and most intensively investigated ceremonial centers in the United States. Sprawling across 300 acres, Moundville overlooks Alabama's Black Warrior River. Three thousand people once lived here, and for centuries, Moundville was the largest center in the American Southeast (see Figure 10-7).

This complex of about 30 earthen mounds was a bustling ritual center between about 950 and 550 BP. Like most **Mississippian** political units, this maize-based society engaged in extensive trade, and its skilled artists worked in stone, ceramics, bone, and copper. Moundville contains 20 major ceremonial mounds—large flat-topped earthen structures designed to function both as artificial mountains (elevating elite residences and possibly temples above the landscape) and as mortuary areas. A stout bastioned palisade protected Moundville's large central plaza. This suggests that warfare was probably a recurring feature of life at Moundville (see Figure 10-8).

Moundville was a major participant in the "Mississippian tradition," a term referring to the hundreds of societies that thrived from about 1200 to 500 BP throughout the southeastern United States. In their heyday, the Mississippian elite presided over breathtaking ceremonial centers (as at Moundville) that were invested with power by the thousands of people who lived in smaller nearby farmsteads.

RAPID REVIEW

Anthropological Concepts Important to Archaeology

Concept	Archaeological Manifestation
Social organization/kinship	Reflected in spatial layout of houses and communities; mortuary goods
Political organization	Reflected in spatial layout of public space in communities; mortuary goods, location of burials, evidence of burial ritual; trade goods
Gender	Reflected in mortuary goods associated with males/females; bioarchaeological data

C. B. Moore (who excavated at Indian Knoll) conducted archaeological investigations at Moundville in 1905 and 1906, digging into both platform mounds and village areas. The Alabama Museum of Natural History then excavated at Moundville from 1930 through 1941. More than a half-million square feet of the village areas at Moundville were uncovered during this 11-year period, in part by workers in the Civilian Conservation Corps. The more than 3000 excavated burials from Moundville provide a unique database for studying Mississippian social structure.

The Symbolism of Grave Goods at Moundville

Christopher Peebles (1939–2012) and Susan Kus (Rhodes College) took advantage of this database and analyzed Moundville's burials with an eye toward reconstructing Moundville's political organization. They began with the grave goods, many of which display the distinctive symbols characteristic of what archaeologists call the **Southeastern Ceremonial Complex** (see Figure 10-9).

During the Mississippian period, artifacts that bore striking stylistic similarities appear in a number of sites and several large centers, including Moundville, across the southeastern United States from Oklahoma to Florida. These artifacts include conch shell gorgets and cups, copper plates, ceremonial axes and batons, effigy pipes, and flint knives—many decorated with one or more of a set of symbols, such as the "forked eye," the cross, the sun circle, the hand and eye, and the bi-lobed arrow. The distribution of these items parallels a trade network of exotic items, as well as basics such as food and salt. But the similarities in the motifs imply more than simple trade; a higher degree of social interaction was at work.

Whatever the Southeastern Ceremonial Complex really was—and archaeologists still debate it—it crosscut the boundaries of many widely separated residential groups. At each major site are artifacts that bear local symbols. At

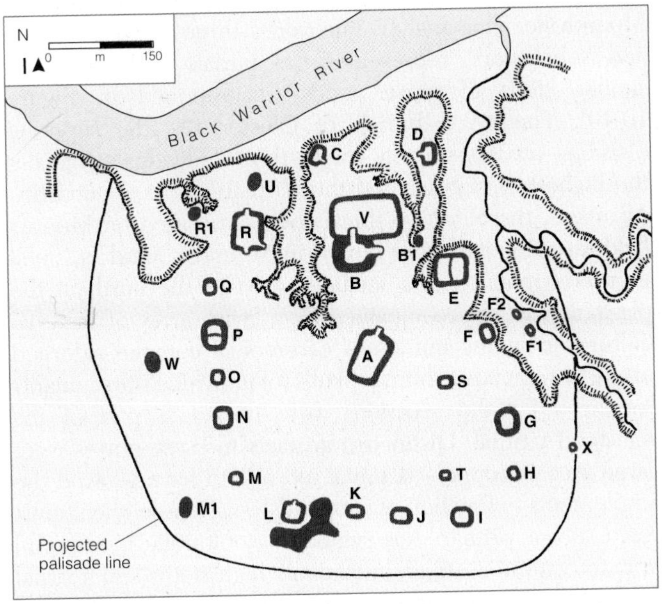

FIGURE 10-8 A map of the site of Moundville; the letters designate mounds mentioned in the text. From *Archaeology of the Moundville Chiefdom*, edited by Vernon James Knight, Jr. and Vincas P. Steponaitis, published by the Smithsonian Institute Press, Washington, D.C.; copyright © 1998 by the Smithsonian Institution. Used by permission of the publisher.

egalitarian societies Social systems that contain roughly as many valued positions as there are people capable of filling them; in egalitarian societies, all people have nearly equal access to the critical resources needed to live.

ranked societies Social systems in which a hierarchy of social status has been established, with a restricted number of valued positions available; in ranked societies, not everyone has the same access to the critical resources of life.

Mississippian A widespread cultural tradition across much of the eastern United States from AD 800 to 1500. Mississippian societies engaged in intensive village-based maize horticulture and constructed large, earthen platform mounds that served as substructures for temples, residences, and council buildings.

Southeastern Ceremonial Complex An assortment of ceremonial objects that occurs in the graves of high-status Mississippian individuals. Ritual exchange of these artifacts crosscut the boundaries of many distinctive local cultures.

FIGURE 10-9 An image in the Southeastern Ceremonial Complex style, pounded in copper. Note particularly the forked eye motif around the eye, which probably represents a symbolic association with peregrine falcons, known for their keen vision and skill as hunters (from Spiro, Oklahoma).

Moundville, these artifacts are specially constructed animal effigy vessels or parts of animals (such as canine teeth, claws, and shells). The local symbols probably functioned as status items within Moundville, whereas the ceremonial complex symbols designated the rank of individuals in the overall region.

Each burial mound at Moundville contained a few high-status adults, as indicated by their grave goods. These included copper axes, copper gorgets, stone disks, various paints, and assorted exotic minerals—such as galena (cubes of natural lead), mica (paper-thin sheets of translucent silicate minerals), and sheet copper. Copper and mica items often depict scalloped circles, swastikas, and the "hand-eye" motif (an open hand with an eye in the palm). Presumably, individuals buried with these artifacts had statuses and reputations recognized throughout the entire Moundville cultural system. Each mound also contained some presumably lower-status individuals who were buried with only a few ceramic vessels. Other commoners were buried in cemeteries away from the mounds with no burial goods (or, at least, none that preserved).

By correlating the presence of higher- and lower-status symbols, Peebles and Kus could infer that social status was ascribed at Moundville. Some infants and children—clearly too young to have accomplished anything noteworthy in life—were buried with lavish grave goods. These children must have been important because of who they were at birth, not because of what they had done in their short lives. This is clear evidence of a ranked society.

Two Axes of Social Patterning

On the basis of ethnographic evidence, Peebles and Kus predicted that the Moundville population may have been subdivided along two major social axes, which they termed the superordinate and subordinate.

The subordinate division recognizes that certain symbols and the energy expended on mortuary ritual reflect the statuses of age and sex. With respect to age, the older the individual, the greater the opportunity for lifetime achievement, and hence the higher the deathbed rank can be. This means that at Moundville (along the subordinate axis, at least), adult burials should be more lavish than those of children, and children should be accompanied by more grave goods than infants. And because the subordinate division is also graded by gender, men and women should not be expected to have equivalent grave goods.

The superordinate division at Moundville is a partially hereditary ordering based on criteria other than age and sex. Among the elite—people whose status was assigned at birth—some individuals will be infants, some children, and the rest adults.

Peebles and Kus predicted that the statuses should form a pyramid-shaped distribution. At the base of the pyramid are the commoners, whose statuses are determined strictly by sex and age. The next step up the social ladder, the next rank, consists of those few individuals with ascribed status. Finally, at the top will be the paramount individuals, those who enjoy all the emblems of status and rank available in the society.

Quantitative Distribution of Moundville Grave Goods

This model was tested by performing a statistical analysis of the grave goods of 2053 of the best-documented burials from Moundville. This analysis uncovered three distinct clusters and subclusters, represented by burials that contained similar kinds of grave goods (diagrammed in Figure 10-10). The seven burials of Cluster IA—the supreme division—are presumably chiefs, those individuals enjoying the highest of statuses and the ultimate political authority. All males, the elite (we think; these are based on Moore's field assessments), were buried in Mounds C and D, small mortuary mounds in a secluded area to the north of the plaza, and were accompanied by a lavish array of material culture, including numerous ceremonial complex–adorned artifacts. Infants and human skulls (of individuals presumably sacrificed for the occasion) were buried as part of the Cluster IA ritual. Distinctive artifacts in these graves were large axes of copper—a metal too soft to have allowed the implements to function as chopping tools. These, then, must have served primarily as symbols, a culturally meaningful way to communicate an individual's high status and a visual reminder of the reasons for differences in people's ranks.

Cluster IB burials, both children and adult males, were interred in the mounds surrounding the plaza and in cemeteries near mounds. They also had a number of ceremonial complex artifacts plus mineral-based paints included in their grave goods. Cluster II, the final cluster of the superordinate division, included adults

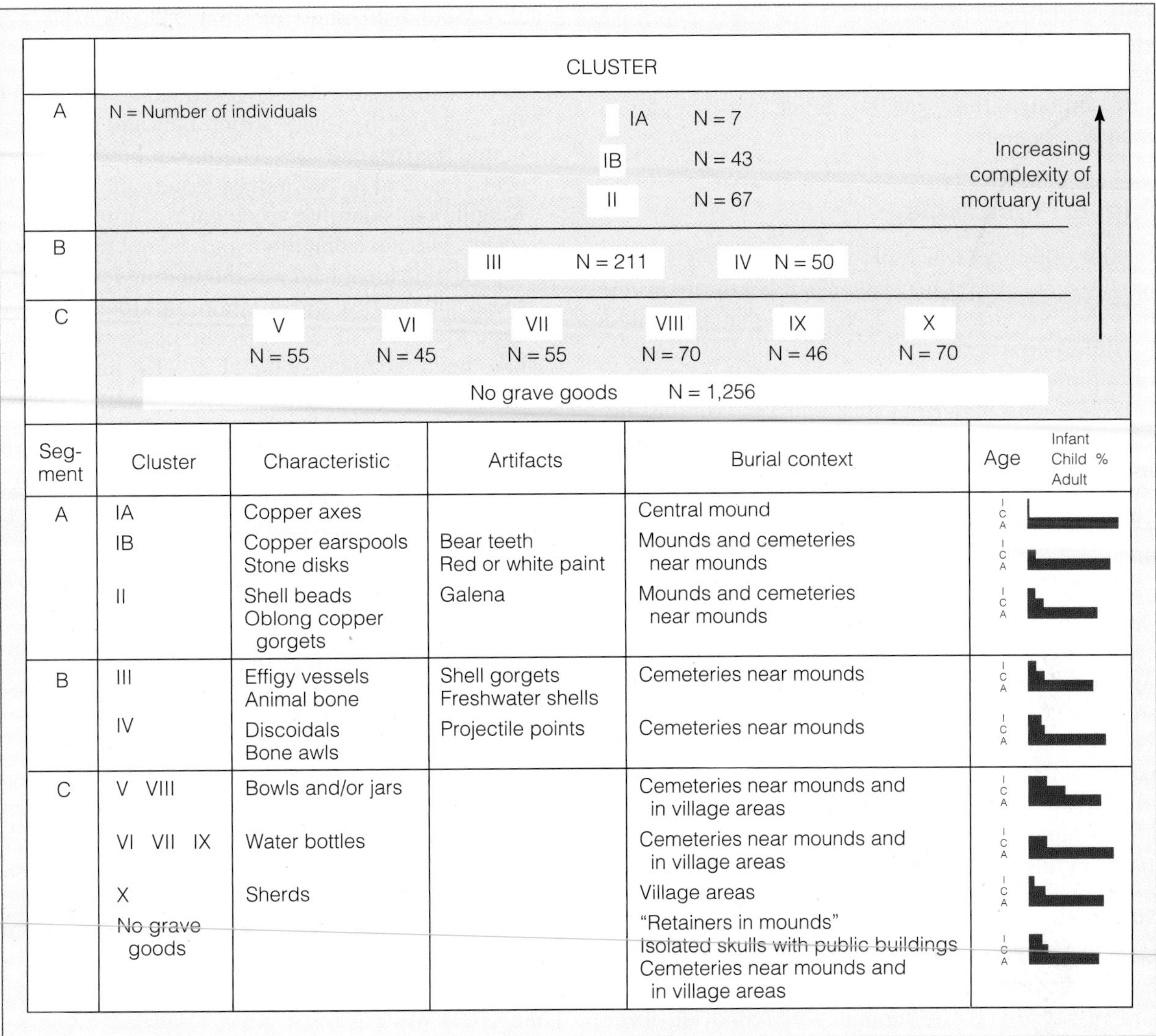

Segment	Cluster	Characteristic	Artifacts	Burial context	Age (Infant / Child / Adult %)
A	IA	Copper axes		Central mound	I C A
	IB	Copper earspools Stone disks	Bear teeth Red or white paint	Mounds and cemeteries near mounds	I C A
	II	Shell beads Oblong copper gorgets	Galena	Mounds and cemeteries near mounds	I C A
B	III	Effigy vessels Animal bone	Shell gorgets Freshwater shells	Cemeteries near mounds	I C A
	IV	Discoidals Bone awls	Projectile points	Cemeteries near mounds	I C A
C	V VIII	Bowls and/or jars		Cemeteries near mounds and in village areas	I C A
	VI VII IX	Water bottles		Cemeteries near mounds and in village areas	I C A
	X	Sherds		Village areas	I C A
	No grave goods			"Retainers in mounds" Isolated skulls with public buildings Cemeteries near mounds and in village areas	I C A

FIGURE 10-10 The hierarchical social clusters represented in burials at Moundville.

and children buried in cemeteries near the mounds and beneath what were charnel houses near the main plaza; their grave goods included chest beads, copper gorgets, and galena cubes.

Hierarchically below the Level A elite are those of subordinate Levels B and C (who enjoyed status largely on the basis of sex and age differences). In Cluster III, for instance, stone ceremonial axes are found only with adult males, whereas infants and children have "toy" vessels, clay "playthings," and unworked freshwater shells. Unworked bird claws and deer and turtle bones were found only with adults. The individuals in the lowest segment, Level C, were mostly buried away from the mounds and major ceremonial areas at Moundville. But some of the burials in this cluster were individuals buried as retainers and isolated skulls placed at the bases of large posts.

Burial context appears to clarify the nature of ranking in the Moundville society. The most elite were buried in a sacred area and accompanied by symbols of their exalted status. The Moundville elite also apparently lived in larger, more complex dwellings than did the commoners. Elite membership was conditioned by genealogy and, because social position was inherited within the elite, even children occupied such social positions.

Farther down the ladder, the villagers' graves also reflected their social status in life at this level, positions conditioned largely by sex and age distinctions rather than by inheritance. Their less glamorous grave goods were distributed in a different way. Graves contained pottery vessels, bone awls, flint projectile points, and stone pipes, all of which were distributed mostly to older adults. Peebles and Kus infer that these individuals were required to achieve—rather than inherit—their social status. More than half of the Moundville graves contained commoners buried with no grave goods at all.

Peebles and Kus suggested that Moundville conformed to a chiefdom model, a society similar to that of Tahiti and characterized by a status framework with few valued positions, although they saw no direct evidence for a redistributive economy.

Kinship at Moundville

Despite the differences in rank, Moundville was still an integrated society. And it may have been bonds of kinship that provided the integrating factor and that prevented extreme differences between the elite and the commoners. Indeed, although chiefdoms are internally ranked, their members commonly understand that everyone is ultimately, albeit sometimes distantly, a relative of the chief, who may even use kinship terms to refer to his followers.

To help reconstruct Moundville's social organization, Vernon Knight (University of Alabama) employed an ethnographic analogy with the nineteenth-century Chickasaw, the Native Americans who lived in the vicinity of Moundville at the time of European contact. Knight noted that there are two major classes of mounds at Moundville. Some of the mounds contain burials; others were residential mounds, with evidence for wattle-and-daub or thatch structures on their flat tops. These mounds alternate around the square plaza so that each residential mound is paired with one and sometimes two burial mounds, forming eight burial/residential mound groups. Knight saw in this pattern a parallel to Chickasaw society.

The ethnographic data are limited, and Chickasaw society had undergone profound changes because of European contact, but Knight found that the ideal Chickasaw village had sets of houses arranged around a square plaza, just as the mounds at Moundville form a square plaza. In Chickasaw society, each set of houses belonged to a matrilocal clan that was the political and land-owning unit. In addition, the clans were grouped into moieties, which lived on opposite sides of the square village layout. The highest-ranking clan of each moiety was located on opposite sides of the north end of the square plan, with lower-ranking clans to the south. Thus, Chickasaw villages spatially mirrored the kinship structure (just as we saw with Mikea hamlets).

Knight wondered if this kinship pattern extended back to the inhabitants of Moundville. Perhaps, he suggested, each of the eight residential/burial mound units represents the high-ranking home of the leader of eight clans. Knight pointed out that the Moundville plaza can be neatly bifurcated by a line passing through Mound B at the north end of the plaza, through the central Mound A, and then between smaller burial mounds K and J (refer to Figure 10-8). Extrapolating from the Chickasaw analogy, the resulting halves might represent two moieties, each comprising four clans. Note also that the most elite burials were recovered in Mounds C and D; although these are not the largest mounds, they are located at either side of the north edge of the plaza.

But Moundville and Chickasaw villages exhibit crucial differences:

- In the Chickasaw camp layout, a large fire hearth in the center of the village structurally and symbolically united the two moieties. There was, however, no central mound or ceremonial structure.
- Knight points out that nineteenth-century Chickasaw society was not a chiefdom and did not possess a central individual who was the uniting focus of the social and political organization. In Moundville, the large Mound B, at the north end of the site, might have been the home of the chief—the highest-ranking individual—and evidence of a tier in the social organization that was not present among the Chickasaw.

In sum, Knight's analysis of Moundville's layout supports the conclusion of the mortuary analysis that Moundville was a chiefdom.

Trade and Political Organization

In our discussion of Moundville, we mentioned the Southeastern Ceremonial Complex, a social phenomenon that included an extensive trade network. All societies—from egalitarian bands to chiefdoms to modern states—exchange goods, ideas, and services. The geographic scale of trade tells us something about the nature of the nonresidential group that a residential group was part of, and how far-flung their political, economic, and kinship connections were.

In archaeological sites in the Great Basin, for example, archaeologists frequently find beads made of the shells of *olivella*, *haliotis*, and *dentalia*—marine organisms that live along the coasts of California and Oregon. Obviously, they point to some sort of interaction between people on either side of California's Sierra Nevada.

These shell beads are not numerous in Great Basin sites. They appear as personal ornaments in some burials, but they are not exclusively associated with men or women, the old or the young. Many are found in residential sites where, because they are small, they were probably lost as they fell off clothing or a necklace. It is more difficult to say if the beads indicate exchange of goods between the peoples of the Great Basin and California or were simply the personal belongings of people (wives or husbands? emigrants?) who moved from California to the Great Basin.

Anthropologists have found that as societies change from egalitarian bands to ranked societies, the formal trade of **exotics** becomes an integral part of the economy. Exotics are artifacts made of raw material or in a style that indicates contact with the people of a distant region. Members of the elite trade or give away exotics at competitive feasts as a way to communicate and maintain the social order. Exotic artifacts, therefore, are symbols of status and prestige—visual reminders of a person's social, political, or religious connections to a larger world. As such, they are signs of power and, consequently, of social and political organization as well.

Tracing Exotics

In some cases, it is easy to determine which objects are *not* locally produced. Recall that at Moundville, for example, some of the elite burials contained copper axes. This copper is not smelted; smelting technology did not exist in North America prior to European contact. Instead, the copper was extracted in its raw form. We know that this kind of copper, known as native copper, is not found around Moundville. In fact, native copper occurs only in the southern Appalachian Mountains and near the Great Lakes. The copper artifacts at Moundville have been traced to a geological deposit in the southern Appalachian source. Likewise, the galena cubes have been traced to geological sources in Missouri and Wisconsin.

Human societies create many different kinds of trade systems, but they tend to be of two major types. The first is **direct acquisition**; as you might guess, this means that you go to the natural source of a raw material and extract the material yourself, exchange goods or services for it or for a finished artifact, or receive an artifact or raw material as a gift. Direct acquisition might entail a special trip, or it may be embedded in a foraging excursion or a visit to relatives.

The second major type is **down-the-line trade**, in which people acquire a particular raw material or an artifact fashioned from that raw material from their neighbors, who have immediate access to the raw material. These people then trade it to others who live still farther away from the source, who may in turn trade it to people living still farther away. Down-the-line trade usually results in a steady decline in the frequency of artifacts made of a particular material in sites farther and farther away from the raw material's source. Occasionally, an unexpectedly high density of the raw material at a site distant from the source may signal that the site is a secondary trading center. Down-the-line trade can move raw materials long distances. For example, archaeologists have found incised Gulf Coast shells in sites along the Missouri River in Montana.

Nobody knows how the copper axes made their way to Moundville—perhaps they were gifts sent between ranking elites—but they clearly signal that only a few people had the authority and power to acquire them or to merit receiving them as gifts. Although the copper axes had no material function—they would have made poor cutting implements—they were powerful symbols of the "connections" an elite individual had and perhaps of his ability to draw upon social, economic, military, or religious sanctions should anyone contest his hold on power.

We mentioned that archaeologists traced the copper axes at Moundville to geological sources in the southern Appalachian Mountains. We do such tracing by "fingerprinting" an object and comparing it to similar fingerprints of known sources of the raw material. Several different methods can accomplish this.

Fingerprinting Obsidian

Obsidian—the volcanic glass that makes such impressively sharp implements—occurs naturally only in geologic deposits of the western United States. So, why do obsidian artifacts appear in **Hopewell** burial mounds and sites in Ohio and Illinois?

Recall from Chapter 2 that Squier and Davis mapped and studied the earthworks of the eastern United States, especially along the Ohio River Valley and its tributaries. We now know that some of the flat-topped pyramid mounds—such as those at Moundville—belong to the Mississippian period. But other mounds—including geometric earthworks and some effigy mounds—are earlier, belonging to the Hopewell culture. "Hopewell" refers to a particular archaeological culture of the American Midwest, especially the Ohio River Valley, between 2200 and 1600 BP. Hopewell peoples were predominately hunter-gatherers, although they also cultivated indigenous plants and small amounts of maize. They lived in small, sedentary villages.

Hopewell culture is known for its elaborate mortuary rituals, which suggests the beginnings of a ranked society. Many goods appear in elite Hopewell graves, including copper ornaments, incised pottery, carved mica, ceramics, and obsidian. The fact that obsidian is found almost exclusively in burials of Ohio Hopewell sites, rather than in middens, suggests that obsidian played something other than a purely functional role in Hopewell society.

exotics Material culture that was not produced locally and/or whose raw material is not found locally.

direct acquisition A form of trade in which a person or group goes to the source area of an item to procure the raw material directly or to trade for it or finished products.

down-the-line trade An exchange system in which goods are traded outward from a source area from group to group, resulting in a steady decline in the item's abundance in archaeological sites farther from the source.

Hopewell A cultural tradition found primarily in the Ohio River Valley and its tributaries, dating from 2200 to 1600 BP. Hopewell societies engaged in hunting and gathering and in some horticulture of indigenous plants. They are known for their mortuary rituals, which included charnel houses and burial mounds; some central tombs contained exotics. They also constructed geometric earthworks as ceremonial enclosures and effigy mounds.

Squier and Davis recorded small numbers of obsidian spear points in five Hopewell mounds, and more have since turned up in Tennessee, Illinois, and elsewhere. At the time, Squier and Davis postulated that the obsidian came from Mexico or the American Southwest, but these were simply guesses. Early in the twentieth century, several archaeologists proposed the Rocky Mountains as the source—specifically the obsidian outcrops in Yellowstone National Park. More than a century after Squier and Davis first reported on the obsidian, James Griffin (1905–1997) used the then new technique of "neutron activation analysis" to source the obsidian in the Ohio Hopewell mounds to Obsidian Cliff in Yellowstone National Park, some 2400 kilometers away. Because of concerns with the accuracy of neutron activation analysis, Richard Hughes (Geochemical Research Laboratory, California)—one of the world's leading authorities on obsidian sourcing—used the current sourcing method, **energy dispersive x-ray fluorescence (XRF)**, to test Griffin's findings.

How can XRF trace obsidian artifacts to their geologic source? Many geological deposits form slowly—over years, decades, thousands, or even tens of thousands of years. But obsidian deposits are produced during a single lava flow, and hence they are created in a geologic instant. A volcano could produce multiple flows, but because each flow forms quickly, it usually has a unique chemical "fingerprint." This fingerprint appears as particular quantities of trace elements, such as zinc, rubidium, strontium, and barium. Different flows contain different amounts of these elements. If we can fingerprint samples from all geologic sources of obsidian—a formidable but not impossible task—and then fingerprint obsidian artifacts, we should be able to match up an artifact with its source.

XRF allows us to accomplish this goal. The analyst shoots an x-ray beam onto a piece of obsidian, causing the electrons to become excited and emit fluorescent x-ray energies. Because different trace elements emit different levels of energy, analysts can measure the spectra of energy emitted from the piece of obsidian and, from this, determine the proportion of each trace element present—defining the sample's distinctive trace element fingerprint. Comparing the sample's trace element composition statistically with all known sources allows analysts to find the best match and, presumably, the geologic source of an artifact. XRF is a very useful technique because it is nondestructive, works well on very small samples (down to 1 millimeter in diameter), takes only minutes to complete, and is relatively inexpensive.

Hughes's analysis confirmed that most Hopewell obsidian came from Obsidian Cliff in Yellowstone National Park. But he also discovered that some obsidian, especially that found in Illinois and Indiana Hopewell sites, came from Bear Gulch in southeast Idaho.

We now know that obsidian from the Yellowstone region appears in small quantities at other Hopewell-age sites in Wisconsin, Iowa, Illinois, and Indiana. Instead of direct acquisition, high-ranking Hopewell individuals probably acquired obsidian through down-the-line trade—the stones' shiny black surfaces serving to remind people not of vacations to Yellowstone, but of the social ties some individuals had to high-ranking people in other Hopewell communities.

energy dispersive x-ray fluorescence (XRF) An analytical technique that uses obsidian's trace elements to "fingerprint" an artifact and trace it to its geologic source.

Conclusion

In reconstructing social and political organizations, archaeologists remember that artifacts were not just utilitarian items, but also carried symbolic meanings—meanings that could be manipulated and that played a role in how those artifacts eventually ended up in an archaeological context. Sometimes these symbolic meanings reflect elements of social and political organization—such as gender roles, kinship systems, trade networks, and political connections. However, it's hard to construct middle-level theory that allows us to infer social and political organization from archaeological remains, and it may forever require well-supported ethnographic analogy. However, new techniques—analysis of physical and chemical properties of artifacts and the use of genetic markers in human skeletal remains—give archaeology ways to test various hypotheses and continue to improve its reconstruction of the past.

In the following chapter, we go into an even more difficult area of archaeology: the analysis of symbols, concepts, and abstract thought. As you will see, reconstructing social and political organization is a walk in the park compared with trying to draw inferences from symbolic systems.

Summary

- What concepts help archaeologists to reconstruct past social and political organizations?
  - Archaeologists think in terms of both residential and nonresidential groups.
  - How these groups operate is a matter of gender (culturally based interpretations of biology), the division of labor, kinship, and status.
  - Bioarchaeological analyses provide clues as to the division of labor, but strong empirical generalizations or historically linked ethnographic analogies are often needed.
  - Kinship is the socially recognized network of relationships through which individuals are related to one another by ties of descent (real or imagined) and marriage.
  - Status refers to the rights, duties, and privileges that define the nature of interpersonal relations. *Ascribed status* is parceled out at birth without regard to personal characteristics; *achieved status* comes from what one accomplishes in life.
  - A society is *egalitarian* if achieved status is the means whereby an individual acquires a high position. In a *ranked* society, ascribed status places people into a ranked order of privilege; ranked societies exhibit a hierarchy, and its members have unequal access to basic resources.
- What archaeological remains are important in reconstructing political organization, especially those involving inherited social inequities?
  - Egalitarian and ranked societies are often studied through patterning in mortuary remains, on the assumption that treatment in death reflects status in life, as well as through public and household architecture.
- What archaeological remains help reconstruct social organization, especially kinship?
  - Social groupings are reflected "on the ground" in terms of house spacing and placement. Genetic distance studies of human skeletal remains provide clues to postmarital residence.
- What techniques help reconstruct ancient trade networks?
  - Trade networks reflect the geographic scale of nonresidential groups, economic patterns, and political authority. Trade is established by determining whether artifacts were made or obtained locally and by determining the source of raw materials for artifact manufacture.
  - Obsidian, clay, and temper sourcing studies demonstrate the geographic scale of an economic and/or political organization.

Media Resources

CourseMate

Access chapter-specific learning tools including learning objectives, practice quizzes, videos, flash cards, and glossaries, as well as web links, and more in your Archaeology CourseMate. Login to www.cengagebrain.com to access the resources your instructor has assigned and to purchase materials.

The Archaeology of the Mind

11

© Bettman/CORBIS

This horse was painted on the ceiling of the cave of Lascaux, in France, some 17,000 years ago.

Learning Objectives

After reading this chapter, you should be able to answer these questions:

- What is the central challenge of "cognitive archaeology"?
- How do archaeologists study ancient religion?
- Can archaeologists learn anything from very ancient cases that have no close cultural descendants?

Preview

AS CULTURAL BEINGS, we all construct the world in which we live. By "construct," we mean that although we physically alter the world—through farming, architecture, trash disposal, logging, mining, and so forth, we also interpret our world symbolically, which can lead to different approaches to the physical world. In this chapter, we will concentrate on these symbolic meanings.

Some archaeologists attempt to infer the symbolic meanings of specific artifact forms, and others try to reconstruct concepts and perceptions about how the ancients viewed the world and the place of humans in it. As you might guess, symbolic approaches in archaeology raise some difficult issues. Although a huge range of human behavior falls under the category of "symbolic," we will concentrate on investigations of ritual and religion, iconography, and the interpretation of prehistoric rock art.

Introduction

When processual archaeology gained prominence in the 1960s, it generated numerous studies of prehistoric demography, settlement patterns, subsistence, technology, and the human use of landscapes, plants, and animals. These approaches relied largely on rigorous scientific methods. The focus was heavily materialistic because processual archaeologists believed that subsistence behavior provided the infrastructure for the rest of the cultural system (see Chapter 2).

Early on, processual archaeologists were optimistic about studying all aspects of the human condition from archaeological data. But through the 1970s and 1980s, most processual archaeologists remained decidedly lukewarm toward **cognitive archaeology**. Many felt that the archaeological record relating to "ideas" seemed too shaky and ambiguous—not to be approached in an explicitly scientific, objective manner. And processual archaeologists assumed that the cognitive aspects of culture—including religion—were "epiphenomena," features of human societies that were merely derivative from the more critical technological and economic basics; as such, they were unimportant to understanding the past.

The appeal of processual archaeology is easy to understand. This research paradigm places priority on just those things that archaeologists are most confident in recovering from their sites—evidence about past environments, technologies, and economies.

But other archaeologists felt that such heavy-handed materialism dehumanized the past. They argued instead for an "archaeology of the mind"—one that emphasizes the values, ideas, and beliefs that make us all human. To be sure, any archaeology of the mind will have a more postprocessual than processual flavor because such an approach will necessarily address recovering *meanings* (rather than law-like statements or generalizations about human behavior). Today, cognitive archaeology remains largely interpretive, but we will demonstrate that such symbolic perspectives can indeed lend themselves to scientific testing as well—if appropriate linkages can be made between the interpretations of ancient symbols and those human behaviors most directly inferred from the archaeological record.

All humans interact with their world through their cultural perception of it, and modern archaeologists can ill afford to overlook the power of symbols. Take food, for example. Economic decisions might appear to be rather straightforward: Eat this food because it is nutritious and efficiently harvested, and avoid that food because it is not. Although such decisions do heavily condition subsistence practices, we also face an ever-changing background of cultural information about what is/is not edible. As we pointed out in Chapter 2, some societies consider dogs to be food, even prestigious feast foods. Yet people in other cultures are repulsed by the idea of eating their "pets" (see "Looking Closer: Food Taboos in the Near East"). And some animals may be highly valued in particular cultures, not because of their nutritional content, but because of their symbolic meaning. Native peoples of New Guinea hunted cassowary birds not for food, but because their feathers were prestigious gifts that were given away at feasts.

Symbolism goes beyond food to permeate all arenas of human life. We saw in Chapter 8 that even firewood,

cognitive archaeology The study of all those aspects of ancient culture that are the product of the human mind: the perception, description, and classification of the universe; the nature of the supernatural; the principles, philosophies, ethics, and values by which human societies are governed; and the ways in which aspects of the world, the supernatural, or human values are conveyed in art.

LOOKING CLOSER

Food Taboos in the Near East

Traditional Jewish and Islamic faiths prohibit eating pork. This prohibition is very ancient, dating back to the Near Eastern roots of both religions. Pork is a perfectly nutritious food, and pigs can be raised quite efficiently. Why, then, did this prohibition arise in these Near Eastern religions? Here we contrast two different explanations for this food taboo—one materialist, the other symbolic.

Following a materialist paradigm, Marvin Harris (1927–2001) argued that pigs were prohibited in the ancient Near East because they are poorly suited for life in the desert. Pigs are forest dwellers, and they do well in wet environments. Harris suggested that any food, even a formerly useful food, will be tabooed when the cost of producing it outweighs its nutritional value. In the desert, the cost of trying to keep pigs alive would indeed be high.

But why would a taboo with supernatural sanctions be necessary if the food was clearly inefficient to produce or procure? Certainly, people are rational enough to see when raising or harvesting a particular food is not worth the effort. And the prohibition against pork is only one of a lengthy list of tabooed foods. This list first appears in the book of Leviticus in the Old Testament, and later in Deuteronomy. In those passages, God prohibits the followers of Moses from eating pigs, but also shellfish, rabbits, camels, insects, and a variety of birds. Many of these, such as camels, are perfectly suited for life in the desert.

Mary Douglas (1921–2007), a symbolic anthropologist, argues that you cannot explain one of these tabooed foods without explaining all of them. She proposes a different explanation based on Near Eastern cultural ideas about animals. The prohibited animals in Leviticus were said to be "unclean," and Douglas focused on the meaning of that term. She pointed out that unclean often means "disorderly." You might say that your house is "not clean" when in fact what you mean is that clothing is lying on the floor and you haven't put the furniture back from last week's party. You might say that dishes sitting beside the sink are "dirty" when in fact you were just eating off of them moments earlier. They are not dirty; they are simply not "in their place" (washed, dried, and in the cupboard).

Taking this approach to the complete list of food prohibitions, Douglas found that virtually all the prohibited animals are ones that ancient Near Easterners saw as violating cultural ideas about the order of creation. Animals were supposed to be those that walk, hop, or jump on all four feet. Thus, insects that "swarm upon the land" are unclean because they are outside the cultural order of life. Likewise, edible animals were supposed to be those that have cloven hooves and that chew the cud—such as cattle, sheep, and goats. Pigs have cloven hooves, but they do not chew the cud. Consequently, they are unclean because they are an anomaly in the "natural" order of animals. Avoiding certain animals, then, had little to do with food, but with a continual affirmation of what constitutes God's order in the world.

Which explanation is right? Douglas's argument is appealing because it provides an explanation for all the forbidden animals. But this raises a new question: If pork was prohibited because it fell outside the natural order, what gave rise to that view of the world?

something apparently mundane and utilitarian, was symbolically loaded for the Inca. And Chapter 10 explained how kinship involves the imposition of different symbolic ideas about kin onto biological relationships. Male and female tasks also differ among societies, depending on what symbolic value a culture assigns to different tasks. In industrial societies, advertising tells us that clothing, houses, cars, hairstyles, tattoos, beer—virtually everything, in fact—carries symbolic meaning.

Humans live in a material world, and nobody can avoid the realities of survival. But people also live in a culturally constructed world, and material decisions are always made against a backdrop of symbolic meanings. This is why a number of archaeologists have turned to an ideational emphasis in their research, examining the active role of symbols in shaping the economic, social, and even technological structure of societies. We discussed the symbolic element of human culture in Chapter 2; now we consider symbols in more detail.

What's a Symbol?

The ability to use symbols goes to the essence of what it means to be human. Language is made possible by symbols; so are stories, art, and poetry. Symbols shape the way that people see, understand, and feel about the world.

To most anthropologists, a **symbol** is an object or act (verbal or nonverbal) that by cultural convention stands for something else *with which it has no necessary connection.* Consider a symbol that is familiar to most Americans: the red circle with a red line running diagonally through it. With a capital "P" in the center of the circle, the symbol tells us "no parking"; with a cigarette in the middle, it means "no smoking." (The "P" and the cigarette, by the way, are not symbols but signs because they actually have a connection to what they signify—the word "parking" itself and a cigarette). Virtually all Americans understand that a red circle with a diagonal line through it forbids whatever is in the circle.

But is there any *necessary* connection between a red circle with a line through it and prohibition of a certain behavior? No. In fact, this symbol might just as easily mean the opposite: Parking *is* allowed here, smoking *is* permitted here. If you were not enculturated into the meaning of the symbol, you would have no way of deducing the symbol's meaning merely from the symbol itself—*because there is no necessary connection between a symbol and the thing it stands for*. Some anthropologists suggest that a few basic symbols might have an inherent meaning genetically programmed into our consciousness; red, for example, the color of blood might carry the meaning of danger. But the vast majority of the symbols we use have no such "natural" meaning. (And if you think they do, rent a car in Paris and figure out the "natural" meaning of French road signs.)

This is why symbols are so powerful. A simple symbolic act can be made to carry enormous amounts of information. In fact, the same symbol can carry different meanings under different situations. Consider a simple wink of the eye. In one situation, it can signal a playful conspiracy between two people against a third; in another, the same gesture is flirting (or harassment). But in another culture, a wink might mean nothing more than that a person has something irritating his or her eye.

Because symbols have no necessary connection to their culturally assigned meaning, they can be used in different ways. Much of the humor, pathos, and poignancy in literature and the arts come from the playful or artful use of symbols (such as the use of the red prohibition circle in the comedy *Ghostbusters*). This is another way in which symbols are powerful.

But these very essential qualities make symbols difficult to study archaeologically. If there is no necessary connection between a symbol and what it stands for, then how does an outsider know what a particular symbol "means"? How would you know that a red circle with a line through it *prohibits* rather than *permits* a behavior? Deciphering these messages is difficult enough today, when we have access to language, informants, and observable behavior. But it is manifestly more difficult—some would say impossible—to understand symbolic behavior in an archaeological context, where the physical symbol survives, but its meaning does not.

Consider, for example, the rock art shown in Figure 11-1—one of the thousands of images found at La María, a complex of rockshelters in Patagonia (a region of southern Argentina). The central figure is a guanaco, a wild camelid once hunted by native peoples of the region. Along the guanaco's back and haunches is a series of white dots, and other white dots are on the body. In the upper right is a hand silhouette, created when the artisan placed his or her right hand on the wall and then blew paint over it. Between the hand and the guanaco runs a red, white, and black line, immediately below which is a line of red dots.

FIGURE 11-1 A panel of art from a rockshelter at La María, in southern Patagonia. The central figure is a guanaco, a wild camelid.

What do these images mean? Was the hand painted as part of ritual? Or is it more like graffiti "tagging"? What do the lines and dots represent? A hunting fence or drive line? Or maybe a map? Does the guanaco "mean" guanaco? Or is it a symbol that stands for something else, like a lineage? What about the dots on the guanaco? Is this hunting or fertility magic, or an appeal to a supernatural being represented by the figure? There are no easy answers to these questions.

Anthropologists might interpret symbols by looking at the various ways a particular symbol is used and its (possibly varied) contexts. They might see which symbols are consciously manipulated and which are not; which can be used for humor (and who finds them funny). They might see if some symbols are exclusively used by or associated with women or men. By viewing a symbol's use in a variety of circumstances, we can construct an understanding of what the symbol means. But this understanding requires the living context of the symbol, something archaeologists do not have. And this means that ancient symbolic systems may remain forever silent as to their specific, detailed meanings.

But many contemporary archaeologists disagree, believing it's still worthwhile exploring human behavior as a system of meanings, rather than merely acts that meet material needs. For some, this means relying heavily on ethnographic analogy or oral traditions (see "What Does It Mean to Me? What Role Do Oral Traditions Play in Archaeology?")—remember how African societies treated

symbol An object or act (verbal or nonverbal) that, by cultural convention, stands for something else with which it has no necessary connection.

WHAT DOES IT MEAN TO me?

What Role Do Oral Traditions Play in Archaeology?

We point out in this chapter that ethnographic and ethnohistoric information can be crucial to an "archaeology of the mind." Some of this information might come from *oral traditions*—accounts of the past passed down by word of mouth from generation to generation. What do archaeologists do if oral traditions—a culture's stories about its past—conflict with archaeological data?

On the one hand, we could say that no one knows a culture's past better than its descendants. On the other hand, we could point out that oral traditions are often selective in what they remember, or that they alter the nature or sequence of events to suit particular political needs. This is not a matter of lying. Oral traditions are a product of current events and sensibilities, and whereas they can contain accounts of past events, they are not always straightforward accounts of what "really happened" in the past.

For example, many European Americans imagine the mid-nineteenth-century settlement of the West as consisting of small, lonely caravans of Conestoga wagons nightly forming a circle to repel the Plains Indians' "wheel of death" attacks. We get this image from Western "oral" tradition—movies and novels. However, John Unruh (1937–1976), a historian who carefully read all surviving emigrant diaries of the years between 1840 and 1860, found virtually no mention of such encounters. Most wagon trains were large, and far more people died of cholera and accidents than from Indian attacks (in fact, more Indians died at the hands of the emigrants than vice versa). And most attacks occurred along the Snake and Humboldt Rivers in Idaho and Nevada, not on the Plains. The popular image was created by the media (as early as 1850) to justify the taking of Native American land; in so doing, they created America's own "origin myth." Oral histories are a product of the time and culture in which they are produced; they are not purely factual accounts of the past.

Oral histories can change with time, and the older the events they describe, the greater is the likelihood that some elements have been dropped and others added. Lakota oral traditions, for example, contain many references to horses, but the Lakota did not have horses (which the Spanish brought to the New World) until after AD 1740. They must be a fairly recent addition to Lakota oral history.

Many archaeologists believe that oral traditions must be corroborated by archaeological data. But many people find this insulting because to test oral traditions is, in effect, to question them. Many Christian fundamentalists feel the same way. If biblical archaeology corroborates the Bible, fine; but if it does not, some would argue, it is because archaeology, not the Bible, is imperfect.

Archaeology has standards of evidence, evaluation, and self-criticism (we've discussed many in this text), but so does the study of oral traditions. Peter Whiteley (American Museum of Natural History), for example, points out that oral histories can be evaluated in terms of their *consistency*—do different people give the same account, and does the same person give the same account over time? Are some elements of a tradition validated by independent sources (for instance, historical documents or archaeology)? Keeping these standards in mind, oral history can contribute some additional data to the interpretations archaeology produces.

pig bones in so many different ways (in Chapter 7). We'll give you two more examples that explore some potential and limitations inherent in an archaeology of the mind.

The Peace Pipe as Ritual Weapon

Writing in the late 1970s, archaeologist Robert L. Hall (1927–2012) used the calumet—the peace pipe—to demonstrate how a cognitive approach could broaden the horizons of archaeological investigations.

Hall focused on the Hopewell culture, which probably included many different peoples speaking different languages and living in various ways, ranging from the lower Mississippi to Minnesota and from Nebraska to Virginia. But during Hopewell times (between 2200 and 1600 BP), these diverse people apparently shared a unifying set of symbols that may indicate a common set of religious beliefs. Archaeologists refer to this common set of symbols found over a wide area as the **Hopewell Interaction Sphere**.

To understand what was going on, let's first consider whether the Hopewell people shared a common religion. Broadly speaking, anthropologists consider **religion** to be a specific set of beliefs about the supernatural. Religion is a society's mechanism for relating supernatural phenomena to the everyday world. It often includes rituals that enlist supernatural powers for the purpose of achieving or preventing transformations of state in humans and nature—in other words, to make sure that good things happen and bad things do not. In some religions, individuals use rituals to influence the course of events;

RAPID REVIEW

Characteristics of Symbols and Their Archaeological Study

- All objects are symbolic to one extent or another.
- There is no necessary link between an object and its symbolic meaning.
- Symbols can be manipulated, and used in different ways for different purposes in different contexts.
- These characteristics make the archaeological study of symbols difficult.
- Specific meanings of ancient symbols may be forever lost to archaeology, but the effect of a system of meanings may not be.

in others, they help novices find their path in a world that they see as beyond their control. All living cultures have some form of religion, and we suppose that was true of past societies as well.

Religious beliefs are manifested in everyday life as **ritual**, a succession of discrete behaviors that must be performed in a particular order under particular circumstances—such as saying prayers at certain times of the day accompanied by particular acts or gestures. Rituals are fundamentally religious acts because they are the mechanisms by which individuals attempt to intercede with the supernatural.

This particular definition of religion is especially relevant to archaeology because of its emphasis on ritual. Rituals are behavioral acts that often entail material culture and therefore can be represented in the archaeological record. The analysis of past ritual behavior is thus archaeology's major contribution to the study of religion.

Some of the highly standardized Hopewell artifacts are perhaps indicative of rituals. One particularly intriguing artifact is the stone platform pipe, some examples of which are shown in Figure 11-2. Hopewell artists fashioned these from pipestone, often ornamenting them with carved mammals, birds, or reptiles that rest on a straight or curved base. The pipes were probably used to smoke tobacco, which is indigenous to the New World; the earliest evidence of tobacco in the eastern United States dates to about 1900 BP.

The effort taken to carve these pipes suggests that whatever rituals the pipes were involved in were a critical aspect of Hopewell ceremonial life. Hundreds of pipes were found in the so-called Mound of the Pipes at Mound City, near Chillicothe, Ohio. Some think that this mound was a monument to a master carver of sacred pipes.

What were the pipes used for? What did they signal to their users?

To try to explain these pipes, Hall looked to historical and ethnographic data. He was especially intrigued by the fact that the "peace pipe" used historically to establish friendly contact almost always took the form of a weapon. He then reasoned that all cultures engage in certain culturally dictated customs whose exact meaning and origin may be lost in time. For example, the rite of toasting with drinks in Western culture originally was the sloshing and spilling together of two people's drinks to reduce the possibility that one planned to poison the other. But how many of us who have toasted friends realize the origin of the custom? Hall suggested that although the original functions of such gestures have lost their practical significance, the acts survive as elements of etiquette or protocol.

Hall applied similar reasoning to the Hopewell platform pipes by calling upon ethnographic data. Throughout historic times in the eastern United States, Indian tribes observed the custom of smoking a sacred tribal pipe. When the pipe was present, violence was ruled out. Moreover, the peace pipe usually was made in the shape of a weapon. The Pawnee peace pipe, for instance, looked like an arrow, and the Osage word for calumet translated as "arrow shaft." Hall suggested that the weaponlike appearance resulted from a specific ceremonial custom. Could it be that, at least during the period of European contact, the peace pipe symbolized a ritual weapon?

Hall then projected his idea back into ancient Hopewell times. Suppose that the distinctive Hopewell platform pipes were also ritual weapons—but made before these people knew of the bow and arrow. At the time, the most common Hopewell weapon was the atlatl, or spear-thrower, like those that appear in Figure 11-3.

Hall suggested that the distinctive Hopewell platform pipe symbolically represented a flat atlatl decorated with an effigy spur. He also observed that the animal on the bowl was almost always carved precisely where an atlatl spur would be. And the curvature of the platform seemed to correspond to the curvature of the atlatl. These correspondences led Hall to conclude: "I see the Hopewell platform pipe as the archaeologically visible part of a transformed ritual atlatl, a symbolic weapon which in Middle Woodland times probably had some of the same functions as the calumet of historic times, itself a ritual arrow."

Hopewell Interaction Sphere The common set of symbols found in the midwestern United States between 2200 and 1600 BP.

religion A specific set of beliefs about one's relation to the supernatural; a society's mechanism for relating supernatural phenomena to the everyday world.

ritual A succession of discrete behaviors that must be performed in a particular order under particular circumstances.

FIGURE 11-2 Hopewell effigy pipes. The bowl for tobacco is on the animal's back. These would have been placed on the end of a wooden stem and may represent the hook on the end of an atlatl.

FIGURE 11-3 Some representations of atlatls in aboriginal North American art.

Hall then proposed that the importance of the Hopewell pipe might well extend beyond symbolism—that the platform pipe was not merely one of many items exchanged between groups, but that "it may have been part of the very mechanism of exchange." Materialist research on eastern United States prehistory has conventionally defined the Hopewell Interaction Sphere primarily in economic and environmental terms. Perhaps, by maintaining relationships between large-scale networks of ritual trading partners, far-flung Hopewell communities joined economic forces, looking to one another for support in lean years.

Hall suggested that a shift away from strictly materialistic thinking—toward a more cognitive approach—could generate a broader understanding of the Hopewell lifeway. Reasoning from Native American ethnographic analogies, Hall contended that peace pipe rituals served to mediate interaction over a vast area of eastern North America. By promoting a common set of symbols—perhaps linked to some common religious ideas—the Hopewell Interaction Sphere tended to reduce regional differences and promote contact and communication between discrete groups.

We pointed out that interpretations of the symbolic meanings of artifacts are difficult to test directly. But we could test the *implications* of Hall's conclusions by assessing whether the archaeology of the Hopewell Interaction Sphere supports the social and political ramifications of Hall's interpretation of the stone pipes. Is there evidence of conflict in Hopewell sites? If so, how does it relate to the distribution of stone pipes and their source areas? How does the distribution of pipes across the Hopewell Interaction Sphere relate to evidence for subsistence stress (from faunal, macrobotanical, and human skeletal remains)? In other words, if we treat symbolic interpretations as hypotheses, then it is possible to test them by linking them to phenomena that are more archaeologically accessible. To see how this might work, let's return to an example that we have used before, the Chavín culture of Peru.

Exploring Ancient Chavín Cosmology

In Chapter 8, we discussed the Chavín culture of the central Andes. Specifically, we looked at the faunal remains recovered from Chavín de Huántar and learned what these finds could tell us about subsistence and trade.

But the term "Chavín" conjures up to most archaeologists much more than llama bones. Archaeologists commonly consider Chavín to be Peru's first highland civilization because of its stratified social and political organization and its achievements in metallurgy, weaving, monumental architecture, irrigation systems, and stone sculpture.

Chavín also left a lasting legacy in Andean **cosmology**. By cosmology, we mean a culture's understanding of how the world works, how it originated and developed, how the various parts fit together, what laws they obey, and, especially, the place of humans in the natural and supernatural worlds. A glimpse of a culture's cosmology can often be found in its **iconography**—its art forms or writing systems (such as Egyptian or Maya hieroglyphs) that symbolically represent ideas about religion or cosmology.

The iconography at Chavín de Huántar established the tone of subsequent central Andean cosmology. All deities of the succeeding generations in the central Andes looked more or less like the gods in the temple at Chavín de Huántar. Archaeologists Richard Burger and George Miller (whose faunal analysis of Chavín de Huántar we discussed in Chapter 8) have explored the nature of Chavín cosmology, looking in particular at the distinctive Chavín iconography that appeared over a wide area of the central Andes nearly 2500 years ago.

Animal Symbolism in Chavín Iconography

Chavín de Huántar has given its name to one of the Americas' most famous art styles. Chavín iconography is derived from stone sculptures at Chavín de Huántar, an example of which appears in Figure 11-4. This art style was reproduced in many villages in the central Andes on locally made ceramics, textiles, goldwork, and stone.

Remember that the community of Chavín de Huántar depended on a range of animals for food, including wild deer, vicuña, llama, and guinea pigs. These were local beasts, probably encountered by local residents on a daily basis.

But the local highland animals of Chavín de Huántar are conspicuously absent from the thousands of known temple sculptures, ceramics, and textiles that display the widespread Chavín style. Instead, the Chavín style drew inspiration for its stylized fangs and talons, feathers and scales from the jaguar, crested eagle, monkey, serpent, and caiman (alligator). These creatures are native to the cloud forests and rain forests of the *eastern* Andean slope, if not the floodplains of Amazonia itself—located several hundred miles to the east, on the other side of the Andes. These same animals play a prominent role in the mythology and religious symbolism of modern people of Amazonia, but they were utterly foreign to the inhabitants of Chavín de Huántar.

FIGURE 11-4 One of the carved stone heads on the temple at Chavín de Huántar, representing a shaman's transition from human to jaguar.

Why did the major animals in Chavín religious art come from places outside the local highland environment?

Where Did Chavín Cosmology Come From?

Archaeologists have proposed several hypotheses to explain this puzzling aspect of Chavín cosmology. One holds that the climate was radically warmer and more humid during Chavín times. If so, then maybe the lowland complex of animals—the jaguar, the caiman, the crested eagle, and so forth—could have once lived in the highlands around Chavín de Huántar.

But this hypothesis is not correct. Several lines of evidence demonstrate that the climate was similar to the modern pattern during the Chavín time period (2900 to 2200 BP), and remember from Chapter 8 that the animal bones recovered from Chavín de Huántar belong to the same species as modern highland animals—camelids, deer, and so forth. Paleoenvironmental change cannot explain the nature of Chavín iconography.

Peruvian archaeologist Julio Tello (1880–1947), discoverer of the Chavín civilization and first excavator at Chavín de Huántar (in the 1930s), and later American archaeologist Donald Lathrap (1927–1990) championed

cosmology The study of the origin, large-scale structure, and future of the universe. A cosmological explanation demonstrates how the universe developed—both the totality and its constituent parts—and also describes what principles keep it together.

iconography Art forms or writing systems (such as Egyptian or Maya hieroglyphics) that symbolically represent ideas about religion or cosmology.

another hypothesis. Plants indigenous to Amazonia—including manioc, bottle gourd, hot peppers, and possibly peanuts—all appear at Chavín de Huántar. Tello suggested that immigrants from the tropical forest introduced the lowland plants and animals to Chavín de Huántar. Lathrap attributed the migration to population pressure in the lowland Amazonian or Orinoco basin that forced the early Chavín folk into the Andean highlands. According to Lathrap, the heavy Amazonian component of Chavín religious art displayed homage and deference to the ancient homeland and subsistence regime that was responsible for the initial success of the Chavín elite.

But this hypothesis also seems to be incorrect. Lowland crops are impossible to grow in the Andean environment, and they could not have been brought with and grown by an immigrant population. Instead, their presence suggests trade or some other kind of contact between Chavín de Huántar and Amazonia. Burger also hypothesizes that if a tropical forest people had moved wholesale into the Andes, their ceramic traditions should show a direct relationship to those of the Amazonian homeland. But the earliest ceramics at Chavín de Huántar show a conspicuous lack of Amazonian characteristics; the pottery looks local rather than imported. It also is clear that the basic high-altitude mixed agricultural subsistence pattern the pioneer population practiced at Chavín de Huántar was not Amazonian at all; it had developed in place—in the highlands—at least a thousand years earlier. The ceramic and subsistence evidence makes it unlikely that a tropical forest group was responsible for the lowland iconography evident on the earliest buildings at Chavín de Huántar.

This is why Burger advocates a third hypothesis to explain the Amazonian elements of Chavín cosmology. Chavín de Huántar occupies a strategic gateway position, in a corridor that extends from the Pacific coast to the highland Andes and down to the lowland rain forest to the east. Burger argues that Chavín's religious leaders deliberately imported Amazonian symbolism, perhaps in the belief that the exotic lowland people had especially powerful esoteric knowledge. This interpretation, supported by ethnographic and ethnohistoric documentation, suggests that shamans and healers may have made pilgrimages to the distant lowlands—viewed as the powerful source of sacred knowledge, medicinal plants, and other ritual necessities. In fact, in many parts of the world, anthropologists have found that people who live outside dense forests often ascribe magical powers or sacred knowledge to their neighbors who live in the forests. Burger argues that the Chavín people imported religious knowledge from the remote, exotic tropics to the Andean highlands.

Analysis of Chavín iconography provides some details that explain the cult's remarkable success. Early sculptural evidence suggests that Chavín ideology held that priests had the ability to turn themselves into mythical beasts to intervene with supernatural forces. Temple sculptures clearly demonstrate that, employing hallucinogenic snuff and beverages, Chavín shamans could transform themselves into jaguars or crested eagles. Specially designed drug paraphernalia—stone mortars, bone trays, spatulas, miniature spoons, and tubes—seem to be part of the Chavín ritual toolkit. Use of similar artifacts can be documented among modern South American people. Burger believes that this analogy—based on sixteenth-century ethnohistoric sources—may explain the singular success of the Chavín cult in uniting previously unrelated cultures throughout the Andean highlands and along the Peruvian coast.

Historical documents also suggest how this religious network might have operated 2000 years earlier. The religious center was a large ritual complex featuring an **oracle**, accessible only to certain cult specialists. Based on the oracle's secret projections, cult members could provide "insider information," offering favorable intervention with the natural elements, protection against disease, and specialized knowledge concerning auspicious times for planting and harvesting.

Under this regional religious system, local communities could establish "branch shrines" by pledging support for the religion. If the pledge was accepted, a local priest was assigned; in return, local communities allotted agricultural lands to produce tribute and promised public labor for farming and herding. In effect, these local branches supported the religion's headquarters with large quantities of cotton, corn, dried fish, llamas, guinea pigs, raw materials (such as gold and obsidian), and manufactured goods (such as fine cloth).

Burger suggests that this ethnohistoric cult provides an analogy for the distinctive regional organization that characterized Chavín civilization. He hypothesizes that the oracle cult center was located at the archaeological site of Karwa, unfortunately looted during the 1970s. Iconographic elements—particularly stylized felines and raptorial birds—woven into textile fragments recovered from tombs at Karwa show unmistakable ties to the sculptures at Chavín de Huántar. Despite the nearly 400 miles separating the two sites, the complex elements of Chavín cosmology seem to have been transported intact, without simplification or misrepresentation.

The Role of Cosmology in Andean Civilization

This model suggests that Chavín iconography was a widespread religion subdivided into a number of localized branches, each sharing in the major elements of Chavín iconography—probably reflecting major deities—but complemented by distinctive localized elements. By this view, the Chavín religion maintained its characteristic regional flavor, but also demonstrated a willingness to incorporate motifs and symbols significant to local constituencies.

Burger emphasizes that the long-standing interest of archaeologists in Chavín iconography has led to a deep understanding of how this distinctive civilization came to be. Had this research taken place within a strictly materialistic framework, Burger suggests, the direction would have been much different and considerably more restricted. He stresses that interregional exchange and tribute in the form of gifts to the religious center, rather than local agricultural production, contributed to the development of Chavín civilization.

The spread of Chavín elements (2500 to 2250 BP) across the central Andes happened at a turbulent time, following the collapse of many early coastal political systems. An unprecedented amount of contact occurred between distant and unrelated groups, producing a previously unknown degree of sharing of ideology and technology, reinforced by the movement of goods and people. For Burger, Chavín culture was a forerunner of the many later attempts in Andean history to create single social entities out of a diversity of local cultures.

So, why did Chavín succeed where earlier attempts failed?

Relying on historical evidence from the sixteenth-century regional ceremonial complex, Burger argues that Chavín was a large-scale religion, transcending political and ethnic boundaries. Chavín ideology and rituals were sufficiently powerful to support a hierarchical organization, with officials overseeing local cult activities and monitoring deviation among local congregations. Although regional diversity was evident throughout the reach of the Chavín cult, a central authority exerted its power and extracted tribute from smaller communities. Thus, Chavín religion spread not because of political expansion, but because of the extension of a powerful shared cosmology, rendered visible in ritual objects and manifested through the growth of complex interregional exchange networks.

According to Burger, by 2400 BP, the centers of the Chavín horizon rivaled the classic Greek cities in size and beauty, with massive public structures of finely cut and polished masonry, and the settlements were home to a complex society, differentiated by both social status and economic activities.

Burger argues that this power came from the original priests of Chavín de Huántar, who focused the growing Chavín mythology emphasizing mystique over the mundane. It would be these mysterious lowland animals that would ultimately determine the long-term success of Chavín society and economy.

One message of Chavín art may have been that the prosperity and well-being of the community depended on maintaining the favor of forces alien to the local habitat and daily experience—forces redolent of the powers of the distant and mysterious tropical forest. The mediation of this relationship required the services of ritual specialists. This explanation suggests that Chavín ideology—heavily emphasizing the exotic tropical forest fauna—ritually reinforced the wealth and power of Chavín de Huántar society.

Current evidence suggests that social stratification may have first appeared in the highlands in association with long-distance exchange—offering local leaders an unparalleled opportunity to control and manipulate the existing socioeconomic system. Burger argues that tribute supplied to regional ceremonial centers by travelers and pilgrims could have been a major source of wealth and power for newly emerging elites.

Religious ideology seems to have played a central role in promoting and legitimizing these profound sociopolitical transformations, suggesting that many of the key ingredients for social complexity existed in the central Andes prior to the Chavín horizon. Although still a hypothesis to be tested, perhaps it was the power of Chavín's symbols—rather than a change in food resources, climate, or population density—that played a key role in the development of the Andes' first civilization.

Blueprints for an Archaeology of the Mind

These two examples, Hopewell and Chavín, share a couple of things. Note that neither tries to interpret the exact meaning of the various symbols involved. Hall doesn't say what the raptors or other animals carved in stone on Hopewell pipes "mean." Burger and Miller don't attempt to explain what the jaguars, caimans, or crested eagles symbolized to those participating in the religion and iconography of the central Andes some 2500 years ago. Archaeologists simply cannot make the inferential leap from an ancient symbol to its past meaning based strictly on the symbol itself. We can only speak in general terms about what the symbols imply about a level of human interaction that differs considerably from a purely material interaction with the environment.

Both examples also rely on solid ethnographic and ethnohistoric data. Hall's idea that Hopewell pipes were part of a peace pipe ritual was based on copious ethnographic data on such rituals among many eastern North American peoples. Likewise, Burger and Miller would have been hard-pressed to generate a viable hypothesis to account for Chavín iconography without access to a rich historical and ethnographic record of the Andes Mountains.

Good researchers will always draw upon imagination and personal feelings to think up testable hypotheses. But thinking about ancient symbolic systems can always run amok. Without some solid way of checking ideas against facts, archaeologists will always run the risk of what Kent Flannery and Joyce Marcus (University of Michigan) call "a bungee jump into the Land of Fantasy." At best, archaeology can capture only certain limited aspects of ancient ideas.

Marcus and Flannery also suggest that cognitive archaeology can (and should) follow relatively rigorous methods, *provided ample historical and ethnographic documentation is available.* Should such data be lacking, they warn that "far less success should be anticipated."

oracle A shrine in which a deity reveals hidden knowledge or divine purpose.

So what about those truly ancient symbolic systems that lack historically linked ethnographic insights? Do we simply shrug our shoulders and turn to some other problem? To answer this question, let's examine how archaeologists have studied one of the earliest symbolic systems, Upper Paleolithic cave art of western Europe.

Upper Paleolithic Cave Art

The lineage that would eventually become *Homo sapiens* split from the rest of the primate lineage more than 5 million years ago. But the earliest evidence for artistic expression appears only in the last 100,000 years and does not become widespread until the last 40,000 years.

The **Upper Paleolithic** (40,000 to 12,000 BP) in Europe is distinguished by the appearance of a complex technology of stone, bone, and antler as well as wall art, portable art objects, and decorated tools—an example of which appears in Figure 11-5. Archaeologists sometimes call this an artistic "explosion," and the metaphor is appropriate. Only a handful of objects from the preceding 5 million years can be called art (and many of these may not be artifacts at all). But many, many Upper Paleolithic sites contain engraved, carved, or sculpted objects, and caves occupied by Upper Paleolithic peoples often contain wall paintings.

Cave paintings occur in 200 French caves, and still more are found in Spain. Much of the painting dates to the **Magdalenian** phase (18,000 to 12,000 BP). However, in the French site of Grotte Chauvet, discovered in 1994, AMS radiocarbon dates on the paintings themselves (the black paint is charcoal, with fat or blood sometimes used as a binder) and some torch marks point to an age of 26,000 to 32,000 BP.

Upper Paleolithic wall paintings have intrigued archaeologists for more than a century. More than simple line drawings, these are masterworks created by talented artisans who knew animal anatomy and behavior well. Careful shading shows the contours of animals' shoulders and haunches. Rutting stags lower their heads to bugle. Some animals may be pregnant. Many of the images were painted with brushes, and hand silhouettes by the hundreds cover some cave walls.

The paintings are deliberately dramatic. The artists understood the principles of perspective, and they sometimes employed the natural topography of cave walls to bring the animals to life. As you walk down one dark, narrow passage in the French cave of Lascaux, for example, two bulls appear to be running toward and to either side of you—a trick made possible by clever use of the cave's contours.

Upper Paleolithic paintings sometimes turn up in the most obscure places, difficult to locate even with modern equipment. The art is often found in the deepest recesses of caves, some at the very ends of passages, showing that a cave's entire passable extent was explored. Imagine entering one of these caves with only a reed torch or stone lamp burning tallow as your source of light. There are pits, pools, and rivers to avoid, narrow passageways to crawl through, and jutting rocks to duck under, and remember, you have to find your way out again. At Lascaux, cave art even appears at the base of a deep pit. Not only does the descent into the darkness require a rope, but also, carbon dioxide accumulates at the pit's base, making breathing difficult.

Upper Paleolithic artisans clearly intended to place their art in places that were difficult to access. This remoteness strongly suggests a connection between the art and religious ritual, a suggestion supported by the occasional finds of bear teeth or ocher-covered flint blades stuffed into cracks in the cave walls, perhaps as offerings of some sort.

The content of the art is also intriguing. Human beings rarely appear, and when they do, they are poorly executed in comparison with the marvelous animal figures. Also, Upper Paleolithic art contains no actual "scenes." Although images often overlap, no one has identified a "story" or landscape. And whereas the cave art provides vivid evidence documenting the range of animals living in Ice Age Europe, certain animals are emphasized, especially horses, aurochs (wild cattle), bison, ibex, stags, and reindeer, with occasional mammoths, bears, rhinoceri, and large cats. The ancient artists sometimes painted some images on top of (or partially overlapping) previous paintings, suggesting that the act of making the art was more important than the final product.

What accounts for the particular forms that the art takes and the locations where these forms were painted?

FIGURE 11-5 Carved from reindeer antler, this bison probably served as the end of an atlatl and is an example of the artistic work that typifies the European Upper Paleolithic.

Art or Magic?

Various nineteenth-century scholars viewed Upper Paleolithic cave art romantically, as an early expression of a growing human sense of beauty and perfection. This "art-for-art's-sake" perspective stressed what humans could accomplish in the leisure time that technology brings. So viewed, the animals had no particular meaning; they were simply artistic expressions of the things that people saw around them. The lack of scenes or stories in the art was taken as evidence that the artistic sense was in a rudimentary stage of development.

David Lewis-Williams (University of the Witwatersrand, South Africa) points out the circularity in this approach: An innate aesthetic sense is inferred from beautiful art, and the presence of beautiful art is evidence of this innate sense. The art-for-art's-sake approach likewise fails to explain why the artists chose such remote locations. If art was something done in leisure time for public enjoyment, why decorate remote, dangerous reaches of caves?

Other anthropologists suggested that the cave art involves **sympathetic magic**, grounded in the principle that "like controls like." In the late nineteenth century, Salomon Reinach (1858–1932) proposed that the images were intended to promote the fertility of game animals, thus ensuring an abundant food supply for Upper Paleolithic hunters: If you draw pregnant animals, then the real animals will become pregnant and the food supply will be ensured. Abbé Henri Breuil (1877–1961) subsequently developed a similar line of thought, suggesting that the images were a form of sympathetic magic designed to guarantee the success of a hunt: If you kill the stylized animal on the wall, you will also kill the real animal out in the valley.

It is true that the artists drew some animals with spears thrust into them (although only a few may represent pregnant animals). But whereas bison and horse are the most frequently depicted animals, most of the food bones recovered from Upper Paleolithic caves in Europe are red deer and reindeer. If this art represents sympathetic magic, then it was not very successful.

The sympathetic magic interpretation assumes that the animals are literal and that they have no symbolic meaning. But other scholars view the Upper Paleolithic cave paintings as a structured code, drawing upon a theoretical paradigm known as **structuralism**. Briefly, structuralism argues that humans understand reality as paired oppositions. The concept of "life," for example, is meaningless without the opposite concept of "death." Likewise, the concept of "male" means nothing without the opposing concept of "female." From a structuralist perspective, culture—and its material expressions, such as art—is played out in terms of such paired oppositions. So viewed, the task of the archaeologist becomes discerning and interpreting these pairs of oppositions.

Following this paradigm, French archaeologists André Leroi-Gourhan (1911–1986) and Annette Laming-Emperaire (1917–1977) argued that Upper Paleolithic cave imagery contained binary oppositions that "stand for" male and female (although Laming-Emperaire backed away from this interpretation later in her life). Criticizing what she saw as simplistic, off-the-cuff interpretations, Laming-Emperaire advocated a more systematic approach to cave art. She sought to identify not merely the animals represented in the images, but also where in a cave particular images were found (the entrance, middle chambers, the rear), their positions (ceiling, wall, and so on), signs of use, archaeological remains, and associations among images. In other words, Laming-Emperaire did what good archaeologists should do: She systematically analyzed both the images and their contexts.

It remained for Leroi-Gourhan to complete the work Laming-Emperaire began. Rejecting previous ethnographic analogies and earlier models of cognitive evolution, Leroi-Gourhan instead assumed that the minds of Upper Paleolithic people were every bit as complex as those of modern people. Based on systematic, quantitative data collected from 66 French caves, Leroi-Gourhan's maps suggested that the various cave elements clustered into four major sets of images:

- Small herbivores (horse, ibex, stag, reindeer, and hind)
- Large herbivores (bison, auroch)
- Rare species (mammoth, deer, ibex)
- Dangerous animals (cat, bear, rhinoceros)

Working in the structuralist paradigm, Leroi-Gourhan associated the small herbivores with "maleness" and the large herbivores with "femaleness." He also defined two major groupings of abstract signs—a set of "narrow" symbols (such as rows of dots, arrow-like representations, and straight lines) that he believed were "male," and a second set of "wide" symbols (rectangles, upside-down Vs, and some curvilinear symbols) that he associated with "female." In this way, the abstract symbols and the animal portrayals were viewed as complementary.

Leroi-Gourhan then looked for patterning in the placement of images within cave settings. Dividing the

Upper Paleolithic The last major division of the Old World Paleolithic, beginning about 40,000 years ago and lasting until the end of the Pleistocene (about 10,000 BC).

Magdalenian The last major culture of the European Upper Paleolithic period (about 16,000 to 10,000 BC); named after the rockshelter La Madeleine, in southwestern France. Magdalenian artisans crafted intricately carved tools of reindeer bone and antler; this was also the period during which Upper Paleolithic cave art in France and Spain reached its zenith.

sympathetic magic Rituals in which doing something to an image of an object produces the desired effect on the real object.

structuralism A paradigm holding that human culture is the expression of unconscious modes of thought and reasoning, notably binary oppositions. Structuralism is most closely associated with the French anthropologist Claude Lévi-Strauss.

caves into entrances, central areas, peripheral areas, and back areas, he discovered that stags (a male sign) tended to appear in cave entrances. Male signs and images (stags, horses, and ibex) were also in the peripheral areas, whereas dangerous animals and carnivores appeared mostly in the backs of the caves. The central areas contained both male and female signs (along with horses, bison, and aurochs).

To some, the presence of a male sign at the entrance might suggest that the caves were regarded as "male" places, a stag being the equivalent of an ancient "No women allowed" sign. But keep in mind that structuralism arrays the world into oppositions. If there is a male, there must be a female. Leroi-Gourhan pointed out that central areas contain male elements placed around female elements (with male elements also found in peripheral areas and at the entrance). Where is the female to balance the male? Leroi-Gourhan said it must be the cave itself.

Armed with these inferences, Leroi-Gourhan could now interpret the "meaning" of the caves: This is where Upper Paleolithic people dealt with the oppositions and contradictions that, according to structuralist theory, are the inevitable consequence of human thought. Inside the caves, they used symbols drawn from the world of nature to create and communicate a cosmology that explained life's fundamental oppositions: male and female, nature and culture, human and supernatural, life and death.

But some empirical problems plague Leroi-Gourhan's analysis. Sometimes he used an image to determine whether a portion of a cave was "central" or "peripheral," and in others he reversed the process, assigning an indistinct painting to a particular species depending on where it was located. Both are instances of circular reasoning. And the associations that formed the baseline of his analysis did not hold up as more caves were investigated. Eventually, his ideas collapsed under the very empirical standards that he had constructed; that's often how science progresses.

Of greater interest (at least today) are the ways in which Leroi-Gourhan interpreted the symbols. To pursue his structuralist paradigm, Leroi-Gourhan needed to define binary oppositions, the most prominent of which were male and female symbols. In so doing, he was required to jump from the symbol to its meaning. Because symbols take on meaning only from culture, there is always the danger that archaeologists will draw upon their own culture, rather than that of the ancient people who created the symbols. This was clearly a problem with Leroi-Gourhan's interpretation of abstract symbols of the Upper Paleolithic. Living in a world where Freudian psychology was popular, Leroi-Gourhan interpreted "narrow" and "wide" symbols as representing male and female genitalia. We see here how a paradigm affects the way that we understand the world. It is unlikely that, in a pre-Freudian world, Leroi-Gourhan would have proposed that lines = penises and rectangles = vaginas.

How did Leroi-Gourhan attribute different animal species to men and women? Like most symbolic anthropologists, he looked for associations in the symbols, focusing on bison and horses. In a limited number of cave paintings and engravings, he found women depicted next to bison and men painted next to horses (although the interpretation of some figures as men or women is dubious, as is the contemporaneity of the juxtaposed images). There were also opposite associations—men with bison and women with horses—or ambiguous ones, such as men *and* women with bison *and* horses.

Recall that the same symbol can be employed in many different ways even in the same culture. Do the opposite or ambiguous associations suggest that Leroi-Gourhan is simply wrong—that bison do not really "stand for" female and horses do not "stand for" male—or are they plays on the symbolic meanings of bison and horses? Maybe the men with bison are berdaches (see Chapter 10), and the women with horses are what the Lakota called "manly hearted women."

Or maybe this is all wrong. Maybe the bison and horses and other animals had different meanings in different caves at different times in the past. Maybe the images are **totems**, symbols of different clans (as Laming-Emperaire eventually concluded).

That Leroi-Gourhan was influenced by Freud and structuralism does not automatically mean that his interpretation of the symbols in the paintings is wrong. The problem is that *we cannot assess whether he was right*.

The most secure way to go from symbols to their meanings is by using some historical or ethnographic information, as Burger and Miller did with Chavín art and Hall did with Hopewell platform pipes. But given that we lack any associated ethnographic data for the Upper Paleolithic, we must ask if there is anything we can do with this art other than admire its beauty and mystery.

Shamanism?

David Lewis-Williams offers an alternative explanation of Upper Paleolithic cave art that, although still speculative, is more firmly grounded in middle-level theory. In brief, Lewis-Williams argues that Upper Paleolithic cave art is evidence of shamanic trances. His explanation does not rely on an interpretation of the images' symbols, and he tries to explain multiple aspects of the art, including the particular abstract elements, as well as the locations of images in caves and their association with animal images.

Lewis-Williams begins by pointing out that virtually all hunting-and-gathering societies known to anthropology practice a form of religion that involves shamanism. **Shamans** are individuals (often men, but including women in some societies) who claim to be able to access supernatural powers, spirits, or deceased individuals and tap into the power and influence that they offer to the world of the living. They do this through trances, brought on by the use of psychotropic drugs or by fasting, dehydration, and sensory deprivation. Shamans culturally interpret the visions seen while in an altered state of consciousness as communication with the supernatural world.

The Lakota, for example, performed **vision quests** in which men would lie for days on a mountaintop until starvation, dehydration, and exposure brought about visions. These visions were a way for men to communicate with the supernatural world and locate their source of power. Africa's Ju/'hoansi used trances, sometimes brought on by hours of physically and emotionally draining dancing, as a way to contact the ghosts of deceased individuals and perform healing rituals on gravely ill members of the band.

After several decades of study, Lewis-Williams argues that much (though by no means all) of the world's hunting-and-gathering rock art is the result of shamanism. The art is a record of what a shaman saw while in a trance, a way to understand and interpret the meaning of the vision. How can Lewis-Williams say this? If anything is archaeologically inaccessible, it would seem to be what somebody saw in a trance thousands of years ago!

Lewis-Williams relies on cross-cultural psychological and neurological research to bolster his argument. According to this research, when individuals go into a trance, they go through three levels of consciousness, each with distinctive "visual" aspects. In the first stage, a person sees dots, grids, zigzags, nested curves (like rainbows), and meandering lines. These may flicker, vibrate, merge, and break apart. Known as entoptic (from the Greek word meaning "within vision") phenomena, these images appear even with your eyes closed because they are a product of the optical nervous system. Because they are a function of the brain's hardwiring, and given that all people everywhere (and we assume in the past, too) have the same neurology, all people should see the same entoptic images. Lewis-Williams thus injects the important element of uniformitarianism, which you will recall is essential to middle-level theory.

In the second, deeper stage of trance, a person's mind tries to make sense of the entoptic images by converting them into forms that are culturally meaningful (meaning that the particular images become culturally biased). Just as a nineteenth-century Lakota might see horses, teepees, mountains, and bison, the mind of an Upper Paleolithic shaman would convert abstract images into things familiar to that culture, including animals such as aurochs and reindeer.

Those slipping into the third and final stage of trance will sense that they are moving through a tunnel or a vortex, with entoptic images swirling around them and merging into culturally intelligible ones. Again, this experience seems to be universal, generated by human neurology.

Shamans in many hunting-and-gathering cultures talk about reaching the "other side" by moving through a hole or cave, an experience sometimes described as "dying." Upon reaching the third stage, a person is often unable to recognize any stimulus outside the visions. The images become more vivid, and although they may merge with one another and with abstract images, a person senses that they are nonetheless real. At this point, the person has entered an altered state of consciousness and no longer understands that he or she is viewing images; instead, they see themselves as having become part of the image.

But does an understanding of the neurological basis of trance (and dreams) help us understand Upper Paleolithic rock art? Let's look at one especially well-known site that Lewis-Williams studied: the French cave of Lascaux.

The Cave of Lascaux

Found by schoolboys in 1940, Lascaux is perhaps the most famous of all the European caves. The Paleolithic artists who painted the images inside Lascaux some 17,000 years ago would not recognize the outside of the cave today. The schoolboys entered the cave through a sinkhole, then crawled down a long rubble-filled tunnel. Today, however, those lucky few who can enter Lascaux (it is closed to regular public visitations) walk through two airlock doors, then step into an antibacterial footbath (to remove any microbes brought from the outside), all the time listening to the hum of an expensive ventilation system designed to maintain the cave's humidity and preserve the paintings inside.

But the inside of the cave remains much as the Paleolithic artists left it. You first enter the Hall of the Bulls, whose ceiling sparkles with calcite (see the chapter's opening photo and Figure 11- 6). You are struck immediately by the immense aurochs and horses, painted in red and black, that circle the roof; at 5 meters long, the bulls are the largest in all of European cave art. Smaller stags are present, some with many-tined antlers, as well as a bear. Many of the paintings take advantage of the cave's natural topography to accentuate a raised head or shoulders. One peculiar animal has two horns sprouting, unicorn-like, from its head. This painting is well executed, and Lewis-Williams suggests that the artist intended to create an ambivalent species.

A narrow natural ledge 5 to 6 feet above the floor seems to form a ground line for the animals (something rarely seen in Paleolithic art). But because the ledge is too narrow to stand on, the ancient artisans must have constructed platforms to reach the ceiling. Beneath these paintings is room for groups of people to have participated in rituals; whether they did so, however, is unknown.

totem A natural object, often an animal, from which a lineage or clan believes itself to be descended and/or with which lineage or clan members have special relations.

shaman One who has the power to contact the spirit world through trance, possession, or visions. On the basis of this ability, the shaman invokes, manipulates, or coerces the power of the spirits for socially recognized ends—both good and ill.

vision quest A ritual in which an individual seeks visions through starvation, dehydration, and exposure; considered in some cultures to be a way to communicate with the supernatural world.

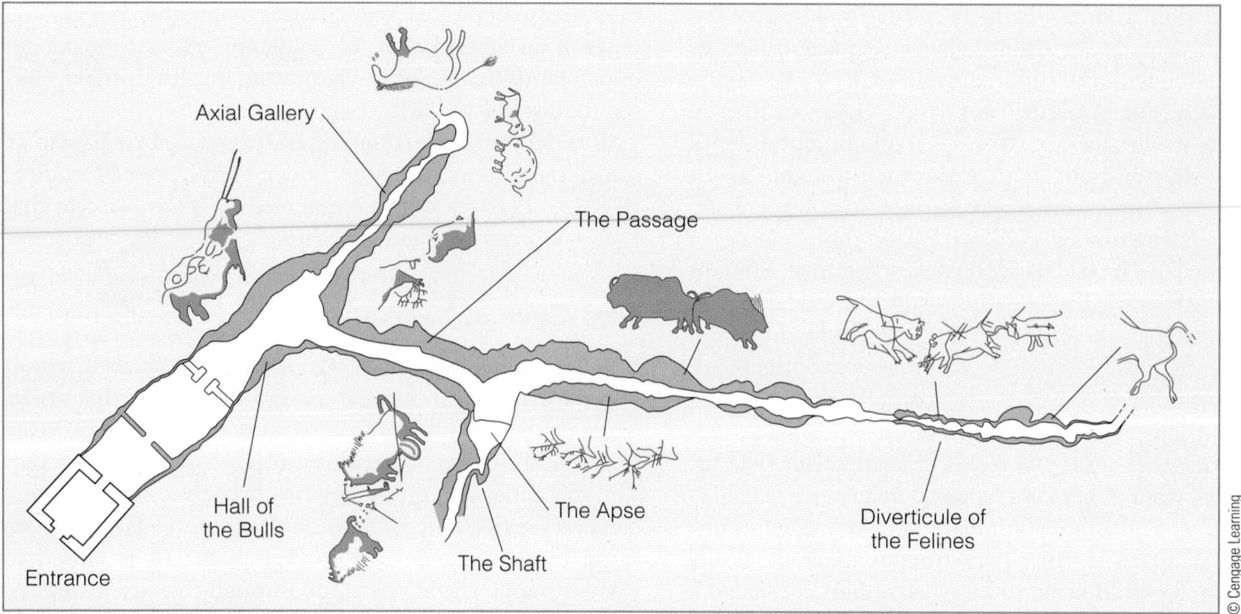

FIGURE 11-6 Map of Lascaux.

Moving straight ahead, you enter the narrow Axial Gallery, which slopes more deeply into the earth. Many horses are on the walls here, with some aurochs and stags. Two of the horses have what appear to be spears or darts shooting toward them. A long line of black dots appear beneath a large stag in a bellowing posture; a horse faces the stag. Lewis-Williams sees these dots as evidence of the merging of abstract and representational images that occurs in trance.

Near the end of the Axial Gallery is one of the most intriguing images in Lascaux. Painted on a jutting piece of rock is a life-size image of a horse, upside-down and apparently falling through the air. This image is not entirely visible until you walk around the bulge in the wall, single file. Several flint blades, covered in ochre and jammed into a crack, were found near this horse image. Walking around the "falling" horse, you encounter another horse, this one upright, and then the end of the passage.

Retracing your steps, you move back through the Hall of the Bulls and to the left. Passing through a low opening, you enter the Passage—this one longer than the Axial Gallery. The original opening was even smaller than it is today, and Upper Paleolithic artisans had to crawl through it.

In the Passage, the walls bear no calcite, and the stone is softer. More horses and bulls are painted and engraved on the walls, although they are not as well preserved as in other parts of the cave. Images are piled up on top of one another, and the art here seems to be less "composed" than in the Axial Gallery and the Hall of the Bulls.

About 15 meters down the Passage, you encounter the Apse on your right, a small domed chamber with walls covered in engravings and a few paintings. Many different species are present—horses, bison, aurochs, ibex, deer, and perhaps even a wolf and lion. These images also overlay one another, producing a confusing jumble. Many engraved lines cut through the images.

Behind the Apse is the "Shaft" or "Well," a 5-meter-deep pit. Stone lamps were found at the bottom—turned upside down, as if the users meant to extinguish them. At the bottom of the pit is one of the oddest images of Upper Paleolithic art, which we show in Figure 11-7: A bison, its head lowered in defensive posture, appears to have a spear through the body. Some interpret the lines

FIGURE 11-7 Bison and "falling man" in Lascaux. It is not known if these images were painted at the same time (as a "scene") or at different times.

emanating from its belly to be entrails. In front of the bison is a stick figure of a man, his penis apparently erect, who appears to be falling backward from the bison's blow. The figure only has four fingers, however, and his head looks more like that of a bird. Beneath the man is a long vertical line, with what appears to be a bird perched on its top. The meaning of this image is the source of endless speculation.

Climbing out of the Shaft, you return to the Passage and continue moving down its length. The walls contain more images for the next 15 meters or so, and then the images cease as the passage narrows and the ceiling drops. You encounter the two charging bison that we mentioned previously—the ones that appear to be running toward and around you. After dropping to your knees and crawling along the cave floor, you encounter the Diverticule of the Felines, with its soft clay walls. If you are a small person, you are crouching; a larger person might be lying on his stomach.

Here there are aurochs and horses and bison, but also large cats—panthers or cave lions. Spears pierce some, others are cut by lines or geometric markings, or they have lines emanating from their mouths and anuses. The images are well composed but seem to have been more hastily engraved than others in the cave. This section of the cave was perhaps rarely visited because otherwise its soft clay walls would not have survived so well.

What Does All This Mean?

Leaving Lascaux, you might turn to look at the Hall of the Bulls one last time, trying to imagine how the scene would appear in the flickering light of a stone lamp. Something significant obviously transpired in these dark places. The aurochs, bison, and horses painted on Lascaux's walls and ceilings were not the fleeting whimsy of a Paleolithic artist. The same images appear in many caves and were used over thousands of years.

We do not know the specific meanings of these world-famous images (and, in truth, we probably never will). Lewis-Williams thinks that this art is somehow related to altered states of consciousness, but the images themselves could not, of course, have been produced while the artist was in a trance state because one would need to be fully conscious to mix the paints, negotiate the cave's twists and turns with a stone lamp, and build scaffolding where needed. But Lewis-Williams thinks that the paintings at Lascaux and elsewhere provide firm evidence of Upper Paleolithic people trying to come to terms with understanding the meaning of altered states of consciousness—dreams and trances.

He sees the larger chambers, like the Hall of the Bulls, as places where communal rituals may have taken place, with people seeking assistance from a spirit world that existed belowground. Although the floor of Lascaux was damaged before it was investigated, the floors at Grotte Chauvet contain many human footprints, some 25,000 or more years old. Some of the prints are big and some are small, telling us that people of all ages visited even remote portions of this cave.

Lewis-Williams also suggests that the distribution of art within a cave may parallel the stages of trances. In the front chamber are animals that figured in the lives of Upper Paleolithic people. Here, too, we find some abstract signs—the rectangles, wavy lines, and rows of dots that appear in the early stages of trance. Deeper inside the cave, the narrowing passageway mimics the movement into the deeper states of trance. Lewis-Williams suggests that the falling horse at the end of the Axial Gallery is not falling at all, but is instead an artist's representation of the vortex that one senses in the deeper stages of trance.

Farther into the cave, we see "confused" images, such as those in the Apse and the Diverticule of the Felines. These, Lewis-Williams suggests, may represent the merging of abstract and natural images in the deepest stage of trance or efforts by one shaman to bond with the power of another by drawing an image over that drawn by another shaman. Although rare in Upper Paleolithic art (and absent at Lascaux), occasional animal images take on human characteristics. They walk on two feet, sometimes hold their front legs in a human way, or turn to stare at the observer with an eerily human gaze. These might record instances where observers entered the deepest stage of trance and were unable to see the difference between themselves and animals.

Lewis-Williams suggests that vision quests may have been held in the deepest cave recesses. Without food or water, the total darkness and silence of a cave is a perfect medium for the production of visions. Perhaps people of the Upper Paleolithic saw caves as one place to access the spirit world.

Recall that some images make use of the bumps and contours of a cave's wall; Lewis-Williams believes this is more than a clever artistic trick. Shamans in hunting-and-gathering cultures often speak of a strong yet permeable membrane between themselves and the spirit world. Lewis-Williams suggests that the nature of trance would have suggested that portions of the spirit world lie belowground. By mimicking the vortex of trance, caves are the closest a person could come to the spirit world; the rest of the journey had to be made through trance. If the cave wall is the membrane between this world and the spirit world, then paintings and engravings were perhaps ways to access that spirit world. By using the cave's contours, the artist makes the painting more a part of the cave wall itself and, in so doing, increases its power. The flints, teeth, and bones left shoved into cracks may also have been similar efforts to break through the membrane and contact the spirit world.

In sum, Lewis-Williams argues that Upper Paleolithic art is not art for art's sake, nor is it fertility or hunting magic. Instead, he argues that the art reflects humanity's effort to come to grips with the perception that their quotidian existence was not all that there was, to answer the question "What is the meaning of life?" And that fact gives us, the denizens of the twenty-first century, a strong link to the artisans who painted bulls on the ceiling of a cave by torchlight thousands of years ago.

Conclusion

An archaeology of the mind attempts to move beyond the more easily accessible matters of diet and settlement patterns to religion, ritual, and cosmology. People respond to their world through culture, an integrated set of symbolic meanings that are communicated through material culture. But given that there is no necessary link between symbols and their meanings, the development of reliable middle-level theory is almost impossible, and so this crucial area of human behavior often eludes archaeologists. Successful efforts rely upon historically linked ethnographic analogies, but these are limited to the more recent prehistory of regions with good ethnographic data. More ancient symbolic systems must be studied in ways that make use of uniformitarian elements of human neurology or perhaps a few symbolic universals (though these remain to be demonstrated).

Summary

- What is the central challenge of "cognitive archaeology"?
    - Cognitive archaeology aims to study the perception, description, and classification of the universe; the nature of the supernatural; the principles, philosophies, and values by which human societies are governed; and the ways in which aspects of the world, the supernatural, or human values are conveyed in art.
    - Studying these ancient modes of thought requires the interpretation of symbols, objects, or acts (verbal and nonverbal) that by cultural convention stand for something else *with which they have no necessary connection.* This means that, without some ethnographic context, there is no obvious way to connect a symbol to its meaning.
- How do archaeologists study ancient religion?
    - Archaeologists attempt to understand past religions—the specific set of beliefs based on one's ultimate relation to the supernatural. Such religious beliefs are manifested in everyday life through rituals—behaviors such as prayer, music, feasting, sacrifice, and taboos. As such, ritual is a material manifestation of the abstract idea of religion and archaeology's easiest portal to the study of ancient religions.
    - Archaeologists also attempt to understand cosmology. This encompasses how past cultures explain their universe—how it originated and developed, how the various parts fit together, and what laws it obeys—and expresses their concern with what the future of the universe holds.
    - Where archaeologists have some ethnographic data available that are closely related to the archaeological case, they may be able to extrapolate backward from the present to the past. Even these cases, however, harbor the chance that a symbol meant something different in the past than it does in the present.
    - Iconography, a culture's expression of abstract ideas in art and writing systems, can also be used to reconstruct the religious and other ideas that stand behind the art.
- Can archaeologists learn anything from very ancient cases that have no close cultural descendants?
    - The study of ancient symbols runs the risk of becoming a free-for-all, with any interpretation being as valid as another. It is perhaps especially important, then, that the study of ancient iconography and other manifestations of a culture's cosmology and religion adhere to the canons of scientific analysis.
    - In instances where ethnographic data are not available, archaeologists must be more restrained in their interpretations, not focusing on the specific meaning of particular symbols but looking to the more general character of thought itself.

Media Resources

CourseMate

Access chapter-specific learning tools including learning objectives, practice quizzes, videos, flash cards, and glossaries, as well as web links, and more in your Archaeology CourseMate. Login to www.cengagebrain.com to access the resources your instructor has assigned and to purchase materials.

Historical Archaeology: Insights on American History

12

Buffalo Bill Historical Center/The Art Archive at Art Resource, NY

Custer's Last Stand *(1899) by Edgar Samuel Paxson (1852–1919). Historical archaeology asks: Is this how it happened?*

Learning Objectives

After reading this chapter, you should be able to answer these questions:

- Why do historical archaeology if we already have the historical records?
- What are the three major areas of historical archaeological research today?
- How is historical archaeology more amenable to the postprocessual paradigm than prehistoric archaeology?

Preview

HISTORICAL ARCHAEOLOGY is currently one of the most important directions in archaeology, but to this point, we have only briefly glimpsed what historical archaeologists actually do (for example, in discussing Thomas's excavations at Santa Catalina on St. Catherines Island, Georgia). In this chapter, we look at historical archaeology in more depth.

Historical archaeology is fundamentally similar to the prehistoric archaeology you've already experienced. Both fields maintain high standards of excavation, dating, and interpretation, but because of its close relationship with the discipline of history, historical archaeology has its own distinctive flavor. Commonly less concerned with grand explanation, historical archaeologists often shed light on lesser-known aspects of the historical past (such as the daily life of slaves), correct mistaken assumptions about history, and use the archaeological record to create views of the past that sometimes contrast with the picture derived from documentary evidence alone. Although historical archaeology is an international field, this chapter will focus on its manifestation in the United States.

Introduction

Archaeologists have been investigating historic period sites for a very long time. In fact, the first bona fide historical archaeology in America took place about 150 years ago. James Hall, a trained civil engineer, was a direct descendant of Miles Standish, who arrived with the Pilgrims aboard the *Mayflower* in 1620 and eventually became a leader in Plymouth Colony. Wanting to learn more about his celebrated ancestor, Hall located the foundations of the Standish homestead in Duxbury, Massachusetts, and in 1853, he conducted detailed excavations there.

For more than a century, Hall's field notes and artifact collection from the Standish house remained unknown to anybody but immediate family members. In the 1960s, however, they surfaced in Mexico and were brought to the attention of James Deetz (1930–2000), a historical archaeologist working at Plymouth Plantation. As he looked over the surviving materials, Deetz was impressed at the high quality of Hall's 1853 excavation.

After carefully gridding the site and establishing datum points to maintain vertical control, Hall made a meticulous site map. He tried to recover artifacts in situ, plotting their locations onto this master site map. He even recorded stratigraphic relationships within the house ruin. After the excavation, Hall cataloged each artifact, carefully numbering each find. In short, Hall's 1853 excavation technique comports nicely with today's standards of acceptable archaeological practice.

Almost simultaneously, a second pioneering exploration in historical archaeology took place in Canada, under very different circumstances.

In 1855, the Canadian government commissioned Father Félix Martin, a Jesuit priest from Montreal, to explore and excavate the site of Sainte-Marie, Georgian Bay (near Midland, Ontario). Sainte-Marie was a tiny mission outpost founded in 1639 to bring Christianity to the local Huron Indians. Although they were 800 miles west of their supply base in Quebec, the missionaries enjoyed some success, and several left the mission proper to work with surrounding Huron communities. But during the winter of 1648–49, the Huron villages in this area came under attack from raiding Iroquois war parties. The resident Jesuit priests refused to flee, and several died martyrs' deaths. In March, the surviving priests abandoned Mission Sainte-Marie. Although it had lasted only a decade, Sainte-Marie became a sacred place in Christian history, what archaeologist Kenneth Kidd would later describe as "the pulsating heart of French missionary effort in America." Father Martin had this heritage in mind when he went to Sainte-Marie in 1855. Seeking to establish a personal link to his own Jesuit past, Martin identified the site's location, mapped and described the ruins, painted several watercolors, and conducted limited excavations. Years later, the Jesuit order purchased the site to encourage its preservation and make it available for religious pilgrimages. Today, the Martyrs' Shrine Church stands nearby, honoring both the Jesuit missionaries and the Christian Huron people who once lived there.

These two mid-nineteenth-century digs illustrate two important themes that eventually came to distinguish the field of historical archaeology. For one thing, both excavators were motivated by a dynamic and personal connection to their own past—Hall to his Pilgrim heritage and Father Martin to the legacy of his martyred Jesuit brothers. For both men, the past had a special relevance to the present.

Both excavators were also familiar with the documentary sources relating to their excavations. This meant that, before looking to the archaeology of their respective sites, they had some knowledge of what to expect: where to dig, what to look for, and generally what kind of material record they should encounter—expectations derived from basic historical sources. By themselves, however, these historical sources were incomplete and not entirely satisfying. Encountering the archaeological record itself—the physical remains of the past—induced Martin and Hall to undertake their own excavations.

So, what constitutes modern **historical archaeology**? Kathleen Deagan, the historical archaeologist profiled in Chapter 1, defines the field as "the study of human behavior through material remains, for which written history in some way affects its interpretation." Although this simple definition certainly captures the field, others point out that, because historical archaeology encompasses the past 500 years, historical archaeology also inherently must address the history of colonialism and capitalism. Next we show you how historical archaeology takes on different flavors depending on which of these definitions you choose.

Why Do Historical Archaeology?

At this point, you might be asking yourself, Why bother with the archaeology of historical sites if they are already described in documentary sources? Won't archaeology, with its problems of context, preservation, and interpretation, always prove inferior to the written sources?

Documentary sources can indeed be superior to archaeology. But they can also be quite selective and biased. Slave owners wrote little about the day-to-day life of slaves because they did not think it important, and slaves only rarely wrote letters or diaries, because most were illiterate (and often forbidden from learning). Most authors of documentary sources were biased toward the interests of their particular cultural, political, or ethnic group, and sometimes the documentary sources are simply wrong. Today, archaeologists look at archaeological and documentary records as *equally valid yet independent* lines of evidence. Rather than discard differences between the two as "exceptions" or "noise," we sometimes look for "ambiguities" between the historical and archaeological evidence, recognizing that *differences between the two are as important as each piece of information alone.* This is why historical archaeology is an essential component to our understanding of the relatively recent past.

Historical Archaeology: Just a "Handmaiden to History"?

In the early days, excavations in historic period sites merely supplemented the "known" documentary view of the past. In the words of Ivor Noël Hume (former director of the archaeological program at Colonial Williamsburg, Virginia), the proper role of historical archaeology was to serve as a "handmaiden to history"; the historical archaeologist was "a historian with a pen in one hand and a trowel in the other."

This perspective was particularly evident in projects closely linked to historical reconstruction and restoration. Archaeologists, for instance, recovered most of the architectural detail necessary to restore and interpret public sites such as Plymouth Plantation (Massachusetts), Jamestown and Colonial Williamsburg (Virginia), and Fort Michilimackinac (Michigan). Such projects in historical archaeology began in America in the 1940s and 1950s, concentrating on a very few selected sites—particularly houses of the rich and famous, forts, and other military sites.

Colonial Williamsburg served as a model for this early stage of historical archaeology. Architectural historians conducted most of the early excavations at Williamsburg, their goal being little more than exposing historic-period building foundations. They did not dig very carefully and showed little interest in the trash middens and smaller structures that would eventually captivate archaeological interest. Only later did historical archaeologists follow the example of their colleagues in prehistoric archaeology and develop independent, artifact-based methods for dating sites and components.

Historical Archaeology Comes of Age

Things changed markedly in the 1960s, partly because of the growing impact of cultural resource management. Federal legislation from the 1960s requires that archaeology be done in advance of construction projects (we discuss this further in the next chapter). This "applied" version of archaeology proved to be a boon for both prehistoric and historical archaeology. In the beginning, most historical archaeologists received their training on prehistoric sites. But today, the field of historical archaeology is highly specialized, with its own journals and professional societies—not just in the United States, but around the globe. Historical archaeologists today study everything from the earliest colonial settlements to nineteenth-century mining camps to World War II battlefields (see Figure 12-1).

Characteristics of Historical Archaeology

Contemporary historical archaeology is every bit as diverse as the rest of Americanist archaeology, but three key factors

historical archaeology The study of human behavior through material remains whose interpretation is in some way affected by written history.

© Lin Poyer

FIGURE 12-1 A World War II plane in the Marshall Islands. Today, historical archaeologists study everything from the colonial past to World War II–related sites.

provide historical archaeology with a slightly different flavor from its prehistoric counterpart.

For one thing, modern historical archaeology often has a postprocessual slant to it. Because historical archaeologists commonly have access to texts, ethnohistoric data, and oral traditions, they can often learn something about the meanings of symbols, ethnic affiliation, income, religion, occupation, family composition, economic network, and political restrictions—even before putting a trowel into the ground. It is not surprising, then, that a preeminent historian of archaeology, Bruce Trigger (1937–2006), argued that the most successful symbolic studies lie in the field of historical rather than prehistoric archaeology. The availability of textual information has also made possible many humanistic inquiries, and although historical archaeologists are hardly wed to a postprocessual agenda, the field is certainly amenable to it.

In addition, historical archaeology, especially as practiced in the United States, deals with time periods that are considerably shorter than are those of prehistoric archaeology. Documentary sources can often provide the precise years that a structure (or site) was used, along with detailed information on how its use changed over time. Prehistoric archaeologists may consider themselves lucky if they date an assemblage to a span of a few hundred years. Historical archaeology tends not to study large-scale processes; instead, the high degree of temporal resolution leads historical archaeologists to focus on the specific individuals and events that were part of those larger processes—for example, how a nineteenth-century frontier fort's trash reflects the development of the world trade system.

Finally, we must recognize that historical archaeology is often very close to us—not just temporally (the past 500 years in the United States), but also emotionally—whether one is of European, Hispanic, African, Native American, or Asian descent. The archaeology of the past five centuries records the time that all these different peoples came together and created the modern world. Discussion of this recent history is thus embedded in the continuing discussion of the modern world, with all its cultural, political, and ethical challenges. Because relatively few members of minority groups are professional archaeologists today, such discussions of the recent past can sometimes become emotionally charged (see "In Her Own Words: Why Are There So Few African-Americans Doing Archaeology?" by Anna Agbe-Davies).

IN HER OWN WORDS

Why Are There So Few African-Americans Doing Archaeology?

by Anna S. Agbe-Davies Assistant Professor of Anthropology, University of North Carolina. Reprinted by permission.

Courtesy Anna Agbe-Davies.

Anna Agbe-Davies

Assistant Professor of Anthropology, University of North Carolina

African diaspora archaeology is indeed a "growth industry" within the field. How do we reconcile that fact with the fact that we still find so few black archaeologists in contract firms, university departments, and museums?

For a social science that thrives on quantitative data, we have very little statistical information to answer this question. Surveys of professional organizations based in the United States suggest that between 0.1 percent and 0.2 percent of archaeologists identify as black or African-American—though many respondents refuse to answer. Recent figures on PhDs awarded in anthropology from U.S. universities indicate that fewer than 5 percent of recipients identify as black or African-American—and anecdotal evidence suggests that many of these people are specialists in subfields other than archaeology.

Like members of many academic and professional fields, archaeologists want to increase the diversity of our discipline. We convene committees and task forces. Our organizations support scholarships for student members of many underrepresented groups—not just African-Americans. Formal and informal networks of mentors and peers nurture those already in the profession.

Archaeologists sometimes use functionalist arguments to explain our slow progress in becoming a discipline that reflects the diversity of our nation and our world. Specifically, that people from marginalized groups who pursue advanced degrees are more likely to select fields with more obvious or predictable potential for financial success. I have only circumstantial evidence, but I disagree.

If we again look to data on PhDs, black participation is high in fields like education, law, and social service professions, but low in business and engineering, supporting my hunch that, far from emphasizing financial success, members of marginalized groups want to do work that is *meaningful* and serves the communities from which they come. Many—though by no means all—of the black archaeologists at work in the United States today emphasize topics associated with the African diaspora in their research. I believe that to the extent that African diaspora archaeology makes significant contributions to the lives of black people in the present day, we will see increased black participation in this subfield.

A more important factor shaping the participation of African-Americans in archaeology generally is the lack of opportunities to study archaeology at historically black colleges and universities (HBCUs) and other minority-serving institutions. This is why the loss of a five-field anthropology department at one of the premiere HBCUs (Howard University) is potentially so devastating. I never would have discovered archaeology as the fascinating and rewarding career it has proved to be if it had not been offered at the college I attended.

As an exception that "proves the rule," I am probably the last person who should be explaining why more black people don't become archaeologists. But I, and many of my colleagues—black and not—care about the answer, so we'll keep asking.

Themes in Historical Archaeology

These characteristics suggest three major themes of research in historical archaeology today. Although these directions hardly capture all of historical archaeology—and each theme exists within prehistoric archaeology as well—they define the dominant research domains within historical archaeology today.

First, modern historical archaeology has shied away from a focus on the "oldest," "largest," and "most historically significant" sites, favoring instead the study of historically disenfranchised groups. Many historical archaeologists are working to uncover the history of African-American and Asian-American cultures, Native Americans during the historic period, and Hispanic-Americans—peoples whose histories are still sometimes ignored, only partially recorded, or related in a biased manner.

Second, historical archaeology commonly tackles questions about the recent past that history books answer unsatisfactorily. In this regard, some historical archaeologists are more like forensic archaeologists (which we discuss in the next chapter), collecting data like crime scene detectives to resolve disputes over the nature of key historical events.

Third, we see many historical archaeologists researching the nature of European colonialism (the developing capitalism of that time) and its effects on indigenous peoples. The postprocessual emphasis on power, for instance, meshes easily with historical archaeology's ample record of a developing capitalist society over the last several centuries. Some archaeologists use this research to challenge standard public presentations of mainstream history, calling into question, for example, the melting pot interpretation of America's past. This approach challenges citizens to think more critically about their history.

Following are examples of each of these themes in historical archaeology.

Hidden History: The Archaeology of African-Americans

African-American history is inextricably linked to slavery, and especially slavery on plantations. Plantation archaeology began in 1931 at Mount Vernon (Virginia), George Washington's home. In his role as director of research and restoration at Mount Vernon, Morley Jeffers Williams—a landscape architect—wanted to locate the various structural remains on the property, so he conducted extensive and systematic archaeological testing. Although hardly up to contemporary standards, these excavations did permit the reconstruction of the first president's garden and outbuildings and kicked off the study of plantation archaeology as we now know it.

Most early plantation archaeology was aimed at architectural reconstruction, and, prior to the 1980s, few restored plantations addressed the issue of slavery explicitly. Instead, the restorations usually emphasized the "big house" and the grandeur of the elite who lived there; guides commonly referred to slaves as "servants." This often melancholy, *Gone with the Wind* perspective focused on the passing of an antebellum way of life (one that many white people saw as genteel, although descendants of slaves hold a different opinion).

Slave archaeology began in earnest in the late 1960s—doubtless connected to, or inspired by, the social upheavals of the time—when Charles Fairbanks (1913–1984) began exploring coastal plantations in Georgia and Florida. Fairbanks was the first to study the institution of slavery from the archaeological record; in emphasizing the richness and diversity of the southern heritage, he was clearly departing from the traditional "melting pot" theme in America. Fairbanks and his students set out to dispel myths concerning the biological and cultural inferiority of African-Americans—myths that were used to legitimize segregation and discrimination.

Today, the field of African-American archaeology is a growth industry, helping to uncover information about aspects of slave life on which the documentary sources are often silent. We demonstrate this by looking at the slave archaeology of Monticello, the home of Thomas Jefferson.

Slave Archaeology at Monticello

Visitors motoring up the serpentine driveway to Thomas Jefferson's Monticello, shown in Figure 12-2, are first struck by the world-famous architecture, the vast gardens, and glimpses of mountains in the sprawling Virginia countryside. Walking through Monticello, polite guides provide visitors with ample details about the life of Thomas Jefferson.

But only recently have we heard much about Thomas Jefferson the slave owner. When Jefferson lived at Monticello, the approach to the main house was called Mulberry Row, and it was lined by 19 buildings—the houses and workshops of Jefferson's slaves, hired laborers, artisans, and indentured servants. The mansion at Monticello still stands, attracting tourists by the thousands, yet today aboveground traces of all but four of the structures along Mulberry Row have vanished.

Historical archaeologists working at Monticello have brought Mulberry Row back to life. Work here was begun by William Kelso (currently director of archaeology for the Association for the Preservation of Virginia Antiquities "Jamestown Rediscovery" project), and it continues under Monticello's archaeology program, directed byFraser Neiman.

Jefferson had mixed feelings about slavery. He had a slave force numbering 200 people at times and knew

FIGURE 12-2 Low-level aerial photograph showing Monticello (at the upper left) and Mulberry Row (the line of trees running diagonally through the middle of the photo).

that, without slave labor, the agrarian economy of the day would collapse. Yet he regarded the institution of slavery as preeminently brutal and immoral—and he personally favored its abolition. Recognizing this dilemma, Jefferson once said that slavery is like holding a wolf by the ears: "We can neither hold him nor safely let him go. Justice is in one scale, self-preservation in the other."

Jefferson reportedly did not mistreat his slaves, but he doubted whether Caucasians and Africans could successfully create a biracial society (despite the fact that he probably fathered six children with Sally Hemings [1773–1835], one of his house slaves). Instead, he favored a plan to transport free blacks back to Africa or elsewhere.

How Well Did Jefferson's Slaves Live?

Research at Mulberry Row is aimed at learning more about the living and working conditions of Jefferson's slaves. Although few ruins were visible, Kelso soon found by exploratory excavation that the subsurface record of Mulberry Row was relatively undisturbed (see Figure 12-3). The residents of Mulberry Row were probably the house servants and artisans, who may have enjoyed a better standard of living than the field hands, who lived in settlements farther down the mountain.

FIGURE 12-3 Excavating slave dwellings built during Jefferson's lifetime at Monticello. Evident in this picture are the remains of Building l, the storehouse (foreground); Building m, the smokehouse-dairy (center); and the rebuilt walls of an 1809 stone slave house (background).

Homes along Mulberry Row contained pig, cow, and deer bones; some of these bones were ground up, suggesting the use of meat in stews. Houses also contained ceramic assemblages, dating to about AD 1770 to 1800, that were probably the remnants of table settings from Jefferson's home. No longer usable in the mansion (perhaps having lost a few key pieces), they were given to slave families. These hand-me-downs reflect the growing consumer revolution of the late eighteenth century and the availability of houseware replacements.

Social Life in Slave Houses

Neiman points out that the archaeology of Mulberry Row helps to answer a question posed by the historical documents. About 1776, Jefferson mapped his plan for buildings along Mulberry Row and included a building, some 17 × 34 feet in dimension, which he labeled the "Negro Quarter." By 1790, this building had burned and, between 1792 and 1793, Jefferson built several smaller homes on the site; these he labeled structures r, s, and t on a map made in 1796. He intended these structures to be slave homes; they were only 12 × 14 feet in dimension and were made of split logs, with dirt floors and chimneys of wood and mud.

In 1793, Jefferson served as President Washington's secretary of state, but he still minded the details of his plantation. Jefferson wrote to his overseer, instructing him to move Critta Hemings (the sister of Sally Hemings) and her family to the new House r. Hemings had been living in Building e—a stone house still standing today along Mulberry Row—and she was part of the house staff. According to Jefferson's description, Building e had two rooms, each about 290 square feet in size. It also had a brick floor, a stone fireplace, and a single entry door decorated with a pedimented portico supported by columns.

Taken at face value, Hemings appears to have been demoted—she had to move to a smaller house with dirt floors and no architectural embellishments—yet she continued as a house servant, normally a favored status. In fact, Jefferson instructed the overseer to place her and her family in House r because "she is wanted around the house." How do we explain this apparent paradox?

The answer comes from the archaeology. The excavations at Monticello retrieved data on nine of the slave houses located on Mulberry

Row. Three of the houses date to the 1770s (based on documentary and archaeological evidence). According to Jefferson's maps, the "Negro Quarter" house contained two large rooms, but only a single entryway. The two rooms had separate fireplaces that shared a single flue. A second building originally had a plan similar to that of the "Negro Quarter." A third structure was a single large room, some 250 square feet in size, with a single entryway and a wood and clay fireplace.

These houses contained what historical archaeologists call "subfloor pits," or cellars. These are rectangular holes, some 3½ × 4 feet, and 1 to 3 feet deep. The early houses at Monticello contain up to four of these pits.

These early houses at Monticello are fairly typical of slave dwellings throughout the Chesapeake Bay area in the eighteenth century (although early slave houses at other plantations usually contain four to ten subfloor pits). The function of the subfloor pits is not clear, but they probably served as places for families to store important belongings. If so, they suggest that multiple families occupied the early slave dwellings. Neiman points out that theft is a real concern in situations where you have little choice over your housemates. The subfloor pits may have helped maintain a semblance of privacy and security in an otherwise open structure, because it would have been difficult to steal something if first it had to be exhumed from a pit.

Beginning about 1790, however, a transition in housing occurs at Monticello and at other plantations in the region (see Figure 12-4). Houses became smaller—about 140 square feet (although they became larger in the early nineteenth century)—and were extremely modest, consisting usually of a single room. But they had only one subfloor pit, not multiple pits, and these pits are smaller. This suggests that only one family lived there, and they did not have much need to stash possessions out of sight. Even where structures had two rooms, the rooms were separated by a solid wall, and a separate door opened into each room, permitting privacy. In fact, no subfloor pits have been found in slave houses that date after AD 1800 at Monticello.

So, when Jefferson asked that Critta Hemings and her family be moved to House r, perhaps this was not a demotion. Instead, Hemings would now live in her own house, with her immediate family, where she could control her own household. A home of her own must have seemed quite a step up in her world.

But it must have been a small consolation—after all, she and her family were still slaves.

New York City's African Burial Ground

When most people think of slavery, they think of the Old South and a cotton-based economy. How many people know that slavery was deeply ingrained in the economy north of the Mason-Dixon Line as well? We were all reminded of this forgotten past when, in 1991, the bones of 427 enslaved Africans, interred by their own community and forgotten for centuries, were discovered beneath a parking lot in downtown New York City at a place now known as the African Burial Ground.

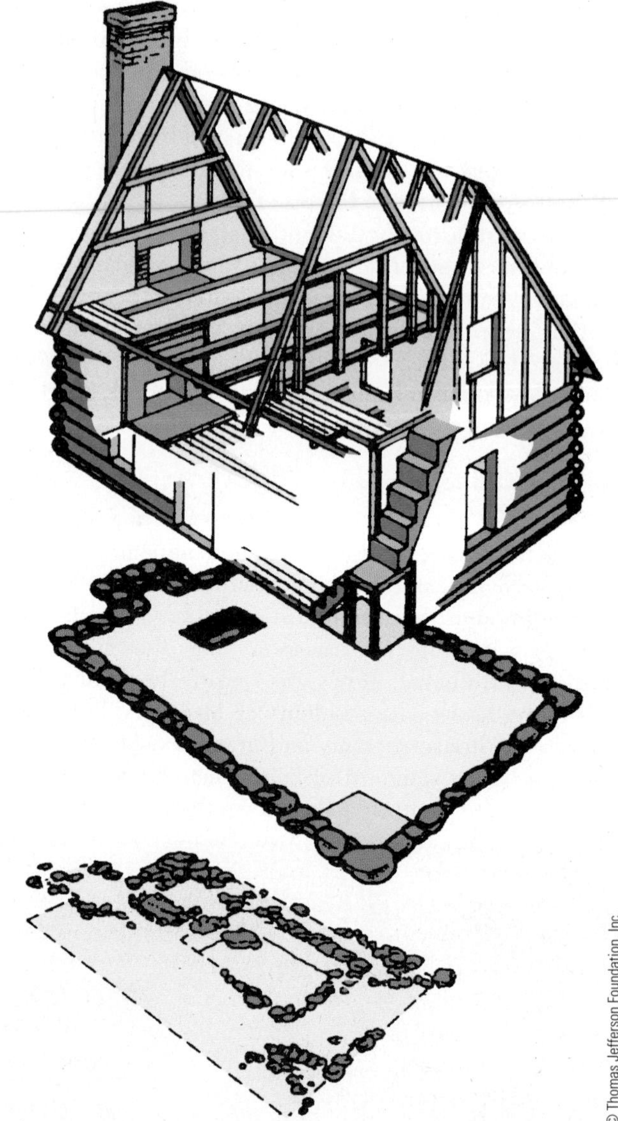

FIGURE 12-4 Artist's reconstruction of post-1790 slave housing at Monticello. This drawing shows a view of a typical slave cabin and its foundation (with a single subfloor pit in front of the fireplace) superimposed over the archaeological plan (servant's House o) at Monticello.

Slavery in Old New York?

The story begins in 1626, when the Dutch West India Company unloaded its first shipment of enslaved Africans in New Amsterdam (today's New York City): 11 young men from what today is the Congo-Angola region of southwestern Africa. Two years later, the Dutch imported three African women "for the comfort of the company's Negro [men]." The Dutch at the time were experiencing a labor shortage in their colonies, and they found slave labor to be the answer to building and maintaining the colony.

Some scholars argue that the Dutch treated slaves better. They point out that some slaves had more rights than

New Amsterdam's Jews, who were forbidden to own land or serve in the militia. Under the Dutch, the Africans were permitted to intermarry with whites, attend white churches, own property, and enjoy the same status as whites in court.

According to this view, the Dutch practiced half-freedom; true slavery was introduced in 1664, when the Dutch ceded Manhattan to the British. At that time, enslaved Africans made up about *40 percent* of New Amsterdam's total population. Everywhere one looked in colonial New York, there were toiling slaves—loading and unloading ships on the waterfront, building the streets, and erecting the buildings to house the people and businesses of this bustling port city crowded onto the southern tip of Manhattan Island.

On the eve of the American Revolution, New York City had the largest number of enslaved Africans of any English colonial city except for Charleston, South Carolina. In fact, New York City had the highest proportion of slaves to Europeans of any northern settlement. Despite what is found in most American history books, it is clear that the African population had a significant hand in the building of colonial New York.

Eighteenth-century New York law prohibited the burial of Africans in Manhattan's churchyards. Left without a place to bury their dead, New York's African population eventually established a cemetery on a deserted tract of land lying just outside the city's protective wooden palisade (the "wall" of modern "Wall Street" fame). There, from roughly 1712 to 1790, the community buried somewhere between 10,000 and 20,000 people (mostly black, but also a few lower-class whites). A 1755 map of downtown New York clearly shows the "Negro Burial Ground" covering perhaps five city blocks.

In 1827, New York abolished slavery altogether. In the meantime, African-American populations had abandoned the downtown area, moving northward in New York City. Over the subsequent decades, the Negro Burial Ground was slowly swallowed up by urban expansion. By the late twentieth century, Manhattan's forgotten cemetery lay buried beneath 20 feet of fill, a scant two blocks north of New York's City Hall.

Archaeology Can Be Contentious

But the Negro Burial Ground was not destined to lie undisturbed. In 1990, the city of New York sold the property to the General Services Administration (GSA), the arm of the federal government responsible for constructing and maintaining federal buildings. The GSA planned to build a 34-story office tower at 290 Broadway, with a four-story pavilion on the parking lot area to house the U.S. attorney's office, a regional office of the Environmental Protection Agency, and a district office of the Internal Revenue Service. Although administrators knew that the pavilion was slated to rise directly above a colonial cemetery, they seriously underestimated its extent and the extraordinary degree of preservation.

As we discuss in the next chapter, the United States has a legal framework to protect its archaeological resources—particularly those on public land. Part of this legislation requires that an environmental impact statement be filed before any construction can begin. Archaeologists and historians routinely participate in preparing such impact statements. The archaeological firm retained for the 290 Broadway historical inventory correctly noted that the "Negro Burial Ground" appeared on historical maps of the area and probably lay nearby. But, recognizing the long-standing construction history of the site, the impact statement concluded that the digging of nineteenth- and twentieth-century basements had probably obliterated any human remains within the historical boundaries of the cemetery. Although the researchers did note that a portion of the old cemetery might have survived beneath an old alleyway, nobody expected much in the way of human remains to surface when construction began at 290 Broadway.

Still, because there remained a possibility of finding significant archaeological deposits in the construction zone, federal law required exploratory archaeological excavations. Those excavations began in September 1991, and human bone was found right away—not just a few scattered remains, but dozens (then hundreds) of intact human burials (see Figure 12-5).

The excavations at 290 Broadway began interfering with construction schedules. Worried that the archaeology might delay the $276 million project, the GSA insisted that the archaeologists work faster, excavating skeletons 10 and 12 hours a day, 7 days a week. Laboratory crew members were reassigned to field excavation duty—anything to

FIGURE 12-5 An artist's reconstruction of a burial at the African Burial Ground.

WHAT DOES IT MEAN TO me?

Archaeology and the Values of Descendent Communities

The African Burial Ground is one of many cases in which archaeologists have tried to take into account the opinions, values, and perspectives of descendent communities. Although admirable, such a stance does raise some ethical questions.

When word of the burials reached African-American leaders in Harlem, they expressed concern over the lack of community involvement in the project. Some people argued that because this was an African find, it should be interpreted from an African point of view. The Government Services Administration (GSA) countered that it had made appropriate notification as mandated by law. "We didn't include the Harlem community board because the project isn't in Harlem, it's in lower Manhattan."

The situation reached a flashpoint when a backhoe operator accidentally destroyed several of the burials. Large-scale protests ensued, culminating in a one-day blockade that shut down construction. To some, the debate surrounding the African Burial Ground became a "microcosm of the issues of racism and economic exploitation confronting New York City." Archaeology never proceeds in a social vacuum.

The GSA eventually commissioned an advisory committee—comprising historians, anthropologists, museum professionals, architects, attorneys, clergy, government officials, and concerned community members—to represent the interests of the African descendent community at large.

Supported by then-Mayor David N. Dinkins (New York City's first African-American mayor), the African descendent community became actively involved in the preservation, dedication, and management of the cemetery site. Michael Blakey's active participation became an overt symbol that the city was considering the African descendent community's wishes. But there were differences of opinion about how the remains should be treated. Some in the descendent community felt that archaeological investigations were disrespectful, adding the insult of grave robbing to the injury of slavery. Others believed that a thorough scientific study was not only a way of honoring the dead, but also of restoring them to their rightful place in American history.

Eventually, the government scrubbed all plans to erect the four-story pavilion. Instead, this piece of prime New York real estate was set aside as a permanent memorial. On February 25, 1993, the New York City Landmarks Preservation Commission designated the site the African Burial Ground and the Commons Historical District. Later that year, the African Burial Ground achieved National Historic Landmark status. Sherrill D. Wilson, an African-American anthropologist, noted that the sudden involvement of black scholars was "very revolutionary. . . . [Such scholarship] is going to set a precedent for what happens to African burial grounds in the future and how African heritage will be viewed by the public."

The African Burial Ground appears to have worked out to the satisfaction of most people. But it raises some questions. First, what defines a descendent community? To our knowledge, no living person demonstrated a lineal relationship to anyone in the African Burial Ground. Who decides who belongs to the descendent community?

And, once that decision is made, what is the appropriate role of descendent communities? Can anyone, with appropriate training, work on any type of site, or is the only valid work on a site done by a member of a descendent community? Can only Native Americans work on Native American sites; African-Americans on African-American sites, European Americans on Euro-American sites? Do we want a world in which there is "my" history and "your" history? Is there a line between empowerment of a descendent community and balkanization of the world of knowledge about the past?

---

speed things up. The cost of the excavation skyrocketed, and the African-American community was upset about the way the project was being handled see "What Does it Mean to Me? Archaeology and the Values of Descendent Communities).

Eventually, a working consensus was forged. A five-year research program was planned, headed by Dr. Michael L. Blakey, a bioarchaeologist and, at the time, director of the Cobb Biological Anthropology Laboratory at Howard University, the nation's premier black research university (he is now at the College of William and Mary). Blakey had already conducted research at the First African Baptist Church Cemetery in Philadelphia, so he was more than qualified to conduct the scientific research at the African Burial Ground.

Blakey's analysis of some 400 individuals from the burial ground is a chilling statement on human brutality. Blakey found that half the population died before reaching the age of 12, with another peak in mortality occurring between the ages of 15 and 20. Some of these deaths were probably due to diseases for which Africans had not developed immunity, complicated by the cold weather. But some people were clearly worked to death. Both men and women had enlarged muscle attachments, demonstrating continual demands on their physical labor, and some had lesions from torn muscle attachments. The bones also showed cranial and spinal fractures—a result of carrying excessive loads on the head and shoulders.

This hard life must have contrasted dramatically with their lives in Africa, for the teeth show little evidence of hypoplasias (see Chapter 9), showing that these African men and women as children had lives relatively free of malnutrition and severe disease. It also contrasted sharply with the life of the other citizens of New York. For example, Blakey found that English settlers were eight times more likely than African slaves to live past the age of 55.

The African Burial Ground Today

Visitors flock to the African Burial Ground center from around the world, and it has become a point of connection for Africans and Americans, white or black. Guided tours and videotapes of the African Burial Ground project are available through the Office of Public Education and Interpretation of the African Burial Ground, which is actively engaged in bringing the findings to a broader public through newsletters, workshops, and lectures. Finally, all the human remains were reburied in October 2003.

The African Burial Ground is a prime example of how archaeology can recover "lost" history. It is also a story about how a descendent community can be empowered through archaeology.

A final note: The artifacts and excavation documents from the African Burial Ground were stored in a basement of one of the buildings at the World Trade Center, along with those from the Five Points Project, another large historical archaeology dig in downtown New York. Most of the African Burial Ground material was recovered after the building's collapse on September 11, 2001; fortunately, the human remains were still stored in laboratories at Howard University. But virtually everything from the Five Points Project (the neighborhood that was the setting for Martin Scorsese's film *Gangs of New York*) was lost.

Beyond Slavery

We have focused on slavery—on and off plantations—because it was a dramatic and key element of African-American history whose full impact is often not communicated in standard documentary sources. But African-American history is much more than slave history, and a number of historical archaeologists have turned their attention to the archaeology of early free black communities in the South and African-American settlements in the West. Still other American historical archaeologists work to recover the history of other peoples by excavating the immigrant communities of early nineteenth-century mining towns, Chinese railroad labor camps, and early Mormon communities.

Correcting Inaccuracies

Historical archaeologists also attempt to correct inaccuracies in the public view of history. Sometimes these inaccuracies are simple mistakes or unintentional omissions, and often they are innocuous and trivial. But other historical inaccuracies are vastly more significant.

What Happened at the Battle of the Little Bighorn?

In the 1850s, American settlers were moving west through land that was the traditional territory of several tribes, including the Lakota on the northern high plains. As long as the settlers were simply moving through, relations were not so violent, but once settlers opted to remain and forts were constructed, hostilities ensued. By the late 1860s, the Lakota had gained the upper hand, and they were prepared to discuss terms of peace.

By signing the Fort Laramie Treaty of 1868, Red Cloud and other Lakota leaders agreed to cease hostilities, and the United States created the Great Sioux Reservation, which included the Black Hills in eastern South Dakota; the treaty agreed that whites would make no settlements or unauthorized incursions into this territory. Still, some Indian leaders refused to sign (among them Gall, Sitting Bull, and Crazy Horse), and they were granted permanent hunting rights in the Powder River region of Wyoming and Montana.

But the legal details of the treaty were difficult to understand (and some are still in dispute). Apparently, the treaty allowed for railroad surveys in the Black Hills, which were conducted in 1872 and 1873. But an 1874 military expedition to the Black Hills to locate a military post may not have been allowed in the treaty. Regardless, what matters is that this expedition discovered gold, and the federal government only halfheartedly tried to stop the ensuing rush of miners. By 1875, the government wanted to reduce the size of the Sioux reservation and also ordered that the nontreaty bands relocate to the reservation. In 1876, the government sent General George Armstrong Custer to find these Lakota and move them to the reservation.

On June 25, with the aid of Crow and Arikara scouts, Custer tracked a large band of Lakota, Northern Cheyenne, and Arapaho to the Little Bighorn River in Montana. Despite his scouts' warnings, he decided to attack. He broke his men into three battalions. One, headed by Captain Frederick Benteen, went to the south to cut off an escape route. Major Marcus Reno led another into the valley to attack the village from the southeast. Custer himself led the third over the river bluffs, eventually reaching a position north of the village. Reno encountered heavy resistance that brought him to a standstill, but his efforts did succeed in creating an exodus from the village. Custer apparently then moved through the low hills northeast of the river, pursuing the women, children, and elderly as they fled down the valley.

No U.S. soldier survived to describe what happened or what Custer's final moments were like. Nonetheless, sensationalist newspaper accounts quickly formed an image of the battle and Custer's gallant "last stand." Years later, that vivid image was immortalized in several paintings. In 1895, Adolphus Busch (the brewery magnate) commissioned Otto Becker to paint *Custer's Last Fight*. The image shows Custer, his men bravely circled around him, almost calmly fighting a huge band of Lakota and Cheyenne. Busch sent lithographs of the image to 150,000 saloons around the country. In 1900, Frederic Remington also painted an image of the battle's final moments in which, again, a cool and collected Custer commands the men clustered around him.

Perhaps the most famous image is that by Edgar Samuel Paxson (see the chapter's opening photo), completed in 1899, which includes 200 individuals (some are recognizable individuals, as Paxson studied all the available photographs of Custer's men as well as those of Cheyenne and Lakota warriors). Here we see Custer calmly standing in a whirlwind of activity, revolvers at the ready, his chest thrust out defiantly. The men of the Seventh Cavalry are gathered around him, disciplined to the end.

Images like these helped to create a fatalistic attitude toward the country's push to the west: Some would have to die in expanding the country westward, but they would die proud, knowing that what they were doing—bringing civilization to the wilderness (or massacring Indians and dispossessing them of their land, depending on your perspective)—was their God-given destiny. And Indians who stood in the way of this destiny should be punished.

But there were other images of the battle. Although none of Custer's battalion survived, many of the 1200 or so Indian warriors did, including such notables as Sitting Bull, Gall, Crazy Horse, and Black Elk (then 13 years old). Many of the Indian survivors were interviewed in the following years, and their accounts were used to draw Indian images of the battle.

The Indian images tell a different story, as shown in Figure 12-6. In the first place, they are far bloodier than the paintings by Paxson and others, who sanitized the gruesome details of hand-to-hand combat. The Indians' images are filled with blood and entrails, decapitation and dismemberment. More important, they show groups of men spread over the battlefield—some firing, others running for their lives. Unlike the images white artists created, the Indians' images show no grand last stand. In fact, there is nothing glorious in their pictures at all; there is only confusion and carnage. Which image is accurate?

An Archaeological Perspective on the Battle

Today, the battlefield is a national monument, but it still remains a lonely and windswept place. In 1983, a brush fire burned the area, which led Douglas Scott (Connor Consulting) and Richard Fox (University of South Dakota) to conduct a survey of the entire battlefield. They checked a sample of the grave markers (individual gravestones marked where bodies were found some time after the battle) and systematically surveyed the battlefield using metal detectors for battle-related artifacts. They found plenty: gun parts, belt buckles, buttons, bridle pieces, human remains, and lots of spent cartridges and bullets. Each item was recorded and its location carefully mapped.

The cartridges and bullets were especially interesting, because they were amenable to forensic analyses. Scott and Fox knew that the cavalry was armed only with .45-caliber

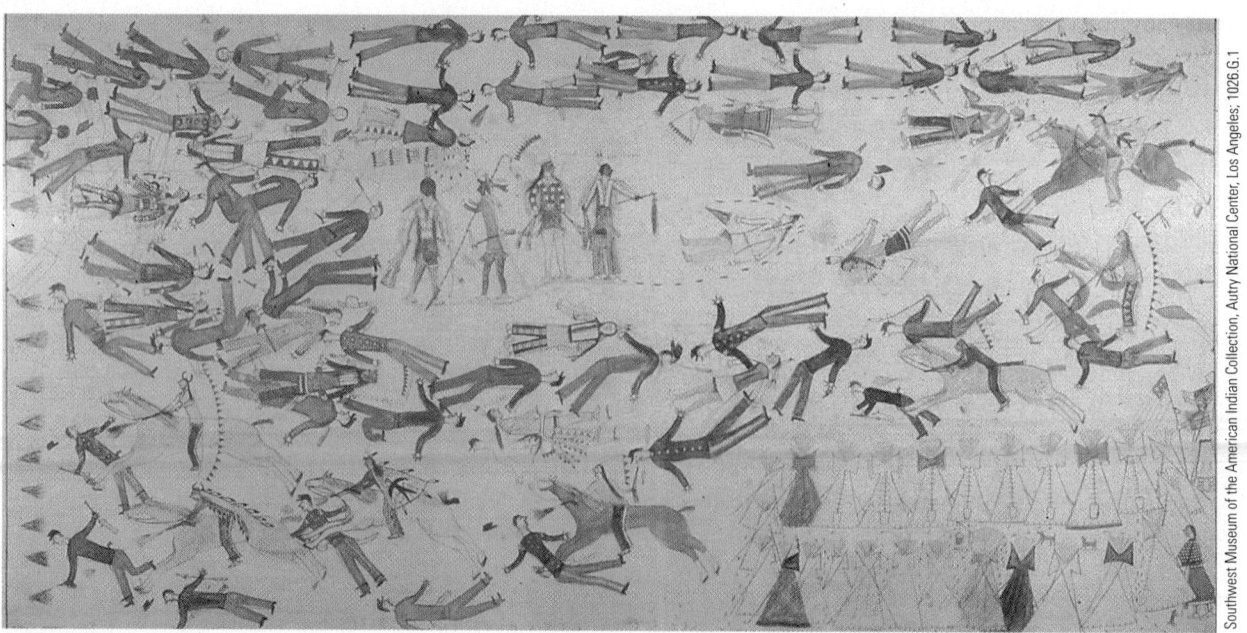

Southwest Museum of the American Indian Collection, Autry National Center, Los Angeles; 1026.G.1

FIGURE 12-6 *Battle of the Little Bighorn* (circa 1898) by Kicking Bear (c. 1846–1904). Kicking Bear made this painting at the request of Frederic Remington; Custer appears in yellow buckskins at the left.

single-shot Springfield carbines and .45-caliber Colt pistols. The Indians had these, too, but forensic studies showed they were also equipped with some 40 other types of weapons, from obsolete muzzleloaders to repeating rifles (acquired through the illegal arms trade of the day). Careful mapping allowed Scott and Fox to ascertain combatant positions (Indian and soldier alike) using cartridge case locations and bullet orientations (which revealed the direction from which the bullet was fired). Most important, in many instances they could use discharged cartridges to trace individual combatant movements by matching the distinctive "fingerprint" that a gun's firing pin makes on the cartridge. What did they learn?

Where Was Custer?

Custer's body was found on the hilltop that today bears his name, surrounded by most of his headquarters staff. But where was he during the battle? We know that Custer's battalion had broken into two wings. Previous scholars argued that Custer was with the right wing because brass cartridges had been found along the path taken by the right wing, and Custer's .50-caliber Remington rifle was thought to be the only weapon on the battlefield that used brass cartridges. But Scott and Fox found many brass cartridges at the site, with firing pin fingerprints indicating that brass cartridges were fired from several different .50-caliber guns (by both soldiers and Indians). The brass cartridges, therefore, cannot be used to pinpoint Custer's personal movements. We don't know where Custer himself fought; we only know where his body eventually came to rest.

Where Were the Indians and the Soldiers?

Scott and Fox also found cavalry cartridge cases on Custer Hill, on the low ridges running to the east and south, and on Calhoun Hill (to the south of Custer Hill). Many more *Indian* cartridges are found in these same places (as well as on the rise coming up from the river—the direction from which the Indians would have attacked). In addition, in some places, expended government bullets were found next to government-issue cartridges. A cartridge drops to the ground as a rifle is reloaded, but obviously the corresponding bullet should appear at the target. Some of the bullets may have resulted from men shooting their horses to use them as shields. But others were probably fired by Indians, using guns they had claimed from Reno's unsuccessful attack or weapons taken from the bodies of Custer's men.

Also telling is the lack of evidence for formal skirmish lines. Army tactics at the time called for companies to form skirmish lines as a defensive measure. To form a skirmish line, a company's men stood about 5 yards apart, with about 15 yards between companies. Such a tactical maneuver leaves a distinctive trace: piles of government-issue cartridges spaced about 5 yards apart. Scott and Fox found only tentative evidence for one skirmish line, on Calhoun Hill. Otherwise, the archaeological evidence fit the Indian accounts of chaos and hand-to-hand fighting.

Eventually, about 100 soldiers made it to Custer Hill, where order was apparently restored, albeit briefly. More Indians slowly arrived. Eventually, about 45 men, 5 of them mounted, made a break down a ridge to the east of Custer Hill. But Scott and Fox found no evidence of a skirmish line there. Instead, the men were perhaps trying to distract the Indians from the mounted soldiers, who were probably trying to reach Benteen. But these men, even the riders, were quickly pursued.

When Custer Hill was overrun, more men ran down the hill to the ravine. Indians recalled that some fired into the air, but others failed even to draw their revolvers. And many did what soldiers before (and after) have done when confronted with death: They froze, with little choice but to accept the inevitable.

The battle lasted less than 90 minutes, and the finale took place not on Custer Hill, as the paintings suggest, but in the ravine, where terrified soldiers who "shot like drunken men," according to Iron Hawk, were hunted down and killed in a terrifying game of hide-and-seek.

Fox argues that Custer was moving confidently in an offensive tactical maneuver when he was caught completely off guard, forcing a rapid transition from an offensive to a defensive posture. But Custer and his men were so rapidly surrounded that they had no time to regroup and carry out formal tactical maneuvers. The coordination of Custer's offensive attack rapidly gave way to chaos. In fact, the distribution of Springfield cases suggests that men clustered together tightly in a nontactical maneuver—something that Indian eyewitnesses recalled years later—firing against the Indians who surrounded them.

To the Last Bullet?

The romantic image of the battle has the soldiers holding off the Indians until their last bullet was fired. In fact, less than a month after the battle, the Helena *Herald* reported the tragedy with the headline "Not Until Their Ammunition Was Gone Were Our Troops Butchered."

But there were almost no Colt .45 cartridge cases found on the battlefield—none, in fact, on Custer Hill. A soldier could fire a revolver six times before he had to reload (unlike the single-shot carbines, from which a soldier had to remove the empty cartridge before reloading). But with their limited accuracy, handguns were only good for close combat. The Indians recalled soldiers using their sidearms, but they said that the soldiers had no time to reload. The distribution of .45-caliber Colt cartridges confirms this account. Close combat came so quickly and with such overwhelming force that soldiers either had no time to use their revolvers or, more likely, had no time to reload them (and the Indians collected the revolvers, still filled with empty or usable cartridges, after the battle).

Romantic images of the battle suggest that Custer and his men were in calm control until the very end. But the archaeology agrees with the Indians' accounts: Custer was caught off guard. Perhaps he didn't expect the warriors to be so motivated to protect their women and children. Perhaps he expected Reno and Benteen to cut through and assist them. We don't know. We do know, however, that the popular images of the battle are inaccurate. The Battle of the Little Bighorn did not end in a "glorious" last stand. Instead, it ended as most battles end: in chaos, panic, horror, and carnage.

The Monument Today

A pillar was erected on Custer's Hill in 1881 as a tribute to the Seventh Cavalry. One hundred and ten years later, Congress recognized the more complex nature of the site's history and changed the name from Custer Battlefield to Little Bighorn Battlefield National Monument. At the same time, it authorized a memorial to honor the fallen Cheyenne, Lakota, and Arapaho warriors. The new memorial, dedicated in June 2003, consists of a low, circular, granite-lined earthwork and contains bronze silhouettes of mounted warriors. Its name: "Peace through Unity."

Reexamining America's History

We now come to perhaps the most divisive aspect of historical archaeology—reexamining history. A national narrative can be contentious, because a nation's history defines who its citizens are and, in no small way, creates their identity. No one wishes to identify with a history of dishonorable acts. This is why slavery was long ignored at reconstructed plantation sites and why revisionist histories of western settlement remain controversial. Going back in time, it seems, is like going deeper into a people's identity and soul. There are many, for example, who do not welcome reinterpretations of Custer's Last Stand, because the myth has become "their" history, right or wrong. Everyone wants their history to be uplifting; scholars also want it to be honest. Here's one example from Annapolis, Maryland.

Historical Archaeology in Annapolis

Working with the Historic Annapolis Foundation, Mark Leone (University of Maryland) has conducted "backyard archaeology" for decades, excavating in basements and backyards, beneath parking lots and pavements throughout Annapolis. By looking at floor plans, dishes, facades, architecture, silverware, furniture, and gardens, Leone is trying to demonstrate the degree to which our history is "constructed"—that is, written and presented for contemporary purposes. And in doing that, Leone has established the relevance of eighteenth-century Annapolis to ourselves and the way we understand not only our past, but also the present and the future.

Because of the explicit political agenda behind Leone's work, it is important to understand his theoretical perspective. Leone works within a postprocessual paradigm called **critical theory**. As applied to archaeology, critical theory emphasizes the importance of archaeologists' understanding of the specific contexts within which they work and of the notion that knowledge is situated within a cultural framework (as we pointed out in Chapter 2) and that it consequently can serve special interests. Critical theory assumes that domination in some form is a central element of modern capitalist society.

"Critical" in this sense means that the relationship between the assumptions and discoveries of a scholarly discipline on the one hand and its ties to modern life on the other is a central concern and subject to examination. Such an approach relates the questions, methods, and discoveries of a science like anthropology to those of the anthropologist's own culture. Critical theorists seek simultaneously to explain the social world, to criticize it, and to empower their audience to deal with it more productively by advocating change.

Pre-1760 Colonial America: The Georgian Order

Before continuing, we must situate Leone's work in a larger context. Folklorist Henry Glassie (Indiana University) and archaeologist James Deetz (1930–2000) both explored the way in which changing cultural ideas were reflected in the material record of the American colonies. As such, they took a decidedly ideational (rather than materialist) approach to the past. Glassie examined early colonial houses in Virginia, whereas Deetz looked at the overall pattern of material culture in New England. Deetz argued that early British colonists in New England had a **medieval mindset** that encouraged a group-oriented, corporate, and relatively undifferentiated lifestyle. He found that by 1660, however, the culture of American colonies had changed. This particular culture is sometimes known as the **Georgian order**.

Material remains of the late seventeenth century, Glassie and Deetz found, reflect a culture of increasing individualism and control. In this regard, American colonial culture reflected elements of the Enlightenment, which focused on progress and on the ability of rational thought to control nature and improve human morality and spirituality. During the late seventeenth century, Deetz argued, Georgian attitudes created material culture patterns that emphasized control, often by partitioning space, and reflected a focus on the individual. These patterns in material culture were strikingly different from the previous "medieval" culture of the colonies. Here is how Deetz saw the differences:

- *Architecture*. Medieval houses had only one or two rooms, with asymmetrical floor plans. All domestic activity took place in these rooms, from sleeping and eating to working and socializing. With the Georgian worldview, houses became functionally structured and compartmentalized, with more balanced floor plans.

- *Ceramics.* The medieval mindset was characterized by plain, utilitarian earthenware. Food was served directly from the cooking pot and consumed from "trenchers," wooden trays that were shared with one or more "trencher mates." During this period, ceramics played only a small role in food consumption. Georgian culture entailed ceramics that were purchased as matched sets of plates and teacups. Serving vessels appeared, and one plate was allotted to each individual around the family table. And whereas medieval ceramics were natural-colored earthenwares, Georgian ceramics became progressively whiter as technology improved.
- *Mortuary art.* Gravestones also became white, replacing earlier green, black, blue, and red markers, and the backs were sculpted smooth, "denying their origin in the native stone." The messages engraved on the medieval tombstones reminded the living of their mortality with engraved death's heads and simple epitaphs such as "Here lies buried . . . ." But in Georgian culture, the typical inscription changed to "In memory of . . . ," and the urn and willow motif was used as a "symbol of commemoration." Georgian epitaphs praised the worldly achievements of individuals.
- *Food preparation.* Medieval diners usually attacked a portion of meat still articulated in joints, "showing in part at least the vestiges of the anatomy of the beast from which they came." But Georgian food was dominated by segmented cuts of meat that were more difficult to identify to anatomical part. Archaeologically, this change is seen as a shift from chopping bones to sawing them.
- Refuse disposal. During early medieval days, trash was simply tossed out of doors and windows, creating a sheet of refuse that domestic animals scavenged. By the mid-eighteenth century, however, trash was deposited in an orderly manner, in square pits up to 7 feet deep. Chamber pots also came into use, reflecting a desire for increased privacy.

These changes in material culture signal a shift to a culture that focused on the individual, rather than the group, and on the control of nature. Glassie and Deetz believe these patterns point to a simple cultural idea: Culture was to nature as order was to chaos. This reflects a general Enlightenment theme: For nature to be controlled, it had to be ordered, and for it to be ordered, it had to be brought into the world of culture.

Capitalism and Power in Historic Annapolis

Leone was interested not just in the operation of the Georgian worldview, but also in how and why it came to exist. He chose to examine these questions in the community of Annapolis.

Annapolis has been a small community since it was founded about 1650. It became the capital of Maryland in 1695, later experiencing a "golden age" of wealth and fame that peaked between 1760 and the end of the American Revolution. In a move designed to symbolically subordinate the military to civil authority, George Washington came to Annapolis to resign his command of the Continental Army. The Treaty of Paris, which officially ended the American Revolution, was also signed there. During the early days of the United States, even though Annapolis remained the state capital, the international, commercial, and industrial potential of nearby Baltimore attracted many of the area's wealthiest residents. Although the U.S. Naval Academy moved to Annapolis in 1845, the nineteenth century signaled an era of "gentle eclipse" for the city. In the 1950s, the beginning of a commercial revival based on yachting, tourism, and new highways defined Annapolis as a suburb of Washington, DC, and Baltimore, less than 30 miles away.

Leone and his team consciously deconstructed the ideology behind the historical development of Annapolis and its environs: Why did some people become rich? Why were some poor? What was the relationship between the two? How did the American Revolution affect these inequalities?

Eventually, Leone developed a "theory of power" to explain the growth of Chesapeake society under the European and American systems. By 1720, a class structure had developed in which a few families of the gentry controlled most of the wealth. The social position of the rest of the population—poorer whites, Native and African-Americans—remained the same before and after the American Revolution.

The Power Garden: Landscape Archaeology as Ideology

Leone paid special attention to the formal landscapes of Annapolis. Recognizing that formal gardens were a new addition to wealthy households, Leone wanted to understand what this piece of material culture had to say about the formation of the Georgian order.

Shown in Figure 12-7, the best known of Annapolis's formal gardens in the late eighteenth century was that of William Paca—a signer of the Declaration of Independence. If we could ask him, Paca would probably say that he built his garden in the style that he did because he "enjoyed" it or because it was fashionable. But this only raises the question of *why* this particular garden style was fashionable.

critical theory A critique of the modern social order that emphasizes exploitative class interests; it aims to change and not simply to understand society.

medieval mindset The culture of the early (pre-AD 1660) British colonies that emphasized the group rather than the individual and in which the line between culture and nature was blurred; people were seen as conforming to nature.

Georgian order A worldview (1660/1680 to 1820) arising in the European Age of Reason and implying that the world has a single, basic immutable order. Using the powers of reason, people can discover what that order is and can thereby control the environment as they wish. The Georgian order is informed by the rise of scientific thought and by the balance and order in Renaissance architecture and art.

© Kevin Fleming/Encyclopedia/Corbis

FIGURE 12-7 The William Paca Garden (Annapolis).

Paca's garden, once described as "the most elegant in Annapolis," was originally built in the 1760s, behind a large, five-part Georgian mansion—which sported a facade and a floor plan exhibiting bilateral symmetry.

The garden is likewise Georgian, with a central axis, and a straight, broad path that descends through several sets of steps as one leaves the house, dividing the space into two parts. These steps lead down over a series of small terraces, creating the same visual effect of bilateral symmetry as that of Georgian architecture.

The garden survived into the early twentieth century, when it was destroyed to make room for a 200-room hotel. When the hotel was torn down in 1968, Stanley South excavated in and around the standing house. Historical archaeologists then moved into the garden area, first testing and then excavating large areas. Original wall footings, documenting the terraces (which could be seen in stratigraphic profile), were found; thus, the garden's basic topography was reconstructed. Trenching and examination of the profiles showed a canal and pond at the bottom of the garden, surrounded by a natural garden (in the terminology of the time, a "wilderness") in the lowest third of the garden. Foundations of a central pavilion and springhouse and of footings for a bridge over the ponds were discovered; 125 paleobotanical samples were recovered from the wet fill. These archaeological data were combined with a few period descriptions and with a contemporary portrait of William Paca that showed the garden as background. The pavilion, bathhouse, springhouse, and Chinese Chippendale bridge all have been restored. Today, the Paca garden is open to the public as both an archaeologically based reconstruction and a horticultural experiment.

Leone first visited the restored garden in the early 1980s, and his impressions remained the touchstone for his subsequent archaeological analyses. He later wrote,

> As I began to walk through the garden from the top, which is 16 feet higher than the bottom, which is 270 feet away, I found it difficult to tell distances; I felt I was being controlled, as paths, precise borders, openings, stairs, and objects that had to be stepped over operated everywhere to control me. This sensation was especially true regarding sight.

This effect is not simply the impact of fastidious design. Paca's sensibilities were affected by larger cultural ideas,

RAPID REVIEW

Three Themes of Historical Archaeology

Theme	Characteristics
Hidden history	Seeks to rectify an injustice by documenting the experiences of minority or subjugated populations whose lack of access to literacy often left their voice out of traditional historical texts
Correcting inaccuracies	Seeks to set historical records of events straight in cases where the records may be biased
Reexamining history	Seeks to determine whether our explanations of the past, or whether national "stories" of how a nation came to be, are accurate or whether the story masks the processes that led to and propagate inequalities

and his garden expresses the Enlightenment idea of the power of Reason over Nature. By putting trees and shrubs into their "proper" places, Paca's landscape architect was demonstrating that nature controlled by culture was more lovely and desirable than wilderness—that is, than nature uncontrolled by culture.

After studying two other large gardens in Annapolis, Leone synthesized what he believed to be the rules behind the design. The Paca garden was constructed following the laws of perspective and used Baroque rules for creating optical illusions. Convergent or divergent lines of sight (to make distances appear shorter or longer, depending on the specific need in each garden) were created, and rows of beds or shrubs were formed into trapezoids and focal points (rather than strictly parallel lines) to manipulate the view. "The gardens are three-dimensional spaces," he wrote, "built consciously using rules which were well understood to create illusions for those who walked through them."

But why the illusion? Leone asked. And why would such Anglo-American gardens proliferate just before the American Revolution and then slowly disappear—like the rest of Georgian material culture—in the decades leading up to the Civil War?

For answers, Leone turned to the general body of materialist theory and formulated a hypothesis to explain governance through ostentatious displays. When money forms the only power base, Leone argued, those governing have little need to demonstrate their right or power to govern; they are in control and intend to stay that way. But ostentatious displays become important when factors other than simple wealth come into play, when it is necessary to convince the governed that those in power deserve to stay there. *Show* becomes important when those in authority do not necessarily control the purse strings or when the wealthy do not control the power structure.

The William Paca garden was built by a wealthy man who lived in a time of contradictions. Although not born to particular affluence, he married into plenty of it. Although a slave owner, he argued for the Bill of Rights. Although descended from planters and tied to merchants, he grew up and lived in economic circumstances in which he and everyone around him were facing serious economic and political change.

Paca could have built his garden anytime during his lifetime, but he chose to do so when his power to protect his wealth was being diminished by Britain. Parliamentary restrictions on trade and local office holding compromised profits and power in the 1760s. Paca was isolated socially and economically by a large and difficult-to-control slave population as well as by poor white farmers and day laborers who were anxious to learn who their future allies would be in the coming war with Britain.

Leone argues that the formal Anglo-American gardens were built deliberately to demonstrate a knowledge of—and control over—the laws of nature. Paca was trying to create the illusion that either (1) he still retained power over his own wealth, or (2) he should be granted the political clout to do so. In this perspective, the garden was not a statement of what existed. Paca's garden both reflected and helped create an ideology, at a time when the wealth and prestige of his class were being undermined and diminished.

Leone points out that the Paca garden illustrates the principles that defined the layout of Annapolis as a whole. The early street patterns and building placements still dominate life in the city. This archaeological study of Paca's garden reveals that perspective and its power to invite attention are still actively used to manage relations of power in the city today. The relations among the prominence of the state capitol, the isolation of the Naval Academy, and the invisibility of the African-American community are all managed using the same spatial principles exhibited in Paca's garden. Together, Leone argues, historical archaeological and critical theory illustrate the origins of modern—and exploitative—social relations that continue to the present.

Taking Critical Theory Public

As discussed in Chapter 2, archaeology's postprocessual critique calls attention to the important role played by local politics in archaeological interpretation—particularly interpretation within the field of historical archaeology.

Critical theorists argue that the proper role of historians is to unearth the beginnings of contemporary class-based ideologies—distortions that rationalize forms of exploitation, such as slavery, sexism, and racism. Applied to historical archaeology, critical theory suggests that once a repressed people can be shown a past in which things were different, they can use this knowledge to challenge and attempt to change the inequities of the present. From this position, responsible historians (and historical archaeologists) should form alliances with members of oppressed classes and work toward social change to better their condition. To critical theorists, capitalism has negative social elements that should be confronted.

Leone grounded his research at Annapolis in the belief that archaeologists and historians should "stand up" against the oppressive excesses of capitalism. In other words, it was not enough for archaeologists simply to learn about abuse of power in the past; it was essential that this knowledge be brought forward into the present.

The call for historical archaeology to become more political comes from two directions. As archaeology becomes more public, individual archaeologists are increasingly called upon to interpret their findings for the public. Such interpretation takes many forms—traditional museum exhibits, outdoor history museums, site-specific tourist facilities, and television and other media interpretations of "the past." But the problem immediately surfaces—which and whose past?

Consider the case of Annapolis, where historical preservation has played a major role in the commercial renaissance of the city. Annually, more than 1 million people visit Annapolis, a city of only about 32,000 people. As in many other small, historical towns, local residents work hard to protect those things that attract visitors.

The encapsulated history of Annapolis has been peddled to generations of tourists who buy guidebooks, listen to tour guides, and saunter through the historic house museums. Prominent are references to the ultimate first tourist, none other than George Washington himself. Discussing his many visits, conventional Annapolis history plays up the social and domestic aspects of Washington's jaunts into the city—going to the racetrack, attending social events and plays, and visiting a host of friends and family members. In effect, the image of Washington in Annapolis largely mirrored the profile of just the sort of visitor that Annapolis wanted to attract—the high-end tourist with some money to spend, but without an attitude.

Through the lens of critical theory, however, Leone and his colleagues noticed something interesting about the tourism process. As the tourists poured through, they were presented the history of Annapolis as a collection of disconnected units from different time periods and institutions. History for the tourist was left in the hands of diverse groups and institutions, some overlapping, some in competition. Annapolis had no unified history to connect the different parts of the city. Black and white populations were presented as unconnected, as were the histories of the city of Annapolis and the Naval Academy.

As written and presented by whites, black history (viewed from the nineteenth-century perspective) was separated from white history (presented from the eighteenth-century perspective). Slavery was not seen as an antecedent to relationships between contemporary groups.

Leone and his associates—notably an archaeologist-cum-lawyer, Parker Potter—designed an on-site program for the 5,000 to 10,000 visitors who stopped by each year. Tourists visiting Historic Annapolis often have a chance to walk through the ongoing archaeological excavations. Well-prepared guides explain what the archaeologists are doing and why they are doing it.

The site excursions were enormously popular with tourists and residents in Annapolis, and they seemed to rally the city's support to protect the archaeological sites of Annapolis. But in regard to social change, Leone and Potter were frustrated with the results. Potter believed that the "Archaeology in Annapolis" tour program failed to effect any significant change in Annapolis. "As far as I can tell," Leone has written, "[the tours] changed consciousness not at all. . . . We were speaking to the wrong audience."

For a historical archaeology of capitalism to be fruitful, Leone realized, "there would have to be a dialogue with those who see knowledge about themselves as a way of dealing with their own oppression or victimization." This was disappointing in a sense because it suggested that critical theory—as a strategy for effecting social change (its avowed goal)—might not work as intended (at least not by itself).

On reflection, Leone still believed that the "Archaeology in Annapolis" program had successfully explored the histories of the white residents who lived there (even if the white tourists to Annapolis did not seem to pick up on the message to "stand up against capitalism"). But he also realized that, in its early stages, the archaeology program had overlooked a major portion of the city by not explicitly addressing the African-American experience through archaeology. This realization led Leone and the public programming effort at Annapolis in another direction—into the contemporary African-American community of Annapolis.

The dialogue between Annapolis archaeologists and the African-American community immediately raised three related questions:

- Was there, indeed, any way to tell whether archaeological material was associated with African-Americans?
- Does the African-American community care about that record? (Some important questions: Can you tell us about freedom, not just about slavery? Is there anything left from Africa?)
- What would an African-American historical archaeology look like?

Faced with this entirely new direction, Leone realized, "We ourselves had to admit we did not know the answers."

So began a new interchange at Annapolis, between white archaeologists and African-Americans. No longer was the archaeologist the "teacher," with the community serving only as "listener." In this dialogue, all participants defined themselves as professionals, informants, scholars, students, and fund-raisers. Everyone involved, according to Leone, admitted ignorance on some topics, but also expressed a willingness to learn. This experiment in historical archaeology is still ongoing.

Conclusion

Historical archaeology is the growth industry of archaeology in the twenty-first century. In part, cultural resource management and the large number of historical sites that are uncovered by the construction activities of a growing population drive this. But it is also driven by a desire to understand the colonial and postcolonial history of the United States and the roles played by all the peoples who have found a home in America. For this reason, historical archaeology will continue to occupy a prominent place in archaeology for years to come. We expect that the processual paradigm will continue to be important, but that postprocessual approaches will play a large and significant role as issues such as power, domination, class, and resistance figure prominently in the world's recent (colonial) history.

For this reason also, historical archaeology will continue to be the source of some heated disputes. Some of these disputes will focus on who has the right to study and interpret the material remains that document the history of various groups—African, Asian, Native, Hispanic, and European Americans. We predict that these debates will be less contentious and more productive if archaeologists maintain a dialogue with the public and descendent communities while at the same time holding fast to their scientific standards of excavation and interpretation.

Other disputes will focus on the proper place of politically motivated interpretations of the past. Leone, for example, suggests that capitalism creates its own view of the past, which masks the formation of inequities that are essential to the operation of capitalism today—a bourgeois class of consumers and an economically and politically repressed group of workers. But some might legitimately argue that any archaeology pursuing a political position is biased from the start, and hence all its interpretations of the past are suspect. Those in historical archaeology who pursue the paradigm of critical theory will have to meet this challenge in the future by combining a passionate desire to use archaeology to effect social change with a dispassionate and thorough scientific analysis of archaeology's data.

Summary

- Why do historical archaeology if we already have the historical records?
  - Historical archaeology looks at material remains from past societies that also left behind some form of written documentation ("history") about themselves.
  - Historical sources can be significantly biased—sometimes intentionally, sometimes not; archaeologists look at archaeological and documentary records *as equally valid yet independent* lines of evidence.
- What are the three major areas of historical archaeological research today?
  - Historical archaeology eschews the "oldest," "largest," and "most historically significant" sites, favoring instead the study of historically disenfranchised groups, including African-Americans, Asian-American cultures, Native Americans during the historic period, and Hispanic-Americans.
  - Historical archaeology tackles questions about the recent past that history books answer unsatisfactorily. In this regard, some historical archaeologists are like crime scene detectives, collecting data to resolve disputes over the nature of key historical events.
  - Many historical archaeologists research the nature of European colonialism (the developing capitalism of that time) and its effects on indigenous peoples.
- How is historical archaeology more amenable to the postprocessual paradigm than prehistoric archaeology?
  - Historical archaeology has been fertile ground for postprocessual interests because texts can provide data with which to place archaeological remains in context.
  - The study of the symbolic meaning of material remains proceeds more comfortably in historical archaeology, where documents can provide interpretations of material culture.

Media Resources

CourseMate

Access chapter-specific learning tools including learning objectives, practice quizzes, videos, flash cards, and glossaries, as well as web links, and more in your Archaeology CourseMate. Login to www.cengagebrain.com to access the resources your instructor has assigned and to purchase materials.

Caring for the Global Cultural Heritage

13

© AP Images/Kirsty Wigglesworth

Archaeology students sieve through earth among the stones at Stonehenge, England, 2008. Though known for hundreds of years, this site continues to provide new knowledge about the past.

Learning Objectives

After reading this chapter, you should be able to answer these questions:

- Does archaeology have practical value in the world today?
- What is the attitude of archaeology toward public education?
- What federal policies help protect cultural resources, including archaeological sites?
- What are the important elements of the 1906 Antiquities Act, the 1966 National Historic Preservation Act, and the 1979 Archaeological Resources Protection Act?

- Is there an international black market in antiquities? If so, what can be done about it?
- Why is the Native American Graves Protection and Repatriation Act of 1990 important to archaeologists? How does it differ from other archaeological legislation?
- As archaeologists become increasingly involved with descendant and stakeholder communities, what associated ethical problems and positive potentials arise?

Preview

THROUGHOUT THIS BOOK, we have tried to paint a realistic picture of what archaeology is all about. We have often reached into the past to demonstrate how today's archaeology has evolved over the last 150 years. Now we will look forward to address two of the key challenges facing archaeology in the twenty-first century:

- How is archaeology relevant to the modern world?
- How should archaeologists share control over knowledge of the past?

As we explore these related issues, you will probably find more questions than answers.

Introduction

We began this book talking about Kennewick Man, an important archaeological find that fostered an equally important legal case. The legalities of the Kennewick case highlight even larger issues surrounding the role of archaeology in modern society. But before we consider those issues, let's first recap some key concepts from earlier chapters.

Throughout this text, we have emphasized the "big picture" of archaeology: the role of archaeological objects in the modern world. We discussed archaeology's contribution to the larger field of anthropology and the different ways that archaeologists "think from things"—the different paradigms that we use to reconstruct and explain the past.

We then addressed the particulars of archaeological fieldwork and analysis: how we find and excavate sites; how we date and analyze artifacts and dirt; and how we interpret the remains of plants, animals, and people. You have seen how archaeologists can extract an enormous amount of information from broken, dirty bits of ancient objects to reconstruct ancient cultural behavior—and archaeology is still a relatively young science, making progress each year. We've only touched on the highlights in this text. The future promises even greater knowledge and understanding—achieved by methods that will be even more remarkable than those we've described here.

We examined historical archaeology, the methods used to understand the more recent past. Here we saw archaeology's special power to correct historical inaccuracies, to recover portions of history unrecorded in documents, and to bring new meaning to the present by reevaluating the past.

In various "What Does It Mean to Me?" boxes, we have reiterated a point first made in the Introduction. Archaeology is not just about the dead; it's also about the living. We will devote part of this final chapter to exploring the implications of that statement.

We will also explore the "business" of archaeology—cultural resource management—and its link to laws that govern the preservation of cultural resources, which accounts for most of modern archaeology. We revisit the Kennewick case and discuss NAGPRA, a law that, instead of protecting the *objects* of the past, is intended to protect the various *interests* in the past. This law explicitly recognizes that archaeologists are not the only ones interested in antiquity and that the past holds different meanings for different people.

Virtually everyone cares about the past, to one degree or another. But people care about history for different reasons. We will always face important issues regarding (1) what is done with our knowledge of the past, (2) who gets to "tell the story," and (3) who controls access to data. We believe that archaeology plays several roles in the modern world, and although each of these functions can be beneficial, some soul-searching is required for professional archaeologists to understand and fulfill their responsibilities.

Archaeological Science: Pure or Applied?

Anthropology is conventionally perceived as a **pure (or basic) science**, as the systematic pursuit of knowledge for its own sake. And it is true that anthropologists, like many other scientists, are commonly motivated more by

pure (basic) science Systematic research directed toward acquisition of knowledge for its own sake.

intellectual curiosity than by the practical applications of what they learn. Anthropologists have traditionally looked for answers to the larger, holistic questions regarding the human condition: How, where, and when did humanity arise? What is the relative importance of nature versus nurture? How (and why) did major social institutions evolve? These are large-scale questions about the basic nature of the human condition, issues without immediate practical application or "relevance."

But anthropologists have long attempted to apply their findings to practical ends—that is, to do **applied science**. During World War II, for instance, some American anthropologists volunteered their services in the war effort. Several collaborated on "national character" studies—detailed memoranda on European and Asian countries that tried to characterize peoples who were either allies or enemies, or who lived in enemy-occupied territory. For example, anthropologist Ruth Benedict (1887–1948) temporarily left her professorship at Columbia University to join the Bureau of Overseas Intelligence of the U.S. War Department during World War II. Here she took on a study of Japanese national character, providing information that would ultimately prove critical for the Allied forces occupying Japan during the postwar period. Today, the Human Terrain Teams in Iraq and Afghanistan include anthropologists that help the military see situations from an indigenous perspective, to help build better relations, ease poverty, and provide protection. (Such projects are controversial; many anthropologists oppose the practice, fearing that anthropological knowledge will be used for military purposes.)

Applied anthropology is a huge field. Applied anthropologists evaluate domestic social programs, improve corporate working conditions, develop culturally appropriate methods of delivering health care or agricultural assistance programs, and devise and implement international development programs, to mention only a few areas. Some cultural resource management archaeologists also see themselves as applied anthropologists.

Modern archaeology likewise attempts to apply its knowledge and insights to the modern world. In this chapter, we will present multiple examples of how applied archaeology (1) brings the techniques of archaeology to nontraditional venues and (2) applies our knowledge of the human past to concrete economic or social problems.

The Garbage Project

Emil Haury (1904–1992) was the senior archaeologist at the University of Arizona for decades. A specialist in Southwestern prehistory, Haury continually taught his students that "if you want to know what is really going on in a community, look at its garbage."

Haury's earthy advice was not lost on his students and colleagues. In 1971, the University of Arizona launched a long-term, in-depth study of a community's garbage. But it must have surprised Haury when the Garbage Project decided to focus on the trash of contemporary Tucson.

The Garbage Project was begun by William Rathje (1945–2012), a Harvard-trained archaeologist who had previously specialized in Maya archaeology. Through the Garbage Project, Rathje applied archaeological methods to the analysis of modern American society.

Rathje was dissatisfied with available research techniques for dealing with contemporary society, particularly the dependence on questionnaires because, like many anthropologists, Rathje realized they can be problematic: Respondents may lie or give answers that they think are truthful, but actually are not.

Archaeologists, of course, have methods designed to reconstruct human behavior from trash. Rathje reasoned, "Why can't we use these methods to study modern human behavior?"

How Do Archaeologists Collect Trash?

Although it would eventually investigate community trash and landfills around the country (see Figure 13-1), Rathje's Garbage Project began in Tucson, Arizona, in 1973. Garbage was picked up from randomly selected households, and a sampling design ensured that different socioeconomic neighborhoods were included. Student volunteers from the University of Arizona sorted the garbage on special tables provided by Tucson's sanitation department.

Courtesy Bill Rathje, photo by Jim Sugar

FIGURE 13-1 At California's Sunnyvale landfill, garbage project coordinators Bill Rathje (center) and Wilson Hughes (to Rathje's left) search for newspapers to date a landfill sample.

Student workers had appropriate inoculations and wore laboratory coats, surgical masks, and gloves. Students sorted garbage items into about 150 categories—under the larger headings of food, drugs, sanitation products, amusement and educational items, communication, and pet-related products—and recorded the data on forms for computer processing. The principles of archaeological classification provided objective, repeatable categories of data retrieval. The Garbage Project has involved hundreds of students and 60 participating organizations, recording more than 2 million items from 15,000 household refuse samples representing some 125 tons of garbage.

The Archaeology of Us

The Garbage Project has studied a number of contemporary social issues, including alcohol consumption. Years ago, the Pima County Health Department conducted interviews with a sample of Tucson households to discover how much beer people drank in a week. The sample was carefully chosen using conventional sociological procedures, and informant anonymity was assured. Many took the health department's information as accurate measures of the rate of alcohol consumption in Tucson.

How did the questionnaires stack up against the material evidence—the beer bottles and cans that Rathje's volunteers recorded? It turned out that a large discrepancy existed between front-door answers given to interviewers and back-door behavior reflected in the contents of the trash. Garbage cans don't lie, and the Garbage Project found significantly heavier beer consumption—in the form of more drinkers and higher rates of drinking—than was reported to the interviewers.

This should astound nobody. Many people drink more beer than they own up to. But the degree of distortion is noteworthy. The skewing, it turns out, correlates with socioeconomic factors. Low-income households typically distorted their interviews by reporting no beer consumption at all (low-income respondents may receive food stamps and, fearing the loss of support, might lie on surveys). Middle-income respondents did admit to drinking beer but significantly underreported the amount they actually consumed. These individuals probably gave an honest, though inaccurate, estimate because they don't perceive themselves to be "beer drinkers." These findings actually provided future studies with a way to correct for this inevitable skewing in the data from health questionnaires.

Myths about America's Landfills

The Garbage Project also has something to say about landfills. Everyone knows that we produce a lot of trash. But it's hard to say how much we're producing and of what it consists. Formal landfills did not become a significant feature on the American landscape until after 1945, when the country's rural population shifted to the industrial cities. Today, more than 70 percent of our garbage—180 million tons annually—goes into some 5500 active landfills across the country. Landfills are the largest human-made structures in the world; some are many times the size of Khufu's Pyramid near Cairo. The twentieth century's lasting monuments for posterity will be places like Staten Island's Fresh Kills Landfill, which even before rubble from the World Trade Center was deposited there, covered 3000 acres and contained 3 billion cubic feet of trash.

But space for landfills around large cities is rapidly dwindling; New York City, for example, trucks some of its garbage as far away as New Mexico. One reason is that old landfills were simply holes in the ground, while new landfills are complex places governed by a host of regulations and technologies to control toxic substances and methane gas. As a result, the cost of garbage disposal is skyrocketing—$15 billion a year and rising. This means that we need to know as much about landfills as possible.

But surprisingly, prior to Rathje's studies, little was known about what is actually in landfills and what actually happens there. Rathje argues that "if we are making such a large contribution to future generations, we should know exactly what we are bequeathing them. The only way to unlock these entombed secrets is to excavate." And so Rathje dug, and his research exposed a number of myths about landfills.

The Garbage Project used systematic archaeological methods to explore nine landfills across the United States, recovering about 12 metric tons of debris deposited between 1952 and 1989.

Landfills are generally covered with layers of earth on a set schedule, so they are conveniently stratified. And these strata can be chronologically ordered using newspapers and magazines. But the size of modern landfills did not allow Rathje to sample them with a trowel and dustpan. Instead, he used backhoe trenches (up to 25 feet deep) and a 3-foot-diameter auger equipped with steel teeth that can cut through anything, including a car chassis. Each auger load was hand-sorted, allowing the Garbage Project personnel to calculate what's in America's landfills.

Let's first consider what Americans *think* is in their landfills. The Garbage Project's surveys showed that people think disposable diapers, plastic bottles, and large appliances take up most space in landfills. But Rathje's excavations show that these three items *together* take up *less than 5 percent* of a landfill's volume. All kinds of plastics take up less than 15 percent of landfills. And the percent volume of plastic appears to be going down over time as manufacturers continually produce more "lightweight" packaging. Similarly, a survey conducted by the Audubon Society concluded that fast-food containers, polystyrene foam cups and packaging, and disposable diapers constituted most of the space, but Rathje's data show that these products *together* take up *less than 3 percent* of a landfill's volume.

applied science Research to acquire the knowledge necessary to solve a specific, recognized problem.

So, what's in landfills? What fills up the 3000 acres at Fresh Kills?

The largest component, it turns out, is *paper*—packaging, newspapers, telephone books, magazines, and mail-order catalogs. Paper takes up *40 to 50 percent* of the volume in American landfills. Despite the growing commitment to local recycling programs, the amount of paper is steadily rising—up from 35 percent in 1970. The rest of a landfill consists of, in descending order of volume, construction/demolition debris, metals, plastics, other materials, food and yard waste, and glass.

And here's the really bad news: Contrary to popular opinion, paper doesn't biodegrade in landfills. The Garbage Project has found 40-year-old newspapers, still fully readable (some with 40-year-old hot dogs wrapped in them). Our landfills are constructed on the belief that the nasty stuff inside will decompose on its own, like some kind of monumental compost heap.

But very little in our landfills actually biodegrades. Compost heaps work only when we chop up the organics, add fluids, and regularly churn the whole batch. This doesn't happen in landfills: Nothing is chopped up, fluids are often prohibited, and debris is compacted, not churned. Methane production, a by-product of decomposition, ceases 15 to 20 years after a landfill is closed, indicating that decomposition has stopped. But Rathje's excavations show that after 20 years, from one-third to one-half of all organic materials are still recognizable. These remaining organics may eventually break down, but only after many more decades, if not longer.

Most of our knowledge about solid waste disposal and landfill design comes from laboratory experiments, but the inside workings of landfills—what actually happens—have remained almost entirely unknown. Plenty of federal policies regulate landfills, but usually government planners work with "logical assumptions" about what landfills "should" contain.

Rathje doesn't assume, he digs. If we are interested in finding sensible ways to dispose of our trash, we need to know *exactly* what is being thrown away and what happens to it after it enters a landfill. By applying some archaeological approaches, Rathje has learned that many of the long-held assumptions about America's garbage are just that—rubbish.

Forensic Archaeology

When Thomas was a first-year curator at the American Museum of Natural History (in the early 1970s), he received a telephone call from a Sergeant McTigue of the New York City bomb squad. At the time, McTigue was working a series of New York City subway bombings. Nearly a dozen such attacks had occurred, killing one person and injuring several others. McTigue suspected that a political protest group was behind the bombings, and he had even identified a prime suspect ("I know the creep who's doin' it.").

Before he could make an arrest, however, McTigue had to establish that, in fact, a crime had been committed. Otherwise, "the perp's lawyer will claim that it was a natural gas explosion, and we can't prove otherwise." To clinch his case, McTigue needed to produce parts of the actual detonating device that had triggered the explosion. Knowing this, McTigue kept sorting through the debris left by each underground explosion. But he never could find what he was looking for. So "the perps" remained free to bomb again, which they did with alarming regularity.

As he was investigating yet another ruined subway station, McTigue finally admitted to himself that he was a cop—trained in standard law enforcement techniques—not an expert in sorting through trash and debris. But if he wasn't, who was? That's what archaeologists do, right?

That insight brought McTigue to Thomas's office. He explained the problem in simple terms: Suppose that he were to treat each crime scene as if it were an ancient archaeological site. What are the systematic, standardized techniques that archaeologists use to recover their data?

So McTigue and Thomas spent three hours working through Archaeology 101: how to establish a three-dimensional grid system and datum point, map surface finds, remove archaeological strata, and use sifters and flotation devices. They went over note taking, photography, and cataloging. Armed with this new investigative strategy, McTigue said "Thanks" and took off.

A few days later, there was the sergeant with his bomb squad on the 6 o'clock news. They were quickly yet efficiently digging and measuring, photographing and sifting the ruins of the latest subway bombing. Except for being a little older (and also heavily armed), the police looked no different from other novices on their first "dig class." After a week or two, Thomas got another call from Sergeant McTigue, and sure enough, they'd found the detonating device they were looking for. An arrest was quickly made, and New York's subway bombings came to an end.

This is an example of **forensic archaeology**—using established archaeological techniques to assist law enforcement agencies. This has become increasingly common in the past 20 years—although, as you will see, for some tragic reasons.

The Archaeology of Mass Disasters

As archaeologists become increasingly involved with criminal investigations domestically, they are also increasingly involved with international investigations. These are sad cases as they involve people who were lost in war, massacres, and assassinations. Professional archaeologists have joined investigatory teams to recover MIAs in Vietnam, excavate mass graves of missing people in South and Central America, and work with United Nations investigatory teams to collect data for tribunals and courts from massacre sites in Croatia, El Salvador, and Rwanda (see Figure 13-2). We'll just look at the last of these.

The violence in Rwanda began in April 1994, shortly after Rwandan president Juvenal Habyarimana was killed in an airline crash (allegedly caused by a missile). An ethnic war

FIGURE 13-2 Forensic archaeologist Clea Koff excavating a mass grave in Yugoslavia.

broke out between the Hutus and Tutsis, and within months more than 500,000 people were slaughtered. Many were rumored to be civilians, including women and children who were mercilessly clubbed, burned, or macheted to death. Seeking to determine whether the deaths resulted from civil war or genocide, United Nations investigators authorized archaeological investigations at key sites in central Rwanda.

One such excavation took place at Home St. Jean, where an estimated 4000 to 6000 people were killed. The Midwest Archeological Center, a branch of the National Park Service, assisted in the investigations at the massacre site. Working with forensic specialists, the archaeological team first mapped and photographed the site. They mapped the locations of surface skeletal materials, numbering each item and collecting it for analysis. Through this process, the team discovered six potential mass graves and began working on the largest. Once the stratigraphy had been determined through hand excavation of several test trenches, the overburden was removed with a backhoe. The archaeologists then exposed human remains by standard archaeological procedures and photographed, mapped, and removed them from the grave.

The archaeologists recovered several hundred sets of remains using these procedures, making this one of the largest exhumations ever conducted in the investigation of human rights violations. Autopsies were conducted to determine sex, age, kind of trauma, and cause of death. Decomposition is rapid in tropical environments, and many of the identifications were made using the techniques discussed in Chapter 9.

Cut marks on bones showed that many individuals were killed by machetes from behind, as if they were fleeing their attackers; cut marks on the bones of hands and forearms showed that some people were unmercifully killed by machete, their arms raised in a desperate effort to ward off the blows. These were clearly unarmed civilians, murdered as part of a program of genocide. The meticulous archaeological documentation provided critical evidence for the United Nations tribunal, which quickly handed down numerous indictments.

Archaeologists are playing an increasingly important role in the investigation and documentation of human rights abuses. In fact, as we write this, teams are at work uncovering mass graves in Iraq that could contain more than 300,000 bodies of people whose deaths Saddam Hussein allegedly ordered.

Archaeology and the World Trade Center

The story is all too well known: On September 11, 2001, two hijacked airplanes piloted by al-Qaeda terrorists slammed into the two 110-story towers. Within hours, the towers and neighboring buildings collapsed into a massive pile of concrete and twisted steel. Rescue efforts, which had begun even before the towers collapsed, continued for days afterward.

Emotionally taxing as the attack was, cleanup efforts had to begin immediately, and they continued, around the clock, for the next 7 months. The steel girders were recycled, but the rest of the debris—more than 1.7 million tons—was hauled off in a continuous stream of trucks to the Hudson River. Here the debris was loaded onto barges and taken to the Fresh Kills Landfill on Staten Island (the same landfill that Rathje had sampled years before).

This was no ordinary cleanup operation. Besides the sheer enormity of the task, the massive rubble pile was the world's largest crime scene. The debris had to be manually searched for the remains of victims, as well as for personal effects that could help identify people whose bodily remains might have simply vanished. The debris was run through sorters to remove large objects, then it was spread out on the ground and manually searched with rakes. Later, a conveyor belt operation sped up the search.

Within days of the disaster, Brooklyn College archaeologist Sophia Perdikaris put out an informal call to archaeologists for assistance. She recognized that although archaeologists usually deal with ancient artifacts, they are also skilled at finding small things in a vast matrix of dirt and rock, at recognizing and identifying fragments of human bone, and at recognizing broken fragments of objects for what they used to be.

Overwhelmed by the response, she asked the Society for American Archaeology for help. The society set up an online registrar and within a week had more than 300 individuals and organizations prepared to volunteer at the landfill. The FBI declined to take advantage of this resource, because they were already overwhelmed with police and fire personnel who had the appropriate clearance and hazardous materials training.

Nonetheless, this effort, and his personal experience with the World Trade Center disaster, inspired archaeologist Richard Gould (Brown University) to develop a volunteer

forensic archaeology The application of archaeological and bioarchaeological knowledge for legal purposes.

archaeological unit designed to assist at disaster scenes (Forensic Archaeology Recovery). Most archaeological excavations are pretty happy affairs, with plenty of banter and good-natured ribbing. The archaeology of disasters is quite different.

What Is Cultural Resource Management?

Archaeologists also have a critical role in helping to conserve the world's cultural heritage. Threats to this heritage come from those who loot archaeological sites for personal gain and from relentless development around the globe. Nearly everywhere you look, you see bridges, dams, roads, and buildings under construction. Pipelines, power lines, highways, and fiber optic cables slice across the global landscape. New roads pave over the past, and as new houses spring up, archaeological remains are carted away in dump trucks. Over the years, governments around the world have passed laws to protect their nations' cultural heritage in archaeological sites, historic buildings, and landscapes.

In this country, the term **cultural resource management (CRM)** describes the brand of archaeology related to compliance with legislation that protects cultural resources. It is difficult to emphasize the importance of CRM to contemporary archaeology. Prior to the 1960s, nearly all American archaeologists worked for universities and museums. Today, the number of archaeologists in the United States vastly exceeds those working in the 1960s. Well over half of them work in the framework of CRM; in fact, CRM projects account for about 90 percent of field archaeology conducted today in the United States.

How did this change come about?

Early Efforts to Protect America's Cultural Heritage

Concern with historic preservation began in the earliest days of the United States. In 1789, for example, wealthy Bostonians formed the Massachusetts Historical Society in response to the destruction of John Hancock's house. The society became a watchdog to ensure that other historically significant properties were not lost. And, in 1813, the federal government ordered the preservation of Independence Hall in Philadelphia. But a *systematic* concern for preserving America's cultural heritage developed rather slowly, coincident with the more broadly based environmental preservation movement. Both movements flourished in the 1960s and 1970s, but their roots extend back another century.

America's environmental movement can be traced to such nineteenth-century writers as Henry David Thoreau, John Muir, and Ernest Thompson Seton, each of whom inspired generations to notice the natural world around them and to respond to increasing human impact on the landscape. Some worked to save the continent's indigenous wildlife, while others worked to preserve wild places.

Archaeology and the preservation of cultural and historic properties were swept along with the conservation movement nearly from its beginning. One of the first sites to be protected was Ohio's Serpent Mound, a 1400-foot-long snake effigy mound. Treasure hunters had heavily damaged the site by the 1870s, and it was probably not pristine even when Squier and Davis (the Moundbuilder investigators introduced in Chapter 2) mapped it some 40 years earlier. Frederic Putnam (1839–1915), of Harvard University's Peabody Museum, realized that the nation would soon lose this unique site. So, with the help of wealthy Bostonians, he saved it the old-fashioned way: He bought it. Harvard University owned the site until 1900, when it transferred title to the Ohio Historical Society, which owns and maintains the site today. (This "old-fashioned" approach still saves sites today through the Archaeological Conservancy, which has preserved more than 400 sites in 41 states.)

Although this concern for preserving the past was certainly sincere, the late nineteenth-century approach was piecemeal, and the looting and destruction of archaeological sites proceeded at an alarming pace. The cliff dwellings in the Mesa Verde area of southwestern Colorado (see Figure 13-3) were especially hard-hit. Tucked beneath massive arches in sandstone cliffs, the large pueblos of the Mesa Verde region—and the tens of thousands of well-preserved artifacts they contain—had been protected from the elements since the dwellings were abandoned in the late thirteenth century. This fact did not escape the notice of skilled pothunters working the area, who tore the roofs off structures and blasted holes through the stone and adobe walls to let sunlight in. Six-hundred-year-old roof beams disappeared in the looters' campfires, hundreds of purloined pots appeared on an expanding curios market, and sacred kivas were damaged beyond repair.

To prevent such destruction, in 1906, President Theodore Roosevelt signed into law the **Antiquities Act**, which contained three important provisions:

- The act made it illegal to excavate or collect remains from archaeological sites on public lands without a permit from the relevant government agency.
- The act stipulated that permits would be granted only to museums, universities, and other scientific or education institutions "with a view to increasing knowledge," and that objects gathered would only be "for permanent preservation in public museums."
- The act invested the president with authority to create national monuments on federal lands containing "historic landmarks, historic and prehistoric structures, and other objects of historic or scientific interest."

The Antiquities Act of 1906 became the foundation of all subsequent archaeological legislation.

Historic Preservation Comes of Age

A larger portion of the American public—many aroused by Rachel Carson's *Silent Spring* (1962)—came to recognize

FIGURE 13-3 The site known as Cliff Palace, in Mesa Verde National Park, was occupied in the late 1200s; it was among the first archaeological sites in the United States to be protected by the government.

that wilderness and wildlife refuges alone could not stem the effects of pollution. By the early 1970s, an environmental movement was in full swing. The voter appeal of these popular movements was not lost on legislators, and many of them became "conservationists" as well. In fact, sufficient power came down on the side of the ecologists for laws to be drafted protecting the *nonrenewable resources* of the nation.

When most people think of nonrenewable resources, they think of redwoods, whooping cranes, and baby seals. Others think of energy-related assets, such as oil, coal, and uranium. But most legislators have a legal background, and in the course of legally defining national resources, they realized that properties of historic value must be included. After all, they reasoned, how many Monticellos do we have? Aren't archaeological sites nonrenewable resources too?

The concern with historic preservation was largely about the destruction of historic buildings through urban renewal and the construction of national highways in the 1950s and 1960s. Nonetheless, archaeological sites were included in historic preservation legislation and are now considered **cultural resources**, to be legally protected just like redwoods, whooping cranes, and shale oil fields. That legal protection came through various laws and established the framework within which archaeology in the United States operates today. The most important of these is the National Historic Preservation Act of 1966.

The National Historic Preservation Act

The Antiquities Act is a short, one-page piece of legislation, intelligible to just about anyone. The **National Historic Preservation Act (NHPA)**, on the other hand, is lengthy, tedious, and shot through with bureaucratic jargon. But every archaeologist working in the United States must be intimately familiar with its details.

cultural resource management (CRM) A professional field that conducts activities, including archaeology, related to compliance with legislation aimed at conserving cultural resources.

Antiquities Act Passed in 1906, this act (1) requires federal permits before excavating or collecting artifacts on federal land, (2) established a permitting process, and (3) gave the president the authority to create national monuments.

cultural resources Physical features, both natural and artificial, associated with human activity, including sites, structures, and objects possessing significance in history, architecture, or human development. Cultural properties are unique and nonrenewable resources.

National Historic Preservation Act (NHPA) Passed in 1966, this act created (1) the National Register of Historic Places, (2) the Advisory Council on Historic Preservation, and (3) State Historic Preservation Offices, as well as (4) a process to mitigate the impact of development; it also requires that government agencies provide good stewardship of their cultural resources.

The NHPA formally stated the policy that lay behind the 1906 Antiquities Act: "It shall be the policy of the Federal Government . . . to foster conditions under which our modern society and our prehistoric and historic resources can exist in productive harmony." Three years later, Congress made this policy even more explicit in the National Environmental Policy Act (NEPA): "It is the continuing policy of the Federal Government" to "preserve important historic, cultural, and natural aspects of our national heritage."

Whereas previous legislation approached historic preservation in a piecemeal fashion and was largely reactive, the NHPA created a systematic, nationwide program of historic preservation. It has therefore had far-reaching effects on American archaeology. The act created State Historic Preservation Offices, headed by State Historic Preservation Officers. Subsequent amendments created Tribal Historic Preservation Offices on Indian reservations as well; many tribes, such as the Cherokee, Hopi, Zuni, and Navajo, now have large and successful historic preservation programs.

Historic preservation offices are tasked with creating state (or reservation) inventories of archaeological and historic properties, assisting federal agencies in complying with the State Historic Preservation Act, evaluating national register nominations (to give select sites special protection), and serving as repositories for resource information, such as state site files. The NHPA also created the national Advisory Council on Historic Preservation, which promotes the preservation of the nation's cultural resources and which advises the president and Congress on preservation policy.

The Archaeological Resources Protection Act

The Antiquities Act made it illegal to collect and/or excavate a site on federal property without a permit, and the penalties for violators were pretty stiff for 1906: "a sum of not more than five hundred dollars" and/or imprisonment "for a period of not more than ninety days." But these sanctions mean little in today's world, where a single Mimbres painted bowl or Mississippian vessel can fetch thousands or even tens of thousands of dollars on the illegal antiquities market. Despite the Antiquities Act's intentions, looting and site vandalism continue to destroy America's cultural heritage. The federal government estimates that of the 2 million archaeological sites presently recorded in the American Southwest, between 50 and 90 percent have already been looted to some degree. And as off-road sports become more popular and open access to remote regions of federal land, large-scale looting of archaeological sites became a major threat to the preservation of America's cultural heritage.

The **Archaeological Resources Protection Act (ARPA)** of 1979 tried to change this, making it a felony "to excavate, remove, damage, or otherwise alter or deface or attempt to excavate, remove, damage or otherwise alter or deface any archaeological resources located on public lands or Indian lands" without a permit. ARPA also made it illegal to sell, receive, or transport artifacts illegally removed from federal lands. The penalty for violating ARPA is a fine of up to $250,000 and/or up to five years in prison. (Collecting arrowheads from the surface, however, was specifically exempted and is not a punishable activity in the act.) The government can also confiscate any equipment used to loot the sites, including vehicles.

ARPA also allows judges to assess civil penalties that can take into account what it would have cost to professionally excavate a damaged site. This can result in large penalties. Looters can move more dirt in a weekend than an archaeologist would excavate in an entire season, or two or three. Add to that the cost of chronometric dates and of faunal, macrobotanical, and geoarchaeological analyses, and the "archaeological value" can be high.

These penalties may seem stiff to some people. But looted sites are lost forever; they cannot be replaced, and it is difficult to put a value on such a loss. Consider also that many looters are often involved in other illegal activities as well—fencing stolen goods, drugs, burglary, and so on. Some have been videotaped looting sites with automatic rifles slung over a shoulder. ARPA, in fact, has proven to be a way to track down some serious criminals.

Even with the added protection of ARPA, it is difficult to police millions of acres of federal land, so looting continues to destroy the nation's cultural heritage. Numerous federal and private agencies have taken aggressive anti-looting measures, such as site monitoring (using motion-sensitive cameras in some cases), substantial fencing, and more diligent law enforcement. The successful "Adopt a Site" program pairs motivated avocational archaeologists with particularly vulnerable sites that benefit from continued monitoring. Still, vandalism and looting continue to be the major threats to American archaeology today.

What about State and Private Land?

ARPA applies to federal land. And some states have laws that cover cultural resources on state land. But these laws do not apply to private land. Many private landowners are wary of archaeologists because they believe that if they find something significant on their property, the government can confiscate the artifacts or even their land. In some countries, this is true. In England or Mexico, for example, so-called treasure laws give the government ownership of all subsurface historical resources. But this is not true in the United States. No matter how significant or remarkable a site may be, if it is on private property, it belongs to the landowner. The government cannot take it away. The only exception concerns human burials. In some states, the *intentional* destruction of a burial, regardless of its age, is a violation of state law—even if that burial is on your property.

The sanctity of private land in the United States can be frustrating because the lack of legislation means that the commercial mining of terrestrial (and underwater) sites for artifacts is often completely legal or subject to only a minor penalty. As a result, important archaeological sites on private land can be rapidly destroyed. Archaeologists in Kentucky learned this lesson the hard way.

FIGURE 13-4 Several hundred burials at the Slack Farm site, a fifteenth-century Mississippian burial ground, were looted and destroyed in the 1980s.

The Slack Farm Incident

Slack Farm sits on a pleasant stretch of rich bottomland along the Ohio River in northern Kentucky. In the fifteenth century, the Ohio River Valley was the center of a thriving chiefdom society, supported by maize agriculture. Several large sites, complete with flat-topped temple mounds such as those we described at Moundville (see Chapter 10), were the centers of large populations. Some of these Mississippian communities may have been even larger than the small towns that lie along the river today.

Prior to 1987, the Slack family knew of and protected a large fifteenth-century Mississippian site on their property. But when they sold the farm, the new owner was uninterested in protecting the site; in fact, he leased the property for six months to two men for $10,000. These two individuals, in turn, subleased portions of the land to eight others. The leasers' intent was not to grow tobacco or maize, but to mine artifacts.

Using everything from shovels to bulldozers, the ten men mined their shares and paraded the skulls and pots they recovered from the 500-year-old cemetery around town. Within a few weeks, the field looked like a war zone—pockmarked with craters (see Figure 13-4). Human skeletal remains were strewn about alongside beer cans as the looters made a mad rush for valuable artifacts.

Someone in town finally alerted the police, but they could only charge the men with "desecration of a venerated object," which at the time carried a penalty of $500 and a maximum of six months in prison. Some of the pots they had found were probably sold on the black market for thousands of dollars, so the fine was a mere annoyance. Archaeologists later determined that although only about 10 to 15 percent of the cemetery had been disturbed, more than 600 graves had been disinterred.

Outrage in the Native American community and the public at large brought a halt to the looting, and archaeologists tried to assess the damage and retrieve some information (all the skeletal remains were reburied in 1988). But because the crime was only a misdemeanor, no one would prosecute, and all ten men walked away. As a result, Kentucky revised its burial laws, upgrading the penalty for intentionally desecrating a grave (including those on private property) from a misdemeanor to a felony.

Sadly, the looting of archaeological sites on private land will continue unabated until the market for artifacts disappears. Given that this is unlikely, the alternative is that an educated public must simply refuse to accept it, as at Slack Farm.

International Efforts to Protect Cultural Resources

Here's the grim truth: Looting of archaeological sites in the United States has reached epidemic proportions, and the international problem is even worse. In fact, illegal trafficking in antiquities *may be second only to the drug trade* in international crime.

The looting of other countries' archaeology has been going on for some time. One well-known example is the **Rosetta Stone**, a large basalt tablet inscribed in three scripts that allowed French linguist Jean-François Champollion to

Archaeological Resources Protection Act (ARPA) Passed in 1979, this act (1) prohibits the excavation or removal of artifacts from federal property without a permit, (2) prohibits the sale, exchange, or transport of artifacts acquired illegally from federal property, and (3) increased the penalties for violations of the act over those of the Antiquities Act.

Rosetta Stone A black basalt stone tablet found in 1799 that bears an inscription in two forms of ancient Greek and ancient Egyptian. By working from the Greek texts, scholars were able to decipher the ancient Egyptian hieroglyphs.

WHAT DOES IT MEAN TO me?

Should Antiquities Be Returned to the Country of Origin?

The world's major museums contain artifacts that come from many different countries. The majority of these were acquired through legal channels. But some pieces have more checkered pasts. Among these are the Parthenon marbles.

The Acropolis is a limestone plateau that overlooks modern Athens. Temples and shrines adorn the plateau, among them the Parthenon, built between 447 and 438 BC and dedicated to the goddess Athena. It has been a sacred place in Greek culture for 2500 years and has served as a Catholic church, a mosque, and even a weapons depot.

The current problem began about 1800, when Thomas Bruce (better known as Lord Elgin) was British ambassador to Turkey (at the time, Turkey ruled Greece as part of the Ottoman Empire). Elgin removed statues and portions of the 75-meter marble frieze from the Parthenon, sending them to England. Elgin was later captured by the French and spent two years in prison, during which time the marbles were kept at his English estate, sometimes in the coal shed. Elgin spent most of his fortune removing the marbles and other Greek art treasures. Divorced, ill, and in debt, he sold the marbles to the British Museum in 1816, for a fraction of what they cost him. He died penniless in 1841.

Greece has demanded the return of the marbles ever since. The late Greek minister of culture, Melina Mercouri, argued that they symbolize Greece itself, and many Greeks feel that the sculptures belong in Greece.

The British Museum has countered that the museum acquired the marbles legally, has done nothing wrong, and that *any* return of antiquities smacks of "cultural fascism." It is true that the museum purchased the sculptures legally, and Lord Elgin always claimed he had permission from the Turkish government to remove them.

But Greece points out that the Turks, as occupiers of Greece, did not have the right to give Greek patrimony away. And, in fact, the surviving paperwork suggests that Elgin had permission only to draw, make casts, and do some small excavations; other evidence suggests that Elgin abused his political position and used bribes to remove the marbles. The British Museum counters that Elgin saved these priceless treasures from the decay that political violence and pollution have visited upon the statues that remain on the Acropolis.

Britain argues that the marbles are now part of global, not just Greek, patrimony and that they deserve to be in the British Museum, where people from around the world can enjoy them. If it returned the marbles to Greece, the British Museum argues, the floodgates would open, myriad countries would demand the return of art objects, major museums would be empty, and the world would have far less access to these cultural treasures.

Greece points out that pollution is now under control in Athens and that conservation measures protect the sculptures (and that, in fact, the British Museum itself damaged them decades ago by using harsh cleaning solutions and chisels on them). The marbles themselves would be housed in a museum at the base of the Acropolis, as open to the world as the British Museum.

Should treasures like the Parthenon's marbles be removed from "your" museum and returned to their country of origin? Should we take into account the (often nefarious) ways in which artifacts were acquired in the past, or are we generating a tidal wave of litigation that will ultimately serve no one well? Do we consider whether the country of origin is capable of caring for artifacts by itself? Do we consider current national borders or those that existed at the time of the taking? Returning treasures to the country of origin seems to encourage a balkanization of the ancient world that will not serve archaeology or humanity well. But consider this: Seeking to defend the British Museum's claim to the marbles, the Parliamentary Assembly of the Council of Europe passed a resolution stressing "the unity of the European cultural heritage." Does keeping the marbles in Britain achieve this goal better than keeping them in Greece?

decipher Egyptian hieroglyphics. It was found by a French soldier in 1799, during Napoleon's conquest of Egypt. Fortunes change quickly in war, however, and by 1801, the Rosetta Stone was in the British Museum, where it is today. Many countries today demand the return of their artifacts; Yale University, for example, under threat of a lawsuit by Peru, has agreed to return artifacts excavated in the early twentieth century from the Peruvian site of Machu Picchu (see "What Does It Mean to Me? Should Antiquities Be Returned to the Country of Origin?").

Because the conservation of archaeology has been linked to the environmental movement, you might think a public sensitive to issues such as global warming, forest conservation, and biodiversity would be similarly aware of the international trade in looted artifacts. But this is not the case. Thousands of graves are looted in China each year (despite the fact that the Chinese government has stiff penalties against looting). Maya stelae are cut apart with rock saws and the glyphs sold individually. Thieves cut or chip rock art off caves and cliffs in North and South America, Australia, and Africa and hustle them away to waiting buyers. Armed looters ransack Peruvian tombs for gold; Spanish shipwrecks are plundered for silver; graves of World War I dead are robbed of medals and military paraphernalia. There is literally no place in the world safe from looting. At the present rate, there will be precious little left by the end of this century.

Responsible museums today refuse to accept artifacts illegally imported from the country of origin or to display illegitimate artifacts already in their collections. Many, in fact, have returned artifacts in their collections that the museum discovered had been acquired illegally. The American Museum of Natural History, for example, forbids curators from authenticating or appraising artifacts, and its Museum Shop does not sell antiquities.

Like the drug trade, the illegal trade in antiquities is hard to stop as long as there is a market. We've learned this lesson many times, including in Iraq, and today, Egypt.

The Thieves of Baghdad

The power of the illegal international antiquities market was driven home on April 11, 2003, a few days after the U.S. military entered Baghdad. Although the Pentagon had promised to protect Iraqi cultural institutions, they left the Baghdad Museum unguarded. The looters smashed some artifacts, and destroyed much of the documentation. Although museum personnel had moved many of the more precious artifacts—most of the gold, for example—to secure bank vaults, many irreplaceable artifacts were stolen.

An investigation headed by Colonel Matthew Bogdanos, United States Marine Corps, concluded that 40 items were stolen from the main galleries, along with more than 13,000 items from storage rooms. As of March 2008, many artifacts had been recovered, most through an amnesty program (and Syria just returned more than 700 pieces), but others were found through raids or customs inspections in Iraq, Jordan, Italy, Great Britain, and the United States. Many of these items were outside of Iraq within days of their theft. And some 4000 to 7000 artifacts are still missing (the precise number is unknown because many records were destroyed).

Although the museum was ransacked by local people looking for anything they might sell, Bogdanos's investigation found evidence of professional thieves with intimate knowledge of the museum—and keys. It was an inside job, and the thieves were selective in what they took. In the basement, for example, the only storage room entered was that containing a huge collection of ancient coins. Fortunately, the thieves dropped the keys to the cabinets and lost them in the unlit room (the electricity was off by this time; Bogdanos later found the keys). The looters lit a fire for light and, before the smoke drove them out, snatched 103 boxes that contained some 10,000 cylinder seals, pins, beads, pendants, and necklaces.

Other Iraqi museums were also hit, and archaeological sites were attacked by armed looters—many now look like bomb-scarred battlefields. One can hardly blame a poverty-stricken Iraqi farmer for exploiting an opportunity to make ten years' worth of wages in a night of digging. Instead, the blame rests with wealthy buyers in developed nations. They are the ones that drive this destruction, who encourage a country to rob itself of its cultural patrimony and to destroy irreplaceable records of human history.

What Can Be Done?

To stop the global traffic in illegally acquired antiquities, many nations (including the United States) have signed the **UNESCO Convention of 1970** with the unwieldy but accurate name of "Means of Prohibiting and Preventing the Illicit Import, Export, and Transfer of Ownership of Cultural Property." The 100 countries that have signed this convention agree, among other things, to put into place the legislation and administration to:

- Regulate the import and export of cultural objects
- Forbid their nations' museums from acquiring illegally exported cultural objects
- Establish ways to inform other nations when illegally exported objects are found within a country's borders
- Return or otherwise provide restitution of cultural objects stolen from public institutions
- Establish a register of art dealers and require them to register

In keeping with the convention, the United States has passed laws such as the 1983 Cultural Property Implementation Act and signed treaties with several countries that specifically prohibit the importing of artifacts without established "pedigrees" into the country. Some of these treaties "grandfather in" artifacts excavated before the treaty's date; this means that an importer must now prove that artifacts were excavated prior to a treaty's date or were otherwise obtained in ways not prohibited by the treaty. As more countries establish such treaties, it will become increasingly difficult for someone to import illegally acquired antiquities. And these treaties do work. In 2003, an appeals court upheld the conviction of Frederick Schultz, an art dealer who had been convicted under the National Stolen Property Act of conspiring to sell artifacts acquired illegally from Egypt, including the head of a statue of Amenhotep III, which he had sold for $1.2 million.

UNESCO Convention of 1970 This international agreement requires that signers create legislation and the administrative structure to (1) regulate the import and export of cultural objects, (2) forbid their nations' museums from acquiring illegally exported cultural objects, (3) establish ways to inform other nations when illegally exported objects are found within a country's borders, (4) return or otherwise provide restitution of cultural objects stolen from public institutions, and (5) establish a register of art dealers and require them to register.

The Native American Graves Protection and Repatriation Act of 1990

So far, we have discussed government responses to the need to conserve cultural resources around the globe. But in 1990, a piece of legislation was passed whose purpose was actually to *rebury* some of those cultural resources that other legislation protects and preserves. The **Native American Graves Protection and Repatriation Act (NAGPRA)** moves cultural resource law away from the area of preservation into the field of human rights legislation.

In 1988, the American Association of Museums told the Senate Select Committee on Indian Affairs that 43,306 individual Native American skeletons were held in 163 museums in the United States. Some of these were skulls removed from battlefields—including heads taken from the 1864 Sand Creek Massacre in Colorado, where soldiers and militiamen massacred some 150 Cheyenne and Arapaho, mostly women and children. Native Americans pointed out that although Indian people represent less than 1 percent of the U.S. population, their bones constitute more than 50 percent of the skeletal collection in the Smithsonian Institution.

Many senators were shocked—as they should have been. Although archaeologists had nothing to do with decapitating fallen Indian warriors, they had been aware for 20 years that many Native Americans were upset by the excavation, analysis, and display of their ancestors' skeletal remains. Walter Echo-Hawk (Pawnee) said "We don't expect everyone to share our beliefs; but it doesn't take the wisdom of Solomon to understand that our dead deserve to rest in peace. . . . All we're asking for is a little common decency. . . . We're not asking for anything but to bury our dead." Such statements spurred the Senate into action and brought an end to decades of wrangling that pitted museums, universities, and federal agencies against Native American tribes. In 1990, NAGPRA was signed into law.

NAGPRA provides for the protection of Indian graves on federal and tribal lands and prohibits the commercial sale or interstate transport of Native American bodies or body parts. It developed some very specific rules about who owns Native American remains excavated after 1990. It also required that all institutions that receive federal funds inventory all human skeletal remains held in their collections. Those inventories showed that American institutions held more than 117,000 sets of human remains, most from Native American burials. This inventory covered not only skeletal remains but also *funerary objects* (objects placed with a body as part of funerary ceremony), *sacred objects* (ceremonial objects necessary for current practice of traditional Native American religions), and *objects of cultural patrimony* (objects that have ongoing cultural importance to a tribe and that were "inalienable" at the time they left the tribe's possession—that is, no one had the right to give them away).

Once the inventories were completed, NAGPRA then required institutions to consult with appropriate Native American tribes determined to be "culturally affiliated" with the remains and objects regarding their repatriation. As of October 2003, 27,777 sets of human remains had been determined to be culturally affiliated and offered to the relevant tribes for repatriation, along with about 636,386 funerary objects, 1185 sacred objects, and 267 objects of cultural patrimony. Critical to the disposition of these remains and those found in the future is the definition of "Native American" and the concept of "cultural affiliation" in the law.

Native Americans and Cultural Affiliation

Once an institution determines that remains and covered objects are Native American, they must decide whether they are to be repatriated. But to which tribe? Many tribes expressed a desire to have only *their* specific tribal ancestors returned to them. The Eastern Shoshone on the Wind River Reservation in Wyoming do not wish their ancestral remains repatriated because they question the accuracy of museum records. The Blackfeet do not want remains returned unless the museum is *absolutely positive* the remains are Blackfeet, because they don't want responsibility for the remains of a traditional enemy.

And tribes have different ideas about what should be done with the remains. The Zuni asked that skeletons identified as Zuni remain under museum curation. California's Chumash, after having reclaimed their ancestral remains through repatriation, elected to preserve them in their own repository. Many other tribes rebury or cremate repatriated remains. These differences of opinion meant that the government needed a procedure to decide which tribes have control over which remains.

That decision rests on the concept of **cultural affiliation**. Tribes that are culturally affiliated with particular burials, funerary and sacred objects, and objects of cultural patrimony are entitled to have those burials and objects repatriated to them. If remains or objects cannot be culturally affiliated under the law, then they are classed as "unaffiliated." NAGPRA does not say what happens to those remains; for the time being, they are in limbo and remain in the museums.

Although some archaeologists remain flatly opposed to NAGPRA, the vast majority recognize that the statute has forced a dialogue that was long overdue. But this does not mean that answers come easily.

Is Kennewick Native American?

NAGPRA's definition of "Native American" is "of, or relating to, a tribe, people, or culture that is indigenous to the United States." According to the courts, the key

RAPID REVIEW

Key Legislative Acts and Their Effects

1906 Antiquities Act

- Made unpermitted collection of artifacts from federal lands illegal
- Approved permits only to scientific or education institutions to increase knowledge; artifacts must reside in public institutions
- Gave the president the authority to create national monuments on federal lands
- Began U.S. protection of archaeological sites

1966 National Historic Preservation Act

- Mandated inventory of sites on government property
- Mandated that federal government consider effects of actions on federal land or federally supported projects
- Created the National Register of Historic Places
- Created State Historic Preservation Offices
- Made site protection the official U.S. policy

1979 Archaeological Resources Protection Act

- Increased penalties for removal of artifacts from federal lands
- Made illegal the interstate transport or sale of artifacts illegally obtained from federal lands
- Added teeth to existing legislation to halt looting and vandalism

1990 Native American Graves Protection and Repatriation Act

- Mandated inventory of institutions' human skeletal remains
- Required that institutions consult with tribes and offer to repatriate culturally affiliated remains, funerary objects, sacred objects, and objects of cultural patrimony
- Gave Native Americans a large role in disposition of artifacts and skeletal remains

word in the definition, believe it or not, is the word "is." The courts argued that the definition requires showing a "general relationship to a *present-day* tribe, people, or culture" (emphasis added). Kennewick, the courts pointed out, had no artifacts associated with it; and, because it had eroded from a riverbank, the nature of any burial ritual, which is a cultural act, is gone. Thus, the judge concluded that the culture of Kennewick Man "is unknown and apparently unknowable."

Recall from the prologue that Kennewick's cranial morphology—the shape of his skull—is quite different from that of later Native Americans. No matter how you measure it, the Kennewick skull looks more like that of southeast Asians, Polynesians, or Japan's Ainu, not other Native Americans. For this reason, and although many archaeologists disagreed, the courts declared that Kennewick was not Native American.

Can Kennewick Be Culturally Affiliated with Modern Tribes?

Assuming that Kennewick is Native American, the next question is whether he can be culturally affiliated with tribes who claim such an affiliation. NAGPRA's definition of cultural affiliation is "a relationship of shared group identity which can be reasonably traced historically or prehistorically between a present-day tribe or Native Hawaiian organization and an identifiable earlier group." This is a more rigorous definition than that of *Native American*.

Cultural affiliation requires that we establish an identifiable earlier group. With only one burial and no grave goods, it is impossible for archaeologists to identify Kennewick's social group. That alone means that Kennewick cannot meet the requirement of cultural affiliation under the law.

In addition, archaeology tells us that the lifeways of Native Americans who lived on the Columbia Plateau for the past 13,000 years have dramatically changed over time—for example, in the style of projectile points and houses that were used, in burial rituals, in economy and trade patterns. In this particular case, archaeology cannot reasonably trace shared group identity over time.

What about Native American oral history? Is it possible that oral traditions preserve eyewitness accounts of the past? For example, oral traditions among Columbia Plateau tribes include tales in which bison turn to stone or mythical beings create valleys and hills by dragging huge fish across the landscape. Clearly, the tales do not relate eyewitness

Native American Graves Protection and Repatriation Act (NAGPRA) Passed in 1990, this act (1) protects Indian graves on federal and tribal lands, (2) recognizes tribal authority over treatment of unmarked graves, (3) prohibits the commercial selling of native dead bodies, (4) requires an inventory and repatriation of human remains held by the federal government and institutions that receive federal funding, (5) requires these same institutions to return inappropriately acquired sacred objects and other important communally owned property to native owners, and (6) sets up a process to determine ownership of human remains found on federal and tribal property after November 16, 1990.

cultural affiliation In NAGPRA, "a relationship of a shared group identity which can be reasonably traced historically or prehistorically between a present-day Indian tribe or Native Hawaiian organization and an identifiable earlier group."

PROFILE OF AN ARCHAEOLOGIST

A Cultural Resource Management Archaeologist

William Doelle is the president of Desert Archaeology, Inc., a cultural resource management firm in Tucson, Arizona, and the Center for Desert Archaeology, a nonprofit corporation that promotes the study and preservation of archaeological sites in the American Southwest. Reprinted by permission.

© William Doelle

William Doelle

"Holy <expletive deleted>!" It was the only appropriate response to the cream-colored stone tool that had just caught my eye.

I was walking the centerline of a half-built road. It had been under construction, but representatives from the Tohono O'odham Nation in southern Arizona had protested when they observed road machinery cutting through a buried Hohokam village ("Hohokam" means "those who have gone" in the O'odham language and refers to village sites dating after AD 700). Work was halted, and the slow process of legal compliance begun.

A competitive bid process awarded an archaeological contract to my young firm. We were in our second week of fieldwork when the cream-colored tool—a Clovis point—was found. Unable to identify any intact Clovis-age deposits, however, we concluded that Hohokam farmers who lived at what we called the Valencia site had encountered this spear point in their fields and brought it back to their village.

This first work on the Valencia site on Tucson's south side took place in 1983. Despite the construction, our excavations yielded some 25 intact Hohokam pithouses. In the last 20 years, I have conducted six additional projects at this site, each one expanding our knowledge of the Valencia community between AD 400 and 1200. An overview of that work provides a cross-section of the diversity in modern cultural resource management, or CRM—the professional area where I have made a living since 1974.

Our 1983 fieldwork was constrained to a narrow strip less than 20 meters wide and some 500 meters long. While we were in the field, we focused on that limited space because we had a great deal to accomplish in a very brief time—the bulldozers were waiting for us to finish. After the fieldwork, three of us volunteered to complete a map that put the site in a fuller context. I had been aware that there was a prehistoric ballcourt just 50 meters from our excavation, but only with the complete map did the full settlement plan make sense. There was an open, central plaza, surrounded by low trash mounds that were the surface indications of residential areas.

It wasn't long before we conducted an intensive surface collection of the entire site, refined our initial map, and did further excavations to define the site's southern boundary. Archaeologists had improved the ceramic typology, and we used it to plot distributions of ceramics by time periods as short as 50 years. It was clear that initial settlement had clustered around the ballcourt and plaza, but around AD 1000 the community became more dispersed, with houses scattered along a mile of the Santa Cruz River. Two decades later, there is still debate about the reasons for this change. Were ballcourts abandoned around AD 1000, or did they last for another century? Regardless, the pattern at the Valencia site has since been shown to hold at all other ballcourt villages in Tucson.

The next big research opportunity came along in 1991. The local community college planned a new campus in an area that we thought was outside the Valencia site, but reexamination showed that to be wrong. So, we carried out a surface collection and testing program to provide information for the college. As it turned out, this area held an earlier, more subtle pithouse site, almost certainly the ancestral village for Valencia. Our work in 1991 helped planners to place high-impact features like new two-story buildings off the main occupation area. In the winter of 1997–98, when we conducted preconstruction excavations, we documented more than 100 early pithouses and projected a total of around 400. The arrangement of houses around a large central plaza provided the excavators with information to develop a refined model of early Hohokam villages.

My company had grown from one full-time employee in 1983 to 35 in 1997. Thus, I was largely an observer in the research process. I work on management issues like an open house for the community college, tours by the cultural committees from the Tohono O'odham Nation, and writing grant proposals so that things like storm sewers do not destroy archaeological sites. I keep watch over the rapid development of Tucson and work with various groups—such as the community college, the city, the Tohono O'odham, the archaeological community, park planners, and landscape architects—to develop plans to preserve archaeological sites.

I have found that the opportunities to be creative are tremendous in CRM, and I plan to pursue at least another decade as head of my CRM firm before retiring. These opportunities are further enhanced through the nonprofit Center for Desert Archaeology. Through grants, endowment building, and a membership program, this institution pursues a mission of preservation archaeology. We balance research, public outreach, and stewardship in our programs in the American Southwest and Mexican Northwest. Archaeology in the private sector presents unique challenges, but I have found it to offer great rewards.

accounts; they could be explanations of how a landscape came to be using observations made on that landscape long after the natural events that formed it actually took place. Oral traditions may be useful in some cases, but in Kennewick's case, they cannot meet the legal standard of tracing "shared group identity" across time.

Taking all these data into account, the judge decided that, under the requirements of NAGPRA, Kennewick cannot be culturally affiliated with the tribes who claimed affiliation.

The Legacy of Kennewick Man

Some archaeologists point out that NAGPRA is problematic because it employs the Western notion that "identity" is fixed at birth (and hence immutable). In Western culture, one is Irish or English, Spanish or Basque, French or German—implying that ethnicity has hard boundaries, both spatially and temporally. Assuming that such boundaries were "natural," the American government created them among Indians through the treaty and reservation process.

Those hard boundaries are now codified in NAGPRA. It was not the judge's place to decide whether NAGPRA was right or wrong in its definition, but only to determine how that definition ought to be implemented in the Kennewick case. Given the law's definition and the available evidence, there is no "preponderance of evidence" to argue in favor of a cultural affiliation between Kennewick and the tribes who claimed identity with him.

But NAGPRA does not define what is meant by "identity," and this creates some discordance between conclusions reached under NAGPRA and Native American sensibilities.

NAGPRA assumes that human groups have a distinct point of formation, yet few actually do. Cultures change over time, even if we ignore the effect of migrations. NAGPRA further assumes that as one moves back in time, one encounters some point at which shared group identity is lost. It is lost not because the archaeological record is too poor to trace it (although that is often the case); it is lost because the differences between the modern tribe and the past group are so numerous or large that members of the modern and ancient groups would not share an identity—the ancient and modern peoples, if they could somehow meet one another in time, would not see each other as being the same.

But what is enough cultural change for the archaeologist to cut the tie of cultural affiliation between the past and the present may not be enough for Indians. Many Native Americans feel affiliated with *any* burial in their traditional territory, no matter the burial's age. In these cases, Indians feel betrayed—given that the purpose of NAGPRA was to allow tribes to bury "their" dead. In a legal sense, feelings of betrayal don't matter; the law is what it is. But such feelings do matter if we see NAGPRA as a way to do the right thing ethically. For this reason alone, Kennewick, and other cases like it, will continue to challenge archaeology and Native Americans alike.

Who Owns the Past?

The NAGPRA legislation clearly reflects the degree to which the authority of archaeology is being questioned. Who has the right to acquire the data of the past? Who gets to analyze it? Who gets to use the remains of the past? We have already considered how these challenges to archaeology arise over the analysis of human skeletal remains; they are also seen in the study of Native American spiritual sites.

A Spiritual Site: The Bighorn Medicine Wheel

Look at Figure 13-5 and you will see the Bighorn Medicine Wheel, an ancient stone arrangement perched atop a 9640-foot windswept peak in Wyoming's Bighorn Mountains. There are actually quite a few medicine wheels in the mountains of the high plains, but the Bighorn Mountains site is by far the largest. Today, you reach it by driving up a gravel road to a parking lot and then walking 1½ miles up the ridge. If you arrive in July or August, you might avoid trudging through snowdrifts.

Courtesy U.S. Forest Service

FIGURE 13-5 An aerial view of the Bighorn Medicine Wheel, surrounded by a log post and rope fence to which are attached many modern offerings.

The modern visitor is first struck by the simplicity of the structure: A stone circle, or "wheel," nearly 90 feet in diameter; in the background stretches the vast Bighorn Basin. Inside the stone circle, 28 stone "spokes" radiate out from a central "hub," which is marked by a stone **cairn** about 4½ meters across. Five smaller cairns lie along the Wheel's periphery.

But who built it (and why) is more controversial. Some suggest that the rock cairns were graves, each marking where a powerful person was buried. The lines of rocks (the spokes) show the different directions in which the departed ranged "on the warpath," recording the deeds of each dead chief. The rock piles at the ends of the lines may represent enemies killed in battle.

Drawing upon the ethnohistoric record, others suggested the site was for vision quests, a Plains Indian ritual in which an individual sought communication with the spirit world. For example, the Crow gave an account of the Bighorn Medicine Wheel based on the experience of Red Plume (also known as Long Hair), a famous Crow chief who visited the Wheel in the late 1700s:

> Red Plume . . . obtained his inspiration and received his medicine and the token which resulted in the application of that name by him at the Medicine Wheel. As a young man, Red Plume visited the wheel in the hope of receiving a strong medicine which would make of him a great warrior and chief. Without food, water, or clothing, he remained for four days and nights awaiting recognition from the spirits. On the fourth night he was approached by the three little men and one woman who inhabited the underground passage to the wheel and was conducted by them to the underground chamber. He remained there for three days and three nights and was instructed in the arts of warfare and in leading his people. He was told that the Red Eagle would be his powerful medicine and would guide him and be his protector through life. He was told to wear always upon his person as an emblem of his medicine, the soft little feather which grows upon the back above the tail of the eagle. This little red plume gave him his name. Upon his death, after many years of successful warfare and leadership, he instructed his people that his spirit would occupy the shrine at the medicine wheel which is not connected with the rim, except by an extended spoke, and that they might at all times communicate with him there.

Several contemporary Native American people say they have used it this way. Upslope winds whistle through countless crevices, creating a babel of moaning and shrieking voices. Some archaeological evidence suggests the rock cairns were protected by small enclosures during the early historic period, perhaps providing a modicum of shelter for those fasting, waiting, and seeking supernatural advice.

But there are other explanations. Astronomer John Eddy suggested that Native Americans constructed the Medicine Wheel as an astronomical observatory, to record the summer and winter solstices. Yet others suggest that it was built to aid travel, the rock piles left as directional aids to newcomers; or that it is a representation of the 28-raftered lodge built as part of the Sun Dance ceremony. Others suggest that the Medicine Wheel may have been a boundary marker, a depiction of a mythical turtle, or an enduring stone marker demonstrating geometrical expertise.

In brief, we don't know what the Medicine Wheel was in the past. But we do know what it is today.

After taking in the simple majesty of the stone structure and the breathtaking view, the modern visitor is soon struck by the number of offerings left at the site, a scene reminiscent of the Vietnam Veterans Memorial in Washington, DC. Scattered among the cairns and stone spokes are medicine bundles, antlers, coins, beadwork, photographs, bundles of sage or sweetgrass, and strips of cloth tied to the heavy wooden fence that now surrounds the site. The prehistoric use of the Medicine Wheel may forever remain an enigma, but to many contemporary Indian people the Medicine Wheel remains a holy place, one of many sacred sites where ceremonies are performed to this day.

Yet many of the most important sacred sites—places like the Bighorn Medicine Wheel—are being overrun each year by thousands of non-Indians: well-meaning tourists, scientific teams, and New Agers seeking a spiritual experience. Indians are greatly concerned that the plants, paths, shrines, rocks, and other aspects of their sacred sites are being destroyed by the curious, and their power diffused by the insensitive.

North American archaeologists agree that the Bighorn Medicine Wheel is one of America's more intriguing ancient sites—and with its stunning setting and puzzling past, the Medicine Wheel is a natural for the heritage tourist. Or is it? Should tourists be encouraged to visit the Bighorn Medicine Wheel?

How do archaeologists balance the dual concerns of bringing American archaeology to the interested public while respecting the wishes of the descendant populations still involved with many of those sites? Some Native Americans claim that all prehistoric sites are sacred. Should they be closed to the public? Should only Indians get to visit these places? Should only Indians study and interpret them?

In the case of the Medicine Wheel, a coalition representing varied interests—tribal, scientific, ecological, and governmental—is trying to protect, preserve, and respect the site. One mutual decision was to close the last mile and a half of the road to the site (allowance is made for the disabled). This solution minimizes the negative impact of tourism, respects the religious freedom of native people, and yet keeps this place accessible to those who wish to see firsthand the structure that has drawn people here for centuries.

William Tallbull (1921–1996), a Northern Cheyenne elder who had a deep and long-lasting personal relationship to the Medicine Wheel, felt it important to keep the site accessible. He believed it inappropriate to exclude anybody. From his perspective, if the educational and contemplative potential of sacred sites can be maintained, then they can offer an important opportunity for teaching tolerance and respect.

Whether considering the Medicine Wheel or any other site, it is impossible for archaeologists to escape a central issue: Who owns the past? This is not a question of who owns a site—that's a simple matter of property law—but who has the authority to uncover, interpret, and present knowledge gained from the past?

The past can be a powerful place to visit, and for many, archaeological sites like the Medicine Wheel are strong symbolic reminders of identity and continuity. But is it appropriate that only "descendants" should be "owners" of their past? Is the descendants' perspective the only admissible one?

Leave aside the sticky issue of defining who is a "descendant," and just consider the extreme case—giving complete power to one group of people, be they white, black, Hispanic, or Indian; rich or poor; urban or rural. Our point is a familiar one: Power corrupts, and absolute power corrupts absolutely. It's true in politics, and it's true in archaeology. The Nazis provide a vivid example of this.

Nazi Archaeology: The Danger of Owning the Past

Gustaf Kossinna (1858–1931) did not live to see Hitler's ascension to power in 1933, but his work was inspirational to the Nazi elite. A linguist turned prehistorian, Kossinna sought to link Germanic culture to particular types of artifacts. Bettina Arnold (University of Wisconsin, Milwaukee) notes that Kossinna's work was intended to help the Germans rebuild their country after the First World War. In fact, his book on German prehistory was dedicated "To the German people, as a building block in the reconstruction of the externally as well as internally disintegrated fatherland."

Kossinna wrote that the presence of allegedly "Germanic" artifacts was archaeological proof demonstrating Germany's prior claim to vast stretches of territory, including large parts of Poland. Kossinna and his acolytes argued that waves of Germanic people had emanated from a northern European core area, carrying with them major cultural achievements such as agriculture, pottery, and metallurgy (none of which fit with the archaeological evidence as we know it). In one of his dinnertime monologues, Arnold notes, Hitler even claimed that the ancient Greeks were Germans who had migrated south.

Prehistory was largely ignored in Germany prior to Hitler's rise to power, and Arnold suggests that it was therefore easy for the Nazis to appropriate the past for their own purposes. From the time Hitler rose to power in 1933 through the end of World War II, eight new chairs of archaeology were established at German universities, and considerable funding became available for excavation. Of course, these new archaeologists were appointed and funded only if they were enthusiastic Nazi party members.

The interest in prehistory went to the highest levels of Nazi political power. Heinrich Himmler—the leader of the SS, Hitler's terrifying personal army—formed a wing of the SS called the *Ahnenerbe* ("Ancestor Heritage"). He looked to prehistory to establish an identity for the SS, using a Germanic-like rune as the source of the unit's double lightning-strike insignia. His archaeologists ventured as far as Tibet and Iceland searching for Atlantis, the Holy Grail, and Aryan kings (providing the inspiration for Steven Spielberg's *Raiders of the Lost Ark*).

During the war, archaeologists were part of the *Sonderkommando Jankuhn*, a military organization led by SS archaeologist Herbert Jankuhn, which looted museums and libraries in conquered lands in the search for artifacts that would demonstrate Germany's ancestral claim on virtually all of Europe. Posters exhorted Germans to preserve and report all archaeological finds to authorities because every potsherd was "a document of our ancestors." (This attitude was not motivated by a love of prehistory, for although allegedly Germanic artifacts were preserved, unrelated archaeological sites in places such as Poland and Czechoslovakia were destroyed.)

Archaeological excavations in Germany were wildly misinterpreted to support claims for Aryan superiority, and contrary evidence was suppressed. Open-air theaters, known as *Thingstätten*, where Nazi propaganda plays were performed, were built only in places where the community could demonstrate prehistoric Germanic occupation. For many of these, Arnold points out, the archaeological data were grossly misinterpreted, if not outright fabricated.

Not all German scholars, however, were complacent; even Hitler thought Himmler sometimes went too far with his archaeological fantasizing. Opposition was nonetheless squashed, books outside the party line were banned, and scientists who would not toe the line were ostracized. There were no open debates, and the Nazi party controlled all discussion of the past.

Nazi archaeology is, to be sure, an extreme case. No form of modern archaeology is in the same pigeonhole. But even extreme cases have value because they warn what can happen when a single group appropriates complete control over the past. It is precisely the issue of power and control that creates conflicts such as that over Kennewick Man. In the prologue, we used the Kennewick case to raise some tough questions: *What gives archaeologists the right to poke into the past, to study the dead? Who owns the past, anyway? And who gets to decide?* We can now return to those questions and consider them in a broader context.

Why We Do Archaeology Affects *How* We Do Archaeology

Henry Ford once said that "history is bunk," but as practicing archaeologists, we disagree. History tells us how we became the people we are today. History contains important lessons about the nature of humans and cultural change—lessons that have practical applications, lessons that help us frame and understand the challenges facing the world

cairn An artificial mound of stones, often constructed as an aid to navigation, as a memorial, or to mark the location of a grave.

today. If we didn't believe strongly that we can learn from, and not just about, the past, then we would not be archaeologists.

Hardcore scientists tend to think that people should be united by a passionate belief in pure science, a passionate curiosity about the world around us. This is a laudable desire, and perhaps the day will come when we can seek new worlds of knowledge just for the sheer thrill of it. But that day is not today. We live in a world partitioned by walls of our own social construction—barriers of race, nationality, ethnicity, wealth, and culture. Listen to the news on any day, and you'll see that this is the greatest challenge facing the world.

In that world, archaeology can ill afford to stick its head in the sand, claim the high moral ground of pure science, and ignore the ways that other people understand or give meaning to the past. Archaeologists often claim that we do archaeology because understanding the past will help us construct a better tomorrow. But if in doing so we tell a group of people that their interests and concerns do not matter, that scientists will tell them what is best, haven't we contributed to the problem—and substantially undermined any reason for doing archaeology in the first place?

For this reason, archaeologists will continue to debate and discuss the past with various groups outside archaeology, and the discussion will not be easy. Passing judgment on anybody's values or beliefs is tricky business. Should we take seriously the Asatru Folk Assembly, a group of Euro-Americans who claim to maintain an ancient Celtic religion, when they argue that Kennewick Man is their ancestor? And what about actress Shirley MacLaine, who claims (quite sincerely from all accounts) that she's a reincarnated Inka princess? Should we negotiate with Ms. MacLaine if she were to launch a repatriation claim for Inka gold held by museums? Should we give equal time in textbooks to Erich von Däniken and the movie *Indiana Jones and the Kingdom of the Crystal Skull*, both of which claim that the pyramids and other architectural wonders of the prehistoric world were built by travelers from other planets?

We don't champion any of these causes. But just because some *individuals* make frivolous claims does not justify setting aside the voices of other *groups*. Shirley MacLaine may have no rights to Inka gold, but the Peruvian government or the Quechua (the indigenous people of the highland Andes) might have very valid claims indeed. Obviously we need a dialogue, and it is important to remember that a "dialogue" implies at least two partners, participating as equals. It does *not* mean that archaeologists should abdicate their responsibility as trained observers and interpreters of the data of archaeology. In fact, it is essential that archaeologists and other interested communities work jointly because when control rests in the hands of one exclusive group—be it scientists or descendants—we run the risk of a Nazi-style archaeology. Professional archaeologists should continue to do archaeology because, if we quit, someone else will surely step in to fill the void and make their own claims about the past. We worry that the vacuum would be filled by groups like the Asatru Folk Assembly or followers of von Däniken—people who do not criticize their own ideas, who fail to adhere to high standards of evidence, and who don't make their data and arguments explicit and public.

Archaeologists can sometimes get lost in the myriad details of archaeological investigations—the intricacies of radiocarbon dating, ceramic petrography, faunal analyses, and the like. A considered dialogue is beneficial because it continually reminds us about why we do archaeology. Many archaeologists, in fact, have already found that there are enormous advantages, both political *and* scientific, to bringing in rather than shutting out other groups.

Seeking Common Ground

A growing number of American archaeologists have developed research programs that incorporate the perspectives of Indian and other descendant communities. Each year, we see more examples of archaeologists using archaeology to help communities reconnect to their past, to establish ties broken by sociopolitical forces. Many archaeologists have worked hard to make participation in field projects financially possible for members of descendant communities. The Society for American Archaeology, for example, annually awards field school scholarships to Native American students.

More archaeologists are tackling projects in close consultation with tribal councils and descendant communities at the beginning, rather than the end, of a project, devising research in such a way that it is useful to the tribe or community.

On Alaska's Kodiak Island, for example, the repatriation of several hundred burials excavated in the 1930s resulted in the formation of a native-driven archaeology program. Kodiak Island is the aboriginal home of the *Alutiiq*, an Eskimo people. The repatriation took years to negotiate, but because it empowered the native community, the result was more—not less interest—in their past. So, while the repatriation struggle was going on, Amy Steffian (then a graduate student at the University of Michigan) was given permission and funding to dig further at the grave site. It's not that the Alutiiq hated archaeology; they just hated an archaeology that implied that they could not be full partners, that their participation was not needed.

Today, Steffian serves as deputy director of the Alutiiq Museum, an outgrowth of the Kodiak Area Native Association's Culture and Heritage division. Recognizing that they were losing a record of their heritage to winter storms, vandalism, and time, the Alutiiq founded the Heritage program in 1987 to create an island-wide strategy of archaeological research and to promote educational programs on Alutiiq culture, language, and arts. Eight

Courtesy Alutiiq Museum, photo by Patrick Saltonstall

FIGURE 13-6 Alutiiq intern April Laktonen excavates at the Outlet site on Kodiak Island, Alaska, during the Alutiiq Museum's Community Archaeology Program.

native corporations today fund and govern the Alutiiq Museum; they also oversee their own archaeological research projects, employing professional archaeologists to work with crews of native people, as shown in Figure 13-6, and community volunteers. The Alutiiq Museum curates the resulting collections and displays artifacts in a native-governed repository. In fact, the repatriated artifacts are today stored and available for study in the Alutiiq Museum.

The museum also provides professional and technical support to the Dig Afognak archaeological program, which is organized and staffed through the Afognak Native Corporation. Dig Afognak offers the opportunity to live and work with native people in the remote wilderness of the Kodiak archipelago. Its purpose is "to regain, restore, and carry forward the light of our culture" and "to make the circle complete" by inviting the interested public to join the effort.

The founding of the museum and the growth of archaeological programs produced new career opportunities for native people. Many of the Alutiiq students involved in the archaeology program are now pursuing college degrees in history and anthropology. One of these, Sven Haakanson, Jr., became director of the museum after completing a PhD in anthropology at Harvard. Several other Alutiiq women, who were once interns on field projects, form a third of the museum's staff.

Other archaeologists who conduct research on Kodiak today follow this example. Ben Fitzhugh (University of Washington), for example, excavated a 135-year-old Alutiiq-Russian site on the south shore of Kodiak with local junior high and high school students. The project discovered a 5000-year-old site beneath the Russian colonial-era one, providing an opportunity to explore changes in Alutiiq heritage unknown without the aid of archaeology. The students later presented the project's findings to the community in a series of conference-style papers. The students left the project not only with knowledge of archaeological methods and strategies, but also with bragging rights: They knew more about Kodiak's deep past than most of their parents.

Later, Fitzhugh and local high school students combined archaeological data on floor plans with the accounts of elders who had grown up in traditional earthen structures to build a replica *ciqlluaq*, or sod house, that today is an educational resource. Through projects such as these, communities take ownership of their heritage and work to promote its protection.

The beginning of this new brand of archaeology on Kodiak Island was NAGPRA. This legislation forced archaeologists to consult with local communities over their research and to do some soul-searching. Although NAGPRA calls for the repatriation of many archaeological collections, the result in some cases has been increased protection of the unexcavated archaeological record. And, ironically, NAGPRA may have engendered changes within archaeology and the Native American community whose end result will be the acquisition of more, not less, information about the past.

Conclusion: Archaeology and the Global Cultural Heritage

In this chapter, we have looked at the role of archaeology in the future. We examined some ways in which archaeology can be of pragmatic value—by using archaeological techniques to understand modern garbage and to gather the data needed to bring criminals to justice.

Perhaps even more important, however, will be archaeology's role in knocking down the walls that so often divide the people of the world. Archaeology can do this in part through the information that it gathers. Archaeology can show, for example, how different environmental and historical circumstances work together to create the diversity of human societies. But archaeology also contributes not only by *what* it learns about the past, but *how* it goes about learning it—the way in which it incorporates different perspectives, attitudes, and concerns of descendant communities and other stakeholders in the past.

Archaeology, as we have said, is not just about the dead; it's also about the living. And, it turns out, archaeology is not just about the past; it's also about the future.

Summary

- **Does archaeology have practical value in the world today?**
  - Although archaeology is conventionally perceived as a "pure" science, many archaeologists are finding ways to apply the techniques of archaeology to new problems, such as the analysis of contemporary garbage and landfills to help solve the nation's trash problem.
  - Others are involved in forensic archaeology, working with law enforcement officials, providing training in the recovery and analysis of material remains, and generating firsthand evidence to be presented in courts of law; still others use archaeology to recover ancient technologies that benefit developing nations.
- **What is the attitude of archaeology toward public education?**
  - One way or another, virtually all archaeological research depends on public support. Particularly within the last two decades, responsible archaeologists have recognized the importance of returning to the public some of the benefits.
  - Consequently, many archaeologists are involved in public education, adding educational components to "pure" research projects.
- **What federal policies help protect cultural resources, including archaeological sites?**
  - Although the United States has been concerned with preserving its cultural heritage for a long time, protection of cultural resources did not become policy until the National Environmental Policy Act.
- **What are the important elements of the 1906 Antiquities Act, the 1966 National Historic Preservation Act, and the 1979 Archaeological Resources Protection Act?**
  - The 1906 Antiquities Act required that individuals acquire a permit from the government before excavating archaeological sites, and gave the president the authority to create national monuments.
  - The 1966 National Historic Preservation Act required that the government inventory cultural resources on its properties and ensure that development projects consider their effects on significant archaeological sites. The act established the National Register of Historic Places and State Historic Preservation Offices.
  - The 1979 Archaeological Resources Protection Act provided further safeguards against the destruction of archaeological sites on federal and tribal land by increasing the penalties for excavating without a permit.
- **Is there an international black market in antiquities? If so, what can be done about it?**
  - Yes, in fact, this problem may be second only to drug trafficking. The United States and many nations around the world are working to stop the flow of illegally acquired antiquities. Although many measures have been put into place, most countries still find it difficult to stop antiquities from entering a country where buyers are willing to pay high prices for them.
- **Why is the Native American Graves Protection and Repatriation Act of 1990 important to archaeologists? How does it differ from other archaeological legislation?**
  - The 1990 Native American Graves Protection and Repatriation Act, often seen as human rights rather than archaeological legislation, ensures that human remains, funerary objects, sacred objects, and objects of cultural patrimony are offered for repatriation to culturally affiliated tribes and Native Hawaiian organizations. This process is still underway for most of the nation's museums and universities.
  - This act differs from others in that it returns materials for reburial, rather than preserving them for the future.
- **As archaeologists become increasingly involved with descendant and stakeholder communities, what associated ethical problems and positive potentials arise?**
  - In the past 20 years, archaeologists have become increasingly concerned with incorporating multiple voices into their research and educational efforts. In some cases, this has created problems, as the various stakeholders in archaeology contest who "owns" the past; this issue is especially prominent for sites that some communities perceive as sacred.
  - In a growing number of cases, archaeologists have created vibrant research and educational programs that create a better understanding of the past with the input of descendant communities' perspectives. In addition, such archaeological programs bring people of different backgrounds together and further break down social, ethnic, racial, and cultural walls that divide the world.

Media Resources

CourseMate

Access chapter-specific learning tools including learning objectives, practice quizzes, videos, flash cards, and glossaries, as well as web links, and more in your Archaeology CourseMate. Login to www.cengagebrain.com to access the resources your instructor has assigned and to purchase materials.

Glossary

absolute date A date expressed in specific units of scientific measurement, such as days, years, centuries, or millennia; absolute determinations attempting to pinpoint a discrete, known interval in time.

accelerator mass spectrometry (AMS) A method of radiocarbon dating that counts the proportion of carbon isotopes directly (rather than using the indirect Geiger counter method), thereby dramatically reducing the quantity of datable material required.

achieved status Rights, duties, and obligations that accrue to a person by virtue of what he or she has accomplished in life.

adaptive perspective A research perspective that emphasizes technology, ecology, demography, and economics as the key factors in defining human behavior.

aDNA Ancient DNA recovered from organic materials in archaeological sites.

analogy Noting similarities between two entities and inferring from that similarity that an *additional* attribute of one (the ethnographic case) is also true of the other (the archaeological case).

androcentric A perspective that focuses on what men do in a society, to the exclusion of women.

anthropology The study of all aspects of humankind—biological, cultural, and linguistic; extant and extinct—employing a holistic, comparative approach and the concept of culture.

antiquarian Originally, someone who studied antiquities (that is, ancient objects) largely for the sake of the objects themselves, not to understand the people or culture that produced them.

Antiquities Act Passed in 1906, this act (1) requires federal permits before excavating or collecting artifacts on federal land, (2) established a permitting process, and (3) gave the president the authority to create national monuments.

appendicular skeleton All parts of an animal excluding the axial skeleton.

applied science Research to acquire the knowledge necessary to solve a specific, recognized problem.

arbitrary level The basic vertical subdivision of an excavation square; used only when easily recognizable "natural" strata are lacking and when natural strata are more than 10 centimeters thick.

archaeological context Once artifacts enter the ground, they become part of the archaeological context, where they can continue to be affected by human action but are also affected by natural processes.

Archaeological Resources Protection Act (ARPA) Passed in 1979, this act (1) prohibits the excavation or removal of artifacts from federal property without a permit, (2) prohibits the sale, exchange, or transport of artifacts acquired illegally from federal property, and (3) increased the penalties for violations of the act over those of the Antiquities Act.

archaeological site Any place where material evidence exists about the human past. Usually, "site" refers to a concentration of such evidence.

archaeology The study of the past through the systematic recovery and analysis of material remains.

argilliturbation A natural formation process in which wet/dry cycles push artifacts upward as the sediment swells and then moves them down as cracks form during dry cycles.

argon-argon dating A high-precision method for estimating the relative quantities of argon-39 and argon-40 gas; used to date volcanic ashes that are between 500,000 and several million years old.

artifact Any movable object that has been used, modified, or manufactured by humans; artifacts include stone, bone, and metal tools; beads and other ornaments; pottery; artwork; religious and sacred items.

ascribed status Rights, duties, and obligations that accrue to a person by virtue of his or her parentage; ascribed status is inherited.

assemblage A collection of artifacts of one or several classes of materials (stone tools, ceramics, bones) that comes from a defined context, such as a site, feature, or stratum.

attribute An individual characteristic that distinguishes one artifact from another on the basis of its size, surface texture, form, material, method of manufacture, or design pattern.

axial skeleton The head, mandibles, vertebrae, ribs, sacrum, and tail of an animal skeleton.

berdaches Among Plains Indian societies, men who elected to live life as women; they were recognized by their group as a third gender.

bilateral descent A kinship system in which relatives are traced equally on both the mother's and father's sides.

bioarchaeology The study of the human biological component evident in the archaeological record.

biological anthropology A subdiscipline of anthropology that views humans as biological organisms; also known as physical anthropology.

bonebed Archaeological and paleontological sites consisting of the remains of a large number of animals, often of the same species, and often representing a single moment in time—a mass kill or mass death.

bundle burial Burial of a person's bones, bundled together, after the flesh has been removed or allowed to decay off the bones.

burial population A set of human burials that come from a limited region and a limited time period. The more limited the region and the time period, the more accurate will be inferences drawn from analysis of the burials.

cairn An artificial mound of stones, often constructed as an aid to navigation, as a memorial, or to mark the location of a grave.

cargo system Part of the social organization found in many Central American communities in which a wealthy individual is named to carry out and bear the cost of important religious ceremonies throughout the year.

caries Cavities.

channel flake The longitudinal flake removed from the faces of Folsom and Clovis projectile points to create the flute.

ch'arki Native South American (Quechua) term for freeze-dried llama and alpaca meat.

charnel house A structure that eastern Native Americans used to lay out the dead where the body would decompose. The bones would later be gathered and buried or cremated.

chiefdom A regional polity in which two or more local groups are organized under a single chief (who is the head of a ranked social hierarchy). Unlike autonomous bands and villages, chiefdoms consist of several more or less permanently aligned communities or settlements.

clan A group of matri- or patrilineages who see themselves as descended from a (sometimes mythical) common ancestor.

classical archaeology The branch of archaeology that studies the "classical" civilizations of the Mediterranean, such as Greece and Rome, and the Near East.

Clovis The earliest well-established Native American culture, distributed throughout much of North America and dating 11,200 to 10,900 BC.

cognitive archaeology The study of all those aspects of ancient culture that are the product of the human mind: the perception, description, and classification of the universe; the nature of the supernatural; the principles, philosophies, ethics, and values by which human societies are governed; and the ways in which aspects of the world, the supernatural, or human values are conveyed in art.

collagen The organic component of bone.

comparative collection A skeletal collection of modern fauna of both sexes and different ages used to make identifications of archaeofaunas.

component An archaeological construct consisting of a stratum or set of strata that are presumed to be culturally homeous. A set of components from various sites in a region will make up a phase.

coprolite Desiccated feces, often containing macrobotanical remains, pollen, and the remains of small animals.

core A piece of stone that is worked ("knapped"). Cores sometimes serve merely as sources for raw materials; they also can serve as functional tools.

cosmology The study of the origin, large-scale structure, and future of the universe. A cosmological explanation demonstrates how the universe developed—both the totality and its constituent parts—and also describes what principles keep it together.

cribra orbitalia A symptom of iron deficiency anemia in which the bone of the upper eye sockets takes on a spongy appearance.

critical theory A critique of the modern social order that emphasizes exploitative class interests; it aims to change and not simply to understand society.

cryoturbation A natural formation process in which freeze/thaw activity in a soil selectively pushes larger artifacts to the surface of a site.

cultural affiliation In NAGPRA, "a relationship of a shared group identity which can be reasonably traced historically or prehistorically between a present-day Indian tribe or Native Hawaiian organization and an identifiable earlier group."

cultural anthropology A subdiscipline of anthropology that emphasizes nonbiological aspects: the learned social, linguistic, technological, and familial behaviors of humans.

cultural disturbance processes Human behaviors that modify artifacts in their archaeological context—for instance, digging pits, hearths, canals, and houses.

cultural resource management (CRM) A professional field that conducts activities, including archaeology, related to compliance with legislation aimed at conserving cultural resources.

cultural resources Physical features, both natural and artificial, associated with human activity, including sites, structures, and objects possessing significance in history, architecture, or human development. Cultural properties are unique and nonrenewable resources.

culture An integrated system of beliefs, traditions, and customs that govern or influence a person's behavior. Culture is learned, shared by members of a group, and based on the ability to think in terms of symbols.

culture history The kind of archaeology practiced mainly in the early to mid-twentieth century; it "explains" differences or changes over time in artifact frequencies by positing the diffusion of ideas between neighboring cultures or the migration of a people who had different mental templates for artifact styles.

data Relevant observations made on objects that then serve as the basis for study and discussion.

datum point The zero point, a fixed reference used to keep control on a dig; usually controls both the vertical and horizontal dimensions of provenience.

deconstruction Efforts to expose the assumptions behind the alleged objective and systematic search for knowledge; a primary tool of postmodernism.

deductive reasoning Reasoning from theory to predict specific observational or experimental results.

de Vries effects Fluctuations in the radiocarbon-dating calibration curve produced by variations in the atmosphere's carbon-14 content; these can cause radiocarbon dates to calibrate to more than one calendar age.

direct acquisition A form of trade in which a person or group goes to the source area of an item to procure the raw material directly or to trade for it or finished products.

dosimeter A device to measure the amount of gamma radiation emitted by sediments. It is normally buried in a stratum for a year to record the annual dose of radiation. Dosimeters are often a short length of pure copper tubing filled with calcium sulfate.

down-the-line trade An exchange system in which goods are traded outward from a source area from group to group, resulting in a steady decline in the item's abundance in archaeological sites farther from the source.

eburnation A sign of osteoarthritis in which the epiphyses of long bones are worn smooth, causing them to take on a varnish-like appearance.

ecofact Plant or animal remains found at an archaeological site.

egalitarian societies Social systems that contain roughly as many valued positions as there are people capable of filling them; in egalitarian societies, all people have nearly equal access to the critical resources needed to live.

electron spin resonance (ESR) A trapped charge technique used to date tooth enamel and burnt stone tools; it can date teeth that are beyond the range of radiocarbon dating.

element In faunal analysis, a specific skeletal part of the body—for example, humerus or sternum.

enamel hypoplasias Horizontal linear defects in tooth enamel indicating episodes of physiological stress.

energy dispersive x-ray fluorescence (XRF) An analytical technique that uses obsidian's trace elements to "fingerprint" an artifact and trace it to its geologic source.

epiphyses The ends of bones that fuse to the main shaft or portion of bone at various ages. Most bones are fused by age 25; this fact can be used to age skeletons of younger individuals.

ethnoarchaeology The study of contemporary peoples to determine how human behavior is translated into the archaeological record.

exotics Material culture that was not produced locally and/or whose raw material is not found locally.

experimental archaeology Experiments designed to determine the archaeological correlates of ancient behavior; may overlap with both ethnoarchaeology and taphonomy.

faunal In archaeology, animal bones in archaeological sites.

faunal analysis Identification and interpretation of animal remains from an archaeological site.

faunal assemblage The animal remains recovered from an archaeological site.

faunalturbation A natural formation process in which animals, from large game to earthworms, affect the distribution of material within an archaeological site.

feature Nonportable archaeological evidence such as fire hearths, architectural elements, artifact clusters, garbage pits, and soil stains.

flake A thin, sharp sliver of stone removed from a core during the knapping process.

floralturbation A natural formation process in which trees and other plants affect the distribution of artifacts within an archaeological site.

flotation The use of fluid suspension to recover tiny burned plant remains and bone fragments from archaeological sites.

flute Distinctive channel on the faces of Folsom and Clovis projectile points formed by removal of one or more flakes from the point's base.

forensic archaeology The application of archaeological and bioarchaeological knowledge for legal purposes.

formal analogies Analogies justified by similarities in the formal attributes of archaeological and ethnographic objects and features.

formation processes The ways in which human behaviors and natural actions operate to produce the archaeological record.

functional type A class of artifacts that performed the same function; these may or may not be temporal and/or morphological types.

gender ideology The culturally prescribed values assigned to the task and status of men and women; values can vary from society to society.

gender role The culturally prescribed behavior associated with men and women; roles can vary from society to society.

gene A unit of the chromosomes that controls inheritance of particular traits.

general systems theory An effort to describe the properties by which all systems, including human societies, allegedly operate; popular in processual archaeology of the late 1960s and 1970s.

geographic information system (GIS) A computer program for storing, retrieving, analyzing, and displaying cartographic data.

georeferenced Data that are input to a GIS database using a common mapping reference—for example, the UTM grid—so that all data can be spatially analyzed.

Georgian order A worldview (1660/1680 to 1820) arising in the European Age of Reason and implying that the world has a single, basic immutable order. Using the powers of reason, people can discover what that order is and can thereby control the environment as they wish. The Georgian order is informed by the rise of scientific thought and by the balance and order in Renaissance architecture and art.

global positioning system (GPS) Handheld devices that use triangulation from radio waves received from satellites to determine your current position in terms of either the UTM grid or latitude and longitude.

graviturbation A natural formation process in which artifacts are moved downslope through gravity, sometimes assisted by precipitation runoff.

ground-penetrating radar (GPR) A remote sensing technique in which radar pulses directed into the ground reflect back to the surface when they strike features or interfaces within the ground, showing the presence and depth of possible buried features.

half-life (of ^{14}C) The time required for half of the carbon-14 available in an organic sample to decay, or 5730 years.

Harris lines Horizontal lines near the ends of long bones indicating episodes of physiological stress.

heat treatment A process whereby the flintknapping properties of stone tool raw material are improved by subjecting the material to heat.

high-level theory Theory that seeks to answer large "why" questions.

historical archaeology The study of human behavior through material remains whose interpretation is in some way affected by written history.

Homo erectus A hominin who lived in Africa, Asia, and Europe between 2 million and 500,000 years ago. These hominin walked upright, made simple stone tools, and may have used fire.

Hopewell A cultural tradition found primarily in the Ohio River Valley and its tributaries, dating from 2200 to 1600 BP. Hopewell societies engaged in hunting and gathering and in some horticulture of indigenous plants. They are known for their mortuary rituals, which included charnel houses and burial mounds; some central tombs contained exotics. They also constructed geometric earthworks as ceremonial enclosures and effigy mounds.

Hopewell Interaction Sphere The common set of symbols found in the midwestern United States between 2200 BP and 1600 BP.

hypothesis A proposition proposed as an explanation of some phenomenon.

iconography Art forms or writing systems (such as Egyptian or Maya hieroglyphics) that symbolically represent ideas about religion or cosmology.

ideational perspective A research perspective that focuses on ideas, symbols, and mental structures as driving forces in shaping human behavior.

index fossil concept The idea that strata containing similar fossil assemblages are of similar age. This concept enables archaeologists to characterize and date strata within sites using distinctive artifact forms that research shows to be diagnostic of a particular period of time.

inductive reasoning Working from specific observations to more general hypotheses.

in situ From Latin, meaning "in position"; the place where an artifact, ecofact, or feature was found during excavation or survey.

kill sites Places where animals were killed in the past.

kinship A socially recognized network of relationships through which individuals are related to one another by ties of descent (real or imagined) and marriage.

kiva A Pueblo ceremonial structure that is usually round (but may be square or rectangular) and semi-subterranean. They appear in early Pueblo sites and perhaps even in the earlier (pre–AD 700) pithouse villages.

krotovina A filled-in animal burrow.

landscape archaeology The study of ancient human modification of the environment.

law of superposition The geological principle that in any pile of sedimentary rocks that have not been disturbed by folding or overturning, each bed is older than the layers above and younger than the layers below.

linguistic anthropology A subdiscipline of anthropology that focuses on human language: its diversity in grammar, syntax, and lexicon; its historical development; and its relation to a culture's perception of the world.

living floor A distinct buried surface on which people lived.

long bone cross-sections Cross-sections of the body's long bones (arms and legs) used to analyze bone shape and reconstruct the mechanical stresses placed on that bone—and hence activity patterns.

low-level theory The observations and interpretations that emerge from hands-on archaeological field and lab work.

macrobotanical remains Nonmicroscopic plant remains recovered from an archaeological site.

Magdalenian The last major culture of the European Upper Paleolithic period (about 16,000 to 10,000 BC); named after the rockshelter La Madeleine, in southwestern France. Magdalenian artisans crafted intricately carved tools of reindeer bone and antler; this was also the period during which Upper Paleolithic cave art in France and Spain reached its zenith.

mano A fist-sized, round, flat, handheld stone used with a metate for grinding foods.

matrilineage Individuals who share a line of matrilineal descent.

matrilineal descent A unilineal descent system in which ancestry is traced through the female line.

matrix sorting The hand sorting of processed bulk soil samples for minute artifacts and ecofacts.

Medieval mindset The culture of the early (pre-AD 1660) British colonies that emphasized the group rather than the individual and in which the line between culture and nature was blurred; people were seen as conforming to nature.

metate A large, flat stone used as a stationary surface upon which seeds, tubers, and nuts are ground with a mano.

midden Refuse deposit resulting from human activities, generally consisting of sediment; food remains such as charred seeds, animal bone, and shell; and discarded artifacts.

middle-level theory Hypothesis that links archaeological observations with the human behavior or natural processes that produced them.

minimum number of individuals (MNI) The smallest number of individuals necessary to account for all identified bones.

Mississippian A widespread cultural tradition across much of the eastern United States from AD 800 to 1500. Mississippian societies engaged in intensive village-based maize horticulture and constructed large, earthen platform mounds that served as substructures for temples, residences, and council buildings.

mitochondrial DNA (mtDNA) Genetic material found in the mitochondria of cells; it is inherited only from the mother and appears to mutate at a rate of 2 to 4 percent per 1 million years.

moieties Two groups of clans that perform reciprocal ceremonial obligations for one another; moieties often intermarry.

molecular archaeology The use of genetic information in ancient human remains to reconstruct the past.

molecular clock Calculations of the time since divergence of two related populations using the presumed rate of mutation in mtDNA and the genetic differences between the two populations.

morphological type A descriptive and abstract grouping of individual artifacts whose focus is on overall similarity rather than function or chronological significance.

mortality profiles Charts that depict the various ages at death of a burial population.

Mousterian A culture from the Middle Paleolithic ("Middle Old Stone Age") period that appeared throughout Europe after 250,000 and before 30,000 years ago. Mousterian artifacts are frequently associated with Neanderthal human remains.

National Historic Preservation Act (NHPA) Passed in 1966, this act created (1) the National Register of Historic Places, (2) the Advisory Council on Historic Preservation, and (3) State Historic Preservation Offices, as well as (4) a process to mitigate the impact of development; it also requires that government agencies provide good stewardship of their cultural resources.

Native American Graves Protection and Repatriation Act (NAGPRA) Passed in 1990, this act (1) protects Indian graves on federal and tribal lands, (2) recognizes tribal authority over treatment of unmarked graves, (3) prohibits the commercial selling of native dead bodies, (4) requires an inventory and repatriation of human remains held by the federal government and institutions that receive federal funding, (5) requires these same institutions to return inappropriately acquired sacred objects and other important communally owned property to native owners, and (6) sets up a process to determine ownership of human remains found on federal and tribal property after November 16, 1990.

natural level A vertical subdivision of an excavation square that is based on natural breaks in the sediments (in terms of color, grain size, texture, hardness, or other characteristics).

Neanderthals (or Neandertals) An early form of humans who lived in Europe and the Near East about 300,000 to 30,000 years ago. Biological anthropologists debate whether Neanderthals were in the direct evolutionary line leading to *Homo sapiens.*

new archaeology An approach to archaeology that arose in the 1960s, emphasizing the understanding of underlying cultural processes and the use of the scientific method; today's version of the "new archaeology" is sometimes called processual archaeology.

nuclear DNA Genetic material found in a cell's nucleus; this material is primarily responsible for an individual's inherited traits.

number of identified specimens (NISP) The raw number of identified bones (specimens) per species; a largely outmoded way of comparing archaeological bone frequencies.

old wood problem A potential problem with radiocarbon (or tree-ring) dating in which old wood has been scavenged and reused in a later archaeological site; the resulting date is not a true age of the associated human activity.

optically stimulated luminescence (OSL) A trapped charge dating technique used to date sediments; it measures the time elapsed between the last time a few moments' exposure to sunlight reset the clock to zero and the present.

oracle A shrine in which a deity reveals hidden knowledge or divine purpose.

osteoarthritis A disorder in which the cartilage between joints wears away, often because of overuse of the joint, resulting in osteophytes and eburnation.

osteology The study of bone.

osteophyte A sign of osteoarthritis in which bones develop a distinct "lipping" of bone at the point of articulation.

paleodemography The study of ancient demographic patterns and trends.

paleoethnobotanist An archaeologist who analyzes and interprets plant remains from archaeological sites to understand the past interactions between human populations and plants.

paleopathology The study of ancient patterns of disease and disorders.

palynology The technique through which the fossil pollen grains and spores from archaeological sites are studied.

paradigm The overarching framework, often unstated, for understanding a research problem. It is a researcher's "culture."

participant observation The primary strategy of cultural anthropology, in which data are gathered by questioning and observing people while the observer lives in their society.

patrilineage Individuals who share a line of patrilineal descent.

patrilineal descent A unilineal descent system in which ancestry is traced through the male line.

period A length of time distinguished by particular items of material culture, such as house form, pottery, or subsistence.

phase An archaeological construct possessing traits sufficiently characteristic to distinguish it from other units similarly conceived; spatially limited to roughly a locality or region and chronologically limited to the briefest interval of time possible.

photosynthetic pathways The specific chemical processes through which plants metabolize carbon. Because the three major pathways discriminate against carbon-13 in different ways, similarly aged plants that use different pathways can produce different radiocarbon ages.

phytoliths Tiny silica particles contained in plants.

Pleistocene A geologic period from 2 million to 10,000 years ago, which was characterized by multiple periods of extensive glaciation.

plow-zone The upper portion of a soil profile that has been disturbed by repeated plowing or other agricultural activity.

political organization A society's formal and informal institutions that regulate a population's collective acts.

pollen diagram A chart showing the changing frequencies of different identified pollens through time from samples taken from archaeological or other sites.

porotic hyperostosis A symptom of iron deficiency anemia in which the skull takes on a porous appearance.

postprocessual paradigm A paradigm that focuses on humanistic approaches and rejects scientific objectivity. It sees archaeology as inherently political and is more concerned with interpreting the past than with testing hypotheses. It sees change as arising largely from interactions between individuals operating within a symbolic and/or competitive system.

potsherd Fragment of pottery.

principle of uniformitarianism The principle asserting that the processes now operating to modify the Earth's surface are the same processes that operated long ago in the geological past.

processual paradigm The paradigm that explains social, economic, and cultural change as primarily the result of adaptation to material conditions. External conditions (for example, the environment) are assumed to take causal priority over ideational factors in explaining change.

projectile points Arrowheads, dart points, or spear points.

proton precession magnetometer A remote sensing technique that measures the strength of magnetism between the earth's magnetic core and a sensor controlled by the archaeologist. Magnetic anomalies can indicate the presence of buried walls or features.

provenience An artifact's location relative to a system of spatial data collection.

pubic symphysis Where the two halves of the pelvis meet in the groin area. The appearance of its articulating surface can be used to age skeletons.

puna Native American (Quechua) term for the treeless, windswept tablelands and basins of the higher Andes.

pure (basic) science Systematic research directed toward acquisition of knowledge for its own sake.

random sample A sample drawn from a statistical population such that every member of the population has an equal chance of being included in the sample.

ranked societies Social systems in which a hierarchy of social status has been established, with a restricted number of valued positions available; in ranked societies, not everyone has the same access to the critical resources of life.

reclamation processes Human behaviors that result in artifacts' moving from the archaeological context back to the systemic context—for example, scavenging beams from an abandoned structure to use them in a new one.

relational analogies Analogies justified on the basis of close cultural continuity between the archaeological and ethnographic cases or similarity in general cultural form.

relative dates Dates expressed relative to one another (for instance, earlier, later, more recent) instead of in absolute terms.

religion A specific set of beliefs about one's relation to the supernatural; a society's mechanism for relating supernatural phenomena to the everyday world.

remote sensing The use of some form of electromagnetic energy to detect and measure characteristics of an archaeological target.

reservoir effect When organisms take in carbon from a source that is depleted of or enriched in ^{14}C relative to the atmosphere; carbon dating of such samples may return ages that are considerably older or younger than they actually are.

reuse processes Human behaviors that recycle and reuse artifacts before the artifacts enter an archaeological context.

ritual A succession of discrete behaviors that must be performed in a particular order under particular circumstances.

rockshelter A common type of archaeological site, consisting of a rock overhang that is deep enough to provide shelter but not deep enough to be called a cave (technically speaking, a cave must have an area of perpetual darkness).

Rosetta Stone A black basalt stone tablet found in 1799 that bears an inscription in two forms of ancient Greek and ancient Egyptian. By working from the Greek texts, scholars were able to decipher the ancient Egyptian hieroglyphs.

sample fraction The percentage of the sample universe that is surveyed. Areas with a lot of variability in archaeological remains require larger sample fractions than do areas of low variability.

sample units Survey units of a standard size and shape, determined by the research question and practical considerations, used to obtain the sample.

sample universe The region that contains the statistical population and that will be sampled. Its size and shape are determined by the research question and practical considerations.

sciatic notch The angled edge of both halves of the posterior (rear) side of the pelvis. Measurement of this angle is used to determine sex in human skeletons. Although its width varies among populations, narrow notches indicate a male and wider notches indicate a female.

science The search for answers through a process that is objective, systematic, logical, predictive, self-critical, and public.

scientific method Accepted principles and procedures for the systematic pursuit of secure knowledge. Established scientific procedures involve the following steps: (1) define a relevant problem; (2) establish one or more hypotheses; (3) determine the empirical implications of the hypotheses; (4) collect appropriate data through observation and/or experimentation; (5) compare these data with the expected implications; and (6) revise and/or retest hypotheses as necessary.

seasonality An estimate of the part of the year a particular archaeological site was occupied.

seasonal round Hunter-gatherers' pattern of movement between different places on the landscape, timed to the seasonal availability of food and other resources.

seriation A relative dating method that orders artifacts based on the assumption that one cultural style slowly replaces an earlier style over time. With a master seriation diagram, sites can be dated based on their frequency of several artifact (for instance, ceramic) styles.

shaman One who has the power to contact the spirit world through trance, possession, or visions. On the basis of this ability, the shaman invokes, manipulates, or coerces the power of the spirits for socially recognized ends—both good and ill.

shell midden The remnants of shellfish collecting; some shellfish middens can become many meters thick.

shovel testing A sample survey method used in regions where rapid soil buildup obscures buried archaeological remains; it entails digging shallow, systematic pits across the survey unit.

sipapu A Hopi word that loosely translates as "place of emergence." The original sipapu is the place where the Hopi are said to have emerged into this world from the underworld. Sipapus are also small pits in kivas through which communication with the supernatural world takes place.

size classes A categorization of faunal remains, not to taxon, but to one of five categories based on body size.

slash-and-burn A horticultural method, used frequently in the tropics, in which a section of forest is cut, dried, and then burned. This returns nutrients to the ground and permits the land to be farmed for a limited number of years.

Smithsonian number A unique catalog number given to each site; it consists of a number (the state's position alphabetically), a letter abbreviation for the county, and the site's sequential number within the county.

social organization The rules and structures that govern relations within a group of interacting people. Societies are divided into social units (groups) within which are recognized social positions (statuses), with appropriate behavior patterns prescribed for these positions (roles).

soil resistivity survey A remote sensing technique that monitors the electrical resistance of soils in a restricted volume near the surface of an archaeological site; changes in the amount of resistance registered by the resistivity meter can indicate buried walls or features.

Southeastern Ceremonial Complex An assortment of ceremonial objects that occurs in the graves of high-status Mississippian individuals. Ritual exchange of these artifacts crosscut the boundaries of many distinctive local cultures.

space-time systematics The delineation of patterns in material culture through time and across space. These patterns are what archaeologists will eventually try to explain or account for.

statistical population A set of counts, measurements, or characteristics about which relevant inquiries are to be made. Scientists use the term "statistical population" in a specialized way (quite different from "population" in the ordinary sense).

statistical sampling The principles that underlie sampling strategies and provide accurate measures of a statistical population.

status The rights, duties, privileges, powers, liabilities, and immunities that accrue to a recognized and named social position.

stelae Stone monuments erected by Maya rulers to record their history in rich images and hieroglyphic symbols. These symbols can be read and dated.

strata (singular, **stratum**) More or less homogeneous or gradational material, visually separable from other levels by a discrete change in the character of the material—texture, compactness, color, rock, organic content—and/or by a sharp break in the nature of deposition.

stratified random sample A survey universe divided into several sub-universes that are then sampled at potentially different sample fractions.

stratigraphy A site's physical structure produced by the deposition of geological and/or cultural sediments into layers, or strata.

structuralism A paradigm holding that human culture is the expression of unconscious modes of thought and reasoning, notably binary oppositions. Structuralism is most closely associated with the French anthropologist Claude Lévi-Strauss.

symbol An object or act (verbal or nonverbal) that, by cultural convention, stands for something else with which it has no necessary connection.

sympathetic magic Rituals in which doing something to an image of an object produces the desired effect on the real object.

systemic context The living behavioral system in which artifacts were originally manufactured, used, reused, and discarded.

taxon In faunal analysis, the classification of a skeletal element to a taxonomic category—species, genus, family, or order.

temporal type A morphological type that has temporal significance; also known as a time marker or index fossil.

testability The degree to which one's observations and experiments can be reproduced.

test excavation A small initial excavation to determine a site's potential for answering a research question.

theory An explanation for observed, empirical phenomena. It seeks to explain the relationships between variables; it is an answer to a "why" question.

thermal infrared multispectral scanning (TIMS) A remote sensing technique that uses equipment mounted on aircraft or satellites to measure infrared thermal radiation given off by the ground. Sensitive to differences as small as 0.1°C, it can locate subsurface structures by tracking how they affect surface thermal radiation.

thermoluminescence (TL) A trapped charge dating technique used on ceramics and burnt stone artifacts—anything mineral that has been heated to more than 500°C.

time markers Artifact forms that, as with index fossils in geology, research shows to be diagnostic of a particular period of time.

total station A device that uses a beam of light bounced off a prism to determine an artifact's provenience; it is accurate to ± 3 millimeters.

totem A natural object, often an animal, from which a lineage or clan believes itself to be descended and/or with which lineage or clan members have special relations.

trapped charge dating Forms of dating that rely upon the fact that electrons become trapped in minerals' crystal lattices as a function of background radiation; the age of the specimen is the total radiation received divided by the annual dose of radiation.

tree-ring dating (dendrochronology) The use of annual growth rings in trees to assign calendar ages to ancient wood samples.

type A class of archaeological artifacts defined by a consistent clustering of attributes.

typology The systematic arrangement of material culture into types.

UNESCO Convention of 1970 This international agreement requires that signers create legislation and the administrative structure to (1) regulate the import and export of cultural objects, (2) forbid their nations' museums from acquiring illegally exported cultural objects, (3) establish ways to inform other nations when illegally exported objects are found within a country's borders, (4) return or otherwise provide restitution of cultural objects stolen from public institutions, and (5) establish a register of art dealers and require them to register.

Upper Paleolithic The last major division of the Old World Paleolithic, beginning about 40,000 years ago and lasting until the end of the Pleistocene (about 10,000 BC).

UTM Universal Transverse Mercator, a grid system in which north and east coordinates provide a location anywhere in the world, precise to 1 meter.

vision quest A ritual in which an individual seeks visions through starvation, dehydration, and exposure; considered in some cultures to be a way to communicate with the supernatural world.

water screening A sieving process in which deposit is placed on a screen and the matrix washed away with hoses; essential where artifacts are expected to be small and/or difficult to find without washing.

zooarchaeologist (also *faunal analyst*) An individual who studies the faunal (animal) remains recovered from archaeological sites.

Bibliography

The following chapter-by-chapter bibliography contains the specific references used in each chapter as well as some additional references that can provide students with more in-depth reading on particular subjects. We've arranged this bibliography by chapter so that students can more easily locate additional readings on a particular subject. Where direct quotes have been used in the text, their source is indicated here at the end of the appropriate entry.

Chapter 1

Binford, Lewis R. 1962. Archeology as anthropology. *American Antiquity* 28: 217–225.

———. 1972. *An Archaeological Perspective.* New York: Seminar Press.

———. 1983a. *In Pursuit of the Past: Decoding the Archaeological Record.* London: Thames and Hudson.

——— (Ed.). 1983b. *Working at Archaeology.* New York: Academic Press.

———. 1989. *Debating Archaeology.* San Diego: Academic Press.

———. 2001. *Constructing Frames of Reference: An Analytical Method for Archaeological Theory Building Using Ethnographic and Environmental Data Sets.* Berkeley: University of California Press.

Binford, Sally R., and Lewis R. Binford (Eds.). 1968. *New Perspectives in Archeology.* Chicago: Aldine.

Caton-Thompson, Gertrude. 1983. *Mixed Memoirs*. Gateshead, UK: The Paradigm Press.

Champion, Sara. 1998. Women in British archaeology: Visible and invisible. In Margarita Diaz-Andreu and Marie Louise Stig Sørensen (Eds.), *Excavating Women: A History of Women in European Archaeology* (pp. 175–197). London: Routledge.

Daniel, Glyn, and Colin Renfrew. 1988. *The Idea of Prehistory.* Edinburgh: University of Edinburgh Press.

Darwin, Charles. 1958 [1859]. *On the Origin of Species.* New York: Dutton.

Deagan, Kathleen. 1973. Mestizaje in colonial St. Augustine. *Ethnohistory* 20: 55–65.

———. 1980. Spanish St. Augustine: America's first "melting pot." *Archaeology* 33(5): 22–30.

———. 1982. Avenues of historical archaeology. In M. B. Schiffer (Ed.), *Advances in Archaeological Method and Theory*, Vol. 5 (pp. 151–177). New York: Academic Press.

———. 1983. *Spanish St. Augustine: The Archaeology of a Colonial Creole Community.* New York: Academic Press.

———. 1987. *Artifacts of the Spanish Colonies of Florida and the Caribbean, 1500–1800: Vol. 1. Ceramics, Glassware, and Beads.* Washington, DC: Smithsonian Institution Press.

——— (Ed.). 1995. *Puerto Real: The Archaeology of a Sixteenth-Century Spanish Town in Hispaniola.* Gainesville: University Press of Florida.

———. 1996. Colonial transformation: Euro-American cultural genesis in the early Spanish-American colonies. *Journal of Anthropological Research* 52: 135–160.

Deagan, Kathleen, and José María Cruxent. 2002a. *Archaeology at La Isabela: America's First European Town.* New Haven: Yale University Press.

———. 2002b. *Columbus's Outpost among the Tainos.* New Haven: Yale University Press.

Drower, Margaret S. 2004. Gertrude Caton-Thompson, 1888–1985. In Getzel Cohen and Martha Joukowsky (Eds.), *Breaking Ground: Pioneering Women Archaeologists* (pp. 351–379). Ann Arbor: University of Michigan Press.

Dunnell, Robert C. 1986. Five decades of American archaeology. In David J. Meltzer, Don D. Fowler, and Jeremy A. Sabloff (Eds.), *American Archaeology Past and Future: A Celebration of the Society for American Archaeology 1935–1985* (pp. 23–49). Washington, DC: Smithsonian Institution Press.

Grayson, Donald K. 1983. *The Establishment of Human Antiquity.* New York: Academic Press.

Irwin-Williams, Cynthia. 1990. Women in the field: The role of women in archaeology before 1960. In G. Kass-Simon and Patricia Farnes (Eds.), *Women of Science: Righting the Record* (pp. 1–41). Bloomington: Indiana University Press.

Kidder, Alfred V. 1924. *An Introduction to the Study of Southwestern Archaeology.* New Haven: Yale University Press.

———. 1960. Reminiscences in Southwest archaeology, I. *Kiva* 25: 1–32.

Kidder, Alfred V., and Samuel J. Guernsey. 1921. Basketmaker caves of northeastern Arizona. *Papers of the Peabody Museum of American Archaeology and Ethnology* 8(2).

Kidder, Alfred V., Jesse D. Jennings, and Edwin M. Shook. 1946. *Excavations at Kaminaljuyu, Guatemala.* Carnegie Institution of Washington Publication no. 561. Washington, DC: Carnegie Institution.

Mayes, S. 1959. *The Great Belzoni.* London: Putnam.

Parezo, Nancy J. (Ed.). 1993. *Hidden Scholars: Women Anthropologists and the Native American Southwest.* Albuquerque: University of New Mexico Press.

Patterson, Thomas. 1995. *Toward a Social History of Archaeology in the United States.* Fort Worth: Harcourt Brace.

Ryan, Donald. 1986. Giovanni Batista Belzoni. *Biblical Archaeologist* (Sept.): 133–138.

Stanford, Dennis. 1996. Hannah Marie Wormington 1914–1994. *American Antiquity* 61: 274–278.

Taylor, Walter W. 1948. A study of archeology. *American Anthropological Association, Memoir,* 69.

Trigger, Bruce G. 1999. *A History of Archaeological Thought,* 2d ed. Cambridge, UK: Cambridge University Press.

White, Nancy M., Lynne P. Sullivan, and Rochelle A. Marrinan. 1999. *Grit-Tempered: Early Women Archaeologists in the Southeastern United States.* Knoxville: University of Tennessee Press.

Willey, Gordon R., and Jeremy A. Sabloff. 1993. *A History of American Archaeology,* 3d ed. New York: Freeman.

Woodbury, Richard B. 1973. *Alfred V. Kidder.* New York: Columbia University Press.

Wormington, H. Marie. 1937. *Ancient Man in North America.* Denver: Colorado Museum of Natural History.

———. 1947. *Prehistoric Indians of the Southwest.* Denver: Colorado Museum of Natural History.

Wylie, Allison. 2002. *Thinking from Things: Essays in the Philosophy of Archaeology*. Berkeley: University of California Press.

Chapter 2

Atwater, Caleb. 1820. Description of the antiquities discovered in the state of Ohio and other western states. *Archaeologia Americana: Transactions and Collections of the American Antiquarian Society* 1: 105–267.

Baldwin, John D. 1872. *Ancient America in Notes on American Archaeology.* New York: Harper.

Binford, Lewis R. 1983. *In Pursuit of the Past: Decoding the Archaeological Record.* London: Thames and Hudson.

Bintliff, John. 1991. Post-modernism, rhetoric, and scholasticism at TAG: The current state of British archaeological theory. *Antiquity* 65: 274–278.

Carrithers, Michael. 1990. Is anthropology art or science? *Current Anthropology* 31: 263–282.

Daniel, Glyn. 1991. Post-processual developments in Anglo-American archaeology. *Norwegian Archaeological Review* 24: 65–76.

———. 1995. Expanding middle-range theory. *Antiquity* 69: 449–458.

Dark, K. R. 1995. *Theoretical Archaeology.* Ithaca, NY: Cornell University Press.

Flannery, Kent V. 1967. Culture history vs. cultural process: A debate in American archaeology. *Scientific American* 217(2): 119–121.

———. 1973. Archeology with a capital S. In Charles L. Redman (Ed.), *Research and Theory in Current Archeology* (pp. 47–53). New York: Wiley.

Gibbon, Guy. 1989. *Explanation in Archaeology.* Oxford, UK: Basil Blackwell.

Harris, Marvin. 1968. *The Rise of Anthropological Theory.* New York: Thomas Y. Crowell.

———. 1979. *Cultural Materialism: The Struggle for a Science of Culture.* New York: Random House.

Hegmon, Michelle. 2003. Setting theoretical egos aside: Issues and theory in North American archaeology. *American Antiquity* 68: 213–244.

Hodder, Ian. 1985. Postprocessual archaeology. In Michael B. Schiffer (Ed.), *Advances in Archaeological Method and Theory*, Vol. 8 (pp. 1–26). Orlando, FL: Academic Press.

———. 1986. *Reading the Past: Current Approaches to Interpretation in Archaeology.* Cambridge: Cambridge University Press.

———. 1989a. Post-modernism, post-structuralism and post-processual archaeology. In Ian Hodder (Ed.), *The Meaning of Things.* One World Archaeology, no. 6 (pp. 64–78). London: Unwin Hyman.

———. 1989b. Writing archaeology: Site reports in context. *Antiquity* 63: 268–274.

———. 1990. Archaeology and the post-modern. *Anthropology Today* 6(5): 13–15.

———. 1995. *Theory and Practice in Archaeology.* London: Routledge.

———. 1999. *The Archaeological Process: An Introduction.* Oxford, UK: Blackwell.

——— (Ed.). 2001. *Archaeological Theory Today.* Oxford, UK: Blackwell.

Jefferson, Thomas. 1787. *Notes on the State of Virginia.* London: John Stockdale (rpt. Chapel Hill: University of North Carolina Press, 1954).

Johnson, Matthew. 1999. *Archaeological Theory: An Introduction.* Oxford, UK: Blackwell.

Kemeny, John G. 1959. *A Philosopher Looks at Science.* New York: Van Nostrand Reinhold.

Knapp, A. Bernard. 1996. Archaeology without gravity: Postmodernism and the past. *Journal of Archaeological Method and Theory* 3: 127–158.

Kroeber, Alfred, and Clyde Kluckholn. 1952. Culture: A critical review of concepts and definitions. *Papers of the Peabody Museum of American Archaeology and Ethnology* 47(1).

Kuznar, Lawrence. 1997. *Reclaiming a Scientific Anthropology.* Walnut Creek, CA: Altamira.

Mcgee, R. Jon, and Richard L. Williams. 2004. *Anthropological Theory: An Introductory History,* 3d ed. New York: McGraw Hill.

Phillips, P. 1955. American archaeology and general anthropological theory. *Southwestern Journal of Anthropology* 11: 246–250 (quote from page 246–247).

Preucel, R. W. (Ed.). 1991. *Processual and Postprocessual Archaeologies: Multiple Ways of Knowing the Past.* Center for Archaeological Investigations, Occasional Paper no. 10. Carbondale: Southern Illinois University.

———. 1995. The postprocessual condition. *Journal of Archaeological Research* 3: 147–175.

Salmon, Merrilee H. 1982. *Philosophy and Archaeology.* New York: Academic Press.

Skibo, James M., William H. Walker, and Axel E. Nielsen (Eds.). 1995. *Expanding Archaeology.* Salt Lake City: University of Utah Press.

Squier, Ephraim G., and Edwin H. Davis. 1998. *Ancient Monuments of the Mississippi Valley,* edited and with an introduction by David J. Meltzer. Washington, DC: Smithsonian Institution Press.

Thomas, Cyrus. 1894. *Report on the Mound Explorations of the Bureau of Ethnology.* Washington, DC: Smithsonian Institution.

Tylor, Edward Burnett. 1871. *Primitive Culture,* Vols. 1 and 2. London: Murray (quote from p. 1).

Watson, Patty Jo. 1995. Archaeology, anthropology, and the culture concept. *American Anthropologist* 97: 683–694.

Wilk, Richard. 1985. The ancient Maya and the political present. *Journal of Anthropological Research* 41: 307–326.

Yoffee, Norman, and Andrew Sherratt (Eds.). 1993. *Archaeological Theory: Who Sets the Agenda?* Cambridge: Cambridge University Press.

Chapter 3

Aldenderfer, Mark, and Herbert Maschner (Eds.). 1996. *Anthropology, Space, and Geographic Information Systems.* New York: Oxford University Press.

Binford, Lewis R. 1964. A consideration of archaeological research design. *American Antiquity* 29: 425–441.

Boyd, Mark, F., Hale G. Smith, and John W. Griffin. 1951. *Here They Once Stood: The Tragic End of the Apalachee Missions*. Gainesville: University of Florida Press.

Crumley, C. L. 1994. The ecology of conquest: Contrasting agropastoral and agricultural societies' adaptation to climatic change. In C. L. Crumley (Ed.), *Historical Ecology: Cultural Knowledge and Changing Landscapes* (pp. 183–201). Santa Fe: SAR Press (quote from page 183).

Donoghue, D. N. M. 2001. Remote sensing. In D. Brothwell and A. Pollard (Eds.), *Handbook of Archaeological Sciences* (pp. 555–564). Chichester, UK: Wiley.

Garrison, Ervan G., James G. Baker, and David Hurst Thomas. 1985. Magnetic prospection and the discovery of Mission Santa Catalina de Guale, Georgia. *Journal of Field Archaeology* 12: 299–313.

Kantner, John. 1997. Ancient roads, modern mapping: Evaluating prehistoric Chaco Anasazi roadways using GIS technology. *Expedition* 39: 4962.

———. 2004. Geographical approaches for reconstructing past human behavior from prehistoric roadways. In M. F. Goodchild and D. G. Janelle (Eds.), *Spatially Integrated Social Sciences: Examples in Best Practice* (pp. 323–344). Oxford, UK: Oxford University Press.

Kelly, Robert. 2001. *Prehistory of the Carson Desert and Stillwater Mountains, Nevada: Environment, Mobility, and Subsistence.* University of Utah Anthropological Papers 123.

Riley, D. N. 1987. *Air Photography and Archaeology.* London: Duckworth.

Sabins, Floyd F., Jr. 1996. *Remote Sensing: Principles and Interpretation,* 3d ed. New York: W. H. Freeman.

Snead, J., and R. Preucel. 1999. The ideology of settlement: Ancestral Keres landscapes in the northern Rio Grande. In W. Ashmore and A. B. Knapp (Eds.), *Archaeologies of Landscape: Contemporary Perspectives* (pp. 169–197). Oxford, UK: Blackwell.

Thomas, David Hurst. 1983a. The archaeology of Monitor Valley: 1. Epistemology. *Anthropological Papers of the American Museum of Natural History* 58(1): 1–194.

———. 1983b. The archaeology of Monitor Valley: 2. Gatecliff Shelter. *Anthropological Papers of the American Museum of Natural History* 59(1): 1–552.

———. 1987. The archaeology of Mission Santa Catalina de Guale: 1. Search and discovery. *Anthropological Papers of the American Museum of Natural History* 63(2): 47–161.

———. 1988. The archaeology of Monitor Valley: 3. Survey and additional excavation. *Anthropological Papers of the American Museum of Natural History* 66(2): 131–633.

———. 1993. The archaeology of Mission Santa Catalina de Guale: Our first 15 years. In Bonnie G. McEwan (Ed.), *The Missions of La Florida* (pp. 1–34). Gainesville: University Press of Florida.

Wheatley, David, and Mark Gillings. 2002. *Spatial Technology and Archaeology: The Archaeological Applications of GIS.* London: Taylor and Francis.

Chapter 4

Collis, John. 2001. *Digging Up the Past: An Introduction to Archaeological Excavation.* Phoenix Mills, UK: Sutton.

Daugherty, Richard, and Ruth Kirk. 1976. Ancient Indian village where time stood still. *Smithsonian* 7(2): 68–75.

Flannery, K. V. 1982. The golden Marshalltown. *American Anthropologist* 84: 265–278 (quote from page 278).

Folsom, Franklin. 1992. *The Black Cowboy.* Niwot, CO: Roberts Rinehart.

Fowler, Brenda. 2001. *Iceman: Uncovering the Life and Times of a Prehistoric Man Found in an Alpine Glacier.* Chicago: University of Chicago Press.

Kirk, Ruth, and Richard Daugherty. 1974. *Hunters of the Whale.* New York: William Morrow.

Lock, Gary. 2003. *Using Computers in Archaeology: Towards Virtual Pasts.* London: Routledge.

Loud, Lewellyn L., and Mark R. Harrington. 1929. Lovelock Cave. *University of California Publications in American Archaeology and Ethnology* 25: 1–183.

McMillon, Bill. 1991. *The Archaeology Handbook: A Field Manual and Resource Guide.* New York: Wiley.

Meltzer, David. 1993. *Search for the First Americans.* Washington, DC: Smithsonian Institution Press.

Purdy, Barbara A. 1996. *How to Do Archaeology the Right Way.* Gainesville: University Press of Florida.

Schiffer, Michael B. 1972. Archaeological context and systemic context. *American Antiquity* 37: 156–165.

———. 1987. *Formation Processes of the Archaeological Record.* Albuquerque: University of New Mexico Press.

Struever, Stuart. 1968. Flotation techniques for the recovery of small-scale archaeological remains. *American Antiquity* 33: 353–362.

Thomas, David Hurst. 1983. The archaeology of Monitor Valley: 2. Gatecliff Shelter. *Anthropological Papers of the American Museum of Natural History* 59(1): 1–552.

Wagner, Gail E. 1982. Testing flotation recovery rates. *American Antiquity* 47: 127–132.

Watson, Patty Jo. 1974. Flotation procedures used on Salts Cave sediments. In Patty Jo Watson (Ed.), *Archaeology of the Mammoth Cave Area* (pp. 107–108). New York: Academic Press.

Chapter 5

Aitken, M. J. 1990. *Science-Based Dating in Archaeology.* London: Longman.

Baillie, M. G. L. 1995. *A Slice through Time: Dendrochronology and Precision Dating.* London: Batsford.

Bar-Yosef, O., and B. Vandermeersch. 1993. Modern humans in the Levant. *Scientific American* 268: 64–70.

Bishop, Gale A., Harold B. Rollins, and David Hurst Thomas (Eds.). 2011. *Geoarchaeology of St. Catherines Island (Georgia)*. Anthropological Papers of the American Museum of Natural History 94.

Bowman, Sheridan. 1990. *Radiocarbon Dating.* Berkeley: University of California Press.

———. 1994. Using radiocarbon: An update. *Antiquity* 68: 838–843.

Cook, E. R., J. Esper, and R. D. D'Arrigo. 2004. Extra-tropical Northern Hemisphere land temperature variability over the past 1000 years. *Quaternary Science Reviews* 23: 2063–2074.

Douglass, Andrew Ellicott. 1929. The secret of the Southwest solved by talkative tree rings. *National Geographic* 56(6): 736–770.

Dunnell, Robert C. 1970. Seriation method and its evaluation. *American Antiquity* 35: 305–319.

Feathers, James. 2003. Use of luminescence dating in archaeology. *Measurement Science and Technology* 14: 1493–1509.

Grün, R. 1999. Trapped charge dating (ESR, TL, OSL). In D. Brothwell and A. Pollard (Eds.), *Handbook of Archaeological Sciences* (pp. 47–62). Chichester, UK: Wiley.

Haas, Herbert, James Devine, Robert Wenke, Mark Lehner, Willy Wolfli, and George Bonani. 1987. Radiocarbon chronology and the historical calendar in Egypt. In Oliver Aurenche, Jacques Evin, and Francis Hours (Eds.), *Chronologies in the Near East: Relative Chronologies and Absolute Chronology 16,000–4,000 BP* (pp. 585–606). British Archaeology Reports International Series 379. Oxford, UK.

Mann, M. E., R. S. Bradley, and M. K. Hughes. 1999. Northern Hemisphere temperatures during the past millennium: Inferences, uncertainties, and limitations. *Geophysical Research Letters* 26: 759–762.

Mann, M. E., C. M. Ammann, R. S. Bradley, K. R. Briffa, T. J. Crowley, M. K. Hughes, P. D. Jones, M. Oppenheimer, T. J. Osborn, J. T. Overpeck, S. Rutherford, K. E. Trenberth, and T. M. L. Wigley. 2003. On past temperatures and anomalous late 20th century warmth, *Eos* 84: 256–258.

Marquardt, William H. 1978. Advances in archaeological seriation. In Michael B. Schiffer (Ed.), *Advances in Archaeological Method and Theory*, Vol. 1 (pp. 257–314). New York: Academic Press.

Mayer-Oakes, W. 1955. Prehistory of the Upper Ohio Valley: An introductory study. *Carnegie Museum Anthropological Series* No. 2. Pittsburgh.

Nash, Stephen E. 1999. *Time, Trees, and Prehistory: Tree Ring Dating and the Development of North American Archaeology, 1914–1950.* Salt Lake City: University of Utah Press.

———. 2000. *It's about Time: A History of Archaeological Dating in North America.* Salt Lake City: University of Utah Press.

Nelson, Nels. 1916. Chronology of the Tano Ruins, New Mexico. *American Anthropologist* 18: 159–180 (Table 5-1 is from p. 166).

Stuiver, Minze, and Paula J. Reimer. 1993. Extended ^{14}C database and revised CALIB 3.0 ^{14}C age calibration program. *Radiocarbon* 35: 215–230.

Swisher, C. C., III, G. H. Curtis, T. Jacob, A. G. Getty, and A. Suprijo Widasmoro. 1994. Age of the earliest known hominids in Java, Indonesia. *Science* 263: 1118–1121.

Taylor, R. E., and M. J. Aitken (Eds.). 1997. *Chronometric Dating in Archaeology.* New York: Plenum Press.

Taylor, R. E., Austin Long, and Renee S. Kra (Eds.). 1992. *Radiocarbon after Four Decades: An Interdisciplinary Perspective.* New York: Springer-Verlag.

van der Merwe, Nikolaas J. 1982. Carbon isotopes, photosynthesis, and archaeology. *American Scientist* 70: 596–606.

Wintle, Ann G. 1996. Archaeologically relevant dating techniques for the next century. *Journal of Archaeological Science* 23: 123–138.

Chapter 6

Binford, Lewis R. 1973. Interassemblage variability—The Mousterian and the "functional" argument. In Colin Renfrew (Ed.), *The Explanation of Culture Change: Models in Prehistory* (pp. 227–254). London: Duckworth.

Cordell, Linda. 1984. *Prehistory of the Southwest.* New York: Academic Press.

Dunnell, Robert C. 1986. Methodological issues in Americanist artifact classification. In Michael B. Schiffer (Ed.), *Advances in Archaeological Method and Theory*, Vol. 9 (pp. 149–207). New York: Academic Press.

Kidder A.V. 1931. *The Pottery of Pecos, vol. 1.* Papers of the Southwestern Expedition, Phillips Academy. New Haven: Yale University Press.

Lyman, R. Lee, Michael O'Brien, and Robert C. Dunnell (Eds.). 1997. *Americanist Culture History: Fundamentals of Time, Space, and Form.* New York: Plenum.

Rouse, Irving. 1960. The classification of artifacts in archaeology. *American Antiquity* 25: 313–323.

Spaulding, Albert C. 1960. The dimensions of archaeology. In G. E. Dole and R. L. Carneiro (Eds.), *Essays in the Science of Culture in Honor of Leslie A. White* (pp. 437–456). New York: Thomas Y. Crowell.

Spier, Leslie. 1931. N. C. Nelson's stratigraphic technique in the reconstruction of prehistoric sequences in southwestern America. In S. A. Rice (Ed.), *Methods in Social Science* (pp. 275–283). Chicago: University of Chicago Press.

Steward, Julian H. 1954. Types of types. *American Anthropologist* 56: 54–57.

Sutton, Mark Q., and Brooke S. Arkush. 1996. *Archaeological Laboratory Methods: An Introduction.* Dubuque, IA: Kendall/Hunt.

Thomas, David Hurst. 1981. How to classify the projectile points from Monitor Valley, Nevada. *Journal of California and Great Basin Anthropology* 3: 7–43.

———. 1983. The archaeology of Monitor Valley: 2. Gatecliff Shelter. *Anthropological Papers of the American Museum of Natural History*, Vol. 59, Part 1.

Willey, Gordon R., and Philip Phillips. 1958. *Method and Theory in American Archaeology.* Chicago: University of Chicago Press (quote from p. 22).

Wissler, Clark. 1926. *The Relation of Nature to Man in Aboriginal America.* New York: Oxford University Press.

Chapter 7

Agenbroad, Larry. 1978. *The Hudson-Meng Site: An Alberta Bison Kill in the Nebraska High Plains.* Washington, DC: University Press of America.

Binford, Lewis R. 1967. Smudge pits and hide smoking: The use of analogy in archaeological reasoning. *American Antiquity* 32: 1–12.

———. 1978. *Nunamiut Ethnoarchaeology.* New York: Academic Press.

Brandt, Steve A., and Kathryn Weedman. 1997. The ethnoarchaeology of hideworking and flaked stone tool use in southern Ethiopia. In K. Fukui, E. Kuimoto, and M. Shigeta (Eds.), *Ethiopia in Broader Perspective: Papers of the XIIth International Conference of Ethiopian Studies* (pp. 351–361). Kyoto: Shokado Book Sellers.

Chaplin, R. E. 1971. *The Study of Animal Bones from Archaeological Sites.* New York: Seminar Press.

Coles, John M. 1973. *Archaeology by Experiment.* New York: Scribner's.

Crabtree, Don E. 1966. A stoneworker's approach to analyzing and replicating the Lindenmeier Folsom. *Tebiwa* 9: 3–39.

David, Nicholas, and Carol Kramer. 2001. *Ethnoarchaeology in Action.* Cambridge: Cambridge University Press.

Efremov, I. A. 1940. Taphonomy: A new branch of paleontology. *Pan-American Geologist* 74(2): 81–93.

Flenniken, J. Jeffrey. 1978. Reevaluation of the Lindenmeier Folsom: A replication experiment in lithic technology. *American Antiquity* 43: 473–480.

Gamble, C. S., and W. A. Boismier (Eds.). 1991. *Ethnoarchaeological Approaches to Mobile Campsites.* International Monographs in Prehistory. Ann Arbor, MI.

Gifford, Diane P. 1981. Taphonomy and paleoecology: A critical review of archaeology's sister disciplines. In Michael B. Schiffer (Ed.), *Advances in Archaeological Method and Theory,* Vol. 4 (pp. 365–438). New York: Academic Press.

Gryba, Eugene M. 1988. A Stone Age pressure method of Folsom fluting. *Plains Anthropologist* 33: 53–66.

Hayden, Brian. 1979. *Palaeolithic Reflections: Lithic Technology and Ethnographic Excavation among Australian Aborigines.* Atlantic Highlands, NJ: Humanities Press.

Hill, Andrew, and Anna Kay Behrensmeyer. 1984. Disarticulation patterns of some modern East African mammals. *Paleobiology* 10: 366–376.

Hodder, Ian. 1982. *Symbols in Action.* Cambridge: Cambridge University Press.

———. 1987. The meaning of discard: Ash and domestic space in Baringo. In S. Kent (Ed.), *Method and Theory in Activity Area Research* (pp. 424–448). New York: Columbia University Press.

Kelly, Robert L., Lin Poyer, and Bram Tucker. 2005. An ethnoarchaeological study of mobility, architectural investment, and food sharing among Madagascar's Mikea. *American Anthropologist* 107: 403–416.

Kelly, Robert, Jean-François Rabedimy, and Lin A. Poyer. 1999. The Mikea of southwestern Madagascar. In R. B. Lee and R. Daly (Eds.), *The Cambridge Encyclopedia of Hunter-Gatherers* (pp. 215–219). Cambridge: Cambridge University Press.

Kramer, Carol. 1997. *Pottery in Rajasthan: Ethnoarchaeology in Two Indian Cities.* Washington, DC: Smithsonian Institution Press.

Kroeber, Theodora. 1967. *Ishi in Two Worlds: A Biography of the Last Wild Indian in North America.* Berkeley: University of California Press.

Lehner, Mark. 1997. *The Complete Pyramids: Solving the Ancient Mysteries.* London: Thames and Hudson.

Longacre, William A. (Ed.). 1991. *Ceramic Ethnoarchaeology.* Tucson: University of Arizona Press.

Longacre, William A., and James M. Skibo (Eds.). 1994. *Kalinga Ethnoarchaeology: Expanding Archaeological Method and Theory.* Washington, DC: Smithsonian Institution Press.

O'Connell, James F. 1995. Ethnoarchaeology needs a general theory of behavior. *Journal of Archaeological Research* 3: 205–255.

Perkins, D., Jr., and P. Daly. 1968. A hunter's village in Neolithic Turkey. *Scientific American* 219(5): 96–106.

Pope, Saxton T. 1974. Hunting with Ishi—the last Yana Indian. *Journal of California Anthropology* 1: 152–173.

Raab, L. Mark, and Albert C. Goodyear. 1984. Middle-range theory in archaeology: A critical review of origins and applications. *American Antiquity* 49: 255–268.

Stahl, Ann B. 1995. Has ethnoarchaeology come of age? *Antiquity* 69: 404–407.

Todd, Lawrence C., and David Rapson. 1999. Formational analysis of bison bonebeds and interpretation of Paleoindian subsistence. In J-P. Brugal, F. David, J. G. Enloe, and J. Jaubert (Eds.), *Le Bison: Gibier et moyen de subsistance des hommes du Paléolithique aux Paléoindiens des Grandes Plains* (pp. 479–499). Antibes, France: Association pour la promotion et la diffusion des Connaissances Archéologiques.

Trigger, Bruce G. 1981. Archaeology and the ethnographic present. *Anthropologica* 23: 3–17.

———. 1995. Expanding middle-range theory. *Antiquity* 69: 449–458.

Tunnell, C. 1977. Fluted projectile point production as revealed by lithic specimens from the Adair-Steadman site in northwest Texas. In Eileen Johnson (Ed.), Paleoindian Lifeways. Lubbock: West Texas Museum Association, Texas Tech University. *The Museum Journal* 17: 140–168.

White, Theodore E. 1953. A method of calculating the dietary percentage of various food animals utilized by aboriginal peoples. *American Antiquity* 18: 396–398.

———. 1954. Observations on the butchering technique of some aboriginal peoples, nos. 3, 4, 5, and 6. *American Antiquity* 19: 254–264.

Wylie, Alison. 1985. The reaction against analogy. In M. B. Schiffer (Ed.), *Advances in Archaeological Method and Theory,* Vol. 8 (pp. 63–112). New York: Academic Press.

Yellen, John E. 1977. *Archaeological Approaches to the Present: Models for Reconstructing the Past.* New York: Academic Press.

Chapter 8

Binford, Lewis R. 1978. *Nunamiut Ethnoarchaeology.* New York: Academic Press.

———. 1981. *Bones: Ancient Men and Modern Myths.* New York: Academic Press.

Brewer, Douglas J. 1992. Zooarchaeology: Method, theory, and goals. In M. B. Schiffer (Ed.), *Archaeological Method and Theory,* Vol. 4 (pp. 195–244). Tucson: University of Arizona Press.

Brothwell, D., and A. Pollard (Eds.). 2001. *Handbook of Archaeological Sciences.* Chichester, UK: Wiley.

Crabtree, Pam J. 1990. Zooarchaeology and complex societies: Some uses of faunal analysis for the study of trade, social status, and ethnicity. In M. B. Schiffer (Ed.), *Archaeological Method and Theory,* Vol. 2 (pp. 155–205). Tucson: University of Arizona Press.

Cummings, Linda Scott. 2001. Phytolith analysis. In R. L. Kelly (Ed.), *Prehistory of the Carson Desert and Stillwater Mountains: Environment, Mobility, and Subsistence in a Great Basin Wetland* (pp. 251–252). University of Utah Anthropological Paper no. 123. Salt Lake City.

Dincauze, Dena. 2000. *Environmental Archaeology: Principles and Practice.* Cambridge: Cambridge University Press.

Evershed, R. P., S. N. Dudd, M. J. Collins, O. E. Craig, and R. J. Sokal. 2001. Lipids in archaeology. In D. Brothwell and A. Pollard (Eds.), *Handbook of Archaeological Sciences* (pp. 331–350). Chichester, UK: Wiley.

Faegri, K., P. E. Kaland, and K. Krzywinski. 1989. *Textbook of Pollen Analysis,* 4th ed. New York: Wiley.

Frison, George C., and Dennis Stanford. 1982. *The Agate Basin Site: A Record of the Paleoindian Occupation of the Northwestern High Plains.* New York: Academic Press.

Gilbert, B. Miles. 1980. *Mammalian Osteology.* Laramie, WY: Modern Printing.

Grayson, Donald K. 1984. *Quantitative Zooarchaeology: Topics in the Analysis of Archaeological Faunas.* Orlando, FL: Academic Press.

Hastorf, Christine A., and Sissel Johannessen. 1991. Understanding changing people/plant relationships in the pre-Hispanic Andes. In Robert W. Preucel (Ed.), *Processual and Postprocessual Archaeologies: Multiple Ways of Knowing the Past* (pp. 140–155). Center for Archaeological Investigations, Occasional Paper no. 10. Southern Illinois University at Carbondale.

Haury, Emil W., E. B. Sayles, and William W. Wasley. 1959. The Lehner mammoth site, southeastern Arizona. *American Antiquity* 25: 2–30.

Hill, Matthew G. 2001. *Paleoindian Diet and Subsistence Behavior on the Northwestern Great Plains of North America.* Unpublished PhD dissertation, Department of Anthropology, University of Wisconsin, Madison.

———. 2008. *Paleoindian Subsistence Dynamics on the Northwestern Great Plains: Zooarchaeology of the Agate Basin and Clary Ranch Sites*. Oxford: British Archaeological Reports, International Series, no. 1756.

Holden, T. G. 2001. Dietary evidence from the coprolites and the intestinal contents of ancient humans. In D. Brothwell and A. Pollard (Eds.), *Handbook of Archaeological Sciences* (pp. 403–414). Chichester, UK: Wiley.

Leroi-Gourhan, Arlette. 1975. The flowers found with Shanidar IV, a Neanderthal burial in Iraq. *Science* 190: 562–564.

Lyman, R. Lee. 1994. *Vertebrate Taphonomy.* Cambridge: Cambridge University Press.

Malainey, Mary E., R. Przybylski, and B. L. Sherriff. 1999. Identifying the former contents of late pre-contact period pottery vessels from western Canada using gas chromatography. *Journal of Archaeological Science* 26: 425–438.

Mehringer, Peter J., and Vance Haynes. 1965. The pollen evidence for the environment of early man and extinct mammals at the Lehner mammoth site, southeastern Arizona. *American Antiquity* 31: 17–23.

Miksicek, Charles H. 1987. Formation processes of the archaeobotanical record. In Michael B. Schiffer (Ed.), *Advances in Archaeological Method and Theory*, Vol. 10 (pp. 211–247). New York: Academic Press.

Miller, George. 1979. *An Introduction to the Ethnoarchaeology of the Andean Camelids.* PhD diss., University of California, Berkeley.

Miller, George, and Richard Burger. 1995. Our father the cayman, our dinner the llama: Animal utilization at Chavín de Huántar, Peru. *American Antiquity* 60: 421–458.

———. 2000. Ch'arki at Chavín: Ethnographic models and archaeological data. *American Antiquity* 65: 573–576.

Moore, P. D., J. A. Webb, and M. E. Collinson. 1991. *Pollen Analysis.* Oxford, UK: Blackwell Scientific.

Pearsall, Deborah M. 2000. *Paleoethnobotany: A Handbook of Procedures.* New York: Academic Press.

Reitz, Elizabeth, and Elizabeth Wing. 1999. *Zooarchaeology.* Cambridge: Cambridge University Press.

Rhode, David. 2001. Macrobotanical remains. In R. L. Kelly (Ed.), *Prehistory of the Carson Desert and Stillwater Mountains: Environment, Mobility, and Subsistence in a Great Basin Wetland* (pp. 254–262). University of Utah Anthropological Paper no. 123.

———. 2004. Coprolites from Hidden Cave, revisited: Evidence for occupation history, diet, and gender. *Journal of Archaeological Science* 30: 909–922.

Sobolik, Kristin. 2003. *The Archaeologist's Toolkit: Vol. 5. Archaeobiology.* Walnut Creek, CA: Altamira.

Solecki, Ralph S. 1971. *Shanidar: The First Flower People.* New York: Knopf.

Sommer, Jeffrey. 1999. The Shanidar IV "Flower Burial": A Reevaluation of Neanderthal Burial Ritual. *Cambridge Archaeological Journal* 9: 127–137.

Stahl, Peter. 1999. Structural density of domesticated South American camelid skeletal elements and the archaeological investigation of prehistoric Andean ch'arki. *Journal of Archaeological Science* 26: 1347–1368.

Sutton, Mark Q., Minnie Malik, and Andrew Ogram. 1996. Experiments on the determination of gender from coprolites by DNA analysis. *Journal of Archaeological Science* 23: 263–267.

Valdez, Lidio. 2000. Ch'arki consumption in the ancient central Andes: A cautionary note. *American Antiquity* 65: 567–572.

Chapter 9

Brooks, Sheilagh, Michele Haldeman, and Richard Brooks. 1988. *Osteological Analyses of the Stillwater Skeletal Series, Stillwater Marsh, Churchill County, Nevada.* U.S. Fish and Wildlife Service Cultural Resource Series, no. 2.

Buikstra, Jane E., and L. Konigsberg. 1985. Paleodemography: Critiques and controversies. *American Anthropologist* 87: 316–333.

Dillehay, Tom D. 1989. *Monte Verde: A Late Pleistocene Settlement in Chile: Vol. 1. Paleoenvironment and Site Context.* Washington, DC: Smithsonian Institution Press.

———. 1997. *Monte Verde: A Late Pleistocene Settlement in Chile: Vol. 2. The Archaeological Context and Interpretation.* Washington, DC: Smithsonian Institution Press.

Eshleman, Jason A., Ripan S. Mahli, and David Glenn Smith. 2003. Mitochondrial DNA studies of Native Americans: Conceptions and misconceptions of the population prehistory of the Americas. *Evolutionary Anthropology* 12: 7–18.

Ezzo, Joseph A., Clark Spencer Larsen, and James H. Burton. 1995. Elemental signatures of human diets from the Georgia Bight. *American Journal of Physical Anthropology* 98: 471–481.

Gilbert, M. Thomas P., Dennis L. Jenkins, Anders Götherstrom, Nuria Naveran, Juan J. Sanchez, Michael Hofreiter, Philip Francis Thomsen, Jonas Binladen, Thomas F. G. Higham, Robert M. Yohe II, Robert Parr, Linda Scott Cummings, and Eske Willerslev. 2008. DNA from pre-Clovis human coprolites in Oregon, North America. *Science* 320: 786–789.

Horai, Satoshi, Rumi Kondo, Yuko Nakagawa-Hattori, Seiji Hayashi, Shunro Sonoda, and Kazuo Tajima. 1993. Peopling of the Americas, founded by four major lineages of mitochondrial DNA. *Molecular Biological Evolution* 10(1): 23–47.

Huss-Ashmore, Rebecca, Alan H. Goodman, and George J. Armelagos. 1982. Nutritional inference from paleopathology. In Michael B. Schiffer (Ed.), *Advances in Archaeological Method and Theory*, Vol. 5 (pp. 395–474). New York: Academic Press.

Hutchinson, Dale, and Clark Spencer Larsen. 1988. Determination of stress episode duration from linear enamel hypoplasias: A case study from St. Catherines Island, Georgia. *Human Biology* 60: 93–110.

———. 1995. Physiological stress in the prehistoric Stillwater Marsh: Evidence of enamel defects. In C. S. Larsen and R. L. Kelly (Eds.), *Bioarchaeology of the Stillwater Marsh: Prehistoric Human Adaptation in the Western Great Basin* (pp. 81–95). Anthropological Papers of the American Museum of Natural History, no. 77. New York.

Kelly, Robert. 2003. Maybe we do know when people came to North America; and what does it mean if we do? *Quaternary International* 109–110: 133–145.

Kitchen, Andrew, Michael M. Miyamoto, and Connie J. Mulligan. 2008. A three-stage colonization model for the peopling of the Americas. *Plos One* 3. www.plosone.org.

Konigsberg, Lyle W., and Jane E. Buikstra. 1995. Regional approaches to the investigation of past human biocultural structure. In Lane Anderson Beck (Ed.), *Regional Approaches to Mortuary Analysis* (pp. 191–219). New York: Plenum Press.

Larsen, Clark Spencer. 1997. *Bioarchaeology: Interpreting Behavior from the Human Skeleton.* Cambridge: Cambridge University Press.

Larsen, Clark Spencer, and Robert L. Kelly (Eds.). 1995. *Bioarchaeology of the Stillwater Marsh: Prehistoric Human Adaptation in the Western Great Basin.* Anthropological Papers of the American Museum of Natural History, no. 77.

Larsen, Clark Spencer, Christopher B. Ruff, and Robert L. Kelly. 1995. Structural analysis of the Stillwater postcranial human remains: Behavioral implications of articular joint pathology and long bone diaphyseal morphology. In C. S. Larsen and R. L. Kelly (Eds.), *Bioarchaeology of the Stillwater Marsh: Prehistoric Human Adaptation in the Western Great Basin* (pp. 107–133). Anthropological Papers of the American Museum of Natural History, no. 77.

Meltzer, David J. 1995. Clocking the first Americans. *Annual Review of Anthropology* 24: 21–45.

Pääbo, Svante. 1993. Ancient DNA: Genetic information that had seemed lost forever turns out to linger in the remains of long-dead plants and animals. *Scientific American*, November, pp. 87–92.

Powell, J., and W. A. Neves. 1999. Craniofacial morphology of the first Americans: Pattern and process in the peopling of the new world. *Yearbook of Physical Anthropology* 42: 153–188.

Price, T. Douglas (Ed.). 1989. *The Chemistry of Prehistoric Human Bone.* Cambridge: Cambridge University Press.

Rothschild, Bruce M., and Larry D. Martin. 1993. *Palaeopathology: Disease in the Fossil Record.* Boca Raton, FL: CRC.

Sahlins, Marshall.1968. Notes on the original affluent society. In Richard Lee and Irven DeVore (Eds.), *Man the Hunter* (pp. 85–89). Chicago: Aldine.

Sarich, Vincent, and Allan Wilson. 1967. Immunological time scale for human evolution. *Science* 158: 1200–1203.

Schoeninger, Margaret. 1995. Dietary reconstruction in the prehistoric Carson Desert: Stable carbon and nitrogen isotopic analysis. In C. S. Larsen and R. L. Kelly (Eds.), *Bioarchaeology of the Stillwater Marsh: Prehistoric Human Adaptation in the Western Great Basin* (pp. 96–106). Anthropological Papers of the American Museum of Natural History, no. 77.

Scott, G., and Turner II, C. 1997. *The Anthropology of Modern Human Teeth.* Cambridge: Cambridge University Press.

Seielstad, Mark, Nadira Yuldasheva, Nadia Singh, Peter Underhill, Peter Oefner, Peidong Shen, and R. Spencer Wells. 2003. A novel Y-chromosome variant puts an upper limit on the timing of first entry into the Americas. *American Journal of Human Genetics* 73: 700–705.

Stone, Anne C., and Mark Stoneking. 1993. Ancient DNA from a pre-Columbian Amerindian population. *American Journal of Physical Anthropology* 92: 463–471.

Szathmary, Emöke J. E. 1993. Genetics of aboriginal North Americans. *Evolutionary Anthropology* 1(6): 202–220.

Tamm, Erika, Toomas Kivisild, Maere Reidla, Mait Metspalu, David Glenn Smith, Connie J. Mulligan, Claudio M. Bravi, Olga Rickards, Cristina Martinez-Labarga, Elsa K. Khusnutdinova, Sardana A. Fedorova, Maria V. Golubenko, Vadim A. Stepanov, Marina A. Gubina, Sergey I. Zhadanov, Ludmila P. Ossipova, Larisa Damba, Mikhail I. Voevoda, Jose E. Dipierri, Richard Villems, and Ripan S. Malhi. 2007. Beringian standstill and spread of Native American founders. *Plos One* 9. www.plosone .org.

Torroni, Antonio, Theodore G. Schurr, Chi-Chuan Yang, Emöke J. E. Szathmary, Robert C. Williams, Moses S. Schanfield, Gary A. Troup, William C. Knowler, Dale N. Lawrence, Kenneth M. Weiss, and Douglas C. Wallace. 1991. Native American mitochondrial DNA analysis indicates that the Amerind and the Nadene populations were founded by two independent migrations. *Genetics* 130: 153–162.

Walker, Phillip L. 1986. Porotic hyperostosis in a marine-dependent California Indian population. *American Journal of Physical Anthropology* 69: 345–354.

Chapter 10

Bailey, Robert C., and Robert Aunger. 1989. Hunters vs. archers: Variation in women's subsistence strategies in the Ituri Forest. *Human Ecology* 17: 273–297.

Beck, Lane Anderson (Ed.). 1995. *Regional Approaches to Mortuary Analysis.* New York: Plenum Press.

Conkey, Margaret W., and Janet Spector. 1984. Archaeology and the study of gender. In Michael B. Schiffer (Ed.), *Advances in Archaeological Method and Theory*, Vol. 7 (pp. 1–38). Orlando, FL: Academic Press.

DeNiro, Michael J., and Margaret J. Schoeniger. 1983. Stable carbon and nitrogen isotope ratios of bone collagen: Variations within individuals, between sexes, and within populations raised on monotonous diets. *Journal of Archaeological Science* 10: 199–203.

Galloway, Patricia (Ed.). 1989. *The Southeastern Ceremonial Complex: Artifacts and Analysis.* Lincoln: University of Nebraska Press.

Gero, Joan M., and Margaret W. Conkey (Eds.). 1991. *Engendering Archaeology: Women and Prehistory.* Oxford, UK: Basil Blackwell.

Houston, S. D., and P. A. McAnany. 2003. Bodies and blood: Critiquing social construction in Maya archaeology. *Journal of Anthropological Archaeology* 22: 26–41.

Hughes, Richard E. 2006. The sources of Hopewell obsidian: Thirty years after Griffin. In Douglas K. Charles and Jane E. Buikstra (Eds.), *Recreating Hopewell* (pp. 361–375). Gainesville: University Press of Florida.

Joyce, Rosemary. 1995. The construction of gender in Classic Maya monuments. In Rita Wright (Ed.), *Gender and Archaeology* (pp. 167–195). Philadelphia: University of Pennsylvania Press.

Knight, Vernon J., Jr. 1998. Moundville as a diagrammatic ceremonial center. In V. J. Knight, Jr., and V. Steponaitis (Eds.), *Archaeology of the Moundville Chiefdom* (pp. 44–62).Washington, DC: Smithsonian Institution Press.

Knight, Vernon J., Jr., and Vincas Steponaitis. 1998. *Archaeology of the Moundville Chiefdom.* Washington, DC: Smithsonian Institution Press.

re, C. B. 1916. Some aboriginal sites Green River, Kentucky: Certain ginal sites on lower Ohio River. *of the Academy of Natural Sciences of Philadelphia,* 2nd series, vol. XVI. Philadelphia: Academy of Natural Sciences.

Nelson, Sarah M. 1995. *Gender in Archaeology: Analyzing Power and Prestige.* Walnut Creek, CA: Altamira.

Orton, Clive, Paul Tyers, and Alan Vince. 1993. *Pottery in Archaeology.* Cambridge: Cambridge University Press.

O'Shea, John M. 1984. *Mortuary Variability: An Archaeological Investigation.* Orlando, FL: Academic Press.

Peebles, Christopher S., and Susan M. Kus. 1977. Some archaeological correlates of ranked societies. *American Antiquity* 42: 421–448.

Rice, Prudence M. 1991. Women and prehistoric pottery production. In D. Walde and N. Willows (Eds.), *The Archaeology of Gender* (pp. 436–443). Calgary: Archaeological Association of the University of Calgary.

Sinopoli, Carla. 1991. *Approaches to Archaeological Ceramics.* New York: Plenum Press.

Smith, Bruce D. (Ed.). 1990. *The Mississippian Emergence.* Washington, DC: Smithsonian Institution Press.

Wason, Paul K. 1994. *The Archaeology of Rank.* Cambridge: Cambridge University Press.

Webb, William S. 1974 [1946]. *Indian Knoll.* Knoxville: University of Tennessee Press (quote from p. 330).

Wright, Rita (Ed). 1996. *Gender and Archaeology.* Philadelphia: University of Pennsylvania Press.

Chapter 11

Bahn, Paul. 1998. *The Cambridge Illustrated History of Prehistoric Art.* Cambridge: Cambridge University Press.

Bender, Barbara. 1993. Cognitive archaeology and cultural materialism. *Cambridge Archaeological Journal* 3: 257–260.

Burger, Richard L. 1992. *Chavín and the Origins of Andean Civilization.* London: Thames and Hudson.

Conrad, Geoffrey W. 1981. Cultural materialism, split inheritance, and the expansion of ancient Peruvian empires. *American Antiquity* 46: 3–26.

Conrad, Geoffrey W., and Arthur A. Demarest. 1984. *Religion and Empire: The Dynamics of Aztec and Inca Expansionism.* Cambridge: Cambridge University Press.

Douglas, Mary. 1966. *Purity and Danger: An Analysis of the Concepts of Pollution and Taboo.* London: Routledge and Kegan Paul.

Flannery, Kent V., and Joyce Marcus. 1993. Cognitive archaeology. *Cambridge Archaeological Journal* 3: 260–270.

Hall, Robert L. 1977. An anthropocentric perspective for eastern United States prehistory. *American Antiquity* 42: 499–518.

———. 1997. *An Archaeology of the Soul: North American Indian Belief and Ritual.* Urbana: University of Illinois Press.

Laming-Emperaire, Annette. 1962. *La signification de l'art rupestre Paléolithique.* Paris: Picard.

Lathrap, Donald W. 1973. Gifts of the cayman: Some thoughts on the subsistence basis of Chavín. In Donald W. Lathrap and Jody Douglas (Eds.), *Variation in Anthropology* (pp. 91–105). Urbana: Illinois Archaeological Survey.

———. 1977. Our father the cayman, our mother the gourd: Spinden revisited, or a unitary model for the emergence of agriculture in the New World. In Charles A. Reed (Ed.), *Origins of Agriculture* (pp. 713–751). The Hague: Mouton.

———. 1985. Jaws: The control of power in the early nuclear American ceremonial center. In C. B. Donnan (Ed.), *Early Ceremonial Architecture in the Andes* (pp. 241–267). Washington, DC: Dumbarton Oaks Research Library and Collection.

Leroi-Gourhan, André. 1968. *The Art of Prehistoric Man in Western Europe.* London: Thames and Hudson.

———. 1980. *Treasures of Prehistoric Art.* Trans. from French by Norbert Guterman. New York: Harry H. Abrams.

———. 1982. *The Dawn of European Art: An Introduction to Palaeolithic Cave Painting.* Cambridge: Cambridge University Press.

Lewis-Williams, David. 2002. *The Mind in the Cave.* London: Thames and Hudson.

Marcus, Joyce, and Kent Flannery. 1996. *Zapotec Civilization.* London: Thames and Hudson.

Mason, Ronald. 2000. Archaeology and Native North American oral traditions. *American Antiquity* 65: 239–266.

Renfrew, Colin. 1993. Cognitive archaeology: Some thoughts on the archaeology of thought. *Cambridge Archaeological Journal* 3: 248–250.

Renfrew, Colin, and Ezra B. W. Zubrow (Eds.). 1994. *The Ancient Mind: Elements of Cognitive Archaeology.* Cambridge: Cambridge University Press.

Von Hagen, Adriana, and Craig Morris. 1998. *The Cities of the Ancient Andes.* London: Thames and Hudson.

Chapter 12

Archaeology. Retrieved June 14, 2006, from www.archaeology.org/online/features/afburial.

Ascher, Robert, and Charles H. Fairbanks. 1971. Excavation of a slave cabin: Georgia, U.S.A. *Historical Archaeology* 5: 3–17.

Beaudry, Mary C. (Ed.). 1988. *Documentary Archaeology in the New World.* Cambridge: Cambridge University Press.

Blakey, Michael L. 1995. Race, nationalism, and the Afrocentric past. In P. R. Schmidt and T. Patterson (Eds.), *Making Alternative Histories: The Practice of Archaeology and History in Non-Western Settings* (pp. 213–228). Santa Fe: School of American Research Press.

Crader, Diana C. 1990. Slave diet at Monticello. *American Antiquity* 55: 690–717.

Deagan, Kathleen. 1982. Avenues of inquiry in historical archaeology. In Michael B. Schiffer (Ed.), *Advances in Archaeological Method and Theory*, Vol. 5 (pp. 151–177). New York: Academic Press (quote from p. 153).

Deagan, Kathleen, and Darcie MacMahon. 1995. *Fort Mose: Colonial America's Black Fortress of Freedom.* Gainesville: University Press of Florida/Florida Museum of Natural History.

Deetz, James. 1977. *In Small Things Forgotten: The Archaeology of Early American Life.* Garden City, NY: Anchor Books.

———. 1988. Material culture and worldview in colonial Anglo-America. In Mark Leone and Parker Potter (Eds.), *The Recovery of Meaning: Historical Archaeology in the Eastern United States* (pp. 219–233). Washington, DC: Smithsonian Institution Press.

———. 1991. Introduction: Archaeological evidence of sixteenth- and seventeenth-century encounters. In Lisa Falk (Ed.), *Historical Archaeology in Global Perspective* (pp. 1–9). Washington, DC: Smithsonian Institution Press.

Fairbanks, Charles H. 1984. Plantation archaeology of the southeastern coast. *Historical Archaeology* 18: 1–14.

Ferguson, Leland B. 1992. *Uncommon Ground: Archaeology and Early African America, 1650–1800.* Washington, DC: Smithsonian Institution Press.

Fox, Richard. 1993. *Archaeology, History, and Custer's Last Battle: The Little Big Horn Reexamined.* Norman: University of Oklahoma Press.

Glassie, Henry. 1975. *Folk Housing in Middle Virginia.* Knoxville: University of Tennessee Press.

Government Services Administration. *Archaeology* online. Retrieved June 14, 2006, from www.archaeology.org/online/features/afburial.

Handsman, Russell G., and Mark P. Leone. 1989. Living history and critical archaeology in the reconstruction of the past. In Valerie Pinsky and Alison Wylie (Eds.), *Critical Traditions in Contemporary Archaeology: Essays in the Philosophy, History and Socio-Politics of Archaeology* (pp. 117–135). Cambridge: Cambridge University Press.

Hume, Ivor Noël. 1964. Handmaiden to history. *North Carolina Historical Review* 41(2): 215–225 (quote from p. 215).

Kelso, William M. 1986. Mulberry Row: Slave life at Thomas Jefferson's Monticello. *Archaeology* 39(5): 28–35.

Kidd, Kenneth E. 1949. *The Excavation of Ste Marie I.* Toronto: University of Toronto Press.

———. 1994. The phoenix of the north. In Stanley South (Ed.), *Pioneers in Historical Archaeology: Breaking New Ground* (pp. 49–65). New York: Plenum (quote from p. 49).

Leone, Mark P. 1984. Interpreting ideology in historical archaeology: Using the rules of perspective in the William Paca Garden in Annapolis, Maryland. In Daniel Miller and Christopher Tilley (Eds.), *Ideology, Power, and Prehistory* (pp. 25–36). Cambridge: Cambridge University Press.

———. 1987. Rule by ostentation: The relationship between space and sight in eighteenth-century landscape architecture in the Chesapeake region of Maryland. In Susan Kent (Ed.), *Method and Theory for Activity Area Research: An Ethnoarchaeological Approach* (pp. 604–633). New York: Columbia University Press.

———. 1988a. The Georgian order as the order of merchant capitalism in Annapolis, Maryland. In Mark P. Leone and Parker B. Potter (Eds.), *The Recovery of Meaning: Historical Archaeology in the Eastern United States* (pp. 235–261). Washington, DC: Smithsonian Institution Press.

———. 1988b. The relationship between archaeological data and the documentary record: Eighteenth-century gardens in Annapolis, Maryland. *Historical Archaeology* 22(1): 29–35 (quotes from p. 32).

———. 1995. A historical archaeology of capitalism. *American Anthropologist* 97: 251–268 (quotes from pp. 261, 262).

Leone, Mark P., Paul R. Mullins, Marian C. Creveling, Laurence Hurst, Barbara Jackson-Nash, Lynn D. Jones, Hannah Jopling Kaiser, George C. Logan, and Mark S. Warner. 1995. Can an African-American historical archaeology be an alternative voice? In Ian Hodder, Michael Shanks, Alexandra Alexandri, Victor Buchli, John Carman, Jonathan Last, and Gavin Lucas (Eds.), *Interpreting Archaeology: Finding Meaning in the Past* (pp. 110–124). London: Routledge.

Leone, Mark P., Parker B. Potter, Jr., and Paul A. Shackel. 1987. Toward a critical archaeology. *Current Anthropology* 28: 283–302.

Orser, Charles E., Jr. 1984. The past ten years of plantation archaeology in the southeastern United States. *Southeastern Archaeology* 3: 1–12.

———. 1995. *A Historical Archaeology of the Modern World.* New York: Plenum.

Potter, Parker B., Jr. 1994. *Public Archaeology in Annapolis: A Critical Approach to History in Maryland's Ancient City.* Washington, DC: Smithsonian Institution Press.

Scholnick, Jonathan, Derek Wheeler, and Fraser Neiman. 2001. *Mulberry Row Reassessment: The Building l site.* Monticello Department of Archaeology Technical Report Series 3. Charlottesville, VA.

Scott, Douglas D., Richard A. Fox, Melissa A. Connor, and Dick Harmon. 1989. *Archaeological Perspectives on the Battle of the Little Big Horn.* Norman: University of Oklahoma Press.

Scott, Elizabeth M. (Ed.). 1994. *Those of Little Note: Gender, Race, and Class in Historical Archaeology.* Tucson: University of Arizona Press.

Shackel, Paul A. 1993. *Personal Discipline and Material Culture: An Archaeology of Annapolis, Maryland, 1695–1870.* Knoxville: University of Tennessee Press.

Shackel, Paul A., Paul R. Mullins, and Mark S. Warner. 1998. *Annapolis Pasts: Historical Archaeology in Annapolis, Maryland.* Knoxville: University of Tennessee Press.

Singleton, Theresa A. (Ed.). 1985. *The Archaeology of Slavery and Plantation Life.* Orlando, FL: Academic Press.

South, Stanley. 1977a. *Method and Theory in Historical Archeology.* New York: Academic Press.

———(Ed.). 1977b. *Research Strategies in Historical Archaeology.* New York: Academic Press.

———(Ed.). 1994. *Pioneers in Historical Archaeology: Breaking New Ground.* New York: Plenum.

Wall, Diane diZerega. 1994. *The Archaeology of Gender: Separating the Spheres in Urban America.* New York: Plenum.

Wilson, Sherrill D. From *Archaeology* online. Retrieved June 14, 2006, from www.archaeology.org/online/features/afburial.

Chapter 13

Arnold, Bettina. 1992. The past as propaganda. *Archaeology* 45(4): 30–37.

Bray, Tamara L., and Thomas W. Killion (Eds.). 1994. *Reckoning with the Dead: The Larsen Bay Repatriation and the Smithsonian Institution.* Washington, DC: Smithsonian Institution Press.

Bogdanos, M. 2005. *The Thieves of Baghdad.* New York: Bloomsbury Publishing.

Brodie, Neil, and Kathryn Walker Tubb (Eds.). 2002. *Illicit Antiquities: The Theft of Culture and the Extinction of Archaeology.* London: Routledge.

Brown, Michael F. 2003. *Who Owns Native Culture?* Cambridge, MA: Harvard University Press.

Cleere, Henry (Ed.). 1989. *Archaeological Heritage Management in the Modern World.* London: Unwin Hyman.

Connor, Melissa. 1996. The archaeology of contemporary mass graves. *Bulletin of the Society for American Archaeology* 14(4): 6, 31.

Crowell, Aron L., Amy F. Steffian, and Gordon L. Pullar (Eds.). 2001. *Looking Both Ways: Heritage and Identity of the Alutiiq People.* Fairbanks: University of Alaska Press.

Echo-Hawk, Roger C., and Walter R. Echo-Hawk. 1994. *Battlefields and Burial Grounds: The Indian Struggle to Protect Ancestral Graves in the United States.* Minneapolis: Lerner.

Echo-Hawk, Walter (Ed.). 1992. Special Issue: Repatriation of American Indian remains. *American Indian Culture and Research Journal* 16(2): 1–200.

Eddy, John A. 1974. Astronomical alignment of the Big Horn medicine wheel. *Science* 184: 1035–1043.

Elia, Ricardo J. 1993. U.S. cultural resource management and the ICAHM charter. *Antiquity* 67: 426–438.

Ferguson, T. J. 1996. Native Americans and the practice of archaeology. *Annual Review of Anthropology* 25: 63–79.

Fowler, Don D. 1986. Conserving American archaeological resources. In David J. Meltzer, Don D. Fowler, and Jeremy A. Sabloff (Eds.), *American Archaeology: Past and Future: A Celebration of the Society for American Archaeology 1935–1985* (pp. 135–162). Washington, DC: Smithsonian Institution Press.

Goldstein, Lynn, and Keith Kintigh. 1990. Ethics and the reburial controversy. *American Antiquity* 55: 585–591.

Grey, Don. 1963. Big Horn Medicine Wheel site, 48BH302. *Plains Anthropologist* 8: 27–40.

King, Thomas F. 1991. Some dimensions of the pothunting problem. In George S. Smith and John E. Ehrenhard (Eds.), *Protecting the Past* (pp. 83–92). Boca Raton, FL: CRC.

———. 2003. *Places That Count: Traditional Cultural Properties in Cultural Resource Management.* Walnut Creek, CA: Altamira.

Klesert, Anthony L. 1992. A view from Navajoland on the reconciliation of anthropologists and Native Americans. *Human Organization* 51: 17–22.

Klesert, Anthony L., and Alan S. Downer (Eds.). 1990. *Preservation on the Reservation: Native Americans, Native American Lands and Archaeology.* Navajo Nation Papers in Anthropology, no. 26.

Klesert, Anthony L., and Shirley Powell. 1993. A perspective on ethics and the reburial controversy. *American Antiquity* 58: 348–354.

Koff, Clea. 2004. *The Bone Woman: A Forensic Anthropologist's Search for Truth in the Mass Graves of Rwanda, Bosnia, Croatia, and Kosovo.* New York: Random House.

Layton, Robert (Ed.). 1989. *Who Needs the Past? Indigenous Values and Archaeology.* One World Archaeology Series. London: Unwin Hyman.

Lynott, Mark J., and Alison Wylie. 2000. *Ethics in American Archaeology: Challenges for the 1990s,* 2d ed. Washington, DC: Society for American Archaeology.

Mansfield, Victor N. 1980. The Bighorn Medicine Wheel as a site for the vision quest. *Archaeoastronomy Bulletin* 3(2): 26–29.

McManamon, Francis P. 1991. The many publics for archaeology. *American Antiquity* 56: 121–130.

———. 1992. Managing America's archaeological resources. In LuAnn Wandsnider (Ed.), *Quandaries and Quests: Visions of Archaeology's Future* (pp. 25–40). Center for Archaeological Investigations, Occasional Paper no. 20. Carbondale: Southern Illinois University.

———. 1994. Changing relationships between Native Americans and archaeologists. *Historic Preservation Forum* 8(2): 15–20.

McManamon, Francis P., and Alf Hatton. 2000. *Cultural Resource Management in Contemporary Society.* London: Routledge.

Messenger, Phyllis (Ed.). 1989. *The Ethics of Collecting Cultural Property: Whose Culture? Whose Property?* Albuquerque: University of New Mexico Press.

Neumann, Thomas W., and Robert Sanford. 2001. *Cultural Resources Archaeology.* Walnut Creek, CA: Altamira.

Nicholas, Lynn H. 1994. *The Rape of Europe: The Fate of Europe's Treasures in the Third Reich and the Second World War.* New York: Knopf.

Rathje, William L. 1991. Once and future landfills. *National Geographic* 25(May): 116–134 (quote from p. 120).

Rathje, William, and Cullen Murphy. 2001. *Rubbish! The Archaeology of Garbage.* Tucson: University of Arizona Press.

Rathje, William L., W. W. Hughes, D. C. Wilson, M. K. Tani, G. H. Archer, R. G. Hunt, and T. W. Jones. 1992. The archaeology of contemporary landfills. *American Antiquity* 57: 437–447.

Richman, Jennifer R., and Marion P. Forsyth (Eds.). 2003. *Legal Perspectives on Cultural Resources.* Walnut Creek, CA: Altamira.

Rose, Jerome C., Thomas J. Green, and Victoria D. Green. 1996. NAGPRA is forever: Osteology and the repatriation of skeletons. *Annual Review of Anthropology* 25: 81–103.

Sabloff, Jeremy. 2008. *Archaeology Matters*. Walnut Creek, CA: Left Coast Press.

Smith, George S., and John E. Ehrenhard (Eds.). 1991. *Protecting the Past.* Boca Raton, FL: CRC.

Swidler, Nina, Kurt E. Dongoske, Roger Anyon, and Alan S. Downer (Eds.). 1997. *Native Americans and Archaeologists: Stepping Stones to Common Ground.* Walnut Creek, CA: Altamira.

Watkins, Joe. 2000. *Indigenous Archaeology: American Indian Values and Scientific Practice.* Walnut Creek, CA: Altamira.

Wendorf, Fred, and Raymond H. Thompson. 2002. The Committee for the Recovery of Archaeological Remains: Three decades of service to the archaeological profession. *American Antiquity* 67: 317–330.

Zimmerman, Larry. 2003. *Presenting the Past.* Walnut Creek, CA: Altamira.

Zimmerman, Larry J., Karen D. Vitelli, and Julie Hollowell-Zimmer (Eds.). 2003. *Ethical Issues in Archaeology.* Walnut Creek, CA: Altamira.

Index